The Path of Mercy

To Patricia Bell, RSM,
with deep gratitude for all you
have done for the Mercy world and
for me. May Catherine always be for
you a strong source of encouragement,
inspiration, and help. Fondly,
May 22, 2012   Mary Sullivan, RSM

The Path of
Mercy

The Life of Catherine McAuley

Mary C. Sullivan

THE CATHOLIC UNIVERSITY OF AMERICA PRESS
Washington, D.C.

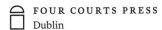

FOUR COURTS PRESS
Dublin

Published in Europe by Four Courts Press
7 Malpas Street, Dublin 8, Ireland
ISBN 978-1-84682-320-6

Published in the rest of the world by The Catholic University Press of America

The paper used in this publication meets the minimum requirements of
American National Standards for Information Science—Permanence of Paper
for Printed Library Materials, ANSI Z39.48-1984.

LIBRARY OF CONGRESS CATALOGING-IN-PUBLICATION DATA

Sullivan, Mary C.
The path of mercy : the life of Catherine McAuley / Mary C. Sullivan.
p. cm.
Includes bibliographical references (p.   ) and index.
ISBN 978-0-8132-1873-1 (cloth : alk. paper)   1. McAuley, Catherine, 1778–1841.
2. Nuns—Ireland—Biography.   3. Sisters of Mercy—History—19th century.
I. Title.
BX4483.8.S86 2012
271'.9202—dc23
[B]   2011044345

Contents

Illustrations

Preface

Numerous black and white portraits of Catherine McAuley, all of them posthumous, hang on the walls of schools, hospitals, social service centers, and dwellings across the world, in places she could never have imagined. The challenge of these paintings and the other portraits and sculptures that have followed them has been to get behind the canvas and the bronze, to see and feel the color and the movement of the nineteenth-century Irish woman who inspired them. W. B. Yeats's remark in "Adam's Curse" about the needed but deceptive appearance of effortlessness in successful lines of poetry probably ought to apply as well to a biography:

> A line will take us hours maybe;
> Yet if it does not seem a moment's thought,
> Our stitching and unstitching has been naught.
> Better go down upon your marrow-bones
> And scrub a kitchen pavement, or break stones.

No biography is inevitably written exactly as it is written. Choices are made along the way, among alternative routes, many of them shaded in uncertainty. Admittedly, at such junctures, the solid kitchen floor or the stone yard has its tangible appeal. Yet I have stayed with this "stitching" of Catherine McAuley's life for a number of reasons.

Over the fifty years since Mary Bertrand Degnan published *Mercy Unto Thousands* (1957)—the most recent full-length, fully documented, public biography of Catherine McAuley—many new resources have become available. Relevant archives the world over are now well organized, and their many holdings on McAuley are better known. New primary sources have come to light. McAuley's letters—in editions by Neumann (1969), Bolster (1989), and Sullivan (2004)—can now be consulted more easily. Many biographical memoirs written by McAuley's contemporaries have been published or are readily available. Moreover, a wealth of new published research in women's history, Irish history, and religious history has now opened up in great detail the several contexts within which this woman lived and acted.

Let me say clearly: this is a biography about a woman who late in her adult life became a nun, a Catholic sister, the initially reluctant founder of the Sisters of Mercy. I have hoped that this fact alone would not be an automatic curtain-closer, a reason in and of itself for some potential readers of the book to put it down. I can only suggest that Catherine McAuley's actual life, as she experienced it and as I have hoped to grasp and portray it, is more attractive and universally encouraging than a generic image or label might seem to imply.

Among the new McAuley resources are problems to be addressed: for example, numerous factual obscurities and inaccuracies in the early biographical manuscripts, the most obvious of which is the claim in some that Catherine McAuley was born in 1787—four years after her father died. There are legends and assumptions that need scrutiny. Certain transcriptions and secondary sources have ascribed to Catherine McAuley words, sayings, and opinions that are different from, or even contradicted by, reliable primary evidence. And there are generalizations that postdate her life or do not fit her case. Reviewing all these materials requires discriminating between speculations and documentable facts, often a risky business. Hence, new burdens of inquiry fall on any would-be biographer.

Yet for all this, McAuley research and writing have significantly developed over the last one hundred fifty years, and a present-day biographer can use the fruits of many scholars. Mary Vincent Harnett, who knew her personally, and Mary Austin Carroll were Catherine McAuley's first published biographers, Harnett in 1864 and Carroll in 1866. Over the ensuing years scholars and other interested parties have searched and found new pieces of McAuley's story. Mary Dominick Foster (1877–1960) was among the first to accumulate new data. She and her Jesuit collaborator, John MacErlean (1870–1950), assembled a large collection of documents and research notes on a wide range of topics which informed Roland Burke Savage's 1949 biography. Mary Bertrand Degnan's extensive research in the 1940s and 1950s, leading to *Mercy Unto Thousands,* and Mary Ignatia Neumann's in the 1960s, leading to the first publication of her correspondence, *Letters of Catherine McAuley,* also contributed new biographical information and primary documents. Mary Eugene Nolan, following MacErlean, secured copies of numerous transcripts of property deeds.

Mary Angela Bolster's extensive research uncovered many further and important early documents such as correspondence to Catherine McAuley, newspaper accounts, and crucial material in diocesan and Vatican archives. Bolster published the *Correspondence of Catherine McAuley, 1827–1841,* several small booklets and books on McAuley's life and spirituality, and a deliberately unfootnoted short biography, *Catherine McAuley: Venerable for Mercy* (1990). The latter is a sympathetic and generally accurate analysis of Catherine McAuley's life, but it could not do justice to Bolster's extended research over many years.[1]

---

1. Mary Angela Bolster's most extensive research—prepared under the aegis of the Congregation for the Causes of Saints in Rome—was assembled in two huge volumes intended for and still restricted to the process of Catherine McAuley's possible canonization. This study is entitled *Documentary Study for the Canonisation Process of the Servant of God Catherine McAuley . . . 1778–1841: Positio super Virtutibus* (Prot. No. 1296).

Embracing all this published as well as available archival material, no contemporary biographer need start from scratch, even though she must find her own way through the sheer volume and variety of these resources and the problems they may individually or collectively pose. For example, Harnett's *Life* was edited and introduced by Richard Baptist O'Brien, a Limerick priest who also knew Catherine McAuley. But it is hard to identify exactly what he may have added, deleted, or perhaps overemphasized in order to strengthen what he evidently wished to present as an "edifying" and "heroic" life: "There are many and edifying reasons for publishing the following Memoir," and its "manifestations of heroic sanctity . . . would seem to demand the present publication." Carroll conducted her extensive research through interviews with Frances Warde and Teresa Byrn, McAuley's contemporaries, and through transatlantic correspondence with well-intentioned but not always exact assistants, before the era of modern research aids. Thus her *Life*, its later edition (1870?) and its many reprints, and her four-volume *Leaves from the Annals of the Sisters of Mercy* (1881–1895) combine hard-won facts with embellishments, faulty transcriptions and dates, and created dialogue in a way that can, unfortunately, raise questions about the accuracy of some of her reports. I have chosen not to cite at all the *Familiar Instructions of Rev. Mother McAuley* (1888), edited, I believe, by Mary Magdalen de Pazzi Bentley, and have cited only very occasionally the *Retreat Instructions of Mother Mary Catherine McAuley* (1952), edited by Mary Bertrand Degnan—for reasons I explain in detail in the appendix.

In this biography, I have tried to question assumptions and received information; to acknowledge areas where the data are not clear or available, and may never be; to avoid a deliberately hagiographical style; and to rely, in general, on primary sources. Some chapters have lengthy notes where I have tried to supply data that will spare future researchers from having to re-plough the same ground.

One specific stylistic matter should be noted here: the use of titles and names. In general, clerical and religious titles are not used in this biography except where needed for clarity. Priests and bishops are identified as such, but their formal titles are not often used. However, in the post-penal era Irish priests were often called "Mr.," a carry-over from the days when their presence in Ireland often had, for safety reasons, to be unadvertised. Bishops and vicars general were usually given the title "Dr.," and I have sometimes used this title for clarity's sake.

The names of Sisters of Mercy present two special problems, calling for complicated solutions. In the narrative, before 1831 or whatever year they became novices and received the religious habit, they are called by their baptismal names and surnames. After their religious names were conferred at their reception of the habit, their religious names and surnames, or a shortened form thereof, are more appropriate. To prevent possible confusion (for example, that two different persons are indicated when it is really the same person), the baptismal name appears in parentheses in the first few references to the woman as a sister.

However, many of these women later wrote important biographical manuscripts about Catherine McAuley which are often quoted in this biography; in these instances, the authors are called by their religious names and surnames, or a shortened form thereof, whenever their writings are referenced in the text or notes. For example, Georgiana Moore became in religion Mary Clare Moore, or simply Clare Moore; when her biographical commentaries are quoted she is always called Clare Moore. Moreover, it was apparently the custom of this period to refer to novices as "Miss," and to refer to professed women religious sometimes as "Mrs.," for example, on the cover of posted letters and in other references. This usage will occasionally appear.

In the case of Catherine McAuley herself, in the narrative she is usually referred to simply as "Catherine," not as "McAuley," which some historians might prefer. To refer to Catherine merely by her surname is not the common practice of present-day sisters or associates of Mercy, or of others familiar with her personality. The title "Reverend Mother"—a designation she did not like and never used of herself—will, however, occasionally appear in quoted material from the period. She signed herself simply "C. McAuley" or "M. C. McAuley," but the affectionate respect in which she came to be held by others nearly always overrode her personal preference.

Another stylistic issue concerns the confusing spellings of family surnames. The family tree provided in this volume may help, but not completely. Catherine McAuley's father signed his name James McGauley. Others, for instance at the Registry of Deeds, often transcribed it as McGauly or McGawley. After his death, Catherine's mother, Elinor, apparently continued to use McGauley as her surname. Although I have not seen a deed or memorial of a deed with her own signature on it, an attested copy of one official transcript of a deed to which she was a party gives her signature as McGauley (though occasionally in transcribing other memorials the scribe wrote McGawley or McGauly). It has been said that Elinor changed her surname to McAuley, which may be true, but I have found no primary evidence of that. After 1822, when we first have Catherine's own signature, or mention of her in a legal document, she always uses McAuley.

To add to the difficulty, in 1804 Catherine's sister, Mary McAuley, married a William Macauley of an entirely different, Protestant family, though he occasionally signed his name MacAuley. Their five children were born Macauleys, but later—it is said, at Catherine's request—changed the spelling of their last name to McAuley. Catherine's brother, James, used both versions of the surname, McAuley and Macauley.

To mitigate this confusion somewhat, I have used McGauley for Catherine's father and mother, and I have throughout used McAuley for Catherine and her brother. Unless I am quoting a primary document, I have used McAuley and then Macauley for her sister, and Macauley for her brother-in-law and their children—except young William, who always used McAuley in his correspondence.

It is helpful to recall that the name McGauley/McGawley/McAuley/Macauley is said to be of Viking origin (meaning "descendant of Olaf"), and derivations of it, in distinct families, are found in Ireland and Scotland. Catherine's father evidently belonged to a very old Irish family some of whom eventually settled in County Westmeath. William Macauley's remote ancestors were Scottish or English settlers who came to Ulster. Early on the names of these several Gaelic families could be and apparently were reasonably transliterated into English spelling in a number of different ways.

Finally, to dispel any mystery, let me say what is probably obvious: I too am a Catholic woman, and a Sister of Mercy since 1951, but a resident of the United States, living far too distant from Ireland to have an instinctive Irish sense or vocabulary. Yet in this biography I have wished to be faithful to the main concerns, experiences, and emphases of Catherine McAuley's life insofar as I understand these, and to give them the weight they seem to have had in her life. I have wished to present her as who and what she was: an ordinary woman, with her human qualities and personal limitations, trying to do her utmost, as a human being, a woman, and a Christian. I have tried not to presume to know her unexpressed feelings and thoughts. I have also tried to see her life in her own historical moment and place, with whatever possibilities and drawbacks that then characterized her Ireland, her church, and her era.

Acknowledgments

In addition to the many McAuley, Mercy, and other researchers, past and present, from whom this biography has benefited, I wish to acknowledge and thank publicly the many archivists, librarians, and others, in Ireland and elsewhere—Sisters of Mercy and other professionals—who in one helpful way or another have assisted this project over the past several years. I think gratefully of Maree Allen, Douglas Appleyard, Franco Azzalli, Kathrine Bellamy, Ethel Bignell, Conrad Borntrager, Mary Jeremy Buckman, Angela Bugler, Damien Burke, Maíre Ni Chonalláin, Caitlín Conneely and the staff at Mercy International Centre, Theresa Delaney, Tom Desmond, the Discalced Carmelites on Clarendon Street, Mary Kay Dobrovolny, Helena Doherty, Mary Doherty, Brenda Dolphin, Glynn Douglas, Noelle Dowling, Raphael Downing, Alan Ennis, Sebastian Falcone, Magdalena Frisby, Agnes Gleeson, Anna Gordon, Marilyn Gouailhardou, Lee Guirreri, Canice Hanrahan, Liam Hogan, Barbara Jeffery, Kate Johnston, Kay Lane, Eleanor Little, Dora Lynch, Mary Lyons, Estelle Martin, Marion McCarthy, Elizabeth McCaver, Mary McEnearney, Robert Mills, Mary Hermenia Muldrey, Susan Nowalis, Fergus O'Donoghue, Paula O'Gorman, Majella O'Keeffe, James O'Neill, Olivia Parkinson, Marian Rankin, Jeanne Reichart, Anne Reid, Mary Reynolds (executive director of Mercy International Association), Patricia Sadler, Barbara Stinard, Rosaleen Underwood, Anne Walsh, Samuel Williamson, and Teresa Worthington. The list is long, but so is my gratitude. I also wish to acknowledge and thank Frances Billee McAuley Morwitch and Richard O'Leary, Australian descendants of Catherine McAuley through her nephew William (Willie) McAuley. Finally, I thank especially Marianne Cosgrave, archivist, and Frances Lowe, staff, at Mercy Congregational Archives, Dublin. A glance at the notes will show how much help I received from Marianne and Frances, for which I am very grateful.

The travel and other expenses associated with preparing this biography have been generously borne by the New York, Pennsylvania, and Pacific West Community of the Sisters of Mercy of the Americas, with significant financial help from the former Rochester and St. Louis Regional Communities, and the Sisters of Mercy in Sunderland, England. The Mercy International Association, who requested the biography, has provided accommodation in Dublin and other assistance. All of these Mercy organizations have been supportive in countless ways, large and small, but none has ever suggested how the biography should be written. To each of them I am, of course, deeply grateful, as I am to the many Mercy communities who provided accommodation and encouragement.

I wish also to thank those who took on the burden of reading and critiquing the manuscript and did so with an amazing cheerfulness worthy of Catherine McAuley: Patricia Brewster, Doris Gottemoeller, and the late Rev. Ernan McMullin read and offered comments on the entire text, including some chapters several times. Bishop Matthew H. Clark, Anne Coon, Elizabeth Davis, and Margaret Mac Curtain read individual chapters. To each of them and to the anonymous scholars of Irish history who reviewed the manuscript for the publishers, I am very grateful for the many corrections and suggestions they offered as well as for the time and care they devoted to this project. Louise Novros typed the entire manuscript and all its many revisions, and I can only thank her sincerely for her patience, late nights, and expertise.

Permission to reproduce certain materials in this biography has been granted with the request that the holders be explicitly acknowledged: the British Library, and the National Archives of Ireland and the Director of the National Archives. I thank these repositories for their extensive holdings and access to them.

Finally, I owe sincere gratitude to David J. McGonagle, former director of the Catholic University of America Press, for his guidance over many years and his persistent attention to this manuscript; to Theresa Walker, managing editor at the press, for her professional skills and her willingness to respond to queries; to Ellen Coughlin, the manuscript's expert and solicitous copy editor; and to Anne Kachergis, artist and book designer. Each has generously enriched this project.

Once again, the Mercy community with whom I live, Gratia L'Esperance and Marilyn Williams, have borne the brunt of my cluttered boxes of notes, preoccupation, and tardiness at meals with a constant understanding and assistance for which I am profoundly grateful.

To all these generous people this book is dedicated.

Abbreviations

Compilations of Primary Sources

CCMcA   Mary C. Sullivan, ed., *The Correspondence of Catherine McAuley, 1818–1841* (Dublin: Four Courts Press, 2004; Washington, D.C.: The Catholic University of America Press, 2004).

CMcATM   Mary C. Sullivan, *Catherine McAuley and the Tradition of Mercy* (Dublin: Four Courts Press, 1995; Notre Dame, Ind.: University of Notre Dame Press, 1995). Texts of biographical manuscripts and letters about Catherine McAuley written by her contemporaries; the original Rule and Constitutions of the Sisters of Mercy, which she composed; and excerpts from the Annals of two early Mercy communities.

PS   [Mary Clare Moore, comp.], *A Little Book of Practical Sayings, Advices and Prayers of our Revered Foundress, Mother Mary Catharine* [sic] *McAuley* (London: Burns, Oates, 1868). The first and most authentic such compilation. Copies are available in the Archives of the Institute of Our Lady of Mercy in London and Mercy Congregational Archives in Dublin.

Archives

AAH   Archives, Apothecaries Hall, Dublin

AIMGB   Archives, Institute of Our Lady of Mercy, London

APF   Archives of Propaganda Fide, Rome

ASB   Archives, Sisters of Mercy, South Central Province, Booterstown, Ireland

DDA   Dublin Diocesan Archives

IJA   Irish Jesuit Province Archives, Dublin. This archives contains MACE/MCAU, a large collection of research notes on Catherine McAuley by John MacErlean, S.J. (1870–1950).

MCA   Mercy Congregational Archives, Dublin

NAI   National Archives of Ireland, Dublin

NLI National Library of Ireland, Dublin

RCPI Royal College of Physicians of Ireland, Dublin

RD Registry of Deeds, Dublin

SMA Archives, Sisters of Mercy of the Americas, Silver Spring, Maryland

Manuscripts in CMcATM, and their archival location

BA Bermondsey Annals (1841), containing a biography of Catherine Mc-Auley composed by Mary Clare Moore, 1814–1874 (AIMGB).

CA Carlow Annals (1837–1841), containing commentary on Catherine McAuley (Archives, St. Leo's Convent, Carlow, Ireland).

CAM "Memoir" of Catherine McAuley composed by Mary Clare Augustine Moore, 1808–1880 (MCA).

CML Five letters about Catherine McAuley written by Mary Clare Moore to Mary Clare Augustine Moore in 1844–1845 (MCA).

DL The Derry Large Manuscript, a biography of Catherine McAuley presumably composed by Mary Ann Doyle, 1801–1866 (Archives, Sisters of Mercy, Northern Province, Bessbrook, Northern Ireland).

Lim The Limerick Manuscript, a biography of Catherine McAuley composed by Mary Vincent Harnett, 1811–1865 (ASB).

MADL Three letters about Catherine McAuley written by Mary Ann Doyle to Mary Clare Augustine Moore in 1844 (MCA).

MVWL Six letters about Catherine McAuley written by Mary Vincent Whitty (1819–1892) to Mary Cecilia Marmion in 1841 (Archives, Sisters of Mercy, Brisbane, Australia).

Rule The Rule and Constitutions of the Religious Sisters of Mercy as composed by Catherine McAuley. Citations give chapter and paragraph numbers (e.g., 8.2), and unless otherwise noted citations of the Rule refer to part 1.

TA Tullamore Annals (1836–1841), containing commentary on Catherine McAuley (Archives, Convent of Mercy, Tullamore, Ireland).

Family of Catherine McAuley

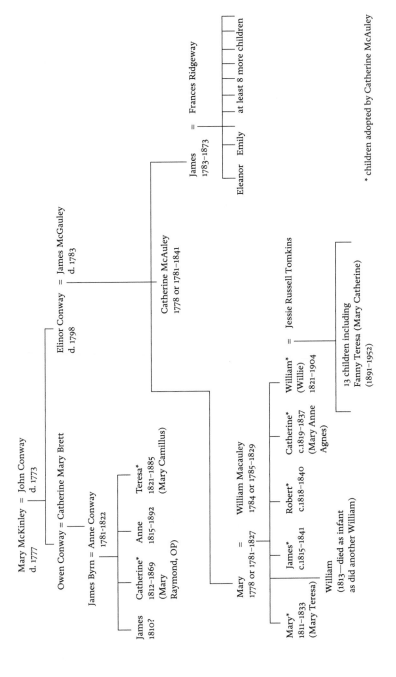

Mary McKinley = John Conway
d. 1777   d. 1773

Owen Conway = Catherine Mary Brett

James Byrn = Anne Conway
              1781–1822

James   Catherine*   Anne   Teresa*
1810?   1812–1869   1815–1892   1821–1885
           (Mary   (Mary   (Mary Camillus)
           Raymond, OP)

Elinor Conway = James McGauley
d. 1798   d. 1783

Catherine McAuley
1778 or 1781–1841

James
1783–1873   =   Frances Ridgeway

Eleanor Emily   at least 8 more children

Mary   =   William Macauley
1778 or 1781–1827   1784 or 1785–1829

Mary*   James   Robert*   Catherine*   William*   =   Jessie Russell Tomkins
1811–1833   c.1815–1841 c.1818–1840 c.1819–1837   (Willie)
(Mary   (Mary Anne   1821–1904
Teresa)   Agnes)

William   13 children including
(1813—died as infant   Fanny Teresa (Mary Catherine)
as did another William)   (1891–1952)

* children adopted by Catherine McAuley

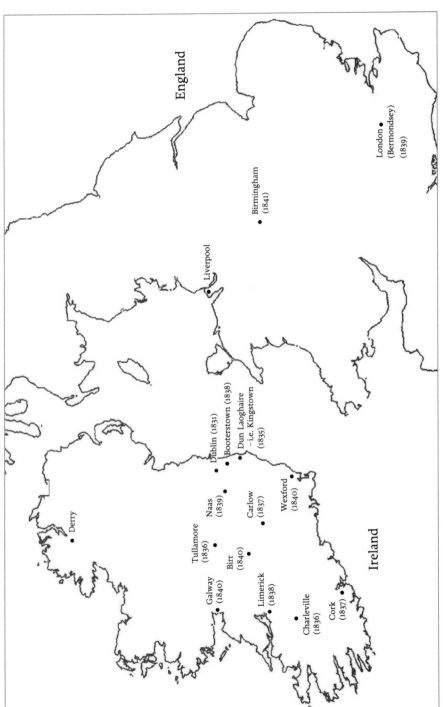

Map of Ireland and England showing foundations by the Sisters of Mercy, 1831–1841

The Path of Mercy

Introduction

In 1829 a priest who severely criticized the house Catherine McAuley (1778?–1841) had built on Baggot Street, Dublin, and the lay community of women who joined her efforts there, is said to have called her a "parvenue" and an "upstart," and evidently thought that the "unlearned sex" could do nothing "but mischief by trying to assist the clergy."[1] Catherine was indeed, in a positive sense that Matthias Kelly did not intend, an "upstart," one who would, in time, reveal the benefits of that "mischief," in her native land and well beyond it.

The multiple Irelands she knew, marked by great contrasts between the prosperity of many and the destitution of a majority in the late eighteenth century and the early nineteenth century, were sustained by profound, undeniable riches of the spirit. One cannot read Ireland's history or Catherine's story without marveling at the goodness and courage of countless celebrated and uncelebrated people, the voluntary charity of hundreds in mansions and one-room thatched cabins, of clergy in all Christian denominations, of Quakers, and many others. One sees the contributions to their neighbors and to church-building of Catholic people who could barely afford to provide potatoes and milk for their own families, and the generosity of scores of priests and bishops who served their people with wisdom and compassion in the most trying circumstances. The resilience and cheerfulness of the Irish people themselves were further national treasures.

Catherine cherished and benefited from this spiritual endowment, but she was also subject to the limitations of her era, with its post-Reformation theologies, its religious prejudices, its limited recognition of women, its fixed class and ecclesiastical attitudes, and its traditional concepts and practices of

---

1. CAM, in *CMcATM*, 208. See chapter 1 for a discussion of the uncertainty regarding Catherine McAuley's birth year.

vowed religious life. Of these she could be a polite, sometimes indirect, critic. She was reverent toward clergy, yet on several occasions contested their decisions. She read the spiritual books available to her, yet developed independent opinions on certain points. She accepted the status and employment that society would allow poor women—generally, domestic service—yet did not tolerate violations of their rights. She was strict about what she took to be essential religious values, but spoke against making "too many laws." She cooperated with the requirements of social and church structures, but did not accept the notion of a "weaker sex." She was silent about matters she apparently felt she could not change, yet vocal about those she felt could and should be changed. In all this she honored her own experience and let it influence her views and actions. The adage "never too old to learn" was, she said, a great comfort to her.

Politically, she lived in a largely post-penal era. After centuries of occupation by English forces and of plantations by Scottish and English settlers sent to hold the land for England, Ireland had endured, beginning in the 1690s, not only continued appropriation of Irish lands, but also a new series of anti-Catholic penal regulations, some having long-term, damaging effects on Irish life. These "popery" laws, as they were sometimes called, were aimed at reducing (if not extinguishing) the leadership potential and influence of Irish Catholics (about 80 percent of the population), by disempowering their clergy and landed laity, politically and economically, and thereby protecting from attack the social, economic, and political power of the English government and the Protestant minority, thus safeguarding their ascendancy.

According to the letter of these intricate laws, most of them passed in the earliest decades of the eighteenth century and only more or less enforced until about the 1750s (though some enforcement occurred after that), all kinds of restrictions were placed on Catholic activity. Diocesan priests already in the country in 1704 had to register, and the geographical scope of their pastoral service, and therefore influence, was narrowed. Priests from the continent were forbidden to enter the country, and unregistered priests were, at least according to the law, subject to arrest and banishment. Catholic chapels for worship could, in effect, be built only inconspicuously, not on main streets or roads. Catholics could not keep weapons. Sponsoring Catholic schools and serving as Catholic teachers were proscribed, and Catholics who went abroad for their education, including priests, could not legally return. Known members of Catholic religious orders could not live in Ireland, and existing bishops and others in high-level ecclesiastical roles were required to leave the country. Bishops who posed as simply parish priests also had to register, and new bishops could not, according to the statutes, be sent to Ireland or be consecrated there. In the early years of the eighteenth century, circumventing these laws often required hiding, a good deal of discretion, and dependence on the good will of Catholic laity and sympathetic Protestants. "Priest-catching" was permissible and rewarded.[2]

Moreover, in what S. J. Connolly regards as "the most important single penal statute," the Act to Prevent the Further Growth of Popery (1704), Catholics were forbidden to buy land or to lease property for more than thirty-one years, and they could not inherit land from Protestants.[3] Catholics, especially gentry who still owned land, had to bequeath it equally to *all* their male heirs, thus gradually reducing the amount of land owned by Catholic families, and their corresponding power and influence as landowners. In 1709, legislation explicitly recognized "discoverers," that is, persons, whether Protestant or Catholic, who, having successfully reported an illegal property or inheritance transaction, acquired the assets involved.

These laws were aimed not directly at the entire Irish Catholic population or, specifically, at their practice of the Catholic faith, but at those who had power or influence. They were, moreover, selectively enforced, at the whim, or occasionally the mercy, of magistrates. But their very presence on the books was a disruption and humiliation with side effects. Agitation to repeal the penal regulations grew by 1760, if not before, and partial "relief acts" were passed in 1778, 1782, 1792, and 1793. However, Catholics were still prohibited from holding the highest governmental offices, including serving as members of parliament, whether in the Irish Parliament, soon to be dissolved, or the British Parliament. By the Act of Union passed in 1800, Ireland was declared a constitutive part of the United Kingdom of Great Britain. However, the remaining penal restrictions on office-holding were not repealed until the Act of Catholic Emancipation in 1829. Until then, Irish Catholics had little voice in legislative decisions affecting Irish life unless legitimately elected members of the British Parliament (men

2. See S. J. Connolly, ed., *Oxford Companion to Irish History*, 2nd ed. (Oxford: Oxford University Press, 2002), 462–63, for a summary of the penal laws; Patrick Corish, *The Irish Catholic Experience: A Historical Survey* (Dublin: Gill and Macmillan, 1985), 123–50; and James Kelly, "The Impact of the Penal Laws," in *History of the Catholic Diocese of Dublin*, ed. James Kelly and Dáire Keogh (Dublin: Four Courts Press, 2000), 144–74.

3. "Penal laws," in Connolly, *Oxford Companion*, 462.

belonging to the established Church of England or the Church of Ireland)
supported their cause. Even after 1829, their voice in Parliament was dis-
proportionately limited by new voting regulations that reduced the number of eligible Irish voters in urban areas to one in twenty-six, and in the
counties to one in 116, far fewer than in England.[4]

Neither the Act of Union nor the repeal legislation, in themselves, directly addressed the persistent and socially and ecclesially damaging effects of the early penal laws. But one consequence of the repeal legislation and the Union was to alarm some Protestants and make them fear
for their privileges. Resentments on all sides, continuing tensions between
Catholics and Protestants, prejudices and habits of discrimination, at least
as Catherine McAuley experienced these in her adult years, to say nothing of Catholic poverty, low literacy in English especially among the poor
in the West, and weaknesses in Catholic knowledge and practice, at least
among many of the poor, continued well into the nineteenth century.[5] All
these factors shaped aspects of Catherine's world.

Economically, she witnessed splendid wealth on the part of some and
severe poverty on the part of the majority, with variations between these
extremes. The slowly arriving industrial revolution in Ireland, the evolving international trade picture, the movement toward larger farms with a
greater focus on livestock than crops, the resulting evictions of small tenant farmers, the parlous state of medical science and practice in the beginning of the nineteenth century, and even the vagaries of weather and crop
failures all played some part in deepening the poverty she would encounter.

The poverty in Dublin in the 1820s and 1830s was augmented by many
factors of varying application and social magnitude: the decrease in the
demand for labor after the Napoleonic wars; shifts in English industrial
production and export and import legislation that rendered certain Irish
manufactured goods almost worthless; recurring epidemics of fever, typhus, and dysentery that often killed the only wage earners in poor families; the poor sanitation and the decaying and vastly overcrowded Dublin
housing stock in the oldest and poorest parts of the city. All this, in turn,
led to renewed cycles of disease and even greater poverty.

---

4. "Franchise," in Connolly, *Oxford Companion*, 215.

5. The 1841 census of Ireland indicated that by then "only a minority—37 per cent of males and 18
per cent of females—could read and write." A fairly straight line from Derry to Cork marks the discrepancy between these skills in the east, and in the west where the poorest half of the population resided.
Cormac Ó Gráda, "Poverty, Population, and Agriculture, 1801–45," in *Ireland Under the Union, I, 1801–1870*,
ed. W. E. Vaughan, 110 (Oxford: Oxford University Press, 1989); and T. W. Freeman, "Land and People, c.
1841," in *Ireland Under the Union, I*, 266, map 4.

The great increase in the numbers of very poor people in Ireland in the first half of the nineteenth century was also due in part to an overall explosion of the general population, with fluctuations in the numbers in various times, places, and classes. By 1841, the year of the first reliable census, the population of Ireland "had topped the eight million mark," up from an estimated four million in 1791.[6] Four-fifths of the population in 1841 were "rural-dwellers," and one-fifth were classified as "town-dwellers," though "this category included any settlement exceeding twenty houses."[7] Some "forty percent of the houses in Ireland" were classified as fourth-class housing, the lowest. In the country or rural areas outside towns this was one-room mud cabins. In Dublin, where the population in 1841 was over 232,700, some 23,197 families lived in fourth-class housing.[8] However, as Jacinta Prunty points out, "a family which had sole possession of a fourth class hovel was possibly no worse off than a family sharing a single room with perhaps two other families and lodgers in what was technically a 'first class' house."[9]

In rural areas, before 1815 and increasingly thereafter, many barely survived at a subsistence level. As Gearóid ÓTuathaigh explains:

The labour demands of some small-farmers were met by the members of their own families. The bulk of the labour force, however, were cottiers and landless labourers. The cottier usually paid the rent of his tiny plot partly in labour, partly by the sale or surrender of his slight crop. . . . The landless labourers, the rural proletariat of the pre-famine economy, were in every respect its most unfortunate victims. . . . A small minority were still housed and fed by their farmer-employer, while yet another group gave their labour in return for access to a potato plot. The most insecure class, however, were the labourers who rented plots for a cash rent and hence were obliged to find adequate wage-paid employment if they were to survive. All of these labourers were in a perilous economic situation in pre-famine Ireland, where the labour market was greatly over-supplied. Some sought wage-paid work through seasonal migration . . . [for instance] seasonal employment in England and Scotland.[10]

To interpret the monetary figures in what follows it may be helpful to recall that by 1826 the former Irish currency had been amalgamated into the British currency.[11] A pound (£) was worth twenty shillings, and

---

6. Gearóid Ó Tuathaigh, *Ireland before the Famine, 1798–1848* (Dublin: Gill and Macmillan, 1972), 129 and 148.

7. Ibid., 146 and 151.

8. Jacinta Prunty, *Dublin Slums, 1800–1925: A Study in Urban Geography* (Dublin: Irish Academic Press, 1977), 42, table 2.3.

9. Ibid., 41.

10. Ó Tuathaigh, *Ireland before the Famine*, 133–34.

11. Robert Heslip, "Money," in Connolly, *Oxford Companion*, 384–85.

each shilling (s) was worth twelve pence (d). The cost of something, or a wage, for instance, was represented as £10.13s.8d, or more briefly, £10.13.8. Amounts less than one pound were recorded simply as 7s or 4d or 1d (one penny).

Citing testimony "given at a parliamentary enquiry in 1838," ÓTuathaigh says that "the wages for unskilled labourers in Dublin" were then about eight or nine shillings a week. However, "agricultural labourers in the rural hinterland could at best look forward to only eight or ten pence per day," that is, about three or four shillings a week if employed five days.[12] Citing an earlier, 1804, document, Maria Luddy provides the following picture for County Armagh:

> The male servant of the farmer or manufacturer will receive about six guineas per annum [about £6.6.0], with board and lodging; the woman about £3. The general employment of the women is spinning. . . .Women's wages are about sixpence per day . . . children's from threepence to sixpence. But at some branches of the linen manufacture, if they had constant employment, they could earn tenpence per day.[13]

Mary Cullen notes that in various agricultural areas, as surveyed in 1835–1836, a male farm laborer constantly employed might earn £12 to £14 a year, sometimes £16. Through raising pigs and poultry, his wife's contribution to the family's annual income might be another £1 to £2, in addition to her help in producing the potato crop.[14] Before the decline by 1820 of textile manufacturing in the home, hand spinning or weaving might add another sixpence a day to a family's income, but this work could not be done all day or every day of the year. Obviously the cash earnings of married women (in addition to the benefit of their unpaid family work) were a necessary part of the household economy of poor families, though in various government reports the women's earnings were often subsumed under their husbands' earnings.

All a family's expenses (rent, food, clothing, turf, soap, candles, tools, etc.) had to come out of its annual income. If the husband was only occasionally employed, or if he was employed at a lower level, or if either partner became ill or died, the family's income was much less.[15] "Few of the laborers had overcoats and their womenfolk and children generally went

---

12. Ó Tuathaigh, *Ireland before the Famine*, 153–54.
13. Maria Luddy, *Women in Ireland, 1800–1918: A Documentary History* (Cork: Cork University Press, 1995), 162. Luddy is citing a statistical survey done by Sir Charles Coote.
14. Mary Cullen, "Breadwinners and Providers: Women in the Household Economy of Labouring Families 1835–6," in *Women Surviving: Studies in Irish Women's History in the 19th and 20th Centuries*, ed. Maria Luddy and Cliona Murphy (Dublin: Poolbeg Press, 1990), 93–97.
15. Ibid., 98–99.

barefoot. Among the very poorest, clothing was little better than rags."[16] Widows with children and single women without immediate family wage-earners were the most vulnerable. Mary Cullen reports that in 1835–1836 "women greatly outnumbered men among the destitute."[17]

The earnings of indoor domestic servants, whether in country estates or townhouses, varied according to the number and level of the servants employed and the wealth and generosity of the employer. At the lowest level, a scullery maid or kitchen maid, employed, for instance, in Dublin in 1899, might annually earn only £11.3.0., though room and board were sometimes provided.[18] Early in the nineteenth century her average wage would have been much lower. Though the "largest source of female employment was domestic service," domestic servants "were the most poorly paid section of the community." Yet this was often the only career for a young country girl migrating to a city or town. Though such a servant might be "better fed and housed than the majority of the working class," she "worked long hours at heavy duties in an age which lacked . . . labour-saving devices," and her free time "was minimal."[19]

The following figures are illustrative of the cost in 1835–1836 of certain food staples in different situations, and they may illumine the poverty of the majority of Irish people and the inadequacy of their wages. If a family with children earned only £10 a year, their daily allowances for food were small, and they could barely manage, if at all. At the Dublin market in July 1836, for example, "inferior mutton" cost five to five and a half-pence per pound; butter was nine- or tenpence per pound; green peas were fourpence, and beans twopence per quart; a hundredweight (112 pounds) of new potatoes or oatmeal cost six shillings or fourteen shillings, respectively.[20] In September of the same year green peas had risen to tenpence per quart, but new potatoes had fallen to four or five shillings per hundredweight.[21]

Potatoes, "the most versatile food known to man," were the primary, if not the sole, food of the poor, and are said to have provided "all the proteins, calories and minerals" they needed, if they could afford them.[22] In Ireland in

---

16. Ó Tuathaigh, *Ireland before the Famine*, 149.

17. Cullen, "Breadwinners and Providers," in Luddy and Murphy, *Women Surviving*, 87.

18. Luddy, *Women in Ireland*, 226–27, quoting data on domestic servants prepared for the House of Commons in 1899.

19. Mary E. Daly, *Social and Economic History of Ireland since 1800* (Dublin: Educational Company of Ireland incorporating Longman, Browne and Nolan, 1981), 105.

20. *Freeman's Journal*, July 20, 1836.   21. *Freeman's Journal*, September 10, 1836.

22. Cormac Ó Gráda, *The Great Irish Famine* (Dublin: Gill and Macmillan, 1989), 26.

the early nineteenth century (and almost unbelievably by present-day habits), an adult male would generally "consume 12–14 lbs. (or 5–6 kilos) of potatoes daily for most of the year, and the rest of the family in proportion."[23] Yet citing the 1835–1836 government inquiry, Cullen reports that in many counties the annual supply of potatoes (for a family who did not grow their own) cost, on average, £8.13.0. The family oatmeal for the same period cost £1.15.0.[24]

It is incorrect, according to Mary E. Daly, "to see Ireland in the 1840s as marked with uniform destitution," yet it was still the case that in rural areas "the living standards of labourers or tenants with less than five acres were close to subsistence," and almost 75 percent of families in the poorest counties of the West lived in "extremely poor conditions." Daly therefore calls the years 1815–1850 an "age of economic crisis."[25] Under these circumstances, migration to Dublin and other towns was often the only recourse, even with the declining opportunities for paid urban employment.

It is therefore not surprising that in Dublin, in her mature years, Catherine McAuley saw many single women, mothers, and others turn to pawning their clothes and public begging. Or that some young women, migrating to barrack towns and port cities such as Dublin, turned to prostitution as a survival strategy. The midsummer months, between the exhaustion of the previous year's crops and the new harvest, as well as the winter months, when estate and townhouse owners dismissed servants and returned from Dublin to the country or to London, were particularly stressful.

Public begging, or mendicity as it was often called, was common. Commenting on pre-famine Ireland, R. B. McDowell notes the distinction in the prevailing laissez-faire economic theory, as expressed in the Mendicity Act of 1772:

The most important piece of social legislation enacted by the Irish parliament in the eighteenth century, the act empowering counties to erect houses of industry [workhouses], is solidly based on these ideas. A clear division is made between the deserving poor and the rest. The helpless poor, "reduced to that state by sickness or misfortune," were to be badged and authorized to beg, or to be cared for in the houses. But "disorderly persons," "strolling vagrants capable of labour," were to be conditioned to honest toil by imprisonment and hard labour.[26]

---

23. Ibid., 25. Ó Gráda's estimate of a male's daily consumption of potatoes (in three meals) is confirmed by other scholars.
24. Cullen, "Breadwinners and Providers," in Luddy and Murphy, *Women Surviving*, 93–97.
25. Daly, *Social and Economic History*, 19.
26. R. B. McDowell, "Ireland on the Eve of the Famine," in *The Great Famine: Studies in Irish History, 1845–52*, ed. Dudley Edwards and T. Desmond Williams (New York: New York University Press, 1957), 31.

The 1772 scheme was never fully implemented, many places relying instead on voluntary denominational charity. Later a government-supported system of workhouses (or "unions") was created by the Poor Law Act for Ireland in 1838. But these places were often intentionally managed, in terms of low diet, crowded lodging, and monotonous work, as to deter every beggar but the most disabled and destitute. Moreover, families were broken up, with "men, women, and children over 2 years of age being assigned to separate wards."[27]

The distinction between the "deserving" and the "undeserving" poor existed in another form. Prostitutes fell into the category of the "undeserving" poor. Treated as an undifferentiated group, they were commonly regarded as morally, socially, and physically dangerous: a contagion. Their presence could induce homeless, unemployed girls and women to follow their example. They visibly intruded on and contaminated public space. And their presumed venereal diseases, certainly not fully understood medically in this era, were infectious. The fact that prostitution among young girls and women in the lower classes might have been, at least initially, motivated by severe poverty was not generally acknowledged. Evidently some attempt was made to distinguish women deliberately pursuing prostitution as a chosen path of paid employment from young women involved in an injudicious act or victimized by incest or rape. But the general presumption was that the woman had freely cooperated with the man, if she had not actually seduced him.[28] Not until later in the nineteenth century were sufficient voices raised about the man's complicity, and not until the twentieth century were there cures for venereal diseases.

Moreover, pregnancy outside of marriage often drew severe condemnation, even in the girl's or woman's family. Thus infanticides and female suicides were occasionally reported in newspapers. In any event, prostitution, if uncovered by the police, was regarded as a crime, subject to arrest, and punishable by consignment to a Lock hospital, or a special area of a jail or prison. Such a woman was, after all, seen as a contaminant. Where some repentance was evident, voluntary or assigned recourse to a magdalen asylum was an option, but she was still regarded as potentially infectious.[29]

Police records for Dublin show 2,849 arrests of suspected prostitutes

---

27. Virginia Crossman, "Workhouse," in Connolly, *Oxford Companion*, 631.

28. See Maria Luddy, *Prostitution and Irish Society, 1800–1940* (Cambridge: Cambridge University Press, 2007), a thorough treatment of the subject.

29. Some magdalen asylums are discussed in chapter 19 of the present book, and in its notes.

in 1838. Not all of them were convicted of soliciting.[30] The brothels were generally on streets in the poorest parts of the old city, near the Liberties in the west, and below and above the Liffey in the east. Upscale brothels that catered to a "superior" class of customer were less often investigated by the police. Maria Luddy, who has published the most extensive research into prostitution in Ireland, reports that in 1838, "there were 402 brothels, or houses frequented by prostitutes, in Dublin."[31]

Apparently, such expressions as "women of good character," and "distressed women," evolved in an effort to distinguish the women so regarded from those suspected of regular prostitution and possibly or actually carrying venereal disease. In Catherine McAuley's day these expressions were commonly used for the residents admitted into the houses of refuge founded and sustained by the philanthropy of Protestant and Catholic laity. Admission committees, where they existed, looked for character references, and prospective employers sought such recommendations. Catherine herself, when she later founded a House of Mercy, insisted that only the director of the house could inquire into the previous personal lives of women about to be admitted, and that only a regular chaplain who served full time, not a series of rotating chaplains, could adequately serve these women's sacramental needs.[32]

These, then, were some of the conditions in Ireland that Catherine McAuley experienced as she entered the nineteenth century, and some of the political, economic, and social attitudes and realities she had to negotiate. But there was another central reality: the Roman Catholic Church in Ireland, still emerging, generally successfully, from the now mostly repealed restrictions of penal days, but also subject to its own structural and theological limitations.

This church, variously described by Patrick Corish, Hugh Fenning, James Kelly, Donal Kerr, Dáire Keogh, Emmet Larkin, Margaret Mac Curtain, and other historians, was hierarchically and clerically focused. This is not to say that Catholic laity, especially the poor, but also the rising middle class and the wealthy, did not very significantly carry the church forward and contribute enormously to its development, but only that it was a bishop- and priest-centered church. In describing the pastoral role of the Catholic Church in the years 1750–1850, Emmet Larkin indexes very few

---

30. Luddy, *Prostitution and Irish Society,* 18.
31. Ibid., 21.
32. Rule 4.4, in CMcATM, 300; letter 53, October 3, 1837, in CCMcA, 96–97.

laymen and mentions only three named women: Queen Anne (1702–1714), whose Parliament framed several of the penal regulations; Mrs. Samuel Carter Hall, a traveler in Ireland; and one Briget Duffy, alias McEleer, who in 1817 brought a legal case against a priest for sexual advances.[33] The official Irish *Catholic Directory,* issued each year beginning in 1836, regularly focused on bishops, priests, and men in high places in the church and society, as might to some extent be expected given the marginal status of women. In church histories of the period, bishops or priests alone were personally credited with having built chapels and founded religious congregations and other beneficial confraternities, lay movements and charities, not the women or laymen who actually endured the personal sacrifices involved in the building and founding. The ecclesiology that underlay such presentations still awaited the emergence of a wider view of ecclesial pastoral life and of events worthy of ecclesial memory.

John Troy, the Catholic archbishop of Dublin from 1786 to his death in 1823, served his people during the difficult transitional period when he and other bishops, after the dislocation of the penal days and in collaboration with Rome, were trying to assist the institutional church in Ireland to move on from certain popular religious devotions and the occasional laxity of the early decades of the eighteenth century to the catechetical maturity and sacramental discipline envisioned by the Council of Trent.[34] It was also a time when sporadic Catholic rebellions and Protestant efforts at proselytizing were equally feared. After the uprisings of the 1790s various English laws against insurrection and against organizations suspected of possible insurrection were passed. Troy supported these, apparently out of a prudent fear that the Catholic relief acts could themselves be repealed. Yet Protestants, still fearing takeovers by "popery" and "papists," found informal and formal ways to maintain their prerogatives, through control of various functions and institutions such as hospitals and cemeteries. Troy's functioning as a Catholic administrator spanned much of this tense and evolving era.

When Daniel Murray was appointed Troy's coadjutor in 1809, and later archbishop (1823), he also, like Troy, was committed to developing the distinctively Irish church while cooperating with Roman regulations and,

---

33. Emmet Larkin, *The Pastoral Role of the Roman Catholic Church in Pre-Famine Ireland, 1750–1850* (Washington, D.C.: The Catholic University of America Press, 2006).

34. Dáire Keogh, "'The Pattern of the Flock': John Thomas Troy, 1786–1823," in Kelly and Keogh, *History of the Catholic Diocese of Dublin,* 219–33.

where possible, with his Church of Ireland counterparts. Loyal though he always was to central Catholic needs and rights, his personality and manner set a gracious tone for relations among the Christian churches and with the British government. While opinions vary on the relative value of his accomplishments and mode of acting, as compared with those of Paul Cullen, his successor (1852–1878), Murray was, according to Donal Kerr, and again like Troy, an example to his flock, a mild, prudent, moderate, and humble churchman who showed courage in many ways that continued the sacramental development and strengthened the education of the Irish Catholic people, even though he did not like to confront others, especially his colleagues and friends, and was "reluctant to interfere."[35]

If one can judge from the sheer volume of spiritual publications available through Catholic printers and booksellers, and the development of personal and parish libraries at this time, Catholics literate in English, at least those in Dublin, displayed considerable interest in reading spiritual books. Many of these—such as Joseph Joy Dean's *Devotions to the Sacred Heart of Jesus* (Catherine McAuley's own prayerbook)—were collections of prayers promoted as a help to private devotion, and for use during Mass, which was celebrated in Latin.[36] The contents of these prayerbooks as well as of the many other available spiritual books were generally of European origin, translations of post-Reformation writings by French, Spanish, and Italian authors. For example, Catherine McAuley read works by Thomas à Kempis, Francis de Sales, Francis Blyth, Louis Bourdaloue, Luis of Granada, Alphonsus Liguori, Alban Butler, among others (see chapter 10). Some of these writers were English, most were French or Spanish, whom she read in translation. She had her own copy of Richard Challoner's edition of *Journal of Meditations for Every Day in the Year* and was particularly attracted to an English translation (1806) of Alonso (Alphonsus) Rodriguez's *Practice of Christian and Religious Perfection*. A prayerbook by Ursula Young, an Ursuline nun in Cork (the only religious book Catherine is known to have read that was written by a woman), and other prayerbooks she used were edited or compiled by Irish writers and were in frequent editions and reprintings.[37]

35. See Donal Kerr, "Dublin's Forgotten Archbishop: Daniel Murray, 1768–1852," in Kelly and Keogh, *History of the Catholic Diocese of Dublin*, 247–67.

36. *Devotions to the Sacred Heart of Jesus*, ed. Joseph Joy Dean (Dublin: Chambers and Hallagan, 1820).

37. [Ursula Young], *The Soul United to Jesus in the Adorable Sacrament* (Dublin: James Duffy and Sons, 1883). While this edition appeared long after Catherine McAuley's death, the third edition is list-

Many of the standard classic works from Europe contained much (not all) which proved to be perennially sound. However, the wholesale attempt on the part of the Catholic Book Society and Dublin printers and booksellers to import into Ireland the spiritual emphases of sixteenth-century to eighteenth-century European Counter-Reformation understandings was evidently not balanced by comparable attempts to secure and make generally available books on renewed and distinctively Irish theological topics and values such as neighborly charity, intense awareness of the presence of God, the value of spiritual pilgrimage, generosity and hospitality to strangers, and mercifulness to the poor, among many other possibilities. Catherine McAuley was a well-read woman, yet she does not seem to have encountered in her reading any expositions of the older Irish religious traditions, for example, of seeing the person who is poor as the primary this-world locus of *alter Christus* (another Christ). What she, and many like her, learned to believe in these matters evidently came to them in other ways—through prayer, meditation on Scripture, and the example and guidance of priests like Thomas Betagh, Edward Armstrong, Michael Blake, James Maher, and Redmond O'Hanlon, and bishops like Bartholomew Crotty, William Kinsella, and Edward Nolan, all of whom she admired and whom we shall meet later.

Finally, Roman ecclesiastical authorities and others of this period were unsure how to treat the emerging apostolic religious congregations of women in Ireland, whose spirituality, as distinct from that of cloistered contemplative orders, was unfamiliar to them. They were apparently unaware of how to benefit from the prophetic presence of these new movements, and unconscious of their lack in this regard.

Into these multifaceted and evolving worlds came Catherine McAuley, a single woman with great intelligence and a certain beauty. Only one lengthy verbal description of her physical appearance has survived. Written by the artist Mary Clare Augustine Moore, it refers to a meeting in 1829 when Catherine was fifty:

She . . . looked at least 10 years younger. She was very fair with a brilliant color on her cheeks, still not too red. Her face was a short oval but the contour was perfect.

---

ed in the "Catalogue of Books" at the end of P. Baker's *Devout Communicant* (York: Cornelius Croshaw, 1834) and in the lists of books published by the Catholic Book Society inserted at the end of the *Catholic Directory* (1840 and 1841). The book contained prayers Catherine McAuley evidently liked (CAM, in CMcATM, 213).

Her lips were thin, and her mouth rather wide, yet there was so much play and expression about it that I remarked it as the next agreeable feature in [her] face. Her eyes were light blue and remarkably round with the brows and lashes colorless but they spoke. In repose they had a melancholy beseeching look; then [they] would light up expressive of really hearty fun, or if she disapproved of anything they could tell that too. Sometimes they had that strange expression of reading your thoughts, which made you feel that even your mind was in her power, and that you could not hide anything from her. Her nose was straight but thick. She wore bands made from her own back hair which were so well managed as to be quite free from the disagreeable look bands of the kind usually give. The color was pale golden not in the least sandy, very fine and silky. She was dressed in black British merino which according to the fashion of the time fitted tight to her shape. She was remarkably well made, round but not in the least heavy. She had a good carriage, her hands were remarkably white but very clumsy, very large with broad square tips to the fingers and short square nails.[38]

Mary Vincent Harnett's published biography (1864) describes Catherine as "a little over the middle height, well proportioned and erect; her eyes grayish-blue and large, with a penetrating, but very benign expression; her deportment dignified and reserved, yet most kind."[39]

Although reproductions of the oil portrait painted after Catherine's death by Clare Augustine Moore, as well as slightly altered copies of it, multiplied and eventually appeared the world over, her early associates, at least those in Limerick, generally felt that even the original did not bear sufficient likeness to Catherine, and "little if any improvement was made in the new ones, save a more intelligent expression!"[40] The woman herself would not have worried much about how she might look in her posthumous portraits, unless, of course, they showed her as careless or slovenly in her dress, a trait she did not countenance.

This account of Catherine's life draws on a wide cast of characters. Among these are her immediate and extended family, her foster parents, her first companions, priests and bishops with whom she worked, women who helped or supported her, directly or indirectly, and her solicitor, ever patient and resourceful. Here also are dozens of others who peopled her life at one time or another, in one way or another—those dying in hovels, an outcast and mentally ill old woman, a young woman needing a leg amputation, the stagecoach drivers and benefactors she thanked, the physi-

38. CAM, in *CMcATM*, 202.

39. [Mary Vincent Harnett], *Life of Rev. Mother Catherine McAuley*, ed. Richard Baptist O'Brien (Dublin: John F. Fowler, 1864), 206.

40. Handwritten "Limerick Annals," 97 (ASB).

cians she engaged for others and, only when forced to do so, for herself.[41]

Finally, a biographer is faced with the impossibility of even perceiving, let alone chronicling, the action of God in Catherine McAuley's life. And yet that action might still be said to be a theme of this book. Although her letters and other writings and sayings provide insights about her, Catherine was generally reserved about what went on within her own spirit. As an associate once claimed: "She was too humble to talk much about self."[42] Another has said much the same: "It is only by her acts we can judge of her mind. She was perfectly silent as to what she thought."[43] Catherine believed strongly in the value of example over words. So in the end the biographer must, it seems, make do with distantly inferring her relationship with her God in her few allusive words, her acts, and the example she gave. This distance allows us to come as close as one ought to her interior life.

Which is not to say that all in this biography will be serious and solemn. That would be not only untrue to Catherine's temperament, but unfaithful to the record she left behind. Here is a woman who played a practical joke on the bishop of Charleston, who wrote teasing acrostics to a pastor in London, who baptized two wounded knees "Cholera and Cholerene," who laughed at her own blunders, who twice plotted with novices to create a "Nonsensical Club." The following pages are replete with simple things she valued: music, "pure sparkling spring water," "plain, simple, durable" buildings, "a good cup of tea."

Drawing on her own metaphors, we may say that Catherine McAuley wished "to be like those rivers which enter into the sea without losing any of the sweetness of the water," and to bestow herself in service of "the fire Christ cast on the earth."[44] May this biography do justice, however inadequate, to her goodness, her sweetness, and her courage.

41. This introduction has aimed only to set the stage and list the cast, as it were. It has not, therefore, seemed the right moment to comment on Catherine McAuley's efforts or those of other Irish women in her era and either side of it to transform, as much as lay in their power, the society of their time. Yet these women, some of whom will appear in the following pages, amply justify the challenging title and thesis of Mary Peckham Magray's comprehensive 1998 book: *The Transforming Power of the Nuns: Women, Religion, and Cultural Change in Ireland, 1750–1900* (New York: Oxford University Press) goes a long way toward highlighting and seeking to account for (though not without an occasional debatable suggestion) the striking historical phenomena that occurred by 1900.

42. CML, in *CMcATM*, 92.

43. Mary Elizabeth Moore to Mary Ann Doyle, November 21, 1841, in *CMcATM*, 255.

44. Catherine McAuley, "Spirit of the Institute" (AIMGB), in *CCMcA*, 460; letter 180, July 28, 1840, in *CCMcA*, 282.

CHAPTER 1

James McGauley's Daughter 1778–1809

Near twilight, in an upstairs room in a large plain house on Baggot Street, Dublin, Catherine McAuley lies dying. Surrounded by many who love her, she asks Teresa Carton: "Will you tell the sisters to get a good cup of tea—I think the community room would be a good place—when I am gone, and to comfort one another, but God will comfort them."[1] The whole desire and effort of her life seem gathered in that one word "comfort," and its twofold expression.

The birth of a girl and the death of the woman bracket the historical and cultural space between these two human moments, a space of decisions, of words and silences, fears and hopes, sufferings and joys—and, mostly, of love. In the end, the beginning assumes new worth because of the in-between. But in the beginning what has not yet unfolded is unlived and unknown; the beginning is unrecognized for what it is, and perhaps, as in Catherine McAuley's case, the birth is even unrecorded, or only partly or inaccurately recorded.

Catherine Elizabeth McAuley was such a child and such a woman, her "in-between" lying hidden before her. She was born on September 29, in 1778 or at the latest 1781.[2] She lived as an infant and very young child with

1. MVWL [November 12, 1841], in CMcATM, 243.

2. The year of Catherine McAuley's birth cannot be identified. No birth record (not required in Ireland until 1864) or baptismal record has been located. The early biographical manuscripts written by her contemporaries, and the published biographies do not agree on the year, though, with one exception (Cork MS 1, now in MCA), they agree on September 29. Clare Augustine Moore's "Memoir," the Bermondsey Annals biography, and Carroll's Life ([Mary Austin Carroll], Life of Catherine McAuley [New

her parents and her younger (or older) sister, Mary—not in the spacious mansion called "Stormanstown House," as many have claimed, but in a house in the townland of Stormanstown just north of Dublin along the Ballymun Road. Her father, James McGauley, had brought his bride, Elinor Conway—about twenty or thirty years younger than he—to this house in the mid to late 1770s.[3]

A recently discovered newspaper advertisement raises significant questions about how long the family continued to reside in Stormanstown. Early in July 1783, James McGauley placed an advertisement three times in *Saunders's Newsletter* (Dublin). The advertisement implies his earlier lease of property in Stormanstown, but it also, and more importantly, suggests that the family now lived at No. 11 Fishamble Street on the south side of the River Liffey in the city, or at least that their father could normally be contacted there. The advertisement reads:

York: D. & J. Sadlier, 1866]) give 1786 or 1787, both of which are impossible since Catherine's father died in July 1783. Derry Large MS gives no year. Roland Burke Savage (*Catherine McAuley: The First Sister of Mercy* [Dublin: M. H. Gill and Son, 1949]), favors 1781, relying on the research of John MacErlean, who did extensive investigation of the issue, though MacErlean, in notes penned for Mary Bertrand Degnan, says, "The writer will have to choose between the different dates assigned for Catherine's birth" (MCA). Cork MS 1 and Cork MS 3 (the latter prepared by Mary Vincent Whitty and now in MCA), the two Limerick MSS, and Harnett's *Life* all give 1778, as does M. Angela Bolster (*Catherine McAuley, Venerable for Mercy* [Dublin: Dominican Publications, 1990]). Mary Bertrand Degnan (*Mercy unto Thousands: Life of Mother Mary Catherine McAuley* [Westminster, Md.: Newman Press, 1957]) and the present biographer note both 1778 and 1781 as possible years. However, in the present biography 1778 will be used in calculating Catherine McAuley's age at various times.

Further confusion arises from the fact that most of the early sources—especially the manuscripts attributable to Mary Ann Doyle and Mary Clare Moore—say that Catherine was the *second* child, born after her sister, Mary. The manuscripts emanating from Limerick and/or attributable to Mary Vincent Harnett, as well as her *Life* and Carroll's *Life*, all say that Catherine was the *eldest*, the first of three children. MacErlean's notes indicate that in Betham's handwritten "Abstract" of James McGauley's will, probated on August 2, 1783, the children are listed as "Mary, Catherine, and James," presumably in the order of their birth as was customary (IJA). However, another handwritten copy of Betham's "Abstracts" lists them as "James, Catherine, Mary," placing the son first, though he was born last (NLI, Go MS 239). It is not possible to identify the exact year of their parents' marriage, or of Mary's birth, and there are conflicting accounts of Mary's age at her death in 1827. For further explanation of this questions, see Burke Savage, *McAuley*, 418–19.

3. Although many early biographical manuscripts, but not all, and the subsequent published biographies of Catherine McAuley, say that she was born "in Stormanstown House," it appears more accurate, in light of the evidence, to say that she was born in a house "in Stormanstown," a townland north of Glasnevin according to *John Taylor's Map of the Environs of Dublin, 1816*. "Stormanstown House" designates one or other of a series of "great houses" on a large estate, each mansion succeeding an earlier one, at slightly different sites on the estate. The second house was probably built about the time of Catherine's birth, on the site of the first, from its materials, on the left hand side of the Ballymun Road as it heads north from the center of Dublin. Today a school and a library are near the former site of these two houses. The third Stormanstown House, now demolished, was probably across the Ballymun Road, on its right side, approximately where the substation of the Electricity Supply Board is now situated. Possibly the McGauley house was a lodge, gatehouse, or smaller house, with eighteen acres of grazing land, on part of a larger Santry or Stormanstown estate. Evidently Catherine's father, a carpenter, with property holdings, who identified himself as a "grazier" in 1778, leased a house and lands in the Stormanstown area sometime in the 1770s (though a deed for this location giving his name as a party to the deed has not been located). Today the Stormanstown area is called Ballymun.

House and Land

A Handsome House, Garden, and Offices, beautifully situated, with eighteen Acres of Land in great Heart, to let at Stormanstown, near Glasnevin, about two Miles from the Linen Hall [an establishment on George's Hill housing the board regulating linen manufacture]; there are all Manner of Fixtures; the Tenant can have immediate Possession. Inquire of James M'Gauley, No. 11, Fishamble-street.

A good House, with a large Shop and Warehouse, fit for any Business that requires Room, No. 10, in Fishamble-street, to let. Inquire as above.[4]

For land to be "in great heart" meant in good condition, fertile, productive, capable of producing what it was intended for. James McGauley's leased grazing land in Stormanstown was not untested.

Fishamble Street is one of the oldest streets in the oldest part of the city of Dublin, to the east of Christ Church; it derived its name from the fishmongers who operated there from at least the fifteenth century. Unless there is a misprint in the advertisement and Nos. 10 and 11 were not separate dwellings—the advertisement is identical in all three issues—James McGauley owned two, probably three, houses here and was now planning to lease ("to let") one of them, as well as the house and land in Stormanstown.[5] He had evidently long been interested in property in this area on the south side of the city, below the River Liffey.[6]

On October 6, 1778, at Kilmainham, James McGauley, "grazier, residing

4. "House and Land," *Saunders's Newsletter,* July 2, 5, and 9, 1783.
5. The difference between "owning" and "leasing" in Irish deeds in this period can be confusing. The land on which a house was built was generally only leased, for a certain number of years; the house itself might be owned or leased. A house built on leased land was owned by the person who built it unless some clause in the land lease restricted this. An unexpired lease could be further leased (sublet) by the current lessee. Moreover, the future annual lease payments (rent) for a house or land could be "redeemed" in advance if the owner would permit this and if the payments, over time or all at once, added up to the owner's sale or lease price. In James McGauley's time and earlier it would have been rare for anyone to *own* land other than the great estate landlords, such as Domville, the Gardiner family, Fitzwilliam, and a few Catholic estate owners (in 1704 only 14 percent of the land in Ireland was still owned by Catholics), certainly not a person of James McGauley's relatively limited means. Deeds of indenture (lease) or assignment (sale of the holding or of the remaining term of the lease) were usually registered, but not always, at the Registry of Deeds (RD). "Memorials" at the registry are handwritten transcripts of the major features of a deed, and occasionally contain inaccuracies or missing information. Each memorial has a number: book number.page number.transcript number.
6. At least nine times over the years 1756 through January 1783, James McGauley had leased, from or to others, properties on the south side of Copper Alley on both sides of Fishamble Street, on Merchants Quay between Adam and Eve's Alley and Skipper's Lane, on the south side of St. Nicholas Street, on Span's Lane, and on St. James's Street. These properties included dwelling houses, stables, warehouses, a brewery malt house, tenements, the sites of taverns once known as the Queen's Head and the King's Head Inn, and, in one case, a house he had partly built. In the memorials of these deeds James McGauley was various identified as a carpenter, a merchant, a timber merchant, later (1779) "of Stormanstown ... Esquire" and, in January 1783, "of Stormanstown ... Gentleman." One of these transactions was with a priest, John Field, attached to St. Audeon's chapel, later to St. Michael's, Rosemary Lane. All these transactions were carefully registered. Memorial nos. 183.439.123399; 201.373.133223; 204.151.134826; 204.162.134864; 223.358.148566; 226.362.147831; 325.508.222032; 331.137.221098; and 350.182.235016, RD.

at Stormanstown," had taken the oath of allegiance to the king recently prescribed by the Irish Parliament, and confirmed by the English Parliament.[7] The first Catholic Relief Act (1778) allowed Catholics reciting this oath to take leases on lands for 999 years and permitted them to inherit property in the same way as Protestants, thus abolishing these commercial restrictions of the penal code.

By a deed of assignment dated April 29, 1783, and registered on May 8, 1783, before the advertisement in *Saunders's Newsletter*, James McGauley sold a property on the east side Fishamble Street, that known by "the sign of the Butler's Arms," to John Dowling, grocer, subject to the payment of £200 by October 29, 1783.[8] McGauley's properties on the east side of Fishamble Street were bordered on the north by Copper Alley, a narrow cobbled lane, now overarched, that takes its name from the copper money once coined and distributed there.[9] In April 1742 Handel's *Messiah* was first publicly performed in the Music Hall next to the alley.

Exactly when the family moved from Stormanstown to Fishamble Street is not known. They probably did so by early 1783, for Catherine's only brother was evidently born here in April. He was baptized James William in nearby St. Michael's chapel, Rosemary Lane, on May 1, 1783.

Perhaps the flurry of leasing in the spring and early summer of 1783 was related to some growing sense in Catherine's father that he was dying, or at least that he was aging, and that he needed to provide his wife and children with regular income. He was probably now in his sixties or early seventies. Then some time in mid-July 1783, James McGauley died. The exact date and cause of his death are unknown. The abstract of his will, where he is identified as "James McGauley of Copper Alley," says his will was dated July 18 and probated on August 2, 1783.[10] Catherine was not yet five years old.

As the years passed, her childhood memories of her father, though faint, are said to have clustered around his religious instructions and charities to poor children in the Stormanstown and Fishamble neighborhoods, carried on against the backdrop of her mother's frequent complaints about

7. Typescript, John MacErlean to Mary Dominick Foster, April 1, 1942, reporting on his discovery of the registration of McGauley's oath in the Catholic Qualification Rolls in the Public Record Office, Dublin (MCA).

8. "Attested Copy of Memorial of Deed of Assignment, James McGauley and John Dowling, April 29, 1783" (MCA). Memorial no. 343.286.236118, RD.

9. C. T. M'Cready, *Dublin Street Names* (Dublin: Hodges, Figgis, 1892), 25.

10. William Betham, "Abstracts of Prerogative Wills, Genealogical Abstracts, 1781–1791," vol. 17, p. 133, Go MS 239 (NLI).

his unreasonably generous gift of his time and resources. Carl Jung claims of his own childhood recollections: "My memories begin with my second or third year. . . . These are nothing but islands of memory afloat in a sea of vagueness, each by itself, apparently with no connection between them."[11] Catherine's memories of her father would have been of this sort.

In later years she came to know not only her father's real-estate talents but his long-remembered building and woodworking skills. While the evidence is sparse and indirect, it is estimated that James McGauley was born not later than the early 1720s, and that he was apprenticed for seven years as a carpenter by the time he was fourteen. He was eventually employed with his future father-in-law in the construction of the new St. Mary's chapel off Liffey Street, on the site of part of the former Cistercian Abbey of St. Mary. The abbey was founded in the early years of the twelfth century on a wide sweep of land north of the River Liffey. It was suppressed by Henry VIII on October 25, 1539, the land confiscated and repeatedly parceled out to various loyalists over the next two hundred years.[12]

In 1707 Edmund Byrne had been appointed archbishop of Dublin. His appointment continued the bold moves, begun by Roman church authorities in the late 1660s, to restore the Catholic hierarchy in Ireland. For Byrne the possibility of arrest, imprisonment, and forced transportation to a distant English colony was ever present. Moreover, small unobtrusive Catholic chapels served by registered priests, though sometimes tolerated, were often peremptorily closed by governmental authority. These realities highlight the courage of Archbishop Byrne when, in the first year of his appointment, he created two new Catholic parishes in the large northern district of Dublin, dividing the existing parish of St. Michan's into St. Paul's, St. Mary's, and St. Michan's. He named John Linegar parish priest of St. Mary's.[13]

Contrary to the letter of the penal laws, John Linegar decided to build a chapel for his St. Mary's parishioners—who were worshipping in private homes or at St. Michan's on Mary's Lane—and he chose to employ for the work Catherine McAuley's future grandfather and father. Catherine McAuley's second cousin, Catherine Byrn, says that her great-grandfather

---

11. Carl Jung, *Memories, Dreams, Reflections*, ed. Aniela Jaffé (New York: Random House, 1963), 6.

12. This paragraph depends for some of its detail on Nicholas Donnelly, "Parish of the Immaculate Conception," in *History of Dublin Parishes* (Dublin: Catholic Truth Society, [1904–1917]), part 12, 71–81.

13. Hugh Fenning, "The Archbishops of Dublin, 1693–1786," in Kelly and Keogh, *History of the Catholic Diocese of Dublin*, 178–80, which summarizes the experience of the Irish Catholic Church in the penal era, particularly in Dublin during James McGauley's life.

John Conway was the "brick and stone" contractor, James McGauley was the contractor for the "wood work," and the oaken pulpit in the chapel was McGauley's work.[14] Presumably he also made the pillars and cornices surrounding the altar, and perhaps even the altar.

Nicholas Donnelly claims that the chapel was "opened" in 1729, but given the political and religious pressures in Dublin at the time it is conceivable that the interior work on it proceeded slowly over many years.[15] A government manuscript in the British Library, dated 1749, describes the chapel as it was by that date:

A chapel in Liffey Street was built in 1729 by collections made among the R.C.'s [Roman Catholics] of the Parish. . . . This Chapel, though small, is neat, altar railed in, steps ascending to it of oak, fore part of the altar covered with gilt leather, and name of Jesus in glory in the midst. . . . The altar piece carved and embellished with four pillars, cornices and other decorations gilt and painted. The picture of the Conception of B. V. M. to whom the Chapel is dedicated, fills the altar piece. . . . Near it is a neat oak pulpit, on the sounding board of which is the figure of a gilt dove representing the descent of the Holy Ghost. In said Chapel is a small sacristy, four decent confessionals, two galleries, several pews for the better sort, and two sprinkling pots of black marble in Chapel yard.[16]

Catherine Byrn claims that "when the old Chapel was being broken up (in 1827 or '28, I think)," because a splendid new St. Mary's church had been built to the east on Marlborough Street, "the pulpit was sent to Baggot Street 'to Mrs. McAuley because it was her Father's work.'"[17] What subsequently happened to the oak pulpit is not known.

In 1784, a year after her husband's death, the young Elinor McGauley (probably then in her early thirties) moved her family further out of the city, setting up in the "new brick and stone house" on the road leading to Glasnevin, on the north side of the city.[18] Then three years later they

14. Mary Raymond (Catherine) Byrn, to Mary Margaret (Anne) Byrn [October 6, 1867] (MCA). The letter is dated "Rosary Sunday," October 6 in 1867.

15. Donnelly, "Parish of the Immaculate Conception," in *History of Dublin Parishes*, part 12, 83.

16. Ibid. The British Library manuscript is quoted by Donnelly. Permission to quote this manuscript has been granted by the British Library.

17. Mary Raymond Byrn to Mary Margaret Byrn [October 6, 1867] (MCA).

18. No birth, baptismal, or marriage record of Elinor Conway McGauley has been located, though biographers have regarded her as possibly twenty or thirty years younger than her husband, a young partner in her father's building endeavors. By a deed of assignment, June 28, 1787, she assigned the house on Glasnevin Road to Dr. Huson Bigger, a Dublin surgeon (memorial no. 389.470.257474, RD). However, this memorial notes that she was assigning the dwelling "together with a certain Indented Deed of Lease of 24th of June 1784 and made between John Moore of the City of Dublin, Esquire, of the one part and Elinor McGauley of the said City of Dublin, widow, of the other part." No memorial of this 1784 deed can be found (perhaps it was never registered). Another memorial (no. 388.260.258072, RD) indicates that by a deed of assignment dated July 7, 1787, and registered on August 8, 1787, Moore seems to make over to

moved again, leasing a house at 52 Queen Street, also on the north side and near a Protestant friend, a Mrs. St. George.[19] Catherine, still a child at the time of this last move, was probably tutored at home by her mother and possibly by Mrs. St. George or a governess. Though she was obviously literate and cultured, no record of her attending a school for girls has been found. Beyond her studies, Catherine did what young girls do: read books at night by the light of a candle in a box, learned to print, played with her young brother, James, who called her "Kitty," and sometimes got him in trouble by doing his school work for him incorrectly. She also began her lifelong habit of writing verses, which was, in her youth, as she later acknowledged, "my pastime, my folly, my play."[20] That she was very close to her sister, Mary, seems evident from the intimate trust Mary placed in her years later.

During these years, while Catherine was growing to be an attractive blonde-haired young woman with a charming, gentle, but determined manner, her mother was evidently growing away from all but the minimum of Catholic practice. A later and close associate of Catherine's says that Elinor McGauley "was a very amiable and accomplished person; her mind was highly cultivated, but her religious principles were defective; hence she considered liberty of conscience so essential that she thought constraint, or the obligation of performing any duties of religion foreign to its spirit."[21] However, she did see to it that her children were confirmed and learned the natural virtues, such as courtesy and truthfulness. Though Catherine's First Communion may have occurred after her mother's death, she was probably confirmed in St. Paul's Chapel, Arran Quay by Archbishop John Troy in 1789–1791 or in 1796. Throughout her life she treasured Confirmation and wanted children to understand "the nature of the Sacrament, the gifts and graces it imparts, which depends so much on the preparation."[22] Perhaps, in retrospect, she saw this sacramental mo-

---

Bigger the same property as described in memorial no. 389.470.257474, RD. Despite research, I have not been able to reconcile this memorial with the one recording Elinor McAuley's deed to Dr. Bigger.

19. Neither the deed nor its memorial for the June 6, 1787, lease of the house at 52 Queen Street has been discovered. However, the memorial of a deed dated August 13, 1796, and registered on August 17, 1796, by which Elinor McGauley leased that house for the residue of the lease (about twenty-two more years) to John Healy for a yearly rent of £24 indicates that her original lease from Elinor Keating for thirty-one years was dated June 6, 1787 (memorial no. 504.14.324940, RD). The 1787 deed may not have been registered, which was not uncommon.

20. Letter 174 [c. June 7, 1840], in CCMcA, 271.   21. BA, in CMcATM, 99.

22. Customarily a child received the sacrament of Confirmation before receiving First Communion. John MacErlean estimates that Catherine was confirmed in 1796 (when she was fifteen or eighteen), or in the period 1789–1791, that is, when she was between eight and thirteen years old, depending on her birth year. No Confirmations occurred in Dublin in the years 1798, 1799, or 1800 because of the unsettled po-

ment in her own young life as having conferred a then-unnamed strength on which she had later depended so heavily.[23]

Elinor McGauley died, probably at the Conways' home (East Arran Street) on or near October 21, 1798, in what some commentators on Catherine's life have called a religiously tormented death, and a searing memory for her daughter.[24] By then, the family was already suffering from what one of Catherine's early biographers called "pecuniary losses": the gradual evaporation, through sales and perhaps overspending, of income from James McGauley's properties in Dublin.[25] Although she is named as executrix of her husband's and relatives' real estate in several deeds in the 1780s and 1790s, managing money was probably more than Elinor McGauley, a fashionable but financially inexperienced widow, could handle. Consequently, at the time of her mother's death, Catherine was living or about to live with her maternal uncle, the surgeon Owen Conway, and his wife, Catherine Mary Brett, on East Arran Street. Here she grew close to her cousin Anne, their only child—in a friendship that would lead, some two decades later, to Catherine's adoption of two of Anne's children.

Owen Conway, born in 1754 and married in 1779, had apprenticed to Israel Read, a well-known Dublin surgeon, one of the founders of the Royal College of Surgeons in Ireland in 1784.[26] Sometime in the late 1790s, when he apparently ceased to practice as a surgeon, Conway's financial resources began to collapse. This reversal was evidently brought on, in part, by his own behavior, if Catherine Byrn's account, written decades later, can be trusted. She says that her grandfather's "apprenticeship to Surgeon Read was the occasion of plunging him into dissipation and recklessness [and] the Sacraments were neglected."[27] In 1794 Israel Read resigned from the Meath Hospital because "my health at present will not permit me to reside in Dublin."[28] He died in 1795. Whether Catherine Byrn accurately described

litical atmosphere, and those in 1797 and 1801 were in outlying regions of the diocese. Archbishop Troy's register gives only the numbers confirmed, not their names or the parishes where confirmed (MACE/CMAU/1, in IJA). If Catherine received First Communion while her mother was living, she did so before late October 1798, probably in St. Paul's on Arran Quay (BA, in CMcATM, 99; Lim, in CMcATM, 140).

23. Letter 52, August 31, 1837, in CCMcA, 93.

24. Burke Savage, McAuley, 22, cites no source for the date of Elinor McGauley's death, but MacErlean indicates that she was buried in the churchyard of St. James (Protestant) church, Church Street on October 23, 1798 (MACE/MCAU/7, in IJA). Catholics were buried in Protestant churchyards at least until October 1829; until then no Catholic parish had burial grounds. William J. Fitzpatrick, History of the Dublin Catholic Cemeteries (Dublin: Published at the Offices, 1900), 1, 16. On the nature of Elinor's death, see Burke Savage, McAuley, 23; Degnan, Mercy, 9; Carroll, Life, 60–61.

25. BA, in CMcATM, 99.   26. "Index to the Kirkpatrick Archive" (RCPI).

27. Mary Raymond Byrn to Mary Margaret Byrn [October 6, 1867] (MCA).

28. Lambert Hepenstal Ormsby, Medical History of the Meath Hospital and County Dublin Infirmary (Dublin: Fannin, 1888), 171–73.

her grandfather's lifestyle or whether Read's influence or death contributed indirectly to Owen Conway's eventual bankruptcy cannot be known. However, of her grandfather Byrn also claims that she often heard Catherine McAuley say: "Amidst all his gaiety and revels, he retained to the last day of his life, the highest reverence for religious things and religious persons."[29] While Owen Conway disappears from public medical records after 1797, he must have survived to his daughter Anne's marriage around 1801 to James Byrn (or Byrne), a Dublin printer, and may have lived through the births of some if not all of the four Byrn children. Certainly the second child, Catherine, born on March 19, 1812, felt she knew him.

Catherine McAuley soon realized that her staying on in the Conway house meant one more person for the family to try to feed. She therefore accepted the offer of the William Armstrongs, relatives of her mother or family friends, to live with them in their home at 34 Mary Street near the Apothecaries Hall on Mary Street. Armstrong was an apothecary, and Catherine's sister, Mary, and her brother, James, were already living with his family. Catherine's move, taken out of concern for the Conways' increasing poverty, was not without serious drawbacks.

The Conways were generally a devout Catholic family, and living among them had allowed Catherine to develop and freely practice her faith. Catherine Byrn argues that "to her living with my Grandfather, by whom she was much beloved, during the greater part of the time . . . which elapsed between her Mother's death and her going to reside with Mr. and Mrs. O'Callaghan [sic]," Catherine McAuley "was, under God, indebted for the preservation of her Faith, which, by being thrown at an early age completely amongst Protestants, her Brother and Sister unhappily lost."[30]

The Protestant and Catholic portions of the Irish and Anglo-Irish populations at this time were sharply, often bitterly, divided. Public and private encounters were often emotionally painful, exacerbated by mutual ignorance of each other's true beliefs, by incendiary public barbs and controversies, as well as by sincere differences of religious opinions and emphases in theology. Moreover, the ease with which Catholics could reasonably ascribe their past and present—indeed centuries-long—political and economic restrictions and suppression to "Protestants," and the understandable insecurity which Protestants experienced as the minority in

---

29. Mary Raymond Byrn to Mary Margaret Byrn [October 6, 1867] (MCA).

30. Ibid. Byrn also suggests that "4 or 5 years" elapsed between Elinor McGauley's death (1798) and Catherine McAuley's moving in with the Callaghans. During this time she lived with the Conways, then the Armstrongs on Mary Street, and then the Callaghans at their home on Mary Street. Exactly when and for how long she lived with the first two families is unclear from the available evidence.

a population now seeking further repeal of the governmental prerogatives and protections against Catholic influences that Protestants had long enjoyed, only worsened the conflict between the two Christian populations. Bigotry and religious rancor were in the air, especially in Dublin. Charges of "popery" and countercharges of "proselytism" were common, and the rhetoric of sermons and letters in the press often inflamed both public debate and parlor conversation.

William Armstrong was an educated Protestant. In his household Catherine, now in her early twenties, enjoyed the generosity of a man trying to do his best for the three McAuleys. But he was also, apparently, intolerant in his assessment of Catholic religious perspectives and "superstitions." Mary Vincent Harnett (who treats Catherine as younger than she was at the time) describes the years spent in the Armstrong home as a time of growth and hospitality, but also of religious tension and embarrassment:

[Armstrong] took compassion on the children and assumed the care and responsibility of their education. Whatever pecuniary means remained to them were vested in his medical establishment [Apothecaries Hall], and the revenue that accrued therefrom was applied as a provision for their instruction and subsistence. In their new position they seem to have been amply supplied with every thing their worldly wants required; but their guardian, whether from any indifference of his own on such an important subject, or not wishing to interfere with the children of Catholic parents, took no interest in their religious instruction. Thus brought up in the midst of a Protestant family, completely separated from all intercourse with the members of the persuasion to which they belonged, hearing day after day the usual misrepresentations of its rites and practices, and having no opportunity of having these misrepresentations removed, the result may be easily conjectured. The brother James adopted the creed of those with whom he lived. His sister Mary lost by degrees the few Catholic impressions that were made upon her mind in childhood. . . . Catherine, the eldest, having been more perfectly impressed with Catholic principles, was more proof against the influence to which she was subjected.[31]

Harnett may have gained her understanding of the Armstrong interlude directly from Catherine McAuley, with whom she lived for two years, or more likely from Catherine's friend Elizabeth Moore, with whom Harnett lived while writing her manuscript. Other early biographers who knew Catherine well are relatively silent about this period in her life. Unfortunately, two of these crucial manuscripts now lack their early pages.

What is certain is that, beginning with her years in the Armstrong household, and continuing for some time afterwards, Catherine endured conversations that either mildly or severely ridiculed her Catholic faith.

31. Lim, in *CMcATM*, 141.

Simultaneously, she searched for greater understanding of its beliefs and more frequent opportunities to follow its practices—without offending the sensibilities of those with whom she lived and for whom she had genuine gratitude and affection.

In the early 1800s, when she was possibly twenty-five, Catherine made the first of three far-reaching decisions that would shape her later life. She accepted the invitation of William and Catherine Callaghan, friends of the Armstrongs, to live with them and then later move with them to their newly leased estate in Coolock, a village northeast of Dublin. The Callaghans had lived for many years at 18 Silver Court, off Castle Street near Dublin Castle, and were probably now living at 31 Mary Street.[32]

The Callaghan couple was childless and had returned, apparently about 1785–1786, from India, where William Callaghan may have served as an apothecary. The only evidence so far discovered that possibly relates to his years in India is the reference to a "William Callaghan" who was the purser in 1777–1778 on an East India Company ship, the *Grosvenor*, which sailed from Plymouth, England, on February 9, 1778, bound for Madras and Bengal.[33] Callaghan was nominally a Protestant (Church of Ireland) in his religious thinking; his wife was a Quaker by upbringing.

Safety concerns could have motivated a peaceable older couple like the Callaghans to want to move from Silver Court, then from Mary Street and out of central Dublin. Horrific reprisals against the largely nonsectarian, anti-government forces who had waged, or were presumed to have plotted, the various uncoordinated and ultimately unsuccessful rebellions of the

32. Exactly when the Callaghans moved from Silver Court to Mary Street is not clear. John MacErlean says Callaghan leased a Silver Court property to Robert Powell in 1799 (MACE/MCAU/25[2], in IJA), but no memorial of such a deed has been found. Moreover, by a deed of assignment dated May 13, 1805, William Callaghan, "apothecary," assigned to the governors and overseers of the Public Works in Ireland for the sum of £100 "that House and premises in Silver Court, Castle Street . . . wherein the said William Callaghan lived" (memorial no. 566.400.384146, RD). Therefore, the Callaghans *may* have lived in Silver Court on the south side of Castle Street until 1805. However, the *Dublin Directory* gives William Callaghan's address as 18 Silver Court only through 1799; thereafter it is listed as "31 Mary Street" until 1814, and then as "38 Mary Street" from 1814 until 1821 (streets were renumbered in this period).

No memorial of a deed by which William Callaghan himself leased a dwelling on Mary Street has so far been found. Probably the Callaghans were by 1800 or shortly thereafter living in premises belonging to the Hall. On May 15, 1798, he had been "appointed superintendent to the Hall" and its laboratory ("Index to the Second Book of the transactions of the Corporation of Apothecaries Hall . . . 2nd May 1796 ending 31 July 1807," AAH). Thus he could have leased *a* house on Silver Court to Robert Powell in 1799, as MacErlean notes. After 1809, when he was clearly living in Coolock (see note 37 below), Callaghan continued to list in the *Dublin Directory* the Mary Street address as his place of business. The official address of Apothecaries Hall in the *Dublin Directory* for these years is simply "Mary Street."

33. Anthony Farrington, *A Biographical Index of East India Company Maritime Service Officers, 1600–1834* (London: British Library, 1999), 126. Given his later financial expertise, our William Callaghan may well have been the "William Callaghan," purser on the *Grosvenor* bound for India in 1778. He may also have gone to India earlier.

1790s, especially in 1798, were commonplace on Dublin streets. Men who had favored separation from England for political and economic reasons—or at least for greater Irish control of Ireland's internal affairs—were often, with the encouragement of Dublin Castle and the English Crown, severely punished, even hanged, in public view, in an effort to show insurrectionists that revolt against English rule and its social, political, and economic regulations would not be tolerated.

Following the Irish Parliament's acquiescent decision to vote itself out of existence, secured in part by bribery, the British Parliament's Act of Union in 1800 formally integrated Ireland into the United Kingdom. It was England's last-ditch effort to preempt Irish nationalist goals that had been somewhat encouraged by the American and French revolutions. The act, taking effect on January 1, 1801, had been accompanied by British Prime Minister William Pitt's promise that full emancipation of Irish Catholics would soon follow, giving them the right to sit in the British Parliament and hold other high offices—a concession intended to mollify them by completing repeal of the remaining penal laws against them. However, the act itself and the promise only enlarged the agitation.

Dublin Protestants, already fearful of the gradual loss of their sectarian privileges, became increasingly angry at the departure to England of many of the Anglo-Irish nobility and of members of the now-defunct Irish Parliament. Loss of income in the Dublin trades and crafts was immediate and widespread. On the other hand, Catholics who had welcomed the earlier repeals of several penal restrictions (in 1778, 1782, 1792, and 1793) became angered as Pitt's promise remained unfulfilled in London, and George III declared against it. When in September 1803 Robert Emmet, a Protestant and a United Irishman, was charged with high treason—following the murder of Lord Kilwarden—and executed by hanging on a Dublin street, the atmosphere only worsened.

Though William Callaghan had no part in any of this violence, and records give no indication that he was directly affected by it, he nonetheless chose, at least by 1809, to move with his wife, Catherine, to more serene surroundings in the village of Coolock, about four miles northeast of Mary Street.[34] He presumably would not have been an advocate of either Catholic Emancipation or excessive English control of Irish life. He was a medical man, an apothecary, a member of the healing profession. Now, probably in his mid-sixties, he deserved and welcomed at least partial re-

34. See note 37 below.

tirement in Coolock, although he continued his very skilled administrative work at Apothecaries Hall.

The Corporation of Apothecaries of Dublin had come into existence through an act of parliament in 1791, although the Guild of St. Luke (apothecaries) had been active in Dublin since its charter in 1745. The impetus for the corporation came from two pressing concerns: the scientific quality, or feared lack thereof, of drugs and potions being dispensed in Ireland, and the qualifications of those preparing and dispensing the medicines, among whom were evidently many self-proclaimed but untrained druggists. Although William Callaghan listed himself in the *Dublin Directory* of 1786 as simply a "druggist," both he and his colleague William Armstrong were experienced, competent pharmacists even before the creation of Apothecaries Hall.

When Apothecaries Hall was formed in 1791, William Armstrong was a founding member and William Callaghan joined by 1793. Initially "Apothecaries Hall" was simply the designation of the organization. However, after several unsuccessful attempts to secure a site, the physical headquarters was eventually located at 38 (later renumbered 40) Mary Street.[35] The key decision makers of the Hall were its governor, deputy governor, a thirteen-member elected Court of Directors, and its secretary and treasurer. The directors, meeting with the governor, often weekly, made yea or nay judgments about the readiness of applicants from all over Ireland to be certified as apprentices or apothecaries. They rigorously upheld the rules formulated at one of the inaugural meetings of the Hall.

William Armstrong and William Callaghan played major roles in the Hall. Both served occasionally as governor: Armstrong in 1802–1803 and again in 1807–1808; Callaghan in 1813–1814 and again in 1819–1820. Armstrong was deputy governor in 1801–1802, and Callaghan in 1818–1819. One or both of them served on the influential Court of Directors nearly every year when they did not hold the posts of governor or deputy governor. Moreover, Callaghan served as secretary of the Hall in the early years and then as both secretary and treasurer for at least twenty-five years.[36]

To Coolock House—the place that would make such an enormous difference in the direction of her life—Catherine McAuley went with the Callaghans in 1809, little realizing what lay in store for her beyond the gai-

35. "Minutes of the Apothecaries Hall, Dublin," vol. 1: 1791–1796; vol. 2: 1796–1807; vol. 3: 1807–1821; vol. 4: 1821–1828 (AAH).

36. "Minutes of the Apothecaries Hall, Dublin," vols. 2 and 3 (AAH). Most of these minutes are written or signed by William Callaghan.

ety and security of a comfortable home.[37] Years later she compared moving from place to place to dancing the Sir Roger de Coverley, a favorite English parlor dance, and claimed that "we have one solid comfort amidst this little tripping about: our hearts can always be in the same place, centered in God."[38] It is doubtful that she felt fully "centered in God" when she went to Coolock, but even in her youth she had had her share of "tripping about." Since her birth, she had lived in at least seven, and now eight, houses, as she gradually grew from the child of a relatively successful carpenter, timber merchant, grazier, and "gentleman" (as her father was variously identified in government documents and deeds), to the teenage daughter of a widowed mother who was unsuccessful in handling the income of inherited properties, to an orphaned young woman dependent for her bed and board on relatives or friends, to one now grateful for a place in her adopted home. While she had never been, literally, homeless, she had known the interior homelessness of constant uprooting. The Callaghans loved Catherine from the start—as the daughter they never had—but she had no way of knowing or even imagining that their affection would lead her, fifteen years later, to the second major decision of her life.

37. Uncertainty has existed about exactly when the Callaghans, with Catherine McAuley, moved to Coolock. By a deed of release dated July 27, 1803, and registered on October 10, 1803, Sir Charles Domville "granted" to Edward Houghton (Haughton?) of William Street, Dublin "that part of the Lands of Coolock . . . in the Parish and Barony of Coolock and County of Dublin containing, by a survey lately made thereof, 22 acres and 31 perches," bounded on the northeast by other Domville lands, on the northwest by the turnpike from Dublin, on the southwest by Mary Land (sic) Domain then also in the possession of Sir Charles Domville, at an annual rent of £151.9.4 (memorial no. 553.537.370915, RD). A perch was normally equal to 1/160th of an acre.

By a deed of release dated April 26, 1809, and registered that day, Edward Houghton and his brother Joseph, both of Dublin (presumably heirs of Edward Houghton), released the same property and sold the dwelling to "William Callaghan of Mary Street in the City of Dublin, Esquire." The annual rent on the land was "£151.1.4 [sic, perhaps a scribal error]," payable to Sir Compton Domville, eldest son of Sir Charles Domville. The "sum of £600 . . . paid by the said William Callaghan" to the Houghtons probably refers to the redemption of the land lease or to the purchase price of (or a down payment on?) the dwelling and other buildings Edward Houghton had erected or improved (memorial no. 607.354.417041, RD).

The memorial of the deed of conveyance by which Catherine McAuley sold the buildings and released the lands to Henry Brooke in 1828 (memorial no. 838.346.562924, RD), refers to "the original lease of said premises . . . bearing the date 27th day of July 1803," but the 1828 memorial does not name Edward Houghton. Whether the house was leased to Callaghan earlier than 1809 is not clear from any of the memorials cited, but unlikely. Douglas Appleyard says: "The ground landlord was Sir Charles Domville, of Santry Court, who, in 1803, leased 22 acres to a barrister by the name of Edward Haughton, with renewals. The lease was dated on the 2nd [sic] July, that year. Mr. Haughton spent the then large sum of £1,800 on his estate over the next year or so. He built the original house (probably the drawing room end of the present house), and the out-offices to go with it.

"In March, 1804, Haughton sub-let a quarter of an acre for £2 per annum to a solicitor. This piece of land was near the avenue at the Brookville House side. Five years and one month later, Haughton finally transferred the land to William Callaghan, a wealthy chemist. As part of his deal, he took over the solicitor as sitting tenant." Douglas S. Appleyard, *Green Fields Gone Forever* (Dublin: Douglas S. Appleyard, 1985), 120.

38. Letter 220 [December 20, 1840], in CCMcA, 332.

CHAPTER 2

With the Callaghans at Coolock 1809–1822

The gardens, orchards, and cornfields of Coolock, the yews, hazel trees, and heather, must have been a delight to Catherine McAuley. Years later, she urged a sickly friend in Birr: "I hope you have the charity to eat some fresh fruit off the trees, walking in the garden—as that is the way fruit is most beneficial to delicate constitutions."[1] The estate with its land, outbuildings, and indoor and outdoor servants was far different from any city dwelling Catherine had ever known, though, in later life, remembering the poverty of her uncle Owen Conway's household, she "often said that she took her rest more contentedly on the boards than when surrounded by luxuries." She "used to conclude that we are much better able to endure hardships . . . than we usually imagine, and that happiness does not depend on the enjoyment of temporal comforts, since many in great poverty are most joyful."[2]

The name Coolock, according to Douglas Appleyard, "is derived from the Irish word *culóg* which is translated as 'little corner.'"[3] It is ironic that Catherine, who is now known as far away as Johannesburg, Papua New Guinea, Santiago, and Perth, should have spent so many formative years of her adult life in a small village with such a name. From the morning room in the house, looking to the east across the meadows of the townland, she could see Dublin Bay and its rolling waves.

1. Letter 306 [September 26, 1841], in *CCMcA*, 441.
2. BA, in *CMcATM*, 100.
3. Appleyard, *Green Fields*, 1.

A present-day reader may wonder why Catherine did not move out on her own, why she continued to live in the homes of whoever offered her a place. If she was twenty years old when her mother died, even older when she left the Conways, and still older when she left the Armstrongs, why did she go with the Callaghans on Mary Street and then to Coolock? What were her options in the early 1800s? Marriage or some form of live-in domestic service or home-teaching. A respectable single woman did not choose to live alone, unless she was a widow. Moreover, even if this were socially acceptable, it required independent financial means, which Catherine did not have. Though no will of Elinor McGauley has been discovered, and though she may have thought of herself as fashionably middle class, it seems that she and her children were classifiable as "poor" even before she died, hence her living with Catherine at the Conways'. That Mary and James were already living with the Armstrongs was an economic necessity. With the Armstrongs' help or Mrs. St. George's military connections or whatever remained of the McGauley financial resources (thus enjoying the prerogative of the only son), James was enrolled in the Royal Hibernian Military School in the late 1790s or early 1800s (while still in his late teens). When Mary wed William Macauley in 1804, it was also time for Catherine to leave the Armstrongs. She might then have lived with her sister and brother-in-law, as an unmarried sister sometimes did, but perhaps that possibility was not offered, or if offered, not accepted. Clare Moore indicates that while Catherine lived with the Conways or the Armstrongs there were marriage proposals: "She had opportunities of settling in life which she declined."[4] Providing a dowry or marriage settlement would seem to have been out of the question, for her, if not also for Mary. Apparently, both economic and social constraints moved Catherine in the direction of the Callaghans' offer.

Though she was deeply grateful to the Callaghans and began to love them as the adoptive parents they wished to be, even to William Callaghan's dying request that she assume the Callaghan name (which she did not embrace), there must have been an inherent tension, at least in the beginning, between her roles as "household manager/companion" and "daughter." Moreover, for a very long time something she treasured was missing. It could not be found at the Callaghan table, as elegant as it was, or at their frequent parties, as pleasant as these were. It was not that Cath-

---

4. BA, in *CMcATM*, 100.

erine was not convivial. She could dance and sing with the best of them, and she later counseled her associates not to take "a gloomy view of passing events," reminding them that the Scriptures do not describe Jesus as "sad or troublesome."[5] But still, on Mary Street and at Coolock, despite the affection which surrounded her, something troubled her spirit. It had to do with religion, with coming to know and understand her Catholic faith, with being able to express it openly, with learning how to pray as an adult, and, when she was alone, with attending to the incomprehensible mystery whom she called God.

A young woman of remarkable charm and good looks, Catherine was also a conscientious thinker, appreciative of the surfaces of daily existence, but not satisfied that they were all there was to human life. Whatever exactly happened in her heart and mind during the nearly twenty years she lived with the Callaghans, three movements can be identified with some certainty. The graciousness, courtesy, and hospitality that characterized her future life were fully developed during these years. Moreover, she eventually sought and received guidance in her religious faith, though not without some difficulty; and she came to share more and more in the Quaker spiritual values and virtues of Catherine Callaghan. These years were lonely but also pregnant ones, involving the kind of purification of needs and desires that can in the end bear fruit. In an unexpected way, they became for Catherine the earthly grounds of her expanding charity and her subsequent reliance "with unhesitating confidence on the Providence of God."[6]

Mary Vincent Harnett attempts to describe Catherine's internal conflict during these years:

Neither the advantages of her new position, nor the comforts she enjoyed, nor the attention of her sincere and anxious friends could relieve the anxiety, or quiet the troubles of her mind on the great subject of religion. She still continued determined in her intention of professing herself a Catholic, and longed anxiously to communicate her sentiments to her friends, and to have an interview with some Catholic clergyman, for notwithstanding all her study and examination there were a few points on which she still required some explanation, and this she felt could not be satisfactorily obtained by a written communication.[7]

Harnett's published biography (1864) acknowledges that when, and even after, Catherine lived with the Armstrongs her "faith and constancy

5. Lim, in CMcATM, 180.   6. Letter 283, July 24, 1841, in CCMcA, 418.
7. Lim, in CMcATM, 142–43.

met a severe and prolonged trial. In her troubles she used sometimes contrive to meet the Very Rev. Dean Lubé . . . who never failed to console and
encourage her."[8] Andrew Lubé was until 1810 a curate at St. Mary's chapel,
Liffey Street, then parish priest of St. James's until his death in 1831. Catherine Byrn, commenting on Harnett's biography, complains (incorrectly)
that Harnett omits "any mention of Dean Lubé . . . who when Miss McAuley came to reside at. . . Mary Street, with Mr. and Mrs. Callaghan, was until his removal to James's St., her Confessor, & by his charitable counsels
contributed *more than any other* to the preservation of her Faith, at times
sorely besieged."[9] Although Catherine Byrn corrects, apparently rightly,
some material in Harnett's biography, and in Carroll's when that publication (1866) became available in Dublin, her misreading of Harnett's *Life*
in this instance raises a question about the reliability of her memory and
critique in other instances.

Prior to his death in 1811, Catherine also sought the theological help of
Thomas Betagh, a revered Jesuit who had remained in Dublin as a diocesan
priest after the suppression of the Society of Jesus by Pope Clement XIV
in 1773. Mary Ann Doyle says: "She told me that in some doubt she had
recourse to the celebrated Dr. Beatie [Betagh] who quite convinced her."[10]
Clare Moore claims: "Being thrown so much among Protestants she read
assiduously the best controversial works, and went often for instruction to
the Very Revd. Father Betagh, whose learning and piety made every one re-
vere his words, and who was also an able controversialist—hence her visits
to him caused some to think she had been a Protestant."[11] Harnett says
simply: "During this time she occasionally sought for instruction from
the late Dr. Betagh. . . . In mind and heart she was a confirmed Catholic
and she only waited for a favorable opportunity to make known her sentiments and give practical effect to her resolve. This did not present itself as
soon as she wished for or expected."[12]

Thomas Betagh (1738–1811) lived at 80 Cook Street, off Winetavern
Street, below Merchants Quay. He was vicar general of the diocese under
Archbishop Troy, and parish priest of St. Michael's, Rosemary Lane, from
1799 until he resigned in 1810. In conversations with him Catherine must
have learned not only theology, but also something of his deep commitment to the plight of poor children, especially their desperate need for

8. Harnett, *Life*, 6–7.
9. Mary Raymond Byrn to Mary Clare Moore, October 23, 1867 (MCA).
10. MADL, in *CMcATM*, 43.   11. BA, in *CMcATM*, 100.
12. Lim, in *CMcATM*, 142.

food, clothing, and schooling. In 1769–1770 Betagh had set up at different locations in the city four or five night schools for mostly poor Catholic boys, "under the auspices of Saul's Court Academy" off Fishamble Street. The academy was founded in 1750 by a venerated Jesuit, John Austin (c. 1722–1784).[13] In his funeral oration for Thomas Betagh on Palm Sunday, 1811, Michael Blake recalled the orphans to whom Betagh served as a parent, and how, "at the age of *seventy-three,* [he] would sit down in a cold damp cellar, every night, to hear the lessons of these children, and contrived to clothe *forty* of the most destitute amongst them, every year, at his own expense."[14]

Catherine's long mental and emotional struggle about openly practicing her Catholic faith led to the rumor, which persisted into the decades after her death, that she had been a Protestant. Edmund Rice told his brother in 1833: "Her parents died whilst she & a brother & sister of hers were left young in care of a Gentleman of fortune in this City. They were all Protestants & [when] Mrs. McAuley [that is, Catherine] was grown up she was converted."[15] Even Richard Baptist O'Brien, editor of Harnett's biography and the author of Catherine's obituary in the *Halifax Register*—as well as the authors of certain obituaries in Dublin and London newspapers, who may have been reprinting one another—regarded Catherine's religious struggle as ending "in her conversion to the Catholic faith."[16] The Limerick Manuscript, an earlier version of Harnett's biography of Catherine, probably describes the situation in the most accurate and existential way: "A Protestant she was not, but yet she could scarcely be called a Catholic."[17] This sentence does not appear in Harnett's published *Life,* perhaps expurgated by O'Brien's unwillingness to admit Catherine's religious struggle.

Why was Catherine McAuley slow to acknowledge her Catholic faith to the Callaghans and their acquaintances, and slow to seek the freedom to practice it openly, even if unobtrusively? The question is blunt; the answer has to be more complex and nuanced.

Dublin in the early 1800s was not the Dublin of today, and Catherine was a sensitive, thoughtful young woman, conscious of the feelings of others as well as her own:

13. E. E. O'Donnell, *The Jesuits in Dublin* (Dublin: Wolfhound Press, 1999), 25–26.

14. Michael Blake, *Two Sermons: The First . . . on the Lamented Death of The Very Rev. Thomas Betagh . . .* (Dublin: Richard Coyne, 1821), 19–20. A copy of this book is in the Royal Irish Academy, Dublin.

15. Letter 20, December 10, 1833, in *CCMcA*, 57.   16. *CMcATM*, 351 n. 24 and 364 n. 48.

17. Lim, in *CMcATM*, 141.

[Her] inward trial was aggravated by difficulties of a worldly and scarcely less painful nature; such as, the giving offence to valued friends; the separation from long
cherished connections; the probability of being exposed to obloquy, and censure,
and ridicule from those whose good opinion it had ever been an object to secure.
Her friends were unaware of her secret partiality for the Catholic religion, and
she, from a feeling that will be easily understood, had a difficulty in making her
intention known. Yet without making it known it was morally impossible to effect
the object she had at heart; for her residence was some miles from the city, and so
strong was the attachment of her adopted parents that they would scarcely permit
her to be absent from them.[18]

As it turned out, the Callaghans would have respected, and later did respect, Catherine's more regular practice of her religion. While they were
opposed to the Catholic Church as such, they seem to have been toler-
ant of the freedom of conscience of others. But some who frequented the
Callaghan home—William Armstrong; Catherine's brother, James, both
before and after his military service at Waterloo; and her brother-in-law,
William Macauley—were, to varying degrees, inflexible with respect to religious affiliation and prejudiced toward what they deemed "popish practices." An overt decision on Catherine's part to attend Sunday Mass and
participate regularly in the sacraments would not have been without pain
and confusion on all sides.

Some time before Daniel Murray left St. Mary's parish, a way forward
came to Catherine. As she later counseled: "The simplest and most practical lesson I know ... is to resolve to be good today—but better tomorrow. . . . Thus we may hope to get on—taking short careful steps, not great
strides."[19] She now saw a "short step," though it involved some subterfuge:

One day she alleged some excuse for going into Dublin alone; she went to a Milli-
ner's shop, and having purchased some trifling articles of dress, desired the servants
to wait with the carriage until she should return. It was not far from the Roman
Catholic church then in Liffey Street, and almost breathless with haste, and trem-
bling from the excitement of her feelings, she applied at the residence of the clergymen, and inquired whether any of them were at home. The answer was in the affirmative, and she was introduced to the presence of Revd. Dr. [Daniel] Murray, then a
curate attached to that parish, and afterwards Archbishop of Dublin.[20]

If, as Catherine came to believe, the ways of God are winding and inscru-
table, even a hat shop will do. St. Mary's was the chapel her grandfather

---

18. Ibid., 143. Here the manuscript is conflating the Mary Street and Coolock years.
19. Letter 241, February 28, 1841, in CCMcA, 365.
20. Lim, in CMcATM, 143.

John Conway and her father had built and adorned so many years before. Her father's oak pulpit with its gilt dove was still there, offering her some token of reassurance. When she explained to the peaceable Daniel Murray the purpose of her visit and "the peculiar circumstances in which she was placed," he "gave her whatever instruction and advice she needed, removed any remaining difficulties she may have had, and appointed a day on which she was, if possible, to return to him again, and commence her preparation for the Sacraments."[21]

Catherine delayed telling the Callaghans until after she had once again received the sacraments, evidently wishing "to put off as long as possible a disclosure which she apprehended would prove so painful to those she sincerely loved." They, though wishing the contrary, did not exert "even the smallest influence, and allowed her the same freedom of choice in the matter of religion, which in similar circumstances they would have desired for themselves." The first long struggle was over—to be succeeded in later years by other, different, struggles. Catherine evidently took the horse-drawn carriage to Mass when she wished, "without any diminution of their mutual esteem and affection," though "their objection to Catholic practices made her. . . deny herself the use of the crucifix and holy pictures."[22] The absence of these external reminders of her faith was not an irreplaceable loss, for Catherine was apparently coming to sense the merciful God beyond all human images.

Coolock House was a place of rich hospitality—for friends and relatives of the Callaghans, for Catherine's own family, as well as for William Callaghan's professional associates at Apothecaries Hall. By the early 1800s, medical practitioners, as rising members of the new gentry, rivaled in social prominence the Anglo-Irish nobility. However, at this period, distinctions in their medical training and practice, but also in their social status, often separated physicians, surgeons, and apothecaries. Physicians generally based their diagnoses on bodily appearance, and when the body fluids were thought to be "impure" or out of "balance," they were regarded as the cause of disease and other maladies. Surgeons were called in to repair fractures, dress wounds, bloodlet, and do the unpleasant work of performing amputations, without anesthesia. Apothecaries, using herbs and chemicals, mixed and dispensed potions the physicians recommended or they themselves prescribed.[23]

---

21. Ibid.   22. Ibid.

23. See the Oath of Apothecaries in James C. McWalter, *A History of the Worshipful Company of*

Eighteenth-century Dublin society generally sought its entertainment outside the home, in music halls and theaters, but in the early nineteenth century the rising middle class, including medical professionals, tended to host parties in their own homes, with guest-filled, candle-lighted dinners, followed or preceded by dancing, singing, and card games such as whist, commerce, and quadrille. Catherine McAuley shared completely in such occasions at Coolock, where the wide, long entrance hall and the large rooms separated only by folding doors were well suited for lines of dancing couples. Many years later she wrote:

I think sometimes our passage through this dear sweet world is something like the Dance called "right and left." You and I have crossed over, changed places . . . your set is finished—for a little time. I'll have to curtsie and bow, in Birr . . . change corners . . . take hands of every one who does me the honor—and end the figure by coming back to my own place. I'll then have a Sea Saw dance to Liverpool and a Merry Jig that has no stop to Birmingham—and, I hope, a second—to Bermondsey . . . and [then] dance the "Duval" Trio, back on the same ground.[24]

Catherine used these dance metaphors to describe her extensive travels in late 1840 and 1841. How did she know so well the intricate movements of English dances? She must have learned them at the Callaghans.

Her repertoire of songs and ballads, manifested to the amused astonishment of her colleagues in later life, would also have been acquired in these years. How else explain what she called her "songs prepared for the journey," her fascination with John Gilpin's escapade, her humorous renditions of "The Lady of Flesh and Bone," and her advice on at least one occasion: "Dance every evening."[25] She "loved music very much" and "tried to have a piano" in every house she founded.[26]

Catherine's family was well represented among Dublin's medical men

---

Apothecaries of the City of Dublin (Dublin: E. Ponsonby, 1916), 70. In William Callaghan's time the divisions between medical professionals were not absolute—some physicians also performed surgeries, and many apothecaries also qualified as surgeons—but at least one exasperated surgeon, Clement Archer, commented saltily on the supposed greater learning of physicians: "We are not the servants or slaves of physicians, trained up to use the knife, the saw, the cautery and the many instruments of the science under the immediate inspection and direction of self-important dogmatical philosophers, too proud or too elevated by luxury to bloody their own fingers." Tony Farmar, *Patients, Potions & Physicians* (Dublin: A. & A. Farmar, in Association with the Royal College of Physicians, 2004), 60–61.

Apothecaries often visited patients and prescribed for them, and in 1780 the Dublin Society of Surgeons sought, through petitioning for a royal charter, to dissolve "the preposterous and disgraceful union of the surgeons of Dublin with barbers." In 1784 the Royal College of Surgeons in Ireland was founded. Charles A. Cameron, *History of the Royal College of Surgeons in Ireland* (Dublin: Fannin, 1886), 111, 112, 123.

24. Letter 220 [December 20, 1840], in *CCMcA*, 332.
25. Letter 36 [June-July 1836], in *CCMcA*, 76; letter 228, January 15, 1841, in *CCMcA*, 348.
26. *PS*, 28.

and the guests at Coolock. Her uncle Owen Conway may have been still alive in the 1810s, though since 1797 no longer practicing as a surgeon and never a member of the Royal College of Surgeons in Ireland.[27] Her brother, James, was certified as an apprentice to an apothecary in 1802. He was admitted as a member of the Royal College of Surgeons (England) in 1810, having been presented for certification as a surgeon's mate (later called assistant surgeon) by the Royal Army Medical Corps in which he had enrolled that year. After service in the wars between England and France, and participating in the Battle of Waterloo in 1815, he returned to Dublin. In 1817 he was appointed assistant surgeon to the Royal Hibernian Military School in Phoenix Park.[28] William Macauley, the husband of Catherine's sister, Mary, was a member Apothecaries Hall; he had apprenticed in 1796, eight years before his marriage, and qualified as a certified apothecary in 1803. In 1819 William was appointed assistant surgeon at the Royal Hospital Kilmainham, where he served aged and wounded veterans under the renowned Dr. George Renny (1757–1848).[29] Catherine Byrn vividly recalled her extended family's presence at events in Coolock House.

During this period and on into the 1820s Catherine McAuley dressed well and lived "in what is usually called good style."[30] At the same time, a deeper aspect of her character began to develop at Coolock, in part through childhood memories of her father's religious instruction to poor children on Sundays and feastdays, in part through the poverty she saw in the surrounding neighborhood, and in part through the daily influence of Catherine Callaghan.

There is no written evidence that Catherine Callaghan attended Friends Meetings on Meath or Eustace Streets in Dublin during these years, and only the barest early reference to the fact that she was a Quaker.[31] In fact,

27. "Index to the Kirkpatrick Archive" (RCPI).
28. "Hall Certificates, 1791–1819" (AAH) and "Index to the Kirkpatrick Archive" (RCPI). Certification of surgical personnel who enrolled in the British army and their relation to the Royal College in London are explained in Cameron, History of the Royal College of Surgeons, 290–302. James William McAuley earned an M.D. from Edinburgh in 1825, and moved from the Royal Hibernian Military School to the Royal Hospital Kilmainham in 1829. Cameron notes that medical degrees from Edinburgh "became the most sought for," and many Irish surgeons and physicians studied there, 110.
29. William Macauley was born probably in 1784, a year later than his brother-in-law. After his marriage to Mary McAuley in 1804, the couple resided at 24 Townsend Street until 1819, and their first children, all except young Willie and possibly Catherine, were born there. Cameron, History of the Royal College of Surgeons, 617, notes that Dr. Charles Henry Leet, a distinguished member of Apothecaries Hall and its governor in 1840 and 1857, apprenticed under William Macauley for five years beginning in 1818. Macauley's name appears often in the minutes of the Hall and of the Guild of St. Luke (AAH).
30. DL, in CMcATM, 45.
31. MADL, in CMcATM, 43 and 351 n. 22.

having married William Callaghan, a non-Quaker, Catherine Callaghan would have been subject to "disownment" or "disunity" by a formal decision of a Friends Meeting, and thus would have been ineligible to attend meetings. The circumstances surrounding their marriage are unknown. In 1979 Mary Nathy O'Hara noted "a marriage license in 1776 showing that [a] William Callaghan and [an] Anna Ryan were married, but whether or not the Mrs. Callaghan who became so attached to Catherine [McAuley] was formerly Anna Ryan is not known."[32] John MacErlean thought the identity of these two women very unlikely, and that the "William Callaghan," a "cooper," mentioned in the 1776 marriage license was not the same William Callaghan who was Catherine McAuley's benefactor.

However, according to O'Hara, a "strange cloud" of some sort hung over Catherine Callaghan, "connected with her marriage."[33] Austin Carroll—who relies in part on the "Memoir" of Clare Augustine Moore, who had contact with a Mary Murphy, a former servant at Coolock—claims that Mrs. Callaghan received, from a young man to whom her husband "had shown much kindness . . . anonymous letters, full of cutting allusions to her early domestic afflictions, and highly outrageous to her feelings."[34] What the "cloud" and the "early domestic afflictions" were, if in fact they do point to some historical circumstance, can apparently no longer be discovered.

If there was some specific irregularity in Catherine Callaghan's marriage to William Callaghan from an eighteenth-century Quaker perspective, it might have been that he was a Protestant, that they were married before a clergyman, or at a registry office, or that she did not have the consent of her parents, presumably Quakers. For any one of these violations of Quaker discipline, each regarded as "marrying out," Catherine Callaghan could have been declared "disowned" or "disunited."[35] This would indeed have been an "early domestic affliction" to her religious sensibility, and a persistent "cloud" hanging over her great affection for her husband.

---

32. Mary Nathy O'Hara, *Catherine McAuley, Mercy Foundress* (Dublin: Veritas Publications, 1979), 3.

33. Ibid.

34. Carroll, *Life*, 75–76.

35. Janet Ruffing first researched the possible Quaker "disownment" of Catherine Callaghan for her essay "Catherine McAuley's Quaker Connection," *MAST Journal* 8, no. 1 (Fall 1997): 36–45. John Rutty's *A Treatise Concerning Christian Discipline, compiled with the Advice of a National Meeting of the People called Quakers, held in Dublin in the Year 1746*, published in Dublin in 1752, cites in detail infractions of the Quaker marriage regulations that merited disownment. Rutty (1697–1775) was a noted Dublin physician and Quaker. Richard S. Harrison's *Biographical Dictionary of Irish Quakers* (Dublin: Four Courts Press, 2008) presents many instances of Quakers who were disowned for "marrying out."

Nonetheless, a great deal of Catherine Callaghan's Quaker faith and spirit can be found in the early biographical manuscripts about Catherine McAuley, especially the references to Mrs. Callaghan's charity and her appreciation of silence. As a Quaker she would also have been profoundly devoted to reading the Christian Scriptures.

In the Limerick Manuscript, one learns something of her charity to the poor, influenced as it was by the social concern of Quakers throughout Ireland. As she aged, the one who increasingly executed her wishes on behalf of those in need was her foster daughter. Although Catherine McAuley had "little of her own to give beyond a kind word of advice, or an affectionate expression of sympathy . . . her adopted parents were good charitable people, and she was, on almost every occasion, the organ of their benevolence." With the Callaghans' permission—indeed, it was their wish—Catherine reached out not only to the material needs of those in the surrounding area, but to "their spiritual ignorance and destitution," just as she faintly remembered seeing her father doing when she was a child:

She collected the poor children of the neighbourhood in the lodge, which was placed at her disposal, and devoted a great portion of her time to their instruction. Her solicitude for the interests of the poor soon drew around her many who hoped to derive from her advice, relief, and consolation. Everyone who had distress to be relieved or affliction to be mitigated, or troubles to be encountered came to seek consolation at her hands, and she gave it to the utmost of her ability.[36]

In the background of all this response to human need was Mrs. Callaghan, willing it and providing for it, even when she became bedridden.

About 1816 Catherine Callaghan became severely ill with what her husband later termed "a lingering and oppressive disease." She was seventy-seven. In her obituary in the *Dublin Evening Post* three years later, William Callaghan (or Catherine McAuley writing on his behalf) says that his wife "was to the poor a generous benefactor, [and] a number of poor families will be now thrown unprotected on the world, who were supported privately by her weekly donations."[37]

Speculation on the nature of Mrs. Callaghan's disease is impossible, given the meager evidence available, but it was a "tedious one and, though not attended by any violent pain, was sufficient for the most part to confine her to her bed." Suddenly Catherine McAuley was faced with a new and time-consuming form of mercifulness—and a call to deeper prayer,

36. Lim, in *CMcATM*, 144.
37. *Dublin Evening Post*, October 9, 1819.

perhaps not unlike her moments with her own dying mother. For three years she watched by Catherine Callaghan's bed in the front bedchamber at Coolock, connected by a door to her own room in the back. She smoothed the pillow on which Mrs. Callaghan's "wasted and restless head reclined," and learned what one learns to do for the sick by doing it. Although none of the books is named, Catherine McAuley "often read for her some book of moral and religious instruction, though this was a matter of no slight inconvenience, for the tender eyes of the invalid could bear no light but that of a shaded lamp placed on the floor." Catherine's nursing service continued until October 1819: "For many weeks the only sleep Miss McAuley had was on a couch in the sick room, during the patient's intervals of repose; yet even then," it is said, "was her mind engaged in visions of charity and mercy to the poor."[38]

In her half-slumber during these nights, Catherine McAuley apparently had dreams of orphan children, of "destitute females, deprived of their natural protectors and deserted by their friends," and of a "crowd of young women" learning employable household skills. She "often started from her slumbers and burst into tears. 'Catherine,' the sick lady would sometimes say to her, 'I almost wish you never went to sleep, you frighten me so much, and seem to suffer such agony.'" Modern psychologists might offer a scientific interpretation of Catherine's dreams. Were they a subconscious effort to embody the growing desires of her presently confined but future conscious life? Or, as one of her early biographers asked, "could it be that God was thus to manifest to her . . . the extended sphere of usefulness, and mercy, and generous benevolence to which a few years later she was to be called?"[39]

Catherine Callaghan died on October 3, 1819. In the days preceding her death, through conversations with Catherine McAuley about the nature of Catholic faith and practices, she began to desire to "die a member of the Catholic Communion." Imbued as Catherine McAuley was with the then-prevalent but limited Catholic understanding of the ways of God's salvific love, she feared that her good friend would die "outside the Church." She urged "that the sick patient should die in the true Faith and receive all the spiritual helps which the holy Sacraments afford."[40]

But Catherine Callaghan hesitated—for reasons not related to herself, but to her husband and to Catherine McAuley. With respect to William, it

---

38. Lim, in *CMcATM*, 145.   39. Ibid.
40. Ibid., 145–46.

would, she believed, afflict him "beyond measure; he had always been attentive to her, and proved himself on every occasion most affectionate and
devoted, how could she thus requite him for all his kindness? They had
lived in peace and harmony together: how could she by embracing another
creed sever, as it were, the bonds that united them together, and embit-
ter his declining years?" But there was another and related reason: "I think
my husband would be so dissatisfied and displeased with your interference
that he would be very likely to deprive you for ever of any portion of his
property, and I cannot consent to any measure that would prove so disastrous to you." Catherine McAuley heard what she may never have heard
so fully: a wife's ardent love for her husband and a mother's self-forgetting
love for her daughter. To the latter she protested, telling the dying woman: "The poorest habitation, and the humblest position in life, would be a
thousand times more acceptable than the wealth of the universe, if it were
purchased at such a price." She assured Catherine Callaghan that "she was
content to live in the meanest cottage for the remainder of her life" if only
Mrs. Callaghan would die a Catholic.[41]

One day when William Callaghan was absent on business, Michael
Bernard Keogh, a Capuchin priest serving in the vicinity, received the beloved eighty-year-old woman into the Catholic Church and heard her confession. He intended to return in a few days for the other sacraments.[42]
Before he did, Catherine Callaghan died—her decision evidently still withheld from her grieving husband, who nonetheless knew the truth of the
sentences included in his wife's obituary: "She bore her sufferings with
truly Christian patience, and resigned her life at a very advanced age to its
Author, departing for a better world. Her death is a deep source of regret to
her afflicted family, and those who knew her best lament her most."[43] She
was buried in the graveyard of St. John the Evangelist Church (Church of
Ireland) in Coolock.[44]

Catherine remained at Coolock House caring for William Callaghan,
himself still spry and serving again in 1819–1820 as governor of Apothecaries Hall. Slowly, over the course of their evening conversations, he and
Catherine McAuley became more than the rich scientist and his adopted

41. Ibid., 146. Mrs. Callaghan's statement and Catherine's are in quotation marks in the manuscript.
42. BA and Lim, in *CMcATM*, 100 and 146. These primary sources conflict in their accounts of the
sacraments Mrs. Callaghan received on her deathbed.
43. *Dublin Evening Post*, October 9, 1819.
44. Appleyard, *Green Fields*, 63.

daughter.[45] The leader at Apothecaries Hall and the increasingly skilled nurse-companion had much in common—not the sciences or pharmacy, but sincerity, straightforwardness, and the precious memory of Catherine Callaghan.

In time, William's health declined. He too was in his eighties and though he had maintained a work schedule at Apothecaries Hall, he was no longer the robust man he had been for decades, and was no longer upheld by the presence of his lifelong soul-mate.

The minutes of Apothecaries Hall in 1820 and 1821 express well-earned gratitude and deference to William Callaghan. When he indicated that he wished formally to resign his duties as secretary and treasurer, a General Council meeting on May 1, 1820, resolved:

That the sincere thanks of this General Court is due and hereby given to our worthy Member Wm. Callaghan Esq., for his eminent & zealous Services as Secretary & Treasurer for the last 26 years during which period he was frequently in considerable pecuniary advance for the Company, yet with a generosity peculiar to himself charged no interest thereon, and we trust the Members of this Hall will long entertain with gratitude the remembrance of his liberal declaration when his health permits.[46]

As respectfully as he deserved, the council sought Callaghan's full accounting of the financial situation of the Hall with any interest owed him ("his liberal declaration"), when it was convenient for him to give it.

On August 1 that year, when he completed his last term as governor, the council again resolved that

the best thanks of this General Court be given to our late [i.e., recent] Governor Wm. Callaghan Esq. for his constant and faithful services to this Company; in him we have seen time, which often seems to lessen human exertions, serves to add to his zeal and ability & we trust nothing but Death can put an end to our esteem & gratitude for his attention and successful efforts for the success of this Hall.[47]

William Callaghan's role as treasurer had been particularly demanding. He had been responsible for collecting all the income of the Hall, for example, the financial penalties for non-attendance at meetings, the penalties levied against uncertified apothecaries, the payment for shares of stock all members were required to hold in the Hall, and the income from

---

45. No evidence supports the claim, in a recent undocumented homily, that William Callaghan proposed marriage to Catherine McAuley. She was about forty years his junior.

46. "Minutes of the Apothecaries Hall, Dublin," vol. 3, May 1, 1820 (AAH).

47. Ibid., August 1, 1820 (AAH).

the sale of certified medicines prepared in its laboratory. He also had to pay all the Hall's expenses: the salaries of its chemist and housekeeper, the purchase of its herbs and chemicals for compounding, and sundry other expenses, including the cost of gifts and monuments for its most distinguished members. While his quarterly reports were reviewed by an audit committee, some of his transactions were always in flux, members often failing to pay the penalties they had incurred or their required shares. Some of the financial status of the Hall was necessarily in his head, if not on paper, and in mid-1821 and 1822 the members were still trying to grasp what he had handled with ease, through their letters and visits to Coolock when he could not come to Mary Street.

In August 1821 Callaghan was asked to return "all the keys" belonging to the Hall. On January 22, 1822, a series of letters began, requesting that he close his treasurer's account by payment of the remaining £699.7.6. An attorney was asked to wait on Mr. Callaghan and "demand payment of the balance due by him to the company." In February the Hall asked him to return "two Thermometers & [a] Hydrometer belonging to this establishment." By March 1, 1822, to help him settle matters with the Hall, Callaghan asked his law agent, John Chambers, to write to the Hall. Later in March the Hall finally recognized William Callaghan's "infirm state" and, if silence in the minutes is indicative, became less officious in its communications with him. It designated temporary treasurers and relieved him of any remaining treasurer's responsibility. The Hall's tenacious assertiveness, even peremptoriness, toward some of its loyal but aging members—William Armstrong was also taxed and commanded—may not have been unrelated to a particular executive style and a declining financial condition.[48]

Toward the end of his life William Callaghan inquired into Catherine's future. What did she plan to do after he died? One evening he asked her frankly: "What shall I leave you at my death, will you be satisfied with £1000?" Catherine, disturbed at the question, told him she "would not know what to do with £1000." Callaghan apparently laughed: "You would not know what to do with £1000 . . . well, I know what you would do; you would do a great deal of good with it at all events."[49] She little suspected how far off the mark her response would prove.

48. "Minutes of the Apothecaries Hall, Dublin," vol. 4: 1821–1828 (AAH).
49. Lim, in CMcATM, 147.

Mary Ann Doyle, who later knew of Catherine's early plans, says that "her benefactor had once spoken of leaving her a thousand pounds, and she thought, if she had that or even a few hundreds, she would hire a couple of rooms and work for and with her protégées. . . . Night after night she would see herself in some very large place where a number of young women were employed as laundresses or at plain-work, while she herself would be surrounded by a crowd of ragged children which she was washing and dressing very busily."[50] Evidently Catherine's activities in the village of Coolock, her dreams in Catherine Callaghan's sickroom, and her need to think of the future were beginning to coalesce. In view of William Callaghan's generous promise, Catherine may have shared with him the project that was developing in her mind.

But a familial storm was brewing. Some relatives of the Callaghans had come to resent the place Catherine McAuley held in the Coolock household. While Catherine Callaghan was alive, she or Catherine McAuley herself had occasionally received anonymous, insulting letters. On one occasion Catherine Callaghan recognized the handwriting as that of a young male, "a connexion of the family," and when his mother later asked her to approach William Callaghan for £300 so the young man could make a down payment on a commission in the army, the wealthy but conflicted older woman turned to the younger Catherine for advice: "Can I exert myself in favor of one who has in so malicious a manner endeavored to destroy my domestic happiness, who has tried without any provocation to wound my feelings and insult me?" Her companion evidently said, "Well, and will you not do so?" or words to that effect. Taking the letters from her drawer and claiming that were she to read them again, "I could not be prevailed on by any solicitations; but I will act nobly and generously towards him," Mrs. Callaghan cast them into the fire, went to her husband, stated the request, and got the money.[51] In later life, Catherine McAuley would remember the liberating benefit of throwing offensive letters into the fire without reading them a second time.

The young man for whom Catherine Callaghan procured the money may have been a Powell. Richard Moore Powell was married in 1816 to Catherine Callaghan's relative Marianne Johnston, but it may not have been he. A man evidently named Powell, perhaps a William or a Robert

50. DL, in *CMcATM*, 45.
51. Lim, in *CMcATM*, 147.

Powell, will figure, to his own harm, in a subsequent, inadvertent encounter with William Callaghan himself.[52] Meanwhile the relatives' jealousy toward Catherine McAuley grew, much of it undercover until it bloomed later in a legal contest. As Degnan comments, the Callaghans' "continued liberality towards the Powells speaks much for Callaghan charity."[53] But it had its breaking point.

As Mr. Callaghan's health weakened, Catherine's worries about his religious state increased, as they had about his wife's in her declining months. Now Catherine was even more reluctant to speak, whether from the burden of the secret she carried about his wife's conversion, or through genuine respect for his evident goodness and blameless relations with others. Although she "enjoyed his confidence and regard to a greater extent than any other person," she could not bring herself to speak with him about religion—until his attending physician told her that "the nature of his illness is such that he may live for a month, and he may die tomorrow." Still, in the days that followed no words could get past her lips. Finally she simply knelt by his bed, "clasped his hands in hers, and overpowered by her emotions burst into an agony of tears."[54]

William Callaghan was rightly startled, and begged her to explain. At last she said, "It is not for myself, it is on your account I am uneasy." What ensued was a back-and-forth discussion lasting several days, in the course of which the sick man tried to reassure her of his own peace: "I have a firm confidence in God, and reliance on His mercy; I have read a great deal on religious matters, and have, I trust, acted uprightly in following, according to my conscience, the religion I profess," though he promised to speak with her again on the topic.[55] More book reading followed, and then Catherine asked him if she might bring a Catholic priest to the house—apparently realizing that her own store of theological learning was no match for William Callaghan's intelligence, and her love for him too vulnerable.

Biographers differ on whether the priest was Edward Armstrong, then serving at the old penal chapel of St. Mary's, Liffey Street, or the much younger Joseph Nugent, then a curate of St. Brendan's in Coolock. Catherine Byrn asserts that Father Armstrong "had never been in the house" and that it was "Rev. Mr. Nugent who . . . devoted himself to the task of

---

52. The Powell connections can be better understood later, in relation to the will of William Callaghan.

53. Degnan, *Mercy*, 39.   54. Lim, in *CMcATM*, 148.
55. Ibid.

Mr. Callaghan's conversion."[56] Burke Savage and Degnan agree, and their view is more likely than Carroll's or Harnett's, though Edward Armstrong would have been the far more experienced counselor.[57] Joseph Nugent was twenty-six at the time, only recently ordained, but evidently a highly gifted man.

William Callaghan was received into the Catholic Church the day before he died on Sunday, November 10, 1822—the church from which, as Harnett remarks, "the circumstances of his birth, together with his position in society, and not any insensibility or obduracy of his own, had hitherto excluded him."[58] Before his death, Catherine must have told him of his wife's conversion, though this is not recorded in any of the early manuscripts.[59] To not have told him would have violated both his own goodness and Catherine's affection for him.

William Armstrong, his old friend, neighbor, and colleague at the Hall, was still living in 1822. He would have been a solace to Catherine if he attended William Callaghan's burial in the graveyard of St. John the Evangelist Church.

In the announcement of his death, which presumably she wrote, Catherine's grief was only barely concealed: "In his admirable character the most prominent features were humility and gratitude. . . . Forgetful only of the favours he conferred, he cherished to his latest moments an affectionate recollection of the most trivial kindness he experienced. 'May he now repose in the Mansion of Eternal Bliss, where no fears shall trouble him, no pains torment him, nor any grief disturb the quiet of his Soul, but perfect security, pure delights, and unspeakable joys shall for ever be established unto him, through our Lord Jesus Christ.'"[60]

Almost thirty years after she first moved in with the Callaghans, when they were both long gone from her life, Catherine McAuley listed their names and others' in the round spaces of the mottled back cover of a copybook in which she transcribed meditations, noting above their names: "Lord Jesus, have mercy on the souls of . . . Cath[erine] & Wm. Callaghan."[61]

56. Mary Raymond Byrn to Mary Clare Moore, October 23, 1867 (MCA).

57. Burke Savage, *McAuley*, 39–40; Degnan, *Mercy*, 39; Carroll, *Life*, 108; and Harnett, *Life*, 22–24.

58. Lim, in *CMcATM*, 149. William Callaghan died on November 10, 1822, not on November 11, as some biographers have claimed (Lim, in *CMcATM*, 149; Harnett, *Life*, 24; and Carroll, *Life*, 109). See his obituary noted further in the text.

59. Carroll, *Life*, 109, develops her version of such a dialogue in some detail.

60. *Dublin Evening Post*, Thursday, November 14, 1822.

61. This copybook is still preserved (MCA).

In the best room in the house Catherine built, the one containing lovely Georgian furniture brought from Coolock, a large oil portrait of William Callaghan still hangs on the wall, in honor of the foster mother and father on whom so much depended.[62]

62. The portrait may have been the one given to William Callaghan in 1806 by the board of the Apothecaries Hall, as was their custom in honoring distinguished members, or a copy thereof. In arranging for the portrait, the board "resolved unanimously that our worthy Secretary William Callaghan Esq. do forthwith sit for his Picture and that it be placed in a conspicuous part of the Board Room at the expence of this Corporation"; and resolved further, that a committee, including William Armstrong, "do have the foregoing Resolution complied with." "Minutes of August 1, 1806" (AAH). This portrait may have been subsequently given to William Callaghan, to Catherine McAuley directly, or to the Dublin House of Mercy. Since Catherine became heir to all the furnishings in Coolock House, she may have brought Callaghan's portrait (painter unknown) with her to the house she eventually built.

CHAPTER 3

The Bequest and Its Use *1823–1826*

When William Callaghan's last will and testament and its codicil were opened, Catherine McAuley discovered, probably to her astonishment, that his bequests to her went far beyond £1000. Some of the Callaghan relatives were outraged. The will read in part:

To my kind and affectionate friend Miss Catherine McAuley who resides with me for her many kindnesses and attentions I give, devise and bequeath the Four several Annuities heretofore mentioned on the lives of Ross Thompson, Lord Howth, Christopher Robinson, and Robt. M. Fishbourne, with the several Policies of Assurance connected with Same and all benefit and advantage arising therefrom together with such arrears of said Annuities as may be due at my Decease. I also leave and bequeath to the said Catherine McAuley all the Grand Canal Stock or loan which I may have at the time of my Death together with all arrears of Interest that may be then Due on same—and It is my request that the said Catherine McAuley do take and assume the Sirname of Callaghan.[1]

In the will William Callaghan had appointed Catherine McAuley and Marianne Johnston Powell, a Callaghan relative, as joint residuary legatees, but his codicil revoked this provision:

Whereas I have by the foregoing Will nominated Catherine McAuley and Mary Ann Powell joint residuary Legatees, I do hereby revoke the said Will in that respect so far as relates to the said Mary Ann Powell and hereby nominate constitute and appoint the said Catherine McAuley sole Residuary Legatee of all my Estate and Effects real or personal subject to the specific Legacies mentioned in my Will

---

1. "Last Will and Testament of William Callaghan," January 27, 1822 (MCA).

and I do hereby publish and declare this as and for a Codicil to my Will and direct same to be taken as such.[2]

The change noted in the codicil to the will (both are dated January 27, 1822) may have been provoked many months before. At some point, perhaps in 1821, through an unsuspected open window in his room, William Callaghan had heard, from a window just below him, a man whose name was apparently Powell complaining about the presence of Catherine McAuley in the house and declaring that "the idea of Miss McAuley's ever being mistress of Coolock House was too absurd to be entertained." Unfortunately for the complainer, "not one word of this was lost on the invalid in the room above."[3] That invalid was not so ill that he could not dictate a codicil to his will, in which he revoked the former arrangement and made Catherine McAuley his sole residuary legatee.

Other specific bequests in the will—to "Richard Moore Powell of Margaret Place," to "Mary Anne Powell, his wife," to "William, their son," to Catherine's brother, James McAuley, to a druggist on Capel Street, to "Bridget Armstrong, daughter of William Armstrong of Mary Street," to Callaghan's "much Esteemed Friends Doctor William Brooke . . . Doctor William Boyton . . . and Surgeon Robert Moore Peile," to his half-sister Mrs. Mary Nash, to a few other persons, and to "the poor of the parish of Coolock"—were all left unaltered by the codicil.[4]

The will also refers to "Mary Anne Powell, wife of said Robert [sic] Powell" (in contrast to the name, Richard Moore Powell, given as her husband's name in the above bequest). William Callaghan then *appears* to designate "the said Robert Moore Powell and the said Catherine McAuley Executor and Executrix of this my will hereby revoking all former will or wills by me heretofore at any time made and declaring this to be my last Will and Testament." Both John MacErlean and the present biographer question the use in the will of the two forenames, "Robert" and "Richard," for Marianne's husband, and think one or other of these is a scribal er-

2. "Codicil" to "Last Will and Testament of William Callaghan," January 27, 1822, both signed in Callaghan's own hand, although the codicil itself is in the hand of his attorney, John Chambers, or Chambers's assistant (MCA). Marianne Johnston Powell's first name is spelled variously, but in the ledger of debentures of Apothecaries Hall, where Catherine McAuley, as an executor, signs for her, it is spelled "Marianne" (AAH).

3. CAM, in *CMcATM*, 198.

4. "Last Will and Testament of William Callaghan" (MCA). Surgeon Robert Moore Peile was a founding member of the Royal College of Surgeons, serving as its president in 1798 and 1816. Cameron, *History of the Royal College of Surgeons*, 305, 328–29. Unfortunately, we do not know the physician or surgeon who attended Callaghan in his own final illness.

ror which occurred during preparation of the final text or the copy of Callaghan's "last" will. If Marianne Powell was the wife of "Richard," as noted earlier in the will, she could not at the same time have been the wife of "Robert" as noted here, and vice versa.[5] In fact, a Richard Moore Powell was married to Marianne Johnston in 1816.[6] That couple apparently had a son William and possibly a living relative named Robert or Richard.

Despite the paucity of well-correlated, extant information on the Powells—a large, extended family with many having the same forenames—two concerns motivate research on them: the discrepancy in William Callaghan's will itself, or in the copy of it available to present-day researchers; and the belief that he would not have named as one of his executors, to serve in this capacity with Catherine McAuley, a man he knew spoke disdainfully of her and resented her place at Coolock. The Powell who had evidently spoken disparagingly of Catherine within William Callaghan's hearing may have been a Robert, a Richard, or even a William, but it would seem unlikely to have been the Richard Moore Powell whom William Callaghan indeed chose as one of the two executors of his will. In the 1820s and 1830s, in records of annual disbursements of dividends on shares in Apothecaries Hall to those to whom Callaghan had bequeathed them, "Richard M. Powell" (sometimes as "RM Powell") signs several of these payments as "Executor of Wm. Callaghan."[7]

There is no record of how Catherine personally reacted to the dramatic gifts to her outlined in William Callaghan's will and its codicil. Undoubt-

5. MACE/MCAU/71 (IJA). Marianne Johnston, apparently a relative of Mrs. Callaghan, had married into the Powell family, which included several apothecaries, and repeatedly used the same forenames in succeeding generations. In minutes of the Guild of St. Luke for October 18, 1769, one finds a "Richard Powell" listed as an "Assistant" in the Guild; a year later he is elected a "Warden." The October 3, 1771, minutes read: "Mr. Robert Powell admitted free of this Corporation by [reason of] Service, having served his years of Apprenticeship to his father Mr. William Powell deceased & his uncle Mr. Richard Powell both freemen of this Corporation." Later in the minutes (October 18, 1771), "Robert Powell" was elected a warden, and on October 18, 1782, he was elected master. In 1795 or 1796, he or a descendant (or forebear?) was addressed as "Robert Powell, Esquire, late [i.e., recent] High Sheriff of the City of Dublin." According to the *Dublin Directory*, a Robert Powell, who lived on Thomas Street was deputy governor of Apothecaries Hall in 1798–1799, and governor in 1799–1800.

6. "Powell, Richard Moore and Mary Ann Johnston. M[arriage] L[icence] 1816 [page 251]," in *Index to the Act or Grant Books and Original Wills of the Diocese of Dublin from 1800 to 1858*, 868 (NAI).

7. "Debentures of Dividends on Shares in Apothecaries Hall" (AAH). In *CMcATM*, 364 n. 43, the present biographer confused "Richard" and "Robert." For the Powells see also Harnett, *Life*, 18–19, 29; MACE/MCAU/25(2) in IJA; Burke Savage, *McAuley*, 37, 48–49; and Degnan, *Mercy*, 39–40. In *Life*, 77, Carroll gives an elaborate account of the gambling and future life of a "Mr. P" whom she regards as the husband of Marianne Johnston. In Catherine Byrn's letter to Mary Margaret Byrn, October 6, 1867, she says: "Were it borne in mind that Mrs. Powell was the daughter of Mrs. Callaghan's first cousin, and that to Mrs. Callaghan dear Mother Catherine was mainly indebted . . . mention of Mrs. Powell's erring, though good hearted, husband's fault might be omitted during the life of any of her family" (MCA).

edly she was stunned, overcome by the culminating generosity of her adoptive parents' love, and deeply grateful not only for their unexpected gifts, but also for the gift of living with them for almost twenty years. The reaction of some unnamed relatives of the Callaghans was different. They apparently set to work contesting the will and codicil in court, perhaps only to clear up the naming of the executors. The legal proceedings may not have lasted long and were finally judged in Catherine's favor, though what, if any, adjustments or corrections were made cannot now be discovered. At least no one could say that William Callaghan was not of sound mind, nor that the will and codicil were not properly executed. The former governor of Apothecaries Hall was too astute for that. A manuscript page of the "Return of Charitable Donations and Bequests Commencing January 1822," as it affects the bequest to "the poor of the parish of Coolock," indicates that probate for this bequest was "granted to Richard Moore Powell . . . and Catherine McAuley of Coolock . . . the Executors named in said will" on November 26, 1822, just two weeks after William Callaghan's death.[8] By November 1, 1823, Catherine was also attempting, by bond, to secure payment of at least half of the loan William Callaghan had granted to Frederick Moore of Mountjoy Square, a barrister. So the full will and codicil must have been proved in court by this date if not on November 26, 1822.[9]

Biographers over the years have expressed various estimates of the monetary value in pounds sterling of Catherine McAuley's inheritance. In addition to the four annuities, with related life insurance policies, and all of Callaghan's Grand Canal stock or loan, with all arrears of interest due, she also acquired Coolock House, its contents and outbuildings, and appurtenances on the land (including "Furniture, Plate, Linen, Carriage, Horses, and Farming Utensils"). As the sole residuary legatee she also inherited, after payment of the other legacies and any just debts, whatever remained of Callaghan's Wide Street certificates, the dividends on a share in the Apothecaries Hall, and whatever income would accrue through lease or sale of "some Houses in Greek Street," situated north of the Liffey and intersecting Mary's Lane.[10]

8. Photocopy of official handwritten page of "Return of Charitable Donations and Bequests" (MCA). In the *Index for Commissioners of Charitable Donations and Bequests, 1800-1858*, vol. 3, 28 (NAI), is the following entry: "Callaghan, William, Coolock, Co. Dublin, Ext. [Extract] Will Prerog. 26.11.1822. Vol. 3, p. 28."

9. "Single or Joint Bond of Frederick Moore with Catherine McAuley" (MCA). A possibly related Frederick Moore, an apothecary, appears often in the minutes of the Guild of St. Luke, 1819-1821, and of Apothecaries Hall, 1822-1823.

10. In deeds registered in November 1803, William Callaghan leased two separate properties on

Estimates of the inheritance by Mary Vincent Harnett, Clare Augustine Moore, Mary Austin Carroll, Roland Burke Savage, Mary Bertrand Degnan, and Angela Bolster range from £20,000 to £30,000.[11] If the figure £25,000 in 1822 is used, the average equivalent in 2007, using the retail price index, would probably be around £1.88 million. If the figure £25,000 in 1830 is used (1830 being the earliest year available for the exchange rate calculator), again using the retail price index and the 2007 exchange rate of £ = $2, then the average U.S. dollar equivalent in 2007 would be about $2.7 million, the range stretching from roughly $1.78 million to $3.65 million.[12] It was indeed a large inheritance. However, only some of this £25,000 was ready money; the majority of it, annual income. The 1822 value and purchasing power of this inheritance, and why it was called a "fortune," may be better understood if one notes that in 1818, when he was both physician and surgeon to the Royal Hospital Kilmainham, the annual army salary of Dr. George Renny, who had served as president of the Royal College of Surgeons in 1793, was £80, though he probably supplemented this income by other earnings and private fees.[13]

But Catherine's life had become complicated, not in a monetary way, before William Callaghan's death. On August 9, 1822, her cousin Anne Conway Byrn died, leaving four children; Catherine, her eldest daughter, was ten. Anne had been ill for at least a year. Having already adopted at Anne's request the baby, Teresa, her godchild, now fourteen months old, Catherine McAuley soon adopted young Catherine.[14] How she had managed an infant at Coolock, especially as William Callaghan was dying, we do not know, though the servants would have helped. In time Catherine McAuley discovered herself well able to care for babies and small children, and before the decade was over she was to become the adoptive mother of

---

Greek Street (formerly Pill Lane), for twenty-four years each, to Gregory Scurlog and Moses Drake, at annual rents of £12 and £5 (memorial nos. 555.276.371667 and 555.276.371668, RD). In 1804 he leased two more properties on Greek Street to Peter Nowlan and Daniel Nunan respectively (memorial nos. 563.137.374811 and 565.513.379215, RD). In a deed registered in May 1809, he leased a house on Greek Street to Mary Drake, widow, for ten years at an annual rent of £35 (memorial no. 607.501.417444, RD).

11. Lim, in CMcATM, 149; CAM, in CMcATM, 198; Carroll, Life, 111; Burke Savage, McAuley, 40; Degnan, Mercy, 40–41; Bolster, Catherine McAuley, 16; Sullivan, CMcATM, 10.

12. Lawrence H. Officer, "Purchasing Power of British Pounds from 1264 to Present," MeasuringWorth, 2009, http://www.measuringworth.com/ppoweruk/; Lawrence H. Officer and Samuel H. Williamson, "Computing 'Real Value' over Time with a Conversion between U.K. Pounds and U.S. Dollars, 1830 to Present," MeasuringWorth, 2009, http://www.measuringworth.com/exchange/; and Lawrence H. Officer, "Dollar-Pound Exchange Rate from 1791," MeasuringWorth, 2008, http://www.measuringworth.com/exchangepound. All accessed on February 14, 2010.

13. Cameron, History of the Royal College of Surgeons, 319.

14. Legal adoption procedures, with some restrictions, were not introduced in Ireland until 1952 and 1974. Connolly, ed., Oxford Companion, 4.

a whole brood of children, in addition to the orphans whom she welcomed to Coolock.

Thus, in 1823 the Callaghan heiress turned rather swiftly from the care of the elderly to the care of the young, in her own home at Coolock and in St. Mary's parish on Liffey Street. Through her friend Joseph Nugent, the young Coolock curate who in 1823 became a curate at St. Mary's, Catherine began to assist in St. Mary's poor school, then located on Middle Abbey Street. Her chief interest was that poor girls learn employable skills and reap some small benefit from their labors. She taught them sewing and other handcrafts and created a shop in which their handmade clothing and other items could be sold. She also gave them religious instructions. Exactly how long she did this is not known, but in 1824 when she contributed £50 to the fund for completing the interior of the new St. Mary's church, the pro-cathedral on Marlborough Street, she gave as her local address (as noted in the newspaper list of subscribers) 102 Abbey Street. This was not her residence—she was still living in Coolock—but the place in the city where she spent the majority of her days and could easily be reached.[15]

It was also here, on Liffey Street, that Catherine encountered a Mrs. Harper, a poor, old, mentally ill woman "who had formerly been in better circumstances, but was now deserted by everyone." Rather than get her into an asylum, Catherine brought her to Coolock and "took care of her till her death," four or five years later. Dealing with Mrs. Harper was not as pleasant as coddling sweet children, for Mrs. Harper "from the perversity of madness . . . conceived an absolute hatred" for Catherine, and "her language in speaking of her was generally virulent and contemptuous." Besides, "her habits were most filthy, and she had an inveterate custom of stealing every thing she could lay her hands on, hiding those things she could not use."[16] Catherine's nephew Willie McAuley later recalled his childhood glee at Coolock when his aunt, attempting to get clean clothes on Mrs. Harper, "had great trouble to procure a larger pocket which the old lady wore and which, when got, was brought into the kitchen and its contents, consisting of tame mice and bread crumbs, emptied on the floor to the delight of the cats."[17]

---

15. *Dublin Evening Post*, January 24, 1824. The address Catherine gave with her donation was not her place of residence, as in Bolster, *Catherine McAuley, Prophet of Mercy* (Cork: D. and A. O'Leary, 1996), 3, and *Venerable Catherine McAuley, Liminal for Mercy* (Cork: D. and A. O'Leary, 1998), 1.

16. BA, in *CMcATM*, 101.

17. William McAuley, "Commentary on Passages in Carroll's *Life* of Catherine McAuley" (MCA). Here Willie comments on chapter 9 of the *Life*, 112, where Carroll discusses the old woman's "inveterate dislike of soap and water." He supplies her name, "Mrs. Harper."

By 1824 many strands of Catherine's life had begun to come together: the legal contesting of the Callaghan will having proved fruitless, she now had money and time at her disposal; and a lamentable incident that occurred in Coolock or Dublin gave concrete shape to her earlier dreams and growing resolve. In the latter instance, a young servant girl came to her seeking a place to live because, as Harnett's manuscript claims, "her virtue was in danger," presumably from sexual advances toward her by the young master in the house where she worked. Not able to receive the girl at Coolock House—where she had retained nearly all the faithful Callaghan servants and where her adopted children, at least three or four, also lived, as well as Mrs. Harper—and wishing to help the girl move away from the harassment, Catherine tried other possibilities. She asked established houses of refuge in Dublin to admit the girl, but encountered rigid procedures against which she would be dead set for the rest of her life. The admission committees of these houses were not resident at them and often convened only once a week or once or twice a month. Any decision about admitting the girl would have to wait until their next meeting. The waiting proved a "calamity" (Harnett's expression) for the young girl, perhaps an abduction or unsought pregnancy, and Catherine never forgot the painful lesson the incident taught her.[18]

Her mind was now made up, and in mid-1824 she began to act on the second major decision of her life (her moving in with the Callaghans having been the first). Many good friends supported her in the project she envisioned: Michael Blake, Joseph Nugent, her close friend Frances Tighe, and Edward Armstrong, then priest-administrator of St. Andrew's chapel on Townsend Street.

On June 22, 1824, she leased for one hundred fifty years from George Augustus Herbert, Earl of Pembroke, a plot of land, 100 feet by 175 feet, on the corner of Baggot Street and Herbert Street, in southeastern Dublin near the Grand Canal circling the south of the city, at an annual rent of £60. The land, formerly owned by Richard Viscount Fitzwilliam, was in a fashionable area of wealthy homes, two long streets east and south of the magnificent Georgian rowhouses surrounding Merrion Square. In the lease Catherine had to promise that she would not use the land for "a Tavern, Ale-house, Soap-boiler, Chandler, Baker, Butcher, Distiller, Sugar Baker, Brewer, Druggist, Apothecary, Tanner, Skinner, Lime-Burner, Hat-

18. Lim, in *CMcATM*, 144. This incident may have occurred earlier, when one or both of the Callaghans were still living. The sharp memory of it was long-lasting.

ter, Silver-Smith, Copper-Smith, Pewterer, Blacksmith or any other offensive or noisy Trade, Business or Profession whatsoever"—a set of possibilities amusingly far from her intentions.[19] Fortunately, a "Place of Service to Very Poor People" was not on the list. On this land Catherine then contracted to build a large house that would serve as a shelter for homeless servant girls and young women, a school for poor female children, and a residence for any lay women who wished to join her in these endeavors, as well as in visiting the sick and dying poor. It was a bold step, but one she had long contemplated. Fearing their disapproval, she did not inform her sister or brother.

The overseeing architect of the building, a "female asylum" he called it, was John B. Keane, a noted Dublin architect. On December 14, 1824, Catherine signed the final deed of agreement, attested by Keane, with Denis Lenehan and John Curran, the builder and carpenter. The building was estimated to cost £3981.2.1, to be paid in installments, and the deed required that the Reverend Edward Armstrong, the Reverend Michael Doyle (a curate at Sts. Michael and John's), and John B. Keane, or another architect he might choose to act in his place, "shall have the superintendence of the execution of the said Building," and upon their individual or collective binding notice in writing any defect in the construction would be corrected, or £981 in required payment would be forfeited.[20] The large four-inch iron keys to the front door of the house are still preserved, and the house itself still stands, as the Mercy International Centre, Baggot Street.

In July 1824—prior to his departure for Rome, where the Irish bishops had asked him to re-establish the Irish College, driven from Rome in 1798 by French revolutionaries—Michael Blake, parish priest of Sts. Michael and John's, laid the first stone of the building. The next month he left for Rome, not to return permanently until late 1828.[21] His departure was a huge loss to Catherine. Not only had he helped her and their mutual friend Edward Armstrong to choose the site and the architect, and to review the architectural plans, but he was also a man after her own heart, devoted to the needs and rights of the poor, and courageous and self-sacrificing in responding to them.

19. Typescript copy of "Deed of Indenture," June 22, 1824 (MCA). It is incorrect to say, as do the Limerick Manuscript, in *CMcATM*, 151, and Carroll, *Life*, 126, that Catherine McAuley "purchased" the ground on Baggot Street "for £4000 [or £5000] subject to the yearly rent of £60." She leased the land for an annual rent of £60, and spent close to £4000 building the house.

20. "Deed of Agreement," December 14, 1824 (MCA).

21. Peadar Mac Suibhne, *Paul Cullen and His Contemporaries*, vol. 2 (Naas: Leinster Leader, 1962), 339–53.

In the early 1810s, when he built the new church of Sts. Michael and John, Blake had had the audacity to put a bell atop the building, "the first bell set up in any Catholic place of worship since the Reformation." This "aroused the fury of the Orange bigots," and legal proceedings against Blake were begun. However, when it was discovered that Daniel O'Connell, the rising Catholic "liberator," was his advocate, the suit was quietly dropped.[22] His annual sharing of Christmas dinner with a crowd of chimney sweeps was also legendary, as was his practice, even years later as bishop of Dromore, of providing breakfast for hundreds of poor children—a massive cauldron of nutritious stirabout.[23] Now when Catherine most needed his guidance, he would be far away. But this loss was not all.

Sometime in May 1825, Joseph Nugent contracted typhus. He had been assigned to Sts. Michael's and John's to help out in Michael Blake's absence, and his name had been added to the architect's deed of agreement as one who could speak on Catherine's behalf. It was days before Catherine discovered he was sick. In his lodgings she "found him in a sad state of dirt and neglect," and "hardly left him till his death."[24]

"After fifteen days of severe suffering," during which she attended him day and night, Joseph Nugent died on May 30, 1825.[25] He was twenty-nine.

Still grieving her friend's death, Catherine went to Maynooth on June 5 for the episcopal consecration of John MacHale as coadjutor to the bishop of Killala. The professor of theology at St. Patrick's College, Maynooth, MacHale was to become the vigorous archbishop of Tuam in 1834, in which role he was commonly called the "Lion of the West." How Catherine knew him or why she attended his consecration is not known. For his part, meeting her that day made a lasting impression, and he often told his biographer about the encounter:

Her appearance as a lady of the world, so calm and so grave, her more than ordinary attractive manner, the intelligent character of her conversation, and the religious earnestness of her manner enlisted his attention, and gained the silent admiration of the young bishop. Many long years after this event he remembered the interview distinctly, and . . . was in the habit of telling the clergymen with whom he used to converse . . . how glad he was that he had seen one who was destined to be like St. Paul, "a vessel of election," . . . a source of blessing in all times to the suffering poor, and to the houseless and ignorant.[26]

22. Donnelly, *History of Dublin Parishes*, part 8, 195–97.
23. Mac Suibhne, *Paul Cullen*, 337–39.   24. CAM, in *CMcATM*, 198.
25. DL, in *CMcATM*, 46.
26. Ulick J. Bourke, *Life and Times of . . . John MacHale*, 4th ed. (New York: P. J. Kenedy, 1902), 72.

Catherine was then nearly forty-seven, and "destined" almost immediately—also like St. Paul, but not as MacHale could have predicted—for further
loss and sorrow, and for public criticism. The calm manner MacHale observed would be tested and deepened over the next five years. That one who
became so famous for his public vociferousness in defense of his people's
needs as he saw them should have so long treasured the memory of Catherine's calmness in similar pursuits perhaps reveals an aspect of MacHale's
fundamental character. He was not a Murray or a McAuley, but beneath
her serenity and courtesy Catherine would later need some of MacHale's
iron will.

Frances (Fanny) Tighe, a young woman from the archdiocese of Tuam,
frequently stayed with her aunt in Dublin.[27] She came to know Catherine
McAuley, often visited Coolock House, and may have worked with her in
St. Mary's parish. They saw things alike and became close friends, despite
the difference in their ages. As Catherine's plans developed she hoped that
Fanny would join her in executing them. Apparently the two accompanied
Catherine's brother, James, and his wife on a trip in 1825 or 1826, perhaps to
France.[28] However, Fanny wished to enter a convent and, having retained
a strong loyalty to the charitable work needed in the West, on May 3, 1827,
she entered the Presentation convent in Galway. Thirteen years later,
Catherine visited her "dear old friend," now Sister Mary Lewis.[29] But that
reunion was not even imagined in November 1827, when she attended Fanny's formal reception into the Galway community and felt the pang of her
irrevocable loss to the Baggot Street project, still in its precarious infancy.

Catherine's family, particularly her brother, were understandably curious about the rising structure on Baggot Street, as were its neighbors.
What was this large building intended to be? Who was building it, and
why? Catherine kept her intention secret because, it is said, "she had reason to know that her family would resent it extremely."[30]

Here she was, a well-to-do though sudden heiress, youthfully attractive
in her late forties, with a spacious home in Coolock. Her family thought
she should marry, and she had some "advantageous proposals."[31] Harnett
dryly comments that after the inheritance was settled, Catherine "was honored with the attentions of many distinguished individuals, who would
scarcely have condescended to notice the poor orphan girl dependent on

27. Degnan, *Mercy*, 356–57, citing a letter (1948) from the Presentation convent, Galway.
28. Letter 2 [1825–1826], in *CCMcA*, 36–37; Burke Savage, *McAuley*, 57; Degnan, *Mercy*, 45.
29. Degnan, *Mercy*, 356–57; Letter 172 [c. May 12, 1840], in *CCMcA*, 266–67.
30. Lim, in *CMcATM*, 151.   31. DL, in *CMcATM*, 45.

the bounty of her friends; but money is able to make great changes." However, Catherine let it be known that she wished to remain single. "This avowal was not at all displeasing to her more immediate friends, in as much as it seemed to secure to them the reversion of her fortune and property after her death, and the partial enjoyment of it during her life."[32] Little did they imagine how her money would be spent.

In 1821, at the age of thirty-eight, James had married Frances Ridgeway, the daughter of Counsellor William Ridgeway and Catherine Ledwich. James was now a surgeon at the Royal Hibernian Military School in Phoenix Park, where he remained until his appointment in 1829 as assistant surgeon at the Royal Hospital Kilmainham, the facility for aged and disabled soldiers. Eventually Frances and he had ten children; the first two, Eleanor (Ellen) and Emily, were born in 1822 and 1824.[33] Sometime in the mid-1820s, Catherine sent a poem to "My Dear James," assuring him that she and Fanny Tighe would be delighted to join him and his wife "for the Trip / That we'll go in a coach, in a car, or a ship." She closed the poem begging James to "give Ellen & Emily each a sweet kiss / and believe me with warm affection and truth / your sincerely attached since the days of my youth."[34] Meanwhile, the building was proceeding.

On August 18, 1804, her sister, Mary, had wed Dr. William Macauley in St. Mark's church. Catherine attended the Church of Ireland ceremony. William Macauley, an apothecary, was a few years younger than his wife. Though their surnames were similar, they were previously unrelated. Through his mother, Elizabeth Nesbitt, William inherited Montgomery family property in Cartrongarrow, County Longford, and in Aghnamallagh, County Monaghan. To the end of his long life, William (Willie), the youngest son of William and Mary, was still inquiring about this property, which he thought was owed to him.[35] By 1826 William and Mary had five living children: James, Robert, and William were probably born in 1815, 1818, and 1821, respectively; their daughters were Mary, born in 1811, and young Catherine, born in 1819. Two other Macauley children had apparently died in childbirth or infancy, for Willie claimed he was his mother's third attempt to name a son William in honor of her husband.[36]

32. Lim, in *CMcATM*, 150.

33. MACE/MCAU/2(IJA); MacErlean's research notes (MCA); Burke Savage, *McAuley*, 33, 57; Degnan, *Mercy*, 51–52, 358 n. 8. A reliable family tree of James and Frances's descendants is currently being researched.

34. Letter 2 [1825–1826], in *CCMcA*, 36–37.

35. See chap. 15 of the present book for a discussion of these properties and Willie's claims.

36. William McAuley to Mary Camillus (Teresa) Byrn, July 9, 1884 (MCA): "It was the third attempt she made in her great love for my fond father to call a child after him."

Catherine was devoted, and not just dutifully, to her sister and brother and their families. She remained unalterably affectionate toward them as long as they lived, and on the day of her death her brother and his wife were at her bedside. The only tension within the family concerned religion, which created a painful gulf between Catherine and her siblings, especially James. Not to speak of her plans for the house on Baggot Street was her way to avoid fresh stings of that pain. James presumably did not go so far as to agree publicly with people in the neighborhood who, having heard that the house was being erected by a "Miss McAuley," could only conclude that "having lately come into the possession of a great deal of money, she did not know what to do with it." He too thought it was "a useless and wasteful expenditure," and is said to have called the building "Kitty's Folly," but he apparently kept his peace: it was her own money and she could use it as she wished.[37]

37. Lim, in *CMcATM*, 152.

CHAPTER 4

New Sorrows and Responsibilities *1827–1829*

In the summer of 1827, sorrow struck the Macauley family. William, Sr., was then serving as assistant surgeon to Dr. George Renny at the Royal Hospital Kilmainham. His appointment to the hospital in 1819 apparently entitled the family to live in a house on Military Road, adjacent to the hospital grounds. Catherine visited frequently, enjoying the children and the time to be with her sister. She had a natural talent for relating to the young and entering their imagined worlds of ponies, dolls, and wooden toys, a talent soon tested. For in 1827 the obvious symptoms of pulmonary consumption (tuberculosis) began to develop in her sister, Mary, to the heartache of her whole family, not least her husband.

Their son William, not yet six, later recalled the harrowing weeks that followed:

About this time my darling mother became very ill with consumption. She was removed to Stillorgan. I remember the removal as though it was yesterday. My fondly loved sister Mary had twenty-two canaries. She took them with her, put them in a small room off the drawing room. The first night a weasel got in and killed every one of them. My father and I, together with my two pet kids, Diana and Venus, in the well of our outside jaunting car, drove out to Stillorgan frequently. . . . However, I was not allowed to stop many minutes with my loving and idolized mother. At last, the news came along, we were motherless. . . . The light of our eyes was eclipsed by the shadow of death, and we silently mourn[ed] in the dark shades of sorrow.[1]

1. William Armstrong Montgomery McAuley to "Dear Revd. Mother" [Mary Augustine Mungovan], Bendigo, Victoria, Australia, July 15, 1903 (MCA). William concludes this letter, "Pray for poor Wild Willie." He claims his mother died of consumption, not of "an internal cancer" as in Lim, *CMcATM*, 153.

Catherine had supported Mary's going to the house in Stillorgan where the fresher air of the Dublin foothills might assist her breathing. Moreover, Mary had given signs of a growing desire to return to the Catholic Church. If this were the case, a priest could more easily converse with her away from the house on Military Road, away from her husband's avowed prejudice against "papists." Mary had not shared the disapproval with which her husband and brother had reacted to her sister's involvement with the poor and to the building being constructed on Baggot Street. While she apparently had no precise information about Catherine's plans, she evidently spoke frequently of "the delight she hoped to experience in seeing the poor enjoying the comforts of that great house."[2] But this sisterly pleasure was not to be.

In the last weeks of Mary's illness, she and Catherine, who nursed her, had many opportunities to talk alone. In these moments they recalled their Catholic upbringing and Catherine's hope that Mary, now somewhat freed from the daily vigilance of her husband, might return to the faith she had once held, before her otherwise very happy marriage into a family long known for its Orange Lodge affiliations and opposition to all things Catholic.

Sometime in mid-July Mary made her decision, and John McCormick, chaplain of the Carmelite nuns in Blackrock, was invited to Stillorgan, where he offered her the sacraments and received her back into the Catholic Church. Mary informed only her eldest child, young Mary, now sixteen, encouraging her to follow her example, and "requiring that the most profound secrecy should be observed in everything relative to the matter as she dreaded the consequences which might befall her sister."[3] Mary Macauley died in August. She was buried on August 13, 1827, in St. Mark's churchyard, to all appearances a Protestant to the end.

Catherine's sorrow at the death of her sister must have been profound. Gone now was the one adult family member with whom she could share her heart's aspirations, with whom, as with her deceased cousin Anne, she could be fully herself. Gone also was any familial tie to the faith of her father and to some appreciation of his merciful efforts. Her brother, James, was a good man, but having been only a newborn when their father died in 1783, having devoted his adult life to demanding medical and military pursuits, both in and away from Dublin, and having now his own grow-

2. DL, in *CMcATM*, 47.
3. Ibid.

ing family to support, as well as his maintaining a distant attitude toward the Catholic Church, meant that their mutual affection was less intimate. Keeping up positive relations required deliberate effort on both their parts.

After Mary's death, Catherine, while still maintaining Coolock House, resided often on Military Road, helping her brother-in-law care for his five motherless children, ranging in age from six to sixteen. It could have been no easy task overseeing the activities of three establishments, including the Baggot Street house, now partially ready for occupancy.

During 1827 Catherine had met a young Dublin woman who was willing to help her at Baggot Street. Anna Maria Doyle, twenty-six years old, was a godsend. Although she had long planned to enter the enclosed Presentation Sisters in Maynooth and serve poor and uneducated children in that way, her parents were now aging, and as she was "the only one of the family left at home, she was loath to leave them." Her older brother James, a Dublin priest, had offered to provide the Presentation dowry, but had died suddenly of typhus in November 1824. Her older and only sister, Catherine, had recently died in the Presentation convent in Killarney, and her brother John, an artist, and his family were living in London. Anna Maria was therefore her parents' mainstay, and while they supported her life's decision, whatever it would be, they hoped she could sometimes visit and assist them.[4]

When Anna Maria was introduced to Catherine McAuley at the house on Military Road and heard plans for the charitable work to be done by those who, Catherine hoped, would join her in the house on Baggot Street, she was relieved. Here was a way she could fulfill both her goals: devote herself to the service of the poor and, when necessary, serve her parents' needs. The fact that Catherine was close to fifty did not diminish her enthusiasm. If this was a welcome solution for Anna Maria, it was even more beneficial for Catherine. Yet Anna Maria was eager to begin. When could she move into Baggot Street? Any hesitation on Catherine's part could have lost her first and, so far, only volunteer.

Catherine was torn. The Baggot Street building was not fully completed, and there was Coolock House to look after. And one way or another, she had nine or ten children to worry about: the five Macauley children, her adopted cousins Catherine and Teresa Byrn (now fifteen and six), and the orphans living at Coolock, including Ellen Corrigan and perhaps Mary

---

4. Bonaventure Brennan, *"It commenced with two . . . .": The Story of Mary Ann Doyle*, (n.p.: Sisters of Mercy, Northern Province, 2001), 3, 10–15.

Quin and Ann Rice. The servants were certainly a help, but Catherine knew that she was already trying to be the impossible: a bi-located mother. Yet Anna Maria's zeal for the work they envisioned persisted. Finally Catherine decided to ask her young cousin to join Anna Maria in opening Baggot Street. Catherine Byrn had thought of becoming a Dominican sister, but was willing to set this hope aside, perhaps just temporarily, no doubt anxious to assist the adoptive mother who had been so good to her since her mother's death five years before.

Events moved rapidly. Anna Maria wished Catherine to set a date, soon, so she did. She picked September 24, 1827. They later realized they had chosen the feast day of Our Lady of Mercy, and together agreed to place the infant establishment under the patronage of the Mother of God, with the title of "the most amiable of her attributes by which she most resembles Him whose mercies are above all His works."[5] It would be a "House of Mercy." Later, when its works of mercy were more fully operational, they would ask Archbishop Daniel Murray for permission to use this name publicly.

Catherine had instructed John B. Keane, the architect, to create two large dormitories for homeless women and servant girls, two large rooms to serve as schoolrooms for poor girls, some very small bedrooms for the residents who would assist her—the "ladies who might choose, for any definite or indefinite time, to devote themselves to the service of the poor"—and a chapel.[6] But the interior construction had proceeded slowly. In August 1827 the building was little more than a shell. However, two small rooms were ready for Anna Maria Doyle and Catherine Byrn, and that would be enough for the present.

The doors of the House of Mercy on Baggot Street opened on Monday, September 24, 1827—a date that would one day be revered. A flaw in the building's construction had been discovered earlier and by chance. Bryan Bolger, apparently now the assigned overseer, had put in a metal grate between the chapel and an adjoining room, such as one might find in a convent of cloistered nuns. When she was inspecting the building and came upon the grate, Catherine was alternately amused and annoyed. Clare Moore says she "laughed at their putting a choir with a grated window in it."[7] Mary Vincent Harnett says, "She was much surprised and amused," for

---

5. DL, in *CMcATM*, 48.   6. Ibid., 45.
7. CML, in *CMcATM*, 88.

"the idea of founding a religious Institute never entered her mind."[8] What Catherine planned was "a society of pious secular ladies, who would devote themselves" to the work she had in mind, "with liberty to return to their worldly life when they no longer felt inclined to discharge such duties."[9] Clare Augustine Moore says that when Catherine visited the building "it was with great surprise and no pleasure that she saw a grating in front of that part of the chapel which she had reserved for herself and her companions. 'What,' she said, 'could be the use of a grating where there never would be nuns?'"[10] But the grate remained until 1838.

The final architect's drawings for the three-story house—signed by "Catherine McAuley, Spinster," on December 14, 1824—are still preserved. Included in the basement were two kitchens (a large one with a dining area for the House of Mercy, and a smaller one for the "ladies"), two storerooms, a coal vault, a pantry, a refectory for the "ladies," and a laundry. On the street floor (as one faced outward toward Baggot Street) were two main staircases, the front one in the center of the building, the back one at the end of its left side, and two smaller ones at either end of the chapel on the right with an outside passage to the street. On this floor there were also a choir (prayer) room, with its unwelcome grate, to the right of the front door, a reception room to the left, a large schoolroom (twenty feet by sixty feet) on the left, a long connecting corridor that ran from the chapel to the schoolroom, and privies outside the schoolroom and back stairs on the left, beyond a small yard. The middle story, again as one faced Baggot Street, had on the right the upper part of the high-ceilinged chapel with its music gallery in the front and an overhanging gallery and stairs at the back, an "Infirmary for Ladies" in the front, a second large "School Room for Female Children" on the left with access to the back stairs, and again a long front corridor reached by the central staircase. The upper story contained a small "W.C." (water closet), eight small "Ladies Cells" across the front, a corridor stretching the full length of the house, and two large dormitories, one for "Young Women" on the right, and balancing it on the left another for "Female Children."[11] The convent language, "cells," had evidently escaped Catherine's critique. When the house underwent its most recent repairs and renovations, the builders remarked on the quality

8. Lim, in *CMcATM*, 151.   9. BA, in *CMcATM*, 102.
10. CAM, in *CMcATM*, 202–3.
11. Transcript copy of draft "Deed of Agreement, Catherine McAuley, Denis Lenehan, John Curran, and John B. Keane," December 14, 1824 (MCA).

and durability of its 1820s construction. Its original slate roof lasted to the twenty-first century.

The presence in the house of certain features that would be desirable from a modern perspective remains a question. Specifically, did the house have water piped in? If so, to where? Or did it, like most Dublin homes built in the 1820s, depend on water buckets carried from an inside tap in the kitchen, or from an outside tap, a well, a cistern, or a reservoir for water collected from elsewhere in the neighborhood? An inside water supply, just to the kitchen, seems possible, but there are no plumbing or sewage estimates in the extant deed of agreement with the builders. Moreover, the sewers and drainage provisions of Dublin, at this time and until late in the century, generally carried away, not water or waste from homes, but only surface water in the streets, which was then dumped untreated into the River Liffey.

The one W.C. on the top floor (as seen in the architect's drawings) did not necessarily have its own supply of water. It could have been, and probably was, a dry W.C. which needed water carried to it in buckets, and human waste carried from it, both daily chores. Chamber pots and individual wash bowls with pitchers would have been standard. The four outside privies and the "dirt hole" (sometimes called an "ashpit" or "cesspit"), beyond the Herbert Street extension in Keane's drawing, would have completed the sanitary provisions of the house. Mona Hearn describes this arrangement, common even in later Victorian homes in Dublin:

For the disposal of human refuse, a privy at the rear of the house, or the bottom of the garden was used. An unpopular part of the housemaid's work was the emptying of all the chamber-pots used during the night into this cesspit. A simple cesspool required frequent emptying by the so-called "night-soil" men [city employees] who came and went by a back entrance . . . (hence the network of little lanes behind some of the older Victorian [and Georgian] streets). . . . It was only after the Public Health Act, 1878, that water closets [with their own water supply and drains] were regularly introduced into houses in Dublin city, and privies and cesspools were done away with. . . .

Until the 1860s, running water was rarely piped beyond the kitchen, and that was only a cold supply. People bathed in a tin bath. . . . In all cases the baths had to [be] filled and emptied by hand, and the hot water heated by the kitchen range.[12]

On September 24, 1827, when Anna Maria Doyle and Catherine Byrn moved in, there could have been few furnishings in the house, beyond

---

12. Mona Hearn, "How Victorian Families Lived," in Mary Daly, Mona Hearn, and Peter Pearson, *Dublin's Victorian Homes* (Dublin: A. & A. Farmar, 1998), 83–84.

the odd pieces of furniture, bedding, dishes, and other utensils Catherine brought from Coolock House. History is largely silent about these practical matters, as if they were not of primary importance to the first or future residents. Eventually Catherine would bring tables, a cabinet, a writing desk, more dishes with green and gold patterns, some rush-seated chairs, and the oil portrait of William Callaghan, all of which have survived to this day.

The school for poor, barefoot young girls was started later that day and the next. Although Baggot Street, Fitzwilliam Street, and Merrion Square contained the well-adorned homes of the wealthy, the back alleys and narrow side streets surrounding them concealed the slum hovels and cellars of hundreds of poor families. In 1799, Dr. Whitley Stokes—a physician at the Meath Hospital, later Regius Professor of Physic at Trinity College (as well as the father of Catherine McAuley's future physician)—wrote of the poverty hidden in southeast Dublin:

I have seen . . . three lying ill of fever in a closet, the whole floor of which was literally covered by a small bed. . . .

The inhabitants of Merrion-square may be surprised to hear, that in the angle behind Mount-street and Holles-street [near Baggot Street], there is now a family of ten in a very small room, of whom eight have had fever in the last month.[13]

These pockets of poverty in back alleys and mews persisted. But in September 1827 poor families suddenly found, in their own neighborhood, free schoolrooms for their female children. Within the week, homeless women and girls and unemployed or barely employed servant girls also came to the door seeking shelter in the House of Mercy. Happily, there was no non-resident admissions committee to delay or turn down their requests. With her niece Mary, Catherine was there nearly every day to receive them, with a kind word and an outstretched hand.

Meanwhile, "Miss McAuley," as they called her, was traveling back and forth in her Swiss carriage between Coolock, Military Road, and Baggot Street—probably with a sense of joy and gratitude that her long-held dream was coming true, but also with fear, doubt, and apprehension. She had two co-workers, but would others join her? The house was big and the expenses would be great. Would the annual Callaghan money be enough? It was one thing to wish to participate wholeheartedly in the ministry of Jesus to those whom society considered "the least." It was quite another,

13. Whitley Stokes, *Projects for Re-Establishing the Internal Peace and Tranquillity of Ireland* (Dublin: James Moore, 1799), 32–33.

humanly, to pay for the needed food and turf and the annual rent on the property. Soon hundreds of children were coming daily to the poor school, many needing clothes to replace their rags. Eventually some women offered to help in the school: Daniel O'Connell's daughters Kate and Betsey came daily from the family home on Merrion Square, and Louisa Costello, Anne Costigan, and others came, though none of these planned to reside in the house.[14]

On Christmas Day 1827, a dinner of roast beef and plum pudding was served to the poor children of the neighborhood, a custom that would continue. Assisted by many Protestant women friends, Catherine was in her element in the midst of the festivities. All the skills of hospitality and solicitude she had developed at the Callaghans were now put to maximum use at Baggot Street, even though she did not yet reside there.[15]

But a menacing cloud was gathering over the house. Some Dubliners began to murmur. Baggot Street homeowners, though accustomed to seeing beggars and poor people on other city streets, complained about the rag-tag people coming to the house in their own neighborhood. Even some clergy, notably Matthias Kelly, now administrator of St. Andrew's chapel on Townsend Street, the parish where the House of Mercy was situated, began to look askance at the charitable endeavors Catherine had instituted without having sought any parish sanction. Who did this "upstart," this "parvenue," think she was? Some of the murmuring was flavored with sexist overtones. Some people announced that Catherine McAuley had "unsexed" herself, and Matthias Kelly is said to have had "no great idea that the unlearned sex could do anything but mischief by trying to assist the clergy."[16]

Michael Blake was still in Rome, beyond consultation. So in early 1828 Catherine turned to her good friend and confessor Edward Armstrong, now parish priest of St. Michan's church on the north side of the city. She had met him through Joseph Nugent, when both were serving at St. Mary's on Liffey Street. Now in waning health, Armstrong was deeply committed to the success of Catherine's efforts. When the Baggot Street project was in the planning stage it was he, with Michael Blake, who advised her to build in that location: "If you would have a public Institution be of service to the poor, place it in the neighborhood of the rich."[17]

14. CML, in CMcATM, 89; CAM, in CMcATM, 201.
15. Lim, in CMcATM, 157. Whether the first Mass celebrated in the chapel at Baggot Street on Christmas Day was in 1827 or 1828 (as in Harnett, Life, 37) remains a question.
16. CAM, in CMcATM, 208.   17. Lim, in CMcATM, 150.

Obviously Edward Armstrong did not share Matthias Kelly's prejudices. On the contrary, he assured Catherine that the work she had undertaken would survive, to the incalculable benefit of many poor women and girls. Yet he realized her isolation and her need for some sign of ecclesiastical support for her pioneering endeavor: a group of lay women living in a community and dedicated to the daily sheltering and service of scores of poor and uneducated Dublin women and children. As chancellor of the archdiocese and confessor to Archbishop Murray, he had some influence, and promised Catherine he would speak to the archbishop and to other clergy who he believed would appreciate what she was trying to do.

As his health worsened, Armstrong wrote on March 16, 1828, to his "dearly beloved" archbishop asking him to assist in executing his will. After requesting that his few remaining personal effects—his books, a painting, his snuff box, and a little money—might be distributed to his maid, relatives, and friends, as well as some money and other objects to Baggot Street, he explained his greatest concern:

The only great solicitude which presses on me is with respect to Miss McAuley. When I shall be taken from her, she will find herself in a great measure bereft of an Ecclesiastical Friend, which is a desideratum for her of the utmost importance. Surrounded on every side by Protestant and prejudiced relatives and acquaintances, she will be much straightened to follow up her good purposes, unless protected and supported by some zealous and religious Friend. Could I pledge myself to her that you would be that good Friend, who would support and uphold her good purposes, there could not be any fear for her.[18]

Meanwhile he was encouraging Catherine in a quite different and, in effect, more profound and lasting way. He recognized her present difficulties and, insofar as her long-range worries were financial, "suggested that if necessary, a subscription could be raised," but he was "above all things solicitous that she should purify her intention, and place all her confidence in God alone."[19] Clare Moore reports that repeatedly and emphatically he said to Catherine: "'Do not put your trust in any human being, but place all your confidence in God alone'—prophesying almost that all human aid would fail, but God's help would never be wanting. She often told me this when oppressed with care."[20] Mary Vincent Harnett also knew the long-term and hard-won effect of Armstrong's advice: "Those who knew her afterwards . . . thought she possessed holy confidence to an eminent degree

18. Letter 5, March 16, 1828, in *CCMcA*, 40.   19. Lim, in *CMcATM*, 153.
20. CML, in *CMcATM*, 92.

... but it was a virtue she did not suddenly acquire." In the early months of 1828, when she was fearful of and exhausted by her many responsibilities, "her friend had often to repeat the lesson to her."[21] Today those who treasure the life of Catherine McAuley also treasure the legacy of Edward Armstrong's simple sentence.

In May 1828, his ill health became irreversible. In his modest quarters at St. Michan's he was dying. Daniel Murray visited him, and again Armstrong repeated his solicitude for Catherine McAuley and the young establishment on Baggot Street. Catherine herself attended her friend "with unremitting care until his death." He told her of the favorable assurances he had received, but, nevertheless, repeated again and again his most enduring words to her. She was present when he died on Thursday, May 15, the octave of the Ascension. The carriage journey from Halston Street back to Coolock or Military Road must have been a lonely one. She did not record her own thoughts and feelings that day, but those who knew her well knew that Armstrong was her "sincere and long tried friend," and that she had relied on him.[22]

For many months after the opening of Baggot Street in September 1827, Anna Maria Doyle and Catherine Byrn were the only staff living there at night. After Edward Armstrong's death Catherine began to stay there frequently though not permanently. She worked in the house almost daily, bringing her nieces Mary and Catherine, as well as her godchild Teresa Byrn. Slowly in 1828 other helpers joined the resident community. In June, Frances Warde, a young friend of Catherine's niece Mary, began to help out daily and reside there occasionally. Now orphaned, Frances was living with relatives in Dublin. In September, Georgiana Moore, herself only fourteen, responded to a call for a governess for young Catherine Macauley and Teresa Byrn, ages nine and seven. On October 13 Georgiana began to reside in Baggot Street, though eight months later poor health forced her to leave for a year.[23] Meanwhile the door knocker sounded often, with a runaway girl or a homeless servant needing help. Twenty or thirty women and girls were sleeping each night in the one completed dormitory. Most of them went out all day to menial work or to search for work, and several very young orphans were mothered in the house.

The poor school was now flourishing, with at least two hundred pupils and resident and non-resident teachers. One may wonder how so many

21. Lim, in *CMcATM*, 153.   22. Ibid., 158.
23. CML, in *CMcATM*, 85.

children fitted into the two large schoolrooms, one on the street floor and one on the floor above. The girls were evidently taught by the Lancasterian system: adult or senior-student monitors, guided by one or two teachers, gathered around themselves small circles of students separated by ability. The monitors guided the students' learning in reading, writing, spelling, arithmetic, religion, Bible study, and handcrafts.[24]

On September 24, 1828, Archbishop Murray, perhaps adverting to Edward Armstrong's dying plea, sent word that the House could be styled "of our Blessed Lady of Mercy," though it remained commonly known simply as the "House of Mercy."[25] On November 22, he privately received Catherine's niece Mary Macauley, now seventeen, into the Catholic Church in the chapel, following her desire to embrace her dying mother's wish. On the same day he gave permission for the "visitation of the sick," allowing Catherine and her companions to visit sick and dying poor Dubliners not only in their slum hovels but also in any hospital where poor Catholics were admitted, and the women could gain access.[26]

Located mostly in western Dublin south of the River Liffey, within walking distance of Baggot Street, the Liberties were the worst slums of the city, especially the region surrounding St. Patrick's church, including Bull Alley Street, Bride Street, and other narrow, crowded haunts as far south as the Coombe and Kevin Street.[27] In his *Miseries and Beauties of Ireland*, the English writer Jonathan Binns describes the Liberties: "Narrow streets, houses without windows or doors, and several families crowded together beneath the same roof, present a picture of ruin, disease, poverty, filth and wretchedness of which they who have not witnessed it are unable to form a competent idea." Binns notes the "miserable beings ... lying half naked, and apparently half dead from cold and hunger, on the parapets and steps of the houses, their nightly resting places."[28] The area around Townsend Street in the east was no better. It is little wonder that the women of the House of Mercy walked in pairs to visit the sick

---

24. Joseph Lancaster (1778–1838), an English Quaker, advocated this system of monitorial instruction in schools with large numbers of children of varying attainments. Mary Clare (Elizabeth) Agnew's pen drawing of such a schoolroom illustrates the system, though she has the clusters of barefoot girls all gathered around Sisters of Mercy. See Agnew's *Illustrations of the Corporal & Spiritual Works of Mercy* (London: Charles Dolman, 1840).

25. CML, in *CMcATM*, 89; BA, in *CMcATM*, 103; Lim, in *CMcATM*, 159.

26. MADL, in *CMcATM*, 42; Lim, in *CMcATM*, 159; CAM, in *CMcATM*, 201.

27. The Liberties were areas of the old city of Dublin exempt, by royal gift, from the jurisdiction of the mayor of Dublin.

28. Jonathan Binns, *The Miseries and Beauties of Ireland*, vol. 1 (London: Longman, Orme, Brown, 1837), 3.

and dying poor in these alleys, and that Catherine later counseled them "to understand perfectly the way they are to go, and if some places cannot be found without making enquiry it will be most prudent to go into a Dairy, Huxter or Baker's shop where the poor are generally known," not as purchasers but as beggars.[29]

To serve and solace such as these, as best she could, had by late 1828 become the consuming goal of Catherine McAuley's life and energies. On June 12, 1824, just before ground was broken for the house on Baggot Street, she had placed an advertisement in *Freeman's Journal* (Dublin) announcing that Coolock House was for lease or sale:

COOLOCK HOUSE, To be Set or Sold, With 22 Acres of Land. The House consists of a Study, a Dining-room, 32 feet long; two Drawing-rooms, 23 feet each; six excellent Bed-chambers, two large Kitchens, with Hot-hearth, Boilers and Oven; Dairy, Pantry, Store-room, good Wine-cellar, and large Coal-vault. In the Farm-Yard, there are three Dwellings for Out-servants, Coach-house, excellent Stabling, Car and Cart-houses, etc. etc. etc. A good Pump.

The House commands a delightful Sea and Mountain View, and the Air is remarkably healthful.

Near Coolock Village, within 30 minutes drive of Dublin.

Whatever inquiries were then made, Catherine delayed selling or leasing—and for good reason. Coolock House and its outbuildings were filled in 1824 with otherwise homeless women and children and several dependent servants, and the house on Baggot Street was only a mental plan.

Now, on September 15, 1828, Catherine registered the deed of conveyance (dated September 13, 1828) transferring the house and property in Coolock to Henry Brooke, Esquire, of the city of Dublin, at a yearly land rent of £151.9.4, payable to Sir Compton Domville. The deed included the "twenty-two acres and thirty-one perches" of land, as well as "the Dwelling house, offices, Yards, Gardens, orchards, Gates, Buildings, Locks, fixtures, rails and other Improvements enjoyed therewith, together with the several crops then growing or cut, saved, or remaining on the premises and all manure and other matters . . . and all the Estate right Title and Interest of her the said Catherine McAuley." It has been said that she sold the house itself and its outbuildings and appurtenances for £1000, but an official copy of the memorial does not mention this or any figure, saying only (and discreetly), as was common in memorials of deeds of conveyance, "for the considerations therein mentioned."[30]

---

29. Rule 3.5, in *CMcATM*, 298.
30. "Attested Copy of the Memorial of the Deed of Conveyance," September 15, 1828 (MCA), and

Surrendered now was the physical centerpiece of Catherine McAuley's former mode of life, the scene of so much she humanly cherished. Gone were the walls and rooms within which she had matured in the grace of the Callaghans' love. Responding to Francis L'Estrange, a Carmelite priest at St. Teresa's church, she had laid out her plan with clarity and decisiveness:

> With full approbation of his Grace The Archbishop, the institution in Baggot Street is to go on according to the original intention. Ladies who prefer a Conventual life, and are prevented embracing it from the nature of property or connections, may retire to this House. It is expected a gratuity will be given to create a fund for the school, and an annual pension paid sufficient to meet the expence a lady must incur.
>
> The objects which the Charity at present embraces are daily education of hundreds of poor female Children, and instruction of young women who sleep in the House.
>
> Objects in view—superintendence of young women employed in the house, instructing and assisting the sick poor as may hereafter be approved.[31]

The resident ladies of the house were lay women, not nuns. They were free to depart, permanently or temporarily, should a family need or other circumstance necessitate their leaving. Catherine herself, now fifty, intended to remain there the rest of her life, taking with her Ellen Corrigan, an orphan who had lived and worked at Coolock House, the other children she befriended there, and her godchild Teresa Byrn, now seven.

Her nieces Mary and young Catherine, ages seventeen and nine, could stay with her as often as their father permitted. His boys, James, Robert, and Willie, now in school, would stay with their father on Military Road, where servants also looked after them. Catherine's dream of serving the poor full time while fulfilling her many other responsibilities could now be mostly under one roof. Perhaps she could soon sell her Swiss carriage.

The 1828 Christmas dinner for poor children attracted wide public support. "Several charitable persons had sent in contributions of beef, fruit, etc.," and "Protestants as well as Catholics of the best fashion came in great numbers" to assist. Daniel O'Connell, ever loyal to the house, carved.[32] He paid special attention to a young orphan whose mother, a nurse at Sir Patrick Dun's Hospital, had died the week before. While many of the visitors focused on the little girls who were beautiful, orphans who had been

---

memorial no. 838.346.562924 (RD). Appleyard, *Green Fields*, 120, mentions the £1000, but does not give his source. Burke Savage, *McAuley*, and Bolster, *Catherine McAuley*, do not discuss the sale at all. Degnan, *Mercy*, 75, mentions only the fact of the sale, as does Carroll, *Life*, 130.

31. Letter 6, September 10, 1828, in *CCMcA*, 41–42.

32. DL, in *CMcATM*, 50.

longer in the house and "had learned to behave prettily before company," O'Connell's pet was the nurse's child, "the ugliest, most ill formed, uncouth being you could fancy." He treated the child to "dainty pieces, said droll things to make her merry, and when she had done eating took her in his arms, kissed her (she was about 4 years) and told her she was his favorite of all the little girls there."[33]

Only one worry preyed on Catherine's mind: the need to tell William Macauley that his daughter Mary had asked to be received into the Catholic Church, and, if it came to this, that his wife had returned to the Catholic Church before her death. She dreaded having to make these disclosures to him. For all his inherited misinformation and resulting prejudice, which she had often witnessed, he was a good and amiable man, ardently faithful to his wife for whom he was still grieving with tears, and affectionately devoted to his five children. A loving husband, he was now a generous father who, despite the daily demands of his surgical duties at the Royal Hospital, always made time for his children's pleasures.

The disclosures occurred in late 1828, though possibly earlier, while Catherine was staying at the house on Military Road. What actually took place has been the subject of conflicting historical accounts—on the part of those who were unlikely witnesses or were possibly in a position to know, as well as later biographers and others who received their information secondhand. Catherine herself left no account of the event, though she may have described it to one or other of her trusted associates. The worst features of versions of the story are not what she would have wanted repeated about her brother-in-law or given misleading prominence as somehow representing his character.

One evening Catherine told William Macauley about his daughter Mary's proposed (or completed?) reception into the Catholic Church. In the heated conversation that ensued, that night or the next day, she also told him that his wife had died a Catholic and of her dying wish that young Mary follow her example. Harnett's Limerick Manuscript says that William "rushed up stairs perfectly beside himself with the fearful paroxysm of his fury, and utterly reckless as to what his anger might prompt him to

---

33. CAM, in *CMcATM*, 202. O'Connell was then the elected but unseated M. P. for County Clare. Four months later the Act of Catholic Emancipation was finally passed, allowing elected Irish and English Catholics to take their places in Parliament, and O'Connell was re-elected unopposed. Catherine McAuley left no record of her political views, perhaps through long-schooled wariness, given her family climate and its British associations, but she apparently admired Daniel O'Connell, at the very least for his devotion to neglected children. She was pleased, a decade and more later, when Frances Warde in Carlow had "a grand breakfast for the Liberator." Letter 279, [mid-July 1841], in *CCMcA*, 413.

do. Perhaps in the rage of the moment some calamity may have been the result, if Miss McAuley, terrified at the storm which she had excited, had not resolved to escape the danger by flight." She fled to the home of an acquaintance where she spent the night, and "when Dr. Macauley returned to the drawing room, it is said with a dagger in his hand, she was gone." In the morning, "some friends undertook the work of reconciliation, and he, ashamed of his violence . . . made an apology for his conduct, and solemnly engaged that the topic which had been the occasion of his anger should never again be alluded to." Catherine accepted his apology and "to the great happiness and joy of the children their beloved Aunt returned to them."[34] Harnett's published biography (1864) says essentially the same thing, including reference to the dagger.[35]

Mary Ann (Anna Maria) Doyle gives a much abbreviated version of the supposed incident. She does not speak of any weapon, but says Catherine "ran down the Military Road to Dr. Cusack's lodgings in the Royal Hospital" in her "dressing gown."[36] In Clare Augustine Moore's account, the dagger is now "a carving knife."[37] In Carroll's 1866 biography—with even more melodramatic language and created dialogue—the dagger has become a "sword unsheathed."[38]

Writing in 1867, Catherine Byrn felt strongly obliged "to defend good, kind Mr. McAuley [sic] from the imputation of violent conduct towards his Sister-in-law." She argues that he was "one of the kindest and most consistent of Protestants, for he allowed to others the same liberty of private judgment which he claimed for himself," and she says she can "attest" that

every 12th of July [young Mary Macauley's birthday and, coincidentally, the day traditionally chosen for the Orange Order's annual celebration of William III's victory at the Battle of the Boyne (1690)] was spent in Coolock at a family reunion. Had such a scene as that described . . . taken place, I could scarcely have been without hearing of it, and I never did, nor of anything resembling it.[39]

In the late nineteenth century, William McAuley (Macauley), his parents' youngest son, reflected on the scene in question (which allegedly occurred when he was only six or seven): "I certainly was not in the drawing

34. Lim, in CMcATM, 155–56.

35. Harnett, Life, 31–34, 42, places young Mary's reception into the Catholic Church after the event of William Macauley's anger, which may have occurred in 1827 or 1828.

36. DL, in CMcATM, 47.

37. CAM, in CMcATM, 200.

38. Carroll, Life, 114–19, 124. Carroll also seems to place young Mary's reception into the Catholic Church after the scene on Military Road, which she places in 1827.

39. Mary Raymond Byrn to Mary Clare Moore, October 23, 1867 (MCA).

room to witness the scene described. If I had [been] I never would have forgotten it. I cannot reconcile the idea of a thorough gentleman, a brave and feeling man, chasing a lady with a naked sword whom he loved and feared, a man who ... when challenged [on another occasion] to meet with pistols refused, showing his hatred to shedding blood."[40] Mary Hermenia Muldrey, Carroll's biographer, argues that in *The Nun of Kenmare* (1889), Carroll's account is corroborated by the author Margaret Anna Cusack (born in 1829), a niece of the surgeon James William Cusack to whose home Catherine McAuley is said to have fled that night.[41]

The significance of the event lies, not in whether there was a weapon—a question that seems best answered in the negative—but in William Macauley's initial anger, illustrating as it does the depth of the prevailing animosity toward "popery," particularly bitter among Scottish Presbyterians. The various accounts also illustrate how even well-intended manuscripts and books may suffer from inaccuracies and embellishments, and from too great dependence on each other. The only person who could have been a reliable written reporter of the event is Catherine McAuley, and she apparently chose not to be.

But even greater disruption and sorrow lay ahead for the family. Sometime in late January 1829, Dr. William Macauley fell ill. Apparently his ailment was at first an ulcerated sore throat. But a fever quickly developed, related to the throat infection. Had there been a remedy he surely would have known of it. William Macauley died on January 25, in his mid-forties.[42] To the deep grief and astonishment of his children, after only three days' illness their father was gone. In the hours before his death, as Catherine attended him, William Macauley gave his children the freedom to choose their own guardian, either their Uncle James McAuley, his brother-in-law, or their Aunt Catherine. All five chose Catherine: Mary, still seventeen; James, thirteen; Robert, ten; Catherine, nine; and "Wild Willie," as he later called himself, seven in the previous December.

Catherine McAuley was now the guardian of at least nine or ten young people: the Macauleys, Catherine and Teresa Byrn, Ellen Corrigan, and probably Ann Rice and Mary Quin, orphans she had brought to Baggot

40. William McAuley, "Commentary on Passages in Carroll's *Life* of Catherine McAuley," referring to p. 116 of Carroll's *Life* (MCA). In later life he spelled his name McAuley.

41. Interview by the author, May 7, 2007. See also M. Hermenia Muldrey, *Abounding in Mercy* (New Orleans: Habersham, 1988), 79–80, 361 n. 31, 362 nn. 32–33.

42. Some early sources say William Macauley died in February, but this is not accurate, in view of the burial record of St. Mark's church.

Street. She was also the founder of a House of Mercy that needed all the help and time she could give. Michael Blake had just arrived home from Rome. Joseph Nugent and Edward Armstrong had died, and Fanny Tighe was gone to Galway. Daniel Murray, installed as the archbishop of Dublin in 1823, was routinely busy, particularly occupied at this time with a clerical dispute over parish boundaries, correspondence with London about his petition for passage of Catholic emancipation, and correspondence with Rome about the appointment of bishops and the election of Pope Pius VIII. Most of the Dublin clergy showed greater interest in the new women's religious congregations, the Irish Sisters of Charity and the Loreto Sisters, than in the anomalous, fledgling community on Baggot Street where a handful of secular women tried to run a poor school and a shelter for homeless women and maintain a regular schedule of visiting the sick and dying poor.

It was relatively easy for Catherine to recall the dying words of Edward Armstrong: "Do not put your trust in any human being, but place all your confidence in God." In late January and February 1829, it was far more difficult to live and act by such advice. Yet somehow Catherine did, remarking often in later years, and referring more to others than to herself:

If we are humble and sincere God will finish in us the work He has begun, He never refuses His grace to those who ask it.[43]

43. *PS*, 3.

Coolock House, the Callaghan home in Coolock, County Dublin

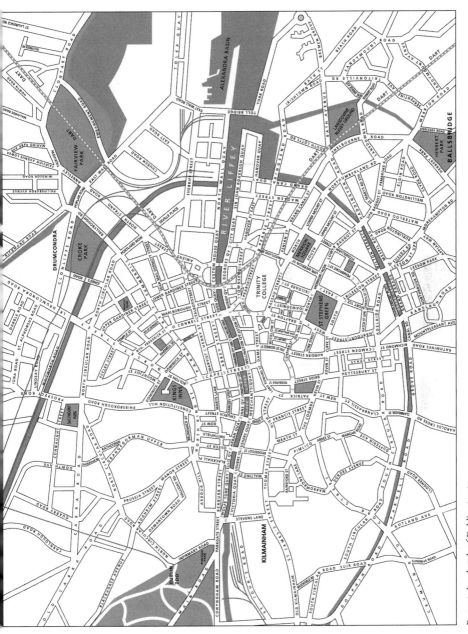

Present-day sketch of Dublin streets

House of Mercy, Baggot Street, Dublin

Portrait of Catherine McAuley (posthumous)

CHAPTER 5

The House of Mercy *1829–1830*

After William Macauley died, the house on Military Road had to be surrendered for someone else's use, probably for his brother-in-law, James McAuley, who succeeded him as assistant surgeon at the Royal Hospital.[1] In February 1829 all five Macauley children came to live in Baggot Street, and Catherine herself moved in permanently. Mary was already a lively help in the poor school, and young Catherine was still being tutored by Georgiana Moore. But what of the boys? For them Baggot Street was, inevitably, a sharp contrast to Military Road.

Fifty years after his father's death, Catherine's youngest nephew, Willie—attempting to identify himself to his cousin Teresa—reminisced, in the present tense, about his father. He recalled, as a child, watching his aunt open the left-hand drawer of a bookcase at Baggot Street: "There is something there I would never be tired looking at (guess). It is a silver case opening at the top and contains a set of lancets. It was my honored, loving and long regretted father's."[2] In 1903, Willie again remembered his affectionate parents and his loss in their early deaths: "From that time forward [i.e., after his mother's death], while my loving and tender father lived, I was always with him day and night, and no other person ever knew the depth of his sorrow as I did when at night taking me in his arms he bathed me with his tears."[3]

1. The *Dublin Directory* (1836) lists James McAuley as living on "Military Road, Royal Hospital."
2. William McAuley to Mary Camillus (Teresa) Byrn, July 9, 1884 (MCA).
3. William McAuley to "Revd. Mother" [Mary Augustine Mungovan], Bendigo, Australia, July 15, 1903 (MCA).

Then, with his mother gone, death "again knocked at our door . . . and seized the head of the house, the guide and protector of his family. . . . With their loss, I lost all my toys, never again to be replaced." Of his years with his parents, he wrote: "As I grew everything I desired was supplied. When taken out of pettycoates, my first suit was a blue military frock coat, vest and trousers to match. I carried my tin sword, my brass cannon, my regiments of horse and foot soldiers, my hobby horse to mount when off parade." That Willie was spoiled may be true; that he was sensitive, tender, and needy is unmistakable—"any unkindness or neglect [was] death to me."[4]

Given Willie's vulnerability at age seven, and the happiness he had known with his parents, one wonders whether his Aunt Catherine now had the time, or perhaps even the patience, to be the kind of adoptive mother he needed. The same may also have been true of James and Robert, still thirteen and ten, though they left no record of their childhood feelings. At Baggot Street, Willie and Teresa Byrn "played in the upper storey over the chapel," but Diana and Venus, his pet kids, which he had "stabled . . . on the carpets in my father's consulting room" were gone.[5] So were his joyous escapades in the well of his father's jaunting car, or in his aunt's carriage pulled by "Dick—one of Aunt's Charabanc [a light carriage] horses, driven by Richard, Aunt's coachman." Years later Willie recalled how once, when he was visiting Baggot Street before his father died, he had nearly scared the life out of the "ladies" living there:

Richard drove Dick over the [canal] bridge to a huxter's shop, I as usual again in the well. Richard . . . pulled the winkers off, away flew Dick to my intense delight, over the bridge with all cars clearing the way, taking the left hand side opposite the new building, full steam on—along the kerbstone of the footpath were a lot of poor women with tables selling apples, oranges, nuts, plums, sugar sticks—bringing the side of the car straight for the tables. Away they tumbled, dashing their contents in promiscuous heaps into the street. A little further on was a horse repository, half the gate open. For this Dick went bolting, up the yard with the shafts, leaving me stuck in the gate in roars of laughter. Very soon all the ladies were across the street to rescue Wild Willie. That was the last time ever Dick drew or Richard drove me.[6]

All three boys had gone to school while on Military Road, and Catherine knew they should be enrolled again. James and Robert were already "well advanced in Classics." Willie later remarked that Robert "would

4. William McAuley to Mary Catherine (Fanny Teresa) McAuley and others, October 28, 1903 (MCA).
5. Ibid.
6. William McAuley to "Revd. Mother" [Mary Augustine Mungovan], Bendigo, July 15, 1903 (MCA).

sooner have a book than all the playtoys, pigeons, guinea pigs, goats, asses, horses, in the world; in short, he was a bookworm." William himself, by his own admission, "did not know my alphabet"—the result, no doubt, of his having often begged to stay with his father rather than go to school.[7]

By March 1829, Catherine had settled on Carlow College, a boarding school for young boys in the town of Carlow, about fifty miles from Dublin. The college also housed a seminary program for young men training for the priesthood. On March 2, James, Robert, and Willie were enrolled and placed under the protective eye of Andrew Fitzgerald, a Dominican priest who had taught there since 1800 and was president of the college since 1814. The annual fees for boarding and educating lay scholars in 1825 were close to £50, and the sons of physicians, military officers, bankers, and merchants came from all areas of the country, but chiefly from Dublin and parts of County Cork.[8] Though the tuition was high, and the vast majority of Irish families could not afford it, the education provided to the young lay students and seminarians enjoyed a well-deserved national reputation.

Mary Bertrand Degnan's detailed review of the Carlow College records tells much about how the Macauley scholars (registered as "McAuley primus," "secundus," and "tertius") fared. James and Robert, whose penmanship was poor, apparently did well in history, geography, reading, Latin, and spelling, though Robert was often "absent from prayers." Willie was weak in spelling, but generally good in "dress," though occasionally, as noted in Latin, *pessime* or *male*. By the time he was eight, he seemed to excel in Latin, but his French ratings were almost universally low. All three boys spent money on combs, silk handkerchiefs, gloves, parties, and barber's services, and had allowances for holiday trips to Dublin "made by Dr. F[itzgerald]—not to be charged."[9]

James and Robert were happy enough at Carlow College, but Willie was not. He later recalled:

---

7. Typescript copy, William McAuley to "Revd. Mother" [Mary Augustine Mungovan], Bendigo, November 24, 1903 (MCA).

8. John McEvoy, *Carlow College, 1793-1993* (Carlow: St. Patrick's College, 1993), 9, says that in the early nineteenth century the "annual fee for Carlow lay scholars was £25 for boarders." In 1825, before a Select Committee of the Houses of Lords and Commons, James Doyle, bishop of Kildare and Leighlin, said the whole annual expense of "the education of a lay boy would cost between forty guineas and fifty pounds a year" (typescript of Doyle testimony, MCA). This testimony is also recorded in M. Imelda Keena, ed., *The Letters of William [Armstrong] Montgomery McAuley* (London: Institute of Our Lady of Mercy, n.d.), 40.

9. Degnan, *Mercy,* 82–84.

There was a boys library to enter which 6d [pence] a week had to be paid; James and Robert were both members; I never was. Again, all the boys were allowed pocket money weekly, some as much as 5s [shillings], as low as 1s. I never had any, nor my brothers, until my last year and then only 6d. The most of the clothes I wore were made in Baggot Street, out of my father's clothes, and they never were as fashionable as those of the rest of the boys. I never complained of those things. All the same I mourned my parents the more.[10]

Apparently the three boys were received into the Catholic Church by Daniel Burke, in the Baggot Street chapel, sometime in 1829. Willie claims to recall "Fanny Warde ushering me into the chapel and asking me to take the name of Joseph, as I was about to be baptized by Father Burke."[11] He also says that "Robert did not wish to turn his religion and argued with his Aunt until, defeated, he gave in, bursting into tears."[12] Certainly William never used the name Joseph. (His brothers may have been baptized earlier in St. Mark's [Church of Ireland] when they were infants, though this is unrecorded. The baptisms there of his sister Mary and one of the Williams who died in infancy are recorded.) Robert's staunch resistance, at age eleven, is entirely possible and understandable, given his upbringing. However, by the time he was fourteen, his Aunt Catherine was telling Archbishop Murray that "my second nephew [Robert] has expressed a strong wish to commence studies for a Priest," and requesting Murray's financial assistance.[13]

Meanwhile at Baggot Street, besides occasionally making a young boy's frock coats and vests, the daily work among the poor went on, and the effects of Edward Armstrong's final generosity were soon evident. With the £50 he had bequeathed to her, Catherine outfitted the second dormitory so she could separate the young women in the House of Mercy from the little girls. However, as Clare (Georgiana) Moore says of the resident community in early 1829: "We all slept in one Dormitory," except Anna Maria Doyle and Catherine Byrn: that is, Catherine McAuley, her two nieces, her godchild Teresa, Frances Warde, Ellen Corrigan, Ann Rice, and "myself."[14] Sleeping in a room with seven others had never been Catherine's experi-

10. William McAuley to Mary Catherine (Fanny Teresa) McAuley and others, October 28, 1903 (MCA).

11. William McAuley to "Revd. Mother" [Mary Augustine Mungovan], Bendigo, July 15, 1903 (MCA).

12. William McAuley, "Commentary on Passages in Carroll's *Life* of Catherine McAuley," referring to p. 143 of the *Life* (MCA).

13. Letter 14, February 19, 1832, in *CCMcA*, 51. Robert subsequently changed his mind.

14. CML, in *CMcATM*, 86. Ann Rice was probably an orphan whom Catherine had taken in while she lived in Coolock or later: "About this period she took charge of a little orphan that she saw cast into the street from a cellar her parents had occupied" (Lim, in *CMcATM*, 153).

ence at Coolock or on Military Road. For a very reserved woman, at least about her own interior feelings, and by far the eldest in the room, the loss of privacy was not negligible.

As he had promised, Edward Armstrong had also bequeathed to Catherine a few objects in his rooms that might be of use to her at Baggot Street: "the large divisional maps and the mahogany case in which they are, together with my Ivory Crucifix and the Calvary in which it stands [a large, carved wooden base], with the Predieux belonging to it, and the pious pictures, prints, to be had in my bed room and study."[15] All but the maps and pictures can still be seen at Baggot Street.

In early 1829, Catherine and her working companions at Baggot Street settled into a daily schedule. She, Georgiana Moore, and sometimes Frances Warde, rose before the others, usually at four. They used to pray "by moonlight" the whole Psalter of Jesus, a prayer Catherine had long favored, read from some spiritual book, such as Luis de Granada's *Sinner's Guide* (a book more gracious and encouraging than its title), and then transcribe passages from religious books that might prove helpful in visits to the sick and dying in hovels and hospitals, a more formal work that had begun in late 1828.[16] One winter morning, when Catherine was looking for some letters in her writing desk, "she held all those sheets of manuscript so close to the candle that they took fire and, before she perceived it, were consumed so far that they could not be saved."[17] Perhaps it was then that she began to say, with an unflappable cheerfulness that amazed others: "Try to view passing events as you will in a year hence, or as if they had happened a year ago."[18]

Their visits to poor Catholics in Dublin hospitals began with a measure of misunderstanding which Catherine did not attempt to correct. She, Anna Maria Doyle, Catherine Byrn, and Frances Warde went one day in Catherine's carriage to Sir Patrick Dun's Hospital on Grand Canal Street, "where the physicians knowing Miss McAuley's family and friends to be all Protestants and probably supposing she and her companions were

15. Letter 5, March 16, 1828, in CCMcA, 40.

16. Two editions of Granada's Spanish work (using the same English translation) were published in Dublin in the 1820s: J. Christie, 1820; Richard Coyne, 1825). Mary Ann Doyle says the work of visiting the sick began on November 30, 1828, a week after Murray's permission for it (DL, in CMcATM, 49); Clare Moore says it began a week later (CML, in CMcATM, 85). Both must mean the regularly scheduled, daily work of visiting the sick poor in their homes and hospitals. Many had been visited in their wretched hovels before this time.

17. CML, in CMcATM, 86.

18. PS, 15.

of that persuasion not only allowed them to speak to the patients, but also gave a general order for their admission in future."[19] At this time Catholic clergy and related social workers were generally not allowed to visit patients, even Catholics unless specifically requested, for the Dublin hospitals were all under Protestant auspices. The first Catholic hospital in the city (and in the country)—St. Vincent's on the east side of St. Stephen's Green—was founded by the Irish Sisters of Charity in 1834; it opened for women patients in 1835, for men in 1836. Following her experience at Sir Patrick Dun's, Catherine's access to poor Catholic patients in Mercer's Hospital, the Hospital for Incurables in Donnybrook, and the Coombe Lying-in Hospital was also gained, presumably by similar means.[20] As Harnett explains, Catherine knew that

the greater number of the patients received into these hospitals were Roman Catholics, [and] she resolved to make an effort to gain access to them for the purpose of communicating instruction and consolation. As she knew that persons would more willingly accede to the request of those who occupied a good position in society, rather than to that made by individuals of humble rank, she resolved for the furtherance of the objects she had in view to make her first visits in her own carriage. This she did, not from any motive of ostentation or display, but from a wish to remove the obstacles the world might raise to the fulfilment of her charitable designs; she wished to vanquish the world's prejudices with its own weapons, and having happily succeeded, she disposed of her carriage in the course of a few months and never resumed it again.[21]

Years later a Kingstown priest called Catherine "cunning and clever," during a protracted controversy with her in which he was the disingenuous party.[22] She was free from guile, but she was also cognizant of the subtle ways by which injustices were perpetuated, and was, when necessary, shrewd in dealing with them.

Catherine also realized that she was fifty, though apparently in excellent health; that all her co-workers were much younger than she and technically temporary; and that she had a large and expensive building on her hands. So on April 8–9, 1829, she established the four-member Baggot Street Trust, which named the Archbishop of Dublin, Catherine Byrn, Anna Maria Doyle, and herself as parties to the trust and effectively assigned the house

19. DL, in *CMcATM*, 49–50.
20. CML, in *CMcATM*, 94. In 1845, after a porter turned the women away from Hardwicke Hospital, Dr. Dominic Corrigan wrote to welcome them. At Sir Patrick Dun's that year they were refused because their request was against the rules of the hospital.
21. Lim, in *CMcATM*, 159.
22. Letter 101, November 15, 1838, in *CCMcA*, 165.

to Archbishop Murray should she and her two companions, or their successors, be unable to fulfill its purposes.[23] Her prudent decision came none too soon.

The murmuring and complaints about Catherine and the house that had begun when it was first opened continued and intensified in 1829, reaching their peak later that year and the next. The nub of the criticism, by some priests and vocal lay Catholics, now seemed to be the character of the community of co-workers who lived in the Baggot Street house. Georgiana Moore had to depart (temporarily) on June 29, 1829, because of health—her sister later claiming that "her lungs were diseased when she was fourteen."[24] But five other women joined that year: Anne O'Grady in January, Marcella Flynn in July, Margaret Dunne in September, Catherine's niece Mary Macauley and Frances Warde's friend Elizabeth Harley in November.[25] By year end there were nine resident helpers, including Catherine herself. Anne was a niece of Father John McCormick who, "ever since he had prepared Mrs. Macauley for death, took a deep interest in her sister's undertaking, and now brought his niece . . . to assist in the good work."[26]

The problem was evidently this: the women dressed and lived simply, wearing plain black dresses in the house; their "going out dress" added "a grey cloak with hood and Black silk bonnet and muslin veil, in summer a Black shawl." They prayed together in the early morning and evening; they walked together to St. Teresa's church for Mass; in fact, they walked all over the poorer areas of the city in twos. They invited the poor girls from the neighborhood to join them for evening prayer, keeping "open house with perfect safety until one day [Catherine] began to boast of it, and be-

23. Typescript, "Baggot Street Deed of Trust," April 9, 1829 (MCA), and MACE/MCAU/66 (IJA). On April 8, 1829, Catherine McAuley assigned to Michael Sullivan as "Trustee" the land lease and House of Mercy on Baggot Street. On the following day, he assigned the house and lease to Archbishop Murray (or his successors), Catherine McAuley, Anna Maria Doyle, and Catherine Byrn as trustees, with no future interest on Sullivan's part. The April 9 agreement ensured that if Catherine McAuley, Anna Maria Doyle, Catherine Byrn, and/or their successors at Baggot Street could not—by death, departure, incapacity, or disinclination—to fulfill the original purposes of the house and its land lease, these would revert to the archbishop of Dublin. If the agreements were ever recorded at the Registry of Deeds, no such memorial has been found. However, on the copy of Catherine McAuley's will (1841) given to Archbishop Murray, her attorney Charles Cavanagh wrote: "I have received from Most Revd. Doctor Murray assignment of premises in Baggot Street from Catherine McAuley to Michael Sullivan, Gentleman, dated 8 April 1829, also assignment of same premises from Michael Sullivan to the Most Revd. Dr. Murray, Catherine McAuley, Anna Maria Doyle & Catherine Josephine Byrn. Charles Cavanagh, 16th November 1841." Murray Papers, file 33/9, no. 23 (DDA).

24. Mary Clare Augustine Moore to Mary Camillus Dempsey, July 7, 1875 (AIMGB).

25. "Baggot Street Register" (MCA).

26. Anne O'Grady joined in January 1829, not December 1828, as in Lim, CMcATM, 160.

fore night the chair on which she was sitting disappeared."[27] So much for her earlier claim: "We have never lost a pin's worth."[28]

Thus they looked like nuns, they acted like nuns, but they were not nuns. Catherine herself was "severely censured and condemned, especially by some among the clergy," for the "singularity of their customs."[29] The house was not enclosed, they had no approved rule, yet they did what nuns did. Such were the overzealous and vociferous public comments leveled against the women on Baggot Street. Mary Vincent Harnett summarized the situation well:

Many well disposed Catholics had taken offence at the strange and unusual appearance which the Establishment presented; it was observed that it had assumed a religious character without having any claim to it; it was neither a convent, nor a private house; neither a religious community, nor yet a public Establishment. Remonstrances were made to the Foundress by friends, as well as by those who were by no means friendly, sometimes in the language of kind and well meant expostulation, and not unfrequently in terms of unqualified disapproval. She often received by post letters written and addressed in the most insulting manner.[30]

The motives for the relatively localized clerical opposition were not solely or even primarily a wish for ecclesiastical clarity. There was, and rightly, strong support in Dublin for the Presentation Sisters, the Irish Sisters of Charity, the Loreto Sisters, and their founders. Though Nano Nagle (1718–1784), their founder, and Teresa Mulally (1728–1803) in Dublin had died long before, the Presentation Sisters on George's Hill, Dublin, and elsewhere in Ireland had won "enormous respect and admiration among the reform-minded Catholic laity" for their education of poor girls.[31] Mary Aikenhead (1787–1858), the founder in 1815 of the Irish Sisters of Charity, with Daniel Murray's and others' financial assistance, drew widespread support for the many charitable works she and her sisters had already established, so similar in many respects to the aims of the Baggot Street community. Teresa Ball (1794–1861), again with Daniel Murray's guidance and financial help, had founded in 1822 the Loreto Sisters, as an Irish branch of the Bar Convent in York. Their boarding school for Catholic girls in Rathfarnham, then the only school in Dublin for children of wealthy and middle-class Catholics, enjoyed deserved Catholic support.[32]

27. CML, in *CMcATM*, 85–86. 28. CAM, in *CMcATM*, 201.
29. BA, in *CMcATM*, 104–5. 30. Lim, in *CMcATM*, 166.
31. Séamus Enright, "Women and Catholic Life in Dublin," in Kelly and Keogh, *History of the Catholic Diocese of Dublin*, 272.
32. Ibid., 278–86.

Catherine McAuley had no wish or intention to compete in any way with these religious congregations or their founders. The poverty in Dublin was wide and deep enough for everyone's efforts. Moreover, her projects were to be like the work of dozens of Protestant charitable societies in Dublin—but Catholic, and without their sometimes overt proselytizing. Baggot Street was not a convent, and its co-workers would take no vows. But nonetheless Catherine was seen by many, not as starting a new mode of merciful endeavor, but as detracting, financially and otherwise, from support of the bona fide religious congregations, especially the Sisters of Charity. Neither Mary Aikenhead nor Teresa Ball appears to have played any role in this growing attitude. In January 1833, Mary Aikenhead, then an invalid with her own sufferings to contend with, wrote to her sisters in Cork about the House of Mercy on Baggot Street:

> Let us take care of every illusion of false zeal or false love of our own Institute. Both are intended for the same great end of promoting the glory of our Heavenly Father and the good of the poor—we cannot promote either, if charity does not reign in our hearts; all other feelings merge in self, and miserable earthly preference of self will banish the Divine Spirit from us . . . and shall we presume to wish His favours to be confined only to ourselves.[33]

Mary Aikenhead's large-mindedness was not shared by some clergy and lay Catholics bent on preventing the supposed competition and on exerting their supposed authority in the matter. These "dreaded lest this new establishment should divert the public attention from those objects in which they took an interest." To many it was "a galling thing . . . that one who had been born their inferior in rank and fortune"—apparently their estimate of Catherine McAuley—"should now occupy a more influential position than rank or wealth had procured for them." What might have counted as Catherine's "influential position" in their minds—whether socially or ecclesiastically—is hard to find, unless it was Daniel O'Connell's and others' support for her work. Mary Ann (Anna Maria) Doyle describes the storm outside the house as cautiously and vaguely as she can manage: "Several of the clergy made no secret of their opposition though obliged to confess that it was grounded not on any mismanagement or misconduct which had come to their knowledge, but on an opinion that hereafter evil consequences would ensue from certain arrangements which were

---

33. Mary Aikenhead to Mary de Chantal Coleman, January 25, 1833, in *The Letters of Mary Aikenhead*, ed. [Mary Padua Flanagan] (Dublin: M. H. Gill & Son, 1914), 19.

not such as they thought advisable."[34] The presumptuous prediction of the "hereafter" proved to be ironic.

On June 4, 1829, in the midst of this criticism, the chapel in the house on Baggot Street was solemnly blessed by Archbishop Murray. Michael Blake preached on the occasion. Clare (Georgiana) Moore notes that his kind feelings toward Catherine "had in no way diminished," and he "never failed to show himself her friend."[35] His sermon that day, preached in the presence of several priests as well as the archbishop, did not mince words. It directly confronted, in a hypothetical way, the criticism swirling around the House of Mercy and its initiator:

I look on Miss McAuley as one selected by Heaven to be specially endowed with benediction; her heart is overflowing with the charity of the Redeemer, whose all consuming fire burns within her. No female has ever done more for sorrowing, suffering humanity than she has done. She may . . . confidently claim a blessing from Heaven on her future exertions . . . and I feel convinced that any individual in society presuming by word or deed to injure her Establishment will draw down on himself the lash, the scourge of the Almighty, even in this world.[36]

Contrary to her characteristic courtesy, Catherine McAuley apparently did not attend the Mass of dedication that day. Early biographical manuscripts say simply that she "was not present, having remained in prayer within the house," or that she "was much affected on that day and would not be present at the ceremonies but remained in prayer."[37] What precisely weighed so heavily on her heart that day: hurt? confusion? doubt? resignation? fear? exhaustion? In later years she would often say, perhaps with some of her own past experiences in mind: "We can never be happy nor feel as we ought until we bring ourselves to the conviction that we are treated by everybody better than we deserve"; and, "Our Divine Saviour's example should be before us under all circumstances, particularly in exercising charity towards our neighbour."[38]

The lunch following the ceremony, where again Catherine was absent, gave at least one priest the opportunity to ask, not pleasantly: Who is "this very extraordinary person Dr. Blake mentioned?" Another declared that "he neither liked the foundress nor the institution." Standing by was William Young, parish priest of Baldoyle. Having "listened in the greatest surprise and confusion to this angry oration," he turned to Frances Warde

---

34. DL, in CMcATM, 51.
35. BA, in CMcATM, 104.
36. Lim, in CMcATM, 163–64.
37. Ibid., 163; MADL, in CMcATM, 42.
38. PS, 1.

and said, with his much-storied kindness, but loud enough to be heard by others: "My dear, have the goodness to assure Miss McAuley of my respect for her and my good wishes for the prosperity of the institution. I am but a poor priest yet I will contribute my mite; I wish I could do more." He then gave her a gold sovereign. Mary Ann Doyle says, "No more [was] said on the subject just then, but a day or two after came an anonymous note directed to 'C. McAuley Esq.' which contained the most mortifying, the most insulting strictures on Miss McAuley's proceedings. She knew the handwriting as that of the priest who had spoken so harshly on the day of the dedication and so did Dr. Blake."[39] Another letter to be burned as soon as read.

On the day he dedicated the chapel, Archbishop Murray did not express any recorded opinion about the house, though he did ask that the chapel be opened to the public, and made two important appointments which indirectly signaled his support. He asked Daniel Burke, a Franciscan priest, to serve as chaplain to the schoolchildren and the women and girls sheltered in the House of Mercy, and he asked Redmond (Raymund) O'Hanlon, the thirty-nine-year-old provincial of the Discalced Carmelite community on Clarendon Street, to be the confessor of the resident coworkers. Daniel Burke turned out to be a constant help in counseling the young girls and homeless women—women who had known more than their fair share of poverty, abuse, and possibly sexual harassment. Catherine certainly knew the Carmelites well, including Francis L'Estrange, then prior, and all the other friars who had taken Baggot Street under their liturgical wing, supplying the house with "vestments and everything almost for the Altar . . . altar breads, Incense, charcoal and other things."[40] The community's debt to these Carmelites, especially to Redmond O'Hanlon, would endure well beyond Catherine's death.

The agitation in Dublin did not abate. People were still opposed to the very existence of the house, and especially to the women's uncustomary mode of life. Finally all the complaints came to a head when Matthias Kelly, priest-administrator of St. Andrew's chapel on Townsend Street, made an unexpected visit to Baggot Street. Kelly was, for understandable reasons, a disappointed man, and Catherine would have easily sympathized

39. DL, in *CMcATM*, 53.

40. CML, in *CMcATM*, 91. The Carmelite community had elections in 1829. By June 4, when the chapel was dedicated and the appointments were made, Francis Joseph L'Estrange may have already become provincial, and Redmond O'Hanlon was free of community office. Transcript, "Tables and Index," Archives, Discalced Carmelites, Clarendon Street, Dublin.

with his situation. He had been trying since 1826, when he succeeded Edward Armstrong, to improve and enlarge the Townsend Street chapel, but sufficient funds had not been collected, the new walls were only half built, talk had surfaced about building an entirely new church on a different site, and he was in debt.[41]

However, seeking Catherine's solace was not the purpose of his visit. He came that day, in 1829 or early 1830, to explore the building and to tell Catherine that "the Archbishop thought of giving the house to the Sisters of Charity, though she might have apartments and a private entrance" for herself.[42] Clare (Georgiana) Moore says he led Catherine through the house "telling her to select a room or two for herself . . . but she could have a private entrance, etc. It was no such thing—he wished it."[43] Mary Ann (Anna Maria) Doyle says Catherine believed him and, recalling the provisions of the Baggot Street Trust, "meekly answered that 'Dr. Murray could do as he pleased with the house for it was his.'"[44]

Catherine's apparent meekness could not have been her only reaction that day. It must have been accompanied by shock, worry, perhaps a sense of impending loss, but also by common sense, which she was wont to say is the "most *uncommon* of all things."[45] She evidently felt she ought not to discuss the archbishop's wishes in front of Matthias Kelly. But when "the revd. gentleman took his leave she immediately wrote to his Grace to say that if such were his determination she should acquiesce in it." Mary Ann Doyle says Archbishop Murray came the next day and "assured her with great warmth that so far from having authorized such a communication he had never entertained the idea of depriving her of her property or putting any obstacle to her benevolent exertions which he was most desirous she should continue."[46] However, Clare Moore, who came to know Catherine's feelings intimately, says Daniel Murray "showed much coldness," and that "when he visited her he said, alluding to the title of Sisters of Mercy being adopted, 'the idea of a Convent starting up of itself, in this manner, never entered my mind.'"[47]

The archbishop's "warmth" or "coldness" notwithstanding—perhaps it was, paradoxically, simultaneously or alternately both—Clare says that

---

41. Donnelly, *History of Dublin Parishes*, part 7, 150–51.
42. BA, in *CMcATM*, 105.   43. CML, in *CMcATM*, 86.
44. DL, in *CMcATM*, 51. In 1832, Matthias Kelly was imprisoned in Kilmainham Jail for building debts running into the thousands. Murray Papers, 31/3–4, nos. 79 and 80 (DDA).
45. *PS*, 27.   46. DL, in *CMcATM*, 51–52.
47. BA, in *CMcATM*, 105.

Dr. Murray's visit was an "affliction" for Catherine, no doubt because it directly raised the question of religious life. True, some members of the community had harmlessly taken to calling one another "Sister"—even nurses did that—but they were a long way from being a convent. Catherine "had imbibed certain Protestant prejudices, which she retained for a very long period. She did not like the idea of Religious vows, and disapproved of Conventual observances, etc., having constantly heard them ridiculed and misrepresented by Protestants."[48] It was not just the laughably inappropriate iron grate in the chapel that bothered her.

However, several of her co-workers in late 1829 and early 1830 had leanings toward religious life. Certainly Anna Maria Doyle and Catherine Byrn did, and probably Marcella Flynn, Margaret Dunne, and Anne O'Grady. Anne had earlier entered the Presentation convent in Wexford, but having caught fever as a novice, her health weakened and she was obliged to leave. Georgiana Moore, now back at her mother's home because of her lung disease, may also have harbored such thoughts.

Mary Ann Doyle says that by 1830, and despite the external opposition to the house

every thing was going on prosperously. The schools were crowded. The House of Mercy had proved an asylum for many young persons. . . . The protection and recommendation of servants was . . . duly appreciated. The visitation of the sick had had the most beneficial results. Still it was evident that both the prosperity and the permanency of the institution must necessarily be insecure if the community whose labours should uphold it were to continue merely an association of seculars bound together by no bond save their mutual regard and an abstract love of doing good; whose fervor or caprice might find sanctuary in a convent or solace in the enjoyment of the world.[49]

In her view, Catherine's original plan would not work for long.

Catherine herself, now fifty-one, shrank from even considering religious life: "She was no longer young, her habits were formed among Protestants, she did not like ceremony, and some of the ceremonies used in convents, [such] as kneeling to Superiors, were particularly distasteful."[50] Ten years later she would write about a series of physical journeys: "We have one solid comfort amidst this little tripping about: our hearts can always be in the same place, centered in God—for whom alone we go forward—or stay back."[51] Now in 1830 she was faced with a formidable

48. Ibid., 102.
50. CAM, in CMcATM, 204.
51. Letter 220 [December 20, 1840], in CCMcA, 332.

49. DL, in CMcATM, 55.

spiritual journey, one she had never planned or anticipated, and it would involve no casual "tripping about." Should she "go forward—or stay back"? Where would her wished-for centering in God, if it was real, take her? How could she, or should she, read the compass of her heart?

She turned to Michael Blake. In her confusion following Daniel Murray's semi-complaint about "a Convent starting up of itself, in this manner"—an idea that had never entered *her* head any more than his—she laid the problem before her friend. He "went on her behalf to Dr. Murray without delay," and, according to Clare Moore, "the result was, that the House would not be suffered to continue in the state it then was"; and the women "should either appear as secular ladies, or become Religious."[52]

Whether Michael Blake reported Archbishop Murray's opinion exactly, and whether Clare Moore had a reliable source for these words, that is, whether Daniel Murray was ever so sharply categorical in his judgment of Catherine's alternatives, cannot now be known, but it is unlikely, given his personality and his long and apparently earnest respect for her vision. Or was the either/or perspective Michael Blake's own analysis? The questions are, in an important sense, irrelevant, for Catherine herself was apparently slowly and silently sorting out her own dilemma and values, with Michael Blake's help and with attentiveness to the views of her companions. What was paramount for her was not her lifelong prejudices against religious life as such, though they were strong, but the stability and continuance of the works of mercy she and her co-workers had begun, and their zealous collaboration with the mercy of God, which, as she would later write, is "the principal path pointed out by Jesus Christ to those who are desirous of following Him."[53] The long-term mission of the house, its merciful service to poor girls, the sick, and distressed women, was everything, more important than her own former views.

Catherine never recorded her own thoughts and feelings as she silently dealt with the situation before her. This does not mean that she did not put the question of religious life before the community, invite them to share their opinions, and listen to them, but only that she did not burden them with her own struggles and fears. In the end they together made the decision which was for her the most demanding but unanticipated decision of her life.

It has sometimes been claimed by present-day commentators that

52. BA, in *CMcATM*, 105.
53. Rule 3.1, in *CMcATM*, 297.

Catherine McAuley was, contrary to her own enduring intention, "forced" by Archbishop Murray and certain priests, including Michael Blake, to accede to founding a religious congregation. At the least such a view does not realistically accept Catherine's historical situation: in Dublin, Ireland, in the early nineteenth century, not elsewhere, nor in a later century. But more importantly and at a deeper level, such a claim does not give Catherine credit for her well-earned maturity, her often demonstrated personal freedom even in the face of opposition, her penchant for prayerful discernment, and the apparent depth of her spiritual life. Nor does it recognize the reality (common in the human experience of others) that, over time, through conversation with those whose opinions she valued, and, when alone, through the mysterious guidance of the God to whose merciful work in this world she was more and more surrendered, her original plan evolved into something surprisingly new and more lasting. The Catherine of 1830 was not the Catherine of 1824 or 1827. She now had a new understanding and a new desire, of something more permanently conducive to her deepest spiritual intention, which had been, and remained, to serve, with her full life and energy, those in her world who were poor, uneducated, and unable to improve their lives without help, as well as those at the edges of society who were sick and dying.

She would "go forward," not "stay back." She would, with her companions, found a new religious congregation of women. Whatever was the turmoil outside the house, inside the house the decision now unfolded as slowly, little by little, as day follows night, which, as Catherine often said, was apparently the way God worked:

See how quietly the great God does all His mighty works: darkness is spread over us at night and light returns in the morning, and there is no noise of closing shutters or drawing curtains.[54]

54. *PS*, 2.

CHAPTER 6

George's Hill at Fifty-Two   *1830–1831*

On September 8, 1830, when she was fifty-two, Catherine McAuley entered the convent of the Presentation Sisters on George's Hill, Dublin, to begin her training in religious life prior to founding the Sisters of Mercy. Recalling that night, she often said that

it was so hard a struggle for her to remain on account of meeting there many things repugnant to her feelings that had she not had the establishment of the Institute most deeply at heart she would (that very evening) have sent for a coach to take her back to Baggot St.[1]

Despite her repugnance, however understandable, there was no going back. No coach was called.

The Presentation convent on George's Hill—an old street on the north side of the city, running perpendicular to the river and north of Mary Street and Mary Lane—is a great old four-story building erected by Teresa Mulally. Here she set up a school in 1789 and founded the Dublin Presentation community in 1794 with two sisters from Cork. Catherine's bedroom was a small, corner room on the south end of the top floor at the back of the convent, looking out on a small garden below and Halston Street. If she opened her window she got the strong odor of whiskey maturing in the yard off George's Hill and the smell of fish from the wholesale market on Bootlane. She could hear the carts rumbling over the cobbles to the potato, fruit, and vegetable markets nearby.[2] In the distance, behind

---

1. CML, in *CMcATM,* 93.
2. Samuel Lewis, *Lewis' Dublin,* compiled by Christopher Ryan (Cork: Collins Press, 2001), 86–87, a

other buildings, she could almost see Mary Street, with all its memories, and nearby, St. Michan's church and the lodgings on Halston Street where Edward Armstrong had died.

Becoming a postulant in the Presentation convent, Catherine did not cease to be who she was: a woman of perceptive common sense who took a long and trusting view of passing events. George's Hill would be a "cross"—she could already surmise that. She could either embrace it as it was, presuming it injured no one else, or "drag" it after her, a gloomy attitude toward unavoidable personal suffering she later discouraged.[3]

By mid-July 1830, after the decision was made to found a new religious congregation of women, further questions had arisen: how? when? who, initially? Not easy questions to answer, given the heavy daily obligations of the twelve co-workers now living and working in the house on Baggot Street. Teaching two or three hundred mostly barefoot young girls in the crowded schoolrooms each day, regularly visiting sick and dying poor people in hospitals or lying on piles of straw and rags in their own hovels, repeatedly receiving homeless girls and women into the House of Mercy, interviewing prospective employers for some of them, and looking after the orphaned children for whom Baggot Street was home—all this needed the time and energies of everyone working there.

In the beginning the women sheltered in the House of Mercy went out all day, to work or hunt for work, and the house was simply a night refuge. But Catherine soon saw that this arrangement was not adequate. The women quickly lost or were advised to give up whatever domestic jobs they happened to get on their own—either because their skills were not sufficient to hold employment in reliable homes or shops, or because the husbands or spoiled sons of otherwise respectable mistresses sexually abused them. After all, they were "servants." Therefore, starting in Lent 1829 most of the women remained in the house all day, receiving breakfast, dinner, and evening tea. They spent the rest of their time learning not only their own personal worth and dignity and the supports for this in their Catholic faith, but also household skills they would need if they hoped to secure suitable and lasting employment.

---

reprint of the section on Dublin in vol. 1 of Samuel Lewis, *Topographical Dictionary of Ireland* (London: S. Lewis & Company, 1837). Today, through a generous Presentation donation, the convent and school on George's Hill provide housing for homeless women and their children; a small Presentation community remains on site.

3. *PS*, 14.

It was a tall order. Catherine's own thimble and sewing basket had not only personal use but an educative role as well, teaching the women how to do plain work, such as mending children's stockings, sewing on buttons, and repairing men's nightshirts and ladies' dresses. Catherine understood the women's plight in a practical way. She later wrote of them: "Many leave their situations not so much for want of merit as incapacity to fulfil the duties they unwisely engaged in."[4]

Then there were all the people like the runaway girl from Killarney and Mary Ann Redmond, sudden emergencies that needed to be addressed. For instance, late one night in 1829 or 1830, after a violent ringing at the door, "the flushed face of a very young girl" appeared. She "implored shelter for the night saying she had traveled on foot from Killarney and knew no one in Dublin." The "wild glare" of her eyes and "the disorder of her hair and dress" aroused suspicions. Was she a young prostitute? The girl said she had gone to the Sisters of Charity refuge on Stanhope Street, but was denied admission, though "as some consolation was told that in Baggot St. a Miss McAuley had a great house where every sort of people were let in." The girl was given bread and milk, but to bring her, at this hour, in this state, into the girls' dormitory without further inquiry seemed unwise. So Catherine took her to an asylum on Little James's Street. The next day Anna Maria Doyle verified the girl's story: yes, her father had married a second time to a woman who was harsh to his older children. So the girl was admitted to the House of Mercy. In time, work was arranged for her, but by then her father had found her, forgave her impulsive escape, and took her home. The whole situation was just part of a night's work at Baggot Street.[5]

Mary Ann Redmond was not poor, but she was in dire straits in 1830. Her parents were dead, and she had been accompanied to Dublin, to seek medical help, by an old country nurse and a young, inexperienced cousin. The best Dublin doctors determined that her leg needed to be amputated, having found no other way to treat her "white swelling on the knee." Michael Blake asked Catherine to visit her in her lodgings, and then asked that Mary Ann be allowed to have the amputation at Baggot Street. Catherine consented. But when the day came, she could not bring herself to be in the infirmary room when Mary Ann's leg, without any anesthesia except possibly a little whiskey or opium, was sawed off. Apparently she just

4. Rule 4.2. in *CMcATM*, 299.
5. DL, in *CMcATM*, 50.

could not face it. Timid Anna Maria Doyle and Margaret Dunne got that terrifying assignment, enduring all the patient's frightful screams. However, Catherine made amends by staying up with Mary Ann night after night in the weeks that followed, watching over her "with the solicitude of a parent."[6]

No amount of "novitiate training" could really prepare the Baggot Street community for the next girl from Killarney or the next Mary Ann Redmond. Yet somehow all this work had to continue, simultaneously, with whatever was entailed in their becoming a religious congregation. So the practical questions—when? how? who, initially?—remained, questions Catherine once thought she had set aside definitively. Her great fear had been "enclosure," which she thought was a required feature of all religious congregations of women, restricting their freedom to leave the convent or walk the streets. Daniel Murray, valuing as he did the "outside" works of mercy in which the community was already engaged, assured her that enclosure, as strictly understood, would not be applied in their case. (Apparently still thinking it was requisite, a few years later Catherine inserted a paragraph outlining a modified form of enclosure, with exceptions, in her draft of the Mercy Rule. Reviewing the draft, Dr. Murray simply deleted the entire paragraph with a large penciled X.)[7]

At first Dr. Murray suggested that Catherine and others whom she would select could receive their novitiate training at the House of Mercy, under the guidance of two vowed members of another, approved religious congregation. It was a considerate offer on his part, but much as Catherine would have liked to remain at Baggot Street for those fifteen months, she instinctively knew that such an arrangement would not work. She and her companions would be distracted from their religious training by the constant work of the house and, in her case, by frequent appeals for her help and leadership. Murray then suggested that Catherine write to the congregations of women in Dublin, asking for copies of their Rules. She and her colleagues could choose the congregation whose life and work seemed most adaptable to their own purposes. They could then request temporary admission into that congregation and subsequently profess their religious vows with his sanction. Michael Blake also thought this was the best plan.

The Poor Clares, Carmelites, and Presentation Sisters quickly responded, but not the Loreto Sisters or the Irish Sisters of Charity. Perhaps the

6. Ibid., 56; CML, in *CMcATM*, 89–90; BA, in *CMcATM*, 104.
7. See *CMcATM*, 314–15.

Sisters of Charity had heard that Catherine McAuley did not approve of having—as they apparently did on Stanhope Street—a non-resident committee deciding, and thereby delaying, admissions to a night shelter; or else Mary Aikenhead herself, having still some prejudices to deal with among her own sisters, decided to leave well enough alone. Why Teresa Ball and the Loreto Sisters did not respond has not so far been discovered. They had close relations with the Sisters of Charity and Daniel Murray.[8]

The choice of a congregation where some of the women at Baggot Street would serve their novitiate was a communal one, which Catherine did not reserve to herself. After all, in 1830, she was twenty to thirty years older than all but one of her co-workers. In her view decisions about the future belonged equally to them. Moreover, as the Carlow annalist, herself a novice, was later to record: "The most amiable trait in her character which we believed we discerned was a total absence of everything in her manner telling, I am the Foundress."[9] So Catherine laid the several Rules before her companions. The Carmelites were eager to "adopt them as a Third Order," but, according to the blunt Clare Augustine Moore, "some of the observances appeared ridiculous and then came the weighty consideration of subjecting [the] community to the Fathers who must change their superiors so often, in which [Catherine] saw great inconvenience."[10] Eventually, "she and they decided that among the Rules submitted to them that of the Presentation order was most in accordance with their vocation, and they were willing to adopt it with modifications suited to the performance of the duties they had undertaken, and which were to form the characteristics of the new Institute."[11] It was a momentous decision they never regretted, Catherine's feelings on the night of September 8 notwithstanding.

For many reasons Catherine would have felt a kinship with Honora (Nano) Nagle, the pioneering founder of the Presentation Sisters in 1775. Nano was born in 1718, long before the dreams of Catherine McAuley. She died in 1784, when Catherine was just a playful child. Yet her name and saintliness were, and still are, legendary in Ireland. In 2005 a program on the major Irish radio station (RTÉ) conducted a poll asking, "Who is Ireland's greatest woman, living or dead?" Nano Nagle emerged as the first

8. Enright, "Women and Catholic Life," in Kelly and Keogh, *History of the Catholic Diocese of Dublin*, 284–86.

9. CA, in *CMcATM*, 230.   10. CAM, in *CMcATM*, 204.

11. Lim, in *CMcATM*, 167–68.

choice, with 23.5 percent of the vote, ahead of Mary Robinson, former president of Ireland, who received 21.4 percent.[12]

Nano Nagle had given her inheritance, money donated by her family, her own home (a mere cottage), and her whole adult life to relieving the poverty, sickness, and educational deprivation of Catholics in penal-era Cork. In 1777 she served Christmas dinner to fifty beggars. She built an almshouse for aged women, opened seven small schools for poor children, and spent her life trying to develop "a way of the religious life that could be fitted to Irish conditions."[13] She once observed that Jesus "came not to be ministered to but to minister."[14] Like Catherine, she was sensible and realistic; she did not want children to be "taught only to say their prayers."[15]

She also resisted the practice of strict enclosure, as unconducive to the real needs of Ireland and to the purposes and external duties of the Sisters of Charitable Instruction (the first title of the Presentation Sisters). She did not live to see her congregation choose enclosure in the early 1800s—to achieve greater stability as a monastic order with solemn vows, and so attract more young women—or to see this decision later reversed by new Roman definitions.[16]

Nano Nagle's letters express sentiments that would one day be echoed in the thoughts and sayings of Catherine McAuley. When Teresa Mulally struggled to establish a Presentation community in Dublin—which became, after Nano's death, the convent on George's Hill—Nano wrote to her: "The best works meet with the greatest crosses. I don't approve of your desponding so much. . . . Though neither you nor I should live to see it prosper in our time, yet I hope it may prosper hereafter and be of universal service."[17] Commenting on the communal prayer schedule of a religious order in France, she wrote: "They have such a number of other prayers that I should imagine they could have little time to attend the sick."[18] Consoling an Irish Ursuline novice in Paris whose novice mistress behaved somewhat harshly toward the Irish in her care, Nano nevertheless said: "Whoever we live with, we must expect to have something to suffer as this world is not to be our paradise."[19] Catherine would have agreed, though she also

12. James Fitzgerald, "Nano Nagle wins title . . . ," *Irish Times*, January 25, 2005.

13. T. J. Walsh, *Nano Nagle and the Presentation Sisters* (Dublin: M. H. Gill and Son, 1959), 105.

14. Ibid., 112.   15. Ibid., 110.

16. Ibid., 173–74, and 180 n. 17. Leo XIII, *Conditae a Christo*, Apostolic Constitution, December 8, 1900, declared that the vows of religious in apostolic congregations are simple, not solemn, and only the measure of enclosure recommended by the local bishop is required.

17. Walsh, *Nano Nagle*, 115.   18. Ibid., 104.

19. Ibid., 78.

claimed, "If everyone would mind their own business, the Convent would be a heaven upon earth."[20] Yet Nano and she shared the same bedrock belief that "divine Providence does everything for the best."[21]

On the morning of September 9, 1830, Catherine tried mightily to focus on that belief. Here she was, in a Presentation convent at fifty-two, under the hourly direction of a novice mistress who was a stranger to her. Though Catherine was not the victim of a precipitate decision, she had certainly laid aside temporarily an enormous measure of personal freedom—if not of thought, at least of movement and action. While she never relinquished her personal feelings of responsibility for Baggot Street and the people there—the orphans, the women, the schoolchildren, her companions—she was at George's Hill, as Edward Armstrong once feared, "bereft," of friends who could easily visit, of her nieces, nephews, and godchild, of the sick and dying, and of access to Michael Blake and Daniel Murray except on their initiative and request. She would have to learn humility, self-denial, and obedience as she had never had to learn these virtues before.

Accompanying Catherine to George's Hill were Anna Maria Doyle, her first co-worker, and Elizabeth Harley, the young daughter of a military officer. Elizabeth had joined the Baggot Street community the previous November, and Catherine thought she would be a great assistance in helping to establish the new congregation.

Then, as now, there were three stages, with their own vocabulary, in the process of a woman's entering religious life. First, one was a "postulant," or candidate; in Catherine's case, this stage would last three months, though normally it lasted six months (today it might last two years). During this period the postulant and the congregation assessed her aptitude for religious life (today these assessments are mutually achieved, not concluded separately as in Catherine's day). Then if the postulant so requested, and the congregation formally approved her request, the postulant was "received" as a "novice," was given the religious garb or "habit" of the congregation, and began her "novitiate," which usually lasted two years; Catherine's novitiate was intended to last one year. Finally, at the end of the novitiate, if the novice wished and the congregation approved her request, a ceremony of "profession" occurred in which she pronounced vows in ac-

20. PS, 5.

21. Walsh, Nano Nagle, 104. Mary Pius O'Farrell's Nano Nagle: Woman of the Gospel (Cork: Cork Publishing, for the Sisters of the Presentation, 1996) is a recent biography of this remarkable woman who served the Irish poor of Cork in the penal era.

cord with the Rule of the particular religious congregation and became a "professed member" of the congregation.

Catherine McAuley, Anna Maria Doyle, and Elizabeth Harley did not intend to remain in the Presentation order, but rather to "found" a new religious congregation. To do so, they had first to serve a novitiate in a congregation whose Rule had already been approved by the church, as the Presentation Rule was in 1805.[22] One major difference between the process followed today and that used in the 1830s was in the duration of the vows: today, a woman would initially profess temporary or "first" vows for a period of three to five years and then profess perpetual vows; in Catherine's day there was only one rite of profession, and the woman professed her vows until "my death." The vows dealt with and were named after three characteristics of her future life, and all that these implied in the Rule of the particular congregation: "poverty," "chastity," and "obedience."

Archbishop Murray formally received the three women into the Presentation community on December 9, 1830. They were now officially "novices" and clothed in the Presentation habit, a garb not unlike what was eventually to become the habit of the Sisters of Mercy. Catherine's days of "good style" and black British merino dresses "which according to the fashion of the time fitted tight to her shape" were over.[23] Her pale golden hair, now beginning to gray, also disappeared behind a white coif and veil. But these feminine losses were the least of it.

Mary Ann Doyle says plainly: "Our Noviceship was severe, being only one year." For a while Catherine was "treated with indulgence and respect, but a change of Superiors taking place," the mistress of novices "left nothing undone for our spiritual improvement."[24] One may wonder exactly how "spiritual improvement" was defined.

When Catherine, Anna Maria, and Elizabeth first went to George's Hill, Mary Clare Angela Doyle was the Presentation superior, and Mary Teresa Higgins, mistress (director) of novices. However, on May 19, 1831, five months into their novitiate, Mary Francis de Sales Knowd was elected superior. Though Teresa Higgins was re-elected mistress, she had now to take her cues in directing the three Baggot Street women from a much stricter woman (though one Catherine later spoke of with admiration).[25] According to Clare Moore, Catherine "felt the change much."[26]

22. Walsh, *Nano Nagle*, 179.   23. CAM, in *CMcATM*, 202.
24. MADL, in *CMcATM*, 42.
25. "Community Chapter Book," Presentation Convent, George's Hill, Dublin, 69–70.
26. CML, in *CMcATM*, 93.

In afteryears, tales of the months at George's Hill must have quietly circulated at Baggot Street, for Clare Augustine Moore, who entered in 1837, claims that, among the Presentation Sisters, Elizabeth Harley was "pronounced a living saint" and Anna Maria Doyle was "the favourite." As for Catherine, "a few of the nuns understood her and valued her highly," but the new superior and the mistress of novices "kept her in perpetual agitation by giving her to understand that they would receive her companions to Profession . . . and postpone hers, or even reject her altogether."[27]

A story also got around, whether based in fact or not, that during a visit from her niece Catherine and godchild Teresa the mistress of novices scolded Catherine McAuley publicly for remaining too long with them. Young Catherine began to cry. Teresa, "unable to control herself, exclaimed: 'Do, dear godmother, come home from that cross lady.'"[28] Evidently Catherine could see through and beyond the crossness, though probably not at first. Years later she often said that "during no time of her life was she so happy as when a novice, and were she permitted to have a choice it would be to continue always living under obedience, rather than to have the government of others."[29] Apparently she did not mind sweeping floors, assisting in the sacristy, or serving in the refectory—these were relatively mindless, uncomplicated, and therefore somewhat restful tasks.

Yet there was one situation in which Catherine spoke up. All of the Baggot Street novices at George's Hill were placed in domestic jobs. Elizabeth Harley "in the discharge of hers had to remain for a long time each day in a very cold damp underground room"—a kitchen, without a fire, where she was "employed cleaning shoes and cooking utensils."[30] Her tendency to consumption apparently worsened under these conditions. When Catherine saw what was happening, she thought it her duty to intervene. But by then it was probably too late. The personal grief at the illness of any young sister that Catherine always evinced over the next ten years must have been piercing in the George's Hill circumstances.

At their reception into the Presentation community in 1830 the three from Baggot Street were given, as was the custom, new names as religious. Catherine was to be "Teresa"; Anna Maria Doyle, "Clare"; and Elizabeth Harley, "Angela." Offering the names of these formidable women saints— Teresa of Avila, Clare of Assisi, and Angela Merici—was a thoughtful ges-

27. CAM, in *CMcATM*, 205.   28. Carroll, *Life*, 165.
29. Lim, in *CMcATM*, 168.
30. DL, in *CMcATM*, 63; CAM, in *CMcATM*, 205.

ture on the part of the Presentation Sisters. They evidently saw in their guests the determination, initiative, and contemplative spirit of the famous reformer, the devotee of voluntary poverty, and the great Renaissance proponent of female spirituality.[31] However, Catherine knew these women as the founders of major religious orders—the Reformed Carmelites, the Poor Clares, and the Ursulines—and she was uneasy about taking their names "lest it might be thought she ranked herself with them." After the reception ceremony when the new names were disclosed, she asked that they might be allowed to retain their own names, preceded by "Mary." She was told this change might be granted at their profession of vows, *if* they were approved for profession.[32]

Unlike many other aspects of religious life at the time, decisions about reception of the habit and profession of vows were made by the consensus of the vowed members of a religious congregation, signified in each case by a secret vote, cast in a meeting called a "chapter." The Presentation Rule provided that two months before a novice's period of probation was scheduled to expire, she was allowed, with the permission of the superior, to present to the chapter her request to profess religious vows:

> If the Chapter accede thereto, a scrutiny shall be made with white and black beans, and if the majority of the votes shall be in [her] favor, [she] shall spend the remainder of the time . . . in prayer and other spiritual exercises.[33]

In 1831 this was the requirement that faced Catherine, Anna Maria, and Elizabeth. The character of their future lives depended on the number of dried white beans.

It was not a foregone conclusion. Several of the Presentation sisters, including the new superior, doubted the wisdom of allowing the profession of women who had no intention of remaining in the Presentation congregation.[34] While history records a long list of saintly women—Teresa of Avila among them—who made their novitiate and professed their vows in one religious congregation, and then, with ecclesiastical approval, left it in order to found another, this prospect did not sit well with some at George's Hill.

---

31. Quericolo Mazzonis's *Spirituality, Gender, and the Self in Renaissance Italy: Angela Merici and the Company of St. Ursula (1474–1540)* (Washington, D.C.: The Catholic University of America Press, 2007) argues that Angela Merici's primary work was her affirmation of women's spirituality. Catherine McAuley probably understood her as a servant of the poor and sick.

32. BA, in *CMcATM*, 105.

33. *Rules and Constitutions of the Institute of the Religious Sisterhood of the Presentation of the . . . Virgin Mary* (Cork: James Haly, 1809), 22.

34. CAM, in *CMcATM*, 204–5.

Meanwhile, back at Baggot Street other troubles arose during the months after Catherine's departure. By late May 1831, Mary Jones had entered, and ten co-workers were now handling all the works of mercy Catherine had left behind. Though Mary Anne Delany, who had joined them in July 1830, was in charge of the house, "superior in effect tho' not in name," and Frances Warde was housekeeper and financial manager, their leadership was not enough to prevent problems, including illnesses brought on by overwork, insufficient sleep, late-night prayer, and unwise and excessive fasting.[35] The absence of Catherine's common sense and seasoned religious understandings left a vacuum of spiritual discretion, allowing several at Baggot Street to adopt acts of mortification that were incompatible with the demands of their daily work.

But there were other illnesses that probably could not have been avoided. The always cheerful, very beautiful, and much beloved Caroline Murphy, who came from Killarney and had somewhat delicate health when she joined the community in June 1830, took on all the worst scrubbing tasks, including the floor of the students' privies. Rapid consumption eventually developed, and she died on June 28, 1831. Having nowhere else to bury her, the Carmelite priests placed her body in their own underground vaults on Clarendon Street.[36]

In the summer of 1831 Anna Carroll entered, and Anne O'Grady began the work of neighborhood "collections," the door-to-door begging of blankets, clothing, and money to assist the poor women sheltered in the House of Mercy and the poor families the community visited. "This exertion made in the heat of the summer months was too great. She sank under it, and in August her case was pronounced hopeless."[37]

Word of Caroline's illness and approaching death, and then of Anne's decline reached Catherine. Deeply afflicted, she was helpless to comfort them or the rest of the community on Baggot Street except by messages sent back through others. The sharp contrast between these human sorrows and some of the piddling things for which she was reprimanded at George's Hill would not have been lost on her.

Catherine had arranged that Redmond O'Hanlon and Daniel Burke would keep an eye on the Baggot Street house while she was away and let her know of any serious difficulty. One such report involved Hannah Fulham. A young woman about whose religious vocation there was some

---

35. CML, in *CMcATM*, 89.   36. Ibid., 91.
37. BA, in *CMcATM*, 106.

genuine doubt, though Frances Warde favored her, Hannah soon settled the question herself. She attempted to steal some silverware from the house, perhaps intending to sell it at a pawnbroker's. Hearing this, Catherine sent word that she was to be immediately dismissed. Not wanting to leave, Hannah suddenly appeared one day shorn of all her lovely hair, claiming that it was cut off by "supernatural agency . . . a sign that she was to remain and be a Nun." Not a single lock of her hair could at first be found. Then some strands were discovered in scissors she had borrowed, and more in the music gallery. Clare Moore, suspecting all along Hannah's alleged "miracle," says simply: "After much to do, she confessed she had cut it off." Poor Hannah "was soon sent off"—with a kind-hearted recommendation to a family in Blackrock where she again showed her unfortunate propensity.[38]

Not all the troubles at Baggot Street during Catherine's absence were tragic. The Presentation Sisters, aware of the illnesses and fatigue at the House of Mercy, made some suggestions intended to be helpful, which Catherine forwarded. Clare Moore recounts the unhappy result of one of them:

The first effects of Revd. Mother's being at George's Hill which we experienced was [sic] an order to change our beds, for . . . we used to sleep on the straw palliasses; those who desired to be comfortable used to cut the stitches, but most of us were quite happy on the hard stitched ones. The Presentation Nuns, however, thought that impossible. So they desired Revd. Mother to have hair mattresses got, and this was I assure you a penance, for to get so many at once was expensive, and some one offering to do it cheap, instead of horse hair, put in cows' or dogs' or something so dreadful that the smell for several months was most sickening.

More helpful than the mattresses was the beer—which the Presentation Sisters recommended—as before they "only had water at dinner."[39]

All in all, fifteen months seemed a very long time—to Catherine, Anna Maria, and Elizabeth, and their companions back on Baggot Street. No amount of solicitude sent back and forth through third parties could fill the gap. Finally October 9, 1831, arrived, the day when the Presentation chapter would make its decisions, using black and white beans.[40]

Sometime before this day, Archbishop Murray intervened in several respectful but crucial ways. He came to George's Hill and assured the Pre-

---

38. CML, in *CMcATM*, 91.
39. Ibid., 94.
40. "Community Chapter Book," George's Hill, 70.

sentation community that any decisions to allow the Baggot Street novices to profess religious vows would, in themselves, be legitimate. He drafted the wording of the Act of Profession that could be used in their case; and, as was required, he examined the three of them, particularly, as Mary Ann (Anna Maria) Doyle later said, on "the new order 'we are about to erect called *of the Sisters of Mercy.*'"[41] Most helpful of all, he comforted Catherine, "telling her to keep her mind in peace for even if what she feared should come to pass, he would himself admit her to holy Profession, if her religious Superiors could assure him that she had been humble and obedient during her novitiate."[42] Catherine, for whom these virtues—maturely understood and practiced—became reliable signs of a genuine following of Jesus Christ, would have been loath to see them in herself in the autumn of 1831, or, indeed, at any time.

On October 9, 1831, the eleven professed Presentation Sisters assembled "to take the votes for profession of the three Sisters of Mercy, Mary Catherine McAuley, Mary Anne [*sic*] Doyle & Mary Elizabeth Harley. The votes were in favor of their Profession," though the exact number of white beans, a majority, is not recorded. "Sister M. F. of Sales Knowd Superioress" signed the entry in the Chapter Book.[43]

Dr. Murray also took on himself the responsibility of seeing that Catherine "had so disposed of her property as to be truly poor at the time of Profession; for which considerate kindness she ever felt most grateful, as it prevented the necessity of making known to others, not concerned [i.e., the Presentation Sisters], the amount and appropriation of the funds of her Establishment."[44] She paid for the board and other expenses incurred by the three of them at George's Hill, but she did not have to present dowries for them to the Presentation Sisters upon profession, nor did she have to disclose to them, in a document forgoing any future personal use of these funds, whatever assets remained from the Callaghan bequest. The Baggot Street Trust also remained in effect, though Daniel Murray would never take advantage of it. Perhaps it was at this time that Charles Cavanagh, a friend of Father Daniel Burke, became the future congregation's voluntary solicitor, financial accountant, and stockbroker for the next thirty years.

In the early morning of December 12, 1831, at a Mass in the convent

41. MADL, in *CMcATM*, 43.
42. Lim, in *CMcATM*, 170.
43. "Community Chapter Book," George's Hill, 70.
44. Lim, in *CMcATM*, 170.

chapel on George's Hill, Catherine McAuley, Mary Ann Doyle, and Elizabeth Harley professed their religious vows of "perpetual poverty, chastity, and obedience." The wording of the Act of Profession that each pronounced in the presence of Archbishop Murray also included the promise
"to persevere until the end of my life in the Congregation called of the Sisters of Mercy established for the visitation of the sick poor, and charitable
instruction of poor females, according to the Rules and Constitutions of
the Presentation Order, subject to such alteration as shall be approved by
the Archbishop."[45]

Their Act of Profession that morning constituted the founding of the
Sisters of Mercy. Much personal courage and resoluteness, as well as trust
in the providence of a merciful God, lay behind their human words. Mary
Ann Doyle was now thirty, Elizabeth Harley was in her early twenties, and
Catherine McAuley was fifty-three. The human journey to December 12,
1831, had not been without its ups and downs, its "joys and sorrows min-
gled, one succeeding the other," as Catherine later concluded the lives of
Sisters of Mercy would often be.[46]

Following the private ceremony, the three returned immediately to
Baggot Street accompanied by Michael Blake, who had attended their profession. Mary Ann Doyle sensed that the Presentation sisters "whom they
left were not a little offended at their precipitate departure," apparently
without even staying for breakfast. But she knew Catherine "was impatient of a longer absence from the Institution which had been the object of
so much solicitude to her and for the sake of which alone . . . she had submitted to the trials and repugnances of her novitiate."[47] Repugnances, yes,
but also, it seems, priceless learning, about herself and about the nature
of the life they had chosen. Years later during a visit to "our old George's
Hill," Catherine kissed "the old rush chair I used to sit on in the novaship
[i.e., novitiate]."[48]

Waiting for them at the front door on Baggot Street were Catherine

---

45. Catherine's Act of Profession was later transcribed into the Presentation community's register,
but this transcription does not contain Catherine McAuley's signature. The original document she must
have signed cannot now be found. See also Burke Savage, *McAuley*, 420–21; letter 12, December 12, 1831, in
CCMcA, 47; and DL, in *CMcATM*, 60.

In addition to the vows of poverty, chastity, and obedience, the Presentation Sisters professed a fourth
vow: to instruct poor girls in the Christian faith (Walsh, *Nano Nagle*, 176–77). In 1831 Catherine McAuley,
Mary Ann Doyle, and Elizabeth Harley did not profess this vow at George's Hill. See chap. 13 of the present
volume for a discussion of the fourth vow later professed by Sisters of Mercy, beginning in 1841.

46. Letter 269, May 28, 1841, in *CCMcA*, 401.

47. DL, in *CMcATM*, 60.

48. Letter 142 [November 17, 1839], in *CCMcA*, 217.

Byrn, Frances Warde, Margaret Dunne, Mary Anne Delany, Mary Macauley, Georgiana Moore, Marcella Flynn, Mary Jones, and Anna Carroll. Running to the windows to catch the first glimpses of the carriage were Catherine's twelve-year-old niece Catherine, Teresa Byrn, Ellen Corrigan, and Ann Rice. In the infirmary, overjoyed, lay Anne O'Grady. Gone now were the faces of Caroline Murphy and the troubled Hannah Fulham. Probably no eyewitness manuscript does justice to what happened when the front door was opened. "Heartfelt joy" must be an understatement.[49]

As they embraced, with smiles and tears, what must have struck them first was Catherine's and the others' religious habit. The long black pleated dress was not unlike the dresses they were wearing themselves. But the white coif surrounding the face, the white linen guimpe covering the shoulders and breasts, and the long black gossamer veil—these would take some getting used to. Sewing them would surely stretch their present skills! Then they noticed the wide leather cincture, looped through a black horn ring at the side and hanging down to the knees, with a large rosary caught in it at the waist. An ebony and ivory crucifix hung from the beads. Then they saw the fitted black sleeves. Finally they saw the silver ring.[50]

A plain band of silver circled Catherine's ring finger on her left hand, and Mary Ann's and Elizabeth's. If you came close and looked very carefully you could see something engraved on them. On Catherine's were the words: *"Ad Majorem Dei Gloriam"* (To the greater glory of God). Later they would learn that inside her ring were the words: *"Fiat voluntas tua"* (May your will be done).

But more compelling than all this was Catherine's face—her smile, her glistening eyes.

The next day, December 13, Daniel Murray came to the house and appointed Catherine McAuley "Superioress and Mother" of the new congregation. This was a formality that was not really needed, as he surely knew. When Catherine objected to the title—"she desired to be called only Sister Superior, and not to have the title Mother amongst us"—Dr. Murray said, probably with what could count as an episcopal twinkle, "there must be at least one Mother."[51] Several years later Clare Augustine Moore remarked:

For a long time she would not be called Revd. Mother but only Mother Catherine. Even to the last she would not allow the least ceremony to be used towards her. . . .

49. Lim, in *CMcATM*, 170.
50. BA, in *CMcATM*, 107 and 108; CML, in *CMcATM*, 95.
51. BA, in *CMcATM*, 107.

She was with us precisely as my own mother was with her family, or rather we used less ceremony than was used at home.[52]

After December 13, Catherine usually signed her correspondence, to all but her family, simply "M. C. McAuley," occasionally "Mary C. McAuley," or more rarely "Mary Catherine McAuley," but never "Reverend Mother" or "Mother Catherine" or "Mother McAuley." Only once, in a petition to Pope Gregory XVI, did she append the title "Mother Superior."

On the same day, Catherine asked Daniel Murray what Rule the community should observe, since revision of the Presentation Rule for their own purposes would take some time. He asked to see a copy of the Presentation Rule. Opening it and pointing to the chapter "On Union and Charity" he said, "If they observe that, it will suffice."[53] It read in part:

"Love one another as I have loved you." . . .

This mutual love and union . . . they should study to maintain, and cherish so perfectly among themselves as to live together as if they had but one heart and one soul in God. . . .

They shall as true followers of God walk in love, as Christ loved us, preserving above all things Charity . . . and in sincerity of heart fervently loving each other. They shall be ready on all occasions to help and assist one another, bearing with patience and charity each other's defects, weaknesses, and imperfections.[54]

In the days that followed Catherine spent time by the bed of Anne O'Grady, holding the hand that had done so much for the poor, and comforting the young woman about whose illness she had been so anxious, even at a distance. The Christmas dinner for all the neighborhood children was held as usual, again with plum pudding, and Catherine once more waiting on the hungry, ragged children she loved.

Then the year ended, as it had always ended at George's Hill, with a retreat on the last three days. At each ringing of the huge brass bell suspended near the central staircase, Catherine entered the chapel. In peace she reflected on the unparalleled promise yet fragility of beginnings, of the small seed sown.

52. CAM, in *CMcATM*, 206.
53. BA, in *CMcATM*, 107.
54. *Rules and Constitutions . . . of the Religious Sisterhood of the Presentation*, 30–32.

CHAPTER 7

The Beginnings—and Cholera *1832*

On January 23, 1832, clamorous confusion and loud indignation reigned outside the front door of Baggot Street.

Daniel Murray had earlier suggested that Catherine McAuley talk with those who remained behind while she was at George's Hill, and when she had selected those ready to become novices, he would preside at the first reception ceremony of the new congregation. The choice of eight women was obvious. Most of them had long lived and acted like Sisters of Mercy: Catherine Byrn, who chose the name Mary Josephine; Frances Warde, who would become Mary Frances; Margaret Dunne, Mary Angela; Mary Macauley, Mary Teresa; Georgiana Moore, Mary Clare; Mary Anne Delany, Mary Magdalen de Pazzi; Anna Carroll, Mary Agnes; and Anne O'Grady, if she were able, Mary Aloysius.[1] Catherine accepted the choice of Clare, Angela, and Teresa, though she must have remembered her own earlier avoidance of these honored names.

Although Anna Carroll was new in the house, having come in July 1831, Catherine knew her aunt in George's Hill, and felt Anna should be received. Marcella Flynn either hesitated herself or evoked some hesitation in Catherine, so her reception of the habit was delayed. The Welshwoman Mary Jones, who had come to Baggot Street in May 1831, was a harder decision, and Catherine chose to delay her reception. Years later she described

---

1. "Frances" is the correct spelling of Frances Warde's religious name, as in Catherine McAuley's letters and certain other primary sources. See *CMcATM*, 218–19, 354 n. 25, and 380 n. 7.

the long-lasting psychological effects of Mary's freely chosen but abrupt conversion to the Catholic faith and entrance into Baggot Street:

> The violent efforts she made to embrace and practice it, and the entire separation from all to whom she was ever known, gave a shock to the whole nervous system which could not be recovered. . . . All her mind turned to England & English manners.[2]

Mary Jones did not wish to leave, and Catherine would not dismiss her.

As the scheduled day approached, Catherine agonized over disappointing Anne O'Grady. Were she not slowly wasting away she should surely receive the habit, but how could she even come to the chapel for the ceremony, let alone put on the black dress, cincture, coif, and white veil. She would have to be a novice in a less visible way, dressed in patience and trust in the greater reception that awaited her.

Catherine resolved to have the ceremony strictly private, for two reasons: the hopeless state of Anne O'Grady, and "on the principle of religious poverty" which she felt was "incompatible with the lavish expenditure of her own reception." At George's Hill, in keeping with Presentation custom, they had been asked to dress in what Catherine regarded as expensive gowns.[3] In later reception ceremonies she would concede to the postulants' wearing plain white muslin dresses as they entered the chapel, with circles of flowers in their hair, but not at this first reception on January 23. As Clare Moore says:

> The expenses incurred during the 15 months of her Noviceship made Revd. Mother resolve on a plan of very strict economy when she came home to Baggot St. . . . Our Postulants dresses were altered and patched up into habits for us to be received in. We had only common brass crosses to our beads. We got their old white veils, only one new one, old guimpes, etc.[4]

The novices-to-be were content to wear the black dresses they ordinarily wore, now re-designed, but the decision to have the ceremony private, with only a few invited priests, proved a huge mistake.

On the morning of the reception, after Archbishop Murray arrived and the ceremony began, such a ruckus occurred on the street outside that it could be easily heard inside—in shrill contrast to the solemnity of the ceremonial music. The clamor of angry voices at the door was hardly a grace-

---

2. Letter 122, May 11, 1839, in *CCMcA*, 194–95. Mary Jones was eventually received as a novice in October 1832 and professed vows on February 11, 1834.

3. DL, in *CMcATM*, 61.

4. CML, in *CMcATM*, 95.

ful accompaniment to the sublime hymn *O Gloriosa Virginum,* sung as the postulants knelt inside.[5]

Catherine had asked the portress to admit no one, including relatives, little realizing how many there would be. Georgiana Moore's sister claims:

> There was such ringing of bells. Friends of the sisters, friends of the Institute, everyone sure that some one else had been admitted, everyone indignant, then the mob that collected round them increased the confusion. But loud above all rose the voice of the junior Postulant's mother who declared she would not allow her daughter to remain in the convent where she herself was so affronted.[6]

Within the week Anna Carroll left at the insistence of her mother. She later entered the Presentation convent on George's Hill, where as Mother Mary Brigid she became a beloved and energetic leader of the community.

Though Catherine had been understandably preoccupied with Anne O'Grady's illness and with properly performing the first reception ceremony over which she would preside, she later advised others: "Every place has its own particular ideas & feelings which must be yielded to when possible," and counseled at least one superior to "avoid all solemn declaration."[7] Yielding to others' wishes "when possible" was a hard, daily lesson to be learned. If she had not fully grasped it before, she certainly learned it quickly on January 23, 1832. Ever after, while she lived, all reception and profession ceremonies, in whatever town or city, were always public and held in the parish church if the convent chapel was not big enough.

Mary Aloysius (Anne) O'Grady died two weeks later, on February 8. Like Caroline Murphy she was buried in the brown Carmelite habit in the underground vaults at St. Teresa's church on Clarendon Street.

But another sorrow was looming. Elizabeth Harley soon fell into rapid consumption, advanced pulmonary tuberculosis. On Ash Wednesday she was well enough to serve in the refectory, but by Easter Sunday (April 22) she could join the community only at the end of dinner "to have a little pudding or something."[8] Elizabeth had begun to show symptoms of the

---

5. *Form of Ceremony for the Reception and Profession of the Sisters of Our Lady of Mercy* (Dublin: J. Byrn, 1834), 3–4. The ceremony, as outlined here, remained almost exactly the same in most Mercy congregations until at least the 1960s. The hymn, *O Gloriosa Virginum,* a melody from the "Harfe David," arranged by P. J. Van Damme, is in the revised Singers' edition, *St. Gregory Hymnal,* edited by Nicola A. Montani (Philadelphia: St. Gregory Guild, 1940), 326–27. Clare Augustine Moore says that the first reception ceremony was held "in the sacristy," not the chapel, but this claim is not verified elsewhere. CAM, in *CMcATM,* 206.

6. CAM, in *CMcATM,* 206.

7. Letter 102, November 17, 1838, in *CCMcA,* 168; letter 103 [December 9, 1838], in *CCMcA,* 170.

8. CML, in *CMcATM,* 96.

disease while at George's Hill, and had nursed Anne O'Grady during the last weeks of her long illness.

From the vantage point of medical knowledge in the twenty-first century it is difficult to imagine a world in which Louis Pasteur had not yet demonstrated the existence of microorganisms (1864), Robert Koch had not yet identified the tuberculosis bacterium (1882), others had not made their stunning discoveries of the causes of other infectious diseases—and a world in which the pharmaceutical breakthroughs of the 1930s–1950s had not occurred. Some sense of "contagion" was prevalent in more advanced medical circles in Ireland, and William Stokes had introduced Laennec's stethoscope in 1825, but neither was widely accepted. Knowledge of the infectious nature of tuberculosis and its aerial transmission from human to human did not generally inform medical practice in Ireland until well after Koch's discovery.

Because of her frequent visits to hospitals as well as her close connections with the medical profession through her family and the Callaghans, Catherine knew who were regarded as the best physicians in Dublin. In 1832 and throughout the following decade she was remarkably astute in securing for her sisters, though only reluctantly for herself, the medical attendance of such highly respected practitioners as Dominic Corrigan, Philip Crampton, Robert Graves, Henry Marsh, James Murray, William Stokes, and Francis White, most of them Protestants.

Once, in 1832, when three in the house "were attacked with virulent scurvy, all the others ill," Catherine called in Dr. Philip Crampton, the surgeon-general since 1813, later appointed surgeon-in-ordinary to the king (queen) in Ireland, and knighted in 1839 by Queen Victoria.[9] Crampton, always a dashing fellow in his blue riding attire and boots with spurs, but even more noted for his acute observation, quickly sized up the situation.[10] "Having always less faith in medicine than management, [he] inquired into their food and occupations, and at once declared that an amelioration of the diet would be the best cure, and especially he ordered beer." He also tried to convince Catherine of the "real unwholesomeness" of the visitation of poor families, but "she never could understand, and always maintained that fresh air must be good, forgetting that it must be taken by us mostly in Townsend St. and Bull Alley"—among the worst slums in the city.[11]

On March 26, Catherine placed an advertisement in *Freeman's Journal*

9. CAM, in *CMcATM*, 206.
10. Ormsby, *Medical History of the Meath Hospital*, 183–90.
11. CAM, in *CMcATM*, 206–7.

announcing that "a Bazaar, promising very great attraction, will be held for the support of the House of Mercy in Easter Week," and noting that "particular circumstances prevented one last Season [in 1831], and the Sisters of the Institution have seen with deep concern many very deserving destitute persons going away, to whom they could not afford protection and relief." After listing over eighty patronesses of the bazaar—including "The Lady Mayoress," over a dozen ladies of the nobility, and the wives of many doctors and military officers, including her own sister-in-law—the ad, which ran through March 31 and again on April 5, noted: "The most trifling Fancy Work will be very gratefully received, as there is not yet sufficient to furnish tables."[12] On Easter Wednesday (April 25), the ad resumed—giving Morrisson's Rooms, Dawson Street as the venue—and ran through April 28, the second day of the bazaar. It promised:

A beautiful Album, with original Compositions and Drawings, a Cabinet, just received from England, of the newest Fancy Work, furnished with a variety of Curiosities, and a very handsome French Screen, will be raffled for.

The Album is to be seen at Mr. Milliken's, Grafton Street, where Tickets may be had.

The Band of the Royal Rifles and of the 28th Regiment will attend at the Bazaar.[13]

Clearly Baggot Street needed money to carry on its work, many fashionable women had been enlisted to support the bazaar, and Catherine had probably drafted her brother to arrange for the military music. In this and other bazaars, she would show herself a skilled public relations and development officer.

Meanwhile, physicians could do nothing for Elizabeth Harley. Early in Easter Week she was dying, loved by all for her charity: "No want of attention ever seemed to give her pain and never by act, word or look did she give pain to others."[14] On Wednesday Catherine could only sit by Elizabeth's bed and pray with her. Then the front doorbell rang, and she was abruptly called away. It was Miss Farrell from Merrion Square, who had carefully read the morning newspaper. Neither Clare Moore nor Mary Ann Doyle knew then that a scolding tirade was in store for Catherine:

12. *Freeman's Journal*, March 26–31 and April 5, 1832. From late March to mid-April, the *Morning Register* ran announcements of the bazaar, with no dates given, but saying it would be "held in Shelbourne House [Hotel]." The venue was then changed to Morrisson's Rooms, Dawson Street, and the dates set: April 27 and 28. The *Morning Register* on April 17 read in part: "The Sisters of Mercy . . . are anxious to express the gratitude they feel to Mr. Burke, proprietor of Shelbourne House, and to the very distinguished Ladies there, who, at great personal inconvenience, offered the use of the Establishment."

13. *Freeman's Journal*, April 26–28, 1832.

14. DL, in *CMcATM*, 63.

It was at the time of the annual bazaar, and poor Mother M. Catherine was called from beside the bed of death to a lady who wanted her in the parlour. Now this was an old lady who was very rich, very charitable and rather odd, having moreover a great dislike to bazaars, and she came to lecture on the impropriety, the utter sinfulness of these ways of raising money for the poor. To all this our dear Mother Catherine listened with exemplary patience which she thought amply rewarded when at length her visitor rising to depart presented her with £15 for the poor.[15]

Catherine was a stickler for politeness, but Miss Farrell must have come dangerously close to outlasting even the bazaar-holder's courtesy.

That evening, April 25, Elizabeth Harley died. Full of sorrow—deeper than the others could realize—Catherine tried to console the community standing near her, repeating to them the short verse from Psalm 118 prayed at Easter: "This is the day that the Lord has made; let us rejoice and be glad in it."[16] As she looked at Elizabeth, she could summon no other words.

A few weeks later, exhausted, Catherine carried home in the dark a newborn baby, wrapped carefully in her shawl, and "put it to sleep in a little bed in her own cell."[17] Another calamity had struck, not Baggot Street, but the whole city of Dublin. The long-feared malignant Asiatic cholera had now arrived from England and Europe. The young mother had just died in the temporary cholera hospital set up on Townsend Street.

In news announcements and placards, issued from Dublin Castle on April 13, 1832, Francis Barker, M.D., secretary of the Central Board of Health for Ireland, had warned the public to seek immediate medical treatment upon experiencing or witnessing "the earliest and most striking Symptoms" of "aggravated forms" of the disease. "Delay, or Concealment for even one Hour, may be the cause of Death."[18]

The first five cases of cholera in Dublin (four of them fatal) had been reported on March 27. On April 24, the Board of Health for the City of Dublin reiterated the plea that patients suspected of cholera be taken immediately to hospital, as there was "little hope" for one "who delays his application for medical treatment beyond six hours." It promised that a temporary cholera hospital would be opened at Grangegorman Lane Penitentiary the next day.[19]

Elizabeth Harley's death on April 25 came as this news was breaking,

---

15. Ibid., 64.   16. BA, in *CMcATM*, 110.
17. CML, in *CMcATM*, 98.
18. "Central Board of Health for Ireland, Dublin Castle, 13th April, 1832" (placard), NAI Board of Health, Cholera Papers Various, 1832–1834, 2/440/10 (NAI). Permission to quote this placard has been granted by the National Archives of Ireland and the Director of the National Archives of Ireland.
19. *Freeman's Journal*, April 25, 1832.

two nights before the two-day Easter Bazaar. Of the bazaar Clare Moore spoke for everyone at Baggot Street: "You may guess how much we felt at being obliged to attend to the different arrangements of it."[20] Although 982 cases of cholera and 360 deaths were soon reported in the city, the duchesses, countesses, and other patronesses of the bazaar, donating sale items as well as purchasing them, may have felt that the epidemic was under control or at least did not affect them.[21] The bazaar was a philanthropic and social event, but now the *Morning Register* of April 28 noted that "at the present time, when pestilence reigns to a certain extent within our city," the bazaar "has claims upon public generosity and public sympathy of no ordinary character," and advised its readers:

If we had no better motive, a principle of selfishness should induce us to aid those who by their devoted zeal and humane exertions possess the power, and regardless of all personal considerations as affect themselves, exert it in visiting the sick, aiding the diseased, and supporting the convalescent; thereby presenting the best and surest specific [i.e., antidote] to the spread of contagion and the extension of mortality.[22]

By April 28, the Board of Health had asked Mary Aikenhead and the Sisters of Charity to assist in nursing at the Grangegorman hospital. On April 30, the board announced that this hospital could receive 150 cholera patients, and that of the 134 patients admitted there on the two previous days, there had been "only fifteen deaths."[23] With everything else on her mind, Catherine nonetheless wrote to Archbishop Murray seeking permission to offer the services of the Sisters of Mercy wherever they were needed. He came to the house immediately.

Dr. Murray had just published a pastoral letter on the cholera visitation, begging Catholics to follow four precautions: avoid intoxicating liquors, since these were thought to weaken physical resistance to the disease; abstain from conducting or participating in wakes for the dead, as these occasions were "most dangerous to the public health"; "procure interment with the least possible delay"; and take suspected cholera victims to the hospitals set up for them, rather than try to treat them at home. Given the unbelievably sudden deaths they had already witnessed, and the high mortality rates, the poor were terrified. Murray tried to assure them that "nothing can exceed the zeal and humanity of the medical attendants"

20. CML, in *CMcATM*, 96.
21. Numbers reported in *Freeman's Journal,* May 1, 1832.
22. *Morning Register,* April 28, 1832.
23. *Freeman's Journal,* May 1, 1832.

in the hospitals, and—speaking of Grangegorman—that a "Priest is on the spot administering spiritual consolation to the sufferer," and "the decencies of Christian burial are provided for—a spot for which, within the enclosure, has been duly consecrated, by my directions."[24]

Daniel Murray endorsed the Baggot Street community's willingness to assist in the epidemic, though there were now only ten of them and they were already running a shelter for dozens of homeless women, teaching hundreds of poor girls in the school each day, and caring for several young orphans. The training of the six novices could be deferred. Yet Murray was concerned about their health:

He came himself to bring the permission, it was evening, we were at Recreation. . . . He did not sit down, but standing at the end of the table spoke a few words about the work we were going to undertake, adding [that] we should take great nourishment, *port wine* and *mutton* chops.[25]

On May 2 the Board of Health reported that it had received a communication "from Mrs. M. C. McAuley, House of Mercy, Baggot Street," which said "the Sisters are most anxious to give all the assistance in their power to the poor Cholera sufferers, and had not heard of any hospital on that side" of the city.[26] Catherine had written her letter just as the board was announcing on May 1 "the immediate opening of the Depot, Townsend-street, for a Cholera Hospital," and promising that it "will be tomorrow capable of receiving fifty patients, and admits of a considerable further increase."[27] So the board immediately and unanimously resolved to send its "cordial thanks . . . to the Sisters of Mercy, and inform them that the Depot in Townsend-street has been opened . . . and that their attendance, co-operation, and consolation will be gratefully accepted."[28]

Preparations at Baggot Street began immediately. Dr. Murray's advice about "port wine and mutton chops" was "literally obeyed for a week or two when it was found to be too troublesome."[29] He had also urged them to "take all due precautions for the preservation of their own health [and] make use of the prescribed remedies against infection."[30]

Mutton chops and port wine or not, the sisters were on the job at Townsend Street by May 4, at the start of one of the most deadly months of the epidemic. They worked in shifts: "We went early in the morning, 4

24. William Meagher, *Notices of the Life and Character of . . . Daniel Murray* (Dublin: Gerald Bellew, 1853), 155–56.

25. CML, in *CMcATM*, 97.

26. *Freeman's Journal*, May 3, 1832.

27. *Freeman's Journal*, May 1, 1832.

28. *Freeman's Journal*, May 3, 1832.

29. CML, in *CMcATM*, 97.

30. DL, in *CMcATM*, 64.

Sisters who were relieved in 2 or 3 hours and so on till 8 in [the] evening. Revd. Mother was there very much. She used to go in Kirwan's car," an open, horse-drawn jaunting car with seats on the sides.[31] Clare Moore remembered that there were "always four" at the Depot "from nine in the morning till eight at night," and that although Catherine "had a natural dread of contagion, she overcame that feeling, and scarcely left the Hospital."[32]

Whatever the community had seen in previous visits to the sick did not compare with the violent cholera ravages they witnessed in the Depot. Inadequate cholera treatment, as it was in 1832, did not offer pleasant sights or sounds or smells. The patients suffered constant diarrhea and vomiting, "resulting in severe dehydration or water loss and its consequences." The diarrhea was followed by severe muscle cramps, "loss of palpable pulse, thickening of the circulating blood, [and] suppression of urination." As the dehydration progressed, the cheeks and eyes of the frightened but conscious patient became sunken, the tongue dry, and the skin withered. A "disastrous fall in blood pressure leading to profound shock" preceded death.[33]

The severe loss of body fluids and electrolytes would today be treated with intravenous therapy and antibiotics. In 1832 treatments such as purgatives and bloodletting were ineffective and further damaging. More conservative Dublin physicians used heating applications, and brandy and laudanum (an opium preparation), usually in half-hour doses, but none of these directly addressed the loss of water and salts in the body leading to severe dehydration. Not until John Snow published his study of the transmission of cholera by contaminated drinking water (1855), and Robert Koch identified the bacterium *vibrio cholerae* as a cholera-producing agent (1883–1884), was the cause and control (and proper treatment) of this dreaded disease set in a sound medical direction. However, some medical hygiene, especially in relation to fecal contamination, was seen as a help even in the Depot: the patients' clothing was burned on entry, and wheel carriages and "cholera-cots" were provided for them. As Clare Moore calmly noted, between shifts "we used . . . *at first* change our habits and use vinegar [as a disinfectant], we then got accustomed."[34]

31. CML, in *CMcATM*, 97.
32. BA, in *CMcATM*, 112.
33. Reinhard S. Speck, "Cholera," in *Cambridge World History of Human Disease*, ed. Kenneth F. Kiple (Cambridge: Cambridge University Press, 1993), 642, 644.
34. CML, in *CMcATM*, 97.

Into this unfamiliar and dangerous setting Catherine McAuley walked at nine o'clock each morning for seven months. She oversaw the eighty poorly paid nurses who worked in shifts and who at this point in nursing history were mostly domestic servants, better at mopping floors than at patient care, and occasionally caught imbibing the alcoholic drams intended for patients. Andrew Furlong, a young doctor who saw Catherine at the Depot each day, reported many years later that the head physician, Dr. Hart (or Harty?) regarded the sisters as "of the greatest use. . . . The hospital could not be carried on without them; they kept the eighty nurses in order—which was hard to do."[35] It may also have been true, as Mary Austin Carroll claimed, that Catherine "would allow no one to be buried till she had assured herself by personal inspection that life was really extinct, nor would she allow the nurses to cover the faces of those supposed to be dead, till a stated time elapsed."[36] The mere presence of the sisters apparently assured patients and their relatives that, contrary to the wild rumors swirling outside, the doctors were not poisoning patients, and that despite appearances and the suddenness of death (within a few hours), no one was deliberately buried alive.

Most of all, Catherine and her sisters consoled and prayed with dying patients and those that survived. When it was possible to give physical relief they did so. From long experience by sickbeds Catherine knew how much small gestures and kind words could help. To those she knew or suspected were Christians, as well as to others who said they were not, she offered hope and confidence in the mercy of a God who looked on them with compassion. The extremity of the situation called for the most thorough consolation she knew how to give: trust in the present and future love of the God in whom she believed. When, according to Carroll, she was accused of "proselytizing," the head physician, a Protestant, defended her.[37]

As if the hundreds of deaths were not enough suffering, in early May the Royal Hospital Kilmainham closed Bully's Acre to any further burials. This ancient, two-acre burial ground at the edge of the hospital lands

---

35. Carroll, *Leaves from the Annals,* vol. 2 (1883), 295. "Dr. Hart" (misspelled?) has not so far been identified. Dr. John Hart (c. 1797–1872), a member of the Royal College of Surgeons in Ireland (RCSI) since 1822, later professor of anatomy at RCSI ("Kirkpatrick Archive," RCPI), may possibly be the "Dr. Hart" who served in the Townsend Street Depot. However, a Dr. William Harty, of 34 Gloucester Street, is listed as a licentiate of the RCPI, *Dublin Directory* (1828), 154, and a William Harty published "On the contagion of cholera," in the *Dublin Journal of Medical and Chemical Science* 3 (1833): 74–86.

36. Carroll, *Life,* 226.

37. Carroll, *Leaves from the Annals* (1883), vol. 2, 295. No further information on the complaint of "proselytizing" or Dr. Hart's (or Harty's?) defense has so far been discovered.

was free: hence, "the destination of most of the Catholic poor." It had long been a site subject to the indignity of midnight body-snatching for the instruction of medical students.[38] Colonel George D'Aguilar, deputy master of the Royal Hospital, told the Board of Health of his "personal and minute inspection of the burial ground" which, over "the last ten days, has already received five hundred bodies (mostly cholera subjects)." He found "the whole place so occupied and encumbered with the dead, that it is impossible to open a fresh grave without encountering at every stroke of the spade some remnant of mortality." Therefore D'Aguilar asked the board "to reconcile the lower orders of the metropolis to other places of interment."[39] Graves in the few churchyards that were still open or in the "poor grounds" of the newly created Catholic cemeteries at Goldenbridge and Glasnevin were the only available possibilities, though in each case there was a nominal fee.

By July 4 the number of cases of cholera in Dublin since commencement of the epidemic reached 5,037, and the number of deaths was 1,478, though many cases and deaths, of those who did not enter hospitals, went unreported.[40] So the board determined to keep open the now enlarged hospital on Townsend Street for the continued reception of malignant cases.

In late October in a report to Sir William Gossett, chairman of the Central Board of Health for Ireland, the Dublin Board of Health listed the expenditures at the Grangegorman and Townsend Street hospitals for the period September 1 to October 13. During these six weeks, the total number of patients served in these hospitals ("three-fifths" at Grangegorman and "two fifths" at Townsend Street) was "1899, of whom 555 died, 1150 were discharged cured," with "167 remaining" (apparently almost twenty-five were unaccounted). The expenditures at Grangegorman were "Furniture—£54.1.5; Clothing & Bedding [to replace what was burned]—£584.15.9; burial expenses—£112.18.3." At Townsend Street the expenditures were "Furniture & Bedding—£32.11.3½; Clothes for Patients leaving Hospital … £355.15.10½; Burial expenses—£169.9.6½." The cost of "Medicines" and "Coals, soap & candles" at the two hospitals was also noted, as were the "salaries and wages."[41] Given the daily needs of these cholera hospitals and

38. Tony Farmar, *Patients, Potions & Physicians*, 56.

39. *Freeman's Journal*, May 5, 1832.

40. *Freeman's Journal*, July 5, 1832.

41. Board of Health for the City of Dublin to Sir William Gossett, October 13, 1832, Board of Health, Cholera Papers Various, 1832–1834, 2/440/10 (NAI). Permission to quote this letter has been granted by the National Archives of Ireland and the Director of the National Archives of Ireland. Burke Savage,

thus the daily duties of the medical attendants, nurses, gravediggers, and others, as implied in this report, the Sisters of Charity and Sisters of Mercy who served gratis were obviously involved in exhausting work.

On November 13 the board reported that of the 12,361 known cases in Dublin since the beginning, 3,668 had ended in death, but the numbers were now diminishing.[42] The Sisters of Mercy remained at the Depot until early December, and the daily public reports on the disease and its fatalities in Dublin ended on December 14, though the epidemic still afflicted other parts of Ireland, and outbursts occurred in the suburbs of Dublin in 1833.

Years afterwards Catherine used to tell newcomers to Baggot Street stories about those extraordinary days in 1832, forever imprinted on her memory. She described "the sisters returning at past 9, loosening their cinctures on the stairs and stopping, overcome with sleep."[43] As Clare Moore recalled, it was on such a night that "a poor woman being either lately or at the time confined . . . died just after of Cholera." Catherine "had such compassion on the infant that she brought it home under her shawl and put it to sleep in a little bed in her own cell," but "the little thing cried all night." The child, of course, needed to be suckled, so "the next day it was given to some one to take care of. I never knew what became of it, for I never asked questions."[44] (Clare later learned to be less reticent.)

Mary Ann Doyle, who worked constant shifts at the Depot, moving from low pallet to low pallet on her knees, carried away from that experience not only lasting swelling and soreness in her joints, particularly one of them, but also a spontaneous treasure in verse. One night after her injury was apparent, Catherine—in an attempt to cheer her and the weary community—cut free the clean inside of a used white envelope, and composed what has remained her most famous doggerel:

> Dear Sister Doyle, accept from me
> for your poor suffering martyrs
> a laurel wreath to crown each knee
> in place of former garters.

McAuley, 150, and others claim that the death rate at Townsend Street Depot (about 30 percent) was lower than at Grangegorman. However, the mortality at the two hospitals undoubtedly resulted from many different factors.

42. *Freeman's Journal*, November 14, 1832.   43. CAM, in *CMcATM*, 207.
44. CML, in *CMcATM*, 97–98.

Since fatal Cholera appeared
you've scarce been seen to stand,
nor danger for yourself e'er feared
when death o'erspread the land.

While on your knees from Bed to Bed
you quickly moved about
it did not enter in your head
that knees could e'er wear out.

You've hurt the marrow in the bone
imploring aid and pity
and every Cardinal in Rome
would say you saved the City.

Now that the story of your fame
in Annals may be seen
we'll give each wounded knee a name
Cholera—and—Cholerene.[45]

Though "Cholera" and "Cholerene" were sore for a long time, no Sister of Mercy contracted cholera in 1832 or during the next sixteen years.

On June 10, 1832, Pentecost Sunday and her twenty-sixth birthday, Anne Moore entered the Baggot Street community. No relation to the other two Moores, she nonetheless brought her own dubious distinction. In January she had been one of those on the street "murmuring" at the closed-door policy of the first reception ceremony. In July she was followed by Frances Marmion, the first of three Marmion sisters to join the community. Presumably fresh and rested, Anne and Frances were quickly pressed into service at Baggot Street and in the cholera Depot. Together with Marcella Flynn and Mary Jones, they were received as novices on October 8 in a ceremony open to the public and happily devoid of outside clamoring. The names they chose were Mary Magdalen (Flynn), Mary Gertrude (Jones), Mary Elizabeth (Moore), and Mary Agnes (Marmion), observing Catherine's apparent preference for feminine names, as Mary Austin Carroll would later claim.[46] Catherine now had ten novices to train, on top of everything else, teaching them more by example than by precept, the method she always favored, attributing it to Jesus in the gospels.[47]

45. Letter 15 [1832], in CCMcA, 52.
46. "Baggot Street Register" (MCA); Carroll, Life, 453.
47. "Spirit of the Institute," in CCMcA, 463.

In June that year Michael Blake, who frequently directed personal bequests he received to Catherine, had turned over to the community a legacy of £715.10.0 in Royal Canal stock. Her annual income from the Callaghan inheritance now far overstretched, Blake's gift was a relief. Catherine also re-instituted neighborhood begging:

Just after the Cholera, Revd. Mother got printed tickets sent to each house begging old clothing, carpeting, bed covering, etc., and the result was that for a long time carriages used to stop and hand in great bundles so that the store room was filled, and the supply lasted a long time.[48]

An earlier door-to-door appeal, in Catherine's handwriting with Daniel Murray's signature, read in part:

Schools and House of Mercy, Baggot Street. . . . In these schools five hundred [sic] poor girls may daily experience the blessing of religious instruction, and being practiced in various branches of industry, come forward . . . prepared as Christians to discharge the duties of the humble state in life to which it has pleased God to call them.

Young tradeswomen of good character . . . are invited to this house at night as their home . . . and guarded against the dangers that surround them.

You are most earnestly entreated to contribute to the support of this Institution.[49]

In August 1832 the community somehow—in the midst of their work at the Depot—made their first annual retreat together, directed by Myles Gaffney, a Dublin priest who later became senior dean at Maynooth (1834) and still later a Jesuit (1856). Gaffney and Catherine evidently thought alike, and while he was a curate at St. Andrew's, Daniel Murray asked him to assist her in composing the Mercy Rule. He apparently spoke so movingly during this retreat, or a subsequent one, that years later Catherine recalled his words in a letter to Frances Warde:

You remember what Father Gaffney said to us when in retreat—"If the entire cross upon which Christ died was sent to this House, how impatient would each Sister be to carry it, and she who was permitted to keep it the longest—would be the most favored. Far better and more profitable for you to receive with all your heart the cross which God will send you in any form or shape He pleases."[50]

The here-and-now-centered Catherine McAuley had reason to follow this advice in December 1832 when Catherine Byrn abruptly departed.

The story of Catherine Byrn may offer a classic example of what can re-

---

48. CML, in *CMcATM*, 98.
49. Letter 4 [December 1827], in *CCMcA*, 38.
50. Letter 269, May 28, 1841, in *CCMcA*, 401.

sult from too great dependence on a single oral or written source, too little questioning of its grounds for credibility, the meagerness of other primary sources, and too little reflection on possible motivations. Roland Burke Savage based his account of Catherine Byrn's departure from Baggot Street on the treatment of this event in the "Memoir" of Clare Augustine Moore, who did not enter the community until 1837.[51] Clare Augustine had written:

Revd. Mother was not without her troubles. Sr. M. Catherine Byrne, one of her first associates, besides a strong preference to the Order of St. Dominic, had a most decided love and talent for manoeuvering, with a most fertile imagination. She had during Revd. Mother's novitiate made acquaintance with a rather wealthy Dominican priest to whom, after her own reception, she gave such a distorted picture of her benefactress and her position that he thought it the most meritorious action in the world to remove her to [the Dominican convent in] Cabra. In the mean time she carefully concealed her project which she effected by means of her office of sacristan, which enabled her to keep one of the orphans, sent to assist her in cleaning the chapel, watching at the visitation entrance . . . till the answers to her notes were brought her by one of the school children. Revd. Mother had not the least idea of what was going on till the Revd. friend came to remove her cousin. She never uttered a single word of remonstrance nor made any effort to shake her purpose though she felt it painfully. . . . It was himself who told me [a] great deal of this; the rest I learned from Revd. Mother herself and the child employed to watch who was, when I came in, a lay sister.[52]

Burke Savage uses the words "love for manoeuvre," "lack of candour," and "surreptitious" in describing Catherine Byrn's conduct prior to her transfer to the Dominican Sisters on December 1, 1832.[53]

Clare Moore says only: "Sister Catharine [sic] Byrn resolved to join the Dominican Order, and effected her purpose under circumstances that were very painful to the feelings of our Reverend Mother."[54] Another early biographer says simply, "Miss Byrne was only withheld by circumstances from entering the Order of St. Dominick, which she eventually did, when these obstacles were removed."[55] One obstacle may have been the need for a dowry, on which women's orders such as the Dominicans usually depended.

Catherine Byrn was then twenty. She had, five years before, made an irreplaceable contribution to the inauguration and early operation of the House of Mercy, but she had apparently clung to her early preference for the Dominican way of life. Writing in 1867 to the Reverend B. T. Russell,

51. Burke Savage, McAuley, 162–63.
53. Burke Savage, McAuley, 162–63.
55. Lim, in CMcATM, 165.

52. CAM, in CMcATM, 207–8.
54. BA, in CMcATM, 112.

O.P., then provincial of the Dominicans, she says that Fanny Tighe, whom she knew through Catherine McAuley, "is one of my oldest and dearest friends, to whom, moreover, I am in great part indebted for my vocation at the age of eleven years, to this holy Order [the Dominicans]."[56] Even when she received the Mercy habit in January 1832, she retained this desire, as Dominican records at Siena convent in Drogheda indicate. A Dominican advisor had early on encouraged her to help out at Baggot Street, noting that "there would be no commitment in doing so because no profession of vows was involved."[57]

But now, on January 24, 1833, if all went well, the first Mercy novices were scheduled to profess religious vows. If standard practice was followed, as one can assume, these novices would be interviewed individually by Archbishop Murray or his deputy, Redmond O'Hanlon, sometime before the end of November, as to their complete freedom in desiring to profess religious vows according to the Rule of the Mercy congregation. At this point Catherine Byrn could have made known confidentially, and possibly did make known, not only her hesitation about remaining, but also the fact—if it was a fact—of her continuing correspondence with Dominican advisors, carried on through messengers and unbeknown to Catherine McAuley.

Why did Catherine Byrn not, as seems the case, present her hesitations, preference, and needs directly to Catherine McAuley, her adoptive mother for ten years and the woman she later always called "dear Mother Catherine"? Perhaps fear of hurting or disappointing her? Perhaps not wanting to ask the financially strapped advocate of poverty for the transportation and dowry she needed? Catherine Byrn had no money. Perhaps reluctance to make a break in the community of sisters who had just endured so much hardship together? Perhaps nursing in the cholera epidemic itself had been too much? Perhaps a feeling, whether based in reality or not, that her cousin Mary Teresa Macauley, just a year older than she, was more beautiful, or more beloved by Catherine McAuley and the community?

In afteryears Catherine Byrn, then Mary Raymond Byrn, O.P., felt free to write to "My dearest" Clare Moore, by then superior of the Mercy community in Bermondsey, London, where Catherine's sister Mary Margaret

---

56. Mary Raymond Byrn, O.P., to B. T. Russell, O.P. [October 1867?] (MCA). Information about Russell as provincial is from Mary Magdalen, O.P., to John MacErlean, S.J., June [July?] 4, 1940 (MCA).

57. Degnan, *Mercy*, 153. See also 154–55.

(Anne) Byrn had professed vows on December 4, 1848. She may also have written, perhaps frequently, to Catherine McAuley herself, but since the elder Catherine apparently destroyed before her death all personal correspondence still in her possession, including letters from Sisters of Mercy, no letter to her from Catherine Byrn has so far been found.

Exactly how or why Catherine Byrn's departure from Baggot Street was "very painful" for Catherine McAuley cannot now be ascertained, despite her earliest biographers' attempts to explain the situation as they understood it. The reserve with which Catherine generally guarded her personal feelings, and the absence of any direct testimony on her part must be acknowledged. One might speculate that she felt guilt, or wounded pride, or disappointment, or uncertainty about her young cousin's future happiness, or simply sorrow at the loss of one whom she had loved since she was a child.

The year 1832—with its joys, mistakes, hard work, and suffering—closed with the three-day retreat. In her *Journal of Meditations for Every Day in the Year,* the prayerbook she had used for the community's morning meditations since 1829, Catherine may have found consolation but also challenge. On December 29 she was reminded that Jesus was not made known to the proud in Bethlehem, "but to Shepherds . . . who were poor, humble, laborious, vigilant, and careful in their office." The next day she was invited to consider "the Infant wrapped in swaddling clothes, and laid in a manger" and asked "whether you can find such signs of poverty and humility in your heart." Finally, on December 31 she would have been urged to remember that "'Mary kept all these words and pondered them in her heart.'"[58]

The past year had offered more than enough to ponder. And on the horizon were Mary Teresa Macauley's increasing doubts. Together, Catherine and her niece would have to weigh these in the new year.

58. [Richard Challoner, ed.], *Journal of Meditations for Every Day in the Year* (Dublin: Richard Coyne, 1823), 66–69. This edition of the *Meditations* is thought to be a reprint of an earlier edition by Challoner (1691–1781), vicar apostolic of London from 1758. The work itself, dating from English penal days, was originally "written in Latin in 1639," presumably by Nathaniel Bacon, a Jesuit (i.e., "Southwell"). The manuscript was "translated into English [and published for the first time] in 1669 by Rev. E. Mico" (i.e., "Harvey"), also a Jesuit. Roger Baxter, ed., *Meditations for Every Day in the Year* (New York: Benziger Brothers, 1884), title page and preface. Catherine McAuley's copy of the *Journal* (Dublin: Richard Coyne, 1823) is now preserved in the MCA.

CHAPTER 8

Her "First-Born" *1833*

On Thursday morning, January 24, 1833, the first profession ceremony at Baggot Street took place, Archbishop Murray presiding. As the hymn *Veni Creator Spiritus* was sung, four novices, each carrying a lighted candle, processed into the chapel, followed by Catherine McAuley and her assistant, Mary Ann Doyle. Near the altar lay the black veil, black domino (a short, inner cotton veil), and the silver ring each novice would soon receive, as well as a pen and ink, and the Act of Profession each would sign after she professed her vows aloud.[1]

As Catherine walked behind the four—Mary Frances Warde, Mary Angela Dunne, Mary Clare Moore, and Mary de Pazzi Delany—joy and gratitude must have filled her mind and heart, as well as memories of the preceding year. Of the eight women who had been received as novices in January 1832, Anne O'Grady had died, Anna Carroll and Catherine Byrn had left the community, and one chose not to profess vows on this day.

In her stall in the chapel was Mary Teresa Macauley, Catherine's elder niece. For months Mary Teresa had been struggling with two conflicting realities: her persistent desire to become a Carmelite, and her weakened health following a burst blood vessel in her lungs. Although her health had been precarious for some time,

her piety often led her to pay but little attention to the suggestions of prudence, and . . . her Aunt was often obliged to use her influence, and to make her moderate

1. The details of the profession ceremony as outlined here, and in the paragraphs that follow, are those prescribed in the *Form of Ceremony* (1834), 21–36, and, with some slight revision of the sequence, in *Form of Ceremony* (London: C. Richards, 1840), 21–34.

her austerities and labors. To her timid conscience this exercise of authority looked like an indication from God that she was not called to the state of life in which she was then engaged.[2]

She began to think that her incapacity for the active works of the Sisters of Mercy was a sign that she should become exclusively a contemplative, in the Carmelite order.

Catherine knew Mary Teresa's commitment to the poor now exceeded her physical strength, and she tried to explain to her that in such circumstances one's goodness was not to be assessed by external activity or by comparison with others. Later she often repeated this principle to professed members of the community: "Although want of health or capacity may hinder a Sister from taking part in the active duties or zealous works of the Institute, she is yet doing a great deal, both for God and her Community, if she is kind and charitable to all."[3]

Instinctively realizing that her niece's health would not be equal to the Carmelite regimen of prayer, fasting, and shortened sleep, yet not wanting her own affection for Mary Teresa to unduly influence her decision, Catherine asked her to consult Daniel Murray when he next visited the house. She did so. He listened "with attention," and assured her that God "required of her only what her strength and constitution enabled her to do." He then suggested that she take a second year of novitiate until she had some "stronger indication" of the life to which she was called.[4]

When Catherine entered the chapel on the morning of January 24, all the tensions borne of their strong mutual affection and efforts to disentangle it must have been in her heart and Mary Teresa's. To let Mary Teresa be Mary Teresa, led as she was led, and to cherish her Aunt Catherine while being true to herself—all this could have been in their eyes if their gazes met across the crowded chapel.

Meanwhile the ceremony proceeded, in Latin. Archbishop Murray blessed the black veils and silver rings. After his sermon in English on the gospel of Matthew (16:24–28)—"If any want to become my followers, let them deny themselves and take up their cross and follow me"—he publicly questioned each novice about her desire to profess the vows of poverty, chastity, and obedience until her death, and asked her whether she considered herself "sufficiently instructed in what regards the vows" and "the obligations you contract." Then the solemn Mass of the Holy Spirit began. Just before she received Communion, Frances, then Angela, Clare,

2. Lim, in *CMcATM*, 175–76.   3. *PS*, 4.
4. Lim, in *CMcATM*, 176.

and de Pazzi pronounced their vows in English and signed their Acts of Profession. After the Mass concluded, the archbishop, setting aside his Mass vestments and putting on a cope, placed a black veil on each woman's head, which Catherine settled as Mary Ann Doyle removed the white one. A silver ring was now put on the third finger of her left hand, a plain band weighing less than a few grams and costing about a shilling. The choir then sang *Regnum Mundi:*

The empire of the world and all the grandeur of this earth I have despised for love of our Lord Jesus Christ whom I have seen, whom I have loved, in whom I have believed, and towards whom my heart inclines.

The newly professed responded antiphonally to the choir, then prostrated themselves on the floor, as the congregation stood and sang the *Te Deum.* At its conclusion, the archbishop blessed the four women, and they then rose to embrace Catherine and the rest of the community. The ceremony ended as the community sang Psalm 132 (133), *Ecce Quam Bonum:* "How very good and pleasant it is when kindred live together in unity. . . . It is like the dew of Hermon, which falls on the mountains of Zion. For there the Lord ordained his blessing, life forevermore."

The solemnity of the profession ceremony now gave way to hugs, kisses, best wishes—and refreshments with friends and families. Apparently no one remarked on the difference between this public ceremony and the closed one the year before.

On Friday morning life at Baggot Street returned to normal. Now there were six professed Sisters of Mercy, each different in her intellectual and social talents and temperament. Mary de Pazzi Delany, thirty-two, was more retiring than the rest and subject to occasional epileptic seizures, especially under stress. Clare Moore described her as having "a horror of vanity" and committed to "unvarying exactitude in the observance of every rule and pious custom."[5] Clare Augustine Moore claimed that Catherine eventually found de Pazzi "too austere a Mistress of Novices and named her Mother Assistant," a position in which she could be more directly subject to moderation.[6] Years later her own sister, Juliana (Ellen) Delany, called her "the prop of the house."[7]

Angela Dunne, now forty-six and the oldest in the community after Catherine, would in a few years become the superior of the distant and

5. "Bermondsey Annals (1872)," vol. 2, [205–6] (AIMGB).
6. CAM, in *CMcATM,* 213.
7. "Bermondsey Annals (1872)," vol. 2, [210] (AIMGB).

very impoverished community in Charleville, County Cork, initially the "sick branch" among the early foundations, where she lived until she was seventy-five.[8] In a house with too few members she would share in the constant poverty of the Charleville people, often living like them on a diet of milk and potatoes. She would endure with them the devastation of the Great Famine, and drawing on her experience in the 1832 cholera epidemic, she would nurse in the local fever hospital when the famine diseases hit.

Clare Moore was the youngest professed sister, not quite twenty, and a good Latin scholar. In the beginning, as she admits, "I scarcely knew how to cut bread and butter."[9] She was reserved and detached at first: "I never asked questions nor concerned myself about what did not concern me; consequently I was ignorant of what was passing around me except when told of something—or when matters were so apparent that I should be not only nearsighted but blind all out not to see them."[10] Eventually, however, she became one of Catherine's closest confidantes. She was a competent, practical help when Catherine turned to the task of preparing the Mercy Rule, and, until she went to Cork (1837) and then Bermondsey (1839), her frequent travel companion. After Catherine's death, Clare told her sister, Clare Augustine: "Tho' you know much about her you did not know her as I knew her."[11] During the Crimean War (1854–1856), Clare with other sisters from Bermondsey nursed in Turkey under Florence Nightingale, becoming her steady help and lifelong friend. In April 1856, Nightingale wrote to her:

Your going home is the greatest blow I have had yet. . . . You were far above me in fitness for the General Superintendency, both in worldly talent of administration & far more in the spiritual qualifications God values in a superior. . . . I have always felt what I have just expressed.[12]

As Clare lay dying, Nightingale wrote: "This we know: She could scarcely be more with God than she was habitually here. . . . It is we who are left motherless when she goes."[13]

Frances Warde was, ever since she joined the community, Catherine's

---

8. Letter 150, December 26, 1839, in *CCMcA*, 231.
9. CML, in *CMcATM*, 97.   10. Ibid., 85.
11. Ibid., 93.
12. Florence Nightingale to Mary Clare Moore, April 29, 1856 (AIMGB). For the story of their work together, correspondence, and friendship, see Mary C. Sullivan, ed., *The Friendship of Florence Nightingale and Mary Clare Moore* (Philadelphia: University of Pennsylvania Press, 1999), where the full text of this letter is given, 72–73. This letter and the following one are quoted through the courtesy of the Henry Bonham Carter Will Trust.
13. Florence Nightingale to "Dear Sister," December 12, 1874 (AIMGB), and Sullivan, ed., *Friendship*, 176.

reliable and capable helper. She was outgoing, not afraid to answer the door or handle financial matters. In fact, the frequency with which Catherine turned to her apparently created some small degree of resentment at Baggot Street.[14] After Frances went to Carlow in 1837, Catherine's letters to her are among the most self-revealing she wrote. She often unburdened herself in detail about problems and annoyances that arose, relying on Frances's understanding and good sense. On one occasion, in a long postscript she labeled "Not fit to appear," that is, not to be shared, Catherine described herself frankly: "Perplexed and weary—out of conceit with everything—I sit down to talk to my own dear old companion and affectionate child."[15] Frances would one day lead a Mercy foundation to Pittsburgh, and then to other cities in the United States.

The early history of Baggot Street was not unlike that of any religious community or indeed of most human organizations. While enormously contributing to the growth of its own members and the good of society, in countless often unacknowledged ways, the community had its little passing squabbles about who was "sweeping the floors" and who was not. Catherine McAuley was not piously exempt from experiencing the occasional small-mindedness of others.

Catherine called these women her "first-born," the ones on whom she relied in the beginning and who with her co-founded the Sisters of Mercy.[16] Not by any stretch all alike or equally endowed with aptitudes that might have seemed needed, each nonetheless gave herself, as she was and would become, to the life and work at hand. With them Catherine did not proceed according to a detailed scheme, prefabricated in the abstract, even though she realized her special responsibility in their formation as a community who would love one another and be wholeheartedly devoted to the works of mercy. She was a realist, and often said: "We all have our imperfections and shall have them till our death. God has never bestowed all his blessings on one person. He did not give to St. Peter what He gave to St. Paul, nor to either what He gave to St. John."[17] Her own novitiate training notwithstanding, she was a democratic, willing learner, who did not assume that she alone would or could understand everything beforehand, or that she even needed to. Eight years later she told Frances Warde: "Our experience in religious life has been so short that a good faithful Sister to whom God has imparted grace may be said to know as much of spiritual

14. CML, in *CMcATM*, 98.
16. Letter 180, July 28, 1840, in *CCMcA*, 283.
15. Letter 89 [late May 1838], in *CCMcA*, 139.
17. *PS*, 3.

life as we do."[18] Her leadership in shaping the first Mercy community was not authoritarian. The shaping was a communal endeavor, accumulating its strength day by day. She led the way more by example than by precept.

At first Catherine could turn to Michael Blake when she was seriously perplexed. But not for long. In 1831 he became parish priest of St. Andrew's, still on Townsend Street. Within a year he had hired an architect and begun building a new St. Andrew's church on nearby Westland Row, laying its first stone on April 30, 1832, during the early months of the cholera epidemic. But on January 13, 1833, he was named bishop of Dromore, and was consecrated on March 17.[19] Now in Newry, County Down, almost eighty miles away from Baggot Street, he was accessible by mail, but only rarely in person. He was succeeded at St. Andrew's by Walter Meyler, a vicar general of the diocese, who soon demonstrated that, whatever other qualities he had that recommended him to Daniel Murray, he had little of Blake's regard for Catherine McAuley and the Sisters of Mercy.

Catherine had no time to dwell on this personal loss, for between April and September five more women entered the community: Sarah Warde (Frances's sister), Amelia White, Elizabeth Magenis, Bridget Gaffney (Myles's sister), and Catherine Jarmy, the widow of a military officer. Sarah and Amelia became two of the future mainstays of the community, Catherine Jarmy was always a steady help, and Bridget died young, but Elizabeth was a far different story. For all her proposed and attractive financial assistance (£1471), she turned out to be just as Michael Blake had subtly, perhaps too subtly, predicted when asked for his recommendation:

As I have no personal acquaintance with the lady herself, and have not seen her but once for a moment, my information has been necessarily borrowed from others. But I have consulted several dispassionate persons, all have agreed in acknowledging the strict morality and religious habits of that lady. All are persuaded that she has means for doing extensive good, all finally regret that one little drawback from the excellence of her other qualities is found in a certain peculiar or a singular mode of thinking & judging by which [she] is distinguished.[20]

In time, as we shall later see, Elizabeth Magenis's "peculiar" attitudes would become unmistakably manifest. Meanwhile, Mary de Chantal (Mary) McCann, a widow, was received in July, and Sarah Warde and Amelia White, taking the names Mary Josephine and Mary Teresa, became novices in De-

18. Letter 255 [April 10, 1841], in CCMcA, 384.
19. Burke Savage, McAuley,166; Donnelly, History of Dublin Parishes, part 7, 151–52.
20. Letter 18 [June 5, 1833], in CCMcA, 54.

cember, on the heels of yet another human sorrow in Catherine McAuley's life—one of the greatest.

Mary Teresa Macauley's health did not improve. It actually worsened after a second lung hemorrhage. Her obvious and rapid consumption finally settled the question of her ever becoming a Carmelite. As her physical condition declined more and more, her desire to profess religious vows as a Sister of Mercy grew stronger. At last Catherine and Redmond O'Hanlon, the archbishop's deputy, following the custom in such circumstances, allowed to her to profess her vows on her deathbed. She did so on November 3, 1833.

In the days that followed, Mary Teresa grew weaker. She asked pardon individually of each sister, if she had ever hurt her or misled her, and each member of the community was "compelled to give forgiveness of offences that never existed."[21] She asked her grief-stricken Uncle James to return to the Catholic faith in which he was baptized. On the morning of November 11, noticing the hot flannels in which she was wrapped, she asked the physician who attended her, and "who had known her from infancy," how many hours he thought she would live. He tried to be evasive. Finally he told her she probably "would not survive the night that was approaching."[22] Mary Teresa died on the morning of November 12, 1833.

At twenty-two, Mary Teresa Macauley was much more than simply her aunt's elder niece, the oldest child of her deceased sister, Mary. She was, in Catherine's view, a beautiful, innocent young woman whom she ever after called "my Mary Teresa" or "our darling Mary Teresa" or "my dear Mary Teresa."[23] Catherine's earliest surviving poem was written to her niece for her seventh or eighth Christmas; it concludes: "But hark, 'tis twelve, I think I hear the clocks / Good night, my love, accept your Christmas Box."[24] In 1840 when Christina Joyce entered the community, Catherine saw her as "a second Mary Teresa . . . in look and manner—all ardor."[25] Later that year, in a poem to Frances Warde's young niece Fanny, a child of about six whose father had just died, Catherine finally parted with an object she had carefully kept for at least seven years. She told Frances Warde: "I promised my little Fanny a brooch to fasten her collar & six kisses on the back. It was my dear Mary Teresa's."[26] In the accompanying verses to the child she wrote:

21. Lim, in *CMcATM*, 176.   22. Ibid., 177.

23. Letter 68, December 23, 1837; letter 102, November 17, 1838; and letter 212, November 24, 1840—in *CCMcA*, 116, 168, and 324.

24. Letter 1 [Christmas 1818–1821], in *CCMcA*, 35.

25. Letter 176, June 30, 1840, in *CCMcA*, 274.

26. Letter 212, November 24–26, 1840, in *CCMcA*, 324.

Though this is very dear to me
For reasons strong and many
I give it with fond love to thee
My doat'y—"little Fanny."[27]

The treasured brooch was gone, but not the memory of her beloved niece.

Throughout 1833 Catherine had evidently been drafting a Rule and Constitutions for the Sisters of Mercy, with Myles Gaffney's help. She intended to use, in revised form, as Daniel Murray had suggested, those parts of the already approved Presentation Rule which were applicable and to add her own chapters on the distinctive works of the Sisters of Mercy. Her time for serious, thoughtful composition was limited, but she kept at it. Finally in late November or early December she had early versions of two new chapters ready—"Of the Visitation of the Sick" and "Of the Admission of Distressed Women."

Catherine had long held a naïve view—or perhaps it was, to her, a logical view—of how ecclesiastical approval of a new religious congregation and its Rule could be secured. As early as 1830, even before the decision to found a religious congregation was made, she apparently thought that if she, or a priest on her behalf, wrote directly to the head of the Congregation for the Propagation of the Faith in Rome (the Vatican department overseeing church affairs in Ireland), asking for a blessing on the House of Mercy and the community working there—presumably to use as a document to counter the clerical opposition they were then experiencing—she would get a direct reply. Of course her early 1830 petition was immediately sent back to Archbishop Murray, and after his qualified comment on it was posted to Rome, a positive reply to her petition and to his comment was sent back to him and, from him, given to Catherine. The whole process, including whatever hand or post delivery was involved, took six months. In December 1833, anxious again for some ecclesiastical approbation of the Sisters of Mercy—in addition to Dr. Murray's now-full endorsement—because requests for convents in other dioceses were beginning to come in, she again tried the direct route, with a similar outcome.

John Rice, an Irish Augustinian priest stationed in Rome, had visited Baggot Street earlier and, hearing Catherine's desire for some sign of approval from Vatican officials, had offered to do what he could to assist. Back in Rome, and not quite clear about the help Catherine wished, he

27. Letter 213 [November 24-26, 1840], in *CCMcA*, 324. "Doat'y" means darling, fond, silly, lovable.

wrote for clarification to his brother Edmund, the founder of the Irish Christian Brothers. On December 7 Edmund Rice visited Baggot Street to find out exactly what Catherine sought. What followed were two letters to John Rice, both on the same large piece of paper: one from Catherine explaining her hopes, and one from Edmund to his brother, vouching for Catherine McAuley and the Sisters of Mercy.

In her letter, written on December 8, Catherine explained, apparently to clear up a misconception: "We do not seek to be engrafted with the good Sisters of Charity, who have only one noviciate [sic], and one general superior—each branch of our Institute will have its own noviciate and be subject to the ordinary [bishop] of the Diocese."[28] She recounted the history of the congregation to date, noted the need for additional Houses of Mercy elsewhere in Ireland, indicated that the Sisters of Mercy had professed their vows "according to the rule and constitutions of the Presentation order—already approved by the Holy See," and then said:

What we humbly beg is to have our two Chapters—one on the visitation of the sick—the other, protection of poor women—added thereto, and that we may be regarded on religious equality with our Sisters of the Presentation order .... and *were* we fully adopted by the Holy See many Houses would soon be established. We have been already invited—and much encouraged—but our first and dearest wish is to obtain the entire concurrence of His Holiness.[29]

After her signature Catherine transcribed the full text of her own Act of Profession, an early version of the new chapter "Of the Visitation of the Sick" and the first three paragraphs of the proposed chapter "Of the Admission of Distressed Women."[30]

Two days later, on the previously blank page three of the large folded sheet, Edmund Rice wrote his own letter to his brother. He gave biographical information about Catherine "as well as I know it." Some of this was inaccurate, including his claim that when she "was grown up she was converted, and practiced her religion a good many years without the knowledge of her Patron." Rice supported what he called her "craving" for his brother's "exertions in [her Institute's] behalf, which indeed it deserves, for already it has cost her a sea of trouble to bring it to what it is at present." He then told his brother:

28. Letter 19, December 8, 1833, in *CCMcA*, 55.

29. Ibid., 56.

30. Catherine McAuley to John Rice, December 8, 1833 (APF, Rome: SC America Settentrionale, vol. 3, f. 197). This letter, once misfiled among papers related to Canada, may now be refiled among those related to Ireland. Letter 19, December 8, 1833, in *CCMcA*, 54–56.

The Monastery, if it can be so called before it gets the sanction of the Holy See, has cost her several thousands of pounds & when I told her Saturday last that you may be able to do something for her at Rome, her heart jumped for joy at the prospect of getting any thing from the H[oly] S[ee]. Now it seems to me that this document of hers is rather a loose thing and should I be right in my conjecture perhaps you may be able to have the matter referred back to Doctor Murray which in my mind would be the best way of doing it; however you must be the best judge, but at all events I hope you will do what you can for the poor Creatures who are sighing for it.[31]

Why Edmund Rice did not tell Catherine immediately and straightforwardly that she should work through Archbishop Murray is not known. He forwarded the letters to his brother John who sent them on to Propaganda Fide together with a formal petition in Italian for papal confirmation of the two chapters of the Rule. John Rice himself apparently drafted the petition, using information in Catherine's letter to him. In May 1834 Propaganda contacted Daniel Murray for his opinion, and Catherine did not hear the final outcome until May 1835, seventeen months after she had met with Edmund Rice.

As she commented years later, about an entirely unrelated and comparatively minor matter: "These good Bishops take their own full time, to consider any little affair, and those that are, like myself, rather impatient for an answer, may just as well make up the mind to wait for one."[32] Seeking papal approbation of a new religious congregation was no "little affair," as she must have realized, but in 1833 her whole concern was the urgency of establishing schools for poor girls and Houses of Mercy for poor women wherever in Ireland they were most needed and had been requested. For this she *was*, given her zeal, impatient. And for this she believed she needed some indication of papal sanction, if only to assure the respective bishops of the bona fide status of the future foundations. She would learn later, as she waited for official word on confirmation of the Mercy Rule, that "these matters seldom go on so rapidly at the Holy See."[33]

At the end of 1833 Catherine could have privately reviewed the last twelve years of her life. She knew well the number of human losses she had endured. Her sister and brother-in-law, Mary and William Macauley, were gone, as were the Callaghans and her close priest friends, Joseph Nu-

31. Letter 20, December 10, 1833, in *CCMcA*, 57–58.

32. Letter 295 [August 16, 1841], in *CCMcA*, 430.

33. Letter 186, August 5, 1840, in *CCMcA*, 291. Today, religious congregations of "pontifical right," such as the Sisters of Mercy, relate directly to the Vatican's Congregation for Institutes of Consecrated Life and Societies of Apostolic Life, and correspondence between the Vatican and the major superiors moves much more quickly.

gent and Edward Armstrong. She saw her brother, James, and his family only occasionally. Absent too, but in different ways, were Catherine Byrn and Michael Blake. Since June 1831 four of the young community at Baggot Street had died: Caroline Murphy, Anne O'Grady, Elizabeth Harley, and now her own Mary Teresa Macauley. Moreover, although her godchild Teresa Byrn, now twelve, and Ellen Corrigan, the orphan for whom she had long cared, were still living at Baggot Street, her niece Catherine Macauley, now fourteen, had left.

As Mary Teresa was dying, her sister, Catherine, expressed a desire to enter the Sisters of Mercy. This alarmed her Uncle James, who felt his niece was overly affected by the happiness with which her sister seemed to die, and by the surrounding affection of the community. He insisted that she leave Baggot Street and live with his family for a while, hoping that

estrangement from the scenes and companions to which she had been until then accustomed, and the attractions of the gay world with which she would be made acquainted, would produce a change in her opinions, and induce her to abandon the determination which, in his opinion, was adopted in a moment of unreflecting enthusiasm.[34]

Young Catherine consented to the experiment as did her aunt, who perhaps felt, as Degnan argues, that living with James and his wife, Frances, would "give her a change of atmosphere in order to learn whether she had a true vocation or whether she had been unduly impressed by the example and loss of her sister."[35] After all, she had lived at Baggot Street, in her aunt's company, at least since she was ten, and on and off before that. Although the elder Catherine knew well her niece's spirit of charity and her devotion to works of mercy among the poor and suffering, she did not wish to presume that young Catherine was called to religious life. Yet her niece was radiantly cheerful and, like her aunt, a great mimic. Her leaving Baggot Street in November or December 1833 was hard.

About this time too, Catherine's nephews James and Robert, then about eighteen and fifteen, were preparing to leave Carlow College at the end of that school year or the next, and hoping to make their own way in the world. They would study law, though where or with whom is not known. James would live for a while with his Uncle James, then briefly in Liverpool, and on his return settle on the family property in Cartrongarrow, County Longford, where he could live off his rents. Robert would

34. Lim, in *CMcATM*, 177.
35. Degnan, *Mercy,* 169.

eventually become a master in the boys' boarding school founded outside of Dublin in 1835 by the Reverend Daniel W. Cahill, a famous preacher. Later he would work for several years as a reporter for the Dublin *Morning Register.*[36]

Willie, age twelve in late 1833, would flounder and be a constant worry to his aunt. He would remain at Carlow College until 1836. He apparently then wanted to join the army: "But where was the money to buy an ensign's commission; it would cost £400 in a foot regiment, in a horse [regiment] £500. . . . I had no hopes of this so said nothing about it." Eventually he would be employed in a doctor's dispensary in Clara, a town northwest of Tullamore—under a Doctor Walsh, a man he "could not respect" because of his treatment of his aged, crippled mother, and his sister, "whom he made a regular drudge." Willie then lived for a while with his brother James in Cartrongarrow. Returning to Dublin, he lived, he says, with the Marmions (the family whose daughters became Sisters of Mercy?) at No. 7 Fleet Street, "spending most of the day at Baggot Street." Later he was bound to a wholesale merchant on Ushers Quay—whom again he "could not respect": "if a blot was in a book, [the merchant] would curse and swear, after every oath throw up his hands and eyes towards Heaven, exclaiming, 'The Lord pardon my soul.'" That, to Willie, "sounded too much like a hypocrite."[37]

Sorting out the details of Willie's early life as well as his brothers' is almost wholly dependent on his scattered recollections penned decades later, recollections that are not always clear chronologically. But that mounting tension developed between him and his aunt during the mid-1830s is evident, both in his own recorded memories and in the biographical manuscripts about Catherine later written by her associates. Recalling one of his frequent visits to Baggot Street after he left Carlow, Willie claims that when he was leaving:

Aunt would paper my hair which curled on the ends. No doubt my dear Aunt's motive was that I should go straight back, and to bed, but her act impeded her desire to keep me from evil, for I was ashamed to have my hair in papers like a girl; I tied a handkerchief round my head and rolled it under my beaver belltopper. Instead of keeping in the respectable thoroughfares, where I might meet some of those who

---

36. William McAuley, "Commentary on Passages in Carroll's *Life* of Catherine McAuley, Chapter 32, page 333," (MCA).

37. Typescript copy, William McAuley to "Dear Revd. Mother" [Mary Augustine Mungovan], Bendigo, Australia, November 24, 1903 (MCA). Here, Willie says he was "taken from college," apparently by Catherine McAuley on the recommendation of Andrew Fitzgerald.

knew me, I traversed byelanes, and low streets, and thus evil befell me. I sinned, and when asked by my master, I acknowledged my sin, which was a breach of my indentures he took advantage of. So I was once more adrift. . . . Through my own fault my sorrows were intensified.[38]

For an Irish mother to roll an adolescent boy's long hair on paper curlers at night was not atypical in the early nineteenth century, or even in the early twentieth century. Yet Willie, despite all his need for affection, was not a lad who could suffer this particular and unwanted maternal solicitude. Catherine had acquired many motherly talents over the years, but she had raised mostly girls, not boys. Though Willie had his own restlessness and insecurities to correct, she could reasonably have regarded herself as a failure in his upbringing, a regret she seems to have carried just below the surface for the rest of her life.

Perhaps it was in late 1833, if not before, that Catherine's tendency to blame herself began to develop more strongly. Those who study her life can know of this propensity only through two or three rare comments in manuscripts later written by Clare Moore who, one can presume, knew Catherine well. In 1844, Clare said of Catherine: "If ever any affliction came to us she attributed the cause to herself. I used to grieve to hear her condemning and blaming herself so much."[39] Later, when Clare wrote the biography of Catherine that is inserted in the Bermondsey Annals, she said of Mary Teresa Macauley's death:

This was a grievous affliction to our dear Reverend Mother, but she submitted humbly, and always ascribed these trials which she felt so sensibly, and which were of frequent recurrence . . . to her own want of fidelity to God's holy inspirations.[40]

Earlier in the Bermondsey biography, Clare speaks of one of Catherine's childhood memories:

She always remembered with bitter regret having once told their Mother of some fault of pride committed by her sister, who was punished for it by being shut up in a dark room, where flames were represented, in order to give her an idea of the horror of eternal torments, for Mrs. McAuley had very strict and peculiar ideas on the education of her children.[41]

One hopes the details of Elinor McGauley's punishments as given in this account are not accurately recorded.

Catherine had long ago suffered the deaths of her parents, but except for others' allusions to her childhood images of her father's faith, his

38. Ibid.
40. BA, in *CMcATM*, 113.

39. CML, in *CMcATM*, 93.
41. Ibid., 99.

charities to the poor, and his fondness for his young daughter (she could not have been even five when he died), her sense of "family" was apparently never invested predominantly in him, nor in her mother. Neither is ever mentioned in her extant correspondence, which dates from about her fortieth year, and the biographical manuscripts written by her contemporaries are silent about her personal relationship with her mother.

Rather, over the years her emotional center, with its deep capacities for affection, loyalty, sorrow, and regret, was gradually shifted from her parents to her foster parents, and then to her foster children, especially her nieces and nephews, and finally to the women gathered around her on Baggot Street and the priests who understood and supported her. With respect to the children, it would be several more years before she would find herself saying: "My earthly joys are cut down," and then: "I have nothing now to draw me for one hour from my religious Sisters where all my joy on earth is centered."[42]

Catherine's loneliness at the end of 1833, though unrecorded, must have been acute. Francis Blyth's *Paraphrase on the Seven Penitential Psalms* was a book she is known to have read often.[43] It contained her favorite psalms, including ones she and the community regularly prayed. Here, in Psalm 129 (130), she may have found a voice for her solitary feelings:

> Out of the depths I cry to you, O Lord.
> Lord, hear my voice!
> Let your ears be attentive
> to the voice of my supplications.
>
> If you, O Lord, should mark iniquities,
> Lord, who could stand?
> But there is forgiveness with you,
> so that you may be revered.
>
> I wait for the Lord, my soul waits,
> and in his word I hope;
> my soul waits for the Lord
> more than those who watch for the morning,
> more than those who watch for the morning.[44]

42. Letter 206, November 9, 1840, in *CCMcA*, 317; letter 265, May 1, 1841, in *CCMcA*, 396.

43. *PS*, 34. A seventh edition of Blyth's *Devout Paraphrase on the Seven Penitential Psalms; or, A Practical Guide to Repentance* was published in Dublin by the Catholic Book Society in 1835.

44. The long Mercy tradition of praying in Latin the "De profundis"—Psalm 129 in the Vulgate numbering Catherine would have known—undoubtedly evolved from her devotion to the penitential psalms, of which this is one.

CHAPTER 9

Daily Life at Baggot Street *1834*

By June 1834 the "big" house on Baggot Street no longer seemed big. Nineteen women lived in the religious community, to say nothing of the women, girls, and orphans sheltered in the House of Mercy. The eight "ladies cells" in the architect's drawings were no longer adequate, so doubling up and dormitory space were needed. Years later, when the house was even more crowded and Catherine was asked where the next sister to arrive was to sleep, she would teasingly respond: "In my lap."[1]

On February 11, Mary Magdalen Flynn and Mary Gertrude Jones professed their religious vows, and Bridget Gaffney and Catherine Jarmy received the habit, taking the names Mary Mechtildis and Mary Genevieve. By June, five more women had entered the community, including Catherine's niece, fifteen-year-old Catherine Macauley. Having given her uncle a two-month trial of "the fascinations of the society to which he took care to introduce her," young Catherine made clear to him that his persuasions were not going to be successful, so he relented. She returned to Baggot Street, entering the community on January 28, 1834.[2] Though young, she knew her own mind and heart.

In early April, the Easter bazaar occurred as usual, this time in the Rotunda at the north end of Sackville (now O'Connell) Street.[3] But with a dar-

---

1. Letter 205, November 8, 1840, in *CCMcA*, 316.
2. Lim, in *CMcATM*, 177, and "Baggot Street Register" (MCA).
3. The "round room," often used for concerts, plays, charitable bazaars, and lotteries, was attached to the Lying-In Hospital Dr. Benjamin Mosse built. It was sometimes called the "Rotundo," but more frequently the "Rotunda."

ing new twist. As Clare Moore later remarked, Catherine's compassion for the poor "made her sometimes adopt plans for their relief which to some appeared beyond the limits of prudence."[4] With polite boldness Catherine wrote a letter directly to Victoria, Duchess of Kent and Strathearn (1786–1861) in England, requesting that she and her daughter, the Princess Victoria, now fifteen, contribute some handmade items for the bazaar in aid of the House of Mercy. Catherine may have included a sentence which later appeared in the *Morning Register* advertisement: "Eight hundred and fourteen most distressed women have been lodged and supported in the House of Mercy since the year 1828—all of whom were deserving of protection, and many quite respectable." To the astonishment of Catherine's associates, a letter from Kensington Palace, dated March 12, 1834, and addressed to the "Sisters of Mercy, Baggot Street," brought this response:

Sir John Conroy is commanded by the Duchess of Kent to acquaint the Sisters of Charity [sic] that her Royal Highness will be most happy to comply with their request to patronize the Bazaar, and to present to it what her Royal Highness fears must be some very trifling work of Hers and the Princess Victoria's.[5]

As was increasingly her practice, whether "beyond the limits of prudence" or not, Catherine had asked the most prominent of the very wealthy to join her in helping the destitute, and her plea had not gone unheard. All Dublin, at least among the ranks of the nobility, was agog. The ads for the bazaar featured "the contributions of bijouterie," the jewelry and decorated trinkets, that had been donated by the "exalted patronage" of the duchess and the princess. On April 4, the final day of the bazaar, *Freeman's Journal* announced that "the doors will be thrown open at an early hour" to accommodate the crowds "attracted by the articles" given by their royal highnesses which "will be brought forward by the Duchess of Leinster," the ranking noblewoman in Dublin.[6] The long list of fashionable attendees increased even more.

Six days after the bazaar, Catherine—seizing the public opportunity to explain gospel charity—inserted the following note of gratitude in *Freeman's Journal:*

As the Ladies Patronesses, particularly those who presided at Tables, are anxious to know the result of their very benevolent exertions, the Sisters of Mercy with joy

4. BA, in *CMcATM*, 112.

5. *Morning Register,* March 31–April 2, 1834. In the press, the Sisters of Mercy were occasionally confused with the Sisters of Charity. The original letter from Sir John Conroy does not appear to be extant.

6. *Freeman's Journal,* April 4, 1834.

and gratitude inform them that the sum of Three Hundred and Four pounds has been received.

If our all-bountiful Redeemer, who came on earth to teach the Works of Mercy by precept and example, has promised that a Cup of Water given in His name shall receive a reward, what may we not hope he will grant to those, who, by the effect of their example, and the influence of their rank in society, have provided a happy home for His afflicted creatures, many of whom have once enjoyed all the comforts of respectable independence.[7]

Three years later, on June 20, 1837, King William IV died, and the Princess Victoria was proclaimed queen of the United Kingdom. That event evidently marked the end of her bijouterie for the annual Mercy bazaar and her royal patronage of "the benevolent exertions of the Sisters of Mercy to relieve the distress that exists . . . in Dublin."[8]

Meanwhile, by mid-May 1834, thirteen postulants and novices at Baggot Street needed to learn the ways of religious life, and the seven professed sisters, in addition to Catherine, still needed help to understand what being "Sisters of Mercy" was all about.[9] As early as 1829, Catherine had worked out a flexible horarium, a daily schedule of prayer, work, instruction, recreation, and meals. The times for communal prayer and the works of mercy were the priorities; the noon meal was often shifted to accommodate the schedule of those teaching in the schoolrooms, walking to visit the sick, and training or serving meals to those in the House of Mercy. It was a juggling act, with many variations over the years.[10]

They arose at 5:30, assembled for morning prayer at 6:00, followed by meditation until 7:00. Mass was at 7:30, and breakfast at 8:00 or 8:15. "Immediately after in the Refectory, Revd. Mother read the Saint for the day." The community re-assembled "near 4:00" for prayer, followed by dinner.[11] After Catherine returned from George's Hill, "supper was at 8, no silence; that only lasted a few weeks. Supper went to 7 and silence."[12] In the early years, Daniel Murray approved all these arrangements, except one: "He desired that there should be recreation [i.e., leisure and conversation] after dinner," which Catherine had omitted, "intending, as she said, that we should labour all day like the poor, and have our rest and recreation after our work was finished," that is, only in the evening after supper (tea).[13]

7. *Freeman's Journal*, April 10, 1834.   8. *Freeman's Journal*, March 17–30, 1837.
9. "Baggot Street Register" (MCA).   10. CML, in *CMcATM*, 90, 97.
11. Ibid., 90. Presumably Catherine read to the community daily portions of Alban Butler's *Lives of the Saints*, a collection of saints' lives laid out according to their feast days in the liturgical calendar. Butler's work was first published in London in 1756–1759.
12. CML, in *CMcATM*, 97.   13. BA, in *CMcATM*, 108.

Silence was observed at meals, except on special feast days, and from nine o'clock at night until after breakfast; in fact, "as much as circumstances admit except at the time for recreation."[14] But silence was not an end in itself. Rather, it was intended to support mindfulness of the true nature of the work they were about. It was not to be stiff or rigid or unaccommodating, and Catherine quickly addressed well-intended, but thoughtless attempts to extend its domain.[15]

Moreover, she often took a flexible attitude toward the daily schedule, adjusting it to crises like the cholera epidemic, extensive illness in the house, and the needs of particular localities. As new convents were founded, new formulations of the horarium were designed, all with the same basic elements, including the *Little Office of the Blessed Virgin Mary* prayed together in English three times a day. As she later told Dr. Thomas Walsh, vicar apostolic of the Midlands (England), the daily schedule was "subject to any alterations that place or circumstances might require" and those "engaged in the visitation are exempt from any choir duty [community prayer] from 10 till 4."[16] Remarking on the sameness of each day, she assured him: "You might suppose the daily and uninterrupted repetition of the duties were tiresome. It is not so. Religious life affords more lively solid lasting happiness than all the variety this world could give."[17]

In spring 1834, correspondence between Rome and Dublin took place about which Catherine may have been unaware. After receiving, through John Rice, her petition for recognition of the Sisters of Mercy as a religious congregation approved by the Holy See, the Congregation for the Propagation of the Faith wrote in May to Daniel Murray. It asked him plainly: "Since Your Grace knows all about this affair . . . what [is] your opinion": did he "think that everything connected with this business is in such a state that a confirmation" of the Sisters of Mercy could be asked of Pope Gregory XVI?[18] On June 21, Murray replied to Cardinal Carlo Pedicini:

They devote themselves earnestly and with great fruit for souls to the pious works which are set down in the petition. And I consider that they fully deserve to receive from His Holiness all these signs of benevolence which may seem suitable for the firm establishing of the good work thus begun.[19]

Murray's response had none of the half-hearted, noncommittal attitude of his letter to Rome on April 17, 1830. Then he had "considered it wise to pro-

---

14. Rule 7.1, in *CMcATM*, 303.   15. CAM, in *CMcATM*, 213.

16. Letters 202 and 203, November 6, 1840, in *CCMcA*, 312, 313.

17. Letter 204 [undated], in *CCMcA*, 314.   18. Letter 22, May 6, 1834, in *CCMcA*, 60.

19. Letter 23, June 21, 1834, in *CCMcA*, 62.

ceed carefully and slowly," and had claimed, correctly, that "these women, in spite of the good works to which they are dedicated, are not organized according to the norms of Religious Life, and I do not presume to ask favours for them which are seen to apply to a Religious Congregation."[20] Much had changed in four years, and Murray was now fully prepared to endorse Catherine's undertaking. However, he would have to wait a full year for the pope's response. Catherine probably never knew the exact character of Dr. Murray's first letter to Rome, and given her other burdens and struggles in 1830 it was just as well.

By the end of 1834 there were twenty-four women in the religious community, including five who entered with the intention of being lay sisters: Susan Walplate, Maria Breen, Mary Carton, Marianne Brennan, and Catherine's own former orphan child from Coolock, Ellen Corrigan. In the history of women's religious orders and congregations, few aspects of religious life evolved so painfully, were so often poorly managed, or provoked so much subsequent resentment as the phenomenon of lay sisters. The attitude toward and treatment of lay sisters varied in different religious congregations, so generalizations can rarely be made. Even within a particular religious congregation, succeeding superiors often behaved very differently toward the lay sisters in their communities. Some drew the distinctions between lay sisters and "choir sisters" too sharply, while others differentiated them in unnecessary ways, with the result that lay sisters, rather than feeling appreciated for what they generously contributed, began over time to feel like, and were in fact treated as, second-class members of these communities. This was not universally the case, but where such situations prevailed, lasting bitterness ensued, and revisionist historical analysis then traced blame for it all the way back to the founders of the congregations in question. The history of the Sisters of Mercy, especially in some countries or in parts of those countries, was not exempt from this pain.

Catherine's own attitude toward lay sisters was straightforward and inclusive. While she lived, the Baggot Street community—at least in view of the available evidence—apparently suffered none of this unwarranted discrimination. Among the women who presented themselves to her, as strongly wishing to be Sisters of Mercy, were some who were illiterate or barely literate, or else lacked sufficient education and refinement of speech. They were not able to read prayers for the sick and dying they

---

20. Letter 9, April 17, 1830, in CCMcA, 44–45.

might visit, or teach poor girls in the schoolrooms, or easily read the *Little Office* with the community, or write what needed to be written.

But these women were very talented in other helpful ways: they could relate well to the residents of the House of Mercy, they could handle household matters with great skill, they could teach sewing and manage large laundry operations, they could cook, often far better than others, and they were reliable messengers. They were, moreover, good women, with generous hearts, which was, for Catherine, the fundamental quality needed. So she accepted them into the community and exempted them from some of the responsibilities of the other sisters, notably from some of their "choir" duties, that is, certain communal prayers. At Baggot Street in her day, the ability to bring a financial dowry of any amount, or the inability to do so, was never a deciding factor. As Clare Moore says, Catherine "never refused any Postulant for want of temporal means when it was at all possible to provide what was essential."[21] Catherine herself once wrote: "We will never frighten a candidate away for not having a bag of money."[22]

Her most explicit statement on lay sisters is the three-paragraph chapter she eventually inserted in the copy of the Mercy Rule and Constitutions she sent to Rome for approval, though no chapter on this topic appears in her first draft of the Rule or in the Presentation Rule. The chapter, which Mary Austin Carroll says was "entirely" Catherine's composition,[23] reads:

Lay Sisters admitted to this religious Institute shall, besides the chief requisites, "vocation, good constitution, and plain education," have manners and appearance suited to religious who must be seen in public, for although they shall be generally employed in domestic work, yet as circumstances may occur which would render their assistance in other situations necessary, they ought to be persons who could occasionally accompany the Choir Sisters without any remarkable exterior difference.

The Lay Sisters shall be distinguished by a white apron which shall receive the benediction of the Bishop together with the Habit, Veil, etc., and be always deemed an essential part of their religious dress, their Habit without train. They shall unite with the Choir Sisters in spiritual exercises whenever their respective occupations do not interfere. They shall breakfast, dine and sup together like the Choir Sisters in the Refectory, after or before the Choir Sisters, as place and circumstances demand.

The state of Lay Sisters is very similar to that which our humble Redeemer made choice of in this world for He was constantly engaged serving others, but never requiring any care or attendance for Himself. It will greatly animate them in all their labors to reflect that they are working for a Heavenly Master who will

21. BA, in *CMcATM*, 114.   22. Letter 242 [early 1841], in *CCMcA*, 365.
23. Carroll, *Life*, 240.

take into account their toil and pain, lighten their difficulties, and most generously reward every exertion which they make for the love of Him.[24]

These three provisions of the Rule, as approved by Catherine McAuley and Daniel Murray and later by Gregory XVI, are in stark contrast to the eight and a half detailed pages on lay sisters contained in the *Guide for the Religious called Sisters of Mercy* written by Mary Francis Bridgeman, then superior of Kinsale, and published in 1866. Catherine's text draws a few distinctions between lay and choir sisters (in her own writings, aside from the Rule, she never uses the term "choir sisters"), for example, in dress and mealtimes as these were necessitated by the lay sisters' duties. However, her wording does not include all the other discriminations between "choir" and "lay" sisters that are explicitly outlined in the *Guide*, an *Abridgment* of which was endorsed by the superiors who attended the March 1864 meeting in Limerick to discuss it, but not by those in Ireland and England who chose not to attend, or were prevented from attending, or by the superiors in North America, South America, Australia, and New Zealand.[25]

Catherine repeatedly demonstrated affection for and reliance on the lay sisters who entered Baggot Street and the other early Mercy communities. Her letters refer often, with gratitude and praise, to each of the five who entered in 1834 and the two who later came to Baggot Street, all of whom subsequently professed vows. Five of the seven are listed as beneficiaries in Catherine's will and its codicil, along with the other professed sisters in the Baggot Street community; one of the seven had died, and the name of another was evidently inadvertently omitted by the solicitor who copied the documents.[26] In countless ways, Catherine signified her appreciation of the presence and work of these women.

24. Rule, part 2, 9.1, 2, and 3, in the hand-printed copy of the "Rule and Constitutions of the Religious Sisters of Mercy" (AIMGB). Evidently another paragraph in this chapter was originally inserted between what are now the second and third paragraphs, but Catherine McAuley apparently deleted it before the document was transcribed and sent to Rome in 1839. It spoke of the titles lay sisters should use in addressing choir sisters, a distinction Catherine McAuley finally would not countenance. The paragraph does not appear in the confirmed Rule (in Italian) eventually returned from Rome in 1841. For a discussion of the far greater importance of this 1841 Rule and Constitutions than of any subsequent treatment of the Mercy Rule—in terms of its representing Catherine McAuley's views (as in her draft of the mid-1830s, in *CMcATM*, 295–328)—see chap. 22 in this volume.

25. [Mary Francis Bridgeman], *A Guide for the Religious called Sisters of Mercy* (London: Robson and Son, 1866), 109–17. Bridgeman's volume, now widely available in Mercy archives throughout the world, has been assumed to have a universal authority it never enjoyed. It is sometimes cited as if it reflected in all its detail the thinking of Catherine McAuley, which it does not. Among the seventeen who attended the 1864 meeting in Limerick and endorsed the *Abridgment* (London: Robson and Son, 1866) were the superiors of four of the autonomous convents Catherine McAuley had founded: Charleville, Cork, Limerick, and Birr, but not the superiors of the other six: Baggot Street (Dublin), Tullamore, Carlow, Bermondsey, Galway, and Birmingham. Handwritten "Limerick Annals," vol. 2, 81–84 (ASB).

26. Veronica (Ellen) Corrigan had died, and Teresa (Maria) Breen's name was accidentally omitted.

The major task facing Catherine McAuley in 1834 was contributing, as best she could, to the gradual spiritual development of the twenty-three women who by year's end were her associates in the Baggot Street family. Each had her own virtues and blind spots, strengths and human weaknesses, as Catherine herself had. Yet somehow she hoped they would together mature into an authentic religious community, animated by the values that would be essential to their character as Sisters of Mercy, not just in name.

Catherine suffered no illusion about her own competence in this regard. She could teach them only what she herself understood, and try to show the way. The result, whatever it turned out to be, depended wholly on their own human efforts in "fidelity to the inspirations of grace."[27] She was convinced that the congregation was "God's work," not her own. Later, when asked to write a short history of the Sisters of Mercy for a priest who needed notes for a charity sermon, she declined, for "the circumstances which would make it interesting could never be introduced in a public discourse. . . . I should write it 10 times at least before it would be fit for his purpose." But still she acknowledged:

There has been a most marked Providential Guidance which the want of prudence—vigilance—or judgment has not impeded—and it is here that we can most clearly see the designs of God. I could mark circumstances calculated to defeat it at once—but nothing however injurious in itself has done any injury.

This is all I could say. . . . It evidently was to go on—and surmount all obstacles—many of which were great indeed—proceeding from causes within & without. . . . We have been deficient enough—and far, very far, from cooperating generously with God in our regard, but we will try to do better.[28]

One way Catherine tried "to do better" involved the daily, as well as periodic, instructions she offered to the community, though these were addressed equally to herself:

Her exhortations were most animated and impressive, especially on the duties of charity and humility. These were her cherished virtues, which she inculcated more by her example than by words. She taught the Sisters to avoid all that might be in the least contrary to charity, even the slightest remark on manner, natural defects, etc., so that they should make it a rule never to say anything unfavourable of each other. . . . Her lessons on humility, being supported by her own unvarying example, necessarily made a deep impression.[29]

27. BA, in *CMcATM*, 111.

28. Letter 110, January 13, 1839, in *CCMcA*, 179–80.

29. BA, in *CMcATM*, 110. See also Lim, in *CMcATM*, 173.

Harnett says that Catherine, "when instructing the Sisters, loved to dwell on those words of our Divine Lord: 'Learn of me because I am meek and humble of heart,' saying, 'If His blessed words ought to be reverenced by all, with what loving devotion ought the Religious impress them on her memory, and try to reduce them to practice.'"[30] She "loved to expatiate on certain words" and used to say: "Our mutual respect and charity is to be 'cordial'—now 'cordial' signifies something that revives, invigorates, and warms; such should be the effects of our love for each other."[31]

A reviver and invigorator herself, Catherine described her own role, or any superior's, as "becoming a pattern to the Community, [that] she may by example more powerfully engage them to the strict accomplishment of the duties of the Institute." To do this she, and every other superior, would have to "tenderly comfort and support the dejected if there be any such, admonish with charity those who may transgress," and "take due care that the Sisters be provided with all necessaries."[32] She apparently never taught that the obedience of religious was to be directed to the person of any superior as such, but rather to the matters described in the Rule they had together espoused, as interpreted, when necessary, by the superior's best judgment. Consequently, she was opposed to what she ironically called "improvements" on the Rule—unnecessary additions to what it already required. When anyone overzealously asked her to make new regulations, she cautioned: "It is better not; be careful never to make too many laws, for if you draw the string too tight it will break."[33] For Catherine, religious obedience was not a net of tight strings, but conscious remembrance of, and fidelity to, what they were about—namely, following the promises, attitudes, and ways of Jesus Christ.

Over and over, she counseled the community: "Be always striving to make yourselves like your Heavenly Spouse; you should try to resemble him in some one thing at least, so that any person who sees you may be reminded of His holy life on earth." This was "her daily resolution, and the lesson she constantly repeated."[34] True obedience, in her mind, had little, if anything, to do with fidelity to small, over-punctilious, ephemeral regulations, but with "the grand precept of the Love of God . . . the plenitude of the Law," and with helping each other to live in fidelity to that enduring vocation.[35]

30. Lim, in *CMcATM*, 181.
31. BA, in *CMcATM*, 117.
32. Rule, part 2, 3.1, 3, and 4, in *CMcATM*, 321.
33. BA, in *CMcATM*, 115.
34. Lim, in *CMcATM*, 181.
35. Rule 8.1, in *CMcATM*, 303.

Mercifulness, therefore, had a central place in Catherine's instructions to the community, for "'Mercy' was a word of predilection with her":

> She would point out the advantages of Mercy above Charity. "The Charity of God would not avail us, if His Mercy did not come to our assistance. Mercy is more than Charity—for it not only bestows benefits, but it receives and pardons again and again—even the ungrateful."[36]

To which she would often add: "How kind and charitable and merciful, then, ought not 'Sisters of Mercy' to be."[37]

The prayer she tried to nurture was shaped by these understandings. "She loved simplicity singularly in others, and practiced it herself," Clare Moore recalls, "telling the Sisters to adopt a simple style of speaking and writing. . . . Even in piety she disliked highflown aspirations or sentences," observing "how much more suitable those simple phrases in ordinary prayers would be."[38] For Catherine, prayer was not primarily words, but remembrance, recollection. It was like a mariner's compass, an inner orientation, that "goes round its circle without stirring from its center" and "our center is God."[39] If the community learned to remember and surrender to the presence of God within them, they would be "shining lamps giving light to all around us," for the "effect meditation should produce . . . is to render you as a lamp kindled with the fire of Divine Love."[40]

A remarkably cheerful person herself, Catherine animated others, "not only by removing whatever could disturb their peace, but also by contributing to the general cheerfulness of the Community especially at Recreation." Although often burdened with many cares, she was "as lively and merry as the youngest Sisters, who used to delight in being near her, listening to her amusing remarks and anecdotes. She had a natural talent for composing verses in a playful style, and would often sing them to some cheerful tune."[41]

Her "Cholera and Cholerene" must have been born on such an occasion. Though she was no Keats, Shelley, Wordsworth, or any other of her famous contemporaries, it is unfortunate that more of her extempore humorous verses were not preserved. In the *Constitutions* Teresa of Avila wrote for the Reformed Carmelites, she claimed that when the Carmelite sisters are given the opportunity to converse together, "the Lord will give

---

36. BA, in *CMcATM*, 117.   37. Lim, in *CMcATM*, 181.

38. BA, in *CMcATM*, 111.

39. [Mary Bertrand Degnan], ed., *Retreat Instructions of Mother Mary Catherine McAuley* (Westminster, Md.: Newman Press, 1952), 154.

40. Ibid., 155, 145.   41. BA, in *CMcATM*, 116.

to one the grace to entertain the others."[42] If this is true, the pre-eminent entertainer at Baggot Street was Catherine McAuley.

However, in October 1834, her cheerfulness was unexpectedly and severely tested. Dr. Walter Meyler, now parish priest of St. Andrew's, the parish in which the house on Baggot Street was situated, suddenly closed the convent chapel to the public. He forbade celebration of the second Mass there on Sundays, the one people from the neighborhood attended. He thus cut off a source of regular income—the Sunday collection—on which the community had come to depend for funds to run the House of Mercy, and to buy clothing for the girls in the school, and food, clothing, candles, and turf for the sick poor. Catherine was evidently upset enough to write to Michael Blake. On October 23 he responded:

I most cordially sympathise with you . . . in the great trial which the closing of your chapel must have caused, although I am sure, from my knowledge of the natural kindness of your revered Archbishop and of his frequently declared sentiments respecting the merits of your Institution, that nothing short of an imperative sense of duty could have induced him to insist on such a sacrifice.

Dr. Meyler must have told Catherine that Dr. Murray approved the closing. Michael Blake knew Murray, he knew Meyler, and he knew they were close friends. He apparently concluded that Walter Meyler was the source of the problem, for he advised Catherine:

If [Dr. Murray] has not explained his reasons to you, be persuaded that they are strong and cogent. . . . It would be right, however, that you should know clearly the will of his Grace . . . and beg as a favour that he would express it directly himself to you.[43]

Whether Catherine ever asked for a meeting with Daniel Murray is not known. Perhaps she did. For his part, Walter Meyler's obvious reason was money. He was engaged in completing a large building project, the new St. Andrew's church. Before Michael Blake was named bishop of Dromore, he "had collected £6,188 and had advanced the building up to the roof." But the interior of the church, which was opened for worship on January 2, 1834, was a long way from finished; eventually it and its related premises would cost another £20,348.[44] Undoubtedly Dr. Meyler hoped that if more people living within the parish boundaries came to St. Andrew's on Sun-

42. Teresa of Avila, *Collected Works of St. Teresa of Avila*, trans. Kieran Kavanaugh and Otilio Rodriguez, vol. 3 (Washington, D.C.: Institute of Carmelite Studies Publications, 1985), 320. For "Cholera and Cholerene" see chap. 7 in the present volume.

43. Letter 24, October 23, 1834, in CCMcA, 63.

44. Donnelly, *History of Dublin Parishes*, part 7, 152–53.

days, his own parish collections would increase. However, mixed into his decision may also have been his unfriendly attitude toward Catherine, of whatever origin, that all her biographers acknowledge. Burke Savage, basing his views on the research of John MacErlean, suggests that Dr. Meyler's "personal difference" with Catherine dated from his days as a curate at St. Mary's, Liffey Street, and that "its memory seems to have rankled and continued to make easy relations between the two almost impossible."[45] Dr. Meyler was known to be strongly partisan toward the Sisters of Charity, and may have been among those who early on saw Catherine's efforts as competition with them. Degnan also claims that Walter Meyler "had been annoyed" with Catherine "in some issue at St. Mary's."[46]

Daniel Murray evidently trusted Dr. Meyler completely, often promoting him to higher clerical positions, their close friendship lasting until Murray's death. Moreover, the archbishop, though he could and frequently did "take a stand," disliked controversy and was, as Donal Kerr admits, on certain occasions "too passive and too anxious to please."[47] Whether this was one of those occasions is hard to say.

Whatever the case, the chapel was now closed to the public. A modest but regular source of income was ended, and Catherine herself was faced with a painful situation involving a priest. For reasons no doubt derived from her previous experiences and her love and respect for the Catholic Church, she had personal reverence for the "sacerdotal character" of priests.[48] As Clare Moore says: "The obedience and respect of our venerated Foundress towards her Ecclesiastical Superiors was that of a humble child; indeed, she often caused herself needless anxiety, through her fear of giving them the least displeasure."[49] Murray, not Meyler, was her ecclesiastical superior, but Meyler seemed to be acting with the archbishop's approval, even though in June 1829 Dr. Murray himself had recommended that the chapel be opened to the public, "saying [then] that the collection would pay the expense and help to maintain the young women" in the House of Mercy.[50]

In 1834 Catherine evidently acquiesced, though in a future disagreement with Dr. Meyler she could not and would not do so. The closing of the chapel hurt the Baggot Street community, the women and girls in the House of Mercy, and the sick and dying poor, but she apparently saw the

45. Burke Savage, *McAuley,* 98.   46. Degnan, *Mercy,* 158.
47. Kerr, "Daniel Murray," in Kelly and Keogh, *History of the Catholic Diocese of Dublin,* 266.
48. Lim, in *CMcATM,* 182.   49. BA, in *CMcATM,* 118–19.
50. DL, in *CMcATM,* 54.

event as one of those moments when, after having represented the problem as clearly as she could, to no effect, "reserve . . . restrains words, looks, and actions and . . . continually whispers 'go back—stop—say no more.'"[51]

Her earlier attempt to run a pension (tuition-paying) school in the refectory at Baggot Street, as a way to support the poor school and other works, had "proved a signal failure and the very few pupils it ever contained dropped off within the year."[52] Obviously, this idea offered no new source of income. That left bazaars, door-to-door collections, an annual charity sermon which she would request in the following year—and even greater poverty within the religious community. Clare Augustine Moore did not enter until 1837, but her frank, perhaps fastidious, description of meals at Baggot Street is probably not far off the mark:

Even when I entered the diet was most unfit for persons doing our duties. Leg of Beef with onion sauce, beef stakes [sic] that seemed as if they had lain in a tanpit, hash of coarse beef, salt beef, and for a dainty, fried liver and bacon, though boiled and roast mutton came in sometimes.

The breakfast table was a trial to one's nerves: sugar of the very blackest and coarsest kind with no sugar spoon, and for that matter the juniors seldom had a little lead spoon apiece, weak tea, very little milk, plates of very stale thick bread with a very thin scraping of butter.[53]

Baggot Street was now providing three meals a day to fifty or sixty people. Of course there was not enough tableware to go around, let alone food.

In Catherine's view, the material poverty of the community was not just a financial reality, but a consequence of fidelity to the purposes of the congregation. It was a necessity if they were to extend the works of mercy to more and more people in need, an implied condition if they wished to live in genuine solidarity with destitute people, and a chosen outcome of their wish to resemble Jesus Christ "in some one thing at least."[54] In itself, as it afflicted poor people, material poverty was an injustice to be alleviated and corrected, if at all possible, but it was also "a most valuable patrimony" bequeathed by Jesus to his followers. As he had suffered "hunger, cold and thirst in the course of His mortal life," so the Sisters of Mercy would be "content with the food and raiment allowed them and willing at all times to give up whatever had been allotted to them."[55] Here Catherine was committed to one clear principle: "The poor shall not be deprived of the comfort that God sent them while we can avoid it."[56]

51. Letter 125 [June–July 1839], in CCMcA, 201.   52. DL, in CMcATM, 56.
53. CAM, in CMcATM, 207.   54. Lim, in CMcATM, 181.
55. Rule 17.1, 2, in CMcATM, 312.   56. Letter 53, October 3, 1837, in CCMcA, 97.

In 1834, joys and sorrows had indeed mingled. Catherine would later say of this mingling, recalling the words of Edward Nolan, bishop of
Kildare and Leighlin, "It is my lot."[57] But it was also a year in which she
had needed great patience, with herself, the newer members of the community, Archbishop Murray—and Dr. Meyler. Patience, a virtue she always believed she lacked, was, in her view, "my great weakness." Perhaps,
then, it was in 1834 that she wrote, on a front flyleaf of her prayerbook, the
following prayer:

I come this day to ask of thee, my God, the virtue and divine gift of patience, which
is so necessary to carry me through the difficulties of my charge and to satisfy
the many duties which are enjoined me by thy command. I here confess my great
weakness in this point—there not being any day which does not convince me how
much I want [i.e., lack] what I now ask, and therefore I earnestly beg of thee that
grace—and according to my necessity, may my prayer so proceed from my heart as
to induce Thee, my God, to grant my petition. May the spirit of the Cross carry me
on and support me under all my trials, and in this same spirit may I surrender my
soul into thy hands. Oh blessed Jesus, stand then by me, shew mercy to thy servant,
and powerfully help me.[58]

57. Letter 124 [May–August 1839], in *CCMcA*, 198.
58. Catherine McAuley wrote this prayer, which I have often titled "Prayer for Patience," in the front
of her copy of *Devotions to the Sacred Heart of Jesus*, edited by Joseph Joy Dean (MCA).

CHAPTER 10

Beliefs and Motivations

The predominant motivations of Catherine McAuley's adult life seem to have been her gradually deepening theological understandings. It is not possible to study her letters, the prayers she is known to have prayed, her recorded instructions to the first Sisters of Mercy, her expressed reactions to events of her life, or her own actions, without recognizing, however fragmentarily, the interior source of her attitudes and actions. While important clues to what moved her can be discerned in previous chapters, it seems necessary to pause here and try to articulate some of the central elements of her theological beliefs as these emerge from the available evidence. In this biography I have hoped to avoid inadvertent misrepresentation of the woman herself (through failing to step back from the daily flow of her life) and yet keep in mind the final inaccessibility of another person's promptings and grounds for action, some of which may not have been known fully or explicitly even to her.

Catherine was deeply engaged, especially in her mature years, in daily interior dialogue between her grasp of Scripture, her knowledge of Christian tradition as it was available to her, and her surrounding cultural experience. Hers was a dynamic, embodied theology. The circumstances of her own life and of the society and church in which she lived constantly shaped and renewed her response to the gospel. In that sense, she was a contextual theologian.

As a serious, intelligent, committed Christian woman, Catherine possessed a working theology that was, to her at least, a relatively complete framework of theological understandings on the basis of which she functioned as a Christian, however little or much she may have articulated this theology thematically and verbally. As Jon Sobrino notes, "Some conception of God underlies every historical [religious] praxis, whether one adverts to it consciously or not."[1]

As one attempts to present what can be surmised of Catherine McAuley's religious beliefs and motivations, two preliminary factors deserve note. Much of the language in which she read, heard, and tried to express what she came to believe was, as is the case for any person at any time, culturally conditioned, and to that extent some of it may seem, in a later era, theologically dated. This is not to say that it is outmoded, but only that much of this language has undergone considerable change over the last two hundred years. For example, professed women religious today would not generally be encouraged to think of their relation to Jesus Christ as to "their Heavenly Spouse," even though in different wording they would understand the complete communion of mind and heart with Christ to which Catherine and they chose to commit themselves.

Secondly, in presenting Catherine's theological views, her own words, as in her letters and other personal writings, would seem to enjoy a greater degree of relevance than the words of prayers composed by others which she is known to have prayed often or the words she transcribed from other sources. Moreover, firsthand accounts of what she said and did, especially the accounts of those with whom she associated and in whom she confided, can be said to have greater authenticity than commentaries by those who were not witnesses (see appendix).

Catherine's experience and theological understandings were highly influenced by what she read, by conversations with those whose lives she admired, by the composed prayers she frequently prayed, and by the multiple conditions that surrounded her in the church and in society, as well as by that most mysterious and perhaps most persuasive influence of all, what she called "the inspirations of grace ... that Divine voice, which silently and constantly whispers to the heart."[2]

The spiritual books Catherine McAuley is known to have read were, generally, in the mainstream of continental Catholic spiritual books dating from the seventeenth and eighteenth centuries. Nearly all of these books

---

1. Jon Sobrino, *Christology at the Crossroads*, trans. John Drury (Maryknoll, N.Y.: Orbis Books, 1978), 181.
2. BA, in *CMcATM*, 111.

were biblically based, with frequent references to the Scriptures as then understood. Catherine read works by Thomas à Kempis, Alonso Rodriguez, Francis de Sales, Francis Blyth, Barthèlemy Baudrand, Louis Bourdaloue, Luis of Granada, John Gother, Richard Challoner, Alphonsus Liguori, Michel-Ange Marin, Alban Butler, and many others. She read some of these works in translations, although two or three members of the community on Baggot Street were proficient in French. William A. Gahan (*A Complete Manual of Catholic Piety*), Joseph Joy Dean (*Devotions to the Sacred Heart of Jesus*), Ursula Young (*The Soul United to Jesus*), and others were the compilers of prayerbooks she is known to have used. All these works, their content largely of European origin, were frequently republished in English in Ireland during the intense flourishing of Irish Catholic publishers, especially in Dublin, that began in the eighteenth century and continued during her adult life.

In theology, as in other matters, Catherine would have felt she was "deficient enough."[3] Yet she was always alert and youthful in her desire to learn. As Clare Moore and Mary Vincent Harnett remarked, she "did not possess worldly accomplishments, but she had read much and well."[4]

Moreover, Catherine's early and wide exposure to Protestant influences occasioned her deeper study of Catholic theology. She read the poems of William Cowper, Hannah More, and Helen Maria Williams. Her long and close associations with other Protestants—mostly members of the established Church of Ireland, and all of them sincere and educated Christians—undoubtedly left within her a wholesome residue of large-mindedness and of reasoned critique of certain convent practices that were not of the essence of Catholic faith. In view of these relations, her choice to remain a practicing Catholic, and then wholeheartedly to embrace religious life, however hesitantly at first, is all the more significant.

Catherine also benefited greatly from conversations with her spiritual advisers. The priests with whom she had in-depth contact on spiritual matters—Andrew Lubé, Thomas Betagh, Edward Armstrong, Michael Blake, and Redmond O'Hanlon—were all men known throughout Dublin for their profound Christian faith, their theological acumen, and their practical, daily efforts to love their neighbors, especially the most destitute. In these friendships as well as others, she explored, not peripheral religious concerns, but the core beliefs of Christian life.

3. Letter 110, January 13, 1839, in *CCMcA*, 180.
4. Lim, in *CMcATM*, 181.

In particular, Catherine felt that the "study of a Religious should be the life and maxims of Jesus Christ; this divine Model should be in her regard like a book continually open before her."[5] Elizabeth Davis has analyzed the many ways in which Scripture, particularly language from the New Testament, is woven into the texture of Catherine's ways of expressing herself. She quoted scriptural texts directly, or cited them "with modified grammar to accommodate the statement she was making"; she alluded "to a verse or theme in Scripture" or echoed one in her own wording—all in an effort to deepen her own understanding and "to shape a community that had 'the same mind that was in Christ Jesus' (Phil 2.5)."[6] The ease and authority with which she used scriptural quotations indicate the extent to which she had personally interiorized the language of Scripture. She encountered it possibly through reading the Bible directly—though no unambiguous evidence of this has yet been found—but also through the spiritual works she read, especially the scriptural texts in the *Office of the Blessed Virgin* which the community prayed in English three times a day, her still-preserved and Scripture-laden *Journal of Meditations for Every Day in the Year* which she read each day, the *Following of Christ*, and Blyth's *Paraphrase on the Seven Penitential Psalms*.

Some insight into her theological understanding can also be seen in the prayers she is known to have prayed often: particularly, the "Psalter of Jesus," Pope Clement XI's "Universal Prayer for All Things Necessary to Salvation," and the two "Thirty Days' Prayers"—"To Our Blessed Redeemer, in Honour of his Bitter Passion," and "To the Blessed Virgin Mary, in Honour of the Sacred Passion of Our Lord Jesus Christ." All of these are found in prayerbooks she is known to have frequently used: for example, Gahan's *Manual of Catholic Piety,* and Dean's *Devotions to the Sacred Heart of Jesus.* The theological formulations in these prayers were among the more frequent theological expressions familiar to her and contributed, at least indirectly and in a contextual sense, to the language of her theological understandings. It was from her copy of Dean's volume, still preserved, that Catherine transcribed the "Act of Consecration" which was once assumed to be her own composition.[7]

5. *PS,* 23–24.

6. Elizabeth M. Davis, "Wisdom and Mercy Meet: Catherine McAuley's Interpretation of Scripture," in *Recovering Nineteenth-Century Women Interpreters of the Bible,* ed. Christiana de Groot and Marion Ann Taylor (Atlanta: Society of Biblical Literature, 2007), 65.

7. See Mary C. Sullivan, "Catherine McAuley's Theological and Literary Debt to Alonso Rodriguez," *Recusant History* 20 (May 1990): 81–105, in which Catherine McAuley's transcription of Dean's "Act of Oblation" as her "Act of Consecration" is also discussed, 103–4.

What one finds in Catherine's instructions, writings, and prayers are verbal representations which embody, explicitly or implicitly, aspects of her personal appropriation of the mystery of God and of Jesus Christ. These words are often cryptic expressions of the topics they address. But where, in addition to her verbal expressions, can we find the fuller representation of Catherine's theological understandings? Where are her other theological expressions out of which some of her verbal expressions emerged and to which they are related?

Whereas theology traditionally described practice as the application of theory acquired elsewhere, many recent theologies understand that the actual practice of the Christian life is the place where faith itself is understood and strengthened in gospel-inspired action. It would appear from the evidence of her life that Catherine's working theology is in some respects more fully expressed in her actions than in her words.

Catherine would not have formulated the evolution of her knowledge of God and of Jesus Christ precisely as present-day theologians formulate their understanding of the relation of practice to theology, but she, too, accorded a fundamental priority to noticing the providential care of God in actual historical circumstances, and to the following of Jesus in the milieu of her actual time and place. Her practical bent, her emphasis on personal example, her characteristic preoccupation with the "example" of Jesus and with "bearing some resemblance to him," and especially her consuming devotion to serving the poor in myriad ways, provide some evidence for this interpretation of her thinking. The three distinctive works of her life—the education of poor girls, the visitation and care of the sick and dying poor, and the sheltering and instruction of orphans, poor girls, and distressed women—are thus necessary sources for reading her understanding of Jesus Christ, as expressed not only in her words but also, and in some ways more clearly, in her actions. Her attempts to "follow" Jesus—in Ireland, in the early nineteenth century—are where she both found and expressed much of her understanding of God and Jesus Christ. Her conscious understandings, therefore, cannot and should not be detached from her cultural and linguistic context, for it is possible to discover in this context the central elements of the beliefs and motivations at the deepest level of her Christian life—in her words and in her daily attempts to search out and follow, during her moment in history, the gospel of Jesus Christ.

So what then did Catherine McAuley believe? What were the central strands of her Christian faith and the central motivations of her life and work, as these may be revealed in her words and actions? These central elements would seem to have been seven: (1) her belief that human life is a spiritual journey, toward God and centered in God; (2) her confidence in the accompanying providence and mercy of God; (3) her understanding of Jesus Christ as the self-bestowal of God, and of the gospel as a call to a corresponding human self-bestowal, to a following of God's generosity in Jesus; (4) her faith in and desire to resemble Jesus Christ as the guiding and beckoning example of this God-inspired and God-provided journey; (5) her focus on the "cross" of Jesus Christ as the fullest human expression of Jesus' own self-bestowal, and on the ongoing historical invitations to participate in that self-bestowal; (6) her belief in the thoroughness of Jesus Christ's compassionate, even "tender," identification with the "least"— with those who were poor and suffering; and (7) her focus on God's mercy as the rendering, in the person of Jesus, of God's love for human beings, and on human mercifulness as "the principal path pointed out by Jesus Christ to those who are desirous of following him."[8] These beliefs and motivations were intimately entwined in Catherine's faith, each one interlaced with the others, such that they cannot be discussed separately— though the following paragraphs attempt to do so—without falsifying to some extent the comprehensiveness of each.

A Spiritual Journey

Throughout her mature life, especially in the period from 1827 to her death for which there are abundant documentary sources, Catherine seems to have been particularly conscious of human life as a swiftly moving journey, a dynamic movement toward death and the promised "joys of a blissful Eternity."[9] Although her spirit is frequently witty and playful, and her respect for "nonsense" is closely related to her detached attitude toward human accomplishments, especially her own, her estimate of human life as a spiritual pilgrimage or journey was surely influenced by her repeated experience of the death of those she loved and served. Even a bare listing of these deaths suggests the more than usual impact of death on her life and thought. Thus she was able to write, with especial poignancy, "the tomb seems never closed in my regard."[10] It was undoubtedly out of such experience that she wrote to a woman whose sister was dangerously

8. Rule 3.1, in *CMcATM*, 297.   9. Letter 241, February 28, 1841, in *CCMcA*, 365.
10. Letter 55, October 17, 1837, in *CCMcA*, 99.

ill: "What is this poor miserable world but a place of sorrow and continued disappointment. God be praised, it is not our fixed abode, only the weary Road that leads to it. Oh, what would we do, if in place of 70 or 80 years, God had appointed three or four hundred for our journey."[11] At the heart of her understanding of human life was her belief in the mysterious movement of the human spirit toward God, a movement centered in God and drawn forward by God. Catherine's God was not "out there," but actively within, bringing "us joyfully on to the end of our journey."[12]

Her "traveling" metaphors and her descriptions of human life as a journey Godward that "draws to a close" in death, imply what others have described as the transcendental movement of the human spirit toward the Holy Mystery that is God. She believed and often said:

Each day is a step we make towards eternity; and we shall continue thus to step from day to day until we take the last step which will bring us into the presence of God.[13]

For Catherine, this movement was constitutive of the human person, and was beckoned forward by God's own self-communication in Jesus Christ. God was close to the faithful traveler, not a distant presence.

Confidence in the Providence and Mercy of God

Catherine's conception of God reveals itself most explicitly in her repeated references to God's providence, and to God's mercy as embodied in Jesus Christ. Her understanding of the mystery of God is the setting and horizon for her understanding of Jesus Christ; it comes to a focus in her understanding of the person of Jesus. She makes only one explicit reference to the "Trinity" in her published letters, and no explicit reference to the "Holy Spirit (Ghost)" or to the "Spirit of God" or "Spirit of Christ" in these letters, though such references appear in the prayers she commonly used.

Catherine seems to have understood confidence or hope in God's providence as the courage to freely commit oneself to the incomprehensible Love who permeates and sustains human existence and is the trustworthy future of that existence. Her notable confidence in God—expressed repeatedly in her letters and implicit in all the prayers that were especially significant to her—was grounded in her faith in God's mysterious but be-

11. Letter 198, October 26, 1840, in CCMcA, 306.
12. Letter 220 [December 20, 1840], in CCMcA, 332.
13. PS, 23.

nevolent providence. God's "providence" is the most frequent reference to God in all her writings.

Catherine saw herself and others as living in God's domain: "The Lord and Master of our House and Home is a faithful Provider. Let us never desire more than enough. He will give that and a blessing."[14] Under the notion of God's "providence" she assumed the whole of created human life: as the object and occasion of God's blessing, as the "moment" of divine visitation, as the circumstance of divine watchfulness, as the "place" of God's consolation or purification, as the offer of participation in the cross of Christ, and so, in Christ's resurrection. She believed wholeheartedly in God's promises as fulfilled in Jesus, and assured Frances Warde, "Nothing can happen to you which He does not appoint. You desire nothing but the accomplishment of His Holy Will. Every thing, how trivial soever, regarding you will come from this adorable source."[15] In a similar vein, she consoled Elizabeth Moore on the death of a lively young Limerick sister:

I did not think any event in this world could make me feel so much. I have cried heartily—and implored God to comfort you—I know He will. . . . Some joyful circumstance will soon prove that God is watching over your concerns which are all his own. . . . Some great thing which he designs to accomplish would have been too much—without a little bitter in the cup. . . . He will soon come with both hands filled with favors and blessings.[16]

A year later she again identified the providence and mercy of God as that which, despite all, shape and guide the Sisters of Mercy:

This is the Spirit of the order, indeed—the true spirit of Mercy flowing on us—that notwithstanding our unworthiness, God never seems to visit us with angry punishment. . . . Take what he will from us, He still leaves His holy peace.[17]

Catherine's emphatic confidence in God's providence pervades all her published correspondence and apparently structured her understanding of the workings of God in individual and corporate human histories. God's providence was for her the manifestation of God's merciful will on human behalf and the mode of God's intimate, active engagement in the forward journeys of human lives. It was hope and trust in this accompanying providence that she apparently had in mind when she prayed daily: "I adore thee as my first beginning. I aspire after thee as my last end. I give thee thanks as my constant benefactor. I call upon thee as my sovereign protector. Vouchsafe, O my God, to conduct me by thy wisdom, to restrain me

14. Letter 242 [early 1841], in CCMcA, 366.   15. Letter 78, February 17, 1838, in CCMcA, 126.
16. Letter 168 [March 21, 1840], in CCMcA, 259.   17. Letter 257 [April 12, 1841], in CCMcA, 386.

by thy justice, to comfort me by thy mercy, to defend me by thy power."[18]

Catherine evidently never spoke of God using other than masculine or gender-neutral images and pronouns. Perhaps she did not conceive of God through any other metaphors than masculine ones. The notion that God might also be equivalently figured—again metaphorically, which is the only way one can speak of "God"—using female images probably did not occur to her. Such language was certainly not the common religious language of her church or culture. However, one suspects she would have welcomed such understanding had it been presented to her, and would have found it in accord with her conceptions of God.

Generosity as Self-Bestowal

Catherine comes closest to an expression of God's action in Jesus in her notion of self-bestowal. She often wrote of God's "bestowing" blessings, and she was particularly insistent to define human generosity as self-bestowal. On July 24, 1841, she wrote to Mary Ann Doyle: "It is not a disposition to bestow gifts, like benevolent persons in the world, that bespeaks generosity of mind for the religious state. It is bestowing ourselves most freely and relying with unhesitating confidence on the Providence of God."[19]

Jesus Christ was, for Catherine, the merciful "Saviour" who came from a provident God into this world to draw all things to himself. She calls him "our Divine Redeemer," "our Divine Master," "our Dear Redeemer," "blessed Jesus," "our heavenly Spouse," but never in her own words, "Son of God." The divinity of Jesus was, for her, presumed and made manifest not so much, it would seem, in his resurrection or in his claims with respect to his Father, but in the love, mercy, humility, meekness, and poverty of his human life and dying.

An important daily locus of her understanding of the divinity of Jesus Christ would have been the "Psalter of Jesus," with its fifteen petitions addressed to him—a prayer she is said to have prayed since childhood.[20]

18. "An Universal Prayer," in William A. Gahan, A Complete Manual of Catholic Piety (Dublin: T. M'Donnel, 1804), 263–64. The prayer texts are the same in all editions of this book, but not the page numbers.

19. Letter 283, July 24, 1841, in CCMcA, 418.

20. CML, in CMcATM, 92. The "Psalter of Jesus" is an old Christian prayer, probably composed by Richard Whytford (Whitford), a priest living near London in the fifteenth century. The version of it Catherine found in her prayerbooks was probably that slightly modified by Richard Challoner (1691–1781). For the complete text, see [Mary C. Sullivan], "The Prayers of Catherine McAuley," in Praying in the

Moreover, in the "Thirty Days' Prayer to our blessed Redeemer, in Honour of his Bitter Passion," Catherine would have frequently prayed:

Hear my prayers . . . by that sweetness . . . of thy alliance with our human nature, when, resolving with the Father and Holy Ghost, to unite thy divine person to mortal flesh for man's salvation, thou didst send thy angel to the holy Virgin Mary with those happy tidings, and clothing thyself with our human nature . . . remainedst true God and true man, for the space of nine months in her sacred womb.[21]

Presumably the expressions in these prayers contributed to Catherine's understanding of the person of Jesus Christ, but her own letters also indicate how she viewed him as the "Divine Redeemer." To Frances Gibson, a prospective Sister of Mercy from Liverpool, Catherine speaks of "our Divine Redeemer who came on earth . . . to bring . . . a Heavenly Sword . . . and thus to draw all to Himself," but she is not explicit about the ontological character of that coming, bringing, or drawing.[22] For her, Christ had simply "come," in a "season of love and mercy."[23] In her thinking the communion of humanity and divinity in the one person Jesus was apparently unexplored, in favor of a, to her, simpler concentration on Jesus' humanity. Yet in "On Union and Charity"—the chapter of the Presentation Rule which she incorporated almost verbatim into the Rule of the Sisters of Mercy—Catherine would have frequently meditated on its analogy between Jesus Christ's union with God and the union of charity within a human community: "This mutual love, our Blessed Saviour desires, may be so perfect as to resemble the Love and Union which subsists between Himself and His Heavenly Father."[24]

The most enigmatic of Catherine's expressions about the nature of Christ's incarnation are her two references to "the fire that Christ cast upon earth," allusions to Luke 12:49.[25] This scriptural reference would seem to represent a special aspect of her interpretation of Jesus' mission. Evidently, his casting "fire upon the earth" and "drawing all things to Himself" were her complementary expressions for the difficult but saving mission of self-bestowal to which she believed Jesus Christ and his followers were called.

Spirit of Catherine McAuley, ed. Doris Gottemoeller and others (Chicago: Institute of the Sisters of Mercy of the Americas, 1999), 57–67.

21. *Poor Man's Manual of Devotions* (Dublin: D. Wogan, 1819), 56–57. This "Thirty Days' Prayer" is included in many prayerbooks used in Catherine's day, including Gahan's *Catholic Piety*.

22. Letter 249, March 28, 1841, in *CCMcA*, 376.

23. Letter 220 [December 20, 1840], in *CCMcA*, 332.

24. Rule 8.1, in *CMcATM*, 303.

25. Letter 173, June [6, 1840], in *CCMcA*, 270; letter 180, July 28, 1840, in *CCMcA*, 282.

Resembling and Following Christ

Among the most numerous Christological references in Catherine's writings and sayings are those to the "example" of Christ, and to "bearing some resemblance to Him." She wrote, for instance, to Elizabeth Moore on Easter Monday, 1841:

I am impatient to send you a few hurried lines, rejoicing that our sorrowful medita-tions are at an end—and humbly beseeching God to impart to us all some portion of those precious gifts and graces which our Dear Redeemer has purchased by His bitter sufferings—that we may endeavour to prove our love and gratitude by bear-ing some resemblance to Him—copying some of the lessons He has given us dur-ing His mortal life, particularly those of His passion.[26]

In the same Eastertide, she wrote similarly to Mary de Sales White:

The impression made on our minds, by forty days meditation on Christ's humilia-tions, meekness, and unwearied perseverance, will help us on every difficult occa-sion, and we will endeavour to make Him the only return He demands of us—by giving Him our whole heart, fashioned on His own model—pure, meek, merciful and humble.[27]

One sees in these expressions not only Catherine's emphasis on following the example of Jesus, but also her view that his life and death invite a cor-responding "return" of love and gratitude.

In the chapter of the Rule on the visitation of the sick, one of the two chapters she composed in their entirety, she writes: "Let those whom Je-sus Christ has graciously permitted to assist Him in the Persons of His suffering Poor . . . ever keep His unwearied patience and humility present to their minds, endeavouring to imitate Him more perfectly every day, in self-denial, patience, and entire resignation."[28] She would also have fre-quently reflected on the description of Jesus' example in the chapter on the vow of poverty, a chapter she copied, with some alterations, from the Presentation Rule:

The Sisters in order to become more conformable to their Heavenly Spouse Christ Jesus . . . should frequently revolve in mind how tenderly He cherished Holy Pover-ty. Born in a stable, laid in a manger, suffering hunger, cold and thirst in the course of His mortal life, not having a place to lay His head, naked on a cross, He conse-crated this virtue in His sacred Person and bequeathed it as a most valuable patri-mony to His followers.[29]

---

26. Letter 257 [April 12, 1841], in CCMcA, 385.   27. Letter 261, April 19, 1841, in CCMcA, 390.
28. Rule 3.3, in CMcATM, 297.   29. Rule 17.1, in CMcATM, 312.

Evidently one of Catherine's persistent hopes for the Sisters of Mercy was that they might follow, and so teach, the example of Christ's thorough self-bestowal, in humility and meekness. As she once wrote to Elizabeth Moore:

May God bless the poor Sisters of Mercy and make them very humble that they may not be unworthy of the distinguished blessings God has bestowed upon them. If one spark of generous gratitude exists in the first-born children, they will labour to impress humility and meekness by example more than precept—the virtues recommended most by our dear Saviour—and chiefly by example.[30]

These expressions suggest that Catherine regarded the example of Jesus Christ as a bequest. His personal qualities and lifestyle were an endowment offered to his followers, as was his pedagogy. For her, humility and meekness were not superficial or passive modes of behaving, but attitudes of heart grounded in her understanding of the extent of Jesus' self-bestowal and solidarity with human beings and of the corresponding self-bestowal and solidarity of those who wish to follow him.

The Cross of Christ

The "Cross of Christ" is the most frequent reference to Christ in Catherine's published letters. For her, the cross was the supreme example of Jesus' complete surrender to and collaboration in the providence of God. In the "Thirty Days' Prayer to Our Blessed Redeemer in Honour of his Bitter Passion" she would have entreated Jesus Christ's help:

By the anguish thou enduredst when the time of thy designed passion drawing nigh, thou prayedst to thy eternal Father, that if it were possible that bitter chalice might pass away from thee; yet concluding with a most perfect act of resignation, "Not my will, but thine be done."[31]

In her references to the cross of Christ, Catherine nearly always moves immediately on to human acceptance of one's "portion of the Holy Cross."[32] She does not, in her own words, explain what she took to be the inherent significance of the death of Jesus as such. However, the wording of the twelfth petition in the "Psalter of Jesus" undoubtedly contributed to her understanding: "Wilt thou be deaf to my cries, who hast laid down thy life for my ransom? or canst thou not save me, who took it up again for my crown."[33]

---

30. Letter 180, July 28, 1840, in CCMcA, 282–83.   31. Poor Man's Manual, 57–58.
32. Letter 269, May 28, 1841, in CCMcA, 401.
33. Gahan, Catholic Piety (n.p.: Agra Press, 1834), Supplement, 102.

From the language of the two Thirty Days' Prayers, one can conclude that at least here Catherine's thought would have focused not so much on the significance of Jesus' death in itself as on his physical and mental anguish: "the welts and sores ... scoffs and ignominies ... false accusation and unjust sentence," as well as "his dereliction on the cross, when he exclaimed, 'My God! my God! why hast thou forsaken me.'"[34] Clare Moore says of Catherine: "Feeling as she did so sensibly for the sufferings of her fellow creatures, her compassion for those endured by our Blessed Lord was extreme, so much so that it was a real pain to her, as she once told a Sister in confidence [Clare herself?], to meditate on that subject."[35] In the wording of the Thirty Days' Prayers, Catherine would also have derived a sense of the death of Jesus as that from which "a flood of grace and mercy has flowed to us."[36] She found a frequent scriptural reflection on the character of Jesus' act of dying in Philippians 2:8, a verse occurring three times in the "Psalter of Jesus": "Jesus Christ for our sakes, became obedient unto death, even the death of the cross."[37]

Much of the "Psalter of Jesus" is prayer to the "merciful Saviour" for the gift of remembrance, not only of "my sins" and "my death," but especially, remembrance of God's mercy and of Jesus' death and resurrection. Forms of the verb "remember" and the nouns "remembrance" and "memory" occur eight times in the course of the "Psalter." Catherine's writings indicate that sheer remembrance of the death of Jesus Christ was a key aspect of her orientation. She seems to have had a vital and fairly constant "memory" of that death and to have regarded it as a living, beckoning power.

In composing the Rule of the Sisters of Mercy, Catherine chose to incorporate almost verbatim the paragraph "Devotion to the Passion of Jesus Christ" in the Presentation Rule. This paragraph speaks not of the salvific significance of Jesus' death, but of conformity to him in his suffering, and participation in his "suffering and humiliation":

The Sisters of this Congregation shall have the most affectionate devotion to the Passion of our Lord and Saviour Jesus Christ. They shall often recall to mind and meditate on the different circumstances of it in order to excite in themselves an ardent desire of conforming themselves to their suffering Redeemer, persuaded that to share hereafter in His glory, they must here participate in His suffering and hu-

34. "Thirty Days' Prayer to the ... Virgin Mary in Honour of the Sacred Passion of ... Jesus Christ," in Gahan, *Catholic Piety* (Dublin: James Duffy, 1844), 524. Again, the texts of the prayers in Gahan's work are the same in all editions.

35. BA, in *CMcATM*, 117.

36. "Thirty Days' Prayer to the ... Virgin Mary," in Gahan, *Catholic Piety* (1844), 524.

37. "Psalter of Jesus," in Gahan, *Catholic Piety* (1834), Supplement, 96, 101, and 105.

miliation. They shall offer the fatigues and labors of their state, the mortifications they undergo, and all their pains of mind and body in union with the suffering of their crucified Spouse.[38]

This text evidently provided the rationale for Catherine's characteristic alertness to each day's "Cross of Christ." In her letters nearly all her references to the cross are references to acceptance of "our portion" of that cross. The historical character of each of these references suggests Catherine's almost daily perception of the continual collaboration called for by Jesus' death. She often reminded her colleagues that "without the cross the real crown cannot come"; that the Sisters of Mercy should be "established on the Cross" and were "founding on the cross now indeed"; that "if they should have a new foundation—it will not be without the cross"; and that in suffering they are "on the secure high road of the Cross."[39]

When a controversy surrounding the denial of a regular chaplain to serve the women and children sheltered at Baggot Street was at its height, Catherine wrote to Frances Warde:

We have just now indeed more than an ordinary portion of the Cross in this one particular—but may it not be the Cross of Christ which we so often pray to "be about us."[40]

Catherine acknowledged not only her own suffering in the midst of difficulties, but also the hesitation that often preceded acceptance of daily portions of the cross. Of the death of the sickly Gertrude Jones she remarked: "I believe she may be truly said to have taken up her Cross—while, in general, we only carry it when it comes—and keep it away as long as we can."[41]

Expressions in the ninth and fifteenth petitions of the "Psalter of Jesus" evidently enabled Catherine to see in painful events the opportunity to participate in the merciful value she saw in the death of Jesus:

Let the remembrance of thy death, teach me how to set a just value on life; and the memory of thy Resurrection, encourage me to descend cheerfully to the grave.

Let the memory of thy passion make me cheerfully undergo every temptation or suffering . . . for love of thee; whilst my soul, in the mean-time, languishes after that life of consummate bliss . . . which thou hast prepared for thy servants in heaven.[42]

---

38. Rule 15.1 in *CMcATM*, 308–9.

39. Letter 168 [March 21, 1840], in *CCMcA*, 259; letter 78, February 17, 1838, in *CCMcA*, 125; letter 175, June 10, 1840, in *CCMcA*, 273; letter 206, November 9, 1840, in *CCMcA*, 316; letter 283, July 24, 1841, in *CCMcA*, 417.

40. Letter 71, January 17, 1838, in *CCMcA*, 119.

41. Letter 122, May 11, 1839, in *CCMcA*, 194–95.

42. "Psalter of Jesus," in Gahan, *Catholic Piety* (1834), Supplement, 100, 105.

Seeing the "Cross of Christ" in other human "crosses" and sufferings apparently had for Catherine the character of a personal *anamnesis,* an effective and present memorial of Christ's death. Remembering his death was an enabling motivation of her desire to "follow" him, and to "bear some resemblance to him."

Jesus' "Tender" Identification with the "Least"

In four passages in chapters 1 and 3 of the Rule, Catherine presents her belief in the presence of Jesus Christ in and with the poor. These passages are the only places where she cites or alludes to Matthew 18:20 and 25:40.

In chapter 1 she states the purposes of the Sisters of Mercy and then notes the sort of animation that could lead to their fulfillment:

The Sisters admitted into this religious congregation besides the principal and general end of all religious orders, such as attending particularly to their own perfection, must also have in view what is peculiarly characteristic of this Institute of the Sisters of Mercy, that is, a most serious application to the Instruction of poor Girls, Visitation of the Sick, and protection of distressed women of good character.

In undertaking the arduous, but very meritorious duty of instructing the poor, the Sisters whom God has graciously pleased to call to this state . . . shall animate their zeal and fervor by the example of their Divine Master Jesus Christ, who testified on all occasions a tender love for the poor and declared that He would consider as done to Himself whatever should be done unto them [Mt 25:40].[43]

In chapter 3 of the Rule, "Visitation of the Sick," she writes:

Mercy, the principal path pointed out by Jesus Christ to those who are desirous of following Him, has in all ages of the Church excited the faithful in a particular manner to instruct and comfort the sick and dying poor, as in them they regarded the person of our Divine Master, who has said: "Amen, I say to you, as long as you did it to one of these my least brethren, you did it to me [Mt 25:40]."

Let those whom Jesus Christ has graciously permitted to assist Him in the Persons of His suffering Poor [Mt 25:40] have their hearts animated with gratitude and love, and . . . ever keep His unwearied patience and humility present to their minds.[44]

When the sisters go through the streets to visit the poor in their homes— a thing not often done by members of women's religious orders in Ireland in Catherine's time—she recommends, here re-interpreting the biblical text:

The Sisters shall always go out together . . . walking in neither slow or hurried pace . . . preserving recollection of mind and going forward as if they expected to meet

---

43. Rule 1.1, 2, in *CMcATM,* 295.   44. Rule 3.1, 3, in *CMcATM,* 297.

their Divine Redeemer in each poor habitation, since He has said: "Where two or three are in my name I will be [Mt 18:20]."[45]

Because these passages are in the Rule which she eventually presented to Rome, they are among her most carefully considered theological expressions. In them we see not only her repeated assertion that the living Christ is to be recognized in the persons of the poor, but her claim that this recognition is "animated," given life, by Jesus Christ himself.

"Tender" and "tenderness" were characteristic words in Catherine's expression. She advocated "great tenderness of all things," and she felt "great tenderness" for the young community in Galway, in the midst of so much poverty.[46] In the chapter on humility in the Rule she illustrated this virtue with the words "tender concern and regard" (though Archbishop Murray subsequently deleted them).[47] She ascribed tenderness to Jesus Christ himself, claiming in the Rule that he "testified on all occasions a tender love for the poor," and that "the many miraculous cures performed by our Saviour, and the power of healing given to the Apostles evince His great tenderness for the sick."[48]

Catherine's desire to resemble Jesus Christ in his "tender love for the poor" underlay both her sense of obligation to the poor and her attitude of solidarity with them. When she heard that the Mercy community in Charleville might have thought of dissolving for want of human and financial resources, she wrote:

Are not the poor of Charleville as dear to Him as elsewhere? . . . Ought we not to persevere and confide in his Providence? . . . Put your whole confidence in God. He never will let you want necessaries for yourself or children.[49]

When after much effort to avert withdrawal, it appeared that another community would have to close, for want of funds to pay a bill wrongfully ascribed to them, she wrote:

Do not be afflicted for your poor—their Heavenly Father will provide comfort for them. . . . I feel that it would give you no consolation were I to say—"God would not be displeased with you—though He may with me." He will not be displeased with me, for He knows I would rather be cold and hungry than the poor . . . should be deprived of any consolation in our power to afford.[50]

45. Rule 3.6, in *CMcATM*, 298.
46. Letter 49, July 27, 1837, in *CCMcA*, 90; letter 230, January 20, 1841, in *CCMcA*, 352.
47. Rule 9.2, in *CMcATM*, 305.
48. Rule 3.2, in *CMcATM*, 297.
49. Letter 67, December 20, 1837, in *CCMcA*, 114–15.
50. Letter 100, November 1, 1838, in *CCMcA*, 163–64.

The concreteness of Catherine's expression, "I would rather be cold and hungry than the poor . . . should be deprived," typifies the depth and extent of her solidarity with them. She saw herself as a participant in their afflictions. On the death of the beloved Edward Nolan, bishop of Kildare and Leighlin, she advised: "To regard it as an individual sorrow would not be right. Our portion of it may well be lost in the lamentations of his poor and destitute people."[51] In her verbal and nonverbal expressions of community with the poor she revealed the conception of Jesus Christ and his mission which underlay and emerged from her works of mercy.

Mercy, the "Practical Rendering" of God's Love

Catherine regarded the ongoing bestowal of God's mercy as the principal work of Jesus Christ, and the daily attempt to collaborate in that mercifulness as the principal work of Christians and so of Sisters of Mercy. In the Rule she identifies mercy as "the principal path pointed out by Jesus Christ to those who are desirous of following Him."[52] In her essay "Spirit of the Institute," where she argues that contemplation and the works of mercy are "so linked together . . . that they reciprocally help each other," she nonetheless emphasizes the priority of the "offices of mercy":

Though the spirit of prayer and retreat should be most dear to us, yet such a spirit as would never withdraw us from these works of mercy, otherwise it should be regarded as a temptation rather than the effect of sincere piety.[53]

In the same essay she urges confidence in the God in whose mission of mercifulness she and her sisters are engaged:

We ought then have great confidence in God in the discharge of all these offices of Mercy, spiritual and corporal—which constitute the business of our lives, and assure ourselves that God will particularly concur with us to render them efficacious as by His infinite mercy we daily experience.[54]

Mary Vincent Harnett reports:

She used sometimes at recreation turn the conversation on the nature and merits of that virtue, comparing it with charity. . . . "The mercy of God," she would say, "comes to our assistance, and renders practical His charity in our regard."[55]

---

51. Letter 55, October 17, 1837, in *CCMcA*, 100.
52. Rule 3.1, in *CMcATM*, 297.
53. "Spirit of the Institute," in *CCMcA*, 458–59 and 461–62.
54. Ibid., 462.
55. Lim, in *CMcATM*, 181.

Similarly, the Bermondsey annalist says of Catherine: "'Mercy' was a word of predilection with her. She would point out the advantages of Mercy above Charity. 'The Charity of God would not avail us, if His Mercy did not come to our assistance.'"[56]

Catherine's description of God's mercy as the "assistance" and "practical rendering" of God's charity was central to her personal interpretation of the significance of Jesus Christ and of the relation of divine and human mercifulness to his person and work. Jesus Christ was the enfleshed "assistance," the "practical rendering" of God's charity. These expressions also describe and explain her own work of mercifulness: her practical daily efforts, on behalf of those in need, to "render" God's love available to them. Many of the actions she took, as noted throughout this biography, are the nonverbal records of this rendering and of her beliefs and motivations as they both informed and emerged from her practice of mercifulness.

56. BA, in CMcATM, 117.

CHAPTER 11

Short Steps and Great Strides *1835*

Aware of the pressing needs of destitute people, and the suddenness with which death could come, Catherine was always conscious of the "shortness of time"—"an ordinary topic with her," according to Clare Moore. She regretted having to take so many mundane pains in such a "fleeting life," saying only half-playfully: "We have scarcely put on our clothes in the morning, when night comes, and we have to take them off again, and then so soon to resume the same task. Oh! how nice it would be if we could make some contrivance only to dress and undress once a month!"[1] This from the woman who wished her associates to "avoid everything bordering on negligence or disorder" in their appearance, and who once called the "thin black gauze" veil of a nun visiting from the United States "frightful."[2]

Though she saw "life and death so closely, so intimately united" that "we have not an hour to spare," Catherine was not headlong or frantic.[3] She often advised: "Let us take one day only in hands at a time. . . . Thus we may hope to get on—taking short careful steps, not great strides."[4] In verses she later wrote for Elizabeth Moore, she counseled:

Attend to one thing—at a time
you've 15 hours from 6 to 9.[5]

In 1835, Catherine's "15 hours" were filled with many short steps, but also a few "great strides." The usual entrance, reception, and profession cer-

1. BA, in *CMcATM*, 116–17.
2. *PS*, 13, and letter 287, July 31, 1841, in *CCMcA*, 422.
3. Letter 205, November 8, 1840, in *CCMcA*, 315.   4. Letter 241, February 28, 1841, in *CCMcA*, 365.
5. Letter 103 [December 9, 1838], in *CCMcA*, 170.

emonies added eight new members to the community. Among those now at Baggot Street were women who would one day found twelve convents of Sisters of Mercy beyond Dublin, one as far away as Perth, Australia.

But in February 1835, Catherine was not looking that far ahead. Instead, she was worried about money—just enough to carry on the work at hand. She had begged her young friend, William Kinsella, bishop of Ossory, to preach a charity sermon at which a collection would be taken up for the House of Mercy. The dates of such sermons, for the various Catholic charitable institutions and societies in Dublin, were assigned by the archdiocese, and the one in aid of Baggot Street was set for Sunday, February 22.[6] Catherine's friendship with William Kinsella went back to March 1829, when she enrolled her nephews in the boarding school at Carlow College, where he taught philosophy and then held the chair of theology until his consecration in July 1829 as bishop of Ossory, with the diocesan seat in Kilkenny.[7] A native of Carlow he returned there often and took an active interest in the Macauley boys' progress at the college, being particularly impressed by young Robert's diligence in his studies.[8] Dr. Kinsella had also visited Catherine at George's Hill.

The sermon on February 22 was set for three o'clock in St. Andrew's church, Westland Row. Dr. Meyler had "tried not to have the Charity Sermon preached in the Parish Church, but the Archbishop decided it was to be so."[9] *Freeman's Journal* announced the sermon, the text of the advertisement undoubtedly written by Catherine McAuley:

> There are many who decline going to Charity Sermons, lest they should occupy the place of others who might contribute more; but the Church in Westland Row is so very extensive, that no considerate feeling of this kind need influence any. Our compassionate Redeemer, who has made the cause of the poor his own, takes particular notice of the widow's mite, and if those who could give only One Shilling will attend the Sermon on Sunday next, he will not fail to bless and reward them.[10]

Journeying through Ireland later that year, with his colleague Gustave de Beaumont, Alexis de Tocqueville visited William Kinsella in Kilkenny and found him "a very likable man, very spiritual, perspicacious, and having enough sense to be impartial (as far as an Irishman can be) and finding

---

6. Some manuscripts of Catherine's associates imply earlier charity sermons on behalf of the House of Mercy, perhaps even one at Baggot Street itself, but as these manuscripts are unclear about dates, and publication of the *Catholic Directory* did not resume until 1836, one cannot be certain that the sermon in 1835 was the first.

7. Michael Comerford, *Collections relating to the Dioceses of Kildare and Leighlin*, vol. 1 (Dublin: James Duffy, 1883), 191.

8. Letter 14, February 19, 1832, in *CCMcA*, 51.   9. CAM, in *CMcATM*, 209.

10. *Freeman's Journal*, February 17, 18, and 20, 1835.

pleasure in showing it." At a dinner Kinsella hosted on July 26, 1835, the anniversary of his consecration as bishop, Tocqueville learned firsthand Kinsella's passion for the sufferings of the poor. Commenting on the need for an Irish poor law, the bishop said:

Who supports the poor in Ireland today? It is the poor. The rich man looks at the poor over the top of the walls of his beautiful park. . . . He does not provide them with work. He has big and fat dogs and his fellow creatures die at his door. Who feeds the poor? The poor. The unfortunate who has 100 bushels of potatoes for himself and his family gives annually 50 to men more unfortunate still who present themselves starving at the door of his cottage. Is it right that this man wears ragged clothes, does not send his son to school, and lays on himself the hardest privations to relieve the misery to which the rich landlord remains insensible?[11]

The destitution in Dublin was, if possible, exceeded by that in the country, and Tocqueville earlier concluded: "If you wish to know what the spirit of conquest, religious hatred, combined with all the abuses of aristocracy without any of its advantages, can produce, come to Ireland."[12] William Kinsella had long wished that Catherine would open a House of Mercy in Kilkenny, but the only available house at the time was apparently one through whose main story a public passageway was cut, so she set his hope aside.[13]

But Catherine *was* thinking of opening another house, outside the sooty air of the city, where sick sisters could convalesce and, if possible, renew their health. Many advocated this, including Dr. Philip Crampton and Redmond O'Hanlon, the Carmelite confessor of the community. However, it was out of the question financially—until Mary de Chantal McCann, a novice and the widow of Dr. John McCann, intervened. Her only child, Kate, had suddenly died of whooping cough in the Loreto boarding school in Rathfarnham. No longer having a child's inheritance to worry about, Mary de Chantal turned her assets over to Catherine before her upcoming profession of vows, explicitly to purchase a small house by the sea. In March, after selling some of the McCann stock, Catherine purchased a house in Kingstown from Patrick Costelloe, a Dublin attorney, and John Burke, then residing in Paris. (Dun Leary had been renamed Kingstown after the departure from its harbor of King George IV in 1821, but since 1921 it is once again Dún Laoghaire.)[14] The house, which cost £700 plus

11. *Alexis de Tocqueville's Journey in Ireland, July–August 1835,* trans. and ed. by Emmet Larkin (Washington, D.C.: The Catholic University of America Press, 1990), 61, 78–79.

12. Ibid., 26.

13. Degnan, *Mercy,* 176–77, and Carroll, *Leaves from the Annals,* vol. 1 (1881), 166–67.

14. "Attested Copy of Memorial of the Deed of Assignment between Peter Costelloe and John Burke to Catherine McAuley, April 10, 1835" (MCA). Memorial no. 1835.6.261, RD.

related fees, was on present-day Sussex Street (then Sussex Place), a street to the northwest of Sussex Parade (now Marine Road), and running from present-day Eblana Avenue to Lower Georges Street.[15]

Kingstown seemed an ideal solution to the health needs of the Baggot Street community, where the past deaths from consumption would not be the last of its ravages. Initially Catherine did not intend that sisters living there would engage in any external works of mercy except visits to the sick. Kingstown was chiefly a resort town for wealthy Dubliners and English landlords, but it was not without its extreme, though largely hidden and unattended, poverty. The slums of the town clustered near York Road and present-day Convent Road. These areas were largely ignored and "remained unsanitary webs of cabins and third-rate dwellings" until the end of the nineteenth century.[16]

In the face of such destitution—which she saw on her visits to the sick—Catherine could not restrain herself. As she later wrote to her solicitor, Charles Cavanagh: "When we went to the convent in Kingstown, I expressed to Revd. Mr. Sheridan a particular desire to have a school for the poor girls whom we every day saw loitering about the roads in a most neglected state." To "encourage a beginning" she offered to give the proceeds of the next bazaar toward the cost of remodeling the unneeded coach house and stable into schoolrooms, though she "distinctly said . . . that [she] had no means to give towards the expence." Two weeks after the purchase of the Kingstown house, the annual Easter bazaar took place (April 22 and 23), and Catherine turned over the £50 proceeds, her promised contribution, to James Nugent, the builder in Kingstown whom Bartholomew Sheridan, parish priest of St. Michael's in Kingstown, had selected. She was happy with the arrangement, and Father Sheridan assured her he would "promote" the renovation and get "from the Board of education a grant nearly sufficient to pay for it."[17] However, the well-known financial shrewdness of Bartholomew Sheridan and Catherine's instinctive generosity toward loitering, neglected girls were, as she would later discover, a bad combination.

15. Ibid. The deed, dated March 4, 1835, and registered April 10, 1835, says the property contained "in front, to a Street then called Sussex Parade, Seventy four feet or thereabouts, and in depth from front to rear One Hundred and forty feet or thereabouts
. . . bounded on the North by the Garden Wall of . . . Anne Drake, on the East by the Stable Lane at the rear of Mallard View . . . on the west by a Plot of Ground in the possession of Lawlor, and on the South by the said Intended Street." Lim, in *CMcATM*, 178; CAM, in *CMcATM*, 210; Burke Savage, *McAuley*, 173–74; and Degnan, *Mercy*, 170, all say the house was on "Sussex Place."

16. Peter Pearson, *Dun Laoghaire: Kingstown* (Dublin: O'Brien Press, 1991), 59–61.

17. Letter 46, June 20, 1837, in *CCMcA*, 86.

The steam railway from Dublin to Kingstown had just opened to the public in December 1834, and Catherine appreciated the ease with which one could go to Kingstown from the terminus on Westland Row in Dublin. A third-class ticket cost six pence, and the trains made "the five and a half mile journey in fifteen minutes." Public opposition to the "noisy, dirty, modern contraption" at first dictated that the seaside station be in Salthill, just short of Kingstown, but by 1836 the line was extended to the bottom of Sussex Parade in Kingstown itself.[18]

The bazaar at the Rotunda, in aid of the House of Mercy, had the usual noble patronage, including once again that of their royal highnesses. The Countess of Howth, the philanthropist Mrs. Richard Verschoyle, Mrs. Cornelius Sullivan, wife of the Earl of Pembroke's agent in Dublin, and dozens of others lent their names to the effort. An advertisement, running fourteen days in *Freeman's Journal,* acknowledged:

The Sisters of Mercy who have charge of this Institution scarcely know how to describe what they feel for the kindness and liberality with which their troublesome applications are received. In returning thanks, they should like to say all that is expressive of the mostly lively and lasting gratitude.

Contributions of Fancy Work will be gratefully received at the House of Mercy, Baggot Street, or Sussex Place, Kingstown.[19]

The £50 proceeds of the bazaar were nowhere near the three hundred pounds of the previous year—when the Princess Victoria's fancy work was first contributed—even though the raffled items included "a most melodious Patent Accordion, a French Clock, a very handsome Gold Watch, and an uncommonly beautiful Reticule."[20] But Catherine immediately gave the money for the school for neglected girls in Kingstown, even though "we were six pounds in debt for things got at Nowlan's on the Bachelor's Walk" along the Liffey.[21]

On April 30, 1835, Catherine read to the community at Baggot Street, as was her custom, the short life of the saint whose feast was celebrated that day. Butler's treatment of Catherine of Siena in his *Lives of the Saints* is hagiography in the medieval sense, filled with the marvelous, the miraculous, the extraordinary. Catherine would have had to search hard, beneath the language she encountered, to discover ways to relate to the holiness of the woman after whom she was named, and whose name she added to the list of saints in the Presentation Rule to whom she wished the Sisters

18. Pearson, *Dun Laoghaire,* 46, 48.
20. Ibid.
19. *Freeman's Journal,* April 7, 1835.
21. Letter 46, June 20, 1837, in *CCMcA,* 86.

of Mercy to have "particular devotion."[22] What must have drawn Catherine of Dublin to companionship with the saint of Siena was probably not Catherine Benincasa's long Lenten fasts or her "visions," but her charity to the outcast—to leprous women, young men sentenced to execution, those afflicted with plague.[23] Catherine of Siena's words and actions foreshadowed Catherine's own desire to live in intimacy with the presence and providence of God, and to honor the sufferings of Christ in the poor, the sick, the afflicted whom she met on the streets of Dublin and Kingstown.

However, on this particular day in 1835 she responded to another, less profound matter. She had received a quatrain from the novices, who included her niece Catherine:

> Dear Reverend Mother, our cook & your namesake
> Wants to compose a most beautiful tea cake
> For materials of which 'twill be needful to pay
> And therefore for cash your petitioners pray.[24]

The playful ringleader, young Catherine, was at it again, wishing to concoct a feastday celebration for her aunt. Having already foreseen the flour, the sugar, and the time her niece would spend hoping the baking adventure would succeed, Catherine immediately responded, also in verse:

> Early this morning on leaving the choir
> I did anticipate this—your desire
> and sent out an order in time—to bespeak
> what I hope you will find—a very nice cake.[25]

The health of Mechtildis (Bridget) Gaffney, also a novice, was declining, and the financial worries of the house were mounting, but one shop-bought cake would not reduce their coffers too much, and would provide a joyous, if temporary, interlude for the whole community—it would also save time, and perhaps prevent a need to mop the kitchen floor.

Unbeknown to her an even greater joy was about to come to Baggot Street. On March 24, 1835, Cardinal Giacomo Filippo Fransoni, prefect of the Congregation for the Propagation of the Faith in Rome, had written a fairly long letter in Latin to Archbishop Murray, at Pope Gregory XVI's behest. Posted mail from the Vatican took weeks to arrive, the slowness

---

22. Rule 16.[5], in *CMcATM*, 311–12.
23. Alban Butler, *Lives of the . . . Saints*, vol. 4 (New York: D. & J. Sadlier, 1846), 187–92.
24. Letter 28 [April 30, 1835], in *CCMcA*, 68.
25. Letter 29 [April 30, 1835], in *CCMcA*, 68.

of delivery increased because such mail passed through England. As soon as the letter reached Dr. Murray on Monday, May 3, he immediately—according to Clare Moore—"brought" it to Catherine.[26] Mary Vincent Harnett says "he without delay informed her."[27] Whether he came to Baggot Street in person or not, May 3, 1835, represented a long-awaited milestone for both Catherine McAuley and Daniel Murray. The letter to Murray, with its ornate Vatican protocol and nomenclature, read in part:

> Your Grace will of yourself understand, without my having to express it in words, how highly the Sacred Congregation [for the Propagation of the Faith] and our Most Holy Lord [Gregory XVI] approve the resolution taken by the very pious lady, Catherine MacAuley, of establishing a society of ladies, called *of Mercy* from the works in which it is to be dedicated. For I need not tell you how deserving of praise that society must be which directs all its efforts and aims to the special end of helping the poor and relieving the sick in every way, and of safeguarding, by the exercise of charity, women who find themselves in circumstances dangerous to virtue. . . . From an Institute of this kind the greatest benefit will result both in civil society and to religion.
>
> The Sacred Congregation has, therefore, praised in the very highest terms the above-mentioned resolution of that very pious lady, and His Holiness, on his part, has not only approved the establishment of that Society, but has declared that it is truly worthy of his paternal benevolence and Apostolic Benediction.[28]

Catherine was far from thinking herself a "very pious lady," but this letter, approving the creation of the Sisters of Mercy as a religious congregation, was, in official language, the formal letter of praise *(litterae laudatoriae)* from the Holy See, giving the support of Rome that she had hoped to receive in some form since 1830.[29] She had not sought "praise," but simply

---

26. BA, in *CMcATM*, 113–14.   27. Lim, in *CMcATM*, 178.

28. Letter 26, March 24, 1835, in *CCMcA*, 66.

29. In 1950, the canon lawyer Joseph F. Gallen, S.J., expressed his view, supported by his extensive analysis, that the letter sent from Rome on March 24, 1835, was not technically, and could not have been, a *decretum laudis* (decree of praise). Rather it was a formal "letter of praise," endorsing and praising Catherine McAuley's resolution (intention) to create a "society of women, called of Mercy." The Latin passage in the letter from Rome (in English in the text) says: "Laudavit igitur Sac. Congregatio amplissimis verbis memoratum religiosissimae mulieris consilium: Sanctitas Sua autem non modo Societatis illius institutionem probavit, sed etiam paterna sua benevolentia atque apostolica benedictione illam dignam vere esse declaravit."

According to Gallen, the distinction between a *letter* of praise and a *decree* of praise is an important and necessary one. A letter "was given when the Institute was of recent origin, had relatively few houses, [and] was without suitable constitutions," as was the Sisters of Mercy in March 1835. "An attentive reading of the 1835 document leads me to believe that it was only a letter of praise." In the Vatican's 1925 declaration that "the Sisters of Mercy were pontifical the only document that is given as proof of the pontifical status is the 1841 document" decreeing the approval and confirmation of the Mercy Rule and Constitutions. Joseph F. Gallen to Mary Bertrand Degnan, April 21, 1950 (SMA).

Gallen's opinion disagrees with, and would seem to correct, the interpretations of Burke Savage, *McAuley,* 171, 263, 414–15, and Bolster, *Catherine McAuley* (1990), 55, namely, that the letter of March 24, 1835, was a *decree* of praise *(decretum laudis)*. However, the distinction may not have been so clearly formulated in the 1830s. Degnan, *Mercy,* 171, avoids calling the letter a decree.

approval; to receive it, expressed as it was in "the highest terms," was probably overwhelming to her, and severely humbling.

In the early morning that day Catherine had read in her *Journal of Meditations* how, one night after the death of Jesus, Peter and the other disciples had gone fishing—"both to relieve their poverty and want," and to avoid the kind of idleness in which they would feel their loneliness. "That night they took nothing." In the morning "Jesus stood on the shore, yet the Disciples knew not that it was Jesus ... at hand in our necessities." When they acknowledge that they have caught nothing, and have no food, he feeds them and "bestoweth his gifts."[30] In her hands Catherine now held the letter from Rome. She must have looked at the Latin words she could not easily read, and simply prayed, Thank you—a prayer Daniel Murray would surely have understood.

Fransoni's letter noted two further points. The pope thought it best that, given the external works of mercy in which they would be employed, the Sisters of Mercy should profess simple vows, not solemn vows as in cloistered religious orders. To Dr. Murray was left the responsibility "to prescribe for the Society of Mercy over and above those Rules and Constitutions" of the Presentation Order which they have "proposed to follow ... such observances as Your Grace will think ought to be decreed, considering the object of the Society."[31] Rome thus left in Archbishop Murray's hands initial approval of the Rule Catherine would eventually submit to Gregory XVI for final confirmation—a task in which Dr. Murray proved to be both judicious and respectful of Catherine's insights.

Catherine had been working on a draft of the Rule since 1833, writing it in her own hand when she had time. Early biographical manuscripts say Myles Gaffney, a priest at St. Andrew's, helped her compose the Rule, but exactly how, in which sections of the text, is not known.[32] Initial versions of the new chapters "Visitation of the Sick" and "Admission of Distressed Women" had seemed ready enough to send to Father John Rice in Rome on December 8, 1833.[33] It was probably during composition of these chapters that Gaffney was most helpful. In 1834 he was named senior dean at St. Patrick's College, Maynooth. Though he remained a good friend, his assistance after that appointment would have been limited.

Basically, Catherine used the Rule and Constitutions of the Presenta-

30. [Challoner, ed.], *Journal of Meditations* (1823), 197–98.
31. Letter 26, March 24, 1835, in *CCMcA*, 66–67.
32. BA, Lim, and CAM, in *CMcATM*, 112, 175, and 208.
33. Letter 19, December 8, 1833, in *CCMcA*, 54–56, and 56 n. 21.

tion Sisters as her guide, often copying it verbatim, but more frequently altering it by adding her own wording or deleting some of its wording and sentences.[34] Her most significant additions were the two chapters "Visitation of the Sick" and "Admission of Distressed Women," the latter devoted to the House of Mercy. She also added an important paragraph to her altered version of the Presentation chapter "Of the Schools." This paragraph reveals her longstanding conviction about the fundamental need and role of women in society:

The Sisters shall feel convinced that no work of charity can be more productive of good to society, or more conducive to the happiness of the poor than the careful instruction of women, since whatever be the station they are destined to fill, their example and advice will always possess influence, and where ever a religious woman presides, peace and good order are generally to be found.[35]

By "religious woman" she did not mean a "woman religious," that is, a nun, but any woman strengthened by personal grasp of God's relation to her life and to this world.

Catherine cannot be called a "feminist" in a present-day sense, but neither was she insensitive to gender biases or androcentric language. In the Rule she frequently deleted Presentation wording that was prejudicial to women. For example, she removed "especially in the female sex" after a reference to "childish humors" that ought to be overcome in the novitiate, and she deliberately did not copy the words "they carry this most valuable treasure in brittle vessels" in her chapter on the vow of chastity.[36] In the same chapter she explicitly omitted the entire second paragraph in the Presentation Rule, which, among other things, counseled the sisters: "When spoken to by men of any state or profession they shall observe and maintain the most guarded reserve, never fix their eyes on them, nor shew themselves, in conversation or otherwise, in the least degree familiar with them, how devout or religious soever they may appear to be."[37] Catherine had been looking men in the eye all her adult life, and she would not write for others a rule she would not herself observe.

Just as the chapters on the education of poor girls and on the sheltering and employment training of homeless servant women were an implicit criticism of the prevailing social system and of sexist householders within

---

34. Catherine's composition of the Rule of the Sisters of Mercy is analyzed in detail in Sullivan, *Catherine McAuley and the Tradition of Mercy,* 258–328.

35. Rule 2.5, in *CMcATM,* 297.

36. Rule, part 2, 6.3, in *CMcATM,* 324; rule 18.1, in *CMcATM,* 313.

37. *CMcATM,* 313 n. 54.

it, her choice of wording elsewhere in the Rule was a conscious though indirect affirmation of women and of their mature capacities. In the chapter "Employment of Time" she would not treat her sisters as children, and deliberately deleted the Presentation injunction: "They shall never be found running giddily thro' the Convent." She wished her companions to be "equally free from restraint and levity," and, given the work they were about, to preserve "recollection of mind," but she would not demean them by words about giddiness.[38]

Catherine copied almost verbatim the Presentation chapter "Union and Charity"—the chapter on mutual love and affection she had long treasured—but she completely omitted, as might have been expected, its final paragraph on the titles to be used in the community in addressing the superior, her assistant, the mistress of novices, and the bursar, both during and after their time in office. Catherine did not see a value in such formality, and she would not require it.[39] However, in this regard she had no control over "improvements" in customs that happened after her death.

She evidently gave her full draft of the Mercy Rule to Daniel Murray some time before May 3, 1835, for on that day he told her "he had carefully collated the copy of the Holy Rule she had sent him, with that of the Presentation Order, that he had changed some points, and that as soon as it was again copied, such as he now gave it to her, he would affix his sanction to it." To Clare Moore fell the task of making the fair copy, under Catherine's guidance, and on it Archbishop Murray wrote "the form of approbation with his signature, dating it from the time that the Institute received the approbation of the Holy See, the third of May 1835."[40]

Daniel Murray was a thoughtful, and restrained, editor of Catherine's manuscript. He inserted only what he thought would be needed to get the Rule approved in Rome—for example, the full Presentation explanation of the role of the "Diocesan Bishop" as ecclesiastical superior of the congregation, a chapter Catherine had condensed to one paragraph covering its essentials.[41] He also made a few wording revisions, some of which seem unnecessary. He obviously had the approved Presentation Rule at his el-

38. Rule 6.2, in *CMcATM*, 302, and 302 nn. 22 and 23.
39. Rule 8, in *CMcATM*, 303-4, and 304 n. 26.
40. BA, in *CMcATM*, 114. On the draft of the Rule in Catherine McAuley's handwriting, on which Dr. Murray made his penciled revisions, he did not sign his name or impress his wax seal. It was from this draft, with his emendations, that Clare Moore made the fair copies for each new foundation. On some of these fair copies Dr. Murray retroactively dated his signature "May 3, 1835," the day the letter of praise came from Rome. However, on at least one fair copy his signature and seal are dated "January 23, 1837" (MCA).
41. Rule, part 2, 1.1-1.6, in *CMcATM*, 317-18.

bow as he read Catherine's document, but his penciled revisions were few in number. He suggested that she divide the first chapter, "Of the Schools," into two, using its first two paragraphs as a short, but important chapter, "Of the Object of the Institute."[42] He deleted, as unnecessary, her modified chapter on enclosure, and her second paragraph on deportment in the chapter "Employment of Time."[43] Most significantly, he did not restore any of the Presentation passages or wording she had consciously omitted, except those on the bishop's role which Roman officials would expect to see. There would be in the Mercy Rule no instruction on not looking directly at men or on religious titles or on the "commands" and "reprimands" of superiors. As one follows Dr. Murray's penciled annotations through the manuscript, one is struck by his evident respect for Catherine's judgment and his general unwillingness to second guess her language or her opinions. Only once, when she used "tender concern and regard" and "affection" to describe the attitude of humility, did he delete her words, and substitute his own, citing St. Paul (Rom 12:10).[44]

Preparing a new draft of the Rule was not all that occupied Catherine's energy in 1835. By May 24, Myles Gaffney's sister, Mary Mechtildis Gaffney, was dying. She professed her vows on her deathbed, and died three weeks later. Once again the pall of loss fell over the community, and a fifth Sister of Mercy was buried in the underground Carmelite vaults on Clarendon Street. As one of Catherine's associates understood:

The greatest trial of all to her were the frequent deaths of the Sisters. While she preserved her health she had a great awe or even fear of death, and she never saw the approach of a Sister's death or spoke of one who had died without great emotion. She had a really tender affection for us.[45]

Meanwhile, scores of poor girls were trooping into the schoolrooms on Baggot Street each day, receiving clothing and food, especially bread, in addition to instruction in reading, writing, arithmetic, and plain needlework, as well as preparation for the sacraments of Confirmation and Holy Communion and guidance in how to pray at Mass. A government-sponsored system of national primary education for all children, including those in Ireland, and regardless of religious background, had been set up in 1831. It was endorsed by Protestants, some hoping it would lead to

---

42. Rule 1.1, 2, in *CMcATM*, 295.
43. [Former chapter 19], in *CMcATM*, 314–15; Rule 6.2, in *CMcATM*, 302.
44. Rule 9.2, in *CMcATM*, 305.
45. CAM, in *CMcATM*, 209.

a "second Reformation"—when Catholics recovered through education from their "popish" and "superstitious" allegiance to their denomination. Most Catholics, including many bishops, saw the system's professed non-denominationalism as a help to poor Irish children and a welcome alternative to proselytizing schools like those of the Kildare Place Society, which the government had previously supported by grants.

To the seven-member Board of Commissioners of National Education who were to oversee the system were appointed two Catholics: Archbishop Murray and a layman, Anthony R. Blake.[46] Murray's attitude toward the system was pragmatic and realistic: "He and others before him had struggled to get for the poor an acceptable, non-proselytizing system of education and, although the National Schools did not meet all their wishes, they went far in that direction and were the best that could be obtained from a state that was officially Protestant."[47] Catholic parishes in Dublin and throughout the country were simply too poor to finance a separate and adequate education for their children. As Patrick Corish comments: "This system was to be non-sectarian, with respect to the religious faith of each child. All were to receive secular education together, and time was set aside for separate religious education." A Catholic parish priest or a Catholic religious congregation could apply for designation as a "national school" and become its "patron" or manager. "Ironically perhaps, the new state system restored to the Catholic church a great deal of control over the primary school system which it had been in danger of losing over the previous fifty years," through its own financial poverty and a decline in adequately trained and voluntary Catholic schoolmasters, especially in rural areas.[48] However, not all Irish bishops approved the system. Notably Archbishop John MacHale of Tuam fulminated against it. This opposition within the hierarchy would fester for years, settled only temporarily in 1841 by a decision from Rome leaving each Irish bishop free to decide for his own diocese.

Siding with Daniel Murray and relying on his oversight as a commissioner, Catherine welcomed the national system, seeing it as a way to get financial help for the education of poor Catholic children. She also felt "the children improve so much more expecting the [external] examination."[49] On July 13, 1834, she had applied for recognition of Baggot Street

---

46. *Catholic Directory* (1837), 223–24, and Kerr, "Daniel Murray," in Kelly and Keogh, *History of the Catholic Diocese of Dublin*, 251.

47. Kerr, "Daniel Murray," 255–56.   48. Corish, *The Irish Catholic Experience*, 165.

49. Letter 124 [May–August 1839], in *CCMcA*, 199.

school as a national school. Her application was evidently tabled until 1839.[50] However, on March 30, 1835, Thomas Osler, assistant commissioner, after a personal inspection of the Mercy school, reported to the Royal Commission on the State of Charitable Education in Dublin: "It would have been difficult to have commended too highly the admirable Convent Schools at Harold's Cross [Poor Clares], in Upper Gardiner Street [Sisters of Charity] and in Baggot Street." Although the exact number of poor girls in the Baggot Street school is variously cited in other early accounts, Osler reported two hundred on the "Rolls" and two hundred "in Daily Attendance," of whom the number of Protestants was "Uncertain," and the number "paying one penny per week" was left blank. He computed the convent's annual expenditure on the school to be £70, and the "annual cost of each girl" to be seven shillings, and noted: "This is the cost of rent and school requisites only: instruction being gratuitous, and food and clothing, which is extensively given, not being computed."[51]

It was all well and good for Catherine to later tell a sister: "Prayer will do more . . . than all the money in the Bank of Ireland."[52] But now there were bread and milk for the children and dried turf to pay for, and the £60 annual rent owed to the Earl of Pembroke was too often in arrears. Years later, when Cecilia Marmion was superior at Baggot Street, she wrote directly to the Honorable Sidney Herbert, asking for a reduction in the rent and forgiveness of some of the arrears. Lord Herbert replied personally: he reduced the annual rent by £10 and decreased the arrears to £55.7.8, one half of what was owed.[53] But all this was in the future. Now, on December 2, 1835, as winter was beginning, Catherine had no ready money. She sent a note down the street to Charles Cavanagh's office on Lower Fitzwilliam Street:

We begin to feel the want of interest due on the Bond—have we any chance of getting it soon. We have so often cautioned all those who supply us—not to give any credit on our account—I doubt would they now, if we were to ask them.[54]

On the same day she made the following notation on a half sheet of paper: "Mr. Cavanagh has lent me twenty pounds this day."[55]

50. Department of Education to Sister M. Imelda Collins, November 8, 1956 (MCA), and Honor M. Tighe (law searcher) to Mary Dominick Foster, January 17, 1957 (MCA). Eventual affiliation of the school with the Board is discussed in chapter 17.

51. Extract from the "Report of the Royal Commission on the State of Charitable Education in the City of Dublin," in Bolster Papers (MCA). See also http://www.eppi.ac.uk, for "Appendix to the First Report from the Commissioners," nos. 9 and 10, accessed on September 19, 2008.

52. Letter 280, July 20, 1841, in CCMcA, 415.

53. Sidney Herbert to Mary Cecilia Marmion, December 13, 1845 (MCA).

54. Letter 32, December 2, 1835, in CCMcA, 70.

55. Letter 33, December 2, 1835, in CCMcA, 71.

CHAPTER 12

The Traveling Begins *1836*

Catherine McAuley had never—except maybe once in 1827, en route to Galway—journeyed by canal boat. It was seven o'clock in the morning on Thursday, April 21, 1836. They had made it to Portobello in southwestern Dublin, with as much luggage as the six of them were allotted and could manage to bring from Baggot Street. Catherine, Mary Ann Doyle, Clare Moore, the novices Teresa Purcell and Anne Agnes (Catherine) Macauley, and Redmond O'Hanlon stood on the dock, waiting to go aboard. Were the boats still drawn by a single horse on a towpath beside the Grand Canal, the women might have been less nervous. The new lightweight fly-boats, drawn more swiftly by two or three horses, were more intimidating, and it would still take eight hours to reach Tullamore, sixty miles to the west in County Offaly. But this was a momentous day. They were setting out to found the first autonomous convent of Sisters of Mercy outside of Dublin, at the request of James O'Rafferty, parish priest of Tullamore.

Tullamore's poverty had been the deciding factor. When O'Rafferty's request was turned down by the Sisters of Charity, Mary Aikenhead realizing the "small means in hands to commence," the priest went to Baggot Street. Catherine "made no hesitation, and when the poverty of the new house was made known to her, it was an additional motive for her to embrace it the more willingly." Apparently, she wished to honor "the poverty of Bethlehem" in their first foundation beyond Dublin.[1]

The house on Store Street near the canal, bequeathed to O'Rafferty in

1. TA, in *CMcATM*, 65.

1835 by the deceased Elizabeth Pentony, was small, the rooms so tiny that, as Catherine joked, "two cats could scarcely dance in them."[2] The curate, Walter Murtagh, later gave them a cow which Catherine dubbed "Madame La Vache," the "first live-stock of the Order." The convent not possessing "even a blade of grass at the time," the famous cow was "sent to the country to graze."[3]

Catherine chose Mary Ann Doyle as the superior of the Tullamore community. To part with her first helper, her trusted assistant at Baggot Street for nine years and the only one now living who had shared the George's Hill experience with her, was not easy. But in Tullamore Catherine began the habit that would characterize her appointments during the rest of her life: the gradual sacrifice, for the sake of the mission of new foundations, of women, one after the other, who were her greatest help and support at Baggot Street. Indeed, this happened to such an extent that, by 1841, she could speak of "our dear old habitation, where I shall never again see all my dearly beloved Sisters—all strange faces."[4]

She remained in Tullamore for over a month, helping Mary Ann Doyle and Teresa Purcell to inaugurate the works of mercy: visiting the sick, teaching poor children—though hoping someday to have a new school to replace the one in the "wretched little garret in Thomas Street"—and instructing adults who came to the door.[5] They welcomed young women who had been waiting to join the community: Elizabeth Locke, the daughter of a man who ran a large distillery nearby (April 30); Mary Delamere (May 12); and Mary Gilligan (May 20). On May 26, Dr. John Cantwell, bishop of Meath, came from Mullingar to welcome the community and to confirm Mary Ann Doyle as its superior.

As became her custom in all foundations, Catherine and the others prayed each day the Thirty Days' Prayer to Mary, the mother of Jesus, asking God to guide their small community and the works of mercy for which they had come to Tullamore. She spent considerable time with Teresa Purcell, giving her final instructions in religious life before her profession of vows. Thinking that a public ceremony of religious profession or reception of the habit was a good way to convey the nature and intentions of the Sisters of Mercy, Catherine scheduled Teresa's profession for 10:00 A.M., Friday, May 27, and invited townsfolk to attend the event. The parish chapel overflowed with the grateful and the curious.

2. Ibid., 66.   3. Ibid., 67–68.
4. Letter 235, February 3, 1841, in *CCMcA*, 358.   5. TA, in *CMcATM*, 67.

After the ceremony Catherine wrote a long poem back to Baggot Street, addressed to Ursula Frayne, then a novice. She described the ceremony, the first of its kind ever to occur in Tullamore. With amused joy she noted the crowd squeezed into the church:

> About thirty priests, and ladies by dozens
> Some of who[m] had got cards of admission
> But their Nieces, their Aunts, and their Cousins
> Came with them without our permission.

She recounted Walter Murtagh's sermon, on Jesus' relations with Martha and Mary, and his words to Teresa:

> The sick and the poor were His constant care
> You are trying His footsteps to trace
> And He will invisibly oft meet you there
> Till you see Him at length face to face.

Refreshments were served after the ceremony, and Catherine admired the hospitality of Bishop Cantwell:

> [He] graciously hearkened to every call
> To carve and to help condescended
> Extending the kindest attention to all
> With grace and with dignity blended.

Then recognizing her occasionally flawed metre and rhymes, she concluded the poem, urging Ursula:

> Read this first alone, in an audible tone,
> Till you gloss over every mistake
> What you can't read you'll spell
> Till you know it quite well
> Do this for your poor Mother's sake.[6]

Tired but exhilarated by the whole adventure, the "poor Mother" returned to Baggot Street on Monday, May 30, bringing her young niece and Clare Moore back with her, Father O'Hanlon having returned earlier. They reached Dublin about four-thirty in the afternoon, Catherine still dwelling on all the Tullamore faces: the poor women in thatched cabins, the cottiers and tillage farmers barely eking out enough potatoes and wheat

---

6. Letter 35 [c. May 27, 1836], in *CCMcA*, 71–74.

for their families, the laborers from the distilleries and limestone quarry, the barefoot children eager to learn, the postulants who came forward, the people intrigued by the black habits and veils they had never seen before. She was eager to return to Tullamore, and even to begin a new community somewhere else. As she later declared: "Nothing like Foundations for rousing us all."[7]

At Baggot Street, Catherine missed, once again, the musically talented Mary Agnes (Frances) Marmion, the first and youngest of the three Marmions to enter the community. She had died of "erysipelas on the brain" in February, two months before they set out for Tullamore.[8] But soon new faces appeared, women who had heard of the Dublin community by word of mouth, often from priests, bishops, or relatives. Teresa (Amelia) White's sister Jane entered from Wexford on June 7; Mary Maher, from Castletown, County Kilkenny, on July 10; and Margaret Thorpe, a Dublin woman, on July 23. By August 1836 thirty-four women were in the Dublin community, including eighteen novices and five postulants, most of them living at Baggot Street though a few were in the branch house in Kingstown where Angela Dunne had replaced Mary Ann Doyle as local superior.[9]

To oversee the House of Mercy, the school, and the visitations to the sick and dying; to think about requests for other foundations beyond Dublin; and to continue to instruct the postulants and novices—all this had become more than Catherine could handle alone, even with rising at five-thirty. Frances Warde and Clare Moore each took on one or the other of the many practical household tasks, but the novices and postulants needed more attention. Catherine regretted giving up the crucial work of directing them, as she had for four years, but in fairness to them she needed to select someone who could guide them full time. So in 1835 she asked Mary de Pazzi Delany to be mistress of novices, hoping she would not be too severe, though given the ease of Catherine's own administrative style, the new sisters were never out of her attention or solicitude. They knew that.

Sometime in late June or July, Catherine wrote to Tullamore, addressing her letter to Mary Delamere, a postulant, but knowing full well that

7. Letter 227 [January 12, 1841], in CCMcA, 344.

8. CML, in CMcATM, 87. In Harnett's *Life*, Mary Agnes Marmion is said to have had erysipelas of the "heart" (118). The disease, caused by a streptococcal infection of the skin and subcutaneous tissues, "usually appears on the face." Ann G. Carmichael, "Erysipelas," in Kiple, *Cambridge World History of Human Disease*, 720–21.

9. "Baggot Street Register of Professed Sisters," supplemented by the list of postulants and novices there who eventually professed vows elsewhere (MCA).

Mary Ann Doyle and the others would read it. She planned to attend their reception ceremony on August 1, and her straight-faced letter, labeled "a preparatory meditation," is so filled with unrestrained humor and nonsense that only those who knew Catherine's playful spirit could have understood it properly. Bishop Cantwell and certainly Father Walter Meyler at St. Andrew's in Dublin would have been puzzled.

Catherine tells Mary that she is "determined not to behave well" in Tullamore, and "you must join me." Mary must "contrive to put the clock out of order," so they will have "till ten o'clock every night not a moment's silence—until we are asleep—not to be disturbed until we awake." Away with the grand night silence and calling bells! Moreover, they will "lock" the "Divine Mother" (Mary Ann Doyle) and Clare Moore (Catherine's traveling companion) in the chapel earlier in the night and keep them there "until after breakfast." If Mary Ann "should complain to the bishop—remember you and I are safe. We are not of his flock, most fortunately"—Mary Delamere apparently coming from the diocese of Kildare and Leighlin, and Catherine herself from Dublin. "We will set up for a week what is called a nonsensical Club. I will be president, you vice-president, and Catherine [probably her niece, who may also come] can give lectures as professor of folly." They will sing "The Lady of Flesh and Bone," with its melodramatic, gruesome refrain: "The worms crawl'd in, the worms crawl'd out." Woven into Catherine's description of their forthcoming escapades is her half-teasing, half-serious claim that these pranks "will shew superiors and their assistants [for instance, Teresa Purcell] that it is necessary sometimes to yield to the inclinations of others, and convince them that authority, however good, cannot always last."[10] No wonder Catherine's sisters loved her. Surely no twentieth-century Mercy postulant ever got such a letter from "Reverend Mother."

Documentary sources do not recount—perhaps wisely?—what actually happened in Tullamore during the four days Catherine was there, except that the ceremony on August 1 was "beautiful," with "solemnity and splendour." Myles Gaffney, now at Maynooth, preached, and the townspeople were proud and "delighted."[11] The new novices, Elizabeth Locke and Mary Delamere, took the religious names Mary Catherine and Mary Clare. Clare Delamere would go to Kells in 1844 and become superior there in 1847. Catherine Locke would one day found a community in Derry (1848),

10. Letter 36 [June–July 1836], in *CCMcA*, 75–76.
11. TA, in *CMcATM*, 68.

and then one in Dundee, Scotland (1859). However, the mischievous idea of creating a Nonsensical Club remained appealing to Catherine McAuley, popping up again in a poem-letter in 1840.[12]

Back at Baggot Street, correspondence and other work were piling up. Three novices were ready for their profession of vows since June, but Archbishop Murray was in Europe with his priest-secretary John Hamilton, en route to Rome for his *ad limina* visit.[13] As vicar general, Walter Meyler was handling affairs in the diocese and felt he could be asked to preside at the ceremony. But Catherine hesitated to invite him. In an otherwise cheerful letter to John Hamilton in Paris in mid-July, Meyler commented on her, while recounting his visits to other communities in Dublin:

I have been to Warren Mount [Carmelites] yesterday for the second time, and once at Rathfarnham [Loreto Sisters]—house at Stanhope St. [Sisters of Charity]—I am told that Mrs. McAuley is keeping 36 *in reserve* for His Grace—only I have just come from the [priests'] retreat, I would say, May she be disappointed.[14]

The "36 in reserve" was clearly a deliberate exaggeration. Relations with Father Meyler were obviously not improving.

Sometime before September, Gerald Doyle, parish priest of Naas, southwest of Dublin, inquired about the requisite characteristics Catherine looked for in prospective Sisters of Mercy. On September 5, she responded:

Besides an ardent desire to be united to God and serve the poor, she must feel a particular interest for the sick and dying; otherwise the duty of visiting them would soon become exceedingly toilsome. She should be healthy—have a feeling, distinct, impressive manner of speaking and reading—a mild countenance expressive of sympathy and patience. And there is so much to be acquired as to reserve and recollection passing through the public ways—caution and prudence in the visits—that it is desirable they should begin rather young, before habits and manners are so long formed as not to be likely to alter.

I beg again to remark that this is what seems generally necessary. I am aware exceptions may be met, and that where there is a decided preference for the order, and other essential dispositions, conformity in practice might be accomplished at any period of life.[15]

Presumably Catherine was thinking of Angela Dunne, Genevieve Jarmy, and herself—none of them exactly "young" in age.

---

12. Letter 174 [c. June 7, 1840], in *CCMcA*, 271–72.

13. A bishop was then, and is still, required periodically to submit a written report on his diocese and make a personal visit to the pope. On March 14, 1835, Dr. Murray was granted a one-year deferment of this journey to Rome. Murray Papers, File 31/4, no. 157 (DDA).

14. Walter Meyler to John Hamilton, July 19, 1836. Hamilton Papers, File 35/6, no. 68 (DDA).

15. Letter 38, September 15, 1836, in *CCMcA*, 77–78.

But a date for the profession ceremony still had to be set. Daniel Murray and John Hamilton returned to Dublin by early October. Hamilton had proved to be an understanding friend, even when he could do little to help, so Catherine wrote to him about her "very perplexing state":

Two Sisters whose noviciate ended in June have been most anxiously awaiting the return of his Grace—who has referred me to the Vicar General. Were it only a Reception, we would not make any remonstrance, though a painful disappointment. But for a Profession, it is extremely difficult to manage. One of the Sisters, a sensible person, thirty-three years old, "fears she will not feel happy, as she confided much in the efficacy of the prayers to be said by the Bishop—and cannot think they could be supplied by a representative."

I was once before in a difficulty of this nature and you, Revd. Sir, forwarded an application to his Grace . . . which he most . . . graciously answered.[16]

John Hamilton intervened, and Dr. Murray set the date for October 22. Mary Cecilia Marmion, Martha (Susan) Walplate, and young Catherine Macauley professed their religious vows that morning, receiving the black veil and silver ring from the man whose accommodating gesture may have been related to his memory of Edward Armstrong. As Catherine heard her "dear Catherine," now seventeen, profess her vows as a Sister of Mercy, she must have been deeply happy.

One week later a founding party headed south to Charleville, in northwest County Cork, south of Limerick. After the pleading of Mary Clanchy, the daughter of a wealthy and socially conscientious family, and Thomas Croke, the parish priest, seconded by Bartholomew Crotty, bishop of Cloyne and Ross, Catherine had agreed to found, sight unseen, a Mercy convent in Charleville (Rath Luirc), a town so poor that many families had "no furniture other than an iron cooking pot."[17] The founding community would be Angela Dunne and two novices, Mary Joseph (Alicia) Delaney and Mary Agnes (Elizabeth) Hynes. Catherine and Clare Moore would accompany them on the long journey, by canal boat, river boat, and coaches.

October 26 or 27, 1836, was the day set for departure.[18] The flurry of preparations centered not so much on packing clothes as on copying the

16. Letter 39, October 14, 1836, in CCMcA, 78.
17. "Early Notes" (Archives, Sisters of Mercy, Charleville, Ireland).
18. In CML, in CMcATM, 87, Clare Moore says: "We set out on the 27th of October, or 26th," but in the biography she says they set out "on the 29th of October" (BA, in CMcATM, 119). She later indicates that the founding party arrived in Charleville on October 31. Possibly they were in Tullamore a full day, October 30, if they left Dublin on the 29th. The whole journey took the better part of three days. Notes in the Charleville Archives indicate *both* that they arrived in Charleville on October 29 and set out from Dublin on that date. The "Baggot Street Register" says Angela Dunne left for Charleville on October 26. Despite these discrepancies, October 29 is regarded as the founding date of the Charleville community.

handwritten Rule, meditations for retreats, prayers for the community and the sick and dying, and passages from spiritual books the new foundation would need to support its life and mission. All hands were pressed into service. Charleville would be far away from Baggot Street, over one hundred forty miles distant. Travel there at the usual rate of six miles per hour, by land and waterway, would take at least twenty-three hours.

Like Tullamore, Charleville would be an independent community, subject only to the bishop of the diocese, not to Catherine McAuley or any subsequent superior at Baggot Street. With practical wisdom Catherine foresaw the difficulty for future superiors of new foundations beyond Dublin if they had to follow guidance from two directions, their own diocesan bishop and Baggot Street. She therefore chose not to centralize the governance of the expanding Sisters of Mercy in a single, possibly remote, bishop or in herself or any of her Dublin successors. It was a generous and trustful decision. Her own continuing contribution would be affection, often-expressed solicitude and prayer, frequent letters, and visits when possible, though these would necessarily be rare. Over 87 percent of her letters after March 1835 were written to or about the sisters in the foundations and branch houses outside of Dublin or, when she was visiting them, to those back at Baggot Street. The surviving letters probably represent only one-third of the total number she must have written to or about the foundations. None of those she undoubtedly wrote to Clare Moore has survived, and only a fraction of those to other founding sisters, for instance to Mary Ann Doyle, Angela Dunne, Elizabeth Moore, and Teresa White, is extant.[19]

The journey to Charleville was "amusing," according to Clare Moore's tongue-in-cheek comment. They went by fly-boat on the Grand Canal to Tullamore where they rested briefly, presumably on the floor in the crowded house. Father Croke met them there, and together at 3:00 A.M. they caught the packet boat on the canal extension to Shannon harbor. Writing in the third person, Clare says:

When they reached Tullamore they found that the boat [to the Shannon waterways] would not arrive until the middle of the night, and that it was a very slow and inconvenient mode of traveling; however [Catherine] was not discouraged, and although she suffered very much from cold and fatigue all that night and the following day (for they did not get to Limerick until nine o'clock in the evening), her patience and

19. Over seventy-five of Catherine McAuley's letters to Frances Warde are extant, though more were probably written.

cheerfulness never failed. The next morning they went on to Charleville [by coach] and arrived there about five o'clock on the Eve of All Saints [October 31].[20]

The convent Mary Clanchy had promised was the center house in a three-dwelling building on what is now Clanchy Terrace. It was "very far from being as convenient as it had been represented ... and, on account of a little stream running close by, extremely damp, so that their clothes were quite wet each morning when they got up." Moreover, Charleville was "a poor small town," with "very little chance of postulants joining them."[21]

Catherine was uneasy. Should they go back to Dublin? Would the community of three ever survive in such a place? Should she risk leaving them there? The town was the severest test yet of her belief that the "truest poverty consists in seeing that our wants are scantily supplied and rejoicing in the scarcity."[22] Charleville was certainly not Coolock, nor even Tullamore. Thomas Croke and Mary Clanchy stressed again the needs of their people, but one poor woman's exclamation, touching Catherine deeply, settled the question: "Ah! it was the Lord drove you in amongst us!"[23]

Though he lived in Cobh (Cove) on the southern coast, well over forty-five miles away even on modern highways, Bartholomew Crotty, the sixty-seven-year-old bishop of Cloyne and Ross, came to welcome them. Recalling his graciousness years later, in contrast to another bishop's aloofness, Catherine remarked: "Poor old Dr. Crotty came to Charleville from Cove—and when I regretted his taking so much trouble, he said, when we did not decline traveling from Dublin to his charge, he could not avoid coming to meet us."[24]

Catherine and Clare returned to Dublin on November 29, worrying about the three they had left behind. Angela Dunne was forty-eight, a wise and generous woman, but could she handle the poverty and the dampness? Would Father Croke help? His hands were already full assisting the widow of his brother to raise their eight children, the eldest just fifteen, the youngest only four. His nieces Margaret and Isabella would one day become Sisters of Mercy, Margaret taking a foundation to Bathurst, Australia, in 1866, and Isabella nursing wounded soldiers in the Crimean War (1854–1856).[25]

The journey back to Baggot Street was as fatiguing as their coming out.

20. BA, in *CMcATM*, 120. See note 18 above.   21. Ibid.
22. *PS*, 6.   23. BA, in *CMcATM*, 120.
24. Letter 230, January 20, 1841, in *CCMcA*, 351.
25. Notes on "The Croke Family" (Archives, Sisters of Mercy, Charleville, Ireland).

Catherine and Clare rose at "two o'clock in the morning to be ready for the stage coach which left Charleville at three." Reaching an inn in Limerick at ten, they declined breakfast, so they could go to Mass and Communion in a chapel some distance away; it was snowing hard, but they walked. From Limerick they traveled the rest of the way by mail coach, avoiding the water route, finally reaching Baggot Street the next morning. John Murphy, bishop of Cork, was there. After celebrating Mass, he pressed Catherine, once again, about opening a convent in Cork. His timing could not have been less opportune, but he was a persistent bishop, and she once more promised a foundation, though "nothing definite was settled."[26] Cork, on the southern coast, was farther from Dublin than Charleville, and wagon wheels were still rumbling in her head.

In early December bad news came from Tullamore. An "epidemic of fever of the worst type" had erupted in the town, and Walter Murtagh, the curate they all loved, was stricken.[27] In reading references to "fever" in Catherine's correspondence and in Mercy annals written in the early nineteenth century, one has to deal with a clinical problem that bedeviled Irish medical practitioners. William R. Wilde, Oscar Wilde's father and "Ireland's leading nineteenth-century medical historian," writing in 1856, "characterized fever as 'the great element of destruction in Ireland.'" He claimed that "the disease had lurked in holes and corners of the island for centuries, and was liable to erupt at any time upon the slightest provocation."[28]

Until William Gerhard distinguished typhus from typhoid fever (1837); William Jenner differentiated louse-borne relapsing fever from both typhus and typhoid (1849); and Pasteur and Koch made their discoveries, confusion about "fever" reigned in Ireland, as elsewhere in the medical world.[29] In Catherine's day these three separate diseases, with their different causes, often went by the same name, "fever." Some symptoms were similar—the fever, rash, fatigue, headache, and body pains. Catherine's references and those in early annals are to be understood keeping that medical climate in mind.

Though Father Murtagh subsequently recovered, the fever in Tullamore was, according to the Annals, a "frightful" epidemic. After the 1817–1819 epidemic, which cost thousands of lives, the government had slowly

26. BA, in *CMcATM*, 120. 27. TA, in *CMcATM*, 70.

28. Cited in Laurence M. Geary, *Medicine and Charity in Ireland, 1718–1851* (Dublin: University College Dublin Press, 2004), 71.

29. Anne Hardy, "Relapsing Fever," and Charles W. LeBaron and David W. Taylor, "Typhoid Fever," in Kiple, *Cambridge World History of Human Disease*, 968 and 1075.

begun to build a system of county fever hospitals, but there was none in Tullamore in 1836 so "the epidemic raged uncontrolled." A severe winter increased the miseries of the poor who "suffered intensely from cold, hunger and disease."[30] The sisters visited them daily, but none were stricken this time.

Another serious illness was on Catherine's mind: Mary Rose Lubé, a novice at Baggot Street, showed "strong symptoms of rapid consumption." Robert Graves (1796–1853), one of the most distinguished physicians in Dublin and an internationally famous proponent of bedside clinical teaching, was attending her. In 1835 he had identified the female disease of exophthalmic goiter, with its protruding eyeballs, the ailment now widely known as Graves's disease.[31] A member of the Royal College of Physicians in Ireland in whose hall on Kildare Street his statue still stands, he also revolutionized the treatment of fever, strongly recommending adequate nutrition.

Dr. Graves's care of Mary Rose's consumption impressed Catherine: "His treatment has been quite different from what we have seen on similar melancholy occasions." Was she thinking of Elizabeth Harley and Mary Teresa Macauley? "So far it has been wonderfully successful, and we have great hope. . . . She is now so much affected by mercury that a decided opinion cannot be given for some days."[32] Evidently Graves had prescribed, as a diuretic or purgative, a small dose of a compound of liquid mercury, a common treatment of various symptoms until later in the century, when the known danger of mercury poisoning from overdose gradually decreased its use.

Catherine concluded her letter to Teresa listing others who were ill at Baggot Street. Noting that Archbishop Murray had visited the Tullamore community, she again teased Mary Ann Doyle with a hyperbolic title: "It was a comfort to her Reverence, I am sure," and then sent her affection "to the Sisters all, including their good Mother."[33]

The year ended peacefully. Perhaps it was the lull before the storm. Catherine was probably glad to be home, in her own bed after two and a half months in unfamiliar ones, or none at all. She had traveled over five hundred miles in 1836, back and forth across Ireland by boat and mail or stage coach. She was fifty-eight, not old by modern standards.

30. TA, in *CMcATM*, 70.
31. Davis Coakley, *Robert Graves: Evangelist of Clinical Medicine* (Dublin: Irish Endocrine Society, 1996), 24, 26.
32. Letter 41, December 13, 1836, in *CCMcA*, 79–80.
33. Ibid.

CHAPTER 13

Suscipe 1837

As beset with illnesses and travel difficulties as 1836 was, it did not compare with what awaited Catherine McAuley in 1837. Five sisters died, three from typhus. With considerable personal sacrifice on her part, new foundations were established in Carlow and Cork. A serious financial crisis unfolded in Kingstown. And the most severe controversy with Walter Meyler erupted. It was a year that would challenge Catherine's faith and virtue as none previously had. Her oft-repeated counsels about patience, charity, humility, and unfailing confidence in the providence of God had now to be more than theoretical, if they had ever been merely that.

At first the year seemed off to a happy start. On January 25, four women received the habit, among them Mary de Sales (Jane) White and Mary Francis (Margaret) Marmion, an indefatigable advocate of poor families. On the same morning, four professed vows: Teresa (Catherine) White, Ursula Frayne, Teresa Breen, and Veronica (Ellen) Corrigan. In early February, twenty-six-year-old Anna Maria Harnett entered the community.

But on February 9, death once again wrenched Catherine's heart. Mary Veronica Corrigan, the orphan she had befriended and cherished since Veronica was a child at Coolock, died of virulent typhus just two weeks after her profession of vows. She was twenty. Then a month later, on March 11, rapid consumption finally claimed the life of Mary Rose Lubé, the sister of Catherine's longtime friend Father Andrew Lubé, who had died in 1831. Rose had professed her vows on her deathbed just three weeks before.

Though still grieving, Catherine had to turn her attention to the future. She had promised to bring a new Mercy foundation to Carlow, a town south of Dublin that had seen its share of political suffering. In the late eighteenth century Irish insurgents were killed in its streets, or captured and executed in retribution. James Maher, a Carlow priest who was soon to become her strong supporter, came by his political passion naturally.

Edward Nolan, forty-four years old and bishop of Kildare and Leighlin since 1834, had received from Michael Nowlan, a recently deceased shopkeeper in Carlow, "seven thousand pounds sterling . . . for the relief of the sick and poor roomkeepers of the parish." Since the "interest amounted to a large sum," the bishop proposed to have it disbursed by a community of Sisters of Mercy, "under the supervision of the trustees of said bequest."[1] Carlow College volunteered to lease a cottage, the old academy at the edge of its property, as a temporary convent.

With no more material assurance than this, Catherine agreed to set out. The departure date was to be Monday, April 10, two weeks after Easter, when the burdens of arranging the charity sermon and the Easter bazaar were over. The sermon was preached in St. Andrew's on Sunday, January 29, by Michael Blake, who would not deny his old friend this support of the House of Mercy, even though he rarely had time to leave Newry, the seat of his diocese in the north. Catherine announced the sermon in the *Morning Register:*

The Sisters of Mercy, in the name of the afflicted poor, most respectfully and most earnestly beg your attendance on this occasion. Many very deserving persons await the result in painful anxiety. Should they remain longer without assistance, their appearance must become so reduced as to render their chance of obtaining a situation nearly hopeless.

Homeless women, out of work, often pawned some of their clothes to buy food, and they, of course, could not bathe. Catherine's request continued:

The Sisters beg leave to add that it would be impossible for them to give a just description of the affliction and sufferings of the Sick Poor, who are now so numerous that they are frequently obliged to give only a few pence, where there is neither nourishment, fire, nor covering.[2]

The size of the collection taken up at Blake's sermon is not known.

The Easter bazaar at the Rotunda on March 29 and 30 was again patronized by over ninety countesses, baronesses, honorable ladies, and oth-

---

1. CA, in *CMcATM*, 225. Whether the bishop and the shopkeeper were related is unknown.
2. *Morning Register*, January 27 and 28, 1837.

ers. The Duchess of Kent and the Princess Victoria, soon to become queen, again sent "work from their own hands (trifles they fear) to evince their sympathy in the benevolent exertions of the Sisters of Mercy." The newspaper advertisement also noted: "The admission money alone would afford great relief, though to each person only One Shilling. Some very pretty and valuable articles will be raffled for."[3] The upper-class women who supported the event with their names and money apparently did not inquire into or advocate against the economic and political causes of the poverty whose effects they sought to mitigate. It was, for them, a fashionable occasion, a socially legitimate way to get out of the house and act on their own, philanthropy being a public sphere open to women.

But now the foundation in Carlow had to be arranged. Ever since the death of Veronica Corrigan, Catherine was torn. Veronica had been a great help at Baggot Street, and Catherine had hesitated to part with her for any foundation. But with Veronica's sudden death, she realized the extent of the self-denial called for if she wished to extend the mission of mercifulness as generously as possible. She could no longer hold back at Baggot Street capable sisters on whom she had personally come to depend. That settled the question of who should be superior in Carlow: it had to be Frances Warde, whatever the pain of parting might be.

The founding party would be Frances and Mary Josephine (Grace) Trenor, a novice, Teresa (Amelia) White and Ursula Frayne (who would stay awhile in Carlow to help the community get started, then return to Dublin), Catherine herself, and Mary Cecilia Marmion, her traveling companion. Six in the coach, with baggage, would be crowded, but the journey would be only six or seven hours, and Catherine was getting used to long, rattling coach rides and fractious horses.

They arrived at the Carlow-Kilkenny Day Coach Office on Duke Street early on April 10, to catch the 9:00 A.M. coach, hoping to reach Carlow by three.[4] Later Catherine sent a long poem-letter back to Baggot Street, addressed to the newest postulant, Anna Maria Harnett, "My Dearest darling youngest Daughter." The problems on the journey were not the horses, but Teresa White—apparently unaccustomed to jiggling travel—and the coach driver:

> I know you would like to hear all in Rhyme
> of our journey—and how we have passed away time

3. *Freeman's Journal*, March 17–30, 1837.
4. *Dublin Directory* (1839), 49.

> We were not two miles and a half on our way
> when Sr. M. Teresa got sick & remained so all Day
> She was moaning & looking as white as a sheet
> almost ready to drop—and lie down at our feet
> About half past 2 we got into the Town
> and passed by our own House—where we should be set down
> at least half a mile taken out of our way
> through the midst of a crowd—on the chief market day.

The coach had overshot their destination and, with the horses attached, could not be turned around, so there they sat, "set up for a shew"—six nuns in black habits in the midst of the pigs and corn brought to market. Finally, someone unlinked the horses, reversed the coach, and they reached their new cottage-convent. Bishop Nolan and Andrew Fitzgerald were there to meet them and took them to the Presentation Sisters for dinner:

> We had plenty of laughing—and cheering & fun
> and music & singing when dinner was done
> The Bishop and good Father Andrew at Tea
> soon after nine we all went away.

Sending love to everyone at Baggot Street, Catherine concluded the poem:

> Write to me soon a poetical letter
> no matter how long—the more nonsense the better
> I hope e'er long to write you another
> and remain your fond and affectionate Mother.

Then she added a postscript: "Don't let this be seen—by any but your little party at home at the fire side."[5] Evidently her iambic-anapestic doggerel was not for visitors' eyes.

At the old College Academy, now convent, Catherine was "suddenly dejected." She "had not asked the Bishop if there was any endowment for the support of the Community, and the residence chosen for the Sisters was a dingy, dilapidated concern."[6] In the Rule, on the vow of poverty, she had advised the sisters not to "keep in their cells anything superfluous, costly or rich, in furniture or decorations. All must be suitable to religious simplicity and poverty."[7] So here in Carlow this was it: "The furniture was scanty, so that when the Sisters went from one room to another, they were

5. Letter 43 [c. April 14, 1837], in *CCMcA*, 83–84.   6. CA, in *CMcATM*, 225.
7. Rule 17.3, in *CMcATM*, 313.

obliged to carry their chairs with them, six being the total number provided." For herself, Catherine was ready to "encounter very considerable inconvenience," but she shrank from putting others "in a position of an embarrassing nature." She told Frances Warde and Josephine Trenor of her "anxiety regarding them, adding that she could only give," from Baggot Street, "the dower of the novice, £100," and then offered "to bring them back to their first convent home, if they wished."[8] Neither Frances nor Josephine would hear of it.

Within days Catherine had to return quickly to Baggot Street, where two novices had suddenly contracted "the worst description of typhus fever."[9] The two recovered, and she returned to Carlow, probably in May, taking with her her young niece Catherine Macauley, apparently then, but unbeknown to her aunt, in an "advanced stage of consumption."[10] Sometime in early May, John Nowlan, brother of the Carlow shopkeeper whose life's savings had enabled the Carlow foundation in the first place, donated to the bishop "two thousand pounds sterling"—the result of his own "persevering industry, for years"—to build a new Mercy convent on the Carlow College property.[11] Bishop Nolan laid the first stone on May 20, 1837. The building, which took two years to complete, still stands.

When Catherine finally returned to Dublin, a financial problem that had been simmering for months began to boil over. On June 7 she wrote to John Hamilton, begging him to come to Baggot Street "any time convenient. I think you could settle a matter relative to the Sisters in Kingstown which has become too serious for me without assistance."[12] Two weeks later she summarized the crisis for Charles Cavanagh, the community's solicitor:

When we went to the convent in Kingstown, I expressed to Revd. Mr. Sheridan a particular desire to have a school for the poor girls whom we every day saw loitering about the roads in a most neglected state, and I proposed giving the coach house, stable, and part of our garden, with some gates, doors, and other materials for that purpose.

Mr. Sheridan seemed quite disposed to promote it, and brought Mr. Nugent of Kingstown [a local builder] to speak about the plan. . . . I most distinctly said in the presence of Mr. Sheridan that we had no means to give towards the expence, but to encourage a beginning I promised to give all the little valuable things we had for a Bazaar that year and to hand over whatever it produced. We got fifty pounds, which I gave immediately to Mr. Nugent. . . .

8. CA, in *CMcATM*, 225–26. 9. Lim, in *CMcATM*, 184.
10. BA, in *CMcATM*, 121. 11. CA, in *CMcATM*, 226.
12. Letter 45, June 7 [1837], in *CCMcA*, 85–86.

While the Building was going on Mr. Nugent repeatedly said he had not any doubt of Mr. Sheridan getting from the Board of education a grant nearly sufficient to pay for it, and always added, "I will only charge what it costs me." Mr. Sheridan also said this was full confidence, and whenever I spoke to him of making application to the board, he answered: "I am waiting for the account."

The letter which I enclose to you, Sir, says the account was furnished to me. It never was, nor could Mr. Nugent have ever—in sincerity—regarded me as answerable to him. The charge seems to be a most extraordinary one for the coarse plain work that is done.[13]

Though the letter she enclosed is not extant, Catherine was now directly charged with the full remaining cost of renovating the schoolrooms, £400, an enormous sum in those days, and Father Sheridan, for all his assurances, was leaving her in the hands of the builder. Nowhere did she have—nor could she acquire—that amount of disposable cash. Apparently neither John Hamilton nor Charles Cavanagh could resolve the issue at this time, so the bill sat, unpaid.

Meanwhile, life at Baggot Street went on. More young women had joined the community: Ellen Leahy from Cork came on May 8, and Frances Boylan and Elizabeth Blake in June. But the long-lasting fever epidemic suddenly struck anew. On June 30, Mary Aloysius (Margaret) Thorpe, still a novice, died, the third death in the community so far that year. Two days later Catherine wrote to Andrew Fitzgerald in Carlow:

We have just sent a fine young Sister to the tomb. She died on the tenth day of violent fever. She was exactly like a person in cholera—cold and purple coloured. Some kind of circulation was kept up by wine, muske, cordials, and warm applications, but no hope of recovery from the first 3 days.

Catherine's heart was heavy, but not just because of Mary Aloysius. Her own niece was also declining. As she told Dr. Fitzgerald: "My poor little Catherine is cheerful as ever, but no symptoms of recovering strength"— adding, "you will not forget to pray for me."[14]

Notwithstanding the burial of Aloysius, ceremonies had to be held on July 1. Daniel Murray had set the date, which could not be changed at the last hour. Besides, the six postulants and novices were looking forward to the day. Mary Xavier (Jane) O'Connell and Mary Vincent (Anna Maria) Harnett received the habit, and four women professed their vows: Teresa Carton, Agatha Brennan, Monica Murphy, and Mary Vincent Deasy. Be-

13. Letter 46, June 20, 1837, in *CCMcA*, 86–87.
14. Letter 48, July 1, 1837, in *CCMcA*, 88, 89.

fore Catherine pinned the black veil on the head of each newly professed, she prayed with them in Latin and, perhaps, in view of the sorrowful circumstances, even more beseechingly than at her own profession: "Uphold me according to thy word, and I shall live, and let me not be confounded in my expectation."[15]

Dr. John Murphy had written earlier to say he had a house in Cork, donated by Barbara Gould (Goold?), where a community could live, and the finances were now in order. He urged Catherine to "make the necessary arrangements to supply" his diocese with "four efficient" sisters.[16] Bishop Murphy was a decisive man, even authoritarian, and as Angela Bolster noted, "the various congregations in his diocese found him less than easy to deal with."[17] Catherine set July 5 as the day for departure, telling Andrew Fitzgerald: "I believe we are to go to Cork on Wednesday. Doctor Murphy has waited for us as long as he could."[18] A power to be reckoned with, John Murphy continued to drive hard bargains, especially where money was concerned. Fortunately, the diplomatic Clare Moore would be the new superior in Cork, even though she was only twenty-three. He was sixty-five, had been bishop for twenty-two years, and was firmly confident of the rightness of his arrangements, even in the face of an experienced woman like Catherine McAuley.

On July 5 the long voyage to Cork, one of the largest cities in Ireland, was by nighttime steam packet from Kingstown, south through the Irish Sea and west on the Celtic Sea to the port at Cobh. This was a shorter and more comfortable route than going overland, the day coach through Clonmel taking about twenty-nine hours, the mail coach through Cashel, over twenty. Catherine later recalled their sleeping on the deck floor en route to Cork: "In the steamer to Cork we lay down altogether / and slept mighty well with blanket or feather."[19]

Cork was a maze of bridges, channels, islands, quays, and the winding River Lee, which divided the city into two sectors, north and south. In or near the city were woolen mills, butter-making factories, tanneries, breweries, and whiskey distilleries. The harbor at Cobh (known as Queenstown from 1849 to 1922, in memory of Queen Victoria's state visit) served the city of Cork and would become infamous during and after the Famine.

---

15. *Form of Ceremony* (1834), 29.
16. Letter 44, April 29, 1837, in *CCMcA*, 84–85.
17. Angela Bolster, *Mercy in Cork, 1837–1987* (Cork: Tower Books, 1987), 4.
18. Letter 48, July 1, 1837, in *CCMcA*, 88.
19. Letter 120 [April 30, 1839], 192.

Here thousands of emigrants, often with only the rags on their backs and already sick, were crowded onto boats bound for North America. Eventually many of these vessels were deservedly called "coffin ships."

The founding party arrived in Cork on July 6: Mary Clare Moore, Mary Josephine Warde, Mary Vincent Deasy, Mary Anastasia McGauley, a novice—the "efficient four" who would remain in Cork—Catherine, and her traveling companion, Teresa (Catherine or Amelia?) White. But two weeks after they had settled in the Rutland Street house in south Cork, Catherine was abruptly recalled to Dublin:

My poor dying child requested I would be sent for—and as she was quite anxious I should remain [in Cork] to the end of the month with Sister M. Clare, etc., I concluded she was drawing near to the end, and hastened back immediately.[20]

Young Catherine Macauley, now eighteen, the last of Mary Macauley's daughters, was dying. Her aunt found her "so much changed that if I had not seen similar cases greatly protracted, I would say she was going very rapidly out of this miserable world." Catherine herself was exhausted, admitting to Elizabeth Moore: "I am weary of all my traveling, and this morning I fell down the second flight of stairs. My side is quite sore, but if ever so well able, I could not leave my poor child." She hoped Elizabeth, now local superior in Kingstown, could care for two more sick sisters there: "You and Sister Chantal might come in the steam [train] tomorrow to see me & the two sisters can return with you. . . . Come in early."[21] Elizabeth knew the emotional need expressed in "come in early."

On August 8, twelve days later, knowing that Frances Warde and the Carlow sisters would be in their annual retreat and not wanting to disturb them with sad news, Catherine wrote to her old friend Andrew Fitzgerald:

Our innocent little Catherine is out of this miserable world. She died a little before twelve o'clock last night. She suffered very little, thanks be to God. Not more than one hour of distressed breathing, and her playfulness continued to the end. . . . She represented Mrs. Deasy, on her arrival from Cork, yesterday morning most perfectly. . . . We feel just now as if all the House was dead. . . . I know you will pray for me.[22]

Young Catherine's spirited mimicking of Mrs. Deasy's Cork accent could have only increased her aunt's grief. Writing to Frances Warde later that month about her niece's "last hours," Catherine confessed: "I have suffered

20. Letter 49, July 27, 1837, in *CCMcA*, 89. 21. Ibid., 90.
22. Letter 50, August 8, 1837, in *CCMcA*, 90–91.

more than usual with my old pain of sorrow and anxiety. My stomach has been very ill."[23]

Catherine McAuley had been a single woman all her life, and a nun for the past six years, but—whether by temperament, circumstances, experience, the gift of God, or all four—she was a mother in the deepest sense. Her children were not just "spiritual" ones, acquired by title—"adoptive mother" or, as Daniel Murray insisted, "mother superior." They were vibrant, sometimes needy, always beloved children, for each of whom, at least for the last sixteen years, she was personally responsible, ever since she had carried home to Coolock the infant Teresa Byrn, and later took Teresa's playmate, Catherine Macauley, into Baggot Street. Their affection birthed new capacities in her heart, even as hers nurtured theirs. Indeed, on August 8, 1837, it did seem "as if all the House was dead." The brevity of her words of grief in the surviving letters of this month was evidently the only way she could handle her tears.

But Cork still needed her time and guidance. As she told Frances Warde in late August:

I expected to be in Cork before this. I am waiting for a packet. One got off without my hearing of it, and my poor Sister Mary C[lare] will be sadly disappointed—indeed I have left her in an unfinished state. She writes, full of fears and doubts. Indeed I know she has too much to encounter until the way was made more easy for her. Please God I will soon go there.[24]

While she and Cecilia Marmion waited for the next steam packet to Cork, Catherine got to know the three women who entered the Baggot Street community in August: Clare Moore's elder sister Mary Clare Moore, an artist, who would one day take the name Mary Clare Augustine; Annie O'Brien from Wexford; and Mary Anne Duggan, a Dubliner. In addition, on August 15, Teresa Byrn, now sixteen, "took the Postulant's dress . . . to fill my dearest child's vacancy."[25]

Catherine reached Cork by August 31, and was soon negotiating, unsuccessfully, with Bishop Murphy about the size of the dowry he required of those entering the Cork community. Some dowry was needed, and, after a woman's profession, as a source of community income to cover her expenses for the rest of her life. At Baggot Street, Catherine had always

---

23. Letter 51 [August 15–30, 1837], in CCMcA, 91.
24. Ibid., 91–92.
25. Ibid. The two Moore sisters are easily confused, especially when Catherine herself, in her letters, calls Mary Clare Augustine simply "Mary Clare." They were apparently unrelated to Elizabeth (Anne) Moore.

carefully considered the financial means of the woman's family. She often asked for no dowry at all, or sometimes for only a pledge of £100 or £200 to be paid in installments over several years. John Murphy required £600, to be promised in advance and paid at the time of profession. Catherine tried but could not budge him. His frequently calling her "Sister of Divine Providence" was apparently not meant wholly as a compliment.[26] As she explained to de Pazzi Delany:

It will not be easy to enter here, the terms are high—and *no abatement*. This is a drawback. . . . All that I could say on the matter—quite fruitless. Sister Mary Clare will not be teased with importunities from Priests or people. Every applicant is to be referred to the Bishop, provided she approves of them, and all settled by him. This will save her from many painful concerns, and to this part of the regulations I could feel no objection. I only wish the terms were not so high—for a beginning.[27]

Someone reflecting on this situation might well be annoyed by Dr. Murphy's intransigence and presumption, his fear of possible financial collapse of the community notwithstanding. Not only were Catherine's personal experience and religious values set aside, but Clare Moore's own role as superior of the new foundation responsible for its finances was obviously not taken into account. Yet this was a young woman who went on to exercise that role highly successfully, administering two Mercy foundations, one after the other, for thirty-seven years.

Moreover, Catherine apparently had to apologize, in "grief," to the "displeased" Bishop Murphy for having on July 23 accepted with a lesser dowry—while he was away, and before she understood his wishes—the first postulant to enter the Cork community. Margaret O'Connell's parents were probably not wealthy. Nonetheless, her energy and wisdom enabled her to serve intermittently, for thirty-five years, as the inspired superior of the Mercy community in Sunderland, England, founded from Cork in 1843 and still vital today. Still Clare Moore, who apparently came to see John Murphy's virtues, claims perhaps too generously that Catherine "revered and loved him as a Father, submitting her judgment to his wise and learned counsels, which she never had reason to regret."[28]

Catherine remained in Cork until October 26—the day after Anastasia McGauley's profession and Mary Aloysius (Margaret) O'Connell's reception—the longest time she had remained with any new foundation to date. There was much to settle besides meeting with Dr. Murphy: inter-

26. BA, in *CMcATM*, 115.   27. Letter 53, October 3, 1837, in *CCMcA*, 95.
28. BA, in *CMcATM*, 121.

viewing prospective postulants; guiding Anastasia and Margaret through final preparations for their ceremonies; welcoming Catherine Mahony, who entered on October 18; and visiting the sick in the southern area of the city. They decided not to open a poor school immediately, since the Presentation Sisters, following Nano Nagle's example, were already involved in that work of mercy, but they anticipated where and how a House of Mercy could be opened early in 1838.

Catherine also visited Barbara Ann Gould at her modest home on the Glanmire road, a retiring and unostentatious woman slightly younger than she, who was the chief benefactor of the Mercy community in Cork. She had given them, through Bishop Murphy, not only the large house on Rutland Street, but also property on George's Quay as a means of regular income.[29] Two years later Catherine was still asking: "How is Miss Goold— give my love to her."[30] In Barbara Gould, she saw the kind of goodness and holiness she had long admired and would see again in other generous but unassuming lay women.

Catherine knew of an emerging chaplaincy controversy with Father Walter Meyler before she left Dublin in late August. She had had at least one conversation with him to try to avert it. Writing from Cork on October 3 to de Pazzi Delany, she attached, to an otherwise pleasant letter which could be read to the whole community, a "private" page for de Pazzi alone, begging her:

My dearest Sister . . . will you relieve me from the distressing business about the chaplain. It is constantly before me, and makes me dread going home. I know it is not possible for me to have any more argument with Dr. Meyler without extreme agitation.[31]

In August, Daniel Burke, O.F.M., the chaplain who had served the schoolchildren and the women and girls sheltered in the House of Mercy ever since his appointment to that post by Archbishop Murray in June 1829, was reassigned to accompany to southern Africa the new vicar apostolic of the Cape of Good Hope, Patrick Griffith, O.P. Burke had also presided at daily and Sunday Mass on Baggot Street, and, utterly generous with his time, used to say: "That House gives work enough for any man."[32]

To Walter Meyler, as a vicar general of the diocese, apparently fell the task of appointing a new chaplain. He proposed that instead of a single

29. Bolster, Mercy in Cork, 4.
30. Letter 131, October 18, 1839, in CCMcA, 209.
31. Letter 53, October 3, 1837, in CCMcA, 96.
32. Letter 76, February 6, 1838, in CCMcA, 124.

priest assigned full time as the regular chaplain, the eight curates at St. Andrew's church would serve on a rotating basis, a day at a time, responding when sent for. Knowing the sacramental needs of the dozens of women in the House of Mercy, and of the hundreds of girls in the school who needed preparation for Confirmation and First Communion, Catherine was "strongly opposed" to Dr. Meyler's plan. As she explained to de Pazzi: "A confessor might be necessary for some days in succession to prepare a person or persons for going into situations [that is, places of employment] and . . . we might want him at night in case of sudden illness, where there was such a crowd of persons."[33] Initially, Dr. Meyler said her explanation of the need "was just," but then changed his mind, insisting on the rotation. For this service, he also required that Catherine would annually pay the parish £50. The most Catherine felt she could scrape together for a chaplain's salary was £40. In her letter of October 3, she urged de Pazzi to speak to Gregory Lynch, one of the curates:

Will you, my Dear, speak to Mr. Lynch and say in the most decided manner that we require a chaplain to the House, *and cannot nor will not* call on any of the Parish clergymen to attend to the Institution—this will imply that no salary will be given—you may add that Mr. [Edward] Armstrong told me it would be injurious—indeed he said if we were a religious community it could not be attempted, and he was deeply afflicted on his death bed that we were not *so* established. . . .

Do get me through this—don't be afraid. I know the Bishop will be rather pleased than otherwise. . . .

Take Mr. Lynch into the parlour and speak with decision. Should Dr. Meyler call, assure him that I will never depart from the advice Mr. Armstrong gave me, that I would sooner leave the parish entirely, and that I am sure the Bishop would not ask me to do what Mr. Armstrong so long and so determinedly objected to.

Then Catherine admitted: "Perhaps one third of what I have said will be more than sufficient—and this is the reason I dread the subject, because I find myself impelled to say too much."[34] Whether de Pazzi ever had the suggested conversations is not known. Catherine was in Cork, could not leave, and could not be in two places at once, but her "dread" remained.

Suddenly, in mid-October, Catherine still in Cork, sad news came from Carlow. Edward Nolan, the widely beloved bishop of Kildare and Leighlin, was stricken with typhus fever while in Maryborough (Portlaoise) visiting a parish. He made it back to his home in Carlow, but the "physician who

33. Letter 53, October 3, 1837, in *CCMcA*, 96.
34. Ibid., 96–97.

first attended him unfortunately prescribed the now obsolete remedy of bleeding, so that the more experienced of the medical faculty, on seeing him, pronounced his case—hopeless." Frances Warde and Teresa White nursed him until his death came on Saturday evening, October 14. Before he died, pointing to the sisters, he said to Father James Maher: "Take care of them."[35]

For Catherine, Edward Nolan's death was more than the passing of a bishop she had met only recently. He had been a good friend to the Carlow community, particularly to Frances Warde. As she wrote to Teresa White:

> To regard it as an individual sorrow would not be right. Our portion of it may well be lost in the lamentations of his poor and destitute people. Yet I can account for my dear Sister Mary Frances feeling so much on this distressing occasion. The good Bishop afforded her the first and chief comfort she experienced on parting me.[36]

Their separation had been difficult for both Frances and Catherine. In a poem she sent to Frances sometime that year, Catherine had tried to assure her that distance did not matter:

> Though absent, dear Sister
> I love thee the same
> That title so tender
> Remembrance doth claim. . . .
>
> O grieve not we're parted
> Since life soon is flown
> Let us think of securing
> The next for our own.
>
> This day of our mourning
> Will quickly be passed
> While the day of rejoicing
> For ever shall last.[37]

Catherine was still in Cork in late October, preparing for the profession and reception on October 25: "The expected ceremony is exciting the greatest curiosity, they fancy it is to be something wonderful. . . . The Bishop says that at least sixty persons must be invited."[38] That meant sixty

---

35. CA, in *CMcATM*, 226.
36. Letter 55, October 17, 1837, in *CCMcA*, 100.
37. Letter 47 [1837], in *CCMcA*, 87. This may not be an original composition on Catherine McAuley's part, but a transcription of another writer's poem. She did not normally use "thee" (as in stanza 1) in her own poems. So far no poem she may have copied has been found.
38. Letter 53, October 3, 1837, in *CCMcA*, 95.

handwritten invitations. Bishop Murphy also suggested that, in the Act of Profession read aloud at profession ceremonies, after the words "poverty, chastity, and obedience" should be added "and the service of the poor, sick, and ignorant"—to better reflect the specific works of the Sisters of Mercy. Apparently Catherine liked this idea, but the new wording was "not generally adopted" until the Rule was approved in Rome.[39]

Things were progressing well in Cork. Josephine Warde was "a Rock— as to propriety and composure"; Anastasia McGauley, "amiable in the highest degree"; and Clare Moore, though "extremely timid" and unwilling to appear without Catherine "on the most trifling occasion," had promised to "overcome this." Catherine was, moreover, "quite surprised to find no remark made as to [Clare's] youth, in any quarter."[40] Her instinct about the young superior's fundamental capability was sound, as history would prove.

Then more sad news came to Cork. Mary de Chantal McCann was dying of "bad typhus fever—Dr. [Henry] Marsh attending her in Kingstown." After the ceremony in Cork was over, Catherine would leave the next day for Dublin, then Kingstown. She promised the still grieving Frances Warde she would stop on the way:

I will return by Carlow to see you, if only for a few hours. I hope to be there by half past 12 o'c on Thursday night. You will have Mary Ann sitting up—but I entreat you may all go to rest as usual. I will not be able to speak till morning. If you can, let me into a room alone to sleep a few hours, and not where I was with my child.[41]

Her sorrow at the death of young Catherine was still too fresh for her to sleep in the room she had shared with her niece in May.

On October 26, Catherine traveled from Cork, on the mail coach departing at noon, passing through Clonmel and Kilkenny. As the coach rumbled along, her heart was heavy. She was, possibly, going toward the fifth death of a sister that year, again from typhus. The wheels of the coach circled and circled as Catherine reflected on the community's joys and sorrows. Dr. Henry Marsh was a highly respected Dublin physician, but could he save de Chantal? And then there was Dr. Meyler. Could she face this continuing disagreement? In Cork she had seen Patrick Griffith and Daniel Burke, then on their way to southern Africa. Even Dr. Griffith, now a bishop, had "said we ought to have a Chaplain *and more*."[42] Alone

39. BA, in *CMcATM*, 122.
40. Letter 53, October 3, 1837, in *CCMcA*, 94–95, 97.
41. Letter 56, October 23 [1837], in *CCMcA*, 100–101.
42. Letter 53, October 3, 1837, in *CCMcA*, 96.

in her thoughts, she also let herself think of her darling young Catherine. The merry light of Baggot Street would not be there when she returned.

Mary de Chantal McCann died in Kingstown on October 27, just as Catherine reached Carlow. She was buried in the Carmelite vault at St. Teresa's on October 29, the eleventh Mercy woman to be interred there since 1831. Catherine was present at Baggot Street, in her white cloak, to see de Chantal's body go out the door. The white cloaks worn for rituals and solemnities did nothing to assuage human grief, but they did signify the community's respect before the deepest mysteries of human life—a woman's courageous yet humanly inexplicable embrace of poverty, chastity, and obedience at her profession, the unfathomable acts of God celebrated at Christmas and Easter, and the passage to greater love and gladness that was concealed in death. Catherine loved to see the community wearing their "church" cloaks, not for the white serge itself, but for what these capes pointed to and meant. They were not work clothes, but celebratory garb.

Going to Kingstown a few days later, to console Elizabeth Moore and the sisters, Catherine was clearly exhausted by all her travels and worries. While there she again fell down a flight of stairs. This time she broke her arm:

When the Angelus Bell rang, I was hastening to the choir from the community room, missed the first step of the stairs, fell forward, and, in endeavouring to save my head from the window, broke my left arm across the wrist, and injured the sinews in the back of the hand so much that I am not likely to have the use of it for months—if ever.[43]

Catherine remained in care of an apothecary for two days without taking off her clothes, and the inflammation was apparently so great that he judged nothing could be done but apply leeches. The bloodletting may have helped somewhat, and when she returned to Dublin, "Surgeon White bound me up in boards," the wooden precursor to modern plaster casts. Catherine made light of her broken arm, telling Frances Warde:

I have great hopes of soon getting my old companion [the arm] on duty again and am happy to tell you from experience that a broken arm is by no means so distressing a matter as I always supposed. The want of its use is the chief inconvenience. . . . Though not proportioned to all the lamentations we hear on such occasions, yet it gives a general shock to the frame that is not easily recovered.[44]

43. Letter 67, December 20, 1837, in *CCMcA*, 114. Many of Catherine McAuley's letters in November and December now exist only in transcriptions available to Carroll and Degnan, so a later autograph is cited here. For other details about her arm, the transcriptions are needed.
44. Letter 61 [November–December 1837], in *CCMcA*, 106, which depends on Carroll, *Life*, 333; Carroll, *Leaves from the Annals*, vol. 1 (1881), 79–80; and Degnan, *Mercy*, 208.

In true style, she was soon joking about her babied arm, telling Frances and others: "I carry my child in its cradle."[45] Mary Ann Doyle claims: "She wrote to me saying my knee was nothing at all to this baby—it had such grand names and was wrapt in new flannel!"[46]

By December 1837, Catherine needed something to joke about. The chaplaincy issue was still not settled, and they were walking to St. Andrew's each morning for Mass. For herself and the community that was no problem: "Twelve couples start as gaily as we did when traveling to Clarendon Street in our first happy days." John McDonough, a curate sympathetic to the work on Baggot Street, waited for them. "We remain for three Masses and are home at nine." But for the women in the House of Mercy and the children it was a different story, especially on Sundays and holy days: "You know how difficult it is to get the poor women and children out and home again on days of obligation, and their confessions are, of course, neglected. The Archbishop does not interfere."[47]

Catherine had asked Andrew Fitzgerald to intervene, and though he did not succeed in getting a meeting with Walter Meyler, he called the whole situation "a wanton unwarranted abuse of Church authority." The longstanding president of Carlow College and alternately its professor of classics, philosophy, theology, and Scripture was not known to spare the truth. Thomas Carroll, a curate at St. Andrew's, had told Dr. Fitzgerald that Dr. Murray had "sanctioned the proceeding to oblige [the community] to take one of the Curates as Chaplain." This, Fitzgerald remarked, was "rather an extraordinary proceeding, seeing all the other Convents had Chaplains, not Curates, to which observation [he] received no reply."[48]

Catherine now wrote to Michael Blake, "stating our grievances."[49] He replied on December 12, urging her to "put your trust in God . . . with perfect resignation to the ways of his providence," but also strongly advising her "to submit your case to his Grace":

It will not be difficult for your wise and benevolent Archbishop to settle the point at issue in a reasonable and satisfactory manner—to give you a distinct chaplain, if you can afford a salary sufficient for his support, or if otherwise, to have such an arrangement made in the parish Chapel, that *one individual* clergyman belonging to it shall have it as his peculiar duty to be an *efficient and regular* chaplain to your community.

45. Letter 62 [December 1837], in *CCMcA*, 106, citing Carroll, *Life*, 334, and Carroll, *Leaves from the Annals*, vol. 1 (1881), 195.
46. "Bermondsey Annals, (1866)," vol. 2, [109] (AIMGB). The Annals, whose pages are here misnumbered, cites a letter from Mary Ann Doyle.
47. Letter 62 [December 1837], in *CCMcA*, 106–7, citing Carroll's texts as in note 45.
48. Letter 58, November 6, 1837, in *CCMcA*, 103.
49. Letter 62 [December 1837], in *CCMcA*, 107.

Dr. Blake interpreted Dr. Meyler's words and behavior as "not absolutely opposed" to their having "a distinct chaplain," and urged Catherine to seek the help of John Hamilton, "whose kindness you have experienced" and who "will not refuse his valuable cooperation in so good a work."[50]

On December 19, her cradled left hand trying to hold the paper so she could write, Catherine penned a two-and-a-half-page letter to John Hamilton, Archbishop Murray's priest-secretary. She summarized the situation as it had developed since his last visit, and transcribed for him her two letters to Dr. Meyler, starting with the one in which she had offered to increase her portion of the salary to £45 if he "would think proper to add five pounds which you give," thus making up the £50 he had requested. She then recorded Dr. Meyler's response, in which he rejected her proposal and said: "I think I feel your friend Mr. Armstrong urging me in this direction." Describing to Hamilton the "disorder" on a recent Sunday, when the women in the House of Mercy did not return from Mass for their Sunday school, at which "my heart became sore and bitter," Catherine then gave him "every word" of the second letter she wrote to Dr. Meyler, which, as she noted, "is proclaimed a threatening one." No doubt the most threatening section was her concluding comment on Father Edward Armstrong:

> When I read . . . that you felt as if my dear respected Mr. Armstrong was urging you to your decision, I thought that in gratitude for the affectionate friendship with which he so long honored me, I ought to mention how he acted towards a religious community. . . . His predecessor in Ann Street [St. Michan's chapel] had been contending with the Sisters in Georges Hill about some temporal matters. When Mr. A. was appointed he immediately visited the convent, gave his most cordial sanction to their two public Masses and a Charity Sermon if they required it—not all this world could give would induce him to harass or annoy a society of women devoted to the service of God and the poor.[51]

According to her letter to John Hamilton, she then told Dr. Meyler that she would prevail on the sisters to accompany her to the archbishop and would represent to him the negative effects of the present situation on the house he had once blessed, which "is now under some kind of condemnation, that even a friendly priest is not permitted to celebrate Mass" and "the poor inmates are deprived of the Sacraments."[52]

Catherine concluded her letter to Hamilton, giving him Dr. Meyler's response to her second letter, and her reaction:

50. Letter 63, December 12, 1837, in *CCMcA*, 107–8.
51. Letter 66, December 19, 1837, in *CCMcA*, 111–12.
52. Ibid., 112–13.

At eight o'clock on Sunday evening a letter was handed me from Doctor Meyler. It began thus: "When is your procession to take place? I should like to see the Theatrical exhibition—the Bishop must be apprised—perhaps you may not admire the reception you will meet, for he is too strait forward a person to be caught by your Juggle."

I read no more and put it out of my power ever to do so by burning the letter. I must now be done with the matter entirely. I will attempt nothing more. The means that contributed to pay a Chaplain is taken from us, and we are to be forced to promise what we cannot be sure of having. We will shew you our accounts, and you will find there is no prevarication in the statement made. I have no one to appeal to.

In a long postscript Catherine said that Gregory Lynch, a curate, came on Monday "but not since," and that while Hamilton had said they were to have Father Paul Farrelly, a Jesuit, "entirely," Dr. Meyler had said they were "to have two." Though "we could not know who to call as a friend . . . even to this we assented, distressing as it is." Finally, denying "that we all dislike the Parish Clergy" (as was "said") and "give freely elsewhere" (as had been claimed) she told John Hamilton that all Redmond O'Hanlon, the Carmelite, ever received from Baggot Street "for his nine years constant attention" was thirty-two pounds—"in all, the entire sum—£32—in nine years."[53]

Though Catherine wrote a cheerful letter to Frances Warde on December 23, the joy of Christmas that year, even with the white church cloaks, was clouded. She believed profoundly in the necessity of true humility if one wished to follow the example of Jesus, and she did not wish, in her reverence for the ordained priestly vocation, to have to contend with Walter Meyler.

To ascribe humility to a person today, especially to a woman, and perhaps even more so to a religious woman, is often suspect, and sometimes rightly so. In a long and often misguided tradition, manifest in some spiritual writers of past centuries, this fundamental and necessary Christian virtue was sometimes inadequately and inappropriately defined. Unthinking submissiveness to others on all occasions and self-denigrating assessments of oneself were advocated in ways that failed to do justice to the presence, gifts, and intentions of God.

Catherine McAuley, though exposed to such descriptions of "humility," seems nevertheless to have aspired to a more thorough, more diffi-

53. Ibid., 113.

cult, and more authentic understanding of humility. For her, true humility was that embodied in and advocated by Jesus Christ and described by the first Christians. It was not immediate submissiveness on all occasions or a superficial mode of speech, appearance, or behavior, but a transparent attitude of mind and heart in the presence of God and of all other humans. Humility was, for her, a truthful selflessness, a selflessness that did not make less or more of one's "self" than one is in the perspective of God. She sought to honor that perspective, that vision and mission of God for the well-being of all humans in this world, as best she was able to grasp and understand it. This humility did not insert an opaque "self" between the desires, the mission, of God and those to whom God evidently wished her to be merciful. When she quoted, as she frequently did, the words ascribed to Jesus, "Take my yoke upon you, and learn from me; for I am gentle and humble in heart" (Mt 11:29), she apparently understood these words as descriptive of Jesus' own self-bestowal, his universal charity, and his complete self-relinquishing embrace of all that the "yoke" of God's mission and charity, and obedience to that mission, would entail in his own personal life, even unto death.

Perhaps her characteristic emphasis on mutual charity and on Jesus' example and command "Love one another as I have loved you" (Jn 15:12) saved her from the kind of pseudo-humility that would have been finally untruthful. Though she would have encountered such views of "humility," she was apparently led—by God, by Scripture, and by friends like Edward Armstrong and Michael Blake—to realizations more in accord with Scripture, and to an understanding of humility based on respect for God's presence in oneself and in one's sisters and brothers on this earth, that is, on the prior and active love and example of God.

As St. Augustine expressed it, the greatest exemplar of true humility is "above": "It is God, 'who descends from heaven by the weight of His charity.'"[54] Thus for Bernard Häring as for Augustine, "the actual dynamic force of humility," the "force of 'gravity'" drawing the human person to deeper humility, "is love," following the example and mission of God in Jesus Christ.[55] The weight of God's charity for human beings constantly pulls God humbly to them, even unto the promise for them implicit in the death and resurrection of Jesus. This humility, as advocated in the Hebrew

54. St. Augustine, *De sancta virginitate,* quoted in vol. 3 of Bernard Häring, *The Law of Christ,* trans. Edwin Kaiser (Westminster, Md.: Newman Press, 1966), 57. Häring cites Augustine's Latin clause: *qui de coelo descendit pondere caritatis.*

55. Häring, *The Law of Christ,* vol. 3, 59–60.

and Christian Scriptures, is the solidarity of God with those who are op-pressed, by their own weaknesses, or by other humans, or by human expe-rience itself. Catherine's attempt to "resemble" Jesus' self-emptying for the sake of this solidarity, in the way he behaved and what he stood for, and her desire "to resemble in some manner"—in her relations with God and with others—"the Love and Union which subsists between Him-self and His Heavenly Father," was, she evidently believed, the way "to be really His Disciples."[56]

She was not over-impressed or put off course by human faults, fail-ings, or defects, her own or others'. On the other hand, she deeply grieved what she took to be her sin (for example, injurious failures of charity or mercifulness), and she was not impressed by what others might have said were her "virtues." She seems to have known only too well her own utter dependence on the virtue of God. When she said, as she evidently did say, that one "should consider her opinion as nothing and herself a nobody,"[57] she apparently meant these words in the wider, deeper context of the "opinion" (the mission) of God, and the incomprehensible humility and gifts of God in the self-bestowal of Jesus, who, for the sake of that mission, "though he was in the form of God, did not regard equality with God as something to be exploited, but emptied himself, taking the form of a slave, being born in human likeness" (Phil 2:6–7).

Catherine seems to have revered the silence, the quiet anonymity, with which God, in her view, came into the world and worked in the world for its sake. She too wished to "shun" drawing attention to herself, to avoid the "noise of closing shutters or drawing curtains." Perhaps these words speak to the kind of transparency of one's self to which she believed she and her companions were called by God's example in Jesus—a transpar-ency of the "self" through which the mission of God's universal love could shine.

Humility for her, therefore, could not be a matter of always deferring to the judgment of others. Her assertions were not assertions of her self as such, but a consequence of what she felt she had to do and of actions she felt she had to take for the sake of others. Like reluctant prophets before her, she often had to be, and was, assertive and firm in judgment, as the Dr. Meyler episode shows. Her humility was her human attempt to resemble the humility of Jesus before the mission of God, Jesus who was strongly

56. Rule 8.1, "Of Union and Charity," in *CMcATM*, 303.
57. *PS*, 1.

assertive on occasions when this was called for. His humility was a transparent emptying of self before the claims and desires of his Father. That sort of selfless humility did not always commend itself to his hearers.

Thus Catherine's humility ran in a very deep channel. It was an assertion of the total dependency of her "self" on something much greater, and a recognition that any "value" she might have was subordinate to and subsumed in the values and demands of God that Jesus illuminated by his example. If publicity occurred through her own presumption or through what she feared was a failure on her part, this grieved her.

Catherine never said or wrote that 1837—with its five deaths, fatiguing travels, human separations, and severe clerical controversies—was one of the hardest years of her life. But one may hazard a guess that it was. Was it then that she began, privately, to compose her *Suscipe,* the prayer that is now sung throughout the world, in many languages, the singers perhaps little realizing what its words once meant to their author:

My God, I am Thine for all eternity. Teach me to cast my whole self into the arms of Thy Providence with the most lively, unbounded confidence in Thy compassionate, tender pity. Grant, O most merciful Redeemer, that whatever Thou dost ordain or permit may always be acceptable to me. Take from my heart all painful anxiety; suffer nothing to afflict me but sin; nothing to delight me, but the hope of coming to the possession of Thee, my God, in Thine own everlasting kingdom.[58]

58. *PS,* 32, and, with slightly different wording, Lim, in *CMcATM,* 188–89. *Suscipe,* a verb, is Latin for "take, receive." Catherine apparently gave no title to this prayer. Clare Moore called it her "Act of Resignation." But *Suscipe,* expressing the intent of this prayer addressed to God, is the title by which it and the musical versions of it are now generally known.

CHAPTER 14

Resilience 1838

With her arm still in boards, Catherine could barely dress herself. The hardest part was the long leather cincture that circled her waist and then had to be looped through the horn ring that also secured her long black-beaded rosary.[1]

Each morning as she put on the cincture she prayed: "Lord Jesus, who for us became obedient unto death, grant me the true spirit of religious obedience."[2] While she believed that "no trouble is too great when obedience is concerned," and that "we need only consider how dear our own will has been to us ... to know how acceptable a sacrifice it is to God," discerning when the moment for obedient sacrifice had arrived, and from whence the moment came, was complicated.[3] For Catherine, discovering what obedience asked of her in the chaplaincy case involved not only coming to understand what Archbishop Murray himself had personally and knowingly decided—an understanding that apparently remained cloudy (at least insofar as no clarifying documents appear extant). It also involved

1. When Catherine McAuley changed the brass crucifix on the rosaries they wore back to the ebony cross with its inset ivory cross and no corpus—which she had received at George's Hill—is not known. Of the habit in early 1832, Clare Moore says simply: "She . . . would only allow of cheap brass crucifixes to [our] Beads, thinking the ebony crosses in use among the Presentation Nuns, and which she afterwards adopted, too expensive" (BA, in *CMcATM*, 108). No primary evidence suggests that Catherine thought Sisters of Mercy should see themselves as the corpus on the ebony and ivory cross.

2. *The Customs and Minor Regulations of the . . . Sisters of Mercy in . . . Baggot Street and its Branch Houses* (Dublin: J. M. O'Toole and Son, 1869), 72. Hereafter: *Baggot Street Book of Customs*. This small book was first published in 1869, but contains "Prayers Used Whilst Clothing" that go back to Catherine McAuley's days.

3. *PS*, 9.

the obedience—in some ways more difficult—of actually listening to the real needs, including the sacramental ones, of the poor women and girls in the shelter and school on Baggot Street, and to the mercifulness toward them required by Jesus Christ's identification with them, as she understood and believed this. All these realities would have been on her mind each morning as she struggled to gird herself with the black cincture that she regarded as a symbol not only of Jesus' obedience unto death, but also of "the true spirit of religious obedience."

Evidently the chaplaincy dispute remained unresolved throughout 1838. Though Catherine gradually learned how to live with it, it continued to be an interior struggle, especially as the Kingstown controversy reached its own humiliating peaks and stretched on into November. However, writing at length to Frances Warde in January, Catherine was peaceful, or at least appeared so in her account to Frances:

If I have inspired you with the melancholy view you take of our situation I assure you I did not intend to do so. We have just now indeed more than an ordinary portion of the Cross in this one particular—but may it not be the Cross of Christ which we so often pray to "be about us." . . . There is no disunion, no gloomy depression of spirits, no departure from charity proceeding from it. The difficulties lessen every day. We get our poor inmates to Confession by six at each time, with Eliza Liston to bring them safe home—and please God we will have all prepared for Holy Communion first Friday.

We get an occasional charitable Mass—and never go out on very wet mornings. I am sure Doctor Meyler would wish the matter were settled according to his own plan—we would have at least three Priests, and never know who[m] to call on as friend or chaplain—and for this must pay or promise to pay £50 per annum, which we really have not, independent of casual events. . . . I offered £40 to Dr. Meyler, and I now believe it is well it was rejected, for if we had not twenty to give at the end of the half year, we would be suspected of withholding it, and all the dispute would be renewed—and whenever I have the happiness of seeing Mr. Maher again, I will tell him—and him only—another strong reason why the proposed connection should be avoided if possible.

I am not unhappy, thanks be to God—nor do I see any disedification likely to arise from the matter. Some think that after having Mr. Burke eight years, we are not now easily pleased—and most of those who know the cause that we go out [to Mass] seem to think we ought to have a distinct chaplain, and only say, Dr. Meyler is a little positive. This is the extent of it at present. It is humiliating no doubt, a smart attack on self-importance, and if this part of it is well managed, it must turn to good account. I humbly trust it will end very well.[4]

4. Letter 71, January 17, 1838, in *CCMcA*, 119.

Earlier in January, after James Maher's visit to Baggot Street, Catherine had written to him, indirectly alluding to the controversy with Dr. Meyler by copying Meyler's language to her in her comment on Maher's services. The whole letter was *not* a serious complaint about Father Maher's failure "to complete the full week's attendance, which according to the regulations of this diocese, would have entitled you to one pound or guinea, whichever you liked best," but a brilliant parody of Dr. Meyler's "regulations" as she must have shared them with Maher. He could not have failed to see the humor in the straight-faced posture and language she preserves to the end, even to her deploring that her "poor infirm hand" had to prepare a final breakfast for him which, in his need to get back to Carlow, he never ate.[5] The parody is Catherine's attempt to be lighthearted about a painful situation, while indirectly expressing her gratitude to Maher.

In the letter to Frances, Catherine also revealed a new development in the Kingstown dispute over payment for renovation of the stable and coach house into schoolrooms. Father Sheridan has, she says, "left me in the hands of Mr. Nugent," the builder:

By giving that £50 Mr. Sheridan says I am, what he terms, committed. . . . I am hiding from some law person who wants to serve a paper on me personally & sent in to say he came from Dr. Murray. I am afraid to remain five minutes in the small parlour [near the front door]. This has caused more laughing than crying, you may be sure, for every man is suspected of being the process man, and kept at an awful distance by my dear Teresa Carton.

So now there is a lawsuit against her—for "4 hundred and fifty pounds"—and a subpoena! Catherine does not comment further on this "animating" development, this second "cross of the Diocese," except to ask Frances: "Pray fervently for me, and you will see me young and handsome at the grand consecration" of Francis Haly, the new bishop of Kildare and Leighlin, in Carlow on March 25. Meanwhile, the House of Mercy was "crowded": "Twenty went to situations in one week—and twenty more came in."[6] Staying out of the small parlour—where she usually received prospective employers and women seeking shelter—and out of range of the law officer delivering the subpoena would have required some careful maneuvering.

<hr/>

5. Letter 69, January 10, 1838, in *CCMcA*, 117–18. Commenting on this letter, Angela Bolster missed its humor: "The stringency of diocesan regulations is seen in . . . references to [Maher's] remuneration for an unfinished series of lectures. . . . [Catherine McAuley's] sense of justice is seen in the . . . postscript." Bolster, ed. *The Correspondence of Catherine McAuley, 1827–1841* (Cork: Sisters of Mercy, Dioceses of Cork and Ross, 1989), 48.

6. Letter 71, January 17, 1838, in *CCMcA*, 120.

On February 6, 1838, Catherine wrote to John Hamilton, the archbishop's priest-secretary. She had evidently not sought to speak directly with Archbishop Murray about the chaplaincy matter, and had felt in December that she had "no one to appeal to." But now the plight of the women and schoolchildren required her to say something more to Father Hamilton:

I feel as if indifference was taking place in my mind when I give up every effort to raise the institution from its fallen state. Since the first of this year, thirty-seven young women went to situations from the House, most of whom merely approached the Sacrament of Penance to obtain a note for admission [before entrance into the house]. We are quite full again of persons under similar circumstances. On such occasions, Mr. Burke attended to the confessional for four or five days together, very often till after four o'clock, to afford them the means of reconciliation, before employment was obtained.

They leave us now, as they came, and there is noise and quarrelling amongst them, which the participation of the Holy Sacraments with due instruction used to cure. The alteration in the school is quite evident. They went to Confession every week in turn, and I assure you, Revd. Sir, Mr. Burke has frequently said he was very tired. . . .

I think it was providential that Doctor Meyler refused the salary, for I still hope God will grant the spiritual assistance required, to meet the expense of which, we would make every exertion and be kindly assisted.[7]

Though she believed that "while we place all our confidence in God— we must act as if all depended on our exertion," some of the exertion she hoped would produce "kindly" assistance yielded little real help.[8] By March she knew the charity sermon, preached by the Reverend John Miley on February 18 (she had tried to get James Maher to preach it) was "very bad," presumably not in its content, but in its attendance and proceeds. And in view of what they had for sale or raffle, the forthcoming bazaar, scheduled for April 17 and 18, also looked "unpromising."[9] At the end of April, she could flatly say it was unsuccessful:

All summed up—after expenses—we will have about forty-five pounds, very unlike past days. Mrs. Sullivan has given us up, and almost all the Protestants. I am told there were not ten Protestants in the room. Mr. Maher, the best purchaser—every one tormenting him. Poor Sister Gertrude made a carpet [blanket or other covering] 5 yards square—which cost us £10. . . . One ticket only was sold. I suppose we are done with Bazaars.[10]

7. Letter 76, February 6, 1838, in CCMcA, 124–25.
8. Letter 212, November 24, 1840, in CCMcA, 323.
9. Letter 80 [March 13, 1838], in CCMcA, 128.
10. Letter 85 [c. April 25, 1838], in CCMcA, 134. Cornelius Sullivan was now land agent for the Earl of Pembroke, from whom Catherine McAuley had leased the Baggot Street property.

Done with bazaars? A risky conclusion she later could not stand by, even if it meant "tormenting" their friend Father Maher, who was notorious for never keeping a penny in his pocket.

Then on May 9 the financial outcome long feared occurred. In the magnificent Four Courts building designed by James Gandon along the Liffey, a magistrate decided the lawsuit brought against Catherine McAuley by James Nugent, builder of the poor school in Kingstown. The verdict was clear and cold: she was liable for the full cost of renovating the coach house and stable she had donated. That day John Martin, solicitor for James Nugent, sent Charles Cavanagh, her solicitor, "the particulars of Mrs. McAuley's case." The "judgment debt" was £360.1.10½, plus "taxed costs" of £15.13.4½, bringing the total she was ordered to pay to £375.15.5, in addition to the £50 she had already contributed.[11] It was not the shillings or pence that alarmed her, but the three hundred seventy-five pounds.

Meanwhile, Bartholomew Sheridan was living at Lodge Park in Kingstown, "a house with elegant stucco additions such as a lion and urns" and "set in extensive grounds" on which three houses and a large orphanage were later built.[12] In 1837, Samuel Lewis called Lodge Park one of the "principal" of the "numerous handsome seats and pleasing villas" in the seaport.[13] Any past thought of soliciting subscriptions or seeking a government grant to pay for the school's construction had apparently disappeared from Father Sheridan's memory. Nicholas Donnelly, himself a bishop, who later acknowledged the "consequence" for the Sisters of Mercy of "an unfortunate financial misunderstanding with the parish priest," wrote of Sheridan: "None can dispute or question the energy of his character, or his zeal or personal piety; but he got the repute of a shrewd and close financier; yet few can show such lasting and prolific results" in the many new churches he built throughout the villages of his large parish.[14] Church buildings evidently trumped wooden schoolrooms for neglected girls.

In February, on the sudden death of Kate Coffey, a Carlow postulant—from a lung hemorrhage triggered by a fall on the snow—Catherine had written to the saddened Frances:

You have given all to God without any reserve. Nothing can happen to you which He does not appoint. You desire nothing but the accomplishment of His Holy Will. Every thing, how trivial soever, regarding you will come from this adorable source.

11. Letter 87, May 9, 1838, in *CCMcA*, 135. 12. Peter Pearson, *Dun Laoghaire*, 50.
13. Lewis, *Lewis' Dublin*, 201.
14. Donnelly, *History of Dublin Parishes*, part 4, 158, 161.

You must be cheerful and happy, animating all around you. . . . the comfort comes soon after a well received trial.[15]

Did those words now apply even more directly to herself? Catherine struggled with their demand. In mid-May, after the court decision, she wrote to Carlow:

Thus we go on, my Dear Sister Frances, flourishing in the very midst of the Cross, more than a common share of which has latterly fallen to my lot. . . . I humbly trust it is the Cross of Christ. I endeavour to make it in some way like to His—by silence.[16]

Patrick Coleman, the senior vicar general of the diocese, had desired Catherine "to regard him as a particular friend." When he died in May, she once again had to come to grips with her own advice. As she told Frances in a private note, Father Coleman had come to Baggot Street "several times" and "went from me to Doctor Meyler." Though he "was then exceedingly weak and the weather most severe," he "used all the means in his power to have [the chaplaincy situation] according to our wishes—and when he could not succeed wrote me a feeling, fatherly letter. I never can forget his great tenderness and most Christian manner of acting . . . and immediately he is called away."[17]

Finally, in mid-June, the depth of what must have been her ongoing interior wrestling came to stark expression in words intended only for Frances:

Pray fervently to God to take all bitterness from me. I can scarcely think of what has been done to me without resentment. May God forgive me and make me humble before he calls me into His presence.[18]

In his *Spiritual Conferences,* parts of which Catherine read often to the Baggot Street community, St. Francis de Sales writes:

The great esteem in which humility holds the gifts of Faith, Hope, and Charity is the foundation of generosity of spirit. . . . Humility looks only to the poverty and weakness which render us incapable of accomplishing any good work; generosity, on the contrary, inspires us to say with St. Paul, "I can do all things in Him who strengtheneth me"—Philippians 4.13. Humility and generosity should always keep pace. . . . These two virtues . . . are so closely interwoven, that they neither are, nor can be separated. . . . Humility which does not produce generosity must necessarily be delusive.[19]

15. Letter 78, February 17, 1838, in *CCMcA*, 126.   16. Letter 88, May 15, 1838, in *CCMcA*, 136.
17. Letter 89 [late May 1838], in *CCMcA*, 140.   18. Letter 90, June 16, 1838, in *CCMcA*, 144.
19. St. Francis of Sales, *The Spiritual Conferences* (London: C. Dolman, 1853), 36. Mary Vincent Deasy,

Francis de Sales then counsels: "It is better to divert the mind from the immediate source of our sufferings. . . . To dwell on our pains not only strengthens our sensitiveness to them, but tends moreover to create an exaggerate[d] impression of their severity."[20]

Before Catherine at this juncture in 1838 lay three "diverting" invitations to new generosity: Booterstown, a laundry, and Limerick. She gratefully accepted the first one, though with some minor difficulty; she enthusiastically seized the second, its considerable difficulty not yet evident; and she embraced preparations for the last.

The people of Booterstown, a seaside parish between Dublin and Kingstown, had long wished to have a religious community there, to minister to the needs of people in the area. In 1812, Richard, Lord Viscount Fitzwilliam, himself a Protestant, had, at his own expense, replaced the old Catholic chapel by a new church "for the accommodation of his Roman Catholic tenants on this part of his estate."[21] His agent at the time was Richard Verschoyle.

After her husband's death and after the Fitzwilliam estates had passed into the possession of the Earl of Pembroke, Barbara Verschoyle herself became a widely generous benefactor. In 1831 she helped bring the Irish Sisters of Charity to Sandymount, and in the mid-1830s she began assisting the committee that was set up in Booterstown to build a convent.

On March 23, 1838, if not before, James Bacon, the agent of the committee and of the recently deceased Mrs. Verschoyle, approached Catherine about "our going to Booterstown."[22] She quickly agreed, evidently realizing that the sisters might one day have to leave Kingstown, if the debt were not somehow resolved. Booterstown with its open spaces and breezes off Dublin Bay would be as good as Kingstown for convalescing sisters, and the town, though becoming a fashionable summer resort, had many unmet educational and spiritual needs among its poorest inhabitants. In addition to her other gifts, Barbara Verschoyle, who died in January 1837 at age eighty-four, had bequeathed £21 per year to support the sisters' efforts in a poor school for girls.[23]

On April 16 and 17, 1838, an appeal appeared in *Freeman's Journal*. Noting the late Mrs. Verschoyle's additional contribution of £100 and her per-

originally from the Mercy convent in Cork, is believed to be the "Member of the Order of Mercy, Sunderland" who translated this edition of Francis de Sales's *Conferences*.

20. Ibid., 40.
21. Donnelly, *History of Dublin Parishes,* part 3, 109.
22. Letter 81, March 24, 1838, in *CCMcA*, 129.
23. Letter 316, October 15, 1841, in *CCMcA*, 451.

sonal solicitation of several other gifts, including £50 from Sidney Herbert, Baron of Lea, the appeal invited further financial assistance toward
the building project:

The Committee erecting the Convent of Booterstown, for the Sisters of Mercy,
have . . . completed their laudable undertaking, but are obliged to request the kind
assistance of the charitable and humane towards liquidating the debts, and finally
finishing it for the reception of the Religious Community, whose attention to the
morals and education of the rising generation, and the comforts of the sick and dying poor, produces the most happy effects in every neighborhood they have been
established.

A list of fifty-seven donations "already received" was appended to the appeal, including sums from James Bacon, Daniel Murray, Patrick Doyle, the
parish priest, and the Dowling family (slate and timber suppliers).[24]

By May 15, Catherine told Frances Warde the plans for Booterstown:
"We have marked out M. Cecilia [Marmion], Superior," Ursula Frayne, Jane
Sausse, Teresa Breen, and Teresa Carton. But "sharp cold" in Dublin and
"sleet this morning" had already affected Cecilia's and Teresa's coughs, so
Catherine delayed departing: "I did hope to have our weak ones in Booterstown this week, but am now afraid to venture, though it is very sheltered
and quite dry."[25] Moreover, Cecilia, though capable, was frequently ill,
and Booterstown would need a strong, healthy sister to manage its several ministries, so Catherine eventually asked Ursula Frayne to be superior
of this house which, like Kingstown but unlike the distant foundations,
would remain directly affiliated with Baggot Street. In time, it would have
a large poor school, and Catherine could then calculate that "600 poor
children in the Archdiocess receive daily tuition from our Sisters."[26]

But in late May, she was "perplexed and weary" and wrote a "Not fit to
appear" letter to Frances Warde. "I have not seen them in Kingstown for a
long time, cannot go—or at least I think so"—because of the lawsuit judgment. Moreover, the "thought of Booterstown is an additional weight on
my mind—I have no happiness in it—& endless difficulty in who will go,
etc." Still she hoped that "God may receive some small portion of glory in
the help that will be given to His poor."[27]

When, by mid-June, the community was finally settled in Booterstown, she was pleased with the "good ground for a garden, quite unmade,"
but not with the shape of the bedrooms:

24. *Freeman's Journal,* April 16–17, 1838.   25. Letter 88, May 15, 1838, in *CCMcA,* 136–37.
26. Letter 290, August 3, 1841, in *CCMcA,* 426.   27. Letter 89 [late May 1838], in *CCMcA,* 140.

All uncomfortable—doors so exceedingly large and in the center of the wall—so that the head of [the] Bed would not fit on either side, and the window as large opposite the door. The only way with room—is across—which scarcely leaves a pass at the foot.[28]

Having lived at Baggot Street for nine years and settled five convent-houses beyond Dublin, Catherine knew a thing or two about the design of small bedrooms. The door should abut a side wall, to leave room for the head of the bed. But no matter. The new parish priest in Booterstown, John Ennis, was "anxious to do all in his power to promote our comfort—he seems to regret the past and says if he lives seven years more it will be atoned for."[29] Evidently Ennis was not the only curate at St. Andrew's saddened by the ongoing chaplaincy dispute.

Booterstown convent was dedicated on July 26, 1838, the feast of St. Anne, after whom it was named, and the committee who erected it could have been proud that the grand old building, now renovated, still stands. It was probably around this time that Catherine sent Ursula Frayne an almost unbelievable poem-letter about her return to Dublin on the steam train.

After waiting for a train in Booterstown, she and Mary Aloysius Scott decided to walk to the "next stand house gate" near Merrion, where they still had to wait. Then seeing a train bound for Kingstown, in the opposite direction, they mistakenly got in, which turned out all right, for in Kingstown "a matter was pending . . . which could not be answered without the Superior":

> It was well I that day appeared on the spot
> and although my old bones were weary and sore
> yet to be there then, I'd have gone through much more.

They left Kingstown the next morning "about half past ten / but—how shall I say it—missed the steamer again." So Aloysius again, "so smart and so airy," suggested they "walk on to Dunleary," apparently to the old village harbor. Warming to her melodramatic tale, Catherine continues:

> By hills and by hollows—through great rocks and stones
> expecting each moment to break my poor bones
> until quite exhausted of temper and strength

28. Letter 90, June 16, 1838, in *CCMcA*, 142.
29. Letter 92, July 3, 1838, in *CCMcA*, 147.

> I gave up to despair and lay down at full length
> on a deep sloping Rock from which the least tip
> would—or I thought so—have caused me to slip.

Finally, finally, they caught a train to Dublin and reached "dear" Baggot Street in time for noon prayers. Presumably Catherine soon learned the wisdom of waiting patiently for trains, though one can be fairly sure she exaggerated the perils of the journey for the sake of provoking laughter in Booterstown. She concluded the poem:

> All things that you've asked for I'm trying to get
> But pray ask no more—my own dearest Pet
> I'll now take my leave—Be a good child
> humble—and merry—diligent & mild.
> Work hard for the poor, love one another
> and believe me your ever affectionate Mother.[30]

What most delighted Catherine in the spring and summer of 1838 was the prospect of finally having a commercial laundry at Baggot Street, which she had long hoped would "render the House of Mercy self-supporting, as the closing of the chapel [in 1834] had so greatly curtailed our resources."[31] In April she told Frances Warde:

We are likely to have the long desired public laundry built this season. Through the Providence of God and the kindness of Mr. O'Hanlon we have got a legacy [£1,000] nearly equal to the expense. What a comfort if I am permitted to see some secure means of supporting our poor women & children established, not to be entirely depending on daily [door-to-door] collections which are so difficult to keep up. We would soon have a valuable laundry as the neighbourhood is so good.[32]

Though Catherine knew little about constructing or running a commercial laundry, she relied on Bernard Mullins, a Dublin architect recommended by Andrew Fitzgerald. The addition to the house would extend from the back, down Herbert Street, and would include another large schoolroom, an additional dormitory for women on the top floor, and the laundry in the basement. In May, Catherine was still enthusiastic about the laundry:

I did hope our Laundry would have commenced by this, but no—delays innumerable. We are leaving it to Mr. Mullins. . . . What would I not go through to see it at

---

30. Letter 93 [mid-1838], in *CCMcA*, 148–50.
31. CAM, in *CMcATM*, 212.
32. Letter 82, April 9, 1838, in *CCMcA*, 132. Arrangements for the addition to the house were made earlier, but the building agreements were not signed until the summer. The £1000 legacy was not used— perhaps could not be—to pay the Kingstown debt.

full work. We have got all information on the matter. You would be surprised to know all that can be earned by this means. New persons coming into the neighbourhood every day. We are asked to take washing. Since the Townsend St. Asylum was removed to Donny Brook, we have constant application. Yesterday it went to my heart to send away a large parcel which would have paid well. In one Institution they earned 7 hundred pounds in 14 months, clear of all expenses. We must give up all the garden for drying ground & grass plot—but there can be a walk round it. God grant it may be soon done.[33]

The building project proceeded slowly. Giving up the garden and grass plot would eventually be the least of its difficulties.

Then, on September 8, Catherine left Dublin to establish a new community in Limerick. The request to found a convent there was among the "endless" invitations she had received. In August, Dr. John Ryan, bishop of Limerick, got her agreement about the foundation, even though in her view: "We are very near a Stop—I should say, a full Stop—feet and hands are numerous enough, but the heads are nearly gone."[34] Elizabeth Moore, potentially a good "head," would be the superior, and Mary Vincent Harnett, still a novice, would remain in Limerick with her. Catherine could spare no more from Baggot Street, but to help out during the first months she would bring Mary Aloysius Scott and Mary Xavier O'Connell.

The September departure was not the best timing for Catherine. She had for weeks "been tortured with my unfortunate mouth"—gum disease, probably scurvy or some form of periodontal disease with painful inflammation. It was only now "getting a little better." Moreover, going to Limerick in the first week of September meant she had to "forfeit the happiness of going to Carlow." As she told Frances: "You may be sure this is sorrowful news to me. . . . I need not bid you pity me and yourself for our mutual disappointment."[35]

The founding party traveled to Limerick by packet boat on the Irish Sea so they could visit the Cork and Charleville communities on the way. Catherine's memories of the long, fatiguing journeys overland from Charleville and Cork in previous years were still too strong to let her face repetition. To avoid the curiosity of other passengers on the boat, Catherine asked her companions not to address her as "Reverend Mother"—as they

33. Letter 88, May 15, 1838, in *CCMcA*, 138. In 1833 the Sisters of Charity took over the Asylum for Penitent Women on Townsend Street which "had fallen into . . . neglect." In 1837, it moved to Donnybrook and was then "known as St. Mary Magdalen's Asylum." [Mary Padua Flanagan], *The Life and Work of Mary Aikenhead* (London: Longmans, Green, 1924), 138.

34. Letter 94, August 23, 1838, in *CCMcA*, 151.

35. Ibid.

invariably did at home, despite her wishes. When motion sickness affect-ed them all, Elizabeth Moore exclaimed: "O Kitty, what shall I do?" James McAuley's favorite name for his sister made them laugh and put an end to worrying about their nausea.[36]

In Cork, Catherine met for the first time Elizabeth Agnew and Ma-ria Taylor, two English women, converts to the Catholic Church, who had come to Cork in April to serve a novitiate prior to founding a community of Sisters of Mercy in Bermondsey, London. Peter Butler, the parish priest in Bermondsey, was a friend of Bishop Murphy, and together they had ap-parently worked out this arrangement with Clare Moore. Catherine found the two women "very pleasing, Sister Agnew particularly so," and all the Cork community "in excellent health and spirits."[37]

On September 12 the group for Limerick went on to Charleville by coach, intending to stay there only a day or two. In the end they remained almost two weeks. As Catherine explained to Teresa White:

I found I could be more useful there than perhaps I have ever been. There was dan-ger of all breaking up—and my heart felt sorrowful when I thought of the poor being deprived of the comfort which God seemed to intend for them. I made every effort & praised be God, all came round.[38]

Illness, financial worries, and lack of postulants still tempted Angela Dunne to think the Charleville community should disband. In December 1837, Catherine had, not too gently, urged her to remain:

What could excuse us before God—for casting off any charge which we had freely undertaken, except compelled by necessity to do so. Are not the poor of Charleville as dear to him as elsewhere—and while one pound of Miss Clanchy's five hundred lasts, ought we not to persevere and confide in his Providence. . . . I am grieved to find such feint-hearted symptoms amongst us.[39]

In the past year Mary Clanchy, now about forty-seven, had married Ar-thur French of County Roscommon, and, at least up to May 1838, had "not fulfilled her engagement for Charleville," though "perhaps she may."[40] At its founding in 1836, Miss Clanchy had promised to give the Charleville community £500, apparently in installments. In July 1838, when Thomas Croke, the parish priest, visited Catherine, she asked him whether Miss Clanchy's marriage would be "any draw back" for the Charleville commu-

36. Handwritten "Limerick Annals," vol. 1, 60–61 (ASB).
37. Letter 96, October 1, 1838, in CCMcA, 156.
38. Ibid.
39. Letter 67, December 20, 1837, in CCMcA, 114.
40. Letter 88, May 15, 1838, in CCMcA, 138.

nity's financial condition. He assured her that even if he "were obliged to go to England to beg for them, they should not feel any loss." Catherine's mind was eased: "This was very strong language, from rather a cold character"—though what she meant by "cold" cannot be guessed.[41]

Now, two months later, Catherine had been in Charleville for twelve days, trying to encourage everyone, for the sake of "the poor of Charleville, as dear to him as elsewhere."[42] Thomas Croke had secured from Lord Cork a grant of land on which to build a new convent, and arranged that the first stone would be laid "on our dear festival, the 24th [of September]," the feast day of Our Lady of Mercy. Later that day, "leaving all in joy and happiness," Catherine and her companions departed on the twenty-one-mile coach journey to Limerick.[43]

What awaited them that night was a large and beautiful old convent enclosed by ivied walls and once occupied by a community of Poor Clares. It was set in a "very bad" section of the city, not far from the ruined castle of King John built around 1200. As Catherine told Teresa White, now the superior in Kingstown: "The poor here are in the most miserable state—the whole surrounding neighbourhood one scene of wretchedness and sorrow."[44] It was "as if our Dublin Convent was in the center of the lanes & courts about Townsend Street."[45]

The big question in Limerick was whether a new religious community could survive there. The Poor Clares had departed in 1831, after the death of their abbess, but left behind three lay sisters. One had died in 1834, but two in their forties, Mary Shanahan and Anne Hewitt, were still there, and Catherine immediately invited them to live in the Mercy community and sit at the head of the table. The Presentation Sisters who had come to Limerick in May 1837 were struggling. "They are in the best part of the city, but are not supported except by words—and a party" of vocal laity. Though everyone "that wishes to show their true love turns away from the S[isters] of Mercy . . . as to patronage," Catherine was cautioned "to take no part, but let it work its own way."[46] She could easily do that because the poor were at the door, and the extensive poor school the two Poor Clares had tried to maintain needed all the energy they could give to it. As the feast of Teresa of Avila (October 15) approached, Catherine begged Teresa White

41. Letter 92, July 3, 1838, in CCMcA, 148.
42. Letter 67, December 20, 1837, in CCMcA, 114.
43. Letter 96, October 1, 1838, in CCMcA, 156.
44. Letter 102, November 17, 1838, in CCMcA, 168.
45. Letter 96, October 1, 1838, in CCMcA, 155.
46. Letter 102, November 17, 1838, in CCMcA, 168–69.

to "implore Saint Teresa who loved foundations to intercede for poor Limerick where no seed has yet taken root. Visitors pray us not to be discouraged by the past failures and promise us it will not be so in our regard. . . . The Bishop [John Ryan] has been here—he was absent when we came. I think he will be very kind."[47]

An amazing but little-noticed feature of Catherine McAuley's leadership was her capacity to develop other female leaders, by the undramatic means of patience, encouragement, and affection. Zealous and experienced herself, she knew she was recommending for episcopal approval, as superiors of the new foundations, women who were much younger than she and unaccustomed to negotiating directly with bishops, priests, or lay people. Skilled at household tasks and ministry among poor people, they were at first fearful and hesitant about business matters. Elizabeth Moore was no exception. As Catherine confided to Frances Warde four weeks after their arrival in Limerick:

I cannot go for a full month. No person of less experience could manage at present—and I am very insufficient for the task. As to Sister Elizabeth, with all her readiness to undertake it—we never sent forward such a feint-hearted soldier, now that she is in the field. She will do all interior & exterior work, but to meet on business—confer with the Bishop—conclude with a Sister—you might as well send the child that opens the door. . . . She gets white as death—and her eyes like fever. She is greatly liked—and when the alarms are a little over and a few in the House, I expect all will go on well.[48]

On October 24, Mary Vincent Harnett professed her vows in the Limerick convent chapel. Though space was limited, all who sought admission to the ceremony "were allowed to take [their] places as best they could."[49] The Sisters of Mercy were a phenomenon in Limerick, where the citizens were used to enclosed religious orders. Now the same woman they had seen stepping across rain puddles and mud on her way to visit the sick, a basket of bread on her arm, stood before them in a white cloak professing her religious vows. It was a fine occasion, in Catherine's opinion—"very good sermon, good private singers—and my most *angelic* Sister Aloysius at the piano." The only drawback was that the unassuming Helena Heffernan, the main benefactor of the Mercy community in Limerick, did not come: "We have never seen the foundress—this is Gospel perfection. She would not even ask for a Ticket to the Ceremony."[50]

47. Letter 96, October 1, 1838, in CCMcA, 156–57.
48. Letter 98, October 25 [1838], in CCMcA, 159.
49. Handwritten "Limerick Annals," vol. 1, 17 (ASB).
50. Letter 98, October 25 [1838], in CCMcA, 161.

Like Elizabeth Pentony in Tullamore, Mary Clanchy in Charleville, Michael and John Nowlan in Carlow, Barbara Gould in Cork, and Barbara Verschoyle in Booterstown, Miss Heffernan had, through a fund she set up, made possible the community in Limerick, and Catherine always considered these women and men the founders of the spreading Mercy endeavors. Helena Heffernan's trust fund yielded £100 to the community annually, and after her death in 1860, £200 annually.[51] On October 24, 1838, Catherine could have little dreamed what would one day be attributed, at least in part, to Helena Heffernan's foresight and mercifulness. Already two women had joined the community: Anne Farrell and Ellen Potter, the latter of whom had briefly entered the Dublin community but left because of poor health. And Catherine expected two more: Joanna Bridgeman on November 1, and Mary Anne Bridgeman, possibly Joanna's cousin, on December 8.[52]

Thus, in the early autumn of 1838, a great deal seemed to be progressing well in the Mercy world. The fever epidemic was over in Tullamore, Catherine Locke and Clare Delamere had professed vows there, hundreds of children and adults were being instructed in the faith and confirmed, and Michael Molloy, a large distiller of whiskey since 1829, was building a new Tullamore convent. In Carlow, their new convent was almost completed, Frances Warde had recovered from a long illness, and the college priests could not do enough for the now much larger community. Andrew Fitzgerald had given them a "piano, a sofa, and chairs for the community room" and £34 to replenish their dwindling funds, and would not call for the rent on the cottage until they could meet it.[53] The sisters in Cork were visiting the city jail, the South Infirmary, and the Cork poor house (Cork Union), and opening a House of Mercy as well as a pension school in a large room of the convent.[54] Charleville and Booterstown were settled, and Limerick was planning to open a House of Mercy on November 19, the feast day of Elizabeth of Hungary. Though Catherine still had fears about Limerick's future, they had "finished the two 30 days' Prayers . . . one in the morning and one in the evening," and were "now going to say the whole Psalter [of Jesus] for 15 days—this is our best hope."[55]

Then, at the end of October, the Kingstown controversy soared to its painful climax.

51. M. Loreto O'Connor, "Helena Heffernan, a True Limerick Woman," in Marie Therese Courtney and M. Loreto O'Connor, *Sisters of Mercy in Limerick* (n.p.: Limerick Leader, 1988), 23–26.

52. "Limerick Convent Register" (ASB). About Anne Farrell, see *CCMcA*, 159 n. 22 and 360 n. 82.

53. CA, in *CMcATM*, 227.

54. Bolster, *Mercy in Cork*, 6, 9.

55. Letter 98, October 25 [1838], in *CCMcA*, 161.

Because the court-assigned debt to James Nugent remained unpaid, the sisters were forced to leave the convent before an eviction notice was placed on it. Perhaps Catherine had already suggested to Charles Cavanagh that the sisters could eventually leave Kingstown, the house could be rented out, and the income used to pay the debt. But the obvious time to rent a house near the sea was spring, not autumn. It is more likely, as becomes clear in February 1839, that Bartholomew Sheridan himself planned to sell the house, which he did not own, to pay the debt to James Nugent. Therefore, "the Sisters had to come into Baggot Street with all haste to avoid being in the house when an execution should be laid upon it"—that is, a document seizing the goods of a debtor in default of a payment assigned by a court of law.[56] On November 1, Catherine, still in Limerick, wrote to Teresa White:

How can I sufficiently thank you for the kind cautious manner in which you communicate the painful news. . . .We have done all that justice and prudence demands—to avert this affliction. If it must come, let us receive it as the Holy Will of God in our regard. It will mortify us and that will be salutary, please God. As to removing the Blessed Sacrament—God will direct you. Be a good soldier in the hour of trial—do not be afflicted for your poor—their Heavenly Father will provide comfort for them, and you will have the same opportunity of fulfilling your obligations during your life.

I charge you, my very dear child, not to be sorrowful—but rather to rejoice if we are to suffer this humiliating trial. God will not be angry—be assured of that—and is not that enough. I feel that it would give you no consolation were I to say—"God would not be displeased with you, though He may with me." He will not be displeased with me—for He knows I would rather be cold and hungry than the poor in Kingstown or elsewhere should be deprived of any consolation in our power to afford—but in the present case, we have done all that belonged to us to do—and even more than the circumstances justified.

May God in His mercy bless and protect you all. Perhaps the next letter will inform me of your removal to Baggot Street.

The Sisters here unite in love—with your ever affectionate

Mary C. McAuley[57]

To de Pazzi Delany at Baggot Street, who was clearly upset by the sudden departure from Kingstown, Catherine tried to explain as fully as possible:

The Kingstown business is a real portion of the Cross. From what you say, I should think you do not know all the circumstances. They were submitted to the Bishop

56. CAM, in *CMcATM*, 210.
57. Letter 100, November 1, 1838, in *CCMcA*, 163-64.

already and I cannot see any use in teasing him with another statement. Indeed, when I think of what my poor Sisters suffered, I do not wish they should return, though I feel very much for the poor souls they have left.[58]

She then told de Pazzi about events that took place in the months since the court judgment in May, and while Elizabeth Moore was local superior in Kingstown:

In my letter to his Grace I mentioned that Father Sheridan said I made myself accountable for the whole debt—by giving fifty pounds—and added, "perhaps, my Lord, I cannot be said to have given it since the builder took it from the table—a heavy parcel of silver." This letter was forwarded to Mr. Sheridan. Mr. Nugent got it to read and conceived it charged him with taking away the bag of silver forcibly. He went to Sister Elizabeth in a violent rage, called me cheat & liar. He did just the same in Mr. Cavanagh's public office in Fitzwilliam Street, and from that time, no proposal Mr. Cavanagh could make would be attended to—and a bitter feeling has existed towards the poor Sisters ever since.

Even Father Sheridan was greatly excited, and said that while I appeared to be a quiet, simple person—I was cunning & clever. These things were never told to me until I pressed Sr. Elizabeth for her reason for disliking Kingstown so much, and for appearing quite in terror lest Mr. Nugent should come whenever I was there. It has been said that not giving the profits of the second Bazaar occasioned the law proceedings—but we never promised it—and one hundred children were then preparing for Confirmation [in Kingstown], for whom 100 dresses were bought.

Two watches were given to that Bazaar for the children, but not for building. Mr. Nugent got £12 each time for putting up the tent—though we had all the trouble of getting permission from Col. Burgoyne—and borrowing sail cloth. In all, Mr. Nugent has got from us eighty four pounds—and ten which Mr. Sheridan sent me for him. I suppose he did not keep a regular account of the expense incurred, for he sent a measurer which he seemed to think we would not allow, for he sent some message the Sisters did not understand—about wanting to know the dimensions, etc.—the plainest work that ever was executed is charged at a high rate—and the promise that was made in the beginning of applying to the board of education—never fulfilled.

Near the end of the letter, after news about Limerick, Catherine commented:

I cannot express the consolation Sister M. Teresa has afforded me by her manner of concluding the Kingstown business—and the few quiet lines she sent to Father Sheridan. Thanks be to God, I find the Sisters can act as well as could be desired when I am not at home—though they cannot write a note then—but I hope to keep them in practice and to rest myself in future.[59]

58. Letter 101, November 15, 1838, in *CCMcA*, 164.
59. Ibid., 165-66. In a preceding year, a second bazaar, in addition to the one in Dublin, was held in Kingstown for which a tent was needed.

At present, there was nothing more to say—or do—about Kingstown. It was over.

Writing to Frances Warde two days later, Catherine was silent about Kingstown. She discussed the upcoming reception of the three Limerick novices and her plan to stop in Carlow on the way back to Dublin. Her only conceivable allusion to Kingstown was her saying she could not remain in Limerick "beyond the 10th—quite impossible, from many circumstances which I will tell you."[60]

Mary Teresa Vincent (Ellen) Potter, Mary Joseph (Anne) Farrell, and Mary Francis (Joanna) Bridgeman received the Mercy habit in Limerick on December 4, and Mary Anne Bridgeman entered the community on December 8. Francis Bridgeman would one day found a community in Kinsale, and in 1854 lead a contingent of mostly Irish sisters to nurse in the Crimean War.[61] On December 9, Catherine departed with Mary Aloysius Scott and Mary Xavier O'Connell. She had been away from Dublin for three months, the longest time she had ever been absent.

She reached Carlow later that day. If she discussed with Frances Warde or Andrew Fitzgerald or James Maher her heartache over Kingstown, no such conversation is recorded. The Carlow community was busy preparing for a reception ceremony the next day, Dr. Francis Haly presiding. Before they were clothed in the black Mercy habit and white veil, the three novices-to-be would each wear "a thick white muslin dress, a home-made lace veil, and a wreath of flowers."[62] Catherine had not instituted this custom at Baggot Street, but may have liked the simple beauty of their appearance as they processed into the cathedral.

Among the new novices was Mary Cecilia (Ellen) Maher, a talented, capable woman. As Catherine watched her receive the Mercy habit, she could not know that in 1849, at age fifty, Cecilia would set out on a long voyage to found at Auckland the first community of Sisters of Mercy in New Zealand. They would journey past the Cape of Good Hope, and learn the Maori language along the way. Crossing the Indian Ocean they would face unusually calm seas and near-starvation.[63]

---

60. Letter 102, November 17, 1838, in CCMcA, 169. This letter was not postmarked until November 26 (Limerick) and November 27 (Carlow).

61. Mary Teresa Vincent's long name was no doubt occasioned by the fact that another "Mary Vincent" was in the Limerick community (i.e., Harnett). St. Vincent de Paul's charitable work among the poor was much admired by the early Sisters of Mercy. The Crimean experience of the Irish sisters is recorded in *The Crimean Journals of the Sisters of Mercy, 1854–56*, edited by Maria Luddy (Dublin: Four Courts Press, 2004).

62. CA, in CMcATM, 228.

63. See Marcienne D. Kirk, *Remembering Your Mercy: Mother Mary Cecilia Maher and the First Sisters of Mercy in New Zealand* (Auckland: Sisters of Mercy, 1998).

On December 11, Catherine returned to Dublin, to the relief of her anxious assistant. During her absence, de Pazzi Delany had been "so frequently ill," presumably with epileptic attacks, especially after the Kingstown affair, that by mid-November Redmond O'Hanlon had asked Catherine to return as soon as possible: "Mr. O'Hanlon has been prevailed on to order me home. I wrote to him and think he will approve my reason for remaining so long—it was as strong [a letter] as it could be."[64] The gentle O'Hanlon was, after all, Archbishop Murray's deputy as the ecclesiastical superior of the Dublin community, and he could easily see that de Pazzi was having trouble dealing with life at Baggot Street. On a later, but similar occasion, "he regretted writing such an imperative letter."[65]

Before leaving Limerick, Catherine wrote a poem-letter of "parting advice" for Elizabeth Moore to read after her departure. Now as she rode home from Carlow to Baggot Street, she may have silently addressed its words to herself:

> Don't let crosses vex or tease
> Try to meet *all* with peace & ease
> notice the faults of every Day
> but often in a playful way
> And when you seriously complain
> Let it be known—to give you pain
> Attend to one thing—at a time
> you've 15 hours from 6 to 9
> be mild and sweet in all your ways
> now & again—bestow some praise
> avoid—all solemn declaration
> all serious, close investigation
> Turn what you can into a jest
> and with few words dismiss the rest
> keep patience ever at your side
> you'll want it for a constant guide
> Show fond affection every Day
> and above all—Devoutly Pray
> That God may bless the charge He's given
> and make of you—their guide to Heaven.[66]

64. Letter 102, November 17, 1838, in *CCMcA*, 168.
65. Letter 267, May 25, 1841, in *CCMcA*, 398.
66. Letter 103 [December 9, 1838], in *CCMcA*, 169–70.

A week after her return, Catherine met with a friendly curate of the Kingstown parish. She asked him to give her a written record of their transaction, and he did so:

Mrs. McAuley has this day handed me the sum of Twenty-Six Pounds Thirteen Shillings and two pence halfpenny being the balance of the Poor Fund in the hands of the Ss. of Mercy at the time of their leaving Kingstown.

William Walsh[67]

Whatever else had happened about Kingstown, she would not hold back the halfpenny.

67. Letter 105, December 19, 1838, in *CCMcA*, 172.

CHAPTER 15

Willie McAuley and His Aunt *December 1838*

The year 1838 ended with another heartache. Catherine McAuley's youngest nephew, Willie, now seventeen, departed from Ireland for good, making no farewell visit to his aunt. He took "passage in the *Clonmel* steamer for London," probably in early to mid-December, with "15 shillings in my pocket. My brothers [James and Robert] came to see me off. As the steamer moved from the Quay my sorrowful eyes fixed on the dear and loving faces of my brothers."[1]

Once earlier, after the death of his sister Catherine in August 1837, William had tried life as an unpaid sailor on the *Millman* brig of Belfast, a ship bound for Demerara, a region in British Guiana, South America, famed for its sugar exports. He then returned to Dublin. Now, in late 1838, since he "did not know just yet" what he was going to do in life, his Uncle James suggested that "as I had gone to sea" before, "I had better follow it up." James told Willie that if he "would go to London and write to him, he would come to London and try to get me entered in a respectable manner to a seafaring life."

At her wish, conveyed by his brothers, William had visited his Aunt

---

1. William McAuley to Mary Catherine (Fanny Teresa) McAuley and others, October 28, 1903 (MCA). In this important handwritten letter to his daughter and others, provoked by his having seen himself made "public property" in Carroll's *Life of Catherine McAuley,* William says he proposes to give a "short sketch of my earliest recollections, and what effect the treatment I received had in the shaping of the course I pursued, in working out my future career. In my statements I will not spare myself; at the same time I will deal as lightly as possible, consistent with the truth, with those I may have to write about." Many extracts from Willie's letter occur in the text that follows. Unless otherwise noted, direct quotations attributed to Willie McAuley are from this source.

Catherine at Baggot Street after his sister Catherine's death and before his first sea voyage to Demerara, but his memory of that visit, as he recalled it decades later, was painful:

The night before I sailed out of Dublin custom house dock, at 8 P.M. we all three went, and on entering the little visitors parlour, I turned to the right, and sat down in the corner, it being the darkest in the room—James on one side, Robert on the other. We were not long seated when Aunt entered the other door and stood facing us. She gave us many good advices, and amongst them, never to marry a woman older than ourselves. . . . That night my Aunt never said she forgave or shook hands with me. . . .

I set sail next day for Demerara. . . . This visit to the convent was my last. I never saw my Aunt again. When I returned to Dublin again I determined not to go there unless I was sent for. There was nothing but my dear brothers to entice me to stop [in Ireland], and I would not be a burthen to them. All the influential friends of my father looked coldly on us because we became Catholics. Often was I told I turned for lucre and gain. I was never introduced into society of corresponding influence with those who turned their backs on me.

So now, in late 1838, there was no farewell visit to Baggot Street. Catherine had been away from Dublin for three months—in Cork, Charleville, and Limerick—but she had returned to the city about December 11 or 12. Perhaps by then Willie had gone to London where, as he again recalls, "I knew no one and [was] penniless."[2] In due time his Uncle James came to him in London "and took me before the Admiralty":

I was too old to enter as a middy. So he found an East India free trader. I signed articles for three years, got a seagoing outfit as a mercantile middy in the *Mary Catherine* barque of London. In this vessel I hauled out of St. Catherine's [Katharine's] dock on the 26th December 1838. I was to be assisted in learning navigation but was not supplied with nautical instruments, a theodolite costing about 12 guineas and a quadrant about 6 guineas, nor was I supplied with any money, so as to be able to cope with the five other young fellows and third mate in our mess. So here I was, armed with self respect, sailing away to extricate myself from two cross fires.[3]

The "cross fires" as Willie felt he experienced them were, on the one hand, the rejection and accusations of his father's Protestant friends, and on the other what he took to be his aunt's and uncle's coldness toward him. In 1903, when he was almost eighty-two, he described the second crossfire:

Those whom I dearly loved showed me the cold shoulder because I sinned. No doubt in time I might have been forgiven, but I could not live upon the air and wait,

---

2. From his account, one can estimate that William was in London at least two weeks.

3. St. Katharine's dock was on the north side of the Thames, east of the Tower of London. A theodolite was a surveying instrument for measuring angles; a quadrant was a quarter-circle instrument for measuring angles and altitudes. *The Compact Edition of the Oxford English Dictionary,* 1971.

and I could not do servile work. If I did my case would be worse. I never [did] and do not now regret that glorious act of my being called through the Mercy of God to the only true Faith of my forefathers, the Holy Roman Catholic Church.

Thus, by the end of December 1838, the youngest of Catherine's nephews was gone, and she never heard from him again. She later assumed he had died at sea or, like his sisters, of consumption, and she died thinking this. Moreover, she apparently never realized—or if she did, she left no word of this—that what Willie most sought in life was her forgiveness, and that her manner toward him at the bedside of his sister Catherine in August 1837 had been, in his young eyes, unforgiving, or reluctantly forgiving. His "sin" may perhaps be interpreted, on the basis of his own veiled reference, as a one-time liaison with a prostitute, or simply as his "wild" floundering, or what he, more vaguely, called his "many grievous faults and sins." In his extant correspondence, as it is known to this biographer, William never precisely named the "sin" or "faults" beyond his saying that, leaving Baggot Street one night after his aunt had rolled his curly hair in papers, "instead of keeping in the respectable thoroughfares, where I might meet some of those who knew me, I traversed bye lanes and low streets, and thus evil befell me. I sinned."

In Willie's sensitive memory, the scene in the summer of 1837 at the bedside of his dying sister Catherine, the one closest to him in age—she then eighteen, and he sixteen—was excruciating on two counts:

My only and dear sister is dying. I was sent for. Sadly I hastened to the convent; I was ushered upstairs to the big room immediately over the Chapel, a large curtained bedstead in the centre of the room, sideways onto the door, the curtains partially opened in the centre. On the opposite side to me sat my Aunt. I looked into the bed, I was so overcome I could not see my sister. I turned my head, looked down the room; my Aunt silently pointed to the bed. I wiped my eyes, and saw the little but fondly loved form of my Angelic departing sister. Now she pleads for her erring brother: Forgive him, dear Aunt, forgive him. The answer came in a low voice, Yes dear; but she never moved from her seat. Oh that terrible interview. Nothing in this world its sorrowful remembrance could ever efface. My only sister gone, let me hope to enjoy Eternal happiness with her dear sister Mary in Heaven. I made up my mind to go to sea. I believed I would not live long; I would never see twenty. This made me reckless, what did it matter where or when I died, better at sea than on shore. I would be less trouble to anyone to bury me.

Apparently his Aunt Catherine's own grief before her dying niece numbed her to Willie's, and his heartache at losing his last sister blinded him to Catherine's. In human terms, it was an isolating, tragic moment for which neither was really prepared, though the aunt might have been expected to be more alert to another's anguish.

A further disappointment troubled William McAuley's long life. After he learned of his brothers' and his aunt's death—in the mid-1840s when he wrote to Baggot Street, and Cecilia Marmion and Mary Camillus (Teresa) Byrn responded—Willie believed that the Macauley family properties in Cartrongarrow, near Ardagh, County Longford, and in County Monaghan, inherited by his father from his maternal grandmother, Nichola Montgomery Nesbitt, should have rightly passed to him.[4] He also believed that, as his guardian after his father's death, Catherine McAuley, and subsequently her executors, had a duty to ensure this. He apparently never knew that long before his aunt's death, his eldest brother, James, having inherited the properties from his father, had sold both pieces of land, with the dwellings on them, and had spent the money on his own and his brother Robert's needs.[5] So there was no property and no "rent" for Willie to inherit, much as he and his large family in Australia would have benefited from such income. He seems to have felt that the Sisters of Mercy at Baggot Street, who were his aunt's executors, had somehow inherited the properties on Catherine's death, everyone there wrongly supposing that "Wild Willie" was dead of consumption or lost at sea and little imagining that he would be eventually living, often in near poverty, in Australia with his wife, Jessie Tomkins, and their thirteen children.[6]

4. In one deed for the Macauley property, eight variant spellings are given for "Cartrongarrow." The first is given here.

5. The eventual sale in 1840, by Catherine McAuley's nephew James, of the Macauley property in County Longford to Laurence Reynolds was relatively straightforward, after the detailed process of deducing James Francis Macauley's title to this land was completed, the family's holding going back to a grant of Charles II in 1668. James's lease of this property for nine years to another person in 1838 also had to be redeemed before the sale occurred. "Attested Copy of Memorial of the Deed of Conveyance, James Francis Macauley to Laurence Reynolds, signed April 23, 1840, and registered on June 9, 1840" (MCA). Memorial no. 1840.12.171, RD.

The sale of the smaller holding in County Monaghan (over eight acres) was more complicated because, unbeknown to James, on December 5, 1828, his father had signed a deed of conveyance to Nathaniel Wright in return for £92.6.0 (partial payment of the £200 sale price). William Macauley having died seven weeks later (January 1829), the deed was never registered, and the rest of the sale price never paid. Finally, on September 20, 1839, James Francis Macauley signed a deed of conveyance with the son of the deceased Nathaniel Wright. "Attested Copy of Memorial of the Deed of Conveyance, James Francis Macauley to Thomas Edmond Wright, registered on September 21, 1839" (MCA). Memorial no. 1839.18.9, RD.

6. William McAuley and Jessie Russell Tomkins were married in Colac, Victoria, Australia, on February 24, 1853. He was then thirty-one, and she a little over seventeen. Their seven sons and six daughters were born over the next twenty-four years. Their first daughter was named Mary Catherine, and died young. Their fifth daughter, Frances (Fanny) Teresa (1871–1952), took the name Mary Catherine when she entered the Sisters of Mercy. Jessie Tomkins, who became a Catholic, is said to have been "disowned" by her family "when she married William McAuley, because he was a Catholic." Jessie died at Colac on June 17, 1896. Photocopy, Mary Dennett, "Family History Report for the descendants of William Armstrong Montgomery McAuley," Melbourne, November 2010.

It was a sad case of lack of communication, made worse by the early deaths of those who knew the situation and could have explained it to Willie in the years up to November 1841, if they had known he was alive and how to reach him. Evidently the letters from Cecilia Marmion and Teresa Byrn in 1845 or 1846, correspondence that is apparently no longer extant, did not address the property issue, probably because they were both ignorant of young James's sales in 1839 and 1840.[7] After an apparently failed attempt to hear from Frances Warde in the United States, Willie finally succeeded in making himself known to Mary Xavier Maguire in Geelong, to Ursula Frayne in Melbourne, and to other Sisters of Mercy in Australia, as well as, again, to his cousin Mary Camillus (Teresa) Byrn, now in Baltimore, and to his cousin Mary Margaret (Anne) Byrn in London. But these, too, did not know, and probably could not have known, of his brother's transactions. This left Willie with the belief that he had been unjustly denied what was rightly due to him. That feeling dogged him until his death on December 30, 1904, at his son Robert's home in Bogan Gate, Parkes, New South Wales.[8]

Another lifelong financial query haunted William Armstrong Montgomery McAuley (who in later life often identified himself this way and

Strong documentary evidence, in records in England and Tasmania, Australia, suggests the following: Jessie Russell Tomkins, who is said to have been born in 1835, was the daughter of Janet (Jane?) Russell before Janet married John Tomkins; the same Janet Russell and John Tomkins were separately convicted in England of crimes involving food, he of burglary and theft, she of theft; they were both transported as convicts to Tasmania, he in December 1828, and she in January 1833; they were married in Hobart Town, Tasmania, on June 27, 1837, and subsequently moved to Deniliquin, New South Wales, Australia. Copies of these records are now in MCA, and more work could be done on them and on related records.

7. William's correspondence with Baggot Street in the 1840s is known only indirectly. In an undated, unfinished letter to Frances Warde (who died September 17, 1884), after noting that he got no response (?) to his earlier letter to her, Willie says that long ago he "had a letter from Mary Cecilia Marmion and Theresa [Byrn]" informing him of his aunt's and brothers' deaths. William McAuley to Frances Warde, [after January 31, 1883] (MCA). Cecilia died at Baggot Street on September 15, 1849. Teresa departed, as part of the New York City foundation, on April 13, 1846. Willie refers again to the 1840s letters in his 1884 letter to Teresa Byrn: "I lost your letter which you wrote in M. C. Marmion's in which you told me you prayed for seven years [1838–1845, or 1839–1846?] for the repose of my soul." William McAuley to Teresa Byrn, July 9, 1884 (MCA). Teresa died on April 8, 1885, in the Mercy convent, Baltimore.

Willie also refers to the letter from Baggot Street—"the only one I ever received from there . . . which was written in 1846" and which "I lost" (i.e., the letter from Cecilia Marmion to which Teresa had appended a letter)—in his 1885 letter to his cousin Anne Byrn. William McAuley to Mary Margaret (Anne) Byrn, September 15, 1885 (MCA). Mary Margaret Byrn, Catherine McAuley's second cousin, professed her vows in Bermondsey, London, on December 4, 1848, and died there on February 26, 1892. "Bermondsey Annals (1848)," vol. 1, 162, and "Bermondsey Annals (1892)," vol. 2, 299 (AIMGB). In this 1885 letter to Anne, Willie also corrects an error in his 1884 letter to Teresa (which she had sent on to Anne): he was *never* a pirate. He had told Teresa that once, in the South Seas, he had "shipped in a brigand" (implying membership in a band of sea robbers). He now tells Anne (who had inquired about this) that he "can only account for your mistake or mine, that the word brigand should be brigantine, a certain kind of vessel, through her rigging being half brig half schooner. I hope you will be pleased to learn you are not second cousin to a sea robber."

8. Dennett, "Family History: William McAuley."

always spelled his surname as Catherine did).[9] What had become of the share—or shares, as he thought—in the Apothecaries Hall which he believed William Callaghan had given to Catherine McAuley *for him*?

In June 1824, when he was not yet three years old, his father had signed a bond to his aunt which stated:

> Whereas William Callaghan . . . by his last will and testament duly executed devised amongst things to the above mentioned Catharine [*sic*] McAuley one share in the funds or stock of the Apothecaries Hall . . . And Whereas the said Catharine McAuley, in consideration of her natural love and affection for her nephew William McAuley Junior . . . and for the advancement in life of her nephew . . . or of such other of the children of the said William McAuley Senior as she the said Catharine McAuley may appoint in the place and stead of the said William McAuley Junior, is minded, and desirous of transferring said share in the stock or funds of the Apothecaries Hall . . . to the said William McAuley Senior in Trust for his son William . . . or of such other of the children . . . as she . . . may appoint.[10]

Because they were not themselves members of the Apothecaries Hall, neither Catherine nor young Willie could have ever personally *owned* the share as such, hence the apparent "transfer" in the bond (or by some other prior legal instrument) of the share to William Macauley Senior who *was* a member. However, in accord with the provisions of William Callaghan's will and codicil, Catherine apparently could personally receive and own the annual *dividends* on this share. By the bond with her brother-in-law, she now transferred the dividends to him in trust for his son Willie or other children.

The bond assigned "the annual dividend or profit" arising from the share for William Macauley's own "proper use" until his young son William was eight years old. After that, the "profit or dividend" was "to be applied by the said William McAuley Senior towards the education and advancement in life of the said William McAuley Junior" or "towards the use" of such other of his children as Catherine McAuley might designate. After young William reached twenty-one, if the share itself could not be given directly to him according to the rules of the Apothecaries Hall (because he was not himself an apothecary and member of the hall), his father or his father's executor was bound to pay and hand over to his son William, or to the other child Catherine might designate, "the full value

---

9. "Montgomery" was the surname of William's distant paternal ancestors, through his great grandmother Nichola Montgomery. He himself explains his use of "Armstrong": "[William] Armstrong of the Apothecaries Hall was my Godfather, and I was named after him, not the good father of that name [Edward Armstrong] whom I saw living." William McAuley to "Reverend Mother" [Mary Augustine Mungovan], Convent of Mercy, Bendigo, Australia, July 15, 1903 (MCA).

10. "Bond, William McAuley [*sic*], Esq. to Catherine McAuley, dated the 21st day of June 1824" (MCA).

and produce" of the share. Should William Macauley or his executors fail to execute the prescriptions of the bond about the dividends, her brother-in-law bound himself and his executors to pay her or her executors "five hundred pounds sterling," a sum presumably based on an estimate of the full value and income of the share over the ensuing years.[11]

When William Macauley died in January 1829, without naming any executor of the will he had apparently drafted, his brother-in-law James McAuley was authorized on March 14, 1829, to take on legal administration of William's property and thus assumed responsibility to execute the bond.[12] The record book of debentures at the Apothecaries Hall lists dividends paid to those who held shares in the hall. William Macauley owned the one share on which he had collected annual dividends up to his death. Thereafter his name remained in the debentures book until the late 1830s, but his brother-in-law drew the dividend, carefully noting his role as "administrator." Then in 1840, in the list of dividends agreed to for the year 1839, James McAuley, also an apothecary, who had gradually increased his own personal shares to three, began to draw dividends on four shares in his own name, and William Macauley's name disappears.[13] This transfer to James of William Macauley's share and its dividends was evidently made possible by Catherine McAuley. On August 31, 1838, before she left for southern Ireland, and when she must have known or suspected that Willie was still unsettled in life, Catherine wrote a short note to her brother:

My Dear James

    I received your two kind notes and trust you will be able to do something for our affectionate Mary's poor spoiled child—and I hereby empower you to apply the Share in the Hall in whatever way you think most useful for him. Should any legal assistance be necessary, Mr. Cavanagh, Solicitor, 18 Lower Fitzwilliam Street, will afford it. Love to all.

Your ever affectionate
C. McAuley[14]

Apparently Willie never knew, or had forgotten it if his Uncle James had ever told him, that in 1838, evidently with Charles Cavanagh's legal

11. Ibid.

12. The County Monaghan deed (see note 5 above) states that William Macauley "departed this life . . . having previous to his death duly made and published his last Will and Testament in writing without naming any executors therein. Whereupon the said James Macauley [his brother-in-law] . . . obtained Letters of Administration with the said Will annexed and was then the legal personal representative of the said William Macauley deceased" (MCA). In signing his name after that of his brother-in-law in the debentures record of the Apothecaries Hall, James McAuley frequently gives the date "March 14, 1829" for his authorization to administer William Macauley's estate (AAH).

13. In these years the debentures record at Apothecaries Hall shows dividends agreed to only "for the year 1837," to be paid in October 1838, and "for the year 1839," to be paid after August 1, 1840 (AAH).

14. Letter 95, August 31, 1838, in *CCMcA*, 152–53.

assistance, his aunt had directed the share once held in trust for him by his father (worth about £100 in 1824) to his uncle for Willie's present needs, to apply "in whatever way you think most useful for him." Presumably James used the dividend on this share to assist Willie to sail from Dublin to London, to repay debts he had incurred while he waited in London, to outfit him as a mercantile seaman, and to get his post on the *Mary Catherine* sailing from London on December 26, 1838—though apparently, if Willie's memory is correct, James did not buy him a quadrant or other nautical instruments.

Given James's and Catherine's solicitude for Willie, the precision of his father's bond with her, her clear intention in her 1838 note to her brother, and the entries in the debentures recorded at the Apothecaries Hall, it is unlikely that James did not claim the share in 1838, with Charles Cavanagh's legal help, and even more unlikely that the share and its dividends were ever simply absorbed into the Baggot Street community's own funds after Catherine's death. Not knowing all this, Willie remained throughout his life—incorrectly it would seem—obsessed with the assumed injustice of his not receiving, after he became twenty-one in 1842, "the three shares [*sic*] in the Apothecaries Hall" (he said his aunt said "three") which "I was always told were mine, from my earliest recollections it was so. I can understand they were a gift to me when born [1821] from Mr. Callahan [*sic*], my Aunt being the trustee."[15] In these comments, written in 1903, Willie was at least partially, but unwittingly mistaken.

A modern biographer of Catherine McAuley must, it would seem, deal forthrightly with the known facts and with the opinions and feelings of her nephew William McAuley, in fairness to her and in fairness to him. Only those biographers writing after the nineteenth century, except Carroll, were in a position to know of the existence of William's several letters from Australia and were thereby freed from the prevailing conjecture that he had been "lost at sea" or had died of tuberculosis as a young man. However, neither Burke Savage (1949), Degnan (1957), nor Bolster (1990) waded into the difficulties of trying to explain the documented details of his brother James's transactions and of the financial relationship between Catherine and Willie.

Willie's is a complicated human story, involving conflicts between his understandings and certain facts unknown to him, as well as between Cath-

15. William McAuley to Mary Catherine (Fannie Theresa) McAuley and others, October 28, 1903 (MCA).

erine's understandings and certain facts unknown to her. It is also a story dependent to some extent on Willie's memories and descriptions, some of which were not wholly accurate. And finally, it is a sad story of misunderstandings made even more painful to him and to his aunt by whatever influence their respective emotions had upon events such as his sister Catherine's death, and their recollections of them, but also by the over sixty years separating their own deaths, time in which no clarifications or reconciliations between them could directly occur.

Catherine did indeed call Willie her sister's "poor spoiled child."[16] Moreover, Clare Moore says that her "hopes" for her three nephews were "greatly disappointed" and that Willie especially "gave her continual uneasiness and trouble."[17] One wants to balance these negative assessments with some recollection of Catherine's care to establish a trust for Willie; her promises of maternal solicitude, made to her dying sister and brother-in-law; her generally realistic understanding of the winding paths of human maturing; her later grief, as we shall see, when her nephew Robert suddenly died in her absence, before her message of "fully given" forgiveness reached him—"a sore trial to her affectionate heart"; and her well-known love of children: "She doted on children and invariably spoiled them," says Clare Augustine Moore.[18]

For his part, William wrote over and over, in his extant letters from Australia, of his "fondly loved guardian and Aunt." The one gift he had most wished to receive from her, beyond all money or property, was forgiveness, a gift he did not experience as forthcoming. Yet near the end of his life he wrote:

In all I have here written I do not wish it to be understood that I blame my Aunt for not forgiving me, but sincerely regret she did not, after my begging so often, and even my sister Kate pleading for me on her death bed. I owed something to self respect, and pride forbade me to persevere. I venerate and love the memory of her departed as fondly as I idolized and revered her in the flesh.[19]

---

16. Letter 95, August 31, 1838, in CCMcA, 152.   17. BA, in CMcATM, 122–23.

18. Ibid.; CAM, in CMcATM, 200.

19. William McAuley, "Commentary on Passages in Carroll's Life of Catherine McAuley" (MCA). This paragraph, the last in the "Commentary," is also in Keena, The Letters of William [Armstrong] Montgomery McAuley, 21. Keena's relatively recent publication attempts to make available William McAuley's six extant letters and his commentary, but its texts of these documents sometimes do not exactly match Willie's original autographs (his handwriting is very hard to read). Moreover, this widely circulated booklet gives only William's views without information from other sources now available. Hence, the need (in this chapter) to present his concerns in the context of facts of which he was evidently unaware. Still, Keena's publication has made him more widely known and loved, despite his unfortunate misunderstandings.

William McAuley's daughter Fanny Teresa (1871–1952) became a Sister of Mercy in Kyneton, Victoria, Australia.[20] She wrote of her father in 1940:

He did get a letter from America or Bermondsey sometime between 1880 [and] 1890. The words, as well as I remember, were: "Darling William, your saintly Aunt forgave you and loved you to the end." My father wept bitterly, and it was his sobs that made me remember, because it was the only time I saw him cry.[21]

As Catherine McAuley faced her sorrow at the end of 1838, she of course did not know the depth of her nephew's own long-lasting sorrow. She little dreamed that he would live to be eighty-three or that she would one day have thirteen grandnieces and grandnephews in faraway Australia—one grandniece, the first, named after her at birth, and another named after her as a Sister of Mercy.

20. She died in the Mercy convent in Kyneton on September 11, 1952.
21. Mary Catherine (Fanny Teresa) McAuley to Mary Dominick Foster, Dublin, May 12, 1940 (MCA).

CHAPTER 16

Loss and Friendship

One word, "bereft," in the 1828 request of Edward Armstrong to Daniel Murray to befriend Catherine McAuley may hint at Catherine's lifelong inner struggle.[1] Though her public life, to an increasing extent, radiated cheerfulness, generosity, gratitude, playfulness, affection, and self-expending mercifulness, inwardly an elegiac residue of constantly renewed grief, due to the frequent loss or death of those she loved, was ever present, managed but never quite dissolved. Her reserve about herself, her insistent rejection of gloominess, her counsels against coldness and stiffness in personal relations were not accidental. Her apparent lack of closeness to her mother; her understandably faint memory of her father; the succeeding deaths of Catherine Callaghan, Anne Conway, William Callaghan, Joseph Nugent, her sister Mary, Edward Armstrong, William Macauley, Elizabeth Harley, her niece Mary Teresa, Ellen Corrigan, and young Catherine; the departures of Fanny Tighe and Catherine Byrn, and now of Willie McAuley; the removal of Michael Blake from Dublin; the gap of understanding in matters of religion between herself and her brother, James: all this repeated loss and privation took its human toll.

Her feelings of self-blame, as witnessed by confidantes; her surface tranquility in the face of the deaths of others; her self-control; her acknowledged and lifelong dread of death; her reliance on the penitential psalms; her advocacy of silence: all these aspects of her quasi-public life

---

1. Letter 5, March 16, 1828, in *CCMcA*, 40. For a longer quotation from Armstrong's letter see chapter 4 in this volume.

had their sound religious explanation, but when set side by side they may also point to the recurring pain in her inner life.[2] Each fresh opening of the scars of her human losses must have deepened and aggravated her personal struggle. All the painful relics of her life's experience were apparently the unspoken, private materials beneath her public self, holding a key for interpreting her daily actions and her half-revealing, half-concealing claim: "We need only consider how dear our own will has been to us from our earliest years, to know how acceptable a sacrifice it is to God."[3] Sacrifice is here conceived not as a voluntary, self-initiated offering, but as a voluntary acceptance of what has happened or is happening beyond one's control; not as a presumptuous seeking or creating of "crosses," but as a wordless embrace of those given, and trust in the mysterious Giver, not of the particulars or in the abstract, but of the evolving shape of her ordinary life.

In 1828, as he was dying, Edward Armstrong had feared, specifically, that Catherine would be "bereft of an Ecclesiastical Friend." It would seem, if one can accept the adequacy of the available written evidence, that Armstrong's fear was somewhat borne out in at least two episodes. In the two most painful crises of an ecclesial nature that Catherine endured—the chaplaincy controversy in 1837–1838 and the Kingstown abandonment in the same years—when she most hoped for Daniel Murray's helpful intervention, the archbishop's assistance was apparently not forthcoming, as far as we know. There may be many human explanations for this—his friendship with Walter Meyler and Bartholomew Sheridan; his other diocesan burdens; his time-consuming efforts to secure passage of an adequate poor law for Ireland (1838) and to avert, against John MacHale's efforts, Vatican condemnation of the national schools system in Ireland; his own health and age (he was seventy in 1838). In other moments he had stood by Catherine. One must also recognize that the content and tenor of their oral communications, if and when they may have occurred, are forever beyond a biographer's reach. Though in early February 1839, Catherine could write of the archbishop that "we have not seen him for thirteen months," he visited Baggot Street in late September of that year, and in mid-November he came again: "We have had long and most kind visits from our poor Bishop."[4] On the Saturday before Catherine died, Daniel Murray

2. On her fear of death, see Lim, in *CMcATM*, 189.
3. *PS*, 9.
4. Letter 114, February 7, 1839, in *CCMcA*, 185; letter 142 [November 17, 1839], in *CCMcA*, 218.

visited her, but who can speculate convincingly on that or any other long past conversation?

However, Michael Blake, Redmond O'Hanlon (the confessor assigned by Dr. Murray and his deputy in regard to the Sisters of Mercy in Dublin), Andrew Fitzgerald and James Maher in Carlow, and John Hamilton (the archbishop's secretary) were her friends to the end, each in his own way. To Fitzgerald she wrote: "I never can forget all the animating lively hope that you created in my mind when we were rising out of nothing."[5] Of James Maher she said: "Indeed I could speak to him with all the confidence of one addressing a long, well proved friend, and such comfort does not often fall to my lot."[6] To John Hamilton she wrote, on one of the darkest days of her life: "The only apology I can offer for all this writing is that it comforts and relieves my mind to declare the truth where I trust I am not suspected of insincerity."[7]

None of the letters Catherine wrote to Michael Blake and Redmond O'Hanlon have survived. Yet they were probably the friends she most frankly trusted, to whom she most revealed her heart, and whose advice she most intimately sought in the last decade of her life. When Michael Blake in Newry received the letter informing him of her death, he said, "My heart was instantly filled with grief," and he spoke of her as "the dear departed friend whom I ever esteemed and reverenced and whose memory I shall ever esteem and reverence until the last moment of my life."[8]

Closer to her than all these priest friends, but in a different way, were her confidantes in the Sisters of Mercy, certain women, all far younger than she, who read her spirit more deeply, and were more explicit in their affection or more ready to share in her hopes and efforts. Among these were, especially, Clare Moore, Frances Warde, Elizabeth Moore, Teresa White, and Teresa Carton, though in her own expressions of love and affection Catherine seems to have striven to be as widely loving as possible. She rarely ever closed a letter to a sister without saying, and meaning: "Pray for your fondly attached M. C. McAuley," or "Your ever affectionate M. C. McAuley" or "Believe me, my very Dear Sister . . . your sincerely attached M. C. McAuley." Eighteenth-century manuals on letter-writing offered stereotypes of such closings, but it is unlikely that Catherine ever consulted them: her clos-

---

5. Letter 92, July 3, 1838, in *CCMcA*, 147.   6. Letter 71, January 17, 1838, in *CCMcA*, 120.
7. Letter 66, December 19, 1837, in *CCMcA*, 113.
8. Manuscript copy, Michael Blake to Mary Elizabeth Moore, November 13, 1841 (MCA). See also BA, in *CMcATM*, 125–26, and Lim, in *CMcATM*, 190–91.

ings expressed not convention, but her own attitude. As she said in the last months of her life: "I have nothing now to draw me for one hour from my religious Sisters where all my joy on earth is centered. Every year's experience of their worth attaches me more strongly."[9]

For Mary Ann Doyle, Catherine never ceased to be grateful—on her collaboration and goodness of heart the whole enterprise had depended in the beginning. But Mary Ann and she had rather different temperaments: Mary Ann was more cautious and more sedate. Yet the few surviving letters between them reveal something of the depth of their friendship. At Catherine's death, the Tullamore annalist wrote, surely quoting Mary Ann:

The death of any one to whom the survivor has been united is a bereavement—it is hard to look the thought full in the face that we shall never see such a one again. But when that one has been light to one's feet, the stay and encouragement of one's very soul in the everyday difficulties and perplexities of life—the removal of such a one is a foretaste of death to those who remain behind.[10]

Some uncertainty as to whether to call her a confidante may also apply to Mary de Pazzi Delany, who became Catherine's assistant in the mid-1830s. Since de Pazzi always lived with her at Baggot Street, Catherine wrote her only two of the extant autograph letters, though there may have been others. A difference of general mood often separated these two women. A certain anxiety on de Pazzi's part led to occasional "frets" surrounding some decisions Catherine felt were needed. Yet Catherine deeply loved and trusted her, and de Pazzi was, as Mary Vincent Whitty reported, "completely" overcome when Catherine died.[11]

Catherine called Frances Warde "my own dear old companion and affectionate child," and envisioned their sitting together at the community table "like old Darby and Joan," the legendary, frail, mutually devoted old man and woman who appear in several English poems and songs.[12] At least one of Frances's letters Catherine "read again and again—as a solace and comfort which God sent me."[13]

Though none of Catherine's letters to Clare Moore have survived, Catherine's reliance on her is well known. She took her as a companion on at least three early journeys, appointed her superior or temporary superior twice, and asked her to assist with copying the Rule and, later, preparing the packet for Rome. She called her, too, "our old beloved companion," and

9. Letter 265, May 1, 1841, in *CCMcA*, 396.   10. TA, in *CMcATM*, 75.

11. MVWL, in *CMcATM*, 243.

12. Letter 89 [late May 1838], in *CCMcA*, 139; letter 64 [November–December 1837], in *CCMcA*, 109 and 109 n. 72.

13. Letter 89 [late May 1838], in *CCMcA*, 139.

lamented, during a typhus epidemic in London, that Clare was "exhausted" and had written: "My heart is gone."[14]

To Elizabeth Moore, who was even more forthright in her affection, Catherine wrote: "Absence has much increased my affection for you—even the new Sisters here are sorry for our mutual disappointment this time, I have talked so much of it."[15] And again: "I need not tell you that it will be a source of great happiness [to visit you]—for which I thank God—a pure heartfelt friendship which renews the powers of mind and body."[16] When Elizabeth sent her, unbidden, a package of fruit and flowers all the way from Limerick, Catherine commented: "The offering of genuine affection has everything to enhance its value."[17]

Clare Augustine Moore says that Catherine once said of Teresa White: "Of all the sisters Sr. M. Teresa has most of my spirit and I trust more to her guiding the Institute as I wish than to any other Sister."[18] Whether this is true or not, Teresa loved Catherine and said of her a few years before her own death: "She was . . . one to whom you could open your whole heart. She was so sweet, so kind, so spiritual; I never met any one like her. She . . . gave each Sister a place in her heart."[19]

To Teresa Carton, Catherine confided the final approach of her last illness, though regretting "to write so much about myself—and give such trouble." She asked Teresa to prepare a bed for her in the infirmary room, and to remain in the room with her—"a little coughing [on your part] will never disturb me."[20]

Friendships appear to have sustained the human heart of Catherine McAuley. Though they did not completely heal the accumulated suffering that the repeated losses of her life had inflicted, or ever completely penetrate her reserve about her own deepest feelings, or ever dissipate her admitted fear of death itself, they did help her to transcend her private pain in response to the pain of others. Death and loss provoked in her a sense of ministerial urgency, and friendship, when it came, seems to have renewed her ability to go forward. At the heart of all this movement, as its center and animation, was what she might have dared to call her friendship with God, and her gratitude for it. As she often said: "We may address God as we would a dear friend to whom we owed a great deal."[21]

14. Letter 206, November 9, 1840, in *CCMcA*, 316.
15. Letter 177, July 1, 1840, in *CCMcA*, 277.   16. Letter 169, March 24, 1840, in *CCMcA*, 261.
17. Letter 126, July 24, 1839, in *CCMcA*, 201.   18. CAM, in *CMcATM*, 212.
19. Carroll, *Leaves from the Annals*, vol. 1 (1881), 49–50.
20. Letter 300, September 6, 1841, in *CCMcA*, 436.
21. *PS*, 10.

So Catherine did not become, or at least did not remain, "bereft" in any more general sense that Edward Armstrong might have feared. Rather, through the empowering strength of friendship, for which she was always deeply grateful, she chose to let herself become dispossessed, to hand herself over more and more freely in daily ways. She chose to give. This was the transformed attitude of mind and heart toward which she seems to have prayed and labored all her life. She apparently did not sequester herself in her sorrow, repeatedly afflicting though it was, but silently altered it, bit by bit, slowly, and not without pain. She turned to the mercy of the God in whom she believed, and to mercifulness toward others, with an empathy and sympathy deepened by the realities of her own life. She did not speak or write of her own inner transformation. Yet somehow her accumulated grief was transmuted into charity, in part by her own efforts, but more, as she prayed would be the case, by the example and help of the Jesus Christ whom she wished to resemble. It was the never-ending human process of bereavement, the gradual, piecemeal yielding to the incomprehensible Mystery whom she trusted as the very ground of human life. As she once wrote: "The Lord and Master of our House and Home is a faithful provider. Let us never desire more than enough."[22] For her, the "House," the "Home," was not primarily a building; it was human life itself, lived in the care of an often obscurely but always compassionate God.

Catherine's learning how to live in this House, how to hand herself over to its daily revelations of joys and sorrows, had begun long before 1839. Yet the last three years of her life called forth this learning and this human effort, in ways she did not anticipate.

22. Letter 242 [early 1841], in CCMcA, 366.

CHAPTER 17

Joys and Sorrows Mingled *1839*

On April 30, 1839, Ursula Frayne sent a pleading poem to Catherine McAuley. Since those in Booterstown could not come in to Baggot Street for Catherine's feast day celebration, would she at least send Cecilia Marmion and Mary Aloysius Scott to celebrate with them. Catherine immediately responded, promising future festivities in the seaside community:

> My own dearest Child, you must eat, laugh & pray
> without Aloysius or Celia today
> and though you're not with us at this little feat
> we are planning to give you a very nice treat
> To this our great feast—an octave we'll add
> and give you a party will make your heart glad.

She and the novices will come in a week for "a nice pick nick dinner": "So merry a party I'm sure was ne'er seen / In parlour or drawing-room—garden or green." They will stay overnight—to do otherwise "would spoil all the fun"—and sleep on the floor "like pins in a row." Recalling how she had slept on the deck of the packet to Cork months before, she promised: "We'll call Booterstown Convent a steamer that day / and wonder there's half so much room on the sea."[1]

But 1839 was not all picnics and playfulness. Until November and December, and the far-reaching events of those months, it was mostly a year

---

1. Letter 120 [April 30, 1839], in *CCMcA*, 192.

of ordinary duties—some hard, some sorrowful, some rewarding, some annoying. And of unexpected joys—flowers from Limerick, success in Carlow, new faces. It was also, at first, a year of hurricane survival, literally in January, and figuratively in February when problems in Kingstown gathered anew.

As the year began, Catherine wrote a poem-letter to her "sweet little poet" in Limerick, admitting that she felt the pressure of time:

> Dear Mary Teresa—Vincent de Paul
> Your names are so pretty—I give you them all
> I hope you don't think I've been very remiss
> In not answering all your nice Rhyme
> I should have done so indeed long e'er this
> Could I snatch but one hour from time
> that monarch who bears us away
> in his chariot of measureless flight
> to whom we can never, oh never, say Nay
> but go with him from morning till night.

She invited the young novice to join her in fresh efforts during the new year:

> The 38th year is now past
> Its cares and its pleasures are gone
> the 39th may be our last
> since the last is so surely to come
> Let us beg for renewed animation
> in discharge of our duties each day.

Conscious as she always was of the shortness of time, and increasingly aware that one's life could end abruptly, Catherine urged Teresa to focus with her on what was most important: "smile under every privation," smother "all coldness and choler," and "cordially love one another."[2] Neither of them realized that Teresa's time would be far shorter than Catherine's.

Then on January 6, late at night, what was subsequently called the "Big Wind" assailed Ireland, a hurricane of such intensity that it blew off roofs, knocked down chimneys, and tore through windows. Before it hit Dublin in full force, Catherine was alone, writing to Frances Warde: "I am come back to my corner after all are gone to Bed—to write a few lines to my poor old child." After noting that a priest from Carlow had "said you were

---

2. Letter 107 [early 1839], in *CCMcA*, 174–75.

pretty well" and that a new postulant from Wexford was coming soon, Catherine sensed the strengthening wind. "It is striking 10, the fire is out and the windows making an awful noise, so I must be done."[3] The main purpose of her writing had been to encourage Frances to trust that Francis Haly, the new bishop of Kildare and Leighlin, would be helpful. So she quickly concluded:

I could not describe the extreme kindness of Doctor Healy [Haly] when he called last. He was afraid I would be uneasy lest the little arrangement he made should occasion any unhappiness to you—and he gave the most full—and unquestionably— faithful assurance of the deepest interest and regard. You have a true Father in him.
Good night, my Dearest Child—affectionate love to all.[4]

Apparently, Dr. Haly did not offer the decisive Frances Warde the same ease of operating as his predecessor, Edward Nolan, had—one of the "bitter- sweets incident to our state," as Catherine euphemistically called such situations.[5]

By the next morning, the hurricane had ravaged many places in Ire- land, including Dublin:

We remained in Bed all night—some in terror, others sleeping, etc. The morning presented an altered scene. . . . The Community Room a compleat ruin in appear- ance, though not much real injury—the Prints and pictures all on the ground— only two broken. The maps and blinds flying like the sails of a ship—the Bookstand down—the cabinet removed from its place, and the chairs all upset—16 panes bro- ken—and such a body of air in the room that we could scarcely stand. The win- dows are still boarded up—it is almost impossible to get a glazier—a fine harvest for them.

In Carlow, "part of their very old roof [was] blown down. . . . The chim- neys of the new Convent in Tullamore blown down. . . . We have not heard from Cork or Charleville."[6] The Limerick convent was apparently unaf- fected.

But Catherine had no time to dwell on boarded up windows or unprec-

3. Letter 108 [January 6, 1839], in *CCMcA*, 176.
4. Ibid., 177. The "little arrangement" Francis Haly had made that might have caused Frances Warde any "unhappiness" cannot be ascertained from the existing Carlow Annals. However, he apparently felt he knew his episcopal prerogatives in relation to the Carlow convent, for in 1842 "he reminded" Frances, who had inadvertently not taken the votes of the chapter, "that she should have conferred with him" on the appointment of Mary Cecilia Maher as mistress of novices "as he only could make the appointment." "Carlow Annals, 1842," 48–49 (Archives, Sisters of Mercy, Carlow, Ireland). In 1843, when Frances's six years (two terms) as Carlow superior expired, he did not seek a rescript from Rome so she could be re- elected, as did other bishops on such occasions. Rather, he appointed Mary Cecilia Maher as superior, and Frances Warde as assistant.
5. Letter 55, October 17, 1837, in *CCMcA*, 99–100.
6. Letter 110, January 13, 1839, in *CCMcA*, 178–79.

edented calls for glaziers. Preparations were needed for reception and profession ceremonies for six on January 21, Michael Blake presiding; the charity sermon by the Reverend Thaddeus O'Malley was set for February 3; two new postulants were entering—Ellen Whitty on January 15, and Annie Fleming on February 5. Meanwhile, affairs in Kingstown, where the debt was still unpaid, had taken a new turn. In a letter to Charles Cavanagh, which he or someone in his office dated "26 January 1839," Catherine told him: "The Sisters are just returned from Kingstown. Mr. Sheridan met them according to his appointment, but said he thought there was a misunderstanding—that we would have to pay four hundred and seventy pounds—before he would make the Choir. This is very different from what he said to you."[7] On February 7, she wrote to John Hamilton, Dr. Murray's secretary:

I beg leave to send you some papers just received. If I were to draw from our fund what would pay the demand [£470], the concerns must be sold to return it, as we have not two pounds a year more than is required for our support, etc.

Mr. Sheridan has the rooms locked—and the furniture may get damp. I never could come to any conclusion as to retaking the charge, without seeing his Grace. If you, Revd. Sir, would be so kind to prevail on him to appoint any time, I would keep the Sisters all at home that they might get his blessing—as we have not seen him for thirteen months.

She added a postscript: "I suppose, Revd. Sir, something must be done to prevent more law proceedings."[8] Catherine was clearly at her wit's end, and not a little frustrated. Sometime in February, she explained the situation to Frances Warde:

Saturday—a new account about Kingstown. Mr. Sheridan told Mr. Cavanagh that if the School House were assigned to trustees—for the children—the debt should be paid & a choir made in the P[arish] church for the Sisters if they would return. Mr. Cavanagh agreed to this. Mr. Sheridan then wrote to me requesting two sisters would go out to select such portion of the church as was deemed necessary. Sister Mary Teresa and Aloysius went on the day he appointed. After taking all their plan, he recalled what he had agreed with Mr. Cavanagh—and said in presence of Mr. Walsh [a curate] that he never invited them to Kingstown and therefore could not be called upon to do what he heard was done for us in other places. I could not describe Mr. Cavanagh's surprise. He said Mr. Sheridan could not speak plainer. He wrote to him expressing his surprise and shewed me a copy of the letter. If it was to me he said it—he would think it was my imagination.

I think it would seem like defiance—if we were to go now, after the Parish Priest saying to two Sisters, in the presence of his curate, that he never invited

7. Letter 112 [January 26, 1839], in CCMcA, 183.
8. Letter 114, February 7, 1839, in CCMcA, 185.

them. Sister Mary Teresa could not avoid saying in reply—that none of them liked to come. It is a perplexing business.[9]

On February 19, William Walsh, a curate in Kingstown, also wrote to John Hamilton—a letter which Catherine may never have seen or known about:

Some one lately told Mr. Sheridan that a Priest commissioned by the S. S. of Charity had been making enquiries at Baggot St. concerning the deserted Convent in Sussex Place. Mr. Sheridan expressed a wish that I should write to ascertain from you whether they have any real intention of settling in Kingstown. He seems very favorably disposed towards them, and says they can have the place at a Dead Bargain—say £500. There would be an ample field here for their charitable zeal. I believe he would be disposed to render them every attention & says they might reckon on a Charity Sermon for the Poor besides Subscriptions [two illegible capital letters]. The convent is now the property of Mr. Sheridan himself & he can sell it for what he likes.

Walsh goes on to lament "the frightful state of the children" and "the excited state of feeling here consequent on the melancholy departure of the Nuns. . . . I hoped to the last, that they might return."[10]

It was, and is, a "perplexing business," as Catherine said, and although all the extant but sometimes undated correspondence on it has been studied, this stage of the Kingstown negotiations remains unclear. In April Catherine wrote again to Charles Cavanagh, suggesting that the house should be rented soon, for the summer season:

May I beg to trouble you again about Kingstown. I hear of places letting all about & fear the season may pass with us. We want knives and many other things in the household way which must be quite spoiled there. Will you in charity conclude the matter for us?[11]

The vacant house on Sussex Place was apparently not rented at this time or later, and it was not occupied by the Sisters of Charity. It is not clear whether, when, or how the debt was paid. Did Father Sheridan pay the debt to James Nugent and then claim, on the basis of this payment, ownership of the house? Did Daniel Murray pay the debt or encourage that it be dropped or paid over a long period of time? Did someone else pay it? Catherine would eventually have known the answers to these questions, but no record of this has so far been discovered. One learns nothing

9. Letter 113 [February 1839], in *CCMcA*, 184–85.
10. Letter 116, February 19, 1839, in *CCMcA*, 187–88.
11. Letter 117 [April 17, 1839], in *CCMcA*, 189.

more about the Kingstown house until March 1840. The best that could possibly be said of the whole Kingstown saga is that more face-to-face conversation between Bartholomew Sheridan and Catherine McAuley might have helped. The worst is that it involved what seems like clerical high-handedness and pastoral insensitivity. The neglected girls "loitering about the roads" in 1835 were not Catherine's children, but the parish's.

At this point, too, relations with Elizabeth Magenis broke down.[12] She had entered from Newry in June 1833, with Michael Blake's mildly expressed caution about her "one little drawback ... a peculiar or singular mode of thinking & judging by which she is distinguished."[13] At the time she had promised a very large dowry. But no amount of money, though sorely needed, could compensate for her gradually more manifest erratic behavior. The Baggot Street community declined to admit her to profession of vows in 1835, but she was unwisely allowed to stay on as a boarder, living in Kingstown until that community was evicted in November 1838. By a letter of agreement dated April 15, 1835, Elizabeth had agreed to transfer £1471.4.0 in new government stock in the Bank of Ireland to Catherine McAuley, Mary Ann Doyle, and Frances Warde as senior members of the Baggot Street community. Following this, Catherine and the others had agreed, by an indented deed, to provide Elizabeth "with board, washing & clothing if necessary during her natural life in either the Convent of Mercy, Baggot Street or the Convent of Mercy, Kingstown." Pursuant to this promise, Elizabeth had transferred the stock.[14]

Now Elizabeth Magenis was at Baggot Street, "so great an oddity" that something had to be done.[15] Finally Catherine did what was necessary. She wrote to Charles Cavanagh on February 14, 1839:

I regret exceedingly being obliged to engage your time and attention so much, but I cannot arrange this matter myself—were it merely personal, I would soon put an end to it, by giving Miss McGuinness [Magenis] what she now violently demands. She is acting in the most rude and unchristian manner—she called me a wretch twice before two or three, and says I prepared a drink for her with something to stupefy her and sent it by Sister White, that you and I got her to sign the deed [transferring the stock] after she had taken this draught. . . . Sister White's father

12. The spelling of her name is problematic. Her signature on a deed is "Elizabeth Magenis." In his letters, Michael Blake uses "Magennis." In references to her, Catherine McAuley writes "McGuinness."

13. Letter 18 [June 5, 1833], in *CCMcA*, 54.

14. Elizabeth Magenis's 1835 letter of agreement is cited in the memorial of the indented deed signed by Catherine McAuley, dated January 28, 1836, and registered on April 28, 1837. Memorial no. 1837.8.71, RD. This memorial also cites Magenis's stock transfer.

15. Letter 223, December 22, 1840, in *CCMcA*, 335–36.

[Laurence White of Wexford] has been appointed a Stipendiary Magistrate and is at present in Town. I was thinking of consulting him—of course he would take up very seriously such a charge brought against his child.

Miss McG. seems to forget entirely that she is to observe any regulations—she interrupts our religious exercises—always saying that she acts by the direction of her Lawyer who, she says, tells her she may go into every room in the Convent—what no religious Sister could do. . . .

If Miss McG. will give a release, I will propose (with permission) returning her one thousand pounds—though we never could consider a person giving four hundred—and paying her expenses—eligible to be admitted as Benefactress. . . .

Will you in charity to all—make the above proposal—and I will get it concluded soon as possible.[16]

Elizabeth Magenis signed a detailed indenture of release on February 25, 1839. On her departure she received from the Baggot Street funds "nine hundred and eighty five pounds fourteen shillings and six pence of Government new three and a half per cent stock equivalent at the price of the day to the sum of one thousand pounds sterling." The community retained only £485 in government stock to cover her expenses during the preceding five and a half years—for "board, lodging, clothing, etc. in Baggot Street Convent or Kingstown," as in the original agreement.[17]

Initiating Elizabeth's departure had been a worrisome but courageous move on Catherine's part, in which she had put the union and charity of the community far above its precarious finances. For herself she could endure being called a "wretch"—James Nugent, the Kingstown builder, had apparently called her even more derogatory names: "cheat & liar"—but she would not allow the peace of the community to be repeatedly injured, if she could help it.[18] On the night of February 25, the community probably breathed a sigh of relief. What became of Miss Magenis is not known. Perhaps she did the "extensive good" for which she seemed to have the means.

When posthumous oil paintings show Catherine McAuley with her hands placidly holding the book of the Rule or serenely writing, these portraits are only half true to life. They do not show the occasional fear or discomfort.

Yet 1839 contained the seeds of much later happiness. Women who joined Mercy efforts in various Irish cities or towns that year would contribute to the future spread of the Sisters of Mercy well beyond Ireland,

16. Letter 115, February 14, 1839, in *CCMcA*, 186–87.
17. "Deed of Release," February 25, 1839, signed by Elizabeth Magenis and Catherine McAuley (MCA).
18. Nugent's words are from letter 101, November 15, 1838, in *CCMcA*, 165.

though Catherine herself could not have imagined this. Ellen Whitty, after serving in other roles, would become the founder of the Brisbane, Australia, community. Mary de Sales (Jane) White, Teresa's sister, who professed vows in January, would eventually take a community to Liverpool. Marianne Creedon, who entered in July, would become the brave and steadfast founder in Newfoundland. Mary Francis Bridgeman, who professed her vows in Limerick, would, as superior in Kinsale, send Mercy communities to San Francisco and Cincinnati. Frances Horan and Mary Angela Maher would one day form part of the founding community in New York City. And among the women who entered, received the habit, or professed vows that year, were also four who would die within five years. This too was, mercifully, beyond Catherine's vision as she struggled with the day-to-day work at Baggot Street.

At midnight on May 9, 1839, Gertrude Jones died in Booterstown at age forty-six, "from no visible cause," as Catherine tried to explain, "but a rending of the heart." Her entry into the Sisters of Mercy nine years before, her remaining, and the sacrifice of all her preferences as an Englishwoman—even, as she saw it, of how to sew and make a pudding—had led to a nervous condition from which she never recovered. She had been confined to bed for a year, and now, as death approached, Catherine and Monica Murphy were sitting up with her. When "the clock struck 12," and "before we could read the departing prayer for her, she was gone," on Ascension Thursday as she had wished.[19] Her death was the long-expected end to a difficult religious life—one Catherine had tried, without success, to spare her, but which, given Gertrude's evident wish, her virtue, and her increasing debility, Catherine had allowed. To let Gertrude profess vows in 1834 had been a difficult decision, with no assurance it was the right one, for Gertrude or the community.

As the summer months approached, Catherine had another nagging worry: when and how to re-open the poor school at Baggot Street. The sisters had been welcoming and teaching destitute girls from the back alleys of nearby neighborhoods, free of charge, ever since September 1827, but the school had been closed since construction of the addition to the House of Mercy began in August 1838. The addition would contain another large schoolroom, above the new laundry in the basement.[20] In a quandary

19. Letter 122, May 11, 1839, in CCMcA, 194–95.
20. In Ireland, then as now, the street floor is the "ground" floor, and the floor above is the "first" floor. Whether the ground- and first-floor schoolrooms of 1827 continued to be used for classes until 1838 is unclear, given the crowded conditions in the community.

about the re-opening, Catherine wrote to the best teacher in the Mercy ranks, Mary Vincent Harnett in Limerick, who had been certified by the Board of Commissioners of National Education, overseers of the system of primary education for all Irish children:

Will you get all the instructions for me as to the school . . . I will rely on your giving every direction possible. You know we are quite unprepared here—we shall be quite perplexed on the New School opening if not ready to receive them in good order. We hope to get a connection with the Board. Our room is a very fine one—with [now, total] space for 400. To begin well is a great point. . . .

This you may consider a real charity, it will so relieve my mind. I dread the crowd rushing in as formerly—without a good arrangement—and such rules as you think may bring about a regular attendance as to hour. Say something of the Infant School. We hope to open on the 1st of August.

Give me all the help you can collect.[21]

Although Catherine had applied to the Board of Commissioners on July 13, 1834, for recognition of the Baggot Street school as a national school, that application had apparently been tabled. Writing now to Elizabeth Moore, Catherine explained that the new application, submitted on July 4, 1839, was introduced by Archbishop Murray, a member of the Board of Commissioners. "Our building is nearly finished—a fine school room & Dormitory—the Laundry not yet opened, but every prospect of its doing well. Our memorial to the board was signed by the most respectable protestants—the Surgeon General [Sir Philip Crampton], Sir Henry Marsh, Mr. [Allen] Hume & several others—it was presented by Doctor Murray and received well. We have great hope of a favorable answer."[22] Up to this point, and like other charitable schools in Dublin, the Sisters of Mercy had borne the full cost of financing the school.

To the "queries" on the application form required by the commissioners, Catherine had responded that instructions were given in the school "5 days each week—four hours and an half each day," and "School commences at 10—closes at half past 2 o'clock." She was "Disposed to use the books issued by the Board." The "Teachers, and their Age" were "Josephine Delaney, 28" and "Elizabeth Scott, 25." Asked whether they could produce "Testimonials . . . of fitness for their office," she replied: "One is acquainted

21. Letter 123 [May–July 1839], in *CCMcA*, 196–97. Mary Vincent's reply is not extant.

22. Letter 126, July 24, 1839, in *CCMcA*, 203. Sir Henry Marsh was president of the Royal College of Physicians of Ireland for four terms. The signature of "Allen Hume, 63 Dawson Street" is on the three-page application for "aid towards fitting up a school, payment of teacher's salary, and supply of school requisites." ED 1/28, no. 75 (NAI). Permission to quote this document has been granted by the National Archives of Ireland and the Director of the National Archives of Ireland.

with the system, the other learning it." When asked, "How many children have been present on an average each week, for the last quarter?" she responded, "about 200 females"; and to the question "Do the scholars pay anything, and what?" the answer was, "One penny per week" (a general rule, but rarely followed). Finally, asked about "the nature and extent of the Aid required," Catherine requested: "Means to provide furniture for an increase of 200 Scholars—and Salary for Teachers."[23]

Certifying the answers to the queries and the request for government aid were the six "Protestants," whose signatures were listed next to those of the six "Roman Catholics." Among the latter were "W. Meyler ... Charles Cavanagh ... J. Kenny, 9 Merrion Square East, James Corballis, Pembroke Road," and "Richard Weldon, 50 Baggot Street." Asked who was "authorized to communicate with the Commissioners," Catherine wrote "Charles Cavanagh."[24]

Her hope for affiliation of the Baggot Street poor school with the Board of National Education was fulfilled on November 14, 1839. From that day, the board (who paid by the quarter, and retroactively) noted that it paid, before year's end, sums amounting to about £9 for school "requisites" (such as books) and £15 for three salaries. Mary Joseph (Alicia) Delaney had returned from Charleville in March 1839; the experienced Mary Aloysius (Elizabeth) Scott taught in the school until she became ill in early 1840; and an Anne Culloe was evidently a hired lay teacher. Further small payments for salaries, and increased payments for "requisites" occurred over the following years, with "assistant teacher, Ellen Whitty" added in October 1840, at an annual salary grant of £8.[25]

On at least one occasion in the summer of 1839, Catherine had needed her old standby, her sense of humor. Though the chaplaincy controversy was probably still not settled to her satisfaction, Dr. Meyler, recently appointed dean of the Dublin Diocesan Chapter, came, in the absence of the archbishop, to preside at the reception ceremony on July 23. Writing to Elizabeth Moore the next day, Catherine slyly casts herself in the third person:

Sisters [Anne] Fleming and [Ellen] Whitty—two very nice young persons—not 21—& Jane Starling were received yesterday by—*Dean* Meyler—gracious as pos-

23. ED 1/28, no. 75 (NAI).

24. Ibid. The sixth Catholic signature is illegible.

25. ED 2/15, folios 112, 208 (NAI). The "Baggot Street Female N.S." is listed in the National School Records as "Roll No. 2018, District 40." Permission to quote these documents has been granted by the National Archives of Ireland and the Director of the National Archives of Ireland.

sible. Mrs. McA a very good child—smiling and praying alternately—attended at table and paid great attention to.[26]

Catherine's well-schooled courtesy and hospitality came in handy. In the same letter she thanked Elizabeth for the "sweet fruit & flowers" she had sent: "Every one who came in since I began—said, oh, the sweet smell, where did you get all the lovely flowers—and when answered, 'from Limerick'—I think they fancied them somewhat out of the common way."[27]

Catherine saw Elizabeth Moore, Frances Warde, Mary Ann Doyle, and others in late August on her way back from Cork where she had gone for the profession ceremony of Mary Clare (Elizabeth) Agnew and Mary Augustine (Maria) Taylor, the Englishwomen who had come to Cork in April 1838 to serve their novitiate, prior to founding a new community of Sisters of Mercy in Bermondsey, London. Establishing a community in London was evidently conceived at first as a foundation from Cork, not Dublin. As Catherine had told Frances sometime that summer:

> I do not yet know how the London House is to commence. The English sisters beg to have Sister M. Clare [Moore]. Dr. Murphy has not given a conclusive answer. . . . They hope to open the Institution on the 24th September—they are to be professed on the 19th of August. I fear I must go to the ceremony. Doctor Murphy says it would be necessary—that every aid should be given to England, we all feel, and every mark of interest shewn—but I get a surfeit of traveling in my old days.[28]

Catherine did not look forward to the long trip to Cork, but it was eventually decided that Clare Moore and she would lead the founding party to London when the convent there was ready. On loan from Cork, Clare would become the temporary superior of the Bermondsey community until Clare Agnew was ready to assume this responsibility.

After the profession in Cork on August 19, the group destined for England traveled to Dublin to await word on the architect Augustus Welby Pugin's completion of the convent in Bermondsey. To break up the long coach journey, but primarily to show the Englishwomen other Mercy communities and their ministries, Catherine had decided to stop in Charleville, Limerick, Tullamore, and Carlow on the way back to Dublin. The added prospect of seeing those she loved evidently made her forget about her "surfeit of traveling."

26. Letter 126, July 24, 1839, in *CCMcA*, 202. In Sullivan, ed., *Correspondence*, 202, "alternately" is incorrectly transcribed as "alternatively."

27. Ibid., 201, 203.

28. Letter 124 [May–August 1839], in *CCMcA*, 198–99.

Usually Catherine was fairly accurate in her assessment of character and astute in her intuitions about a person's future development. But her skills seem to have failed her with respect to Clare Agnew. During the months they waited for word from London, she was increasingly impressed by Clare, the already celebrated author of an autobiographical novel, *Geraldine: A Tale of Conscience,* to which she had added a third volume during her novitiate in Cork.[29] In September, Catherine spoke glowingly of her:

Sister Agnew is a delightful addition—every day more pleasing & amiable. She is evidently selected for a great work—always recollected, but never too solemn—no shew of any kind—yet all that is valuable shews itself continually. She yields to the opinion of others like a little child, and you find yourself irresistibly drawn to hers— by the very manner in which she submits. Had I met her as she is now—10 or 12 years since—I might have been greatly benefited indeed, and even now, she teaches me by her example what genuine meekness and humility are. The adage—"never too old to learn"—is a great comfort to me.[30]

This adage may have been true of Catherine McAuley, but probably not of Clare Agnew.

Frances Warde and the Carlow sisters were departing on September 23 for a new foundation in Naas. Catherine was disappointed that she could not join them: "Many circumstances unite to keep me from you—it would have been a very particular gratification to me. A young Priest is to celebrate his first Mass—Mr. O'Hanlon [is to] bring home a new Sister— and if I were to desert them [here] it would not do well at present for the poor old House."[31] Four days later, she also regretted that she could not "have the happiness of being with you and dear Sister Josephine [Trenor] at the joyful blessing of the [Naas] Convent which of all things I delight in." This time she had to forgo traveling to Naas because Dr. Murray had chosen October 3 for a profession ceremony at Baggot Street. But since Naas was near Dublin, she dared to hope that Frances could come to Baggot Street the night before the profession, "after all your ceremony ended," and "perhaps Dr. Fitzgerald & Mr. Maher, but I suppose this is all too much to think of."[32] It was.

The climax and the most far-reaching event of Catherine's life during 1839 occurred just before and during her trip to London: the final preparation and submission to Rome of the completed manuscript of the "Rule

---

29. Elizabeth C. Agnew, *Geraldine: A Tale of Conscience,* 3 vols. (London: Dolman, 1837–1839).
30. Letter 128, September 27, 1839, in *CCMcA,* 205.
31. Letter 127, September 23, 1839, in *CCMcA,* 204.
32. Letter 128, September 27, 1839, in *CCMcA,* 204.

and Constitutions of the Religious Sisters of Mercy" and the formal petition for its papal approval and confirmation. The transcribing and correspondence associated with this endeavor were enormous, and Clare
Moore, now temporarily in Dublin, was Catherine's right-hand assistant.

The process began in October when Clare made a fair copy of the final draft of the Rule, and Catherine requested letters of endorsement from
bishops familiar with the life and work of the Sisters of Mercy. Michael
Blake responded immediately, once again advising her to follow the normal route of having "your petition sanctioned and corroborated by the
joint request and signature of your venerable Archbishop. Whatever is
asked in this way, if it be at all reasonable, is usually and almost as a matter of course, granted."[33] Blake's guidance, over the past fifteen years, was
invaluable, as were his experience and knowledge of protocol.

The episcopal letters began to come in, but by early November, Catherine had to turn her attention to Bermondsey, for the departure date had
been set: Monday, November 18. Three days before they were to sail, a new
and unrelated problem arose. She began to suspect that the public laundry in the new addition to the house, in which she placed such hope, was
being completed with little or no provision for laundry equipment, and
no flow of water in or out. All she could do at this late date was write to
Charles Cavanagh:

Will you be so kind to send me the contract to look at the words relative to the
Laundry, as it seems now as if we only expected a Room capable of being made into
a Laundry. I most distinctly repeated—that a *perfect* Laundry was the chief object
in view. Certainly Mr. Brophy is bound to that.[34]

Her ever faithful solicitor would deal with Thomas Brophy, the builder,
and Barnard Mullins, the architect, in her absence.

No doubt the laundry was on Catherine's mind as she wrote to Frances
Warde the day before departure. But any worries about it were offset by
the elation of the group about to found in London the first community of
Sisters of Mercy outside Ireland:

I need not tell you all the difficulties I have to meet in getting away from this poor
old charge—which would, and will do as well without me.

The six travelers leave dear Ireland tomorrow, all in tolerable good health—and
more than tolerable spirits. Sister Agnew rejoiced, Sister Taylor in rapture, and their
Mother [Clare Moore] all animation. Sister M. Cecilia [Marmion] greatly improved

---

33. Letter 133, October 30, 1839, in CCMcA, 210.
34. Letter 141 [November 15, 1839], in CCMcA, 216.

and Mary Teresa [White] smart as a lark. I have my songs prepared for the journey.[35]

Always the songs—as essential baggage—for amusement en route or in London, and an emblem of the joy with which this woman always anticipated and accompanied new Mercy foundations, for the sake of the people about to be served.

In the same letter she told Frances she had taken the English sisters to visit George's Hill: "They were delighted and so was I, said I would kiss the chairs & tables—but by some mistake I kissed a grand new chair in the Parlour. . . . I took it back and brought it up to the old rush chair I used to sit on in the novaship [novitiate]." A flood of memories must have surrounded her first recorded visit to the Presentation convent in eight years. Perhaps thinking of the anxious de Pazzi Delany, she also acknowledged to Frances, that for some of those left behind at Baggot Street, the "excitement of my going [to London] will last a few days—I trust only a few." Dr. Murray had visited Baggot Street, and Redmond O'Hanlon had been reading too many London newspapers:

We have had *long* and most kind visits from our poor bishop, a cordial leave taking—and fervent prayers for our safe return. . . . I am sure Mr. O'Hanlon is a little alarmed at the angry things which are said in the English papers—he gave me 10,000 cautions yesterday.

Catherine herself seems not to have feared the anti-Catholic rhetoric still rife in the English press; she had experienced that before—in Dublin. Yet she did add a postscript: "Get all the prayers you can for poor me. Written in the greatest haste on the eve of departure."[36]

The sea voyage from Kingstown to Liverpool, the train to London, the evening arrival at the convent near the commercial docks, warehouses, and horrible slums along the southern bank of the Thames, and all that followed seem to have exhilarated Catherine, as her three long, surviving letters from Bermondsey attest.[37] She was sixty-one years old, but her spirit, if not her body, was more than equal to the whole adventure, our "grand journey" she called it.

They left Kingstown harbor at six in the evening on November 18,

35. Letter 142 [November 17, 1839], in *CCMcA*, 217.

36. Ibid., 217–18. Catherine frequently used the word "novaship" for "novitiate."

37. The letters were written to Elizabeth Moore, Angela Dunne, and Josephine Warde. Catherine McAuley undoubtedly also wrote from London to Mary Ann Doyle and Frances Warde, as well as to de Pazzi Delany at Baggot Street, but these letters have not survived.

aboard the *Queen Victoria*. Catherine thought "Friend Catherine" (drawn from her Quaker memories) was a better traveling name than "Kitty"—"an improvement, you will say."[38] Arriving in Liverpool at dawn, "not one of us sick," they had breakfast at the Mersey Hotel. The day train to London was "a most comfortable conveyance—it was just like 6 very cosy arm chairs"—a step up from the cramped Irish mail coaches.[39] She marveled at the distance covered in so short a time: "What [an] extraordinary expedition—we dined in Baggot Street Monday—and arrived in London time enough to take refreshment, say our prayers, and go to bed early on Tuesday night. Very different from our travels in Ireland—we were 16 hours going from Limerick to Tullamore."[40]

Peter Butler, the Bermondsey priest Catherine would soon admire and tease, could not meet them at the train station the night they arrived. When she finally met him, he was recovering from a broken blood vessel, but he looked "so badly . . . though going about," that she doubted "very much his getting through the Spring."[41] Father Butler had asthma, and later dropsy, but he lived until 1848. The zealous pastor of the mission parish of Bermondsey and Rotherhithe to the east, he had learned the skills of a good carpenter growing up on an Irish farm. These proved useful in his attempts to get the still unfinished convent ready. But he had exhausted himself in the effort.

Dr. Thomas Griffiths, vicar apostolic of the London District since 1836 (the English hierarchy as such was not restored until 1850), could not do enough for the Mercy community. He came the day after their arrival to welcome them, and despite Catherine's saying they had enough money, pressed a £50 note into her hand. At forty-eight, he was striking in his episcopal attire, unlike Irish prelates who, remembering the dangerous penal era, tended to downplay their episcopal insignia. With an eye for such detail, Catherine noticed his "gold chain and large cross outside his dress [cassock] and purple stockings." She found him "exceedingly kind," "remarkably gentle" and deferential. With her typical, self-deflating hyperbole she commented on her role in his eyes: "Every application [for admission into the community] is referred by the Bishop to Kitty—who is major domo."[42]

38. Letter 148, December 17, 1839, in *CCMcA*, 222.
39. Letter 149, December 24 [1839], in *CCMcA*, 226.
40. Letter 148, December 17, 1839, in *CCMcA*, 223.
41. Letter 149, December 24 [1839], in *CCMcA*, 228.
42. Letter 148, December 17, 1839, in *CCMcA*, 223, 224.

The convent building itself was a failure in Catherine's eyes—not in its location, next to the new parish church Butler had built, but in its design. On the spot she conceived a lasting dislike for the renowned Pugin's neo-Gothic architectural preferences. She commented on them in all three surviving letters from London, as well as in letters she wrote later:

I do not admire Mr. Pugin's taste, though so celebrated—it is quite the old heavy monastic style. He was determined we should not look out at the windows—they are up to the ceiling—we could not touch the glass without standing on a chair. We have got one good room finished, with brown walls and a long table.[43]

For a light-hearted woman who valued sunshine this was all too much. She estimated the building would "not be finished for another year, nor dry in three years."[44] And the allocation of space was off: "The refectory is very neat—with tables like Cork—novaship very small. Kitchen fit for a castle—ovens, boilers, etc.—I am sure Mr. Pugin likes to have Dinner well dressed. It is boarded—and nearly the best room in the House." She was not alone in her opinion: "Mother Mary Clare often says she likes Rutland Street Convent [in Cork] much better, and so do I."[45] Too many plaster cornices, and ornamental works! What was needed was a "plain, simple, durable building" with "well lighted" corridors, small sleeping rooms, other rooms much larger.[46]

Presumably Catherine did not make her disappointment so clearly known to the well-meaning Peter Butler. In the midst of one of London's most impoverished and dingy areas, immortalized by Charles Dickens, he had sacrificed his own needs and struggled mightily to raise money, mostly from wealthy Catholic friends and patrons, to construct a large church and convent to serve his people. Alas, a century later, on March 2, 1945, late at night, both buildings were effectively destroyed by a German V2 rocket.

On November 21, 1839, the feast of the Presentation of Mary, Dr. Griffiths came again, celebrated Mass with them in the parish Church of the Most Holy Trinity, and then blessed the convent building, thus marking the foundation day of the Sisters of Mercy in Bermondsey. Acting on Catherine's recommendation, he installed Clare Moore as the first superior of the community, intending that she would serve until August and then return to Cork.

Six women—all but one of them converts—had been waiting in Ber-

43. Letter 149, December 24 [1839], in CCMcA, 227.
44. Letter 148, December 17, 1839, in CCMcA, 223.
45. Letter 149, December 24 [1839], in CCMcA, 227, 228.
46. Letter 160, February 4, 1840, in CCMcA, 250–51.

mondsey to join the new community and working in the poor school of the parish under Peter Butler's guidance. Bishop Griffiths agreed with Catherine that their postulancy could be greatly shortened from the normal three months. As "their sincerity was not to be questioned," and as they had been led to believe that the community would be founded on September 24, "it would not have been fair to keep them longer in expectation."[47] Dr. Griffiths appointed December 12, Catherine's own profession day, for the first Mercy reception ceremony in London. A considerate accommodation to local needs and wishes, it meant that a good deal had to be accomplished in three weeks: making religious habits for six, sewing new dresses for the two hundred poor girls in the school who would attend the ceremony, sending out invitations by the hundreds, to say nothing of instructing the six women in the essentials of religious life they would need to develop as novices. This last endeavor fell to Catherine, but she also helped with the sewing and writing, admitting, "We have been 'Busy Bodys.'"[48]

The ceremony day was splendid, carriages clogging all the nearby streets, and "thousands" of guests, it is said, squeezed into every inch of the church. Members of the nobility, Catholic and Protestant, were seated in the front; Dr. Griffiths in full regalia, with priests from near and far, in the sanctuary. Everyone who wished to come, came—the families of the sisters to be received, the children from the school, the proud, and the inquisitive. It was a far cry from the secluded ceremony at Baggot Street in January 1832. Dr. Griffiths had asked that the reception itself follow the Pontifical High Mass so latecomers would not miss any of the ceremony.

Those who were to receive the novices' habit were the Lady Barbara Eyre, daughter of the deceased Earl of Newburgh and sister to the present earl; Jane Latham, "who had been a professed nun in France for twenty-five years"; Susan Weller, a friend of Jane's; Mary O'Connor, who had been working in the poor school and living in the old parish chapel for two years; and Elizabeth Boyce and Sarah Hawkins, who asked to be lay sisters.[49] It was a mixed group of very different backgrounds, from the wealthy to the very poor. All were dressed in long white gowns when the procession entered the church, but Barbara Eyre, allowed to choose her own, and her last, "worldly" attire, was clearly the most striking figure.

47. Letter 148, December 17, 1839, in CCMcA, 223; letter 149, December 24 [1839], in CCMcA, 226.
48. Letter 148, December 17, 1839, in CCMcA, 223.
49. On Jane Latham, see "Bermondsey Annals (1839)," vol. 1, 9 (AIMGB).

She "wore a full court dress worth 100 guineas—besides valuable diamonds—her train went below the last step when [she was] at the top."[50] The dress was "a white satin petticoat covered with white crape richly embroidered in gold down the middle and at the bottom—a satin body and train of violet hue—embroidered all round—full half yard deep—the train from the waist 3 yards long." Catherine was agape: "I never saw such a splendid thing."[51] So were those who read her descriptive letters in Limerick and Cork. By the time she wrote to those in Charleville she was speaking of the "very valuable diamonds which soon will belong to the poor"![52] Basically Barbara was a humble and good woman, and generous in countless ways, so Catherine had gone along with her wishes, up to a point—only asking her, finally, in view of the religious character of the occasion and place, to wear a lace shawl over her bare shoulders. When Barbara declined, Clare Moore, "taking the shawl to her, merely said, 'Sister, you will wear this,' and she did so without replying a word."[53]

Early that Thursday morning, at the request of her friend the Countess Constantia Clifford, Lady Barbara had her hair and headdress arranged by the court couturier. Before Mr. Trufitt arrived at the appointed hour of nine, Catherine went to Barbara's door and disguised her voice: "Please, your Ladyship, Mr. Trufitt is come." Not seeing who it really was, Barbara answered, somewhat peremptorily: "Take down that box with my feathers & diamonds."[54] Discovering her mistake, she was understandably distressed, but Catherine's laughter dispelled her embarrassment, and Barbara eventually appeared with her hair "dressed with long lace lappets—feathers and most valuable diamonds"—the first and probably the last Sister of Mercy in history to so approach her reception of the Mercy habit.[55]

The procession into the church was led by Teresa White, carrying an "immense" cross. She was followed—"one by one, to make the most of a few"—by Cecilia Marmion, Clare Agnew, Mary Augustine Taylor, the six postulants, Clare Moore, "and her valuable assistant, 'Friend Catherine' or your 'Kitty,'" as Catherine described herself. At various points in the clothing ceremony, Clare and Catherine, accompanying each postulant, had to ascend the sanctuary steps:

50. Letter 148, December 17, 1839, in CCMcA, 224.
51. Letter 149, December 24, [1839], in CCMcA, 227.
52. Letter 150, December 26, 1839, in CCMcA, 230.
53. "Bermondsey Annals (1849)," vol. 1, 172 (AIMGB).
54. Letter 148, December 17, 1839, in CCMcA, 225.
55. Letter 149, December 24 [1839], in CCMcA, 227.

The altar is the highest I ever saw—9 steps—2 platforms—the Bishop at the top—in very rich episcopal dress. Kitty had to go up and down eighteen times—3 times with each—indeed I might have said, poor Kitty.[56]

Poor Kitty, indeed, in all this ecclesiastical splendor, but well known privately in the Mercy community for her too frequently mended undergarments.

What mattered most to her were the postulants' public answers to the bishop's questions, principally this one: "Have you a firm intention to persevere in Religion, to the end of your life—and do you hope to have sufficient strength, to carry constantly the sweet yoke of our Lord Jesus Christ, solely for the love and fear of God?" The reply: "Relying on the mercy of God, I hope to be able to do so." And then the bishop's prayer: "What God has commenced in you, may he perfect."[57]

Months later, two of the six novices, Jane Latham and Susan Weller, "expressed much discontent," though they were "the persons chiefly in fault" in his view, so Bishop Griffiths ordered them to be dismissed before the year passed. The other four remained until their deaths, ardent and self-expending to the end. Mary Ursula (Mary) O'Connor died of typhus fever the following November, after visiting an afflicted family. It took Mary de Sales (Barbara) Eyre a while to adjust, but she did so, with joy. Mary Teresa (Elizabeth) Boyce became a stalwart, generous woman on whom Clare Moore could always count. Clare once told her: "Nothing makes such peace in a community as to look on everything in a cheerful way, as you do."[58] Mary Joseph (Sarah) Hawkins lived to 1882, all innocence and simplicity, her most striking traits. She nursed in the Crimean War, and Florence Nightingale officially commended her for "single-heartedness," and "unwearied devotion, patience & cheerfulness . . . judgment and activity."[59] Though their futures were unknown to Catherine, such virtue must have been her hope for them on December 12, as they put on the Mercy habit and way of life.

After the ceremony a luncheon was provided for the bishop, families, sisters, clergy, and other guests. Mrs. Agnew, Clare's mother, had sent in a turkey for which she had "paid thirteen shillings"—to Catherine, an astounding price. In her conversation with Mrs. Agnew, an Anglican woman she immediately liked, the widow of Sir Andrew Agnew and "much more

56. Letter 148, December 17, 1839, in CCMcA, 224.
57. Form of Ceremony (1840), 6.
58. Mary Clare Moore to Mary Teresa Boyce, June 11, 1869 (AIMGB).
59. British Library, Add. MSS 43402, f. 10, cited with permission of the British Library.

animated than her daughter," Catherine was amused to encounter the first of many instances of upper-class English prejudice toward the Irish.[60] "Mrs. Agnew particularly pleased with 'the young Lady Superior' [Clare Moore]—acknowledges she did not expect her daughter would meet such a companion in the South of Ireland." She was, in Catherine's view, "evidently astonished to find such wild Irish—nuns," and had initially come to the convent "privately, but seeing we were more respectably formed than she expected, came ever after in her own carriage to the public entrance."[61]

Catherine would soon play on this ethnic and religious prejudice in a teasing acrostic to the innocent Peter Butler:

> **F**or wild Irish did you take us
> **A**s some English folk would make us
> **T**hinking we just ran away—from
> **H**irish houses made of clay
> **E**ver glad to change our station
> **R**ushing to another nation.[62]

The Irish in the founding party had certainly never lived in clay and wattle cabins back home, though they had brought solace to many a one.

The English press at the time often featured derogatory comments about the increasing influx of poor Irish immigrants. Their emigration from the land they loved and would always call "home" was actually abetted by land tenure policies and English import and export regulations that drastically reduced employment opportunities in Ireland. But Catherine was also trying to deal with her own latent prejudice. Although she was in some ways more English than Celtic culturally, she admitted: "We cannot avoid preferring our sweet Irish Sisters every where." Speaking of their having "High Mass every Sunday," she confessed: "I like the Irish piety better—it seems more genuine—though not near so much exteriorly."[63]

Finally, after the solemnity of December 12 had passed, the community got down in earnest to the reasons for their being in Bermondsey in the first place. As Catherine told Elizabeth Moore: "There is great work here for the poor Sisters—2 large hospitals, Guy's and St. Thomas's—4 work houses—endless converts."[64] In addition there were the children in the

60. The description of Mrs. Agnew is found in letter 149, December 24 [1839], in CCMcA, 228.
61. Letter 148, December 17, 1839, in CCMcA, 225; letter 150, December 26, 1839, in CCMcA, 231.
62. Letter 153 [December 1839-January 1840], in CCMcA, 235.
63. Letter 148, December 17, 1839, in CCMcA, 225, 226.
64. Ibid., 224.

poor school who would remain in the basement of the old parish chapel for another year, until a school could be built adjoining the convent.[65]

As they walked the streets of Bermondsey, and Southwark to the west, to visit the poor and sick in hospitals and workhouses, they may have passed by the original site of the once-celebrated Tabard Inn or of the infamous Marshalsea debtors' prison. With her literary interests Catherine may have recalled some of the notables who once passed that way: Chaucer, Ben Jonson, Goldsmith, Keats, and Dickens. Dickens visited his father in the Marshalsea, and Keats had studied medicine at Guy's Hospital. But pressing much more immediately on her would have been the area's suffering and squalor.

Because they could not have a chapel in the convent for at least a year, the community prayed together in the parish church, a setting Catherine found "cold & bleak" when they were there alone. The biting cold, the heavy rain, the dampness of the convent, all had an effect on their health. Cecilia Marmion was "extremely delicate ever since we came . . . confined 3 & 4 days at a time to her Bed." Teresa White was "coughing—all the rest traveling on."[66] In her letters, Catherine never mentioned her own illness, but years later Teresa White claimed:

Our dear mother had a miserable time of it, being almost constantly ailing. I always thought the Bermondsey foundation was the beginning of her death-sickness, for she was never perfectly well after. . . . While she was very ill and confined to bed in London, one morning I prepared her breakfast and brought it to her; and because I brought the best I could get—white sugar, china tea-pot and cream-ewer—she said: "My heart, why did you not bring me a little tea in a mug, as you would to a poor person?"

When the whole tray accidentally spilled on the bed, Catherine joked: "Now you are punished for not remembering that your old mother is only a poor nun."[67]

Although she had planned to return to Dublin about January 20, seeing that things were well in hand in Bermondsey—except for the still unfinished rooms and the continued lack of sufficient furniture—Catherine decided to leave London on January 13. Clare Agnew had been appointed assistant to Clare Moore, and several more women were preparing to enter the community. Clare Moore's time away from Cork would expire on Au-

65. "Bermondsey Annals (1840)," vol. 1, 13 (AIMGB).
66. Letter 149, December 24 [1839], in CCMcA, 229.
67. Carroll, Leaves from the Annals, vol. 2 (1883), 58.

gust 22, and, according to the plan, Clare Agnew would that day be named superior. Bishop Griffiths had asked Catherine to announce this before she departed. But speaking privately to her of Clare Moore, he "said he never saw such maturity in so young a person—that she had judgment in her countenance."[68] Catherine knew this, but was pleased to hear him say it. Griffiths had plenty of administrative experience on which to base his opinion, having been president of St. Edmund's College and its adjacent seminary for fifteen years, during which he had had to overcome morale problems, declining enrollment, and financial mismanagement.

Before Cecilia, Teresa, and she departed for the long journey home, Catherine left the community an altered transcription of lines from a poem by the English Protestant Helen Maria Williams (1762–1827), a paraphrase on words in the gospel of Matthew: "Do unto others as you would they should do unto you" (7:12).[69] The poem as Catherine amended it— removing the masculine wording, deleting its reference to "tyrants," and tilting its pronouns to first person—represented her hope and prayer for the young community she was leaving behind and would never see again:

> Precept divine, to Earth in Mercy given
> oh sacred rule of action worthy Heaven
> wert thou the guide of life, we all should know
> a sweet exemption from the worst of woe.
> No more the powerful would the weak oppress
> but all would learn, the luxury to bless
> and av'rice from its hoarded treasures give
> unasked the liberal boon that want might live.
> Thou righteous law—whose dear and useful light
> sheds o'er the mind a ray divinely bright
> condensing in one line whate'er the sage
> has vainly taught in many a laboured page
> May every heart thy hallowed voice revere
> to justice sacred and to nature dear.[70]

68. Letter 158, January 30, 1840, in CCMcA, 248.

69. Helen Maria Williams, "Paraphrase," in vol. 1 of Poems (London: T. Cadell, 1791), 187–90, and in Poems on Various Subjects (London: G. and W. B. Whittaker, 1823), 288–90.

70. Letter 152 [November 1839–January 1840], in CCMcA, 233–34 and nn. 68–69.

CHAPTER 18

The Rule Goes to Rome *Early 1840*

Catherine arrived back in Dublin from Bermondsey on Tuesday, January 14, 1840. Four days later she started a letter to Elizabeth Moore, but stopped after the first two sentences:

After I had written the above ... Mr. O'Hanlon ordered me to Bed—and a Doctor to be sent for. I suffered much in the passage from Liverpool—my stomach continued very sore—and he thought—from my looks and feel—that there was some inflammatory symptom. I am now quite well but weak, of course, after passing through the hands of a Doctor.[1]

Blood-letting or purging medications were probably not what Catherine wanted after all she had been through in the last two months—the cold and dampness of London, the meticulous work of preparing and sending the Rule of the Sisters of Mercy to Rome, the sudden death of her nephew Robert during her absence, and then the rough sea voyage from Liverpool.

Her major accomplishment in late 1839 and early 1840 was submitting the Rule and Constitutions of the Sisters of Mercy for approval and confirmation by Pope Gregory XVI. Her original draft had already been slightly amended and then approved and signed in the mid-1830s by Daniel Murray.[2] The packet now sent to Rome—to the Congregation for the Propagation of the Faith, which had jurisdiction over religious congregations in Ireland—contained a fair copy of the Rule (part 1) and Constitu-

---

1. Letter 157, January 18, 1840, in *CCMcA*, 246.
2. Catherine McAuley's manuscript of the Rule and Constitutions, with Daniel Murray's revisions, is transcribed in *CMcATM*, 295–328.

tions (part 2) handwritten by Clare Moore in the fall of 1839 as she waited in Dublin for departure to Bermondsey.[3] In addition, the packet included the formal petition for papal approval, signed by Catherine McAuley with the names of the other Mercy superiors in Ireland and London, and formal letters of endorsement from Archbishop Murray, six other Irish bishops familiar with the life and work of the Sisters of Mercy, and Thomas Griffiths, vicar apostolic of the London District.[4] The packet was carried to Rome through arrangements evidently made by Dr. Griffiths. The Rule and Constitutions and Catherine's petition were written in English; some, but not all, of the episcopal letters in Latin. Reading the letters of Archbishop Murray and Dr. William Crolly, archbishop of Armagh and primate of All Ireland, and of Bishops Blake, Griffiths, Haly, Kinsella, Murphy, and Ryan, one can surmise Catherine's feelings of gratitude.

Here was not the language of the Reverends Kelly, Meyler, and Sheridan over the previous decade, but of appreciative men with whom she had worked and would continue to work to extend the mercy of God to suffering people. Some of these letters, all for forwarding to Rome, were addressed to Catherine herself; some to Cardinal Giacomo Fransoni, prefect of Propaganda Fide; others to Pope Gregory. Michael Blake told Catherine: "I could not say too much in praise of your Institute."[5] John Ryan spoke of "the edifying conduct and valuable exertions of . . . the Sisters of Mercy" in Limerick.[6] To the pope, William Kinsella claimed, "from an abundant experience of their labours," that the Sisters of Mercy had "produced the most fertile fruits of charity and piety."[7] William Crolly assured Catherine that he felt "much pleasure in stating" that "the Order of the Sisters of Mercy is calculated to render important services to the poor of Ireland."[8] John Murphy told Gregory XVI that the sisters in the "eight convents" he knew were "glowing with charity," and he described in some detail their "help to the sick poor . . . . the faithful . . . convalescents . . . young girls" and "poor servant maids."[9] Francis Haly, noting the two Mercy convents in his diocese (Carlow and Naas), assured Cardinal Fransoni he had "seen with joy this Congregation bringing much fruit" as they "instruct the ignorant . . . encourage and uplift the needy and miserable, visit and console

---

3. Clare Moore's fair copy of the Rule and Constitutions is discussed in CMcATM, 270–72, 292–93.
4. Letter 145 [November or December 1839], in CCMcA, 220–21.
5. Letter 133, October 30, 1839, in CCMcA, 210–11.
6. Letter 134, October 30, 1839, in CCMcA, 211.
7. Letter 135, November 5, 1839, in CCMcA, 213–14.
8. Letter 137, November 8, 1839, in CCMcA, 214.
9. Letter 143, November 18, 1839, in CCMcA, 218–19.

the infirm, assist the dying."[10] Thomas Griffiths, grateful to have a Mercy convent in Bermondsey, told Cardinal Fransoni that the congregation of the Sisters of Mercy had "already for six [sic] years been of the greatest help to the poor of Ireland, as is apparent from the letters of its superiors [i.e., the other bishops]."[11] He wrote a second letter to the pope, begging confirmation of the Rule.[12]

Archbishop Murray's formal letter of approval and recommendation, in Latin, was addressed to Gregory XVI. Written before Catherine left for London, and handed to her to place in the packet for Rome, the letter beseeched the pope

to confirm by your Apostolic authority the Rules already approved by me for the government of the Pious Congregation which is called by the name Sisters of Mercy, and which is spreading more and more every day, far and wide throughout Ireland, to the great benefit of souls and the great consolation of Pastors.[13]

In these letters, over the space of five weeks, Catherine read the largest outpouring of episcopal praise and approval she and her sisters had ever received.[14] It did not carry her away. She was too honest for that, too aware that "we are treated by everybody better than we deserve," too conscious that "those things do not depend on any one in particular, but on the continuance of God's blessing."[15] She was also too convinced that

none can attribute to themselves the success that may attend their exertions, because it is the fruit which God intended to produce when he instituted the order and granted the means to propagate it.[16]

Indeed, she had written earlier, in 1839:

There has been a most marked Providential Guidance which the want [lack] of prudence—vigilance—or judgment has not impeded—and it is here that we can most clearly see the designs of God. . . . We have been deficient enough—and far, very far, from cooperating generously with God in our regard, but we will try to do better—all of us—*the black heads*—will try to repair the past.[17]

---

10. Letter 144, November 22, 1839, in *CCMcA*, 219.

11. Letter 146, December 3, 1839, in *CCMcA*, 221.

12. Letter 147, December 3, 1839, in *CCMcA*, 222.

13. Letter 138, November 12, 1839, in *CCMcA*, 215.

14. Apparently Dr. John Cantwell, bishop of Meath, where Tullamore was located, also wrote a letter, but if it has survived, it has not been located. See letter 231, January 20, 1841, in *CCMcA*, 352–53. No record so far discovered indicates that Dr. Bartholomew Crotty, bishop of Cloyne and Ross, where Charleville was located, wrote a letter, though he was a kind supporter of the Sisters of Mercy. Perhaps his age prevented his writing, or his letter was lost, or misfiled at Propaganda Fide.

15. *PS*, 1; letter 90, June 16, 1838, in *CCMcA*, 142.

16. Letter 324, "Spirit of the Institute," in *CCMcA*, 462.

17. Letter 110, January 13, 1839, in *CCMcA*, 179–80. The "black heads" were the professed sisters, in black veils, not the white-veiled novices.

Still, in the privacy of her heart and prayer, Catherine must have been consoled. Deficiencies notwithstanding, somehow, despite their failings, mercifulness and charity had been shown to those most in need, and God would finish the work God had begun.

Now back at Baggot Street, Catherine's illness lingered for at least two weeks:

I have been chiefly confined to bed since my return—not down until yesterday. First, an affection of my stomach, etc., for which I was obliged to have a Physician—and then my old mouth complaint to a great degree which has kept me on Infants diet for more than 10 days.[18]

It is unfortunate that other January 1840 letters to her confidantes have not survived, beyond those to Elizabeth and Frances, for Catherine came home to a family sorrow: the sudden death of her nephew Robert Nesbitt Macauley.

Robert, now about twenty-one, died, apparently of consumption, on January 4 at his quarters on Monck Place, Dublin, on the north side of the city. Catherine's associates say that his death caused her great anguish, though they differ as to its circumstances. Clare Moore claims that before her November departure for England, Catherine "not only left him in a very precarious state, but had quitted Ireland in displeasure with him on account of some foolish conduct; and the poor youth died during her absence, with expressions of deep regret for not having obtained forgiveness, which was a sore trial to her affectionate heart."[19] Mary Vincent Harnett, who may have had her information from Elizabeth Moore, says Robert, "a young lad of great promise,"

after a course of study of no ordinary distinction, was preparing for the bar; but owing to the indiscretion of youth he had the misfortune of incurring the displeasure of his Aunt, and for some time mutual estrangement was the consequence. During her absence . . . in England, he was seized with an alarming illness, the most fatal consequences threatened to be the result, he became a penitent and sought a reconciliation with her whom he had so deeply grieved. It is needless to add that pardon of the past was at once and fully given, but before it reached the poor sufferer for whom it was intended, death had put an end to his existence. He had received the last Sacraments, been attended by the Sisters of her community in Baggot St., and expired in great sentiments of sorrow and repentance; but the fact of his departing this life without having received her letter or having known her altered sentiments

18. Letter 158, January 30, 1840, in *CCMcA*, 247, and 247 n. 11 on scurvy and pyorrhea.
19. BA, in *CMcATM*, 123.

was beyond measure afflicting to her who had loved him even in his errors with all the fond affection of a mother.[20]

Clare Augustine Moore says, whether correctly or not, that Robert's "consumption" was "brought on by reckless dissipation," and that Catherine "had by every means in her power striven to keep [her two elder nephews] in the right path and afterwards to reclaim them; how much she grieved for their errors few knew so well as I."[21] In her one surviving letter of January 1840 in which she refers to Robert's death, Catherine herself says only, "How can I sufficiently express my gratitude for your tender charitable remembrance of my poor Robert." Ten months later she reminds Frances Warde that "Robert's last wish was that the Sisters would pray for the repose of his poor soul."[22]

Whatever Robert's "errors" or "dissipation" may have been, his obituary in *Freeman's Journal* claimed:

We feel considerable pain in communicating to our readers the death of [Robert N. Macauley, Esq.] who was a long time connected with the *Morning Register,* in the capacity of Reporter. In private life everyone who had the pleasure of his acquaintance valued him as a sincere friend and agreeable companion, and in the discharge of his professional duties he was not to be surpassed.[23]

Robert was buried in Prospect Cemetery, Glasnevin, in grave J.D. 82 in the garden section, on January 6, 1840. In 1940 the superintendent of the cemetery informed John MacErlean that the grave had never been paid for in perpetuity and therefore had no stone marker over it.[24] No record indicates that Catherine ever visited the graves of any of her family members, and it is doubtful that she would have had the funds to provide permanently for her nephew's grave. Yet her grief was evidently profound, and probably threaded with haunting questions: How could she have been a better mother? How should she, or could she, have been more merciful to Robert? Whatever answers came to her, she never shared them in a surviving letter. There remained to the adoptive mother of nine now only James, her eldest nephew, Teresa Byrn, and the orphan Ann Rice. Three of her sister's children (Mary, Catherine, and Robert) and Ellen Corrigan were dead, and Willie was gone from her—as was Catherine Byrn, now in the

20. Lim, in *CMcATM*, 185–86.

21. CAM, in *CMcATM*, 211.

22. Letter 157, January 18, 1840, in *CCMcA*, 246; and letter 206, November 9, 1840, in *CCMcA*, 317.

23. *Freeman's Journal*, January 6, 1840.

24. J. W. Nolan to John MacErlean, May 10, 1940 (MCA).

enclosed Dominican convent on Lower Mount Street, not far from Baggot Street.

But in Ireland a new epidemic of typhus was taking hold. By early March it had afflicted sisters in Tullamore, Carlow, Charleville, and Limerick. Moreover, two sisters were now dying of consumption: one in Cork and another at Baggot Street. Those in Tullamore, Carlow, and Charleville recovered, but there was eventually little hope for the others, and three deaths occurred within twelve days. Mary Francis Mahony died in Cork on March 8, just a month after she professed vows. In Dublin, the second of the Marmion sisters, Mary Francis, died on March 10. She had been an indefatigable advocate of the poor families she visited, and as Catherine sat by her bed for nine long hours, she hoped Francis would speak again: "It is melancholy consolation to look for, yet I think we would all like to hear her gentle voice again."[25] This did not happen.

Then on March 14 word came from Limerick that Catherine's "sweet little poet," Mary Teresa Vincent Potter, had typhus. Catherine was hopeful she would recover, but by March 19, fearful: "No words could describe what I felt—on reading the first line of your letter. . . . I will be in great anxiety to hear—though I will be agitated at the sight of the next letter."[26]

Teresa died on Friday, March 20. Receiving Elizabeth Moore's letter the next morning, Catherine wrote immediately:

My Darling Sister M. Elizabeth

I did not think any event in this world could make me feel so much. I have cried heartily—and implored God to comfort you—I know He will. This has not been done in anger. Some joyful circumstance will soon prove that God is watching over your concerns which are all his own—but without the cross the real crown cannot come. Some great thing which He designs to accomplish—would have been too much—without a little bitter in the cup. Bless and love the Fatherly hand which has hurt you. He will soon come with both hands filled with favors and blessings.

My heart is sore—not on my account—nor for the sweet innocent spirit that has returned to her Heavenly Father's Bosom—but for you.

You may be sure I will go see you—if it were much more out of the way—and indeed I will greatly feel the loss that will be visible on entering the convent.

Earnestly & humbly praying God to grant you His Divine consolation—and to comfort and bless all the dear Sisters—I remain

your ever most affectionate
M. C. McAuley[27]

25. Letter 164, March 10, 1840, in *CCMcA*, 256. See Mary Francis Marmion's poetic exchange with Catherine McAuley, letter 73 [January 25, 1838], in *CCMcA*, 121–22.

26. Letter 167 [March 19, 1840], in *CCMcA*, 258–59.

27. Letter 168 [March 21, 1840], in *CCMcA*, 259.

Catherine had previously told Elizabeth that she could not come to Limerick, neither before nor after her trip to found a community in Galway: "It would add fifty miles to my travelling—who am journeying fast enough out of this world. Every day I am weak at some time. My stomach has never recovered its last attack—frequent swelling and soreness."[28] But now she resolved to do so, even if Limerick "were much more out of the way."

Earlier that year Charles Cavanagh had begun to address the problem in the laundry that Catherine suspected as she was leaving for London. Basically, there were no plumbing fixtures. The bare laundry rooms (the washing room and the drying and mangling room above it) were nearly completed, but no water troughs or sewage outlets had been installed for incoming wash water or outgoing drainage.

In late January, Cavanagh or Catherine received a supplemental contract from Bernard Mullins of the architectural firm of Henry, Mullins, and MacMahon. The new contract itemized the "extra work" required to rectify the laundry situation, as well as certain deductions for previously designed work not to be executed, and then set forth the final cost. Including the plumber's bill, it now totaled £1836.18.6, more than £90 over the original contract of £1743.16.7.[29] Apparently, Catherine complained directly to Mullins about the extra charges and other defects in the new building, for on February 26 she wrote to Cavanagh:

I enclose you a copy of the two notes I wrote to Mr. Mullins, which he terms "graciously offensive." . . . Complaints must necessarily be addressed or referred to him. The man called the contractor [Thomas Brophy] could not alter the most glaring defect without his permission—and repeatedly said "he got enough to starve" on— by the engagement.[30]

The door keys for the laundry had been turned over to her, and Brophy was looking for the final payments promised in the original contract.

"Graciously offensive" or not, of the whole fiasco Catherine could only say flatly: "It is an unkind unjust transaction. I have good reason to say so."[31] Three days later she lamented: "The new Laundry is all loss so far, but we must work on—a year, please God, will bring it forward."[32] Actually another half year at least, but now at a total expense almost double

28. Letter 166, March 14, 1840, in CCMcA, 257.
29. "Admeasurement & Valuation of Extra Work done by Mr. Brophy in the Erection of New Addition to the House of Mercy, Baggot Street—Materials & Workmanship," January 20, 1840 (MCA).
30. Letter 161, February 26, 1840, in CCMcA, 251.
31. Ibid.
32. Letter 162, February 29, 1840, in CCMcA, 254.

the original legacy of £1000 that, two years before, she had so cheerfully invested in building the addition to the House of Mercy and the "long desired public laundry."

In presenting the bill for the "extra" work, Bernard Mullins also indicated that, like the old connection of the original building, the new sewage connection would be inadequate:

I consider the Sewer leading from the Wash House along the area of that building & across the court yard of the front building & thro' it into the main Sewer in Baggot Street too small & insufficient for the purpose & that the part constructed by Mr. Brophy is in this respect as defective as the old House Sewer previously built into which the new part discharges.[33]

Despite her growing architectural acumen, Catherine knew little about designing plumbing, and apparently neither she nor Charles Cavanagh had scrutinized the original contract for the addition to the House of Mercy. However, in this neither she nor Bernard Mullins was fully to blame. The whole city of Dublin lacked an adequate water-borne sewage system until well into the second half of the century. Too late for Catherine McAuley, but not for the house.

Yet the prospect of a successful commercial laundry remained for Catherine a comforting promise of practical assistance to those in need. In her mind's eye she could see the large, future bundles of incoming laundry—even though, as Clare Augustine Moore later acknowledged: "The expense of the building greatly exceeded her calculations, and the building itself was a continual worry. Neither were the returns when it was built at all equal to her expectations; in fact, for long enough after her death they were miserably insignificant."[34] For those who study Catherine's life the laundry remains a touching symbol of her naiveté, yes, but perhaps also of her eager self-expenditure.

Fortunately, it would seem, Catherine appears not to have known that in Rome, during the month of February, the Rule and Constitutions of the Sisters of Mercy was undergoing minute examination by Gavino Secchi Murro (1794–1868), a Servite priest and consultor for the Congregation for the Propagation of the Faith. The procurator general of the Servants of Mary since 1835, and a respected academic theologian, he was a consultor for several Vatican departments, in addition to Propaganda Fide: the Congregations on Bishops and Regular Clergy, the Index of Forbidden Books,

---

33. "Admeasurement & Valuation of Extra Work," January 20, 1840 (MCA).
34. CAM, in *CMcATM*, 212.

and Sacred Rites. He was also an examiner, in the presence of the pope, of bishops and Roman clergy, and the personal theologian of three cardinals. In 1853, when Pius IX named him confessor of the Sacred Apostolic Palace, he moved to the papal residence.[35] As might be anticipated, given his background, Secchi Murro was meticulous in his scrutiny of the Mercy Rule and Constitutions, which had been translated into Italian, the working language of Propaganda Fide.

Clare Moore says the translator was Richard Colgan, O.C.C., an Irish Carmelite priest working in Rome.[36] Mary Vincent Harnett also says that Colgan, who was returning to Rome, "offered to present the Rule for confirmation" and promised "to translate it into Italian in order that it might be examined by . . . Propaganda Fide."[37] However, the Carlow Annals for 1843 says that Michael O'Connor prepared the translation while he was in Rome.[38] But O'Connor had completed his studies in Rome by 1834, then served as vice-rector of the Irish College until 1836 or 1837 when he returned to Ireland. In 1839 he went to Philadelphia to teach, and by 1840 was bishop of Pittsburgh. He may have translated the two chapters of the Rule Catherine sent to Rome in December 1833, but probably not the final 1839 text.[39]

Secchi Murro found errors in the translation but did not identify them, and they were probably never corrected.[40] Twenty months later, Catherine regarded them as "mistakes," though the "mistakes" she saw included changes deliberately made in Rome at Secchi Murro's suggestion, with or without Daniel Murray's input as Secchi Murro had hoped.[41]

The consultor's overall reaction to the Rule proper (part 1) was positive, "on account of the truly evangelical doctrine taught" there, "the maxims of solid piety inculcated," and "the spirit of most perfect charity which

---

35. Gabriele M. Roschini, *Galleria Servitana: Oltre mille religiosi dell'Ordine dei Servi di Maria* (Rome: Pontificia Facoltà Teologica "Marianum", 1976), vol. 1, 543–44; and Antonio M. Vicentini, *Il Confessore del S. Palazzo Apostolico e L'Ordine dei Servi di Maria* (Venice: Tipografia Pontificia Vesc. S. Giuseppe, 1925), 59–62. I thank Franco Azzalli and Conrad Borntrager of the Servite Order for sending me excerpts from these works, and Sebastian A. Falcone for his translations.

36. BA, in *CMcATM*, 123.

37. Lim, in *CMcATM*, 187.

38. "Carlow Annals, 1843" (Archives, Sisters of Mercy, Carlow, Ireland).

39. Mac Suibhne, *Paul Cullen*, vol. 1 (1961), 195–96, 237.

40. In her research for the *Positio* "on the heroic virtues of the Venerable Servant of God Catherine McAuley," prepared under the aegis of the Congregation for the Causes of Saints, Bolster says that Secchi Murro refers to errors in the translation of the original into Latin, that Italian and Latin translations were given to him, and that the work of translation was done by Redmond O'Hanlon. She gives no source indicating that O'Hanlon did either a Latin or an Italian translation. In fact, there does not appear to be *any* Latin translation of the document.

41. See letter 314, October 12, 1841, in *CCMcA*, 449.

is manifested."[42] As to the Constitutions (part 2 of the document), Secchi Murro commended the decentralized governance of the congregation that Catherine had proposed—under the jurisdiction of the respective diocesan bishops—as opposed to the custom of "quasi-monarchical" *(quasi monarchico)* governance under a single superior general. However, he looked for more prescriptive detail:

> There is not much detail given, nor does one find in the proposed rules that methodical positive prescription of actions and other things, which serve to regulate at all times and in every place the conduct of the individuals in a religious community—for which reason these rules could not be properly called a constitutions.[43]

Here Secchi Murro was implicitly, though unwittingly, contradicting Catherine's intention and her oft-stated advice and belief: "Be careful never to make too many laws, for if you draw the string too tight it will break."[44] He supported his view by citing Saint Francis de Sales's comment in his preface to the Constitutions of the Visitation Sisters: "The Rule teaches what is to be done, the Constitutions teach how it is to be done."[45]

Among the particular regulations Secchi Murro wanted to see in the Mercy Constitutions were "fixed" times for the mental prayer and Hours of the *Office of the Blessed Virgin* that the Rule itself prescribes; and "an orderly distribution of hours and of duties, distinguishing feast days from working days, and assigning to all the Sisters in particular and respectively the occupations to which they should attend." He claimed that "Constitutions cannot be said to be complete which lack that detailed method and those positive prescriptions for the observance of the Rule which are so necessary for religious communities, especially of women [*specialmente di donne*]." Here Secchi Murro followed the gender stereotyping that had long compromised some ecclesiastical regulations for women's religious orders: he noted women's supposed "uneasiness and perplexities of mind," their need for "limits" on the authority of their female superiors, the "discords" and "complaints" which "may so easily happen where the law is silent and the motives of the superior's actions are not known."[46] Presum-

---

42. *Voto del P. Secchi Murro Consultore*, S.R.C.G. (1840), num. IX and X, ff. 225r–227r (APF), and the English translation (typescript) by John MacErlean, 3 (MCA). In citing Secchi Murro's views, I have followed MacErlean's translation, with frequent reference to Secchi Murro's document as *printed* in Italian in S.R.C.G. *(Scritture Riferite Congressi Generali)*, not Secchi Murro's *handwritten* document, which MacErlean followed and which is extremely hard to read. The latter is S.O.C.G., vol. 957 (1840), ff. 307r-313r (APF).

43. MacErlean translation, 3 (MCA).

44. *PS*, 21; BA, in *CMcATM*, 115; and Lim, in *CMcATM*, 179.

45. MacErlean translation, 4 (MCA).

46. Ibid., 4–5.

ably such precautionary regulations were less needed, or not needed at all, in religious orders of men.

Secchi Murro then proceeded with "detailed observations" on particular chapters of the Rule that he felt lacked the necessary prescriptions. Among the revisions he suggested were a more detailed curriculum for the schools; removal of the bishop's authority in particular situations to dispense with the requirement of a two-year novitiate; insertion of a fixed horarium for each house of the institute; the addition of regulations about who, how, and when non-sisters might enter the convent building; and references to the reasons and conditions for "expulsion of those [sisters] who are incorrigible."[47]

In speaking of the omissions he noted, Secchi Murro recommended that, if the Congregation for the Propagation of the Faith wished to "complete" the document, it could "be committed to His Grace the Archbishop of Dublin, who would readily satisfy you by introducing those regulations ... which he may have considered superfluous for setting down in the Rules sent by him to Rome for approval."[48] Nevertheless, Secchi Murro registered his vote that the Rule and Constitutions of the Sisters of Mercy "are worthy of all praise, and deserve for that reason the higher approbation of this Sacred Congregation" (i.e., the Congregation for the Propagation of the Faith).[49] This vote would have pleased Catherine McAuley had she known of it, but not some of his recommendations for additions.

Why burden communities with a formal Rule statement of "fixed" times, when the horarium of each house—as Catherine later told Bishop Thomas Walsh of Birmingham—was "contained in our observances, not in our Rule, and therefore subject to any alteration that place or circumstances might require"?[50] Perhaps it would have been wise to state the conditions for dismissal ("expulsion") of professed members from the congregation, to avoid arbitrariness, but she had always hoped such occasions would never arise. The discretion she had given to the respective bishops to shorten the novitiate to one full year specifically allowed each new foundation to have, as soon as possible, a chapter of seven professed sisters who could conduct community elections and make the formal deci-

47. Ibid., 5–7.
48. Ibid., 8–9.
49. Ibid., 2. Nowadays, the proposed Rule and Constitutions of a religious congregation is reviewed by the Vatican Congregation for Institutes of Consecrated Life and Societies of Apostolic Life, which then makes a recommendation to the pope.
50. Letter 202, November 6, 1840, in CCMcA, 312.

sions about admission of new members to reception of the habit and profession of vows.

As for a system of penances to be imposed for infractions of the Rule,
Secchi Murro felt that the lack of such prescription was sufficiently supplied, in general, in the chapter on the office of the mother superior and
that specifics should be left to her discretion—except in cases of "expulsion." As was well known among her sisters, Catherine could barely even
listen, and not without great discomfort, to any sister's expression of failure with respect to the Rule: "She could not be prevailed on to hold the
prescribed Chapter of Faults for a very long time after being made Superior, and was pained when the Sisters manifested their faults to her in private."[51]

Gavino Secchi Murro's vote and his long, accompanying document,
all in Italian, were delivered to the Congregation for the Propagation of
the Faith on March 3, 1840. They were subsequently given to the cardinals who composed the congregation, for consideration at their meeting
scheduled for July 20, 1840. After that meeting several weeks would pass
before Catherine heard the outcome, and then not officially, but only
through informal comments of those who had been in Rome. It would
be well over a year before she heard officially what recommendation concerning the Mercy Rule and Constitutions the cardinals had in fact made
to Pope Gregory XVI, and his response.

Meanwhile, early 1840 presented plenty of other projects and troubles
to claim Catherine's mind. The charity sermon on Sunday, February 23,
was a failure. Advertising it in *Freeman's Journal*, Catherine had cited the
community's swelling need for financial help:

From the increased price of provisions, and the very small collection of last year,
the Sisters have been most reluctantly obliged to reject many reduced persons,
whose respectable character and extreme necessity gave them the strongest claim
for protection. . . . The Sisters feel assured this appeal would not be fruitless could
they give a just description of their feelings on those occasions, as well as in the
visitation of the sick poor; how heart-rending it is to witness such extreme affliction, and not to have it in their power to afford even some trifling relief.[52]

---

51. BA, in *CMcATM*, 111. For a discussion of the Chapter of Faults, see *CMcATM*, 281, which notes
sentences added in Rome to part 2, chapter 18 of Catherine McAuley's text. Catherine had dealt with
this matter, in a more general fashion, in her chapter on the Office of the Mother Superior, part 2, 3.8,
in *CMcATM*, 322. The chapter numbers and sequence in her text, as given in *CMcATM*, 295–328, differ
from those in the copy presented to Rome. See *CMcATM*, 292–93, for outlines of the respective chapter
sequences.

52. *Freeman's Journal*, February 19–22, 1840.

The celebrated preacher, the Reverend Daniel W. Cahill, commenced his sermon on the parable of the prodigal son "so as to attract great attention." But "in less than 10 minutes [he] became so ill as to give up. £25 collected—of which he got 3 and the printer 4. The few old friends gave as usual—all the rest went away disappointed—not a word had been said of the charity." However, afterwards, "better . . . than usual" donations came in, and Catherine was advised to publish the sermon. She was herself "curious to hear how the connection was joined—between us and the Prodigal Son."[53] She did not regard the women they served as "prodigal," but would have hoped that she and the community had the unconditional mercifulness of the prodigal father.

Financial resources were dangerously low, but human help was increasing. On February 27 a large ceremony took place at Baggot Street. Five sisters professed their vows, including Clare Augustine Moore, and two more received the habit. By May seven additional women entered the community, five of them destined for a new foundation in Birmingham.[54]

On February 1, Thomas Walsh, vicar apostolic of the Midland District in England, had requested "the establishment of a branch of the Order" in Birmingham, an industrial center to which many Irish immigrants flocked for work. If Catherine agreed, he promised to send "two respectable females from this country" to serve their novitiate at Baggot Street. John Hardman, a highly successful Birmingham manufacturer of buttons and other metal work, would give land and "offers at his own expense to build and to furnish a small convent." The elderly Hardman also wished to place in the care of the sisters the orphans he had long supported in his home. In addition, John Talbot, the Earl of Shrewsbury, would provide "two thousand pounds, the interest of which—£100 per annum" would support the sisters.[55]

Catherine responded immediately, suggesting that the two women come to Baggot Street for a period of fifteen months. "They could then return, accompanied by one or two well acquainted with our regulations. The pension for each during the novitiate is twenty-five pounds per annum," but "if circumstances required a reduction, it would be made." However, she also put forward another option: if the women "would rather

---

53. Letter 162, February 29, 1840, in *CCMcA*, 253. If Cahill's sermon was ever published, it has not so far been found.

54. "Baggot Street Register" (MCA).

55. Letter 159, February 1, 1840, in *CCMcA*, 249. For information on the Hardmans see Barbara Jeffery, *Living for the Church . . . The Hardman Family Story* (n.p.: Sisters of Mercy, [2010]).

not come to Ireland," they could join two sisters from Baggot Street "on their arrival in Birmingham, which would save expense—and having the ceremony of reception at home" might "animate others to follow" their example. She left the choice to Dr. Walsh: "Whatever you think best suited to the views" of those in Birmingham "shall be met in every possible way."

Catherine's most forthright and specific opinions in the letter concerned construction of the convent building. She had learned her lesson in Bermondsey and did not wish to see that convent's flaws, or Booterstown's, repeated:

My Lord—as to building—I beg leave to suggest the advantage of not doing so on a very limited scale. We should hope that an Establishment in Birmingham would be productive of others. Your Convent should have at least twenty cells—10 feet by 7—a small window—and small door made so close to the partition wall as to leave a sufficient space for the Bed's head—a novaship—about 18 feet by 14—a Community room—Refectory—and Choir [chapel]—each to be 25 feet by 19—a good room for Infirmary—and a small reception parlour. It is very desirable there should be only two floors above the basement story. The refectory should be close to the Kitchen—all executed in the plainest style, without any cornice—cheap grates and stone chimneypieces.

This could be completed in ten months—and would not cost more than a smaller building where ornamental work would be introduced. . . .

The Convent in Bermondsey is not well suited to the purpose—the sleeping rooms are too large—the other rooms too small—the corridors confined and not well lighted—all the gothic work outside has made it expensive. A plain simple durable building is much more desirable.[56]

Thomas Walsh had not mentioned or even alluded to Augustus Welby Pugin, but Catherine was ready for him.

Though she was often obliged to live from day to day, from one contribution to the next, from one crisis to the next, from one "design of God" to the next, taking "one day only in hands at a time," Catherine had a practical instinct about the needs of the future, or at least a hope that the Sisters of Mercy would somehow, in God's providence, endure.[57] She was, therefore, particularly careful not to set unnecessary precedents that would encourage her successors to add new and crippling regulations to the Rule and customs—what she sardonically called "improvements"—saying once, for instance, that "if she added prayers herself some very devout successor would add more, and another more, till, especially in poor convents, the

---

56. Letter 160, February 4, 1840, in CCMcA, 250–51.
57. Letter 241, February 28, 1841, in CCMcA, 365.

sisters would be incapable of the duties of the institute."[58] Catherine's ideal in all aspects of the congregation, not just convent construction, was what was "plain, simple, durable."

Later that spring, Bishop Walsh sent not two, but five young women from Birmingham. Juliana Hardman, the donor's daughter, Anne Wood, Lucy Bond, and Marianne Beckett arrived on April 29, and Eliza Edwards came on May 17.[59] Catherine hardly had time to get to know the first four. The annual Easter bazaar took place in the Rotunda at the end of Sackville Street on Wednesday and Thursday, April 29 and 30. Then she and others were scheduled to depart for a foundation in Galway.

The bazaar, with a new feature this year, was advertised with the usual appeal for funds penned by Catherine herself:

The Sisters of Mercy, in the name of Him whose favorite attribute is Mercy, and on behalf of their poor, friendless, and unprotected charge, the inmates of the House of Mercy and Sick Poor, most earnestly beg your kind support and attendance at their Bazaar.

In honor of Queen Victoria, the advertisement also announced: "Her Majesty's Marriage [February 10] will be beautifully represented by at least Forty Figures in appropriate Costume. A Raffle Ticket will be given Gratis at the door."[60] Who made or organized the making of the forty figurines and costumes is not known, though this artistic work may, for weeks, have occupied all hands at evening recreation on Baggot Street. Whatever the difficult sewing involved, it was a relaxing diversion from walking slum streets and teaching barefoot girls.

In April, at Archbishop Murray's request, the sisters returned to "ill fated Kingstown."[61] Their leader, Clare Augustine Moore, claims, perhaps correctly, that "the debt was paid by the Institute." She records, with distress, that while she was there:

A truly pious, charitable lady called … and said, "You see after all, your clever Mrs. McAuley had to pay that £400." She never reflected that every talent and every penny that our dear foundress possessed had been devoted to the poor. But she endured ingratitude and even insolence so sweetly that those who behaved ill towards her never felt they were doing wrong.[62]

58. CAM, in *CMcATM*, 213.

59. "Baggot Street Register" (MCA).

60. *Freeman's Journal*, March 31–April 29, 1840. "Inmates" did not have its present-day restricted meaning (e.g., prisoners, or patients). It referred to those living in a given residence.

61. Letter 169, March 24, 1840, in *CCMcA*, 260.

62. CAM, in *CMcATM*, 210–11.

Kingstown now re-opened, the bazaar over, the first four of the Birmingham women settled in the care of Cecilia Marmion, the newly appointed mistress of novices, Catherine turned her mind and remaining time to quickly packing for Galway. Father Peter Daly had wanted them to arrive by Low Sunday (April 26), an impossible date given her other obligations.

On the eve of departure, Catherine was tired and out of sorts. As she eventually confessed to Frances Warde, whose brother John had just died in England:

I was so hurried and so cross preparing for this foundation, that I was obliged to put off writing to you. Five English sisters entering—the bazaar—my poor little sister Mary [Liston] carried down from her bed, to be removed to Booterstown—Sister M. Teresa [Amelia or Catherine White?] very ill—so much in every direction to press upon my mind, that I became quite weary. Sister M. Josephine [Warde] sent me some turkey eggs, with a note, saying: "I send you some of your favorite eggs." I do not remember ever speaking about them; but of course I did. . . . If possible, I would have written to your poor brother's widow, but in real truth, I was not able.[63]

Probably the last thing Catherine needed that final weekend in Dublin was turkey eggs—except as an expression of love, well meant by the temporary superior in Cork.

By Tuesday, May 5, Catherine and the founding sisters, with all their baggage, had departed for Galway, well over one hundred thirty miles away in the west of Ireland. They would travel by canal boat, post-chaise, and "car" (a two-wheeled, horse-drawn wagon for transporting luggage).

Catherine was sixty-one years old. She was tired, but, as she told Elizabeth Moore, she still hoped to return to Dublin by way of Limerick—even though this would add more than a hundred miles to her trip:

Ah, if my weary head was beside my darling little Poet—under the sweet inviting willow. When I think rest is coming—business only seems to commence. The prospect of my visit to Limerick will animate me. I need scarcely tell you that it will be a source of great happiness—for which I thank God—a pure heartfelt friendship which renews the powers of mind and Body.[64]

63. Carroll, *Life*, 369. No autograph of this letter has been found. It is not in the editions of McAuley's correspondence by Neumann, Bolster, or Sullivan.
64. Letter 169, March 24, 1840, in *CCMcA*, 260–61.

CHAPTER 19

"100 Miles to Meet This Cross" *1840*

In Galway, Catherine and her companions had to cope with carpenters still pounding nails, a controlling presence in the person of Father Peter Daly, an unexpected death, and "endless" alarming letters from Mary de Pazzi Delany at Baggot Street. But first there was the arduous journey to the west, which Catherine humorously described in verse.

They had traveled on May 4 or 5 by canal boat to Tullamore where they were joined by Redmond O'Hanlon, who planned to accompany them to Galway in part because he was concerned about Catherine's health. Besides Catherine the travelers included Mary Teresa White, who would be the temporary superior in Galway; Mary Catherine Leahy, just professed in February, who could be Teresa's successor in six months; and Mary de Sales White, Teresa's sister and Catherine's traveling companion for the return journey.

After one or two nights in Tullamore, where the Mercy community was recovering from three cases of typhus, the five set out by coach (or canal boat to Shannon harbor at Banagher and then on by coach) to a planned stop in Loughrea, east of Galway, where Father O'Hanlon had arranged a stay at the Carmelite women's monastery.[1] Catherine's long poem back to Baggot Street recounts this last phase of the journey, the visit to the Presentation convent in Galway, and finally their arrival at the convent on Lombard Street:

1. Their exact route to Loughrea is not indicated in any of the primary sources.

Stopped on Mount Carmel on our way
And passed a most delightful day
Sweet simple nuns.
Got lamb and salad for my dinner
Far too good for any sinner
At tea, hot buns. . . .

Next morning we had Mass in choir
To the very heart's desire
Our own dear Father.
Then we had breakfast nice and neat
Tea and coffee, eggs & meat
which we'd rather.[2]

The Carmelites in Loughrea went out of their way to give the Sisters of Mercy foods they probably never enjoyed themselves.

Catherine's gratitude gives way to humor after they depart from Loughrea with a young coach driver whose brogue she attempts to imitate:

At eight o'clock we started fair
One car and horse, one chaise and pair
The car went first.
Not long we traveled 'ere a wheel
Mounted by illtempered steel
Completely burst.

A youthful driver naught dismayed
A real Irish fearless blade
Said: "Sorra fear
The forge is just below the river
We'll get it minded, smart and cliver,
The place is near."

When to the expected forge he came
And no assistance could obtain
Aloud he said,
"Oh such a forge, no nails, no sledge
Pat Lurgan wouldn't take the pledge
He drank his bed."[3]

---

2. Letter 172 [c. May 12, 1840], in CCMcA, 264–65.
3. Ibid., 265–66. "Sorra fear" means roughly "don't worry"; "minded" is "mended"; "cliver" is "clever."

Without the imbibing Lurgan, the coach driver remained cheerful, whether or not his passengers did:

> "I'll mind the wheel now, I'll be bail
> I've got a stone and fine long nail
> Yees needn't fear.
> I'll give the horses male and water
> That mare, I'm sorry sure I brought her
> She's down lame near."
>
> The wheel well mended, horses fed
> First-rate for Galway now we sped
> All blithe and gay
> Dashing in true John Gilpin style
> The post boy calling every mile—
> "Clear the way."[4]

Jolted but still in one piece, like the fictional Gilpin on his runaway horse, they arrived at the Presentation convent in Galway.[5] Here Catherine met again, after a gap of thirteen years, her old friend from Coolock and Dublin days in the 1820s, Fanny Tighe, now Mary Lewis Tighe:

She is all affection, but changed from a fine young girl of twenty-six to a middle-aged woman of forty. It seemed so short a period since last I saw her that I looked eagerly for my dear Fanny, when to my surprise a new figure with a new face ran forward to meet me. Alas! how many loved faces have vanished from my poor sight in life and death.[6]

To Fanny, Catherine too must have looked different, much older and more careworn, now in the Mercy habit, not the good-looking dresses of Coolock days. Yet their friendship was unchanged:

> My dear old friend, sweet Sister Tighe
> By every tender means did try
> Her joy to prove.[7]

---

4. Ibid., 266. "I'll be bail" means "I'll take responsibility; I'll do it." "Male" is "meal."

5. See William Cowper's amusing poem "The Diverting History of John Gilpin; showing how he went farther than he intended, and came safe home again," in *Cowper Poetical Works*, edited by H. S. Milford (London: Oxford University Press, 1971), 346–51.

6. Carroll, *Leaves from the Annals*, vol. 1 (1881), 379. No autograph of this letter has been found. It is not in the editions of McAuley's letters by Neumann, Bolster, or Sullivan.

7. Letter 172 [c. May 12, 1840], in *CCMcA*, 266–67.

The next morning, May 8, the party went on to the convent prepared for them on Lombard Street, not far from a bridge over the Corrib. Writing to Carlow, Catherine described the situation:

We have a very large house, not yet in conventual order. Sisters are entering sooner than I expected. . . . I scarcely know what I am writing, with the noise of carpenters and painters. . . . I am now in the kitchen, the room I was in is being painted. I feel the turf smoke.[8]

Among those who soon entered the community were Anne O'Beirne, Margaret Curran, and Mary Bourke, a somewhat older woman of "good means, and great Galway consequence."[9] Also planning to enter were Ismena McDonnell, daughter of "an estated gentleman" in Westport, and Christina Joyce of the Joyces of Merview (Mervue), whose father "commonly drives four horses in his carriage."[10] Three of these came from families with considerable money, a circumstance which turned out to be necessary—not in Catherine's view, nor the bishop's, but in the rigid requirement of Peter Daly, the priest who with the concurrence of George J. P. Browne, bishop of Galway, had arranged for the Sisters of Mercy to come to Galway.

Though Catherine said at one point, "we all love him," Peter Daly was, in her opinion, "the greatest master we ever met," by which she rightly implied a controlling figure.[11] He insisted that a £500 or £600 dowry was "absolutely required" of entrants, and even opposed a request of Bishop Browne himself. Catherine was shocked: "The Bishop asked me would it be possible to take a person most anxious to come, with whom he would give two hundred pounds—it could not be done." Daly's inflexible attitude toward dowries went against all her instincts: "I am sure there would be fifteen in the Convent before six months, if two or three hundred pounds could be taken."[12] His requirement effectively eliminated, at least for a time, the possibility of any poor women entering.

8. Carroll, *Life,* 369. Again, no autograph of this letter has been found, and it is not in the published editions of McAuley's correspondence.

9. Ibid. Catherine McAuley refers in other letters to a fourth Galway postulant. In letter 172 [c. May 12, 1840], in *CCMcA,* 267, she mentions a Bridget, whose surname is not known. At the Galway reception ceremony in October 1840, Catherine speaks of an unnamed lay sister, already a novice; this may be Bridget. Letter 193, October 12, 1840, in *CCMcA,* 300. Early Galway records are unclear about the names and dates of those who entered in 1840 and 1841.

10. Letter 173, June [6, 1840], in *CCMcA,* 268–69. A modern typescript of the Galway Register says Christina's father was Pierre Joyce, but in this letter Catherine says he was "Walter Joyce of Merview." The Joyces were landed gentry in Galway.

11. Letter 176, June 30, 1840, in *CCMcA,* 274; letter 177, July 1, 1840, in *CCMcA,* 276.

12. Letter 173, June [6, 1840], in *CCMcA,* 268–69.

Daly seemed to have his reasons. The women he had earlier recruited, provided training for in Paris, and called "Sisters of Charity," had not flourished in the house on Lombard Street where he was now putting the Sisters of Mercy. But he also had a personal desire for money and power, ecclesiastical and civil, as well as for dominance. A town commissioner, he "practically ran the town—chairman of the corporation, of the gas company, of the Mechanics' Institute, [and] owner of the Corrib Steam Company," a line of ships sailing from Galway to North America.[13]

Daly's role in the politics of Galway and his relation to the Mercy community there were considerable.[14] However, three matters need to be addressed here: his eventually getting himself appointed "Superior and Father-for-life" of the Sisters of Mercy in Galway, his alleged misuse of their funds, and the last years of his career as a priest.

Some time before Dr. Browne was reassigned to the diocese of Elphin in 1844, Peter Daly persuaded the bishop to appoint him permanent overseer of the Mercy community. This was an extraordinary arrangement, contrary not only to the Mercy Rule and Constitutions, which clearly recognized the current bishop of the diocese as the ecclesiastical superior of the community, but also contrary to the rightful authority of whatever diocesan bishop was in office.[15] While a bishop could appoint a priest to serve as his deputy in relation to a Mercy community, that appointment was understood to be temporary, limited in its range of jurisdiction, and subject always to the wishes of the current bishop and his successors. (Redmond O'Hanlon's role in Dublin, under Daniel Murray, and Peter Butler's in Bermondsey, under Thomas Griffiths, were appointments of this

13. Corish, *Irish Catholic Experience*, 216.

14. Peter Daly's political and religious zeal and his eagerness for ministry to the poor were well known, but these attributes were complicated by hostility toward the men's religious orders in Galway, disputes with bishops and the diocesan clergy, and contentious efforts to control money. At various points he enjoyed a good reputation in England and Rome for his opinions and fundraising abilities, and had the support of Bishop Browne.

When the diocesan see became vacant in 1844, he aspired to the role of bishop of Galway. With only one vote, he was second in the recommendations of the clergy. In their own recommendation to Rome, the bishops of the province said of Daly: "Though he may be inspired by a certain zeal, he is of rough disposition, and is so impatient of authority and labours under such a desire for dominance that he has rendered almost all priests hostile to him. . . . Under the governance of such a bishop, the former discords, now quiescent, would break out again and peace and order would be overthrown." James Mitchell quotes the bishops in his detailed essay, "Father Peter Daly (c. 1788-1868)," *Journal of the Galway Archaeological and Historical Society* 39 (1983-1984): 46. Similarly, in 1855, Archbishop Cullen sent word to Rome that Peter Daly, were he to become bishop of Galway, "would be a real calamity, because he is presumptuous and violent." Emmet Larkin, *The Making of the Roman Catholic Church in Ireland, 1850-1860* (Chapel Hill: University of North Carolina Press, 1980), 326.

15. Rule, part 2, 1.1, in *CMcATM*, 317.

sort.) Daly's seeking and acquiring such authority in his own name, and "for life," was unprecedented among Sisters of Mercy. His motive was apparently not unrelated to his wish to control not only the money but the activity of the Galway Mercy sisters. Having had generally positive experiences with bishops and priests in other dioceses, and being only superficially acquainted with Peter Daly, Catherine McAuley was perhaps too trusting in agreeing to come to Galway at his behest, though she did not live to see the full effect of it. However, she had not come for his sake, but for the poor he described.

Eighteen years after the arrival of the Sisters of Mercy in Galway, Dr. John MacEvilly, then bishop of Galway, and not as fearful of Peter Daly as his predecessors occasionally were, submitted a grievance to Rome. He cited Daly's having treated the Sisters of Mercy "most barbarously"—for example, by using "their money to purchase an estate at Salthill," apparently for himself, and refusing "to admit this"; and by using their resources to build a parish chapel adjacent to the convent near the Salmon Weir Bridge to which he had moved them in 1842. Not only was St. Vincent's chapel "too large and, consequently, very cold in winter, but [Daly] now claimed that he had been authorized to declare it a public chapel, by a papal rescript—which, however, he declined to submit to the bishop."[16]

This is not the place to adjudicate these complaints against Peter Daly, except to note historian James Mitchell's summary with respect to the Mercy funds:

With regard to the alleged misuse of funds belonging to the Sisters of Mercy, a lawsuit had in fact been initiated on their behalf in February of that year, 1858, but was not proceeded with. A letter of the bishop in the following year refers to "mistakes on the part of their attorney" and states the matter had proved "too complicated to unravel."[17]

Old but undated annals in the Mercy archives in Galway indicate that, when Teresa White left Galway in 1855 to found a Mercy community in Clifden,

her successor in office was Mother Gertrude Corcoran. From the beginning the Very Revd. P. Daly, who was guardian and trustee of the Sisters, had charge of the pecuniary affairs of the Convent. Mother Gertrude who wished to get the business in her own hands asked for a "statement of account." Father Daly did not find it easy to

16. Mitchell, "Peter Daly," 70–71. Here Mitchell cites the letter of John MacEvilly to Tobias Kirby, rector of the Irish College, Rome, April 7, 1858. The documentation in the archives of the Sisters of Mercy, Galway, related to this matter is sparse.
17. Ibid., 72.

comply with this request so that for some time there existed what may be described as "strained relations.". . . Eventually the affairs of the Community were given into the hands of the Mother Superior which was of course as things should be.[18]

In January 1862, Peter Daly refused the bishop's entreaty that he withdraw from civic involvements, in which he had accused his political associates of lying and had used "language unbecoming a Clergyman or Gentleman." So Dr. MacEvilly reluctantly "suspended him from ecclesiastical office."[19] After further conflicts and despite insufficiently informed support for Daly on the part of John MacHale, archbishop of Tuam, Pope Pius IX on June 5, 1864, formally approved Dr. MacEvilly's act of suspension. Father Daly did not accept this judgment, and since, despite all, "his [civic] reputation still stood high," he was returned to the Town Commission "unopposed" in September.[20]

After further communication between Daly and Rome, MacEvilly and Rome, and MacEvilly and Daly, the suspension was lifted on December 24, 1864.[21] However, Daly's contention with Dr. MacEvilly continued even as his influence in the town gradually waned. On September 20, 1868, he became ill and asked to see Bishop MacEvilly. The *Galway Vindicator* reported that "the reconciliation between them was complete." The bishop himself is said to have written, "Poor man, I frequently saw him before he died." Peter Daly died on September 30, 1868, at his residence adjacent to St. Vincent's Convent of Mercy, apparently nursed at the end by the Sisters of Mercy.[22]

In May and June 1840, Catherine McAuley could not have guessed at the future career of Peter Daly, though she may have had an inkling. When the time came for her to leave Galway, she recalled that Daly had earlier said to her: "You shall not go—not a vehicle in Galway should carry you. I will not suffer the foundation to be injured," presumably by her departure. He assented, as we shall see, only when Redmond O'Hanlon wrote him an urgent letter from Dublin. Prior to that Catherine felt she "really could not leave . . . without his full concurrence, except I were to become angry or stiff."[23] The situation was, it would seem, a telling omen of the domineering behavior that would characterize Peter Daly's later life and relationships. But Catherine apparently did not fully grasp what it portended. That

18. Handwritten "Annals" (Archives, Sisters of Mercy, Western Province, Galway).
19. Mitchell, "Peter Daly," 85. 20. Ibid., 99, 101.
21. Ibid., 104. 22. Ibid., 113.
23. Letter 177, July 1, 1840, in CCMcA, 276–77.

twenty-eight years later Sisters of Mercy would nurse Peter Daly as he was dying would have seemed only right to her.

The women who joined the community immediately after Catherine arrived in May 1840 were ready by June to receive the habit. Their life and charitable work on Lombard Street under Peter Daly's direction apparently counted in Catherine's mind as their postulancy. She was particularly impressed by Anne O'Beirne, a "very, very nice person."[24] And she admired Mary Bourke, who "never thought of religious life till she heard of the Sisters of Mercy coming to Galway," and "embraced the inspiration the moment it came"; she had been "enjoying the gay world in all its fashion to the week of our arrival."[25] By June 6 or 7, Catherine could tell Frances Warde: "We have four postulants . . . to be received on Thursday next [June 11]." (This number included Margaret Curran, and perhaps a woman named Bridget.)[26] Moreover, Christina Joyce, the daughter of "the Richest man in the Co. Galway," whom Catherine regarded as "a second Mary Teresa McAuley in look and manner" was scheduled to come on June 18. Ismena McDonnell, who "plays the Harp & sings—we expect she will bring one," planned to arrive on July 1.[27]

On Pentecost Sunday, in her joy at these signs that the Galway foundation would take hold, Catherine could not resist writing another poem back to Baggot Street, this time to Marianne Beckett, one of the Birmingham postulants:

> Tho' so long I've delayed to reply to your note
> I never unmindful could be
> of the metre so varied—so sweet that you wrote
> and so kindly to gratify me.

Admitting that she had been writing poems since her "youth"—"'twas my pastime, my folly, my play / and so it is still in good truth"—Catherine told Marianne her secret wish for a nonsensical club in the novitiate on Baggot Street:

> I sometimes wish that we could form
> A little foolish party,

---

24. Letter 176, June 30, 1840, in *CCMcA*, 275.

25. Letter 175, June 10 [and 11], 1840, in *CCMcA*, 273.

26. Letter 173, June [6, 1840], in *CCMcA*, 268, and 268 n. 12. "Margaret" (Curran), "Bridget," and "Nanny," who is undoubtedly Anne O'Beirne, are included in Catherine's poem, letter 172 [c. May 12, 1840], in *CCMcA*, 267.

27. Letter 176, June 30, 1840, in *CCMcA*, 274–75.

who common sense would loudly scorn,
and aim at laughing heart'y.

She then warmed to the plot and, by code-abbreviations, implicated several other like-minded postulants and novices in her mischievous scheme:

Even now, I can select a few
would suit our purpose well
V[eronic]a—J[ulian]a-too
M[ary] A[nn]—and I[sabe]ll

A President we next should seek
of folly a Professor
Try Sister V[incen]t for a week
we'll soon get a successor.[28]

Had the conscientious Gavino Secchi Murro in Rome read these lines he might have had second thoughts about the Mercy Rule, or at least about its author now off in western Ireland writing nonsense poems—to postulants and novices no less. At Baggot Street, de Pazzi Delany must have simply rolled her eyes.

Catherine concluded her poem "with a prayer which I promise to say / from this till we meet—at least twice a day":

May the Spirit of fervor, of light, and of love
which descended from high in the form of a Dove
our dear Postulants visit at this Holy time
and prepare them to enter a life so Divine.
May the fruits of this Spirit each evil efface
and infuse in their hearts an abundance of grace.[29]

Then suddenly, that very Sunday night (June 7), the shadow of "a large portion of the cross" fell on the Galway community and on Catherine's happiness. Mary Bourke, who was slated to receive the habit on June 11, was anointed at eleven o'clock, her apparently minor illness now judged to be typhus. Starting a letter on June 10, Catherine said Mary "was a little heavy on Monday week [June 1]—like a slight cold—on Thursday was prevailed on with difficulty not to get up . . . and yesterday, Tuesday—the

---

28. Letter 174 [c. June 7, 1840], in *CCMcA*, 270–72. Those named by abbreviations are Veronica Cowley, Juliana Hardman, Isabella Corbett, Marianne Creedon, and Mary Vincent (Ellen) Whitty. Marianne Beckett's poem to Catherine McAuley has not been found.

29. Ibid., 272.

9th day [of her illness]—her death expected, sinking all day. . . . 4 physicians are attending. . . . it is quite a public matter." Then she laid down her pen, not finishing the letter until the next day: "a sudden bad change took place—I stopped writing. This morning at quarter past 3 o'clock she expired." Catherine was evidently stunned:

We are founding on the cross now indeed—only eight days since she was forced to stay in bed, not thinking herself seriously ill. . . . God has certainly accepted her offering, and she is—I have no doubt, gone before him—received & professed by Himself. . . .

I traveled 100 miles to meet this cross.[30]

Because of Mary's illness and funeral, and the consequent delay in sewing the needed religious habits, the ceremony set for June 11, the day of her death, was postponed to June 25. Mary de Chantal (Anne) O'Beirne was received, as was Margaret Curran, who subsequently left and whose name in religion is unrecorded, and probably Bridget, whose last name is unknown. Bishop Browne "said a few nice words and wore grand ornaments just arrived to him from France—which he said he would not wear until our ceremony." Father Daly, who ever since Mary's death had been "making it his study to comfort and oblige us," announced: "The root has struck."[31]

While in Galway, Catherine had letters from Charleville, Tullamore, and Bermondsey—each with its own kind of trouble. Angela Dunne had recovered from "severe fever," but now a novice had "caught it." Mary Ann Doyle had invited Theobald Mathew, the widely known advocate of temperance, to preach at an upcoming ceremony in Tullamore, a town whose charitable endeavors rested in no small measure on the wealth of its successful distillers. Bishop Cantwell had intervened, and Mary Ann now had to disinvite the man who was currently administering the pledge of total abstinence to thousands all over Ireland. From Bermondsey, Clare Moore wrote to say that Bishop Murphy of Cork intended to come for her in August, but the bishop of London wished her "to stay another year." Clare herself was unconcerned: "Let their Lordships settle it between them. I feel no anxiety."[32]

The most troubling of the letters came from Baggot Street, where de Pazzi Delany, Catherine's assistant, could not carry on in her absence. She sent "alarming" reports about Mary Aloysius Scott's illness after a hem-

30. Letter 175, June 10 [and 11], 1840, in CCMcA, 272–73.
31. Letter 176, June 30, 1840, in CCMcA, 274.
32. Ibid., 274–75.

orrhage in the lungs. Catherine requested that Aloysius be sent to Carlow "without delay," but de Pazzi replied: "Dr. [Dominic] Corrigan thinks Booterstown as good air for her [as] any other. She is gone there."[33] Mary de Pazzi herself also "had a most severe attack," presumably of epilepsy.[34]

Finally, Redmond O'Hanlon, now back in Dublin, took matters into his own hands. Knowing Peter Daly's obstinacy, he wrote directly to him. On July 1, Catherine broke the news to Elizabeth Moore:

Revd. Mr. Daly had a letter from Mr. O'Hanlon—which he would not shew me—but informed me I was to return immediately. Our places [in the coach] are engaged for Sunday. In Mr. O'Hanlon's letter he promises Mr. Daly that if I am not detained longer (for Mr. Daly would not suffer me to go)—I should return in a few weeks. You may be certain Galway will never see me again but from Limerick.[35]

Gone now was any hope of visiting Limerick on this trip west. A month later Catherine still recalled her disappointment:

I could not recollect any circumstance that inflicted such painful disappointment on me as not going to Limerick before my return, and I suppose it is for this very reason I was not permitted to go—because I desired it too ardently—and I rejoice now at my mortification, for it was a real one.

Aware that she would have to go to Galway again, for the reception of Christina and Ismena, an "*absolute* necessity," Catherine vowed: "If I am to travel—Limerick must be the road that will lead to Galway, and there I will remain until Father Daly comes for me."[36]

She and de Sales White left Galway by coach on July 5 at 4:15 P.M. They rode all night, arriving in Dublin at 7:00 the next morning. If Catherine looked for rest, there was none. Aloysius Scott's illness was not so dire as de Pazzi had indicated, but she was "exceedingly thin and pale," and Catherine hoped to get her to Carlow soon. Others were also ill. And then there was the laundry, now finally operational, though barely. Agatha Brennan was head laundress, "very diligent" and "getting on pretty well," so Catherine tried to be optimistic:

These things take time. The expense of coal is very great—sometimes a ton a week. You may suppose the work must be very great that would leave much surplus after this—soap, etc., etc.—but the fire will not cost more when the work is much encreased—as the hot closet must be prepared for a large or small quantity. We have not lost anything of consequence and only a few borders of fashionable night caps torn, etc., etc.[37]

33. Ibid., 273–74.
34. Letter 180, July 28, 1840, in CCMcA, 282.
35. Letter 177, July 1, 1840, in CCMcA, 276.
36. Letter 180, July 28, 1840, in CCMcA, 282.
37. Letter 182, July 30, 1840, in CCMcA, 285.

So now there were tons of coal to purchase.

On July 23, Margaret Polding, the sixth English postulant, arrived. Whatever exhaustion Catherine felt, the women from Birmingham enlivened her:

They renew my poor spirit greatly—fine creatures fit to adorn society, coming forward joyfully to consecrate themselves to the service of the poor for Christ's sake. This is some of the fire He cast on the earth—kindling.[38]

Notwithstanding her fatigue and her "real old man's cough night and morning—old woman is entirely exploded from the new fashionable vocabulary," this "kindling" for the sake of the poor was the hope underlying all her efforts. In July when Michael Fleming, the vicar apostolic of Newfoundland, visited Mary Francis (Marianne) Creedon, the postulant he had sent to Baggot Street, Catherine spoke of him as "my Bishop."[39] Apparently she thought she would accompany the founding sisters to St. John's, Newfoundland, on the long transatlantic journey which she anticipated would occur in May or June 1841.[40] She may even have thought of remaining there herself. But now there were entrances, receptions, and professions to schedule at Baggot Street.

The most pressing was the reception of Anne Gogarty, an Irishwoman, and the first group of Birmingham postulants: Juliana Hardman, Marianne Beckett, Anne Wood, Lucy Bond, and Eliza Edwards. In the minutes of the chapter of professed sisters held on July 10, all except Marianne are listed as having requested and been approved to receive the habit.[41] Undoubtedly this was an error in recording, for Catherine's letters throughout the summer continue to refer to the "five English and one Irish" who are on retreat and will soon receive the habit.[42]

Daniel Murray had promised to preside at the August ceremony, but had set no date, and was now traveling throughout the archdiocese administering Confirmation. Finally in late July, when priests in Birmingham became anxious to set the date for their travel to the ceremony—one of them Juliana's uncle, Dr. William Wareing, soon to be consecrated vicar apostolic of the newly created Eastern District in England—Catherine asked John Hamilton to contact the archbishop. Dr. Murray responded immediately, offering

38. Letter 180, July 28, 1840, in *CCMcA*, 282.
39. Letter 179, July 27, 1840, in *CCMcA*, 279, 281.
40. Letter 205, November 8, 1840, in *CCMcA*, 315. In the end the community in St. John's, Newfoundland, was founded in 1842.
41. "Baggot Street Chapter Book" (MCA).
42. Letter 186, August 5, 1840, in *CCMcA*, 291.

August 8 as "the earliest day I could promise," but if she preferred August 10, he would hold himself "in readiness."[43] She chose August 10, even though it came in the middle of the annual retreat. This fact and the fact that she still planned to get the ailing Aloysius Scott to Carlow as soon as possible upset de Pazzi Delany: "Poor Sister de Pazzi . . . is now (as you may well know) in great agitation at the retreat being interrupted and parting Sister M. Aloysius. May God preserve her from any return [of epilepsy]."[44]

A year later Catherine recalled that when she first wanted to send Aloysius to Carlow, "as near her native air" in Kilkenny, de Pazzi had "cried and grieved—begging she would be sent to Tullamore." Of this episode, Catherine commented to Teresa Purcell: "For what reason I know not, but she objects to a move anywhere else. . . . I believe she thinks there is more of our first fervor there than anywhere else. It will amuse you to hear that when she & I have a little fret—it is followed by a wish—'that she [de Pazzi herself] was in Tullamore.'"[45] Frets or no, Catherine had need of patience.

She herself guided the annual retreat that began on August 7, half expecting that Myles Gaffney "will give us some instructions, but you know he disappoints sometimes."[46] Early in August Frances Warde had sensed her weariness, and invited her to Carlow, at least for a visit. In a long, solicitous letter Andrew Fitzgerald also urged her to come for "our good air." At seventy-seven, he was not afraid to express his affection for his longtime friend:

I must beg of you to think sometimes that you carry the treasure of God in a fragile vessel, liable to break and chink, and requiring frequent repairs. To effect those, you cannot have leisure amidst the various intrusions of all immediately about you. Break from them, and come to the quiet and calm residence of your dear children here. A few days with us would renovate both body and mind, and send you home fresh for new toils and labors. Now, dearest Friend, may I in union with all here earnestly beg of you to have compassion on yourself and on so many interested in you to come down here as soon as possible. Remember, God has given you in charge [of] your health, which you employ in his service. Come to us, and we shall send you back loaded with that blessing. Remember, I hate that cough which annoys you, but here we have a cure for it. . . .

Though almost blind, I can scarcely give up scribbling to you, as long as the sheet permits. I will conclude with earnestly repeating to you, your obligation of coming down to our good air. . . .

43. Letter 183, August 1, 1840, in *CCMcA*, 287.
44. Letter 186, August 5, 1840, in *CCMcA*, 291.
45. Letter 251 [c. March 30, 1841], in *CCMcA*, 379.
46. Letter 186, August 5, 1840, in *CCMcA*, 290.

With all the affections of my heart, I remain, my dearest, your ever attached in Christ

Andrew Fitzgerald[47]

Catherine could not go to Carlow this time, but the great old Dominican's letter probably did her more good than all the balmy air in the south could have done.

The large reception ceremony on August 10 evidently took place without a hitch. The "Annals" in the next *Catholic Directory* reported it at some length:

At one o'clock, a most interesting ceremony took place in the chapel, attached to the convent of the House of Mercy . . . the clothing or reception of six Catholic young ladies. Five from England, and the sixth a native of Ireland. After they shall serve in this, the parent convent, their one year of noviceship, they are to proceed to Birmingham, there to form the foundation of another community, in a most extensive nunnery, built under the direction of the celebrated Mr. Pugin for which Mr. Hardman, father of one of the young ladies, bestowed the site, with £1000. This house is capable of accommodating 20 nuns and 40 orphans.[48]

As was typical of a narrow conception of church history, the *Catholic Directory* named all the leading clergy who attended, in addition to Archbishop Murray (John Moore from Birmingham, who preached, Walter Meyler, John Spratt, Myles Gaffney, John Miley, Andrew O'Connell, and the visiting Bishop Michael Fleming), but none of the women who received the habit or any Sister of Mercy who officiated.

By early September, Catherine had other things on her mind. She was still worried about Aloysius Scott, now in Carlow, and "Mother de Pazzi [was] very nervous." Two more postulants had entered: Caroline Borini, another woman for Birmingham, and Anna Maria McEvoy, who would eventually go to Birr. Word had also come from Galway setting the date for the ceremony there: "It is decreed that I am to be in Galway on the first of October for what Mr. Daly terms the grand reception" of Christina Joyce and Ismena McDonnell. However, Dr. Murray had scheduled the next profession ceremony at Baggot Street—of Mary Agnes O'Connor and Mary Frances Boylan—for September 24, "from which I dare not be absent."[49] Thus Catherine could not go to Limerick on the way to Galway, so she revised her fragile plan, telling Elizabeth Moore:

47. Letter 185, August 4, 1840, in *CCMcA*, 289–90.
48. "Annals," *Catholic Directory* (1841), 387–88.
49. Letter 191, September 7, 1840, in *CCMcA*, 296.

I will not venture even to hope that I shall return by Limerick, but my Dear Sr. M. E., do not speak of my going. . . . I have had a most pressing letter from Mr. Croke [in Charleville] to go see the Sisters in their new Convent. He will be quite offended if he hears I am in Limerick—and indeed I am not able to add forty miles to my long journey—by going & returning to Charleville. Could I not steal in and away—would Father Fitzgibbon [of Limerick] publish me?[50]

Ever since Richard Colgan returned to Dublin and Paul Cullen came for a holiday, word had been traveling around that the Congregation for the Propagation of the Faith in Rome had approved the Mercy Rule and Constitutions at its meeting in July and sent its recommendation on to Gregory XVI. But no official notice had come. Frances Warde may have suggested that Paul Cullen, a nephew of James Maher in Carlow, could move the matter along when he returned to Rome, for Catherine responded:

I am not surprised at what you say as to the confirmation of our Rule—though we have been led to expect it all the past month—but these matters seldom go on so rapidly at the Holy See. It is however certain that the process of examination has been gone through—and most strong promises made for the conclusion, so much that a Priest [Colgan?] coming to Ireland was asked could he wait a few weeks to carry it with him. Yet I suppose all possible interest and attention may be necessary to prevent its being delayed.[51]

If her letters are any indication, Catherine was not anxious about the confirmation. Word would come in time.

In late September, with de Sales White and Teresa Mary (Catherine) White, Catherine set out for Galway. The reception of Christina Joyce and Ismena McDonnell on October 1, surrounded by the wealth of the two families, was "splendid." Theobald Mathew preached:

Mr. Mathew arrived at the church in Mrs. Redington's carriage—and three more of her carriages, following close with different members of her family. . . . We came next—the two beautiful postulants and my poor self in Mr. Joyce's carriage. Sister Mary Teresa [White], M. Catherine [Leahy] and Teresa Mary [White] in Mr. McDonnell's carriage. Sister de Sales, Sr. M. de Chantal [O'Beirne] and a lay Sister [Bridget?] in the Bishop's carriage. Miss McD had a white satin dress from Dublin—so made up as to turn into a cope. We saw it all in pieces before we left. . . . Miss Joyce had white satin & lace dress over. Both wore white wreaths on their hair. . . . The families of both Sisters supplied a grand *déjeuner.*[52]

50. Ibid.
51. Letter 186, August 5, 1840, in *CCMcA*, 291.
52. Letter 193, October 12, 1840, in *CCMcA*, 300. Mrs. Redington was perhaps the wife of Sir Thomas N. Redington, the popular M.P. for Galway. She was possibly a supporter of Theobald Mathew and a friend or relative of the Joyces or McDonnells.

Though she had a good eye for fashionable attire, the satin dress capable of being dismantled was for Catherine a fitting symbol of the true import of the ceremony, the commitment the new novices had spoken: "The empire of the world, and all the grandeur of this earth, I have despised for love of our Lord Jesus Christ . . . towards whom my heart inclineth."[53]

In Galway Catherine was ill for a day or two: "my stomach & just as when I was here before . . . I find it is the spa-kind of water which affects me." But she was delighted at the House of Mercy: "They are going to commence a laundry. Two go to situations today & 2 more come in. . . . The inhabitants [of the town] say it is the best Institution that ever was in Galway."[54]

In addition to the House of Mercy, there was also a "magdalen" asylum in Galway which eventually came under the auspices of the Sisters of Mercy. In 1821–1824 or thereabouts, on the initiative of Peter Daly, a Mrs. Lynch and her daughter opened a house of refuge which evolved into a magdalen asylum or "penitentiary" (in the parlance of the time), an institution for the apparently voluntary admission of women who had recently separated from what was regarded as immoral sexual behavior. This was not the "House of Mercy" or the laundry to which Catherine McAuley refers in October 1840. However, the asylum started by Mrs. Lynch in the early 1820s and operated by Miss V. Lynch was also initially on or near Lombard Street. In 1845, when Miss Lynch retired to France, she left the "small Penitentiary," and a legacy to support it, in the care of the Sisters of Mercy, probably at Peter Daly's behest. The asylum was moved at least once—in 1870 to College Road, to a site on the part of the road currently called Forster Street. It was permanently closed in 1984.[55]

53. *Form of Ceremony* (1840), 15.

54. Letter 192 [c. October 5, 1840], in *CCMcA*, 298.

55. The history of this magdalen asylum has not been compiled. However, references to it occur in several present-day sources. See Mitchell, "Peter Daly," 28–30; Caitriona Clear, *Nuns in Nineteenth-Century Ireland* (Dublin: Gill and Macmillan, 1987), 105–6; Maria Luddy, *Women and Philanthropy in Nineteenth-Century Ireland* (Cambridge: Cambridge University Press, 1995), 22, 122–23; Luddy, *Prostitution and Irish Society, 1800–1940*, 79, 83, 93, 105–7, 113; and *Convent of Our Lady of Mercy, St. Vincent's, Galway, 1840–1940*, 16–17, 18, 22–23.

The *Guide for the Religious called Sisters of Mercy* (1866) cannot provide an apt description of how the magdalen asylum in Galway was operated. The *Guide* was written by Mary Francis Bridgeman, superior in Kinsale, and her *Abridgment* of it was endorsed by those Irish superiors who wished to and did attend a meeting of Mercy superiors in Limerick in 1864. However, Catherine Leahy, the superior in Galway at the time (1861–1867), did not attend the meeting, nor did Teresa White, by then the superior in Clifden. The regulations in the *Abridgment* were endorsed for magdalen asylums operated by Sisters of Mercy attending the meeting (of which there was then one, in Tralee).

In 1864 magdalen asylums were also operated by Sisters of Mercy at Glasthule in Kingstown (a branch of the Dublin community) and Belfast. However, the Dublin and Belfast superiors did not attend

After the October ceremony in Galway, Catherine did manage to "steal" into Limerick as she had long hoped and promised. There she found a Mercy community and its many works of mercy "now fully and regularly established." When she returned to Dublin she spoke "so romantically of Limerick" that the Birmingham novices pleaded to see it. The "Rational" and "Irrational powers" immediately began a vigorous debate in Catherine's head about whether the £18 expense to take them to Limerick would be justified. The Rational argued: "Would not so much money accomplish some [other] good & useful object?" and "could they not be told of it?" But the Irrational claimed: "What we are told by unquestionable authority inspires confidence—but what we see confirms it." Then the Rational countered: "Where would they lie down at night?" Undaunted the Irrational simply said, "Anywhere."[56] In the end the Rational apparently won the mental contest, for the Birmingham novices never visited Limerick.

While Catherine was in Limerick, from which she hoped to visit Carlow on her way back to Baggot Street, travel plans were, once again, suddenly altered:

Just as our journey to Galway drew near, I received a most interesting letter from the Bishop of London—asking for two professed Sisters, to forward some views—which he does not fully explain, but asks the favor so much in the name of God that it would be impossible to refuse.[57]

Thinking there was no particular rush involved and planning to loan de Sales White, her companion on the trip to Galway, as one of the two for Bermondsey, Catherine had gone on to Galway and then Limerick. But "a letter was sent after us to Limerick—pressing a speedy return, lest the weather would change, which Mr. Butler dreaded so much." The sickly Peter Butler had already come to Dublin to accompany the two to London. He was waiting patiently at the Shelbourne Hotel "in great terror lest the Irish air would disagree with him. Poor man, he is in a very precarious state."[58]

So leaving the ailing Teresa Mary in Limerick to renew her health, Catherine and de Sales took the next coach straight back to Dublin, dashing—if it can be called that—across the one hundred thirty miles at about six miles an hour, stopping along the way only to change coaches or hors-

---

the meeting in Limerick. The *Baggot Street Book of Customs* (1869) contained no chapter on magdalen asylums, only this sentence in its chapter on the House of Mercy: "Penitentiaries are never attached to Convents or Branch Houses, where a House of Mercy is established," 97.

56. Letter 195, October 18, 1840, in *CCMcA*, 301–2.

57. Letter 193, October 12 [and 13], 1840, in *CCMcA*, 299.

58. Ibid., 299–300.

es. Then on October 12, with only a day or two intervening, she went with de Sales, Mary Xavier O'Connell, and Peter Butler to Kingstown, where the three boarded the night boat for England. Catherine still did not know why de Sales and Mary Xavier were needed for a year in Bermondsey. She suspected the community was thinking of founding another house "more central in London," but, as we shall see, the need was more serious.[59] Clare Moore had already been asked to stay on as temporary superior until the following Easter. Dr. Murphy of Cork, "tho' determined to bring her back," had been "prevailed on."[60] It would be almost a year before Catherine understood, though never completely, the emerging issues in Bermondsey.

On October 13, the founder of the Sisters of Mercy could say: "I feel quite deserted this morning—dear Sister de Sales has been my mother for some time, plaiting my coifs, etc., etc. May God bless them and receive the offering to His greater glory." But she could also confess, to Frances Warde at least:

Thank God I am at rest again and now I think the name of another foundation would make me sick—but they say I would get up again. Indeed the thought of it at present would greatly distress me. On this late occasion I traveled one hundred miles a day, which is very fatiguing except on Railways.[61]

But there were Birr and Birmingham and Newfoundland, foundations already planned—and Carlow was founding a community in Wexford in December. The trickle was fast becoming a flood.

So, on October 14, Catherine "got up again." She settled at her writing desk, and sent a letter directly to Cardinal Giacomo Fransoni in Rome. In her most formal language she told him of "ecclesiastical authorities who are anxious to establish more Houses [of the Sisters of Mercy] in England and Ireland, which they think would be greatly facilitated by the full approbation of the Holy See, as all orders of the Clergy would then cooperate in promoting an order which they deem very conducive to the Interests of Religion." She noted that "when the petition was presented—in December, there were twelve Houses in full operation. Two have since been added," and "one hundred and forty-two Sisters are now devoted to God and His poor in this order." They "have been advised to solicit the valuable aid which your Eminence can afford, and which they most humbly and most respectfully beg for the greater glory of God."[62]

59. Ibid., 299.
60. Letter 191, September 7, 1840, in *CCMcA*, 296.
61. Letter 193, October 12 [and 13], 1840, in *CCMcA*, 300.
62. Letter 194, October 14, 1840, in *CCMcA*, 301. Catherine McAuley's counting of houses (14) in-

Whether Daniel Murray was among those who "advised" her to "solicit" the cardinal's aid in hastening final confirmation of the Rule is not known, but improbable. Perhaps Paul Cullen did, or the bishop of Galway or Limerick. Dr. Murray was currently at Rahan Lodge, the O'Brien family retreat near Tullamore, where he had gone to recuperate from his round of administering Confirmation to hundreds of children and adults in the archdiocese.[63] Catherine's letter to Cardinal Fransoni, written on thin blue-gray paper, got no personal response, which she would have saved had she received it, but Cardinal Paolo Polidori inserted it, with an Italian translation, in a dossier of letters about Ireland, perhaps to accompany her petition to the pope, before whom the recommendation evidently now lay.[64]

As Catherine had feared, de Pazzi Delany fell into a melancholy slump. With Aloysius Scott in Carlow, Clare Augustine Moore in Kingstown, and de Sales White now gone to London—three sisters whom she particularly prized—de Pazzi began again to spend her spare time sitting alone in the "bishop's parlour," sighing. At last Catherine, who thought "our divine Redeemer . . . was always pleasing to behold and never sad or troublesome,"[65] found a perfect remedy for her assistant:

Mother de P. and I have kept up a regular concert of sighing and moaning since the Sisters went—but this day I was resolved not to be outdone, or even equaled, so commenced groaning for every sigh she gave, and our sorrows have ended in laughing at each other.[66]

Catherine must have liked her clever "concert" for she repeated the story in a letter to de Sales: "Mother de Pazzi and I have kept up the most musical sighing or groaning. . . . I thought she was far surpassing me—and yesterday I determined not to be outdone and commenced such a moaning as brought all to an end."[67]

Cheerfulness was not a superficial posture for Catherine. It was intimately related to gratitude. In her understanding, a cheerful countenance and cheerful words were the consequence of realizing all the gifts one had received from God. She did not deny feelings of sorrow and suffering— the "sighs" of human experience—but located them in the larger reality of God's constant generosity:

---

cludes nine "in full operation" by December 1839, then Kingstown again in April, Galway in May, Wexford and Birr set for December 1840, and probably also Birmingham or Newfoundland to which commitments had been made. To the 142 sisters she noted, the seventeen who had died by October 1840 could be added.

63. Daniel Murray, Rahan Lodge, to John Hamilton, September 18–November 8, 1840. Hamilton Papers (1) (1840), nos. 107–16 (DDA).

64. S.R.C., Irlanda, vol. 27, f. 340 rv (APF).   65. *PS*, 15.

66. Letter 195, October 18, 1840, in *CCMcA*, 303.   67. Letter 196, October 18, 1840, in *CCMcA*, 304.

As the most acceptable return a benefactor can receive from those on whom he bestows favours is a countenance testifying the gratitude of the heart, how acceptable must it be to God when we make Him this return, shewing to all by our cheerful, happy countenance, the gratitude with which our hearts overflow towards Him for His many favours in this life and His great promises for the life to come.[68]

Actual heartaches and sufferings were all too real, and "crosses" certainly came and were often heavy. But they were not the whole picture or the end of the human story. Through her playfulness and teasing, Catherine tried to encourage this fundamental cheerfulness. Evidently for long stretches de Pazzi Delany needed such encouragement, so her beloved "Reverend Mother" would go on having "concerts" with her.

By the end of October, Catherine had more serious matters to address. In Dublin, Teresa Carton was "coughing very much," and Redmond O'Hanlon was ill, "confined to his room for some days."[69] In London, two novices and a postulant had "bad typhus fever," and there was "a bad case also in Tullamore." In Galway, Peter Daly was objecting to admitting "a very nice person to whom an uncle had left £300—because previous to that she was, for a few months only, at a respectable dress & millinery warehouse.... He said the Co. Galway people would find out anything, and that it would be a certain injury." Working in a respectable dress and millinery storeroom was injurious? In Carlow, Frances Warde had not yet found a Mercy convent with enough funds to accept Anna Maria Maher, with her small dowry and her too numerous Maher relations in the Carlow convent. And, most painful of all to Catherine, her nephew James was "in the last stage of decline in Kingstown. I am as much there as possible."[70]

James's consumption dragged on for many more months. He was cared for by a friend and eventually by the sisters living in Booterstown and his aunt. But the situation in Bermondsey grew immediately more grim: one novice, Ursula O'Connor, died of typhus on November 1, and a second, Scholastica Burroughs, on November 5. Anna Marie Ross recovered, and subsequently left the community. They had contracted the disease while visiting "a poor woman in great misery" whose seven children were all stricken with typhus.[71] When the London epidemic first struck, Catherine worried about the exposure of de Sales, Mary Xavier, and the others. All

68. *PS*, 14.

69. Letter 196, October 18, 1840, in *CCMcA*, 304.

70. Letter 197, October 26, 1840, in *CCMcA*, 305. Mary Teresa (Anna Maria) Maher eventually entered the Kinsale community, and in 1858 founded the Mercy community in Cincinnati, Ohio.

71. "Bermondsey Annals (1840)," vol. 1, 18 (AIMGB).

she could do from so great a distance was pray—and counsel them: "Use all prudent precaution. To act otherwise would bespeak confidence in our prepared state which we have but weak foundation for. Duty only should bring us in the way of contagion."[72] She was also troubled by Clare Moore's evident exhaustion. After the second burial, she had written: "My heart is gone."[73]

Yet in the midst of all this worry, one newspaper clipping lightened Catherine's heart. Daniel O'Connell had made a speech in Carrick-on-Suir in which he had all too dramatically praised the devotion of the Sisters of Mercy to the sick poor dying in hovels:

Look at the Sisters of Mercy, wrapped in coarse black cloaks . . . gliding along, persons apparently poor—while a slight glance at the foot shews the educated Lady. They are hastening to the lone couch of some sick fellow creature fast sinking into the grave with none to console, none to soothe. They come with consolation and hope.

Catherine found O'Connell's tribute entertaining: "As a test of my humility, I have it in my desk—to look at occasionally. . . . The Foot has afforded great amusement at recreation, each claiming for her own foot the compliment paid to all."[74]

Late November and December unfolded with other human needs: three new postulants to welcome; a reception ceremony for the last two Birmingham postulants, Mary Magdalen (Margaret) Polding and Mary Angela (Caroline) Borini; and the profession of Mary Rose Lynch. Offsetting these joys was Catherine's grief for the two unemployed women she could not receive into the House of Mercy, now already "crowded to excess": "Their dejected faces have been before me ever since. I was afraid of hurting their feelings by offering them food & had no money." With upper-class summer residents now "leaving Dublin, dismissing servants and few engaging any, we have every day most sorrowful applications from . . . confectioners & dress makers, who at this season cannot get employment and are quite unprotected."[75]

Then there was the hard fact she had to face in Kingstown: the obvious failure of its tuition-paying school, which she had hoped would help finance the community and poor school there. Finally, on December 22, she wrote a long letter to Archbishop Murray:

72. Letter 200, October 31, 1840, in *CCMcA*, 308.
73. Letter 205, November 8, 1840, in *CCMcA*, 315.
74. Letter 210, November 13, 1840, in *CCMcA*, 321. This letter quotes O'Connell's speech.
75. Letter 211 [c. November 18, 1840], in *CCMcA*, 322.

I am exceedingly sorry to inform your Grace that our little plan of a pension school in Kingstown has not yet succeeded. At anytime during the summer we had not more than six—now only three. Before we were proceeded against for building the poor school—my Lord—the extra expenses incurred by every distinct establishment were defrayed by a Miss McGuinness [Magenis] from Newry—who not being found eligible for a Sister remained as a Benefactress, but was so great an oddity we were obliged to part.

We would not have returned to Kingstown—my Lord—had not Mr. Hamilton expressed very strong desire on the part of your Grace, that we should do so—saying that a portion of some means left at your disposal was allotted to this purpose. I have made every exertion in my power, my Lord, to keep it up for eight months, but cannot go on without some assistance. It would not add more than fifty pounds a year to have the Sisters with us here. It will be more than one hundred to keep them there. If we had even what would sustain it during the winter months, we might make another trial of the school—in spring.[76]

Looming on the immediate horizon was also the journey to Birr in the southern midlands of Ireland, a schism-damaged town where Catherine had promised Theobald Mathew she would found a Mercy community, even though there would be no endowment to support them. She had set December 26 for their departure.

A striking irony characterized Catherine's 1840, the last full year of her life. As her health diminished, her responsibilities, outreach efforts, and numerous obligations increased. As she aged, she became more and more youthful in her desire to respond to human needs. As her cough and stomach ailment became more troublesome, the calls on her mercifulness expanded. As her fingers grew more stiff, there were more letters to write. As her financial resources became more and more reduced, she made new plans to give away more. It was all the mysterious paradox of being "centered in God—for whom alone we go forward—or stay back."[77] It was the humanly inexplicable generosity of "bestowing ourselves most freely and relying with unhesitating confidence on the Providence of God."[78]

76. Letter 223, December 22, 1840, in CCMcA, 335–36.
77. Letter 220 [December 20, 1840], in CCMcA, 332.
78. Letter 282, July 24, 1841, in CCMcA, 418.

CHAPTER 20

"The Business of Our Lives" *Early 1841*

"What a time it would be to desert my post."[1] Catherine was speaking of circumstances at Baggot Street in July 1841 that prevented her visiting Carlow. But her post also had a larger meaning. It pointed to her evolving sense, from 1822 until her death, of her call, her personal vocation in life. Over the years, many interior and exterior promptings seem to have led her to discover and then steadfastly pursue a course of life that was worth all she had and was. There was no "voice" in any literal sense, just a slowly deepening awareness.

Her calling in life, wholly dependent on the gifts of God, was, she evidently felt, to be as faithful as she could to the two greatest commandments: to love God with all her heart, all her soul, and all her mind, and to love her neighbor as herself (Mt 22:37–39) and as Christ does (Jn 15:12). She seems to have heard this twofold call as a profound and mysterious unity. The desire to love God and the desire to love her neighbor were, in her view, "so linked together . . . that they reciprocally help each other." This call became for her the "end and object" of her own life first, and then of the Sisters of Mercy.[2] The effort, the prayer, the work, the self-bestowal, the travels, the crosses, the suffering, even at times the weariness involved in such loving, became, as she said, "the business" of her life:

God never calls any person to any state or for any end without giving the means and necessary helps to carry them through all the difficulties of it. . . . We ought

---

1. Letter 278 [July 15, 1841], in *CCMcA*, 413.
2. Letter 324, "Spirit of the Institute," in *CCMcA*, 458–59.

then have great confidence in God in the discharge of all these offices of mercy, spiritual and corporal—which constitute the business of our lives—and assure ourselves that God will particularly concur with us to render them efficacious as by His infinite mercy we daily experience.[3]

Her confidence in God had nothing to do with thinking that she ever fully embodied such loving. She believed that she was unfinished, that she was only a pilgrim on the way, that she could merely make "a resolve for tomorrow," that she was "far, very far, from cooperating generously with God in [her] regard," but still she persevered in her desire.[4]

So in 1841, Catherine went on walking to the sick and suffering poor. Walking, yes, on her own human feet, but moved and carried forward by her desire to love—even when she felt "the frost most acutely in my right side from my hip to my ankle. I have put on a great flannel bandage with camphorated spirit—and trust in God it will, like a dear good old acquaintance, carry me safe back."[5]

The term "walking nuns" was not a compliment, but a complaint when it was first used in Ireland in the late eighteenth century. Nano Nagle and her early Presentation Sisters often experienced this criticism. They were not regarded as "real nuns" because they chose to walk the streets of Cork to aid the sick and dying, poor families, and poor children in need of education. But Nano felt Ireland desperately needed "walking nuns," not just members of enclosed religious orders, as most orders were in the Ireland of her day. She was encouraged to bear this criticism by a priest who reminded her that Jesus was also sent to the poor, and he too was a walking minister. When she died, the Presentation Sisters were still "walking nuns," but in the early 1800s they chose, for reasons related to being "real nuns," to adopt strict enclosure. Mary Aikenhead's Sisters of Charity, founded in 1815, were also "walking nuns," who worked publicly and visited the poor and sick in their homes and hospitals. Catherine McAuley strongly agreed with Nano Nagle's vision about how poor Irish people needed to be served, beyond schools conducted within strictly cloistered convents. So when she founded the Sisters of Mercy, they too were "walking nuns." They too were criticized for not being "real nuns."

However, the vast majority of Irish laity and clergy slowly came to realize the benefit of women religious who could and did walk the streets to those in need, and "walking nuns" gradually gained a positive meaning and

3. Ibid., 462.
4. Letter 241, February 28, 1841, in *CCMcA*, 365; letter 110, January 13, 1839, in *CCMcA*, 180.
5. Letter 236, February 5, 1841, in *CCMcA*, 359.

was expressed with gratitude. Toward the end of the nineteenth century, the Catholic Church began the long process of sorting out the needed distinctions between women who were members of enclosed, primarily contemplative religious orders (strictly speaking, "nuns") and those who were members of primarily apostolic religious congregations (strictly speaking, "sisters").[6] The Presentation Sisters were by then no longer a strictly enclosed congregation.

Catherine McAuley herself walked to city hovels, to hospitals, to thatched cabins, to any place where people were suffering. She walked in dirty slum alleys and through snow and mud. She walked to neglected people even when she had difficulty walking, her right side weak and her left wrist broken. And she was convinced that she and her sisters would "meet their Divine Redeemer in each poor habitation."[7]

So on Saturday, December 26, 1840, Catherine set out for Birr—a place where there would be plenty of walking—taking with her the now recovered Aloysius Scott to be superior, Mary Rose Lynch, Anna Maria McEvoy, a postulant, and Teresa (Catherine) White, her traveling companion. Birr was about ninety miles from Dublin, and they hoped to break the trip overnight in Tullamore if they could depart the next day for Birr. In mid-December, Catherine wrote to Mary Ann Doyle, asking her to "answer quickly—plainly & briefly." A telegram-style note of invitation and assurance came back from the dear woman she did not think could be so humorous:

"Céad Míle Fáilte"—good dry lodging, entertainment for man and beast—Coffee for teetotalers—Mass at 8 o'c, Breakfast 9½—visit the new Convent at 10—2 first rate chaises from head Inn—at the door at 12—refreshments with the P. P. of Eglish (Father Murtagh) half way—arrive in Birr—4 o'c P.M.—no fog till 5.

Catherine apparently laughed. If Aloysius had not read the letter herself "she would be certain it fell out of my poor head."[8]

After eight hours in the flyboat on the Grand Canal, they arrived in Tullamore at three in the afternoon.[9] How the community "contrived to get us five beds" in their small old convent Catherine could not imagine.[10] Earlier she had teasingly called the Tullamore community "creep-mouses" for not

---

6. Leo XIII, Apostolic Constitution, *Conditae a Christo,* December 8, 1900, in *Acta Sanctae Sedis,* 33 (1900), cited in Catherine C. Darcy, *The Institute of the Sisters of Mercy of the Americas* (Lanham, Md.: University Press of America, 1993), 22–23.

7. Rule 3.6, in *CMcATM,* 298.

8. Mary Ann Doyle is quoted in letter 222, December 20, 1840, in *CCMcA,* 334.

9. Canal Boat Schedule, *Dublin Directory* (1839), 184.

10. Letter 224 [early January 1841], in *CCMcA,* 338.

making any foundations themselves, and had promised: "I will give a bitter scolding, and 3 cheers for Carlow," now well into its second foundation.[11] Of course there was no "bitter scolding" in Tullamore, only good-natured bantering. Mary Ann Doyle "might have been too cautious" at first, preferring to err "on the safe side," but in due course Tullamore sent founding communities to Kells (1844) and Derry (1848).[12]

On Sunday, James O'Rafferty, the parish priest in Tullamore, accompanied the group to Eglish. John Spain, the pastor in Birr, met them, and after dinner with Catherine's old friend Walter Murtagh, they went on to Birr. Catherine found the convent prepared for them "a good old house—delightfully situated—fields or garden all around it. . . . It must be particularly healthy. Ten or twelve Sisters could be very well accommodated."[13] But now in the dead of winter, Birr was bitterly cold. "Here we are surrounded by Newfoundland ice—obliged to keep hot turf under the butter to enable us to cut it."[14]

The next day they did the practical things that needed doing: requested "our tables, entrance bell, teapot, chairs, etc.," and met a prospective postulant.[15] That night they commenced their year-end retreat of three days, having received from generous visitors "2 turkeys, a leg of mutton, bowl of butter—provision for retreat."[16] As she began the retreat, Catherine was obviously at peace:

How sweet, how blessed is our life, which affords much consolation and enjoyment when all that the world values is shut out from us. Everywhere I thought the sun was shining even too much. I do not think any one in the midst of all the Christmas festivities was so happy as we were.[17]

True, for Catherine there was the usual adjustment to yet another "strange habitation—how many beds have I rested in. When I awake in the morning, I ask myself where I am—and on the last two or three foundations, I could not recollect for some minutes."[18] Still, there was something about Birr that exhilarated her, leading her to exclaim often over the next month: "Hurra for foundations, makes the old young and the young merry," and "Nothing like Foundations for rousing us all."[19] Was it "the pure

11. Letter 219, December 17, 1840, in *CCMcA*, 331.
12. TA, in *CMcATM*, 73–74.
13. Letter 225 [January 2–3, 1841], in *CCMcA*, 339.
14. Letter 226, January 4, 1841, in *CCMcA*, 341.
15. Letter 224 [early January 1841], in *CCMcA*, 338.
16. Letter 225 [January 2–3, 1841], in *CCMcA*, 340.
17. Letter 224 [early January 1841], in *CCMcA*, 338.
18. Letter 225 [January 2–3, 1841], in *CCMcA*, 339.
19. Letter 226, January 4, 1841, and letter 227 [January 12, 1841], in *CCMcA*, 343-44.

sparkling spring water," or the renewed health and enthusiasm of Aloysius Scott as she entered into the Birr mission, or the demanding mission itself, in this conflict-ridden town?[20] Or all three?

The retreat ended New Year's morning. The four professed sisters— Catherine, Aloysius, Mary Rose, and Teresa—renewed their vows publicly during Mass in St. Brendan's parish church, using the Renewal of Vows Catherine had composed:

Omnipotent and Eternal God, I, Sister _____, do ratify this day in the presence of the Heavenly Court the vows which I made at my profession, and promise faithfully to observe Poverty, Chastity, and Obedience according to the rules and constitutions of this Institute of our Blessed Lady of Mercy, and under her Protection. I most earnestly supplicate thy Divine goodness through the merits of Jesus Christ to grant me grace to fulfill these obligations.[21]

Catherine had frequently told the early Sisters of Mercy: "When we first make our Vows, it is not surprising if we feel anxious, and pronounce them in a timid faltering voice, being as yet unacquainted with the full extent of His infinite goodness, to Whom we engage ourselves for ever—but when we renew them, it ought to be with that tone of joy and confidence which the experience of His unceasing mercies must inspire." As Clare Moore recalled, "this feeling was easily discerned" in Catherine's "manner of reading the Act of Renewal, and also in the joyful way she announced the usual *Te Deum* afterwards."[22]

Apparently Dr. John Spain heard no timidity or faltering that morning, for after Mass he told all those in the church: "My dear people, I have a new year's gift for you—I have a present to make you, such as is most gratifying to a Pastor's feelings. I present you the 'Sisters of Mercy.'"[23] Later, at breakfast, the postulant Anna Maria dramatically complained, "quite in a whining melancholy voice—'He might have kept us a little longer, he need not have given us away so soon.'" The antic of the young actress amused Catherine: "She did it so well that I really thought she was distressed. She is all life and spirits—nothing like foundations for bringing forth."[24]

But the mission of the Sisters of Mercy in coming to Birr was no blithesome affair, except in the joy they chose to bring to it when they began in earnest on Monday, January 4. To describe the history of repeated violence, the harsh and mutual accusations, and the confirmed animosities of the fif-

20. Letter 228, January 15, 1841, in *CCMcA*, 347. 21. Rule 14.2, in *CMcATM*, 308.
22. BA, in *CMcATM*, 118.
23. Letter 226, January 4, 1841, in *CCMcA*, 342–43.
24. Ibid.

teen-year-old religious "schism in Birr" requires the long chapter Ignatius Murphy devoted to it.[25] It was into this still boiling cauldron that Catherine was asked to come, with healing if possible, by Father Theobald Mathew, the celebrated crusader for temperance.

Mathew had preached a charity sermon in Birr in early 1840, but even before that he was well aware of the all too public conflicts among Catholics in Birr, caused by the behavior of two popular priest-cousins, Michael and William Crotty, and aggravated by a measure of clerical and episcopal mishandling. He urged John Spain to induce the Sisters of Mercy to come to Birr, hoping their visits to the sick and poor and their education of the children would somehow, if not cure, at least assuage the longstanding hostilities between the supporters of the Crottys and the supporters of a series of bishops and parish priests. Dr. Patrick Kennedy, the bishop of Killaloe, and John Spain were the present targets of Crottyite hostilities. The two Crottys and about fifteen hundred lay persons, just under a third of the Catholic population in Birr, were said to be in formal schism from the Church, for repeatedly and often violently refusing to submit to the pastoral decisions of their leaders.[26]

Catherine admired Theobald Mathew's temperance work. In October 1839 she wrote that his "fame has reached the most remote corner of this land—the walls of Dublin covered with placards proclaiming the good he has accomplished. . . . All wish he could extend his influence to every place."[27] She had met or heard from him certainly by June 6, 1840, when she was in Galway: "The Revd. Mr. Mathew made me promise that immediately after Galway was done—I would endeavour to make up a branch for Birr where the unfortunate Crottys have done so much injury to religion. He said they must be truly spiritual souls—confiding entirely in Divine Providence as there was no foundation fund. The Revd. Mr. Spain, P. P., proposed giving up his House and garden, he is so very anxious."[28] In June, or in early October when she was again in Galway and Mathew was there, Catherine herself had taken the pledge of total abstinence, no doubt to support the efforts of others, though she evidently did not want this fact talked about.

However in late October, when Mathew was in Carlow, he announced, with several priests present, that "Revd. Mother had taken the pledge and one of her daughters in Galway." Mary Aloysius Scott, then in Carlow, was

25. Ignatius Murphy, *The Diocese of Killaloe: 1800–1850* (Dublin: Four Courts Press, 1992), 100–133.
26. Ibid., 119.
27. Letter 131, October 18, 1839, in *CCMcA*, 208–9.
28. Letter 173, June [6, 1840], in *CCMcA*, 269.

mortified. Catherine simply commented: "What an affliction for those who still love their freedom far as it may be enjoyed. I did not know till now that Sr. M. A. was an anti Mathewite."[29] But by December she evidently felt free to discuss the pledge she had made and had allowed others in Dublin to make, if they wished:

Sister Teresa [Carton] is much better since she took the pledge. I suppose the wine that I thought so necessary was not good for her. Twenty-one Sisters now belong to the total temperance society. . . . Sr. M. Cecilia was first in the last Batch though she was determined not to be one. Mary Duffy, a most ardent aspirant—Ann Quin, who attends the door, would not take it—she thought it quite awful—and we did not urge her.[30]

What attracted Catherine to Theobald Mathew's efforts was not so much his administering the pledge of total abstinence to thousands of people all over Ireland—though she deplored the increased poverty and ruin to families that excessive resort to alcohol created—but his implicit illustration of what could be accomplished through the instrumentality of *one* person:

You can scarcely form an idea of the moral improvement throughout the country. We passed through populous towns on fair and market days without hearing one angry voice. . . . All so peaceable and happy. This proves to us what the special grace of God can produce—tho' bestowed but on one man—yet so as to go forth amongst millions, through the agency of his touch.[31]

Some Irish bishops were relatively cool in their support of Mathew's work, but others whom Catherine admired were not, including Michael Blake.

So now, in January 1841, Catherine and the handful of sisters in Birr set out, at Theobald Mathew's and John Spain's behest, hoping that through their visits to Crottyite families God might bestow greater peace and charity among them:

Sister Mary Rose & I walked one mile and a half yesterday in all the snow to visit an unfortunate family who were followers of Crotty. Our excuse for going uninvited was that they had a son, 26 years old, killed by a fall from a House since we came. . . . I did all I could to awaken the poor people to a sense of their state . . . schismatics for eight years. . . .

They had been deluded by the false charity of the unfortunate fallen priest—who used to distribute amongst them all that was collected at the church—tho' not his to bestow. . . .

29. Letter 200, October 31, 1840, in *CCMcA*, 308.
30. Letter 215, December 7, 1840, in *CCMcA*, 327.
31. Letter 209, November 13, 1840, in *CCMcA*, 319–20.

I asked them, would it not seem that Saint Paul feared we might mistake such conduct for charity—when he said, If you give your goods to feed the poor, etc., etc. I asked—did they not think our Blessed Saviour had tender charity for the poor—and yet when he dwelt amongst them in our mortal state, He did not take any money to give them.[32]

Catherine's letters from Birr over the next six weeks speak repeatedly of encounters on the streets and of long walks through mud and snow in the surrounding countryside. Their conversations with those who had been or were still followers of the Crottys were often tearful. William Crotty was now a declared and proselytizing Presbyterian, and his cousin Michael, having married, was now in England seeking affiliation with the Established Church, but hoping to return to Birr and reclaim his following. Catherine was saddened: "These unhappy people will not raise the hand" to make the sign of the cross, "or even suffer you to help them; and while they pour out dreadful curses on the miserable man that deluded them, they will not move one step to obtain reconciliation. It seems as if they could not. I never saw schismatics before."[33]

Despite her distress in these conversations, Catherine often found a way to see, or at least record afterwards, a certain light side to her travels:

I have a little secret to tell you—don't proclaim it. I have my morning cloak on for a petticoat—the end of the sleeves sewed up to make Pockets. All my wardrobe is washing. I came home yesterday—with at least half yard deep of mud—melted snow—and I have not a cold in my head. I was out 5 hours.[34]

Ten days later, she could still write: "My clothes are not dry yet—the morning cloak still as a substitute & the sleeves as pockets keep me in mind of John Gilpin's belt—with 2 jars meeting behind. No fire drying here—the turf ashes spoil every thing. Flannel never dries in frost."[35]

Obviously, sparing her clothes on these visits was not a priority. But there were other causes of amusement. Mary Rose and Teresa "had been visiting an old man who has deserted his religion. He is becoming quite penitent":

He said to Sr. M. Teresa, "Well, since the first day I saw you I never had you from my thoughts, you are the most heavenly young woman I ever met." In another

32. Letter 226, January 4, 1841, in CCMcA, 341–42.
33. Letter 227 [January 12, 1841], in CCMcA, 345.
34. Letter 226, January 4, 1841, in CCMcA, 343.
35. Letter 228, January 15, 1841, in CCMcA, 347. See Cowper, "The Diverting History of John Gilpin," in Milford, Cowper Poetical Works, 346–51, with the bottles of wine slung from Gilpin's belt and shattering as his snorting horse breaks into a gallop. This saga struck Catherine McAuley's sense of humor, and she refers to it twice in surviving letters.

place they were standing together, when an old sinner said, "Well, if God did not send his ministers to convert me, sure he sent his little ones." They could scarcely keep from laughing, when they looked at each other [neither was exactly "little"]. In another place—a woman who came from a neighbouring cabin to look at them said, "Such purty little jewels—as fair as an Egg." Sister M. Rose cannot avoid laughing, but says she holds her head down and keeps her handkerchief to her face.[36]

Whether it was the relative youth of some of them, their unfamiliar black habits, their flowing veils and cloaks, their apparent good looks and rosy complexions, or their kindness, the Sisters of Mercy were slowly welcomed in Birr. Catherine recalled one "sweet looking old country woman" who stopped her one morning, "putting 6 pennys into my hand. I said—'for the sick poor.' 'No, honey, for the Sisters, for yourselves.'"[37]

Catherine was coming to love Birr, its people, its many calls to mercifulness, its fresh air. In fact, echoing Cecilia Marmion's comment, she admitted: "Birr appears to be my Pet foundation."[38] Though she felt the frost acutely, and was often "so frozen, so petrified with cold, I can scarcely hold the pen," something about the poverty and need in Birr enlivened her.[39] The smallness of the Mercy community there, in contrast to Baggot Street, was also a surprising pleasure: "I am beginning to cherish the Primate's opinion, 'that too many women living together engenders troublesome humours of mind and Body.'" Aloysius Scott was "in excellent health ... up at 5 o'c—and out visiting in the snow, when she would have been in Bed in Baggot Street"; Teresa, "cheerful and active, always employed"; "Sr. Rose, as usual. Sister A[nna] M[aria], most zealous."[40]

But Catherine had one complaint: the size of the tea cups. Thanking Cecilia Marmion for sending an account of the long-awaited consecration of the new St. Andrew's church on Westland Row, she added:

It came when we were at breakfast and supplied the want of a real Baggot Street drink of tea—which I begin to long for. The cups were provided when we came—they are baby toys compared to ours. I am ashamed to ask for five [servings], and six would not supply the deficiency.[41]

Clearly, for a tea-lover, Birr was not perfect, even if it was her "pet foundation."

Anna Maria McEvoy received the habit on February 2, taking the name Mary Magdeline, and two other women entered: Mary Anne Heenan from

36. Letter 229, January 19, 1841, in *CCMcA*, 349. 37. Letter 228, January 15, 1841, in *CCMcA*, 347.
38. Letter 232, January 21, 1841, in *CCMcA*, 354. 39. Letter 235, February 3, 1841, in *CCMcA*, 358.
40. Letter 228, January 15, 1841, in *CCMcA*, 347, 346.
41. Letter 233 [c. January 30–31, 1841], in *CCMcA*, 355.

Borrisokane on January 22, and Susan Egan on February 2, in effect running away from home. She had come to the reception ceremony, and despite messages from her reluctant parents sent through her younger sister, she would not leave the convent. Catherine knew this was going to happen. Two days before, she had written to Cecilia in Dublin: "Pray that we may get through the runaway on Tuesday—I dread it—'My Mamma could give a scolding,' etc. etc."[42] In time, the "great battle" ended, the Egans relented, apologized for resisting not Susan's wish but the timing of it, and became strong supporters of the Birr community. But Catherine was cautious at first, telling Cecilia: "Don't say a word of Miss Egan—where it could be mentioned outside (I mean of any difficulty). Mr. Egan has a sister in Dublin who knows every Priest—and half the world." In Birr, he "keeps 7 clerks, some of them brothers to the curates."[43]

After instructing the postulants, she was anxious to get back to Dublin, where Cecilia Marmion was carrying the load, and had reported that at least one bishop had complained about Catherine's long absences. The bishops were in Dublin for the consecration of St. Andrew's church on January 29, and five had visited Baggot Street, including Dr. Nicholas Wiseman. Then coadjutor to Dr. Thomas Walsh in Birmingham, he was naturally solicitous, perhaps overprotective, of the Birmingham novices. During their time at Baggot Street, Catherine had gone to Galway twice, and now Birr. On February 3 she told Frances Warde:

I leave this on Monday [February 9] ... Sr. M. C. wrote to me pressingly. Some remarks have been made on my being absent twice during the short novitiate of the English Sisters. The English Bishops think superiors should be with their charge.[44]

They wanted "foundations" all right, but they did not want the "founder" to be away from home.

Leaving Birr was not as easy as she thought. When she mentioned her travel plans, Aloysius Scott became upset, and Catherine "found her crying."[45] So two days later she wrote to Cecilia: "Sr. Aloysius was greatly agitated, and although I have these feelings always to encounter, yet in her case I was afraid of excitement and gave up. We have spoken quietly and rationally on the subject—and she is satisfied I should return Monday week [February 15]."[46] (Aloysius was prone to hemorrhage of her lungs, and died of consumption three years later.)

---

42. Letter 233 [c. January 30–31, 1841], in CCMcA, 356.
43. Letter 236, February 5, 1841, in CCMcA, 359.   44. Letter 234, February 3, 1841, in CCMcA, 357.
45. Ibid.   46. Letter 236, February 5, 1841, in CCMcA, 359.

Catherine knew she was loved, and that partings from her were difficult. It was of a piece with who she was and an inevitable aspect of "founding" new communities she might visit again only rarely. Though she tried
to strengthen the confidence and independence of those she left behind,
she understood that her departures were initially wrenching. She had felt
that herself, ever since Tullamore. It was the human price of extending the
works of mercy, and it took its emotional toll, on her and on others. As she
wrote from Birr to Teresa White in Galway:

I will not expect a letter from you till I return to our old dear habitation, where I
shall never again see all my dearly beloved Sisters—all strange faces. They all say
that the first separation from kindred, etc. was a joyful sorrow, but that the separations in religion are bitter sorrows. What must it be to me who never met one
unkind Sister yet.

This is a gloomy subject—will we all meet in Heaven—oh what joy—even to
think of it.[47]

Gone now from Baggot Street, to death or to the new foundations, were all
the earliest Sisters of Mercy except de Pazzi Delany and Magdalen Flynn—
most of the "first-born," women whom Catherine loved and on whom so
much depended: Elizabeth Harley, Mary Ann Doyle, Angela Dunne, Frances Warde, Clare Moore, Elizabeth Moore, and Teresa White. Elizabeth
Harley had died early on, and later Catherine's nieces and Gertrude Jones.
Catherine would never again see Teresa or Angela, and maybe not Frances.

In the end, she left Birr on February 10 or 11. The coach journey back
to Dublin was long, over ten hours, and she was alone, having left Teresa
Mary White to help out in Birr:

I could scarcely do justice . . . to the kindness of the 2 coach men. The first, from
the time we left Birr, at every stage was quite compassionate to me, offering to carry me into the Inns, to get to a fire, really uneasy about me. When changing, he
recommended me to the second, who was equally kind & neither sought any payment. . . . I never met anything of the sort before.

When we arrived in Dublin my "weak side" was stiff, and I was quite bent or
sunk [shrunk?] in size. A car was waiting for me, with a very small man as driver.
The good coach man said, "is this little man come for this little woman?" Yes. "Oh
then I'm glad—she's lost with cold and hunger."[48]

Clare Augustine Moore and de Pazzi Delany were waiting for her in a
jaunting car at the Hibernian Hotel on Dawson Street. "I was not able to
laugh then, but we all have laughed plenty since at my good hearted coach

47. Letter 235, February 3, 1841, in CCMcA, 358.
48. Letter 238, February 13, 1841, in CCMcA, 361.

man. I would really like to see them again." In the first coach James Carlile, a Presbyterian minister who had come to Birr to join William Crotty's
efforts and later abandoned him, was a passenger. Catherine had studied
his face: "If I can judge of a countenance, his spiritual influence will not
be extensive."[49] Evangelical Presbyterians apparently thought otherwise.
Carlile's tenure on the national education board, like Archbishop Murray's,
was an important appointment, and he was also a leader of the successful
Presbyterian outreach to poor Catholics in the midlands and the west and
south of Ireland.[50]

Spring in Dublin brought mild weather, daffodils, fuchsia, the season
of Lent, and an unforgettable St. Patrick's Day parade that Catherine apparently saw near Merrion Square, its beautiful horses and coachmen bril-
liantly decked out in blue, crimson, and gold. For her, spring also brought
the prospect of a foundation in Liverpool, resumed direction of the novices, a persistent cough, and the final decline of her nephew James, now
living near Booterstown. Though she claimed a few days after her return
from Birr that she was "as usual weary of foundation work," she immediately added, in the same sentence, "and ready for more."[51]

Ash Wednesday was February 24. Writing to de Sales White in Bermondsey, who was always only "skin & bone," Catherine repeated her understanding of true self-denial, the inconspicuous kind that is neither self-
willed nor noticeable.[52] "I hope you are exceedingly cautious as to the fast
of Lent—remember, obedience is above every sacrifice, and you will be far
more mortified in taking that which you do not like to take, than in ab-
staining from it. You have not sufficient strength for that." In addition to
dinner, "take a good collation in the morning, the usual allowance here—
and some light supper. Take in the day a crust—or something—if you have
a long walk. Sister M. Xavier will I know take care . . . I lay this obligation
on you."[53] Catherine put more stock in "small acts of mortification" such
as "trifling acts of humility, charity, patience, etc., of which the daily oc-
currences of life present occasions, and which from their very nature and
unobtrusive character are unlikely to attract human applause."[54] Most of

49. Ibid.
50. Carlile believed in employing lay evangelists who preached "the doctrines of salvation more to
the level of [the people's] capacities." Finlay Holmes, *The Presbyterian Church in Ireland* (Dublin: Columba Press, 2000), 87, 90–91, 98–99, 102.
51. Letter 239, February 16, 1841, in *CCMcA*, 363.
52. Letter 305, September 25, 1841, in *CCMcA*, 439.
53. Letter 241, February 28, 1841, in *CCMcA*, 365.
54. Lim, in *CMcATM*, 174.

all, she hoped that de Sales and she would "endeavour to make these days such as we should wish the past to have been . . . making this to us a truly penitential season, mortifying the pride of self opinion, performing all with an humble heart, keeping the first Lenten admonition engraved on our heart—'you are but dust, and unto dust will soon return.'"[55]

About Clare Augustine Moore's superb artwork, Catherine had to mind her own advice, and often failed. She could not, whether owing to her temperament or artistic ignorance, get it into her head that professional-grade calligraphy and illustration took time. Her comments on Clare Augustine's painting would be humorous if they were not so ill-informed:

She teased and perplexed me so much about the difficulty of copying the two pages, that I was really obliged to give up. . . . She said it would take the entire Lent— indeed you can have no idea how little she does in a week—as to a day's work, it is laughable to look at. She will show me 3 leaves, saying, I finished these today—3 rose or lily leaves.[56]

Clare Augustine had other daily tasks and could paint her "rose or lily leaves" only in odd moments and at evening recreation. Yet in Catherine's view they took too long! However, once, having spoken "rather sharply" to Clare Augustine, Catherine "knelt down" and apologized to her before all who had been present.[57]

At the same time that she complained about the pace of Clare Augustine's artwork, Catherine was a bit testy about other things as well, for instance, an overly timid prospective postulant who "is not half alive and wishes to hide her little head. . . . She has been in a Carmelite convent six months and has indeed got the holy art of custody of eyes, for she seldom opens them." If the young woman were to enter, "I shall have a nice task opening the eyes of the little Carmelite. However, I will have all the talk, for she is as meek as a Dove," and she would "give me so much to do & undo in future."[58]

Conceivably Catherine was now, in March 1841, more ill than she realized, or at least would admit to others. Having sent Cecilia Marmion to

---

55. Letter 241, February 28, 1841, in *CCMcA*, 365.

56. Letter 243 [March 5, 1841], in *CCMcA*, 368. In a remarkable, but undated letter addressed to a "Sister M. Teresa," now among the Bolster Papers (MCA), Clare Augustine speaks about the painstaking process of calligraphy and illustration on parchment. She was no amateur. In 1854 she may have been asked by the Irish bishops to illuminate the memorial, in Gaelic, they wished to send Pius IX in honor of his proclamation of the Immaculate Conception of the Virgin Mary, though no primary evidence of this has so far been located.

57. BA, in *CMcATM*, 119.

58. Letter 243 [March 5, 1841], in *CCMcA*, 368.

Birr to recover *her* health, lest she succumb to the consumption that had stricken her blood sisters, Catherine had temporarily taken over Cecilia's duties of directing the postulants and novices. But she told Cecilia: "Father O'Hanlon came yesterday & he advised me [to] take off the cloak"—one she was wearing indoors for extra warmth—and "drive out to Booterstown today. I have done both, tho' half an hour before I would not have cut off 2 inches for a pattern, I felt so afraid of making a patient of myself again. I think I am much better, not coughing much."[59]

Catherine did not dwell on her cough, but her surviving letters over the next few months refer to it occasionally, nearly always in a nonchalant way. She told Aloysius Scott: "I have the old man's cough yet, tho' as cautious as possible—never go to the choir at 9 o'c [at night]."[60] To Cecilia: "My old cough is tormenting me, some stings in my chest."[61] And she was careful to say very little about her cough to Frances Warde, after her March account of doctoring herself:

I am sorry to find by your letter this morning that they are saying too much about my loss of health. My rather new visitant, a cough—has been with me very constantly since the first Sunday after my return [from Birr]. To please my kind tormentors, I took one large bottle of medicine and put on a small blister from which I (for want of faith perhaps) did not receive any benefit. I am now doctoring myself as I have Sister Teresa [Carton]—very warm flannel entire dress—mellow barley water, old fashioned sugar candy—a little Hippo at night—and I think—*Mr. Time* taken into account—I am doing very well. I do think that a cough has made a resting place with me—and will be no unusual visitor in future. I am now going to hide from the Doctor who is gone up to four influenza patients.[62]

She asked Mary Vincent Harnett to get her "the name of the wine Mr. O'B [Richard Baptist O'Brien?] gave me."[63] She told Aloysius: "Now for my old cough—very frequent since 9 o'c last night. I will use the Crotty oil again—and the Iceland Moss."[64]

59. Letter 244, March 11, 1841, in CCMcA, 369. Catherine's saying she would not have wanted to "cut off 2 inches for a pattern" apparently means that she was so cold that she would not have shortened her cloak for any reason, let alone take it off.

60. Letter 245 [c. March 19, 1841], in CCMcA, 372.

61. Letter 260 [April 1841], in CCMcA, 389.

62. Letter 243 [March 5, 1841], in CCMcA, 367–68. "Hippo" was evidently a honey-based expectorant, named after Hippocrates, who was thought to have praised honey's medicinal benefits. *Freeman's Journal,* December 10, 1832, advertized "Pectoral Lozenges, of Hippo and Squill." Farmar, *Patients, Potions & Physicians,* 75, names among expectorants used in the 1800s "the astringent Hippo (*Euphorbia corolla*)."

63. Letter 258 [April 12, 1841], in CCMcA, 387. Presumably the Reverend Richard Baptist O'Brien had offered her a particular wine to ease her coughing. Otherwise "Mr. O'B" remains unidentified. Drinking alcoholic beverages for medicinal purposes was not contrary to early versions of the pledge of abstinence: "I promise to abstain from all intoxicating drinks, except used medicinally, and by order of a medical man." Paul A. Townend, *Father Mathew, Temperance and Irish Identity* (Dublin: Irish Academic Press, 2002), 22.

64. Letter 267, May 25, 1841, in CCMcA, 399. I have not identified "Crotty oil" with any confidence,

Before widespread acceptance of germ theory and knowledge of specific bacteria, and hence of more precise medicines, physicians and patients alike had only folk remedies or apothecaries' compounds to use. Other potions, the products of quackery but widely advertised, gave only illusory help. The remedies to which Catherine resorted were apparently not without some positive effect, on her symptoms at least, if not on the causes. Self-dosing was common in this period, and often no more unpromising or harmful than the available remedies a physician or apothecary might recommend.[65]

Whatever her health, Catherine's most demanding and enjoyable work in March and April, while Cecilia Marmion was recuperating in the "good air" of Birr, was instructing the novices and postulants, helping them to grow in their understanding of what it would mean to be a Sister of Mercy. In the early spring of 1841 at least twenty such women were in Baggot Street, including the six now destined for Birmingham. Marianne Beckett, a Birmingham novice, had voluntarily left, having doubts about her earlier conversion to the Catholic Church, but she kept in touch with Catherine. (With the help of the Reverend George Spencer, her spiritual director in England, himself a well-known convert, Marianne returned to Baggot Street in 1842 and was sent to Birr, where she eventually became the superior from 1860 to 1894, and again from 1897 to 1900, dying there in 1905.)[66] Perhaps recalling her own religious struggles as a young woman, Catherine was understanding as Marianne found her way. In January she had written: "I feel very much for poor Miss B[eckett]—and wish I knew what to do," but by late spring she could tell Cecilia: "I know the note from Miss Beckett will be consoling to you. I wrote to express the great pleasure it gave me."[67]

Catherine obviously enjoyed being with the novices and postulants. She had a natural affinity for the young, but she also saw them as the leaders of future merciful endeavors wherever they were needed, as some of "the fire Christ cast on the earth—kindling."[68] In her letters to Cecilia and others, she liked to exaggerate how strict a mistress of novices she was trying to be, and to dramatize the good job she was doing among them. It was all part of her effort to divert attention from her health, and to assure

---

unless it was "croton oil," which "was formerly used as a drastic purgative and counter-irritant in human and veterinary medicine but is now considered too dangerous for medicinal use." *Encyclopaedia Britannica*, 15th ed., s.v. "croton oil." "Iceland Moss" is a lichen still advertised as a herbal medicine used to alleviate coughs and other chest ailments.

65. See Farmar, *Patients, Potions & Physicians*, 124–28.
66. Pius O'Brien, *The Sisters of Mercy in Birr and Nenagh* (Ennis: Sisters of Mercy, 1994), 137–38.
67. Letter 232, January 21, 1841, in *CCMcA*, 354; letter 260 [April 1841], in *CCMcA*, 389.
68. Letter 180, July 28, 1840, in *CCMcA*, 282.

her correspondents that nothing had changed, that they need not fear. As she told Cecilia, in her conversations with the novices she "got into many of the secrets of your holy office, and acquitted myself like anything but a new beginner." (She had, after all, directed all the novices and postulants from the beginning until at least 1835.) She promised Cecilia, "I will have all in great order for you."[69] She told Aloysius Scott, with some understatement as well as hyperbole: "I am doing Mother Cecilia's business—well as I can. I think some would wish her safe home when they come on private concerns—in future I will have the Poker in my hand."[70] Prodding and discipline, yes, but she could not fool the novices, who saw through her occasional rigor to the affection she had for them, and her faith in their future service. To Cecilia, she offered a reassuring report, again both exaggerating and underplaying her methods:

The Sisters of the Novaship are truly edifying, and admirably formed—so far as they are advanced. . . . It is my greatest happiness to be with them. Their tempers are regulated so that they seem always prepared for humiliating remarks—which you know I am not sparing of. It comforts me more than I can express to find them so initiated in the real spirit of their state—may God continue to bless them.

I am doing my share—regularly, thank God, novices and postulants in turn, the Rule every evening with scolding, coaxing, etc., etc.[71]

To prepare future Sisters of Mercy, women who would long survive her and would carry needed works of mercy she knew not where, and perhaps under very trying circumstances, was, understandably, Catherine's "greatest happiness" at this stage of her life. She could not foresee, or even imagine, Tonga, Peru, and Nigeria, New Orleans during a hurricane, the Philippine Islands during typhoons and militant rampages, England during World War II, or even Ireland during the coming Famine. If there were "scolding" and "humiliating remarks"—and presumably there were in some sense—they were not reminders of the frailties common to all human beings, but of the quiet but "mighty" work of "the great God" who "will finish in us the work He has begun," the work of God on which, in her view, every human work depended, and to which it, unaccountably, contributed.[72]

On April 24, Mary Vincent Whitty, a novice, was "in fever—slight, thank God—now up. Another has thrown up blood—three times in one day—she

69. Letter 244, March 11, 1841, in CCMcA, 369–70.
70. Letter 245 [c. March 19, 1841], in CCMcA, 372.
71. Letter 254 [April 6, 1841], in CCMcA, 382.
72. PS, 2–3.

is better. A third—one of the English—erysipelas in the head and face—good symptoms." Then, "in the midst of all this alarm," a note came from Genevieve Jarmy, now living in the convent in Booterstown: "Come as fast as possible. James is dying and wants to see you."[73]

In November 1840, Catherine's nephew James had been, as she then thought, "getting nearer to the grave each day."[74] In January he had "rallied a little." Genevieve was "his constant nurse" in his quarters on the Blackrock road, giving him, on Catherine's behalf, "all her affectionate care," and, if necessary, going again in the evening.[75] Catherine had visited him many times during the last six months. He was her sister's eldest son, and though he had not come to see her much before his illness—not for seventeen months at one stretch—they were close for the last year, ever since Robert's death. When she returned from Birr in February, he was "much changed."[76] Now, in April, the end was near, and she went immediately, though her cough was "very severe" and "the door & window [of the coach] were obliged to be open." His spell of "weakness passed away" temporarily, and Catherine feared "my poor child will have many such."[77]

Then, on April 29, 1841, his death came: "My poor dear James is in Eternity. He died like a saint. Though parched with thirst, he would not take a drop of water without making the sign of the cross. . . . He never was impatient for five minutes, tho' six months without being up one entire day. . . . Tell this to Doctor Fitzgerald . . . the religious impressions did not pass away."[78]

Only in this one surviving letter, to Frances Warde, who knew James as a young boy riding his pony on the Royal Hospital grounds, did Catherine speak of this last heartache, the death of the person she thought was her only remaining adopted son. James was twenty-five. He was buried in Glasnevin Cemetery, next to his brother. Thinking Willie was dead, Catherine believed her "earthly joys" were now "cut down."[79]

73. Letter 262 [April 24, 1841], in *CCMcA*, 391.
74. Letter 206, November 9, 1840, in *CCMcA*, 316.
75. Letter 227 [January 12, 1841], in *CCMcA*, 344.   76. Letter 238, February 13, 1841, in *CCMcA*, 362.
77. Letter 262 [April 24, 1841], in *CCMcA*, 391.   78. Letter 265, May 1, 1841, in *CCMcA*, 396.
79. Letter 206, November 9, 1840, in *CCMcA*, 317.

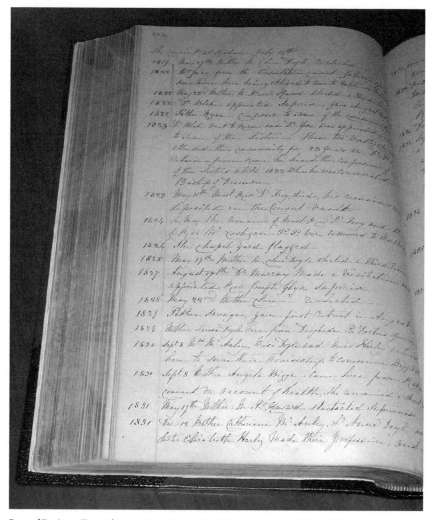

Page of Register (December 12, 1831), Presentation Sisters, George's Hill, Dublin

Wake of Catherine McAuley, November 1841

Grave of Catherine McAuley, Mercy International Centre, Baggot Street, Dublin

Tomb of Catherine McAuley, Mercy International Centre, Baggot Street, Dublin

CHAPTER 21

"Providential Guidance" *May–August 1841*

Riding home in the cramped coach from Tullamore on May 24, 1841, Catherine was relieved and happy. The whole journey to and from Birr had been successful. Father Theobald Mathew had finally agreed to preach at the Birr community's first public reception ceremony. He set the date, May 20, and Mary Anne Heenan and Susan Egan received the habit, taking the names Mary Joseph and Mary Vincent. The Egan family was fully involved and helpful. Even Bishop Patrick Kennedy, who Catherine felt was "no great patron of nuns," went through the ceremony "as if he performed it every week" and was "very kind and pleasing."[1]

Taking Mary Aloysius Cowley with her, Catherine had gone to Birr two weeks early, to help with preparations.[2] She had offered—partly as an excuse for going early—to conduct the retreat for the two prospective novices. Her artful inquiry was meant to co-opt Aloysius Scott:

I really think a few drinks of the waters of Birr—hot and cold—will cure me. Do you not think it absolutely necessary that I should conduct the retreat? Sister M. Cecilia is out of office—and you are not capable.[3]

Aloysius was surely "capable." But since she had wept at Catherine's departure from Birr in February, and had feared she was thinking of going

1. Letter 230, January 20, 1841, and letter 269, May 28, 1841, in *CCMcA*, 351 and 401.
2. Elinor Cowley had taken the name Mary Veronica at reception, but asked to change it to Mary Aloysius before her profession on May 4, 1841, and Catherine had agreed. Letter 232, January 21, 1841, in *CCMcA*, 354.
3. Letter 263, April 28, 1841, in *CCMcA*, 392.

permanently to Newfoundland, Aloysius could only be glad of any ruse to get Catherine back.

On May 23, the first leg of the homeward journey, from Birr to Tullamore—with Aloysius Cowley and Cecilia Marmion, now well enough to return to Baggot Street—was surprisingly easy. They "got excellent horses at Birr" and "a most attentive driver," reaching Tullamore in the early afternoon. But Catherine was saddened by the poverty of the lad who helped them:

The fine little boy who brought the great Trunk would not take any payment—"ah sure, ma'am, I'll be ped [paid] at home." It distressed me to hear him say—ped— he is such a fine creature. Offered him 6d [6 pence] for himself—"ah no, ma'am— haven't I a shillen—to get my supper and my bed and my breakfast."[4]

After a night in Tullamore, Cecilia balked at the idea of going on to Dublin by canal boat, expressing "so much alarm or dislike to the canal that we arranged to go on posting." At first all went well: "Got an excellent roomy chaise, drove 28 miles in 4 hours—had then only 19." Then trouble began. "At 12 o'c started, but met a cross driver, slow horses—and broken harness—kept us five hours & quarter on that short stage—a confined carriage." The young Aloysius Cowley, "who sat at our feet has not stood up quite well yet." But Catherine had had ten days of the "waters of Birr," and was refreshed. She still had her "old cough," especially frequent at night, but she promised to use the Crotty oil and Iceland Moss.[5]

Redmond O'Hanlon had accompanied them to Birr, even though he was then recovering from severe influenza.[6] Perhaps no priest in Catherine's life from 1829 onwards was so frequently present, yet so completely self-effacing, as this Carmelite friar, now in his early fifties. O'Hanlon figures, but always in the background, in many of Catherine's letters and in all the biographical manuscripts written about her by her contemporaries. That he was a help to her is, in view of the evidence, an understatement.

On June 4, 1829, at the dedication of the chapel at Baggot Street, Archbishop Murray had appointed Father O'Hanlon as confessor of the resident community. When these women became a religious congregation, O'Hanlon seems to have been given a second role. If one can judge by the way he functioned over the next ten years, indeed over the next twenty or more, and by the obvious absence of any other priest in this role, he must

---

have been named Archbishop Murray's personal deputy as ecclesiastical superior of the Dublin community.

In the Rule and Constitutions of the Sisters of Mercy which Catherine sent to Rome for approval in late 1839 or early 1840 and which incorporated the revisions Daniel Murray had requested, the first chapter of part 2 is entitled "The Superior and the Visitation of the Convent." The "superior" referred to here is not the "mother superior," but the ecclesiastical superior. Paragraph 1 of this long chapter (a chapter which replaced the single summary paragraph Catherine had originally proposed) states:

This religious congregation of the Sisters of Mercy shall be always subject to the authority and jurisdiction of the Diocesan Bishop . . . as their first Superior after the Holy See. If on account of his many avocations he should not have leisure to attend immediately to the direction of the Community, a Priest shall be appointed by him on whose prudence, piety and experience he can depend to govern and direct under him and to whom he will give the necessary faculties.[7]

Paragraph 2 says further:

The Priest thus appointed shall duly attend to the government and good order of the Community in spirituals and temporals; he shall watch over the exact observance of the Constitutions for the purpose of maintaining good order, peace and charity, and shall also assist the Mother Superior with his advice in all weighty matters. Nothing of moment shall be attempted by her without consulting him nor any matter of importance relating to the House or Community be undertaken without the consent of the Bishop.[8]

These paragraphs and the rest of this chapter of the Mercy Rule and Constitutions were, at Archbishop Murray's request, transcribed verbatim from the already confirmed Rule and Constitutions (1805) of the Presentation Sisters. In the 1830s, and for the rest of the nineteenth century, the jurisdiction of the diocesan bishop in relation to a Mercy community, or of the priest he appointed as his deputy, was the pattern that prevailed. However, the title "ecclesiastical superior," though technically correct, does not fittingly describe the unobtrusive manner in which Redmond O'Hanlon performed this duty.

He was, from all one can learn of him, a respectful, humble, good man. He did not substitute himself for Catherine McAuley. On the contrary, he seems to have acknowledged and affirmed her authority and vision. His conversations with her were unrecorded, or, if ever recorded, not surviv-

---

7. Rule, part 2, 1.1, in *CMcATM*, 317.
8. Rule, part 2, 1.2, in *CMcATM*, 317.

ing, except in the instances where she refers to him in her letters. Most of these concern her health, about which he became increasingly solicitous, especially in the last two years of her life. He "ordered" her to bed when she returned sick from Bermondsey in January 1840. He accompanied her and the others to Galway in 1840, to Birr in May 1841, and to Birmingham later in 1841, apparently only to assist her with the difficulties of travel. He visited the various new foundations when she was not free to do so, presumably just to encourage them as she would have. And it was he who from time to time advised her to see a physician. When she was ill, she often avoided him, knowing full well what his advice would be.

As becomes more apparent as 1841 unfolds, Catherine relied on Redmond O'Hanlon's help, and confided in him as her confessor, though knowledge of that aspect of their relationship is beyond any biographer's reach. Over the last decade of her life, whenever she speaks of him, it is with gratitude and affection: "Mr. O'Hanlon has been the most generous friend."[9] And in 1839: "There scarcely ever was so disinterested a friend."[10] When he has influenza in May 1841, she remarks: "I thought we were going to part [with] him, he looked so badly. Thank God he is recovering."[11]

It is not that Redmond O'Hanlon had nothing to do beyond assisting Catherine and the Mercy communities. Among his Discalced Carmelite colleagues at St. Teresa's church, he was also highly treasured. He was elected prior, vicar provincial, or provincial of that community regularly from 1820 to a few years before his death on February 7, 1864, serving in one or other of these roles in 1820–1823, 1826–1829, and 1832–1856.[12] His Carmelite responsibilities may have been, in 1835, the reason that he considered resigning from his post at Baggot Street. Writing to John Hamilton in November of that year, Daniel Murray says: "It appears that Revd. Mr. O'Hanlon is about to give up his charge of Confessor at Baggot Street. Doctor Meyler should take care that his Friend Mrs. McAuley should suffer no inconvenience from this occurrence."[13] If Dr. Murray's information was correct, and Redmond O'Hanlon was contemplating such a move, it

9. Letter 66, December 19, 1837, in CCMcA, 113.

10. Letter 124 [May–August 1839], in CCMcA, 199.

11. Letter 265, May 1, 1841, in CCMcA, 395.

12. "Discalced Carmelites in Ireland," typescript, Discalced Carmelite Archives, Clarendon Street, Dublin, 26, 27, 29, 30, 31, 32, 35; Phelim Monahan, O.C.D., archivist, interview by the author, Dublin, November 13, 1992. Redmond O'Hanlon and Francis L'Estrange purchased for £400 the life-size sculpture by John Hogan that is often called "The Dead Christ," but that he preferred to call "The Redeemer in Death." This masterpiece still lies under the main altar in St. Teresa's church. "Discalced Carmelites in Ireland," 28.

13. Daniel Murray to John Hamilton, November 24, 1835, Hamilton Papers, 35/1–2, no. 38 (DDA).

is fortunate that he changed his mind. Catherine's letters do not indicate she was aware of the possibility of losing him. If she was, she dealt with it privately.

Reviewing the early years of the Sisters of Mercy, one can easily conclude that it was beneficial for them, especially in an ecclesial sense and particularly for Catherine, that Redmond O'Hanlon was the priest who fulfilled the role of "superior" on the archbishop's behalf, and that Daniel Murray had the wisdom and foresight to appoint him and not someone else. Moreover, it was singularly propitious for the early development of the congregation that it was founded during the long episcopacy of Archbishop Murray (1823–1852) rather than that of his successor, Paul Cullen.[14] Its character and spirit might have evolved quite differently, and its founder might have suffered more. When Catherine wrote, in January 1839, that "there has been a most marked Providential Guidance . . . and it is here that we can most clearly see the designs of God," she could not have known the full aptness of her words.

Back at Baggot Street in late May 1841, Catherine turned her renewed energies to new events: welcoming the postulant Frances Gibson, who had arrived from Liverpool during her absence; receiving her "old beloved companion" Clare Moore briefly back to Baggot Street prior to her return to Cork;[15] negotiating a future foundation in Liverpool; entertaining Bishop John England of South Carolina; planning reception and profession ceremonies to be held in August; instructing the ten postulants and novices preparing for these ceremonies; and arranging her subsequent departure for the new foundation in Birmingham. Twenty-four of Catherine's letters survive from this period, though she may have written double that number—testimony to the dogged zeal with which she functioned during these four months. In mid-July she reassured Frances Warde: "When Father O'Hanlon called here on his return from Carlow—he said to me, 'Oh my dear, I am delighted to see you so much recovered, you are looking quite yourself'—by this you will judge, he does not urge me to change of air."[16] Looks were deceiving.

14. Historians seem divided in their evaluations of the two archbishops who served in quite different periods of Ireland's development. Cullen seems, to some, to have had a penchant for controlling pastoral work in Ireland, centralizing the decision-making of bishops, frequently invoking the involvement of officials in Rome, and eschewing collaboration of the church with the government. Murray is seen as less confrontational, more cooperative with government and Protestants where he could be, more appreciative of the authority of other bishops, and more supportive of the initiatives of particular Irish priests and bishops who collaborated with Catherine McAuley in the extension of the works of mercy.

15. Letter 270 [June 3, 1841] and letter 272, June 19, 1841, in CCMcA, 403 and 404.

16. Letter 279 [mid-July 1841], in CCMcA, 412.

While she was in Birr, she had asked the novice Juliana Hardman to welcome Frances Gibson to Baggot Street when she arrived on May 16, telling Juliana, with roguish advice, to give Frances a "favorable impression" of her absent "superior":

Don't tell her I give severe lectures or sharp reproofs—speak of me as a quiet easy simple goodnatured person, such as you know I am. Tell her how I simpathise [sic] with poor Sisters addicted to crying, how tenderly I compassionate their weakness, in fine, tell her all that will make a favorable impression at first. If I should—unfortunately—fail to realize it . . . she will perceive the kindness of your intention, and admire the charity with which you speak of your superior.[17]

The sensitive, often homesick and tearful Juliana could only laugh at Catherine's pose.

To see Clare Moore again after eighteen months was pure joy—the only time in Catherine's life up to now when one of the "first-born" could come back to Baggot Street for an extended visit. Finally Bishop Murphy had persuaded Bishop Griffiths to let Clare return to Cork as originally planned. On Saturday, June 12, Dr. Griffiths appointed Mary Clare Agnew the superior of the Bermondsey community, and two days later Clare Moore—"Paddy," as Catherine quipped—accompanied by Peter Butler, set out for Dublin. Clare Agnew was the senior professed member of the Bermondsey community, moreover an Englishwoman, and thus the apparent preference of the community. As Catherine later told Frances Warde: "Amongst the most amiable, we could clearly discover—a desire that John Bull should be the head on all occasions."[18] The remaining Irish sisters, de Sales White and Xavier O'Connell, still on loan, would be returning to Baggot Street in September.

It does not appear, from information in surviving letters, that Clare Moore gave Catherine any inkling of problems that could possibly develop—and later did—in the London community, beyond the plain fact Catherine had seen for herself: the English sisters preferred English leadership. In June Catherine told de Sales White—perhaps putting a positive face on it for one still in the scene—that the "report" Clare gave "of the dear Bermondsey convent is consoling indeed. She says it is going on so happily, and Revd. Mr. B[utler] thinks it is most permanently established."[19] Clare Moore was intimate with Catherine, but also fair. She would give Clare Agnew a chance, and spare Catherine any predictions or premature surmises.

Clare remained at Baggot Street about a week and then departed with

17. Letter 266, May 13, 1841, in CCMcA, 397.
18. Letter 305, September 25, 1841, in CCMcA, 440.
19. Letter 274 [June 24, 1841], in CCMcA, 405.

Peter Butler for Cork where, against her personal wish but in accord with Bishop Murphy's, she resumed the role of superior. They stopped in Carlow and Limerick on the way, and Clare had the pleasure of reunions with Frances Warde and Elizabeth Moore, her old companions through the sufferings of the early years. Together they had known the deaths, the cholera, the typhus, and the hard work of maintaining the House of Mercy and the poor school when they were so few in number. Though Catherine found Clare "very thin, and while here had not any appetite," she trusted that "when the excitement of parting and meeting is at an end, she will get a little stronger."[20]

However, by the end of July, Catherine began to get "some unfavorable reports" about the Bermondsey community.[21] Moreover, bishops in England, at least Dr. George Hilary Brown, vicar apostolic of the Lancashire District where Liverpool was situated, began to learn of some "little difficulty" in Bermondsey, which they attributed to the fact that the foundation there had been made from Cork, not from "the chief or Mother House, as they term it, in Ireland." Catherine had to admit that "certainly in that instance more experience" than Clare Moore possessed in 1837–1839 "was required, to take down some of Sr. Agnew's self-importance as to opinion and bring her well through a noviciate."[22]

Catherine wrote immediately to Peter Butler, "begging him to tell me the real state." She sent his response to Frances Warde, seeking her opinion and commenting:

2 left [Bermondsey] under angry circumstances. . . . Sr. Agnew is fond of *extremes* in piety, that is her greatest error. She wrote to me in the greatest alarm—about a most trifling matter—if you and I were to write on such subjects—we would never be done.[23]

But by August 3, Catherine could tell Teresa White in Galway: "Most satisfactory letters from London, all going on remarkably well."[24] And in September, after her return from Birmingham with de Sales White and Xavier O'Connell, who had come to Birmingham from Bermondsey, she was further reassured: "Bermondsey is all alive since 'Paddy' left—such has been the promise given by some unknown letter writer. . . . I am sure they will go on now with great ardor."[25]

20. Ibid.
21. Letter 284 [c. July 26–27, 1841], in *CCMcA*, 419.
22. Letter 282, July 24, 1841, in *CCMcA*, 417.
23. Letter 284 [c. July 26–27, 1841], in *CCMcA*, 419.
24. Letter 290, August 3, 1841, in *CCMcA*, 424.
25. Letter 305, September 25, 1841, in *CCMcA*, 440.

It is highly unlikely that Catherine ever knew the full story of what was happening in Bermondsey. Those who knew also knew of her failing health and may have wished to spare her worry over emerging problems there, about which, from a distance and having no authority in that community, she could do nothing. It was left to Bishop Thomas Griffiths to assess the situation with Peter Butler's help. In December 1841, Griffiths acted. He deposed Mary Clare Agnew and asked Bishop Murphy to allow Clare Moore to return as superior, which she did on December 10. She remained the much loved leader of that community, except for fifteen months in 1851–1852, until her death in 1874.

What exactly happened in Bermondsey in the summer and autumn of 1841? Clare Moore herself wrote most of the yearly entries in the Bermondsey Annals, at least until 1873, and the only available primary source on this topic seems to be her discreet commentary in the Annals for 1841 and 1842:

When Sister Mary Clare Agnew became Mother Superior, she was very anxious to introduce certain customs which she desired to see established in the Community, and changed many of the regulations, which had always been observed, without consulting the feelings of the Sisters, or even apprising them that such alterations would be made—which caused much dissatisfaction among them. In other ways too she gave umbrage, and estranged the minds of the Sisters from her, so that she found her office very insupportable, and being naturally of an enthusiastic temper, and fond of novelty, she turned her attention to other Orders, where she hoped to find greater satisfaction. She fixed her thoughts principally on the Order of La Trappe, and went so far as to enter into a correspondence with the Superiors of it, without acquainting those appointed to guide her or seeking their advice. Revd. Father Butler having discovered this requested the Bishop to permit application to be made for the return of the former Mother Superior, Sister Mary Clare Moore, and having obtained Bishop Murphy's consent, he set out for Cork early in December [1841], and returned to Bermondsey on the 10th of that month, with Revd. Mother Mary Clare Moore who was again appointed to the office of Mother Superior of this Convent.[26]

The Annals notes that in 1842 all in the Bermondsey community worked "cheerfully to discharge the various functions of the Institute, except Sis-

26. "Bermondsey Annals (1841)," vol. 1, 26–27 (AIMGB). According to Carroll, Clare Agnew encouraged the members of the community who felt an attraction to extended contemplation to "live between their cells and the choir." The others would be "pious workers rather than real religious." In the refectory she placed the long narrow tables against the walls so the sisters seated for meals, each facing the wall, would not be distracted by the sight of one another. Though it seems preposterous, Carroll also claims that Clare Agnew disliked seeing the various heights of the sisters as they sat "at office or lecture," so "she wished the shorter ladies to put a sort of padding under their veils to raise themselves to the height of their taller companions." *Leaves from the Annals*, vol. 2 (1883), 88. Carroll may have had a reliable source for reporting these "eccentricities," but no extant primary source reports them.

ter Mary Clare Agnew whose desire for change continued unabated." On one occasion she interpreted the "shining spots" she saw in a "glass which covered a print of St. Clare" as "a vision of the Most Holy Sacrament, directing her to establish perpetual Adoration in the Community."[27] Apparently Clare Agnew wished the Sisters of Mercy to be not a religious congregation devoted to the spiritual and corporal works of mercy, but a fully contemplative order which would, appropriately, make prayer within the cloister its dominant characteristic and priority. In the end she voluntarily departed from the Bermondsey community in October 1842.[28]

Catherine's July 1841 claim that Clare Agnew's fondness for "extremes in piety" was her "greatest error" was evidently prescient, though she did not then, or probably ever, realize the full consequences of this tendency. Catherine's hunch that it is better "not to make too many laws, for if you draw the string too tight it will break," was borne out for six months in Bermondsey.[29] The very nature and purpose of the first community of Sisters of Mercy in London was thus nearly destroyed, a situation that would have deeply grieved her had she known of it—which she would have, except, apparently, for the discretion and charity of those who knew.[30]

27. "Bermondsey Annals (1842)," vol. 1, 98–99 (AIMGB).

28. Clare Agnew's plan to depart, quietly and alone, from Bermondsey having been discovered, Bishop Griffiths advised Clare Moore and Peter Butler to help her "go where she pleased." A temporary place at Stape Hill, a Trappist convent in Dorsetshire, having been offered to her, Peter Butler conducted her there on October 5, 1842. "She remained only nine months." Writing earlier to Father Butler, she said she wished to withdraw "from active life to the seclusion I have long desired." "Bermondsey Annals (1842)," vol. 1, 99–102 (AIMGB).

While with the Trappists, Clare Agnew sought in 1843 to spend "a time" in the Baggot Street community, prior to "establishing our [Mercy] Order in the Western District" of England. She said this was the wish of the recently deceased Bishop Peter Baines. Mary de Pazzi Delany, then the Baggot Street superior, immediately replied that "it will not be in my power to make a vacancy for you." Mary Clare Agnew to Mary de Pazzi Delany, July 30, 1843 (MCA), and draft, Mary de Pazzi Delany to Mary Clare Agnew, August 6, 1843 (MCA). Writing to Dr. Thomas Brindle, de Pazzi said: "It will be quite out of my power to receive Miss Agnew, even for a time, our Convent is at present very much crowded." Draft, Mary de Pazzi Delany to Thomas Brindle, August 6, 1843 (MCA). Clare's letters to Archbishop Murray did not alter de Pazzi's decision.

Clare made other attempts to enter or found separate Mercy or other congregations in England and Europe, but failed. She apparently died in 1881. Degnan, *Mercy*, note 9, 378–79. Carroll's accounts of Clare Agnew—*Life*, 407–21, and *Leaves from the Annals*, vol. 2 (1883), 87–94—are a mixture of negative elaboration and what may be sound data. A brief biography of Elizabeth Agnew's sad, because apparently misguided, life would prove helpful.

29. BA and Lim, in *CMcATM*, 115 and 179, and *PS*, 21.

30. The community in Bermondsey still thrives on the same site, having survived bombing during World War II, though its original Pugin building did not. As a convent of the Institute of Our Lady of Mercy, it houses, in addition to its other ministries, one of two extensive Mercy Heritage Centres in England. The other is in Birmingham.

There appear to be no grounds for claiming that Catherine McAuley's undated "Spirit of the Institute" essay, also called "The Mercy Ideal" (letter 324, in *CCMcA*, 458–63 and 458 n. 85), was intended as a response to the crisis in the Bermondsey community, as in Bolster, *Catherine McAuley* (1990), 74–75. The untitled manuscript now in AIMGB is a thin, re-bound volume of five sheets (eight and a half pages in Catherine McAuley's handwriting) that were removed from an earlier, also re-bound, notebook of

Seeking accurate information about Bermondsey was just a small portion of Catherine's correspondence that summer of 1841. While continuing to write to Tullamore, Carlow, Galway, and Birr, and presumably to the other foundations, she also had to write to Thomas Youens, vicar general in Liverpool, trying through him to persuade Bishop George Hilary Brown to let the Liverpool foundation come from the Carlow community, for which Frances Warde was eager and ready. She also wrote to Bishop Walsh in Birmingham, trying to get him to set the date, as he had promised, for the reception and the profession in Dublin of sisters destined for Birmingham; and to Archbishop Murray, through John Hamilton, to set the date if Dr. Walsh, now somewhere in Europe, could not attend. To John Hardman, Jr., in Birmingham, she wrote, outlining, with drawings, the furniture needed in the new convent that awaited them: a "straw and hair mattress" for each bed; in each bedroom a "small press, not too high, that will answer for a wash hand stand with a small drawer and cupboard for linen"; and chairs and tables for the refectory, community room, and novitiate. Not completely trusting Pugin to get it right, she specified the length, width, and height of several of the tables, those in the refectory to be made "of plain deal, not painted."[31]

In the midst of all this came the unexpected visit of John England seeking a foundation of sisters for his diocese centered in Charleston, South Carolina. He celebrated Mass at Baggot Street and "in a loud voice" pleaded: "Fear nothing. Follow Paul in peril, pestilence & famine, that you may be his glorious associate for time & Eternity." Catherine had no real fear of peril or famine, but neither did she have a community ready to go. So she staged a playful demonstration of that fact, using a very petite young postulant as her accomplice:

> After breakfast we assembled all the troops in the community room, from all quarters—Laundry, Dining Hall, etc.—by chance 2 were in from Kingstown. We made a great muster. The question was put by his Lordship—from the chair—who will come to Charleston with me to act as Superior & the only one who came forward offering to fill the office was Sr. Margaret Teresa Dwyer—which afforded great laughing. I had arranged it with her before, but did not think she would have courage. His Lordship was obliged to acknowledge that we are poor dependants on the

---

other transcriptions in Catherine's hand (selections from the "Meditations" of Peter Kenney, S.J.), also in AIMGB. The watermark on the sheets of the "Spirit of the Institute" is "Superfine 1836"; that on the sheets of "Meditations" is "Bath 1824." The "Spirit of the Institute," an altered transcription of parts of an essay by Alonso Rodriguez, whose writings Catherine read at George's Hill and throughout the 1830s, could have been written any time in or after 1836, and was probably intended not precisely for Bermondsey, but as a general description of the purpose and spirit of the Sisters of Mercy.

31. Letter 276 [July 1841], in CCMcA, 410.

white veil & [postulants'] caps—we certainly look like a community that wanted time to come to maturity, reduced to Infancy again as we are.[32]

In Rome on June 6, Pope Gregory XVI gave his final approval and confirmation to the Rule and Constitutions of the Sisters of Mercy. On July 5 Cardinal Giacomo Filippo Fransoni, prefect of Propaganda Fide, signed a decree to that effect, but as he wished to publish the decree in bound copies of the approved Rule, printed in Italian, and as the printing was still in process, no official word reached Dublin until after Catherine sailed for Birmingham. By early August unofficial word had begun to reach various people in Ireland including Paul Cullen's uncle, James Maher in Carlow. On August 16, Catherine told Frances: "I was aware the confirmation of the Rule was granted, but I have not received it yet—probably his Grace may bring it on Thursday to the ceremony."[33] That did not happen.

As was the custom of the Vatican, all official correspondence was directed to the bishops or vicars apostolic of the respective dioceses. So the woman who had founded the Sisters of Mercy in Dublin in 1831 and, so far, eight additional autonomous communities elsewhere in Ireland and England, and who had worked late at night—when she was fatigued from the daily works of mercy—to compose their Rule and Constitutions, now had to wait.

But she did not wait with her hands resting idly, as posthumous portraits might suggest. Seven novices were preparing for profession of vows, and three postulants were ready to receive the habit. Over the summer Catherine had been giving them daily instructions, in separate groups. Of her time with the Birmingham novices, she said: "Speaking does not injure me. I am giving them instructions every day for more than a month— thanks be to God, they love instruction—and are most anxious to profit by it." In the same letter, she declined Frances Warde's invitation to come to Carlow for rest and the August retreat:

32. Letter 275, June 30 [1841], in *CCMcA*, 407. Catherine McAuley called Margaret Teresa Dwyer a "sweet little Dove" and "Queen of the order." Eventually Bishop England's hope for Sisters of Mercy in his diocese (North and South Carolina and Georgia) was fulfilled. In 1841, he formed in Charleston a sisterhood known as the "Sisters of Our Lady of Mercy." They formed other communities—in Savannah, Georgia, in 1845, and Wilmington, North Carolina, in 1869. By 1892, the Wilmington group had moved their motherhouse to Belmont, North Carolina, and the Savannah group, seventy in number, had become part of the Mercy community in Mobile, Alabama, whose superior was Mary Austin Carroll. In 1913 the Belmont women became an autonomous Mercy congregation. In 1991 they joined the Institute of the Sisters of Mercy of the Americas. Today Sisters of Mercy serve throughout Bishop England's old diocese. Mary Josephine Gately, *The Sisters of Mercy: Historical Sketches, 1831–1931* (New York: Macmillan, 1931), 360–65, and Darcy, *The Institute . . . of the Americas*, 160–61, 172–74.

33. Letter 295 [August 16, 1841], in *CCMcA*, 430. The letter from Fransoni to Murray (letter 288, July 31, 1841, in *CCMcA*, 422), together with "ten copies of the Rule," presumably reached Dublin after August 20, the day Catherine McAuley departed for Birmingham.

I am sure I need not say that it would be delightful to me to accept the invitation
... but think of all that must be left behind. They would feel it very much indeed. It
is quite impossible for any one in my situation to think of pleasing themselves. My
pleasure must be in endeavouring to please all.[34]

She complimented Frances on getting Father Thomas Furlong, professor
of rhetoric and belles lettres at Maynooth, to give the August retreat in
Carlow. Baggot Street—alas, in her view—would have only herself: "I need
not wish you a holy & happy retreat. Father Whitty told me Dr. Furlong
had 23 lectures or explanatory discourses prepared for you. Father McAuley conducts the retreat in poor Baggot St."[35]

Catherine's playful pretense to a clerical title aside, her retreat guidance
that August and the instructions she gave throughout the summer were
the last formal advice she gave to any groups of Sisters of Mercy, except
what she expressed in her remaining letters or on her deathbed. Though
the exact content of her teachings in these months cannot be identified,
these instructions were treasured long afterwards. The twenty-two-year-
old Mary Vincent Whitty, professed that August, later had the "consolation," she says, to be with Catherine when she died and to "close her eyes &
that mouth, from which I have received such instruction. May God grant
us all grace to remember & practice it."[36] In Mary Liguori (Frances) Gibson's retreat notes made that August are unmistakable signs of the topics
Catherine must have emphasized: universal charity, cheerfulness, humility, purity of intention, zeal, and fidelity in one's ordinary actions.[37] Justina
Fleming, who professed vows that August, died of consumption in December. Those who were received or professed vows at the last ceremonies
over which Catherine presided carried the inspiration of her final instructions with them to England, Newfoundland, and Australia. Their future
works of mercy were the vibrant memorials to her words.

At long last, the date for the ceremonies was set: Thursday, August 19,
with Archbishop Murray presiding, Bishop Walsh being unable to attend.
Catherine regretted his absence and Dr. Wiseman's: "All the dear English
Bishops disappointed."[38] As usual, the Catholic Directory, in listing the
event in its annals, mentions the names of only the two bishops present,
Dr. Murray and Dr. Fleming (Newfoundland), the eighteen priests, including Dean Meyler and Fathers O'Hanlon, Gaffney, and Maher, and the

34. Letter 291 [August 4, 1841], in CCMcA, 427.
35. Letter 289 [early August 1841], in CCMcA, 423.
36. MVWL [November 12, 1841], in CMcATM, 242–43.
37. Carroll, Leaves from the Annals, vol. 2 (1883), 366–67.
38. Letter 295 [August 16, 1841], in CCMcA, 430.

Anglican Dr. Edward Pusey—not of "the superioress and her assistant" or of any of the ten Mercy Sisters whose reception and profession were the whole point of the event.[39] Catherine herself preferred to be "hidden and unknown" and advocated not "bringing ourselves into notice," but, once again, in its overemphasis on clerics, the *Directory* missed its opportunity to illustrate and contribute to an adequate account of church history.[40]

The next evening, August 20, Catherine departed for the Birmingham foundation, her last. Boarding the boat at Kingstown, bound for Liverpool, were the newly professed Juliana Hardman, Mary Xavier Wood, Mary Vincent Bond, and Cecilia Edwards, and the novices Magdalen Polding and Angela Borini—all destined to be members of the new community. Accompanying them were Redmond O'Hanlon; Myles Gaffney, who knew the Hardman family; the new novice Mary Liguori (Frances) Gibson, who would be Catherine's companion on the return trip; and Cecilia Marmion. Taking the young Liguori Gibson as her traveling companion was a gesture of compassion for her grieving family in Liverpool, who had just lost their eldest daughter. Catherine hoped they could visit them.[41] Asking Cecilia Marmion to come was Catherine's first clear concession to the uncertainties of her failing health. If she was not physically able to stay in Birmingham for the full time the young community needed guidance, the experienced Cecilia could remain for one or two months more. The day before their departure Catherine posted a short note to Frances Warde:

The ceremony just over—the poor Bishop very much fatigued, had 10 Sisters to officiate for. . . . We had the celebrated Dr. Pusey & his daughter, who engrossed all Dr. Murray's attention. We sail tomorrow. . . .

I am very uneasy.

Dr. Murphy of Cork received an account of the confirmation of our Rule. Dr. Murray has not yet & is much surprised.

Pray for me. God bless you.

Your affectionate
M. C. M.[42]

"Uneasy" about what? Perhaps, chiefly, her own physical capacity to make the trip and get back to Baggot Street.

39. *Catholic Directory* (1842), 419.
40. Catherine's words can be found in *PS*, 2–3.
41. Letter 305, September 25, 1841, in *CCMcA*, 440.
42. Letter 296 [August 19, 1841], in *CCMcA*, 431.

CHAPTER 22

"'Tis Come to a Close" *September–November 1841*

On August 30, Catherine wrote from Birmingham to Dr. George J. P. Browne, bishop of Galway, expressing regret that she would be unable to attend the profession ceremony of Mary Joseph Joyce and Mary de Sales McDonnell in Galway on October 1:

> Even in this very warm weather, my Lord, if I remain any time in a room with a window open, I am coughing all night and disturbing the poor Sisters who are near me. I propose returning to Baggot Street on the 20th of September, and expect to be confined to a close room, as the least blast makes me very troublesome for several days together, but to travel in October would be very imprudent indeed.[1]

This was Catherine's first written acknowledgment of the reduced state of her health at this point. A few days earlier she had written to Frances Warde without mentioning a word about it, except indirectly admitting that she could not go to Bermondsey: "Mr. O'Hanlon most kindly went to London to bring Sisters de Sales & Xavier to me."[2]

Augustus W. Pugin had partially redeemed himself in Catherine's eyes. When the group arrived in Birmingham, by train from Liverpool in the late afternoon of August 21, she found the new convent large enough for twenty and "beautiful." He "would not permit cloth of any kind on the rooms—rush chairs and oak Tables—but all is so admirable, so religious, that no want can be felt. The whole building cost but three thousand pounds. I would say 6—without hesitation."[3] To her delight, there was

---

1. Letter 299, August 30, 1841, in *CCMcA*, 433. 2. Letter 297 [c. August 25, 1841], in *CCMcA*, 432.
3. Ibid.

"not one rib of stucco, or one panelled door, except in the chapel. I have never seen so plain a building."[4] She had at last got her "plain, simple, durable" convent building,[5] from the man who was "a general favourite . . . in this part of England. Nothing is perfect that he does not plan and execute."

But she had two complaints, one practical and one spiritual: "I do think some of his plans would admit of improvements; for example, he has brought the [sleeping] cells close to the chapel-door, which will, I fear, be attended with some inconvenience." Moreover, "I do not admire his gilded figures of saints; they are very coarse representations, and by no means calculated to inspire devotion."[6]

If ever any woman's faith and spirituality were far from being moved by gilded representations of human holiness, Catherine's were. She believed that "Jesus Christ became for our example and imitation the outcast of the world and the last of men," and she saw, in his washing of his disciples' feet, his body "bent to show us how our spirit should be bent to everyone."[7] She therefore put no coarse gilt or veneer on the ways saints had striven to resemble him. Voluntary poverty, simplicity, humility, mercifulness, charity—these unglossed virtues were what beckoned her in those whose example had always inspired her: Catherine of Siena, Angela Merici, Teresa of Avila, Vincent de Paul, Francis of Assisi, and others.

But now, in Birmingham, she had to begin to learn a new (for her) ungilded virtue: how to be a patient, waited on by others. It was not easy. On September 6, writing to Teresa Carton at Baggot Street, she asked that an iron bedstead, with its legs cut down, be prepared for her in the infirmary:

Have the Infirmary very well cleaned. Move your bed to where Sister M. Clare's [i.e., Clare Augustine's] is, and clear out your corner for mine, where I will not hear the noise of the street. I will want a fire. . . . Do not have any hurry about getting the Bed done. It will be time enough—the 3rd Bed to be taken away.

Wistfully she added: "It is strange to me, my Dear Sr. Teresa, to write so much about myself—and give such trouble."[8]

Later that month, still in Birmingham, she told Aloysius Scott in Birr: "I have been very weak and sick for the last 12 or 14 days. . . . Endless visi-

---

4. Letter 298 [Late August 1841], in *CCMcA*, 433.
5. Letter 160, February 4, 1840, in *CCMcA*, 251.
6. Letter 298 [Late August 1841], in *CCMcA*, 433. The Birmingham convent on Hunter's Road, Handsworth, now slightly renovated, currently houses an active community and the Heritage Centre of the Sisters of Mercy of the Union, Great Britain.
7. Degnan, ed., *Retreat Instructions*, 76, 116.
8. Letter 300, September 6, 1841, in *CCMcA*, 436. Mary Clare Augustine Moore had gone to Cork in June to assist Bishop Murphy with some unidentified project.

tors coming in here & I cannot leave the one aired room without coughing violently."[9] Four days later she acknowledged: "I could not go" to Bermondsey "nor ever go out, even to the Garden."[10] The "endless" visitors
included the Hardman family, Bishop Thomas Walsh, and his coadjutor
Dr. Nicholas Wiseman, who had welcomed them to the new convent on
August 21 and "in full pontificals recited the *Te Deum*" in gratitude for their
arrival.[11]

Soon after they reached Birmingham, Catherine had managed to visit
the ailing John Hardman, Sr., the chief benefactor of the convent: "Old
Mr. Hardman whose death was expected has rallied wonderfully."[12] The
sight and embrace of his daughter Juliana, soon to be named superior of
the convent he had built and the orphanage he had endowed, were clearly
the medicine he needed after his long sacrifice of sixteen months.

The journey back to Dublin was more strenuous than usual. Catherine,
Liguori Gibson, de Sales White, and Xavier O'Connell, presumably with
Redmond O'Hanlon, left Birmingham early on September 20. In Liverpool, Dr. Thomas Youens took them to see "the place where he intends
to build a Convent." Catherine found the site "very well suited, quite close
to the Town with 3 good approaches to it." Since "the Packet [to Kings-
town] did not sail till near eight" that night, they dined at Father Youens's
home, where he had arranged for Mrs. Gibson to meet them. Her husband, Liguori's father, was "now in London, after some severe operation,"
and Catherine was glad she had had the foresight to bring their daughter
to England when they were facing such "great family afflictions."

Although they were wearing traveling attire—a black bonnet with a
short veil, black gloves, and a black cloak sufficiently long to conceal the
habit—and were thus unidentifiable as religious, they "dressed for dinner."
Thomas Youens "and some of his Priests have now seen the full costume
which they like very much."[13] Not that their approval really mattered—
except that Catherine herself "loved to look on the religious habit."[14]

Later that night the party embarked. They had "a weary passage from
Liverpool—kept 3 hours waiting for water & did not arrive in Kingstown
until 9 o'c" the next morning. The sisters there "had comfortable Tea, etc.
for us"—plentiful hot tea, not tea laced with whiskey as some interpreters

9. Letter 302 [September 17, 1841], in *CCMcA*, 438.
10. Letter 303 [September 21, 1841], in *CCMcA*, 438.
11. Letter 297 [c. August 25, 1841], in *CCMcA*, 432.
12. Ibid. John Hardman, Sr., died in 1844 at the age of seventy-seven.
13. Letter 305, September 25, 1841, in *CCMcA*, 439–40.
14. Lim, in *CMcATM*, 182.

of "comfortable" have supposed.[15] It was, after all, nine A.M.! They rested until noon, then set out by train for Westland Row. The short ride in a jaunting car or coach to Baggot Street—she could not have walked—was probably Catherine's last through the streets of Dublin.

Primary sources contain many opinions and descriptions of Catherine's last illness. Her own fullest account is in a letter she wrote at the end of September, though it is sprinkled with humor and throwaway lines obviously designed to prevent any alarm in the reader. Redmond O'Hanlon was clearly concerned and had insisted that Catherine see Dr. William Stokes (1804–1872), a medical practitioner widely known for his classic work *Diseases of the Chest* (1837). He is still regarded, with Robert Graves, as one of the two most distinguished and influential Irish physicians in the early nineteenth century.

In late September, Catherine wrote at length to Aloysius Scott about Dr. Stokes's visits and her reaction. After urging Aloysius not to try to send any more fruit—one "could never send it such a journey without its being greatly injured"—and hoping instead that she would "have the charity to eat some fresh fruit off the trees, walking in the garden," she gives her tone-downed version of the medical report:

My cough very variable—one night bad, another good. Five minutes in a room with a window ever so little open brings on an hour's coughing, great expectoration, yet I am not weak—tho' I cannot say I have any appetite.

Mr. O'Hanlon particularly requested I would consult Dr. Stokes. I have seen him twice. On his first visit he looked like a person who had made a great discovery. On his second—Mother de Pazzi conducted him out and returned with such sorrow in her countenance that I entreated her to tell me his opinion.

My Right Lung was "diseased"—I have now less confidence than ever in the [medical] faculty, and you know my stock was small enough. I do not think my lung is affected. I am now dead to the poor children—not to read, speak—give out Office, etc. I tell you all these particulars—to give you the benefit of experience. If my lung is actually engaged, the progress will not be checked, and the fact of no debility—not half so much as I have had when my gums were inflamed—shews that it cannot be.

Ordering a linament to be applied to my chest—he desired my Servant to do it. Mother de P has got that appointment. I call every night for my Servant. Sister M. Catherine administers medicine & Sr. L[ucy?] Vincent is head cook—making nice rennet whey, light puddings, etc., etc. I am very sure her Majesty is not attended with half so much care, often most ungraciously received by a poor unfortunate peevish old sinner, who never required any particular care or attention before, and

15. Letter 305, September 25, 1841, in *CCMcA*, 439.

who is more weary of it than of the delicacy that occasions it. To the affectionate often repeated question—Revd. Mother, what could you take—the best answer is—My heart, you teise [tease] me very much.

As we should carefully examine the motive of our actions—I here humbly confess that my chief motive—just now—is to shew that one of the most distinguished amongst our medical professors may be mistaken—and that we should not immediately take up their opinions.

God bless you and all with you, my ever dear Sister M. Aloysius.

Pray for your affectionate
M. C. McAuley

I should add that it was not the Dr. desired me not read, etc.—it was Fr. O'Hanlon. The Dr. in a melancholy tone—left me to my own wishes—I might take any thing I liked. He seemed evidently to regard the case as hopeless.[16]

That letter was the account given by the "poor unfortunate peevish old sinner" herself. What Dr. Stokes exactly meant by "diseased" is not known.

Mary Vincent Harnett, basing her view on information from Elizabeth Moore, says that Catherine endured

very frequent and violent pain in the stomach, perhaps the beginning of that disease which terminated her existence. She was also subject to inflammatory attacks, accompanied by extreme soreness in her mouth, yet she would go on reading the public lectures, and reciting the Office until absolutely incapable of uttering a word.[17]

Clare Moore says essentially the same thing, though she speaks of "inflammatory attacks in the head."[18] Clare Augustine Moore, in Cork during these weeks, claims, no doubt giving the views of others, that when Catherine returned from Birmingham,

the sisters could no longer deceive themselves: she was evidently dying. An abscess had formed internally; her debility was most painful so that to walk from room to room fatigued her, she coughed incessantly, her appetite was gone, she could not sleep. The highest medical advice was procured but it was useless.

Later, Dr. Stokes told a sister who was caring for Catherine that "he expected the abscess would burst and that would be the immediate forerunner of death."[19]

Interestingly, Mary Ann Doyle provides a different opinion. In 1866, the

---

16. Letter 306 [September 26, 1841], in *CCMcA*, 441–43, and 441 n. 23. Catherine may have started to confuse Mary Vincent (Lucy) Bond, now in Birmingham, and Mary Vincent Whitty, and then corrected herself.

17. Lim, in *CMcATM*, 188.   18. BA, in *CMcATM*, 124.

19. CAM, in *CMcATM*, 215.

year of Mary Ann's death, Clare Moore inserts in the Bermondsey Annals a letter she had received from Mary Ann shortly after Catherine's death. Here Mary Ann says of Catherine:

> She came to Tullamore on her way home [from Birr], which was the last time, six months before her death. Her cough was constant. I was told that one of her lungs was gone before her death, although this was not the cause, but inward inflammation, I think, of the kidneys from what I heard.[20]

Today physicians would probably conclude, from a study of Catherine's symptoms, as given in the various early biographical accounts and as described by Catherine herself, that she suffered from advanced pulmonary tuberculosis aggravated by an empyema. She may also have had tuberculosis in another tissue or organ.[21]

Though limited in some of her activities at Baggot Street, which she now left in the hands of de Pazzi Delany—leading communal prayer and reading spiritual lectures to the community—in other respects Catherine went on as usual, as if there had been no reliable diagnosis, and still pretending, for the sake of others, that she would prove the famous Dr. Stokes mistaken. Her business obligations in late September and October were weighty. She asked Mary Ann Doyle in Tullamore to receive the dying Justina Fleming, who thought "she would receive benefit from change of air which has been prescribed." Amazingly, given her health, she proposed herself "as Deputy to Dr. O'Rafferty in the guardianship" of Tullamore convent, apparently to counteract Bishop Cantwell's erroneous belief that financial resources at Baggot Street could assist the Tullamore community: "Your good Bishop was *much* mistaken as to property here—we have ever confided largely in Divine Providence—and shall continue to do so."[22]

To Dr. Nicholas Foran's request for a Mercy foundation in Waterford, she promised: "If your Lordship . . . could meet three, four, or five educated persons with marked vocations—good constitutions, young if possible," and send them to Baggot Street, "I would have every hope of returning them to you—acquainted with their state as Religious—and well practiced in the corporal and spiritual works of Mercy."[23] Replying to Dean Bernard Burke in Westport, to whom she had already promised a foundation, she said with characteristic understatement: "Many thanks . . . for the kind

---

20. "Bermondsey Annals (1866)," vol. 2, [109].
21. An empyema is an accumulation of pus in a bodily cavity.
22. Letter 304, September 24, 1841, in *CCMcA*, 439.
23. Letter 307 [late September–October 1841], in *CCMcA*, 443.

concern you express about my health. I am really quite a fine lady, doing nothing but looking on, keeping up the little remnant for the foundations, and, above all, for Westport."[24]

But this "fine lady" had two bigger problems to try to solve. When she studied it, with help, she found "evident mistakes" in the now confirmed and published copy of the Mercy Rule and Constitutions. And she had to deal with the threat of law proceedings intimated by a supplier of timber and slates for the Booterstown convent.

After she returned from Birmingham, Catherine received from Daniel Murray, to whom it was sent from Rome on July 31, a printed copy of the papally approved Rule and Constitutions of the Sisters of Mercy, published in Italian and bound in black leather with gold tooling, *La Regola e Le Costituzioni delle Religiose nominate Sorelle della Misericordia*.[25] That the now-church-prescribed Rule for a totally English-speaking congregation of women religious would be presented to them in Italian is, on the face of it, inexcusable. When she had somewhat recovered from the trip, Catherine tried to study it, but of course could not do so without the help of someone fluent in Italian. Presumably Redmond O'Hanlon or another priest assisted her. On October 12, she wrote to Frances Warde:

> The Very Revd. Dr. Kirby, V[ice] P[resident] of the Irish College, Rome, called here the day before he sailed. I mentioned to him some evident mistakes in the Copy of our Rule. He told me to select them and forward the document to him, with Dr. Murray's signature, & said we would without any more trouble obtain permission to rectify the evident mistakes. . . .
> I was cautioned not to speak of any mistake in the R[ule].[26]

On November 21, 1841, Elizabeth Moore concluded a letter to Mary Ann Doyle:

> Get no translation of our Holy Rule till I have time to explain further; our dear Revd. Mother did not sanction the alterations with the exception of one or two— not certain how they crept in, but I have my suspicions.[27]

What were the "mistakes" or "alterations" Catherine found, and what were Elizabeth's "suspicions" as to their origin? Did she think Daniel Murray had been contacted about alterations of the text after the document had

24. Letter 313, October 8, 1841, in *CCMcA*, 448–49.
25. Letter 288, Giacomo Fransoni to Daniel Murray, July 31, 1841, in *CCMcA*, 422–23. The Dublin copy of *La Regola e Le Costituzioni* is preserved in MCA; the Bermondsey copy, in AIMGB.
26. Letter 314, October 12, 1841, in *CCMcA*, 449.
27. Mary Elizabeth Moore to Mary Ann Doyle, November 21, 1841, in *CMcATM*, 256.

been reviewed in Rome? It is unlikely that Elizabeth would have known anything about Gavino Secchi Murro's detailed review of the document in Rome in early 1840, unless Catherine knew and told her.

After his earlier penciled emendations on Catherine's original draft, there is no written evidence so far discovered that Dr. Murray requested, after the document was submitted to Rome, any other alterations in that text, though he may have made oral requests about which Catherine would have known. However, there are references in the material sent to the ten members of the Congregation for the Propagation of the Faith, prior to their meeting on July 20, 1840, about "minor changes" and "modifications" to be made in the Rule with Daniel Murray's concurrence. The formal documentation given to the cardinals read in part:

The distinguished Consultor [Gavino Secchi Murro] agrees fully that the required approval [of the Rule and Constitutions] should be implored, except for some minor changes, which are to be sent, together with related instructions, to Monsignor Archbishop of Dublin—and, so, the Most Eminent and Most Reverend Lords are asked to resolve according to their wisdom the following

Doubt [i.e., question]:
Should His Holiness [Gregory XVI] . . . be implored for the approval with only those modifications proposed by the Reverend Consultor?

At that meeting (July 20, 1840), "their Eminences responded *Affirmative,* and left it to the Cardinal Prefect [Giacomo Fransoni] with the Cardinal Petitioner [Paolo Polidori] to have certain things in the Constitutions, to which attention has been drawn, appropriately emended or more accurately expressed."[28] No archival material so far discovered indicates that Daniel Murray was ever contacted to make the requested changes.

In Ireland and England the task of translating the Rule and Constitutions into English and inserting (or deleting) wording was generally undertaken in a sensible way over the next year or two. Since each foundation had its own handwritten copy of the Rule in English as Daniel Murray had earlier approved it, these communities evidently went through the Italian version, with linguistic help, and where they found added, altered, or deleted wording, they corrected their English text accordingly. Some of them then had this new English version, which still preserved Catherine's original wording where it could, copied by hand or set in printed form so they could have multiple copies of the approved text. At least this was the case

---

28. Letter 178, To the Cardinals of the Congregation for the Propagation of the Faith [July 20, 1840], in *CCMcA,* 278-79; *Acta,* Anno 1840, vol. 203, ff. 206r-208r (APF).

in Charleville, Limerick, Westport (founded in 1842), Bermondsey, and Birmingham, and probably elsewhere. The Birmingham text was published in print in 1844; that in Bermondsey in 1856. In each case this biographer has seen, there was a conscientious attempt to record the Italian alterations correctly, and with episcopal approval.

However, this method of publishing an English translation of the Italian text was not used in Dublin. The Dublin translation, finally published in 1863, with the approval of Archbishop Paul Cullen, was made directly from the Italian text, apparently without any reference to the wording in the English text Catherine McAuley had submitted. It thus suffered from the serious problems inherent in double translation.

Many "modifications" appear in the approved Italian copy of the Rule and Constitutions, as these were later worded, for instance, in the 1863 Dublin translation. Nearly all of the changes bear some relation to the recommendations for more detail and more prescription that Gavino Secchi Murro had made in March 1840. For example:

• In the chapter "Visitation of the Sick," two long sentences are added, requiring that the sisters "dexterously avoid" taking part in any family conversation about "disposal of property"—as if the poor families in their slum hovels had any significant property to dispose of.

• In the chapter "Admission of Distressed Women," words are inserted requiring that, before any women are admitted into the House of Mercy, "the Parish Priest shall always be consulted, in order the better to know their dispositions, for the guidance of Superiors"—a prescription requiring at least one non-resident decision-maker, which Catherine had always felt was detrimental to the women's urgent need for safe housing.[29]

• In the same chapter, the religious obligations of the women in the House of Mercy are expanded from "approaching Holy Communion on First Fridays," to also doing so on all "Feasts of Obligation" and all "Solemnities of the Blessed Virgin"; and changed from confessing to the "Chaplain" of the House of Mercy, to confessing to the "Confessor appointed by the Ordinary"—an impossible burden for Redmond O'Hanlon, and an alteration of the pastoral work Daniel Murray himself had assigned in 1829 to the full-time chaplain. Did those who altered the wording in this important chapter on a central work of the congregation think it was about women entering the religious congregation, not about destitute women

29. *The Rule and Constitutions of the Religious called Sisters of Mercy* (Dublin: James Duffy, 1863), 10, 12, and 13.

needing shelter and employment training as well as rudimentary instruction in the basics of Catholic faith and practice?[30]

• In the chapter "Reception of Postulants, their Clothing and Profession," the time of the novitiate is now to be "two entire years," with no qualification. Catherine's sentence: "The Bishop can, however, in extraordinary cases reduce it to one year," was now removed.[31] This prevented an adjustment that she and the respective bishops had always approved: when a new foundation was in its formative stage, the first novices were required to make only a one-year novitiate until there were seven professed members in the community, enough to constitute a decision-making chapter functioning as the Rule elsewhere prescribes.

To Catherine these were probably the most troubling alterations because of the limitations they placed on the spread and exercise of the works of mercy. But there were other changes which would have seemed to her to violate the spirit and conduct of the congregation. In the chapter "Correction"—now moved from the back of part 2 to part 1, ahead of "Humility"—two specific sentences on the Chapter of Faults were added:

Once every month each Sister, kneeling in public Chapter, shall, for the exercise of humility, accuse herself of her public faults and transgressions. The Superioress shall lovingly correct and sweetly admonish the Sisters on these occasions, without lessening the gravity of their faults.

These sentences replaced Catherine's milder and less specific references in that chapter and in the chapter on the office of the Mother Superior, in neither of which had she mentioned the term "chapter of faults." In addition, the "assistant" to the superior is now called the "Mother Assistant," a title Catherine had deliberately excluded from her composition of the Rule.[32] And, despite Catherine's regard for silence at most meals, it was now necessary that "a spiritual lecture shall be read," not just at dinner, but also "at supper, except when there shall be recreation." Finally, the chapter "Spiritual Retreat and Renewal of Vows" was narrowed by defining the focus of the annual retreat as the "Spiritual Exercises," presumably those of Ignatius Loyola—thus, in effect, eliminating retreats designed by Catherine herself, the superiors of the various convents, or any priest not trained in presenting the "Spiritual Exercises."

Many other changes, too numerous to mention, appear in the Italian

---

30. Ibid., 17.
32. *Rule and Constitutions* (1863), 48, 37, and 20.

31. Rule 20.3, in *CMcATM*, 315.

text, some minor and some undoubtedly reflecting the personal preferences of whoever handled the document in the course of its final approval.
Perhaps most painful to Catherine, though not sufficiently problematic to
warrant calling it an "evident mistake," was the substitution in the chapter
"Union and Charity" of a prescriptive clause—"they shall be solicitous to
repair the smallest offence, by promptly asking pardon, which should be
immediately granted, without contention, and without reserve"—for her
more inviting and more widely applicable sentence, which she had taken
directly from the Presentation Rule.[33] The original reads:

They shall as true followers of God walk in love, as Christ loved us, preserving
above all things charity, which is the bond of perfection, gaining over souls in the
obedience of charity, and in sincerity of heart fervently loving each other.[34]

Perhaps it was the phrase "fervently loving each other" which someone did not appreciate—because he did not know the heart of Catherine
McAuley. Moreover, the single, short clause "Charity is patient, etc., etc."
now replaced Catherine's complete quotation of 1 Corinthians 13:4-7.[35]
That was a scriptural passage on which she particularly "loved to expatiate,
most earnestly striving to reduce it to practise herself, and induce all under
her charge to do the same":[36]

Charity is patient, is kind, envieth not, dealeth not perversely, is not puffed up, is
not ambitious, seeketh not her own, is not provoked to anger, thinketh no evil,
beareth all things, hopeth all things, endureth all things.[37]

Whether, before June 1841 when Gregory XVI considered the document, Daniel Murray was ever asked by Roman authorities to incorporate
these or any other alterations has not so far been discovered in any written
documentation in Dublin or Rome. Nor is it known whether, after October 12, 1841, any list of corrections to be made was ever submitted to Tobias Kirby in Rome—by Catherine, Frances Warde, Elizabeth Moore, or
anyone else. The pressure of events in October and November 1841 soon
overshadowed what would have amounted to a painstaking and lengthy
process of securing such revisions.

Sick or not, Catherine—allegedly "doing nothing but looking on"—had
immediately to address another serious problem. On October 13, M. and
M. Dowling, merchants in Poolbeg Street, Dublin, wrote to her:

33. Ibid., 34.
35. *Rule and Constitutions* (1863), 34.
37. Rule 8.4, in *CMcATM*, 304.

34. Rule 8.3, in *CMcATM*, 304.
36. Lim, in *CMcATM*, 173.

Booterstown Convent is indebted to us for the last 4 years about £130 for Timber & Slates supplied for its erection. We have waited expecting some arrangements would have been made to pay off the debt & have on several occasions called on Revd. Mr. Ennis but as yet nothing has been done.[38]

The Dowlings knew that the late Barbara Verschoyle had "left twenty guineas [£21] a year to the convent," and they had "offered Revd. Mr. Ennis to accept . . . that sum as security until our debt would be discharged." John Ennis, the parish priest in Booterstown, had referred them to Catherine, and the Dowlings now told her that "in the event of your refusing to accede to our terms, we will be obliged (very much against our inclination) to issue an execution and attach the Convent where our property is." They were confident, they said, that "from your well known benevolent disposition you will at once enter into an arrangement for the liquidation of our just claim and spare us the trouble of proceeding."[39]

Catherine, too, wished to be spared the trouble of legal proceedings or an eviction, but the twenty guineas annuity bequeathed by Mrs. Verschoyle was the only regular income the Booterstown community had: "It is small—but not so to us." On October 15, admitting that she would have written sooner, but had "not been well for some days," she referred the Dowlings to James C. Bacon, agent for the Verschoyle estate, who, she was sure, "never expected any circumstance of this nature." But in sentences that must have caused her untold worry and fear, she proposed:

As to any legal proceedings, there is no occasion to have recourse to them. The Sisters can return here, and whoever has a just claim may take possession of the House until their demand is satisfied, if there is no other means of providing for it.[40]

Perhaps she could mentally see the frugal way the Booterstown sisters lived, and the hundreds of barefoot children who would be neglected, but there was no other alternative if James Bacon could not help. She did not have £130 cash. On October 18 she begged Charles Cavanagh to secure the £20 bequeathed to her by a Mrs. Ryan who had lived at the Shelbourne Hotel, and a few days later repeated the same urgent request, perhaps thinking she could use the bequest to buy time with the Dowlings.[41] The second letter to Cavanagh is her last surviving letter.

Ursula Frayne, superior in Booterstown, may have negotiated with John Ennis and James Bacon. On Sunday, October 17, in an event that was prob-

38. Letter 315, October 13, 1841, in CCMcA, 450.
39. Ibid., 450–51.
40. Letter 316, October 15, 1841, in CCMcA, 451–52.
41. Letter 317, October 18, 1841, in CCMcA, 452; letter 318 [October 1841], in CCMcA, 452.

ably planned before the Dowling ultimatum, the Reverend William Meagher of the pro-cathedral preached in St. Anne's church in Booterstown "in behalf of the Sick and Suffering Poor visited ... by the Religious Sisters of Mercy." In a newspaper article on December 15, John Ennis expressed thanks for this "impressive and successful appeal," and invited any "benevolent gentry whose charitable attention has not been duly called to the above, now almost exhausted, funds ... to forward their donations" to him, or to James Bacon, "treasurer" of the "Committee of the Catholic Church, Booterstown."[42] Evidently the Dowling debt was paid by these or similar means. The sisters were not evicted, and Mercy communities live in the Booterstown convent to this day.

In June 1838, when the sisters first moved into Booterstown and he became parish priest, John Ennis, formerly at St. Andrew's, had recalled his acquiescence, however silently, in Walter Meyler's treatment of Catherine, and had promised, "it will be atoned for."[43] Now three years later he apparently made good on his word, with James Bacon's help, and Catherine was spared the spectre of another law proceeding or eviction befalling the Dublin community.

Her other surviving letters, written earlier in October, betray no anxiety about money. Writing to Sisters of Mercy she is all encouragement and cheerfulness, though she often drops clues, usually mild ones, to alert them to her declining health. She reminds Juliana Hardman of her nursing help in Birmingham: "I am not yet quite comfortable, in the Community room or refectory. What would I not give to see my dear nurse coming with her whey," but tells her: "I kept for the last what I know you will like to hear— that every person who has seen me since my return thinks I look much better."[44] She teases the younger members of the Birr community: "Why do they never write a line to their grandmother?" Only at the end of this mostly playful, newsy letter does she pen two mutually contradictory sentences:

Pray, who gave you such a false account of me, I am just as you saw me. Pray fervently that God may grant me the grace of a holy penitential preparation and the grace of a happy death.[45]

She congratulates Teresa White and the Galway community on the profession ceremony that she and de Sales White had to miss. Since de Sales, Teresa's sister, "is my constant affectionate nurse, it was well for me, and in-

---

42. *Morning Register*, December 15, 1841.
43. Letter 92, July 3, 1838, in *CCMcA*, 147.
44. Letter 308, October 2, 1841, in *CCMcA*, 444–45.
45. Letter 310 [October 4, 1841], in *CCMcA*, 446–47.

deed I am a troublesome child. I have felt the last heavy days very much—great increase of cough. Thank God this mild day has revived me." She adds at the end: "I must try to write a few lines to my grandchildren."[46] To Mary Joseph Joyce, one of the two just professed in Galway, she is full of encouragement: "What a sweet and blessed union you have formed . . . going hand in hand with your Divine Redeemer. . . . May He grant you every grace and blessing, and make you one of His dearest and best beloved."[47]

Slowly the "grandmother"—who often called herself this, in relation to the newest members of each foundation—is making herself dispensable to those she loves and who love her. Saying her farewells in the gentlest way she knows how, affirming their goodness, and receding from their need for her presence. Cecilia Marmion in Birmingham—who regretted that she "tore [Catherine's] last dear letters, they were so kind and amusing"—says Catherine told her she was "stronger though getting thin," and believed she would "be a bony old woman."[48]

Only to Frances Warde is she somewhat more straightforward. On October 4 she tells her of the cemetery now laid out in the Baggot Street garden, suggesting (in a comment that is ironic in hindsight) that the consumptive Justina Fleming will be the first to be buried there. She admits:

I would indeed like much to go to you—if I could do so without a journey of 80 miles. If ever any poor creature got—what is called a surfeit [of traveling]—Irish & English—I have.

Singing just beside me or all the noise they make in the Community room [damaged, illegible words] at my hour of retiring would not [disturb] me, tho' close to them, but the sound of a carriage's wheels rouses me at once—I have but little appetite.

She closes the letter with a request: "You will not forget your ever affectionate M. C. McAuley."[49] In a later letter to Frances, the one about "mistakes" in the Rule, she says:

I have felt the last bad change in the weather very much. Father O'H brought your affectionate note. I humbly hope I am done with traveling for some time. If ever any poor sinner got a surfeit of it I have.

Then, in what is probably a postscript to this letter, she expresses sorrow over Andrew Fitzgerald's present illness (he was seventy-eight), and tells

46. Letter 311, October 7, 1841, in *CCMcA*, 448.
47. Letter 312 [October 7, 1841], in *CCMcA*, 448.
48. Mary Cecilia Marmion to Mary Vincent Whitty, November 21, 1841 (Archives, Sisters of Mercy, Brisbane, Australia).
49. Letter 309 [October 4, 1841], in *CCMcA*, 445–46.

Frances: "I have just received your welcome letter. How grateful I ought to be for all your anxiety. We shall meet again, please God, but not at present."[50] Or probably ever again in this life. This is Catherine's last extant letter to any Sister of Mercy. There may have been others, perhaps too fragile to survive the personal handling, folding, and pocketing they probably received.

Catherine became bedridden about October 29, but apparently very few, if any, of her close acquaintances sensed or admitted that she was actually dying. A certain ignorance of the facts, with some measure of denial, appears to have limited their grasp of the situation. Even when she was anointed by Redmond O'Hanlon on Monday night, November 8, those at Baggot Street felt that the anointing, "without the usual Ceremony," was "more to hasten her recovery than that she was thought in immediate danger."[51] Elizabeth Moore in Limerick had been "sent for," apparently by de Pazzi Delany who needed her support.[52] Even Elizabeth was "full of hope till Wednesday morning [November 10] about 11 o'clock ... had I then known what I since heard, I would not have been so unprepared for the shock." As she discovered, Catherine had all along known the end was near:

She was herself well aware she was dying for the last six months & since her return from Birmingham cautiously avoided anything like business; it is only by her acts we can judge of her mind. She was perfectly silent as to what she thought, arranged all her papers etc., about a month or six weeks since & said to Sr. Teresa [Carton] on leaving the parlor that now they were ready.[53]

Catherine saved whatever documents she had from Rome, all the financial papers from Charles Cavanagh, all the building deeds and construction agreements, even one poem she had transcribed.. But she apparently destroyed, perhaps to preserve confidentiality, all the letters she had in her possession from Sisters of Mercy.

Torn between sharing her realization of her approaching death with those she loved, and sparing them what she evidently felt would grieve them, Catherine chose the latter:

Cautious as she was from bringing herself into notice unnecessarily in Health she was still more so in sickness; waiting on herself even in her last agony, preserving to the last moment the same peace & serenity of mind which so eminently distin-

50. Letter 314, October 12, 1841, in *CCMcA*, 449 and its note 61 referring to Carroll, *Life*, 427.
51. Moore to Doyle, November 21, 1841, in *CMcATM*, 256.
52. Mary Elizabeth Moore to Mary Angela Dunne, December 10, 1841, in *CMcATM*, 257.
53. Moore to Doyle, November 21, 1841, in *CMcATM*, 255.

guished [her] through Life, omitting not an iota of what was essential, and totally disregarding all but what was of moment.[54]

Everyone, even those in the foundations, knew that Catherine was very ill, but as Mary Ann Doyle and the Tullamore community put it: "They heard she was ailing, breaking down fast, but it would appear as if they never contemplated death in reference to her at all." The Institute was "still in its infancy and, as it were, but rudely formed," and they "almost thought she could not, would not die so soon."[55]

In the afternoon of November 10, Ursula Frayne, who had come from Booterstown to be one of those who sat up at night, sent all the foundations the first, short official word that Catherine was "past hope of recovery":

With feelings of the deepest and most bitter regret it devolves on me to announce to you that our very dear and much beloved Revd. Mother is considered to be past hope of recovery.

May Almighty God in His Infinite Mercy prepare us all for the heavy affliction that awaits us.[56]

These letters could not have reached their destinations until at least November 11 or 12.

Sometime during the night of November 10–11, Catherine asked Teresa Carton for brown paper and twine. She then wanted Teresa to take the bundle to the fire in the kitchen, "and when it blazed strong to put the parcel in it and turning her back to it remain till it was quite consumed." Fearing the dark kitchen "where the cockroaches would be crawling about her," as well as the "prohibition under obedience," Teresa hesitated.[57] So Catherine sent for Mary Vincent Whitty, inquiring first whether Elizabeth Moore was "out of the way, as the only one she supposed would venture to open the Parcel."[58] Mary Vincent took the bundle and burned it.

They all soon learned that the package contained Catherine's "boots," her worn-out handmade shoes. Only many years later—sometime in the 1850s, and on the advice of Vincent Grotti, a Passionist priest, who apparently encouraged this intrusion into Catherine's privacy—did Mary Vincent reveal that the parcel also contained instruments of corporal penance that she assumed Catherine had used.[59] Clare Augustine Moore, writing

54. Ibid.
55. TA, in *CMcATM*, 75.
56. Letter 319, November 10, 1841, in *CCMcA*, 453.
57. CAM, in *CMcATM*, 216.
58. Moore to Doyle, November 21, 1841, in *CMcATM*, 255.
59. CAM, in *CMcATM*, 216.

after this date, emphatically disapproved of Mary Vincent's revelation, whatever its truth:

She hinted to me of a haircloth, but as I could not approve of a breach of trust under any circumstance, I asked her no questions. She told Fr. Vincent, the Passionist, she saw a discipline. However that be, she returned to the infirmary, was asked if she had done as she was required, answered in the affirmative, and received the thanks of her dying Superior.[60]

Earlier in her "Memoir" Clare Augustine mentions—again based on the reports of others—a haircloth and another instrument of penance she thinks Catherine used:

Besides the internal abscess [apparently related to the tuberculosis] she had a hideous ulcer on the lower part [of] her back, brought on by the use of haircloth and a large chain. This she had concealed. Her brother, how I know not, became aware of it and wanted to see it, which she refused to allow, but consented to let the Sister [Teresa Carton] who slept with her in the infirmary dress it. She told me it was almost as large as the palm of her own hand, with green matter in the middle.[61]

Exactly why Catherine felt the need, if she did, and perhaps only in the last months or year of her life, to use instruments of penance is a question that ought never have been raised, and its answer will probably never be known. Her use of them, which would have been undertaken only with the approval of Redmond O'Hanlon, her confessor, was contrary to all the advice she had ever given to her community about mortification, at least so far as the written evidence indicates. Repeatedly she had advocated small, inconspicuous acts of mortification,

for example, in the Refectory, saying that they ought never let any meal pass without denying themselves something (being careful not to injure their health) and that these mortifications were often of far greater value before God, and caused Him to bestow more abundant graces, than rigid austerities which might spring from, or occasion vanity.[62]

In the Rule, she wrote no chapter on mortification, though self-denial of an ordinary sort is implied in many chapters, including "The Perfection of Ordinary Actions," where she says plainly: "The perfection of a religious

---

60. Ibid. See also CMcATM, 339 and 385 n. 11. A 1911 affidavit by Mary Liguori Keenan, attesting to Mary Vincent Whitty's conversation with Vincent Grotti, is preserved in MCA. Liguori Keenan entered in 1856 and was one of Mary Vincent Whitty's novices.

61. Ibid., 215. The ulcer on Catherine McAuley's back may have been simply a bad bedsore. If there were a "chain" involved, it would not have burned in the parcel. Why, if it existed, was it not found afterwards, by someone, somewhere?

62. BA, in CMcATM, 111–12.

soul depends, not so much on doing extraordinary actions, as on doing extraordinarily well the ordinary actions and exercises of every day."[63]

For Catherine the "purest intention of pleasing God" was the essential. "Without this, the most laborious duties of the Institute, the greatest austerities, the most heroic actions and sacrifices are of no value . . . while on the contrary, actions the most trivial when accompanied by it become valuable and meritorious of Everlasting Life."[64] In general, she believed that "God asks for our heart," not for extraordinary deeds, and "we must offer it to be mortified, crucified and humbled. Do we offer it generously to God, or do we not rather seek to shelter it from whatever might afflict it."[65]

The last day of Catherine's human life approached. She was sixty-three. Mary Vincent Whitty was one of those who nursed her. Because she felt an obligation to keep Cecilia Marmion, the mistress of novices still in Birmingham, informed of Catherine's condition, she wrote an almost daily series of letters for over a week, occasionally giving hourly descriptions of what occurred.

At nine o'clock in the morning on November 11, Mass, with Redmond O'Hanlon presiding, was celebrated in Catherine's infirmary room, and she received Communion. "All were present with white cloaks & lighted tapers—she wished for this." The sisters from Kingstown and Booterstown had come, and each sister received "her blessing and a parting advice." When asked to bless the absent superiors and their foundations:

She went over every name—saying, oh, I remember them all—May God bless them—May the Holy Ghost pour down His choicest blessings—Make them truly good Religious—May they live in Union & Charity & May we all meet in a happy Eternity.[66]

Elizabeth Moore recalled that "her first and last injunction to all was to preserve union and peace amongst each other—that if they did they would enjoy great happiness such as that they would wonder where it came from."[67]

In recounting the above scene, Mary Austin Carroll says that Catherine said, "My legacy to the Institute is charity."[68] Not only was Carroll not present, but for Catherine to speak of *her* "legacy" to the Institute would have been entirely out of keeping with her estimate of herself and

63. Rule 5.1, in *CMcATM*, 300.   64. Rule 5.3, in *CMcATM*, 300–301.
65. *PS*, 16–17.
66. MVWL [November 11, 1841], in *CMcATM*, 242.
67. Moore to Doyle, November 21, 1841, in *CMcATM*, 256.
68. Carroll, *Life*, 435.

her view of God's role in the Sisters of Mercy. She would not have thought of herself as having a "legacy," as such, to give or leave—advice, yes, about union and charity, the essence of their life together that underlay all their desired mercifulness, but no self-referential endowment. However, unhistorical claims have a way of perpetuating themselves.

Each goodbye must have been painful to the recipient, none more so than to the twenty-year-old Camillus (Teresa) Byrn, Catherine's godchild and adopted daughter since she was a baby. Camillus had professed her vows on May 4, 1841. As she approached the bedside, Catherine told her "to kiss her and go away, that she would see her again, as if to prevent her from weeping."[69] And to prevent Catherine's own weeping? In 1846, Camillus went to New York City, as part of the founding group. She lived forty more years, dying in Baltimore, a servant to urchins, prison convicts, and whoever was sick or poor and crossed her path.[70]

At noon Catherine's brother, James, and her sister-in-law, Frances, came, with their young daughters Eleanor and Emily. To James, she said: "'Tis come to a close." When he asked the sisters to leave the room, they did so, briefly, for she was "in great pain." The bond between brother and sister had never been severed, chiefly because, for her part, Catherine had never allowed it to be. Frances McAuley remained to the end. Fathers O'Hanlon, Walsh of Kingstown, Gaffney, and Meyler, Quin, O'Carroll and O'Grady from St. Andrew's also visited her, as did Dr. Stokes, to whom she said, "Well, Doctor, the scene is drawing to a close."[71] Myles Gaffney later recalled that her fear of death was gone: "To the sisters attending her she would often say: 'Oh! If this be death, it is very easy indeed.'"[72]

During the day Charles Cavanagh came with the text of a codicil to her will. The codicil changed nothing in the provisions of the will, but added to its list of beneficiaries the name of every professed member of the Dublin community (in Dublin, Kingstown, or Booterstown) whose name had been omitted in the will she had signed on August 20, the day she sailed for Birmingham. Catherine signed the codicil, witnessed by Charles Cavanagh and his partner Arthur O'Hagan.[73]

69. Moore to Doyle, November 21, 1841, in *CMcATM*, 256.

70. Carroll, *Leaves from the Annals*, vol. 4 (1895), 106–9.

71. MVWL [November 11, 1841], in *CMcATM*, 242, and Moore to Doyle, November 21, 1841, in *CMcATM*, 256.

72. [Myles Gaffney], "*La Regola e le Costituzioni delle Religiose nominate Sorelle della Misericordia*, Roma: 1846, The Order of Mercy and its Foundress," *Dublin Review* 22 (March 1847): 24.

73. Letter 320, August 20 and November 11, 1841, in *CCMcA*, 453–55 and 454 nn. 77–80. The only name still missing in the codicil, apparently inadvertently, is Mary Teresa Breen's.

The next day Mary Vincent Whitty wrote again to Cecilia Marmion. Midway through the letter she says of Catherine:

She begged Dr. Meyler's pardon yesterday—if she ever did or said any thing to displease him—he said she ought not to think of that now & promised, I will take care & do all I can for your spiritual children—she looked at him so pleased & said, will you—then may God help & reward you for it.[74]

Once, toward evening, while the last prayers for the dying were prayed, she said to Elizabeth Moore, who thought it might be necessary to pray "a little louder": "No occasion, my darling, to speak so loud, I hear distinctly." Afterwards, Elizabeth reflected: "I did not think it possible for Human Nature to have such self-possession at the awful moment of Death, but she had an extraordinary mind in Life and Death."[75]

Catherine gave no directions for events after her death, beyond her earlier hope that she would "be buried in the same way as poor people, in the earth."[76] When someone asked her "to name the sister whom she would like to succeed her, she answered, 'The Constitutions give the Sisters liberty of choosing for themselves, and I will not interfere.'"[77] However, not knowing exactly when she would die, perhaps thinking it might be after 9:00 P.M., and fearing that de Pazzi Delany might not think it permissible for the sisters to speak with one another after the customary night silence began, she made one request, for their sakes:

She told Sr. Teresa [Carton] . . . will you tell the Srs. to get a good cup of tea—I think the community room would be a good place—when I am gone & to comfort one another—but God will comfort them.[78]

Many later writers, again following Austin Carroll's biography (1866), speak of Catherine's asking that the sisters have "a comfortable cup of tea."[79] There is no firsthand witness or primary source for such wording. It was to be "a good cup of tea."

They were all with her from six until seven o'clock that evening. Then some of them went to supper and began Matins. But they were soon sent for. Mary Vincent says that "Mother de Pazzi, Mother Elizabeth, Srs. Magdalen, de Sales, Lucy, Martha & I were in the room." When death came, "calmly & quietly," she, the youngest among them, had the "pleasing

74. MVWL [November 12, 1841], in *CMcATM*, 243.
75. Moore to Doyle, November 21, 1841, in *CMcATM*, 256.
76. BA, in *CMcATM*, 127.
77. *PS*, 29.
78. MVWL [November 12, 1841], in *CMcATM*, 243.
79. Carroll, *Life*, 437.

though melancholy consolation" of closing Catherine's eyes and mouth.[80]

About ten minutes to eight that Thursday night, November 11, 1841, Catherine McAuley died in the front room at Baggot Street that is now called "Catherine's Room."

On Friday morning, Ursula Frayne wrote a brief announcement to the superiors of all the foundations outside of Dublin:

Our dear and much beloved Revd. Mother is gone to receive the rewards of her good works. She departed this life after receiving the last Sacraments, between the hours of 7 and 8 yesterday evening. May Almighty God strengthen us all, and enable [us] to submit with calm resignation to this heavy affliction. The Office and High Mass for the repose of her soul will take place on Monday at 11 o'clock.[81]

80. MVWL [November 12, 1841], in *CMcATM*, 242–43. "Lucy" has not been identified.
81. Letter 321 [November 12, 1841], in *CCMcA*, 455.

Epilogue

Catherine McAuley's face and hands were washed, probably with vinegar and water as was the custom. The mattress and bed linen were removed, and a check quilt was laid over the straw palliasse and pillow. Her body clothed in the full Mercy habit was then laid on the bed, to remain there in the infirmary room until Saturday or Sunday. On a small table nearby, a crucifix and two lighted wax candles were placed. At least two sisters watched by the bed through the night and the next days.

On Saturday or Sunday, November 13 or 14, Catherine's body was placed in a plain wooden coffin. Later Mary de Pazzi Delany removed Catherine's cincture from the coffin and replaced her large rosary and crucifix with a smaller rosary and crucifix. The silver ring of her profession of vows was also removed from her left finger, to be given in time to another, newly professed sister. The parchment of Catherine's vows may have been placed in her clasped hands at this time. Then, at night, the black veil was drawn over her face, and the coffin was probably closed.

About half-past eight the coffin was taken to the chapel and placed in the center, on a catafalque covered with black drapery. Tall lighted candlesticks were set beside it, and the community then prayed Vespers for the Dead. Catherine's coffin remained in the chapel until Monday morning.[1]

On Sunday, the cemetery in the garden behind the convent was consecrated by her friend Dr. William Kinsella, bishop of Ossory, at Archbishop Murray's request. Dr. Murray had visited Catherine on Saturday, Novem-

---

1. *Baggot Street Book of Customs*, 113–15. Contrary to the custom as stated in this 1869 publication, Catherine McAuley's silver ring was removed before her burial. It was later given to Mary Juliana (Ellen) Delany, Mary de Pazzi's sister, who entered the Baggot Street community on August 15, 1841, professed her vows on March 19, 1844, and died in Belfast in 1900. It is now on exhibit in the Heritage Room of Mercy International Centre, Baggot Street. The family name is spelled both Delany and Delaney in early Mercy records, but their father spelled it "Delany" in County Laois records. On Saturday, November 13, Mary Vincent Whitty says that Catherine's body "is to be put in the coffin tonight and brought to the choir where she will remain until Monday." MVWL [November 13, 1841], in *CMcATM*, 244.

ber 6.[2] The contents of their last conversation were, understandably, not recorded. He was now seventy-three, ten years older than Catherine, and in the course of the following week became "too ill . . . to officiate himself" at the consecration or to preside at the Solemn Office for the Dead and the Requiem Mass on Monday morning, November 15.[3] Dr. Kinsella spoke to the community after the consecration ceremony, but Mary Vincent Whitty admitted: "I cannot tell you what he said for indeed I can only think of our dear dear Parent for she was truly such to each of us."[4]

At the liturgies on Monday, apparently William Kinsella presided, and he may also have preached. The other bishops present, according to newspaper and other accounts, were Dr. Michael Slattery (archbishop of Cashel), Dr. Frances Haly (Kildare and Leighlin), Dr. George Browne (Galway), and probably Dr. Michael Blake (Dromore) and Dr. John Murphy (Cork).[5] Some sixty unnamed priests also attended. Redmond O'Hanlon, the long faithful guardian and confessor, sang the High Mass, assisted by the two vicars general of the archdiocese: Dean Walter Meyler and the Very Reverend William Yore of St. Paul's parish. The deacon was Paul Far-

2. MVWL [November 12, 1841], in *CMcATM*, 243.

3. BA, in *CMcATM*, 128.

4. MVWL [November 14, 1841], in *CMcATM*, 244–45.

5. Apparently, according to the *Catholic Directory* (1843), 386, the synod of Irish bishops was scheduled to meet in Dublin on November 15–20. Discovering who presided at Catherine McAuley's Solemn Office and Requiem, what bishops were present, and who, if anyone, preached encounters the many discrepancies in the sources. The obituary in *Freeman's Journal* (November 16, 1841) and the "Miscellaneous Registry" of the *Catholic Directory* (1843), 387, say that Dr. Haly "presided" and that Archbishop Slattery was "present." Mary Vincent Whitty says Dr. Haly and Dr. Browne were present (*CMcATM*, 245). Elizabeth Moore does not mention who was there (*CMcATM*, 256), nor do the obituaries in other Dublin newspapers or the *Tablet* (December 25, 1841).

However, in 1868, when she added to her life of Catherine McAuley, Clare Moore said: "Bishop Kinsella officiated, being assisted by the aged Bishop Murphy of Cork, Right Revd. Dr. Blake of Dromore, Right Revd. Dr. Browne of Galway and about sixty of the Clergy" (BA, in *CMcATM*, 128). Harnett's *Life* (1864) says: "Dr. Kinsella presided . . . with four other bishops" (198).

In her *Life*, Carroll, who like others gives the wrong date (November 13) for the requiem, says there were "five bishops," with "Dr. Kinsella, Bishop of Ossory, presiding" (438). In *Leaves from the Annals*, vol. 2 (1883), 370, she attributes the following to Liguori Gibson, who was present: "Archbishop Slattery, Bishops Ryan and Haley [sic]; the crowd so great that the forty Sisters . . . were obliged to retreat to the gallery; here they listened to Bishop Kinsella, who . . . expatiated on the virtues of his cherished friend." Burke Savage, *McAuley*, 380, says there were "five bishops" and that "Dr. William Kinsella . . . presided and preached." Degnan, *Mercy*, 347, says "Bishop Kinsella . . . officiated." Bolster, *Catherine McAuley*, 113, also says "Bishop Kinsella . . . presided."

In the end it seems fair to conclude that Dr. Kinsella presided (as he had at the consecration of the cemetery). He knew Catherine McAuley better than Dr. Haly, was in the same ecclesiastical province (Dublin) as Haly, but was senior to him. Though he is infrequently mentioned, and not at all in November 1841, one can imagine that Dr. Blake attended. On November 13, 1841, he wrote a long letter about Catherine's death to Elizabeth Moore. It appears in at least two of the early biographical manuscripts, BA and Lim, in *CMcATM*, 125–26 and 190–91.

Dr. Kinsella preached at the consecration of the cemetery on Sunday, November 14, and perhaps at the funeral on November 15 or at the one-month anniversary Mass at Baggot Street. John Ryan scheduled an anniversary Mass in Limerick on December 9. MVWL [November 16, 1841], in *CMcATM*, 246.

rally, S.J., who in recent years had occasionally served as chaplain of the House of Mercy; the subdeacon was William O'Callaghan (O'Calahan?), a Discalced Carmelite priest.[6] As Mary Vincent Whitty wrote: "The Priests I think look upon her death as an universal loss."[7] One imagines the presence of John Hamilton and James Maher, and possibly Andrew Fitzgerald. There is no mention of James McAuley and his family, though this does not mean they were absent. At the end of the Requiem Mass, the clergy and the sisters with their "white cloaks on & lighted tapers" followed the coffin to the garden cemetery where it was buried, a small white wooden cross marking the grave.[8]

Elizabeth Moore of Limerick was there, as was Teresa White of Galway. As soon as Teresa heard by post that Catherine was dying—from her sister de Sales, who was nursing Catherine, or from Ursula Frayne—she set out for Dublin. The journey by coach would have taken at least thirteen or fourteen hours, and the trip partly by canal was no faster. A reason for coming, less important than her great love, was evidently the fact that Catherine had initially intended her to be the superior in Galway only temporarily, until Catherine Leahy was ready to assume that responsibility. But whether or when she was to return to Dublin had apparently never been clarified. The question was not answered, for Teresa arrived at Baggot Street after midnight on Thursday, November 11. Forty years later, now in Clifden at the western edge of Connemara where she had founded a new Mercy community in 1855, she expressed the sorrow of that night:

I saw her in death, and was one of those who placed her in her coffin.

I . . . came to Dublin hoping to see and speak to her for the last time; but she had departed four hours before I arrived, and I never felt such grief before or since. I cried for many hours without ceasing.[9]

Nothing in the extant primary sources indicates that the superiors or any sisters from Tullamore, Charleville, Carlow, Cork, Birr, Wexford, or Naas came earlier to visit Catherine or attended her funeral. Elizabeth Moore says: "None of the old Sisters were with her but Mother de Pazzi, Sr. M. Magdalen [Flynn], and your humble servant."[10] The presence of one or other of them may simply have been unrecorded, though that seems very unlikely. Ursula Frayne's letter of November 10 would not have reached

---

6. These names and roles are given in some of the obituaries cited in note 5 above.
7. MVWL [November 12, 1841], in *CMcATM*, 243.
8. MVWL [November 16, 1841], in *CMcATM*, 245.
9. Carroll, *Leaves from the Annals*, vol. 1 (1881), 49–50, quoting an undated letter from Teresa White.
10. Mary Elizabeth Moore to Mary Angela Dunne, December 10, 1841, in *CMcATM*, 257.

them until November 11 at the earliest, and her second letter, giving the time of the funeral, might not have reached some of them until Sunday or the day of the funeral itself. Those in England could not have come. As for the others, there may well have been an unwritten understanding that they would not travel to one another's funeral and burial, given the long distances and the difficulty and expense of travel. Otherwise, it would be difficult to account for the apparent absence of so many of the leaders of the Mercy communities in Ireland: Mary Ann Doyle, Angela Dunne, Clare Moore (still in Cork), Aloysius Scott, Josephine Trenor (Naas), and Mary Teresa Kelly (Wexford).

In particular, what of Frances Warde? Her bishop, Francis Haly, came for Catherine's requiem. Perhaps she could have traveled from Carlow with him, or with James Maher, who more than likely was among the sixty priests who came that morning. Was her shock or sorrow too great, or did she refrain, in view of some understanding?[11]

Mary Austin Carroll claims that when Catherine learned, during her last days, that de Pazzi Delany had sent for Elizabeth Moore, she asked: "Sister, have they sent for my child?" meaning Frances. "Receiving a negative reply," she "said nothing." Whether this is an accurate report one cannot know.[12] On November 13, Mary Vincent Whitty makes a poignant comment which may indicate the extreme suddenness with which Catherine's final hours overtook both her and Frances: "Some of Mother Frances's notes remain unopened."[13] There is, of course, the possibility that Frances did visit Catherine sometime in October or early November and that her visit, with whatever mutual understanding they reached about the future, is simply unrecorded by anyone.

In the collection of manuscripts of retreat instructions in the years 1832–1834, Catherine apparently commented, at least twice, on the place of the individual in the larger picture and history of the community—the community which "is not our own work but God's, who could cause the Institute to be formed and to exist without our being created":

11. Some feeling about Frances Warde existed at Baggot Street, possibly only in de Pazzi Delany, who was severely affected by the prospect of Catherine's dying. This attitude, perhaps unconscious, went back to the years when Frances "was always with Revd. Mother, even when a Novice, so that some little feeling was excited as she never took her turn in the duties which the other Novices had." But as Clare Moore explains, Catherine needed Frances's outgoing manner and business acumen: "I remember some complained to Revd. Mother, but I believe it was necessary she should attend to other business, for Mother M. Ann was of such a retiring disposition that she could not bear to see strangers." CML, in *CMcATM*, 98. Catherine visited Carlow, usually en route from somewhere else, but these visits were less frequent than her visits to Tullamore, also generally occasioned by her travel elsewhere.
12. Carroll, *Life*, 433–34. Healy, *Frances Warde*, 48, 134–35, speculates on this situation at some length.
13. MVWL [November 13, 1841], in *CMcATM*, 244.

Let us not therefore suppose, however virtuous, talented or useful we may be in the community, that our loss would be felt even for a moment. After we are gone, everything will go on, no duty will be omitted, just as if we had never existed. . . .

We should . . . remember, whether we are noticed or not, the time will come in a few years, when we & our actions will be forgotten & unknown.[14]

Though almost two centuries have passed since Catherine made this last prediction, it has not been true in her case. She and her actions are not "forgotten and unknown." However, implicit in her words was, it appears, another hope that was fulfilled: "Everything will go on . . . just as if we had never existed"—though not without God's continuing creation, as she would have contended, nor without her own initial agency, as she would have declined to acknowledge.

Mary Ann Doyle continued her work among the afflicted in Tulla-more, founded a community to do the same in Kells (1844), then went to assist Catherine Locke in the founding in Derry (1848), from which a community was sent to the poor Irish Scots in Dundee, Scotland (1859). She died in Derry on September 11, 1866, a frail and sickly invalid, but still the cheerful spiritual center of that community.[15]

Angela Dunne remained in Charleville until her death on November 12, 1863, at age seventy-five. She and the community served, as best they could, through all the worst ravages of the Great Famine, nursed victims in the fever hospital in its aftermath, and sent two sisters to nurse in the Crimea in 1854. In 1866 the community sent sisters to Bathurst, Australia.[16]

Frances Warde founded from Carlow the community Catherine had promised in Westport (1842), then led Mercy communities to Pittsburgh (1843), Chicago (1846), Providence, Rhode Island (1851), Rochester, New York (1857), Manchester, New Hampshire (1858), Portland, Maine (1873), and elsewhere. In 1851, replying to Camillus Byrn's comment on her changed appearance, she said "it was time for her now to look old and care-worn."[17] But "careworn" or not at age forty-one, she ministered in New England for another thirty-three years. She died in Manchester on September 17, 1884, beloved by the Penobscot Indians of Maine, who called

14. "Instructions of Revd. Mother M. Catherine McAuley, 1832, 1833, 1834," 89–90 and 180 (MCA); and corresponding passages in Degnan, ed., *Retreat Instructions*, 78 and 170.

15. Bonaventure Brennan's *Mary Ann Doyle* is a well researched full-length biography. See also Dolores Walsh, *Grow Where You Are Planted: A History of Tullamore Mercy Sisters, 1836–1996* (Ferbane: Brosna Press, 1996); CMcATM, 37–40; and TA, in CMcATM, 65–76.

16. Accounts of the Crimean experience of the Charleville sisters were written by Mary Francis Bridgeman, Mary Aloysius Doyle and Mary Joseph Croke. See *The Crimean Journals of the Sisters of Mercy, 1854–56*, edited by Luddy.

17. Mary Camillus Byrn to Mary Ann Doyle, Easter 1851, Archives, Sisters of Mercy, Northern Province, Bessbrook, Newry, Northern Ireland.

her the "Great Mother." Two years earlier, still urged on by the example of Catherine McAuley, she wrote: "How full of joys and deep sorrows my life has been, none can tell. It is a long time in which much good could have been accomplished, and I fear much neglected."[18]

Clare Moore went back to Bermondsey in December, founded at least eight more Mercy communities in England, nursed the blind and dying Thomas Griffiths (1847) and the dying Peter Butler (1848), served as a nurse in Scutari during the Crimean War, and in countless ways assisted Thomas Grant, the first bishop of Southwark (1851–1870). She died on December 14, 1874, of pleurisy aggravated by exhausting trips to Eltham, where the community had assumed responsibility for a deplorably mismanaged industrial school for "25 neglected looking girls."[19] As she wrote, "We have been obliged to take from our own barely sufficient quarter's income almost half ... to buy necessary furniture ... clothing for the poor children ... bedcovering and food, besides begging three months' credit from butcher, baker, grocer, etc."[20]

Elizabeth Moore returned to Limerick three days after Catherine McAuley's burial, taking with her Catherine's cloak and one of her prayerbooks. She remained superior there until 1862, nursing cholera victims in two hospitals during the epidemics that struck in 1849 and again in 1854. She founded twelve houses from Limerick, including Glasgow in 1849 and Edinburgh in 1858. She died on January 19, 1868, evidently of "congestion of the heart and liver" and a final paralyzing stroke.[21]

Teresa White went back to Galway, and then, in 1855, deeper into the poverty and desolation of Connemara. She died in the Mercy convent in Clifden on October 10, 1888, at that time the oldest living Sister of Mercy who had been an early associate of Catherine McAuley. In 1881 she described Catherine's voice and manner as if she could still see her:

There was something about her so kind yet so discerning that you would fancy she read your heart. If you came to speak to her on the most trifling matter, although occupied with the most important affairs, she would instantly lay all aside and give

18. Typescript, Frances Warde to Mary Austin Carroll, January 27 [1882] (MCA). The original letter, once said to be in the Archives, Sisters of Mercy, Wexford, Ireland, is now said to be no longer there. Healy's *Frances Warde* is a full-length biography. For shorter treatments see *CMcATM*, 217–25, and CA in *CMcATM*, 225–34.

19. See Sullivan, ed., *The Friendship of Florence Nightingale and Mary Clare Moore*. For shorter studies, see Penny Roker, "M. Mary Clare Moore, RSM," in *English Catholic Heroines*, ed. Joanna Bogle (Leominster, England: Gracewing, 2009), 213–29, and *CMcATM*, 77–84.

20. *CMcATM*, 31–32, quoting the "Bermondsey Annals (1874)" (AIMGB). See also Sullivan, ed., *Friendship*, 174–75.

21. "Limerick Annals," vol. 2, 254 (ASB). For essays on Elizabeth Moore, see Courtney and O'Connor, *Sisters of Mercy in Limerick*, and *CMcATM*, 247–55.

you any satisfaction in her power. . . . I feel very sad to have outlived her and all my early friends.[22]

Aloysius Scott died of tuberculosis in Birr on May 31, 1844. With her community she had created a school for over four hundred fifty poor children and had somehow restored a measure of spiritual peace to that afflicted town, though not without great cost to her own health. The historian Ignatius Murphy claimed: "The fact that the Mercy Sisters were newcomers to Birr and untouched by the controversies of the previous fifteen years undoubtedly helped"—as did, it would seem, their willingness to trudge through rain and mud to cabins in the country.[23]

Juliana Hardman was superior in Birmingham for thirty-five years. She died on March 24, 1884, at age seventy, having founded at least nine new communities or works of mercy, including a larger House of Mercy, a new orphanage at Maryvale, convents in Nottingham and Wolverhampton, and several poor schools in Birmingham. John Henry Newman corresponded occasionally with her, sometimes celebrated Mass in the convent, and knew well the new Mercy orphanage in the old Oscott College building in Maryvale. He once sent £4 to Juliana "if she will kindly accept it for the enlargement of your Poor School House."[24]

Josephine Warde, Frances's older sister, carried on as superior in Cork until 1857, and then for two more six-year periods until her death on December 15, 1879. With the Cork community she founded the convent in Sunderland, England (1843); food distribution during the Famine; Mercy Hospital in Cork, the first Mercy-sponsored hospital in Ireland (1857); and a new and enlarged House of Mercy (1863).[25] In 1871 the community assumed responsibility for the workhouse hospital of the Cork Union. Like the poor, they too were "decimated at various times by famine fever, cholera, small-pox and consumption."[26]

22. Carroll, *Leaves from the Annals*, vol. 1 (1881) 50. See also Majella O'Keeffe, "Mother M. Teresa White, 1809–1888," in *Beyond Catherine: Stories of Mercy Foundresses* (Dublin: Mercy International Association, 2003), 92–95. This volume contains brief biographies of many early Mercy women. A full-length biography of Teresa White (1809–1888) is needed.

23. Murphy, *The Diocese of Killaloe: 1800–1850*, 164. For further treatment of Mary Aloysius Scott's life, see O'Brien, *The Sisters of Mercy of Birr and Nenagh*, 11–28.

24. John Henry Newman to "My dear Sister in Christ," May 3, 1872, Archives, Sisters of Mercy of the Union, Birmingham, England. Extensive information on Juliana Hardman is in these Archives, and in Carroll, *Leaves from the Annals*, vol. 2 (1883), 308–54. See also Barbara Jeffery, *Living for the Church . . . The Hardman Family Story* (n.p.: Sisters of Mercy, [2010]).

25. The first Mercy-sponsored hospital in the world was Mercy Hospital in Pittsburgh, founded by Frances Warde in 1847, followed by Mercy Hospital in Chicago in 1853. The next (after one in San Francisco in 1855) was St. Elizabeth's Hospital, later renamed St. John's and St. Elizabeth's, founded in London by Clare Moore and Mary Gonzaga Barrie in 1856.

26. Carroll, *Leaves from the Annals*, vol. 1 (1881), 245. This volume, 212–65, deals at length with Josephine Warde and the Cork community. See also Healy, *Frances Warde*, passim.

At Baggot Street the professed members of the community elected Mary de Pazzi Delany—Catherine McAuley's old "concert" partner—superior on December 2, 1841.[27] In fidelity to Catherine's plans, she sent the foundation to Newfoundland in 1842. In August 1843 she accompanied the foundation to Liverpool, and remained there over a month. When her three-year term at Baggot Street expired in 1844, she declined to be re-elected. Increasingly regarded as a "saint" of the Baggot Street community and a custodian of Catherine's memory, she died of a stroke on January 13, 1872.[28]

Cecilia Marmion returned from Birmingham in late December 1841, and on January 2, 1842, was elected assistant to de Pazzi and mistress of novices.[29] Elected superior of the Dublin community in 1844, she remained so until she died of malignant typhus on September 15, 1849. She worked to convene a meeting of Mercy superiors at Baggot Street in 1847–49, a project that proved unfeasible, but that eventually led to publication of the *Baggot Street Book of Customs* (1869).

Mary Vincent Whitty succeeded Cecilia, serving as the Baggot Street superior until 1855. She bought the land and initiated the building of the Mater Misericordiae Hospital in Dublin, which remains one of the great hospitals of Ireland. It opened for patients in 1861, but by then Mary Vincent, after pleading that she was at heart a missionary, was on the long sea voyage to found the Sisters of Mercy in Brisbane, Australia, where she died on March 9, 1892.[30]

Ursula Frayne accompanied the foundation to Newfoundland in May 1842, and remained there for over a year, some of it spent contending with the bishop of the colony, Dr. Michael Fleming, over aspects of the Mercy Rule.[31] She and Mary Rose Lynch then returned to Baggot Street, and in September 1845 she set out for Perth in western Australia, as the founding superior of the first Mercy community in the Southern Hemisphere. There she experienced the financial and other difficulties of dealing with an inexperienced and insecure bishop and his coadjutor. Some prelates and many laity called it "persecution." In 1857 she and two of the community moved eastward, at the invitation of Bishop James Goold, to found the first

27. "Baggot Street Chapter Book," 3 (MCA).
28. For the life of Mary de Pazzi Delany (1802–1872), see "Bermondsey Annals (1872)," vol. 2, 195–204 (AIMGB), Carroll's *Leaves from the Annals*, vols. 1–3, and materials in MCA.
29. "Baggot Street Chapter Book," 4 (MCA).
30. Mary Xaverius (Frances) O'Donoghue, *Mother Vincent Whitty: Woman and Educator in a Masculine Society* (Carlton, Victoria: Melbourne University Press, 1972) is a full-length biography. See also *Mercy Women Making History, from the pen of Mother Vincent Whitty,* ed. Kath Burke and others (Ashgrove, Queensland: Sisters of Mercy, 2001).
31. See Kathrine Bellamy, *Weavers of the Tapestry* (St. John's, Newfoundland: Flanker Press, 2006), 54–73.

Mercy community in Melbourne. The voyage, on three different ships across the Southern Ocean, took over seven weeks. In Melbourne, Ursula thrived as did the community and its works of mercy. She died of cancer on June 9, 1885.[32] Two years earlier, she had invited to Nicholson Street a sixty-two-year-old man who said he was Catherine McAuley's nephew. As soon as she saw William's face, she wept. Willie's daughter later claimed that Ursula said to him: "Oh, if I could only tell your beloved Aunt that I have found you."[33]

In Newfoundland, Mary Francis Creedon became superior in November 1843, of a community of two, her brother-in-law's sister Maria having joined. They carried on as best they could, visiting the sick in St. John's and instructing poor children in the school they had begun. Then in June 1847, Mary Joseph (Maria) Nugent died of typhus. Now Francis was the only Sister of Mercy in Newfoundland. Sisters elsewhere urged her to return to Ireland or go to New York City, where Mary Agnes O'Connor had invited her. But Francis stayed on in St. John's, working alone for ten months. Finally in 1848 others began to join her, to form a Mercy community once again and open an orphanage. In mid-1855, Francis collapsed, and died on July 15, worn out by her labors. From her lonely steadfastness, the Newfoundland congregation grew in size and zeal.[34]

Mary de Sales White became the founding superior of Liverpool in 1843. She was to have stayed there only temporarily, but became so devoted to the city's poor Irish laborers, its orphans, and those afflicted by the 1847 typhus epidemic, that she remained. In 1848 she began to suffer from a severe spinal condition, brought on, it was said, by her physical exertion in lifting and turning the dying Thomas Youens (who had typhus). Her spinal ailment, complicated by rheumatism, eventually left her paralyzed. She went briefly to Dublin for treatment, but to no avail. Having resigned as superior in July 1849, she died in Liverpool on October 5.[35]

Mary Liguori (Frances) Gibson succeeded de Sales in Liverpool. She was elected superior on July 17, 1849, and served in that capacity, except for six years, until her death on July 6, 1881. Apparently she shared Catherine

32. See Catherine Kovesi Killerby, *Ursula Frayne,* and Anne Walsh, *The Story of Ursula Frayne: A Woman of Mercy* (Mulgrave, Victoria: John Garratt, 1997).

33. Mary Catherine (Frances Teresa) McAuley to Mary Dominick Foster, November 28, 1937 (MCA).

34. Bellamy, *Weavers of the Tapestry,* provides a biography of Mary Francis Creedon and a history of the Newfoundland congregation. See also Kathrine Bellamy, *The Steadfast Woman: The Story of Sister Mary Francis Creedon* (St. John's, Newfoundland: Sisters of Mercy, n.d.).

35. Archival materials on Mary de Sales White, including the "Liverpool Annals," are now in AIMGB. See also Carroll, *Leaves from the Annals,* vol. 2 (1883), 374–88.

McAuley's sense of humor and her insistence on charity. She once wrote to a sister named Myrtle: "My dearest Evergreen of Fifty-three Years," and signed herself, "M. Liguori—not an Evergreen!" Repeatedly she wrote of charity: "Often it is more in little things than in great that we need generosity, because they are so frequent and escape our attention."[36] The Liverpool community sent out many new foundations, in England as well as to the Isle of Man and Sydney, Australia. Two of their sisters died while nursing in the Crimea: Winifred Sprey, in 1855 of cholera, and Elizabeth Butler, in 1856 of typhus.

Teresa Carton tried to carry on, remembering Catherine's last advice and assurance: "to prove to the world that her exertions for the poor" were "not for Revd. Mother's sake [i.e., Catherine's] but only for love of God, and . . . Jesus would assist her."[37] She became a choir sister by vote of the chapter held in August 1844. However, over time she became, it was said, "weak minded" and in 1865 left the Baggot Street community "under very painful circumstances." She died in 1890, some of her expenses over those years and her funeral expenses paid by the Baggot Street community.[38]

Clare Augustine Moore, the best artist and calligrapher of the Sisters of Mercy over the next forty years and probably of the nineteenth century, painted the first posthumous oil portrait of Catherine McAuley and pioneered the first collection of early biographical manuscripts about this woman she always called "Foundress." In 1856 she began teaching in a school associated with Goldenbridge, a refuge in Dublin for women prisoners about to be released, and in 1870 became supervisor of the refuge. She died at Baggot Street on October 7, 1880.[39]

Catherine's strongest episcopal, clerical, and lay supporters in the 1830s lived after her, some by only a few years. Andrew Fitzgerald, O.P., died on September 14, 1843, still president of Carlow College. William Kinsella, at age fifty, died in Kilkenny in 1845 after a brief illness. Daniel O'Connell died in 1847. Daniel Murray was "seized with total paralysis" on February 24, 1852, and died on February 26, having endured disagreements with Archbishop Cullen, and negative views of himself lodged in Rome.[40] As arch-

36. M. Aquinas Smith, "A Liverpool Pioneer in Mercy's Path," 18–19 and passim, undated typescript (AIMGB). See also Carroll, *Leaves from the Annals*, vol. 2 (1883) 374–453.

37. MVWL [November 16, 1841], in *CMcATM*, 246.

38. "Baggot Street Register" (original draft), with hand notations by Mary Genevieve Bourke (MCA). The "painful circumstances" are not identified. Choir sisters and lay sisters are discussed in chapter 11 of the present volume.

39. See short biographical sketch in *CMcATM*, 193–97.

40. See Donal A. Kerr, "*A Nation of Beggars*"? *Priests, People and Politics in Famine Ireland, 1846–1852* (Oxford: Clarendon Press, 1994), 282–309.

bishop, he had supported Catherine fully in all the ecclesiastical ways that were essential, if not always, it would appear, on other occasions when she personally wished for or would have appreciated his pastoral intervention. Yet they had much in common. As William Meagher said of Dr. Murray in his commemorative oration: "The De Sales of Ireland has passed away. The Borromeo of Dublin is no more."[41]

Michael Blake lived until March 6, 1860, still indefatigable in his advocacy and care of the poor, though now in his eighty-fifth year and "bent low by infirmity and old age," according to Dr. David Moriarity, bishop of Kerry, who preached his funeral oration.[42] He, too, was not always appreciated by Paul Cullen, with whom he disagreed on some key issues. In 1850 Archbishop Cullen wrote of him, not sympathetically, to Cardinal Fransoni in Rome: "The Bishop of Dromore is totally deaf and is not fit to govern his diocese."[43]

John Hamilton died in May 1862, as parish priest of St. Michan's, Dublin, now somewhat out of favor in the diocese, in view of his long association with Dr. Murray. He became blind toward the end, but widows, orphans, servant girls, impoverished old men, and needy priests still turned to him for almost daily help. Charles Cavanagh died in 1862 or 1863. His law partner, Arthur O'Hagan, assumed responsibility for the Baggot Street community's financial and legal affairs, apparently without evincing Cavanagh's generosity. As Mary Vincent Whitty wrote from Brisbane: "I was grieved to hear of Mr. O'Hagan's immense bill of Costs. . . . Poor Mr. Cavanagh. God will reward him for his kindness to Baggot Street for indeed he never charged in that way." She recalled the joy of his and Catherine's "countenances in olden times when trying to arrange for, and speaking over the most difficult circumstances and emergencies."[44]

Redmond O'Hanlon, O.C.D., died at St. Teresa's on February 7, 1864, in his seventy-fifth year. He had guided Catherine McAuley from the sidelines for over twelve years, and remained a faithful friend to her associates until his death. James Maher died at age eighty in Carlow-Graigue on Holy Thursday, April 2, 1874. "At his last visit to his friends in Meath," according to a memoirist, "a lady gave him a large wrapping shawl. A few days after his return to Graigue, he made two parts of it for two poor old women."[45]

41. Meagher, *Notices of the Life and Character of . . . Daniel Murray,* 7.
42. David Moriarity, "Right Rev. Dr. Blake," in *Catholic Directory* (1861), 277.
43. Larkin, *The Making of the Roman Catholic Church in Ireland,* 42.
44. Burke and others, *Mercy Women Making History,* 74–75, 79.
45. Patrick Francis Moran, "Memoir," in *The Letters of Rev. James Maher,* ed. Patrick Moran (Dublin: Browne & Nolan, 1877), xcix.

At Baggot Street, after November 15, 1841, a few tangible human objects connected to Catherine McAuley remained, prosaic reminders of her workaday life. Her thimble, her white coif, her leather cincture, the two priedieux Edward Armstrong gave her, the large keys to the front door, her hourglass, the brass candlestick in her room, prayerbooks she used, her crucifix, her work basket, her bed jacket, a few locks of her graying blonde hair—these common mementos remained.

But there was also a poem.

One poem she had transcribed, only one, was found among her papers after she died. It is based on a poetic narrative by Richard Monckton Milnes (1809–1885) of a monk's reflection on Titian's painting *The Last Supper,* which hung on the refectory wall of the Escorial in Madrid. In December 1839, Mary de Sales (Barbara) Eyre in Bermondsey had given Catherine a small handwritten book of transcriptions which contained Milnes's poem.[46] From this booklet Catherine must have made her own somewhat altered transcription of the poem. Was it the content and feeling of the poem that moved her to save it, even as she destroyed so many other letters and papers?

In the last few stanzas of Catherine's transcription (which copy almost verbatim the last four stanzas of Milnes's poem), the speaker, looking at the faces surrounding Jesus at his last meal with his friends, comments to an onlooker:

46. Richard Monckton Milnes, "A Spanish Anecdote," was evidently first published in some form in 1838 or 1839. It was later collected in *Poetry for the People and Other Poems* (London: Edward Moxon, 1840); *Poems, Legendary and Historical* (London: Edward Moxon, 1844); and *Poetical Works of (Richard Monckton Milnes) Lord Houghton,* vol. 2 (London: James Murray, 1876). Barbara Eyre copied the poem into a small notebook, noting that it was written by "R. M. Milnes." Now in MCA, the booklet bears the inscription: "For Dear Revd. Mother Mary Catherine from Sister Mary De Sales—December 23rd 1839. Convent of the Most Holy Trinity, Bermondsey." Below this, Catherine McAuley wrote: "This little Book was given by The Lady Barbara Ayre [sic] (now an humble Sister of Mercy) to her faithful attached Sister and Servant in Christ—M. C. McAuley."

Milnes may have known the Eyres socially, and may even have been among the Protestant nobility who attended the December 12, 1839, ceremony in Bermondsey at which Barbara Eyre and others were received into the Mercy community. (A member of the Church of England, using the pseudonym "Hierophilos," wrote a poem about the ceremony which was apparently published in the *Orthodox Journal,* December 28, 1839. That poem is also in the handwritten booklet Mary de Sales Eyre gave to Catherine McAuley.)

In "A Spanish Anecdote," a monk explains to "a painter of far fame" (whom Milnes, in a footnote, identifies as "Wilkie") standing near him in the Escorial the lasting effect on his personal life of the vibrancy they witness in Titian's *Last Supper.* Sir David Wilkie (1785–1841), a Scottish painter, had visited Spain in 1827–1828.

When the *Correspondence of Catherine McAuley, 1818–1841* was published in 2004, I had not yet discovered Eyre's booklet containing Milnes's poem. Therefore, in presenting Catherine McAuley's transcription (letter 322, in CCMcA, 455–56), I incorrectly suggested that the original poem might be one by William Wordsworth. Moreover, because it was difficult to tell which side of the single sheet of the autograph was the front and which was the back, I placed the last four stanzas of Catherine's transcription ahead of the first four stanzas. Having Milnes's poem in hand (it is only seven stanzas) has corrected my reading of her autograph.

Stranger, I have received my daily meal
In this good company now three score years
And thou, whoe'er thou art, canst hardly feel
How time these lifeless Images endears.

Lifeless ah no, both faith and art have given
That passing hour a life of endless zest [rest?]
And every soul who loves the food of Heaven
May to that Table come a welcome guest.

Lifeless ah no, while in my heart are stored
Sad memories of my Brethren changed or gone
Familiar faces—now not round our board
And still that silent supper lasting on.

While I review my youth, what I was then
What I am now—and you, beloved ones all
It seems as if these were the living men
and we the coloured shadows on the wall.[47]

After transcribing Milnes's last quatrain, Catherine then added her own final stanza, evidently still seeing in the faces around Jesus Christ not his first-century disciples, but the "good company" of her life, her own "beloved ones all," and the Mercy women, her sisters, now "changed" by death or "gone"—yet their "good effect" lasting beyond her own "weak efforts":

Their good effect remains unchanged by time
In every view they teach, excite—inspire
while our weak efforts always in decline
extinguish more than kindle holy fire.[48]

If there was any small, tangible token Catherine McAuley deliberately left, any little gift, this modest, borrowed poem of love and gratitude for her companions' zeal—left among the financial, real estate, and other needed papers—may have been it.

47. The changes Catherine McAuley made in these lines from Milnes's poem, as she found them in Barbara Eyre's booklet, are few. In line 22 of his poem (line 6 here) she may have changed Milnes's "rest" to "zest," which would fit the spirit of her transcription, though her lettering of this word is not fully decipherable. In line 25 of the poem (line 9 here), she substitutes "my" for "mine"; in line 26 (line 10 here) she substitutes "changed or gone" for "dead and gone"; in line 27 (line 11 here), "faces now not round" for "places vacant round"; and in line 30 (line 14 here), "you" for "ye." She also adds her own eighth (and final) quatrain.

48. The autograph of Catherine McAuley's untitled, mostly transcribed poem—which I have sometimes titled "Lifeless, ah no"—is in the archives of the Sisters of Mercy, Brisbane, Australia. At the foot of page 1, Mary Vincent Whitty wrote: "Our venerated Foundress M. C. McAuley's writing—found amongst her papers after her death. Nov. 1841. S. M. V. W."

A Note on Sources

Readers of the foregoing biography of Catherine McAuley will note that it relies principally on primary sources, but that certain supposed primary sources are used very rarely or not at all. This fact deserves some explanation, especially with respect to McAuley's sayings and instructions. The explanation hinges on which sources can be viewed as authentic, and which ones cannot, in the judgment of this biographer. Hence, this rather extended appendix.

The "instructions" and "sayings" of Catherine McAuley can be distinguished by a simple criterion: her instructions are her extended commentary on a topic—for example, God's mercy; her sayings are usually single sentences on a topic—for example, on confidence in the providence of God. Implicit in what has just been said are all the issues to be discussed here: the question of *authorship*—on what grounds can we claim that these are her sayings or instructions; the question of *accurate texts*—to what extent have her words, as we have received them, been transformed by changed vocabulary or suppression of qualifiers, context, or audience references; the question of *sources*—to what extent are the words Catherine's own original formulations, or were they transcribed from previously published works by other authors, and if so did Catherine or someone else choose the sources to be transcribed; the question of *witnesses*—did someone who lived with Catherine hear her speak these instructions and sayings, or did we receive them from an anonymous source or one who was not a witness. Related to all these questions, of course, are questions about *dates*.

My goals in recent research on these questions have been threefold: (1) to establish accurate texts of those instructions and sayings that we can confidently ascribe to Catherine McAuley—because we have a text in her own handwriting, or a transcription made by her or under her supervision of a document she evidently thought was important, or because a known witness—a contemporary of hers—said that she said these words or gave these instructions; (2) to discover the previously published sources and authors from whose writings Catherine selected instructions and sayings she made her own; and (3) to point out the dis-

tance between Catherine McAuley and some of the instructions and sayings occasionally ascribed to her.

My experience in finding the previously published sources of Catherine's
"Spirit of the Institute" essay (Alonso Rodriguez's treatise in volume 3 of *The
Practice of Christian and Religious Perfection*), her "Act of Consecration" (a prayer
found in her own prayerbook, *Devotions to the Sacred Heart of Jesus*),[1] and three
of her poems,[2] as well as my knowledge of the numerous transcribed books in
the earliest Mercy convents, has taught me that while Catherine was an engaging writer and speaker, and confidently expressed herself on many topics, she often deferred to the writings of others. She read aloud from them to the community, or transcribed them in notebooks, or had them transcribed by others, just
as she had already transcribed some of Rodriguez's three-volume work while she
was at the Presentation convent on George's Hill.

If we want to discover what indeed were her authentic instructions and sayings, we have several published and unpublished sources to consider, not all of
them of equal merit. Her own letters are the most authentic source and provide
the most authentic texts of her sayings. There we see in her own handwriting
what she said, and as she said it, if the published texts of her letters have been
accurately transcribed.

Three other published sources can be regarded as yielding numerous authentic texts of her instructions and sayings: (1) the Rule and Constitutions, which
she composed, consciously choosing or not choosing the wording in the Presentation Rule and deliberately adding her own chapters and an original paragraph;[3]
(2) the "Spirit of the Institute" essay, which is also in her own handwriting (see
above); and (3) the sayings and instructions frequently ascribed to her, often
with quotation marks, in the biographical manuscripts and letters written about
her by her contemporaries in the Sisters of Mercy—for example, by Mary Ann

1. The "Spirit of the Institute" essay (in *CCMcA*, 458–62) is an altered transcription of parts of Alonso Rodriguez's first treatise in volume 3 of his *Practice of Christian and Religious Perfection* (Kilkenny:
John Reynolds, 1806). His three-volume work was originally published in Spanish (in 1609), but was
frequently translated, into French and then English, over the next three centuries. Rodriguez's treatise
is titled "Of the End and Institution of the Society of Jesus," and Catherine McAuley primarily uses passages in chapters 5–8 of the treatise. Her manuscript called "Act of Consecration" (in Bolster's edition
of Catherine's *Correspondence*, 7–8, where the text is inexact, and in Mary Ignatia Neumann's edition of
Letters, 392–93) is an altered transcription of "An Act of Oblation" in Joseph Joy Dean's *Devotions to the
Sacred Heart of Jesus* (Dublin: Chambers and Hallagan, 1820), 267–70. Both transcriptions are discussed at
length in Sullivan, "Catherine McAuley's Theological and Literary Debt to Alonso Rodriguez," *Recusant
History* 20 (May 1990): 81–105.

2. Catherine McAuley's "Precept divine, to Earth in Mercy given" (*CCMcA*, 233–34) is an altered
transcription of a section of a poem by Helen Maria Williams, titled "Paraphrase . . . Matt. vii.12," in volume 1 of the second edition of her two-volume *Poems* (London: T. Cadell, 1791), 187–90. Catherine McAuley's "Trifles" (*CCMcA*, 457–58) is an altered transcription of various lines in a section of Hannah More's
much longer poem titled "Sensibility: An Epistle to the Honourable Mrs. Boscawen," in volume 1 of her
four-volume *Works of Hannah More* (Dublin: D. Graisberry, 1803), 85–96. Catherine McAuley's poem that
can be titled "Lifeless, ah no" is an altered transcription of Richard Monckton Milnes's poem "A Spanish
Anecdote" in volume 2 of his *Poetical Works* (see the references at the end of the Epilogue in the present
volume).

3. "Rule and Constitutions of the Religious Sisters of Mercy," in *CMcATM*, 294–328.

Doyle, Clare Moore, Mary Vincent Harnett, Clare Augustine Moore, Elizabeth Moore, and Mary Vincent Whitty.[4]

Occasionally one can also find presumably authentic sayings and instructions in the early portions of the Annals of the earliest convents, whose superiors were Catherine's contemporaries and friends.[5] They had lived with her, were her first novices, had frequent contact with her, and loved her. They and the authors of the earliest biographical manuscripts were all in a position to hear, remember, and cherish her most characteristic oral instructions and sayings.

Finally, *The Practical Sayings of . . . Catherine McAuley*, published in London by Mary Clare Moore in 1868, can be regarded as containing authentic instructions and sayings. Clare was one of Catherine's earliest associates: she entered in 1830, became superior of Cork in 1837, temporary superior of Bermondsey in 1839, and superior there in 1841. The Bermondsey Annals for 1868, written by Clare herself, describes the process of compiling *Practical Sayings*. Following her August retreat that year, Clare says, she conceived "a determination to collect even a few of the maxims and practical sayings of our revered Foundress." When she had completed the manuscript, Thomas Grant, bishop of Southwark, advised her to send it to Baggot Street "as suggestions or additions might be made which would prove useful." This she did. Living at Baggot Street in 1868 were at least three of the earliest Sisters of Mercy, Catherine's contemporaries: Mary de Pazzi Delany, Clare Moore's sister Mary Clare Augustine Moore, and Mary Aloysius Cowley. The manuscript was "returned with expressions of satisfaction, nothing was remembered additional, except the wish which our revered Foundress had expressed, that those who came on business, or even visitors to the Convent & the poor, should not be kept waiting either at the door or in the Convent longer than necessary."[6]

When *Practical Sayings* was published and sent to some of the existing foundations, several more of Catherine's contemporaries responded, affirming the accuracy of the collection. Ursula Frayne wrote from Melbourne: "How exactly dear Reverend Mother's words are noted down, I could almost fancy myself listening to her once more." Josephine Warde wrote from Cork: "I remember almost all the dear little 'sayings' of our ever loved, blessed Foundress."

One unpublished source of at least the spirit of Catherine's sayings and instructions is Mary de Pazzi Delany's handwritten manuscript, which she titled "Extracts from the Instructions of the Venerated Foundress on the observance of the holy Rule, and the objects of the Order of Mercy, given at divers times to her Religious."[7] Mary de Pazzi entered in July 1830 and lived ten years with Catherine

---

4. Their respective biographical manuscripts and letters are in *CMcATM*, 41–64, 85–129, 139–92, 198–216, 255–57, and 241–46.

5. See, for example, the excerpts from the TA and CA in *CMcATM*, 65–76 and 225–34, as well as the many original Annals in MCA and AIMGB, and in convents, congregational archives, and provincial archives elsewhere in Ireland and England.

6. "Bermondsey Annals (1868)," vol. 2, 124.

7. This manuscript is in MCA.

McAuley at Baggot Street, serving for several years as her assistant. In a letter to Clare Moore on December 8, 1868, she speaks of this manuscript, which she had apparently composed before 1868, and says she fears Clare "will be disappointed" when she receives it, for "on reopening [it] I see there is not as much of loved Mother's writing as you might expect."[8] However, while de Pazzi's manuscript does not directly quote Catherine McAuley, it explicitly alludes to her views at least six times. The manuscript is a long commentary on the chapters of the original Rule and Constitutions and frequently exhibits views and sentiments that correspond with Catherine's idealism and her practical good sense.

Before I proceed to other possible sources of Catherine McAuley's sayings and instructions, a word about the transcriptions made by the earliest Sisters of Mercy is necessary. By "transcription" I mean a handwritten copy of a previously existing book or parts of a book or a copy of a previously existing manuscript or transcription. The copy may be exact—a verbal facsimile of the parts it transcribes—or it may be more or less exact. That is, the copy may slightly alter some of the wording; it may leave out words, phrases, sentences, even paragraphs or pages; it may occasionally alter the punctuation; it may transcribe only a few parts of the source; it may sometimes insert linkages between passages taken from the source. Nonetheless, there is no mistaking that even an inexact copy is a transcription of a particular source: the argument, the sequence of topics, and the flow of the language follow the original, and much of the wording is the same.

The first Sisters of Mercy made numerous transcriptions of long portions of books, both at Baggot Street and in the earliest foundations. Catherine McAuley was a strong believer in the value of spiritual reading, public and private, and of lectures and instructions to the community. She was also modest enough to know that she too had to learn about religious life; that she was not herself, at least initially, an experienced theologian of the spiritual or religious life; and that she should be providing the community systematic instruction, not just her own developing impressions, as crucial as these intuitions ultimately proved to be. Moreover, printed books were expensive and therefore scarce at Baggot Street and in the early convents. Therefore, Catherine herself copied, for instance, parts of Rodriguez's volumes at George's Hill, and when she returned to Baggot Street she transcribed in the early morning by candlelight. Novices and other sisters at Baggot Street also transcribed books she had evidently selected.

Besides the cost of printed books, there was another motive for the numerous transcriptions one can find in the archives of the earliest convents—transcriptions that were made not just while Catherine was alive, but also in the ensuing decades. The Rule and Constitutions which she composed and her own practice in directing new sisters required that postulants make a private retreat of one month before reception of the habit, and that novices make such a retreat

---

8. Mary de Pazzi Delany to Mary Clare Moore, December 8, 1868 (AIMGB).

for two months before profession of vows.[9] These "distant" or "remote" retreats usually included prescribed, daily, private meditations. Then, in the last eight or ten days, daily oral instructions or meditations were offered to the groups preparing for reception or profession. At Baggot Street, these group meditations or instructions were regularly led by Catherine herself; in the foundations, and at Baggot Street after her death, they were often led by the mistress of novices or the superior. A version of this same pattern prevailed at the community's annual retreat (if there was no priest-director), on retreat Sunday (the first Sunday of each month), and in the three-day retreat at year's end.

The basis for both the private reflections of those on retreat and the oral instructions to groups was transcriptions. The archive of every early convent of the Sisters of Mercy contains numerous small copybooks with the title "Meditations for Retreat before Reception" or "Meditations for Retreat before Profession," as well as other titles. I have found such copybooks all over Ireland and England, and they can also be found throughout the Mercy world. Often these transcriptions were re-copied before a foundation was scheduled to depart so that the founding community would have a "starter" collection. But two characteristics mark all these transcriptions. First, the transcribers were often more interested in the content of the work than in its provenance, so the title and author of the work transcribed are usually omitted, especially in the "Meditations for Retreat." Moreover, the transcriber's name (by which one might date the transcription— for instance, to the 1830s? or the 1860s?) is only rarely given, and the handwriting often cannot be identified. The result is that present-day researchers have available to them many transcriptions, as well as multiple copies of the same transcriptions, whose dates are not always known and whose original sources have not yet been identified. Moreover, sometimes several different transcriptions were newly compiled into a single copybook. These facts are relevant to any serious study of documents of instructions said to be "of Catherine McAuley." Her intellectual and spiritual influence on the early formation of the Sisters of Mercy was enormous and long-lasting, but exactly where and how we can identify the content and the documentary location of this influence is not an easy research project.

Familiar Instructions

One supposed source of Catherine McAuley's sayings and instructions is the book *Familiar Instructions of Rev. Mother McAuley,* first published in 1888 and reprinted in a "revised" edition in 1927.[10] But to rely on this work as an authentic source is very problematic.

The editor named in the first edition of this book is the "Sisters of Mercy,

9. See Rule 20, in *CMcATM*, 315–16.

10. *Familiar Instructions of Rev. Mother McAuley,* ed. Sisters of Mercy, St. Louis, Mo. (St. Louis: Ev. E. Carreras, 1888); rev. ed. (St. Louis: Vincentian Press, 1927). Except for the front matter, the pagination and content in the two editions appear identical.

St. Louis, Mo.," but resources in the archives of the Sisters of Mercy of St. Louis, by whom the book was published, suggest that the person responsible for the publication was Mary Magdalen de Pazzi Bentley (1822–1910), superior of the St. Louis community from its founding in 1856 to 1868, and again from 1869 to 1909. Bentley entered the Baggot Street community in 1850, was sent to the New York foundation as a novice in 1851, and then to St. Louis in 1856. In her history of the first fifty years of the St. Louis foundation, Mary Constance Smith claims that before its publication "the Community had submitted" *Familiar Instructions* "to a rigid examination to prove its authenticity," though Smith does not say exactly by whom it was examined for this purpose.[11] According to Mary Isidore Lennon's biography, Bentley arranged for or commissioned the publication of *Familiar Instructions* while she was superior in St. Louis.[12]

The preface to *Familiar Instructions* says that "these Precepts have been used in manuscript form in many convents in Ireland," that a copy of the manuscript can be found in Rochester, New York (which is no longer the case), and that "one [sister] in the novitiate, Baggot Street Convent, Dublin, and who is at present a member of a Community of Sisters of Mercy in America, remembers having heard these same Instructions read from a manuscript for lecture in the novitiate, Baggot Street."[13] It is reasonable to assume that this sister is Magdalen de Pazzi Bentley, who spent thirteen months at Baggot Street before her departure for New York.

The preface also claims *not* that the instructions were composed or transcribed by Catherine McAuley, but that the manuscript "was duly examined and declared authentic, as Mother McAuley's spirit, that is, the spirit of a Religious Sister of Mercy, is breathed in every line." The preface further claims:

The editors have spared no pains to *render* these precepts of their Revered Foundress *acceptable* in every point to those who are so fortunate as to obtain a copy, and sincerely trust that all within whose sphere they come may not fail to appreciate and profit by the many beautiful, spiritual lessons, so simply and so lovingly offered by the "Saintly Foundress."[14]

It is unclear what "render" and "acceptable" mean here, and whether the rendering involved alteration of or additions to the original wording of a manuscript.

Familiar Instructions does indeed frequently convey something of the "spirit" of Catherine McAuley, and when it quotes the original words of the Rule and Constitutions she composed in the 1830s, these words are certainly hers, but I do not believe it is accurate to think that the wording of every line is her wording or in her spirit. There are several reasons for my view, one obvious and others more subtle. The obvious reason is that well over half of the contents of the book is

11. Mary Constance Smith, *A Sheaf of Golden Years, 1856–1906* (New York: Benziger Brothers, 1906), 85–86.

12. Mary Isidore Lennon, *Mother M. de Pazzi Bentley* (St. Louis: n.p., 1980), 17.

13. *Familiar Instructions* (1888), vi.

14. Ibid., emphasis added.

quotations, with or without quotation marks, from many other authors on the spiritual life, and we have no clear grounds for believing that Catherine herself selected these particular passages for transcription, that she supervised the preparation of the manuscript in question, or that it was even prepared during her lifetime. A minor but revealing point is that on page 87 *Familiar Instructions* quotes Frederick W. Faber (1814–1863), whose first notable book, *All for Jesus,* was not published until 1853—twelve years after Catherine's death and two years after Magdalen de Pazzi Bentley left Baggot Street.

The more subtle reasons for my not regarding pages 1–130 of *Familiar Instructions* as a completely reliable and authentic source for Catherine McAuley's sayings and instructions involve the organization of the book itself, the range of its quotations from other authors, and the stringency of much of its language. The book is very tightly designed: nearly every chapter quotes sentences from the original Rule and Constitutions, expatiates on the meaning of that section of the Rule, and then presents such topics as the "motives," "means," "advantages," "marks," "degrees," "practices," and sometimes "obstacles" in fulfilling this portion of the Rule. Whether this organization was in the original manuscript or added to it when the manuscript was "rendered acceptable" for publication is not known. The editor's preface to *Familiar Instructions* indicates that there was some reorganization of material in the manuscript, but that "no material alterations have been made."[15]

Beyond the authors of the sacred Scriptures, the writers directly cited in *Familiar Instructions* include, among many others, Saints Augustine, Gregory, Ambrose, Bernard, Thomas Aquinas, Teresa of Avila, John of the Cross, Ignatius Loyola, Bonaventure, Francis de Sales, Jane Frances de Chantal, Philip Neri, Mary Magdalen de Pazzi, Alphonsus Liguori, and Vincent de Paul. Other authors directly quoted include Thomas à Kempis, Balthasar Alvarez, and Alonso Rodriguez. The most frequently cited saint is Francis de Sales, followed closely, and interestingly, by Mary Magdalen de Pazzi.[16]

While I do not, at this point, claim that either of the following books is the direct source of *Familiar Instructions,* I have found in that work dozens of passages and many sequences of passages that are exact or nearly exact quotations from Alonso Rodriguez's *The Practice of Christian and Religious Perfection* (published in Spain in 1609, but available in English in Ireland, for example, in 1806), and from Alphonsus Liguori's *The True Spouse of Jesus Christ* (published in Italy in 1760 and evidently available in English in Ireland in the early 1800s).[17] Francis de Sales (1567–1622) and Mary Magdalen de Pazzi (1566–1607), among others, are not cited in Rodriguez's work because they wrote only at or after the time of its

---

15. Ibid., v.

16. Saint Teresa of Avila is cited eleven times, Saint Ignatius about eight times, whereas Saint Mary Magdalen de Pazzi is cited at least fourteen times and Saint Francis de Sales, eighteen times.

17. Rodriguez, *Practice of . . . Perfection* (Kilkenny: John Reynolds, 1806). The earliest English translation of Liguori's work that I have been able to study is Alphonsus M. Liguori, *The True Spouse of Christ; or The Nun Sanctified by the Virtues of her State,* trans. "Catholic Clergyman" (Dublin: James Duffy, 1860).

composition; but these and *all* the other writers noted above are cited in Liguori's work. However, the classic comments and explanations of the best-known saints and spiritual writers were frequently cited by many other spiritual writers. Thus the exact source of the transcribed manuscript that is said to have become *Familiar Instructions*—if there was a *single* source for the parts that elaborated on the chapters of the Rule—has not so far been identified. At present, Rodriguez and Liguori are simply strong possibilities for the sources of some of the supplementary comments the "author" or transcriber used in her commentary on the Rule.

Finally—and this is an impression based on my experience of reading texts known to have come from Catherine McAuley's hand, such as her letters, the Rule, and the "Spirit of the Institute" essay, or from her oral instructions as presented in the early biographical manuscripts written by her contemporaries—the language of much of *Familiar Instructions* does not appear to accord with Catherine's mode of thought or manner of speaking. It is often severe in its descriptions and overly focused on the actions of the superior; it is often cut-and-dried in its many numbered lists of "characteristics," "advantages," and "obstacles." Some sentiments expressed in it are indeed reminiscent of Catherine's concerns, but the manuscript from which the published book is said to have come (if it was a distinct manuscript or transcription) cannot have been one whose wording Catherine McAuley supervised, let alone composed. This manuscript is said to have been copied from one in Rochester, New York (which is now apparently no longer extant). Rochester was founded by Frances Warde from Providence, Rhode Island, in 1857, six years after Magdalen de Pazzi Bentley left Baggot Street, and the manuscript, if it ever existed in Rochester, could have come from Providence. Providence was founded in 1851, while Magdalen de Pazzi Bentley was still at Baggot Street. If the manuscript on which Bentley relied originated from one composed or transcribed by Frances Warde, in Dublin, Carlow, Pittsburgh, or Providence, we now have no means of knowing this, and as presented in *Familiar Instructions* it does not reflect the personal language of Catherine McAuley or, it would appear, of Frances Warde, Catherine's close associate. (The missing manuscript may, in fact, have come from the sisters in New York City who, early on, sent help to Rochester.)

At this point all I can say about pages 1–130 of *Familiar Instructions* is that I have no evidence that these pages were based on a manuscript prepared before November 11, 1841, by Catherine McAuley or under her supervision, or after that date by one of her contemporaries who witnessed her instructions. Therefore, except for pages 132–34, and the direct quotations from the Rule and from certain authentic sources in the "maxims" on pages 135–49 (see below), I do not regard the book as a reliable source of Catherine's sayings and instructions.

It is necessary here to comment on Mary Austin Carroll's *Life* of Catherine McAuley, first published in 1866 and frequently reprinted; and on the four volumes of her *Leaves from the Annals of the Sisters of Mercy* (1881, 1883, 1889, and 1895). In her preface to the *Life*, Carroll meticulously lays out the primary source material she received, mostly from abroad, and used (she could not travel to Ireland until 1890). Mary Hermenia Muldrey also recounts how Carroll got and used her sources.[18]

One fact stands out. Except for the original letters of Catherine McAuley in Frances Warde's possession, which Carroll could have directly seen in Manchester, New Hampshire, when she was there from 1859 to 1864, and the memoir on Catherine McAuley prepared for Carroll by Mary Camillus (Teresa) Byrn (apparently unwittingly destroyed after Carroll's death), nearly all the material Carroll used in writing the *Life* and the first three volumes of the *Leaves* was hand copied from materials in Ireland and England and mailed to her. Some of Carroll's correspondents sent firsthand personal reminiscences, and as such these have whatever accuracy can be attributed to those authors' recollections, although Carroll does not in her texts identify their particular contributions. As for other material, some of Carroll's correspondents may have accurately transcribed the material they sent her, but it is evident that others loosely copied and edited what they sent, with the consequent loss of the wording in the original documents. This is especially noticeable in the collection of Catherine McAuley's letters in the appendix of Carroll's *Life,* but it is also true of other documents she received and quoted.[19] Carroll was a diligent researcher, but she could not enjoy the benefits of modern photocopying, and her publications suffer from this disadvantage.

Consequently, to the extent that the "Maxims and Counsels" of Catherine McAuley listed in the back of *Familiar Instructions* (135–49) are drawn, for example, from Catherine McAuley's letters as presented or quoted in Carroll's works, they are usually imperfect recordings of Catherine's exact words, even in letters to Frances Warde, for which Carroll may have used only hand copies. Hence, to treat those maxims which are imperfect renditions of wording in Catherine's autograph letters as authentic sayings is not accurate.

On the other hand, some of the "Maxims and Counsels" appear to have been taken directly from *Practical Sayings* (as do pages 132–34), and thus enjoy the authenticity I have ascribed to that publication. Interestingly, by the time *Familiar Instructions* was first published (1888), Austin Carroll had already issued, in 1877 and 1878, American printings of Clare Moore's 1868 compilation, which Carroll titled *A Little Book of the Sayings, Instructions, and Prayers of the Foundress of the Sisters of Mercy, Catherine McAuley.*

However, in 1878 and 1879 Carroll began to compile her own editions of this little book to which she added "sayings" from her correspondents' copies of Catherine McAuley's letters and from other documents available to her. It is not possible, in the space here, to discuss all the problems that ensued as more and more editors over the next century and a quarter began to put out more and more editions, under various titles, that claimed to contain reliable "sayings," "maxims," or "thoughts" of Catherine McAuley even though, unwittingly, these

18. Muldrey, *Abounding in Mercy: Mother Austin Carroll,* 54–58.
19. Carroll, *Life,* 465–85.

were based on faulty transcriptions and printings or on texts of "retreat instructions" the origin and nature of which were not then understood (see below).

A study of "Maxims and Counsels" in the back of *Familiar Instructions* (pages 135–49) reveals an interesting list of sources. Among the ninety-five maxims listed, only thirteen are accurate or almost accurate quotations from *Practical Sayings;* forty-two are copied directly from the front pages of *Familiar Instructions* itself; sixteen are from Catherine McAuley's letters, though not accurately recorded; and fourteen are quoted from Carroll's *Life* (1866), though Carroll herself did not ascribe four of these to Catherine McAuley. Finally ten are so far unidentified, though some of these may be paraphrases of wording in the various notebooks of "retreat meditations," some of which were published in 1952 as *Retreat Instructions* (see below). Of those taken directly from *Familiar Instructions* itself, four are quotations from other authors, not Catherine McAuley: St. Thomas Aquinas, St. Bonaventure, St. Philip Neri combined with St. Teresa of Avila, and Frederick Faber.

One of the fourteen "maxims" taken from Austin Carroll's *Life* is a direct quotation of Carroll's combined version of Catherine's words to Richard Baptist O'Brien and to Mary Liguori (Frances) Gibson. Four of them are Austin Carroll's own words in her *Life* or a quotation from someone other than Catherine McAuley. Those who value Catherine McAuley's teachings will be particularly interested to discover that two favorite and frequently quoted "maxims" in *Familiar Instructions* are not Catherine's words at all. Grammatically, Carroll ascribes the saying "It is better to relieve a hundred impostors—if there be any such—than to suffer one really distressed person to be sent away empty" to Mary de Chantal McCann, not to Catherine McAuley.[20] And the maxim "There are things the poor prize more highly than gold, tho' they cost the donor nothing; among these are the kind word, the gentle, compassionate look, and the patient hearing of their sorrows" is Austin Carroll's own wording, which she does not ascribe to Catherine McAuley.[21]

I recognize and respect the power and tenacity of sound oral traditions, and I acknowledge that a very few of the "maxims" (in *Familiar Instructions* and other publications) for which I have found no earlier and authentic written source may indeed be oral sayings of Catherine McAuley, long remembered and treasured for their striking common sense and practical compassion. However, we cannot at the present time know of which saying, or sayings, this may be true.

Retreat Instructions

Retreat Instructions of Mother Mary Catherine McAuley was published in 1952.[22] Its title page indicates that the volume was compiled or written "by Sister Mary

20. *Familiar Instructions*, 136; in Carroll, *Life*, 331.

21. *Familiar Instructions*, 138; in Carroll, *Life*, 87.

22. *Retreat Instructions of Mother Mary Catherine McAuley*, ed. Mary Bertrand Degnan (Westminster, Md.: Newman Press, 1952).

Teresa Purcell, 1834–1853, Dublin and Tullamore," and that it was "edited by Sisters of Mercy, Albany, New York." The actual editor was Mary Bertrand Degnan of the Albany community; her initials "S. M. B." appear at the end of the foreword.[23]

Unlike *Familiar Instructions*, we know a great deal, though not everything, about the composition of *Retreat Instructions*. Hence the volume can be regarded as a more reliable source of Catherine McAuley's instructions, but with very important cautions and limitations. The introduction of the volume is said to have been written by "a Sister of the Institute [Sister M. Teresa Purcell]."[24] Mary Teresa (Bridget) Purcell entered the Baggot Street community on February 2, 1834; received the habit on July 3, 1834; and professed her vows on May 27, 1836 in Tullamore, as a member of the Tullamore founding community.

The introduction makes a number of claims about the instructions which are very problematic when viewed against other available information. In this introduction, and in the manuscript on which it is said to be based, and which is now in the Mercy Congregational Archives in Dublin (MCA), the author says, among other things: "The following instructions were given by our Venerated Foundress extempore at lectures and were written from memory afterwards by the sisters." "Most of these instructions were given to novices in successive years during their remote preparation for profession." "As [they] were given at different times on similar occasions, they are repetitious," but "differ in details." In addition, the author states:

In writing up the instructions, some sisters attempted to arrange them according to subject; others merely recorded them under date after hearing them. We [i.e., the compiler of the manuscript or the compilers of the instructions included in it] set them all down as they were written by the different sisters. . . . We attempted no further arrangement and made no corrections.[25]

This introductory commentary raises many serious questions, especially if we interpret it as written, as it says, by "a sister of the Institute" who was in a position to know the origin of the manuscript instructions she presents. When one examines *Retreat Instructions* one cannot see how it could be humanly possible for Catherine McAuley to have presented these instructions completely "extempore"—in a style of language and thought quite different from her own—with no previously prepared text at hand, or how novices or others could then have "written [them] from memory afterwards," again with no previously written text at hand. The instructions are simply too detailed and too dependent on the views of previously published spiritual writers to allow us to believe that Catherine McAuley presented them orally without notes or that the sister-scribes wrote them down afterwards from memory.

Four further and crucial facts complicate our reaching a clear understanding of the origin of the published *Retreat Instructions*: there are many copybooks

23. Ibid., 13.   24. Ibid., 16.
25. Ibid., 16–18.

of "retreat meditations" in archives throughout Ireland and England, as well as elsewhere in the Mercy world; a manuscript in the Mercy provincial archives in Bessbrook, Northern Ireland (where many of the Tullamore and Derry archival documents are now located) is identical to the first portion of the published *Retreat Instructions;* other "retreat" manuscripts—in Bermondsey (London), Dublin, Birmingham, Liverpool, and Naas—are also identical to portions of the published *Retreat Instructions;* and many sections of the published *Instructions* either quote from or are clearly based on the language and analysis found in the writings of Alonso Rodriguez, Louis Bourdaloue, and Michel-Ange Marin, or other spiritual writers not yet identified.

All these facts indicate that the manuscripts on which the published *Retreat Instructions* (1952) was based were not unique and were not original compositions (oral or written) of Catherine McAuley. Rather, they co-existed with, or were even preceded by, other identical manuscripts in the earliest Mercy convents. All of these manuscripts were transcriptions from, or copies of transcriptions from, some earlier published sources not yet fully identified.

My conclusions about the published *Retreat Instructions* are therefore at present fourfold: given the dates noted in the manuscript (1832–1834), Catherine McAuley gave these instructions orally using previously made transcriptions of parts of works by some earlier published author or authors, but possibly and occasionally adding her own thoughts; the sisters on retreat did not record them from memory, but rather used the transcriptions Catherine had used, and later re-copied them, perhaps adding from memory some of her additional oral comments; the manuscript is a compilation of transcriptions; and the author of the introduction, the "sister of the Institute," wrote the introduction and compiled the manuscript published as *Retreat Instructions* perhaps as late as the early 1850s (Teresa Purcell died in 1853), but certainly after the death of Catherine McAuley (1841)—whom the introduction calls "our Venerated" Foundress (an adjective never used of her before her death).

Implicit in this last conclusion is my belief that the author of the introduction was not present when these particular retreat instructions, or at least not all of them, were given. She may not have been Teresa Purcell (who entered Baggot Street in February 1834), as Degnan assumes. The manuscript in MCA on which the published *Retreat Instructions* is based does not identify in any way the "sister of the Institute." Whoever she was, she may simply have been working with the set of copybooks of retreat meditations available to her.

Mary Bertrand Degnan, the editor of the volume and a scholar whose work I admire, says of Teresa Purcell in her foreword, "While still at the motherhouse [i.e., Baggot Street], she collected notes other novices had made from Mother Catherine's instructions and at the new mission, St. Joseph's, Tullamore [in April–May 1836], she came under the foundress' personal direction in the retreat preceding profession of vows."[26] All of this is correct if we interpret the words

26. Ibid., 7–8.

"collected notes other novices had made" as Teresa's act of re-copying, or collecting re-copied transcriptions of, existing copybooks of retreat meditations to take
to Tullamore, which became common practice before founding parties set out
for new Mercy foundations.

According to the Tullamore Annals, Catherine McAuley did indeed prepare
Teresa for her profession of vows in Tullamore on May 27, 1836, and "some notes
of these precious lectures, carefully penned by Mother M. Teresa, have been preserved in this house amongst its greatest treasures."[27] But here again we ought to
understand "notes . . . penned" by Teresa Purcell as copies of retreat instructions
made by her before leaving Baggot Street or new copies of these transcriptions
made by her in Tullamore (from copies Catherine had brought with her from
Baggot Street), possibly with some of Catherine's additional oral comments inserted. The "notes" cannot possibly be Teresa's completely remembered texts of
completely extempore instructions based on no previously written texts. The introduction to the "notes" in the manuscript at MCA (and in *Retreat Instructions*)
was probably written much later, as I have argued above, possibly by Teresa Purcell, but more likely by someone else who was not familiar, as Teresa would have
been, with the exact origin of the transcriptions she was compiling into a single
manuscript.[28]

But what of the "retreat instructions" themselves, their content and the language used to express it? I can only repeat that I have found whole sections of *Retreat Instructions* that are dependent upon the thought and even the wording in
Alonso Rodriguez's *The Practice of Christian and Religious Perfection* published in
English translation in Ireland in 1806. For example, pages 47–53 and 142–45 in the
published *Retreat Instructions*—all on the vow of obedience—are a pastiche of
sentences and images on pages 210–63 of Rodriguez's treatise "On Obedience," in
volume 3 of the 1806 edition. The scattered quotation of his treatise is typical of
the way the works of spiritual writers were transcribed by the earliest Sisters of
Mercy: some sentences were transcribed exactly, others were omitted, still others

27. TA, in *CMcATM*, 67.
28. In both the published *Retreat Instructions*, and in the manuscript in MCA on which it is based,
the initials of a sister, presumably a transcriber, are given in the text, after a parenthetical comment. They
are "Sr. M. C." in the published version (page 160), whom Degnan identifies in a footnote: "Tullamore
annalist, also mistress of novices." In the handwritten manuscript the initials are "Sr. M. C. S." (page 172).
No "M. C. S." has been identified in the early Tullamore community. However, if the manuscript is a later
copy of an earlier manuscript, it is possible that the copyist mistook a cursive capital "D" for a cursive
capital "S," and that the correct initials are "Sr. M. C. D.," in which case the transcriber or copyist of at
least this much of the instructions could well be Sister Mary Clare Delamere. Mary Delamere entered
the Tullamore community in May 1836 and took the name Mary Clare at her reception on August 1, 1836.
She was indeed the first annalist of the Tullamore community until her departure for Kells in 1844. In
fact, she is not to be ruled out as the possible author of the introduction in *Retreat Instructions*. If the
handwritten final initial in the manuscript is intended to be a cursive "L," as it may be, then the compiler
may have been Mary Catherine (Elizabeth) Locke, who entered Tullamore on April 30, 1836, and founded
the community in Derry in 1848. However, in Tullamore records she is not referred to as an annalist, as
Degnan seems to believe the compiler or transcriber was (*Retreat Instructions*, 160), though the compiler
need not have been an annalist, and she may not have lived in Tullamore. However, if the final initial "S"
is correct, then it is unclear who the transcriber was, and when and where she transcribed this portion
of the instructions.

were simply paraphrased; whole treatises were, as far as I have seen, never transcribed exactly or completely.

Other dependencies on Rodriguez's thought and wording occur in the sections of *Retreat Instructions* on pages 56–64 and 145–55: these quotations and paraphrases are taken from his treatise "Of Union and Fraternal Charity," in volume 1 of his work. I have found identical or very similar language to his on pages 60–63 of the *Retreat Instructions* (corresponding to wording on pages 158–61 of Rodriguez's text), and I am confident that there are many other references here which I have not yet correlated. Rodriguez is talking about the union and charity of the Society of Jesus, but as we have seen in Catherine's transcription of the "Spirit of the Institute" essay, she was never above appropriating his language to the needs and spirituality of the Sisters of Mercy.[29]

In addition, the "prayer is a plant" metaphor; the mariner's "compass" image for those who remain recollected in the presence of God while serving others; and the need for Sisters of Mercy to be "shining lamps giving light to all around us"—can all be found in various chapters of Rodriguez's *Practice of Christian and Religious Perfection*.[30] The compass image occurs in his chapter on true contentment in God, in his treatise "Of Conformity to the Will of God."[31] Moreover, the passage in *Retreat Instructions* on banishing "gloom and sadness" (pages 94–95) contains nearly identical wording, including the reference to St. Bernard's views, to wording in Rodriguez's treatise "On Joy and Sadness."[32] However, the reference to "St. Francis [of Assisi]" in Rodriguez's work was miscopied as "St. Francis de Sales" in the manuscript that underlies *Retreat Instructions*.

In presenting *Retreat Instructions* in published form in 1952, Degnan says that she did not copy the wording or punctuation exactly as she found it in the manuscript she was using (just as that collection of manuscripts did not transcribe Rodriguez's or other texts exactly). As she explains in her foreword: "These notes remain much as they appear in manuscript . . . with some modification. . . . Transitions have been supplied and antecedents clarified for this printing. Occasional changes have been made [in wording and word order]." Moreover, in some instances, she says, the "end of the sentence has . . . been changed." However, "archaisms . . . have been allowed to stand as peculiar to the period."[33]

A great deal of research remains to be done to correlate the writings of Rodriguez with *Retreat Instructions*, to discover other sources if Rodriguez was not the only or the direct source (Rodriguez was regularly quoted by other spiritual writers), and to discover the other books which Catherine arranged to have

29. See note 1 of this appendix.
30. *Retreat Instructions*, 90, 108–9, 154, and 145 and 155.
31. Rodriguez, *Practice of . . . Perfection*, vol. 1, 405.
32. Rodriguez, *Practice of . . . Perfection*, vol. 2, 320–38. In the Mercy archives in Birmingham, England, is a three-page, unfinished manuscript that appears to be in Catherine McAuley's handwriting (using the right-slanted style she attempted briefly at George's Hill). The manuscript is a series of direct quotations from chapters 6 and 7 of Rodriguez's treatise "On Joy and Sadness," vol. 2, 333–37. Many of them match the wording, exactly or by paraphrase, in *Retreat Instructions*, 94–95.
33. Degnan, foreword to *Retreat Instructions*, 11–12.

transcribed, as evidenced by the many extant copybooks of "retreat meditations" used before reception and profession. For example, strong possibilities in this research are Michel-Ange Marin's 1747 book *The Perfect Religious* and Louis Bourdaloue's *Spiritual Retreat,* for which I have established a number of correlations.[34] While considerable time has been spent on these endeavors, the task is still not completed.

One further manuscript in the Mercy Congregational Archives, Dublin, may be discussed in relation to *Retreat Instructions.* It is a hand-printed manuscript that may be in Catherine McAuley's hand: the formation of many printed letters in the text matches the formation of the same letters in Catherine's cursive handwriting as seen, for example, in her autograph correspondence. If the manuscript was indeed printed by Catherine McAuley, as I suspect it was, it is a rare example of her printing.

This manuscript is in a small, bound book of transcriptions that was formerly in the Baggot Street convent archives. The first entry, which is in Catherine McAuley's cursive writing, is an incomplete "Preparatory meditation for the first retreat after entering Religion"; it is over forty pages long, may have been transcribed while Catherine was at George's Hill, and is a transcription of parts of Rodriguez's chapter "The great Value we ought to set on Spiritual Things."[35] The second entry is the hand-printed "Meditations after Reception," which I believe is in Catherine's hand. The other entries, all on "retreats," are not in Catherine's handwriting.

A source for the hand-printed "Meditations after Reception" has not yet been identified, and most of its content is not similar to wording in Rodriguez's *Practice of ... Perfection.* The text is punctuated by prayers to "my divine Saviour," "points" for meditation, "considerations," and occasionally the title "Visit to the holy Sacrament," which may suggest Alphonsus Liguori's work *Visits to the Blessed Sacrament,* though the manuscript does not generally match the editions of this work that have been studied.

However, what is most significant about this hand-printed manuscript, which seems to be largely paraphrases, is that passages from it show up in the

---

34. M. A. Marin, *The Perfect Religious,* translated from the French (Dublin: Repository of St. Mary's Asylum, 1845). Carroll, *Leaves from the Annals,* vol. 1 (1881), 240, says Mary Vincent Deasy, an early Sister of Mercy, did an English translation of Marin's work. The Naas collection, in part housed in MCA, and the Dublin collection, also in MCA, have handwritten transcripts of parts of Marin's book in English, as does AIMGB. A copy of Marin's work in the British Library indicates that English translations of it were published as early as 1762.

Louis Bourdaloue (1632–1704) was a famous French Jesuit preacher whose *Oeuvres complètes* were frequently published in the eighteenth and early nineteenth centuries. In 1810 William A. Gahan published in Dublin a second edition of his translation of Bourdaloue's *Spiritual Retreat.* In 1833 a "Catholic priest" published, again in Dublin, a "revised" edition of Gahan's translation, with additional contents. Passages from both English editions appear to be in *Retreat Instructions* (1952), and transcriptions from these editions are also in some early Mercy convent collections.

35. Rodriguez, *Practice of ... Perfection,* vol. 1, 9–13. The chapter on "Spiritual Things" is the first in Rodriguez's first treatise in vol. 1. Catherine also copied parts of other chapters in the treatise, which deal, in general, with the "perfection of our ordinary actions."

published *Retreat Instructions*. Some similarities to the manuscript are in the section of the *Instructions* on prayer—for example, "A religious should be a child of prayer," and the "best means" is "recollection." The "prayer is a plant" metaphor in *Retreat Instructions* uses similar wording to that on pages [83] and [84] of the hand-printed manuscript; and the sections on Holy Communion—for example, the injunction to "Live by Holy Communion" and the overall advice about frequent Communion—correspond to scattered wording on pages [87] through [92] of the manuscript.[36]

The closest correspondences found so far between *Retreat Instructions* and the hand-printed manuscript are the following two sets of quotations. In Catherine's manuscript, which is probably a free transcription of another writer's work, we read under the subtitle "Study Jesus Christ":

Consider that the study of a Christian & religious soul should be that of the life & maxims of Jesus Christ. This divine Saviour should be in her regard like a *Book* that is continually open before her eyes in which she learns the conduct she should observe to become holy. He should be like a *glass* in which she should incessantly contemplate herself to know what she should reform & correct in her interior sentiments & exterior actions. He should be like a *seal* strongly applied to her to imprint his image there. ([65], emphasis added)

In the published *Retreat Instructions,* we read:

The life and maxims of Jesus Christ should be as a *book* always opened before us from which we are to learn all that is necessary to know, as a *glass* in which we will clearly see our defects, and as a *seal* whose image we are to impress on our hearts.[37]

A second correlation concerns the "evangelic spirit." In Catherine's manuscript we read:

Consider that as much as it concerns a religious soul to acquire the evangelic spirit to arrive at the perfection of her state so much also it is dangerous for her to take a contrary spirit which is capable of making her lose that of her state and of making her worldly under her habit of sanctity, if to her misfortune she ceases to think according to the maxims of the Gospel. She would soon pass to hold subjection, humiliation & the mortifying practices of her rule in contempt; far from loving humility & practising it, she will only be ambitious to be first & to distinguish herself from others; she will despise simplicity, poverty will be a burthen to her, she will shake off as much as she can obedience, and reject all that contradicts her self love; she will be neither meek, patient or peaceable, for her state displeases her. Let this detail inspire you with a salutary fear of losing the spirit of the Gospel. . . . It is this evangelic spirit, as the same great saint [Paul] said, that will make us live like citizens of heaven. ([80]–[81], [82])

In the *Retreat Instructions* we read:

To arrive at evangelical perfection, we must endeavor to imbibe the spirit and maxims of the Gospel. . . . If we do not conform our lives to the maxims of the Gospel, we can never reach evangelical perfection but shall retain a worldly spirit under the religious

---

36. "Live by Holy Communion": *Retreat Instructions*, 89, 90.
37. Ibid., 87–88, emphasis added.

habit. Then our duties will become unimportant in our eyes, poverty painful, our charity wanting the force of life which religion gives to those who have its true spirit and which makes us even on earth live as citizens of heaven.[38]

Clearly parts of *Retreat Instructions* reflect parts of Catherine McAuley's hand-printed "Meditations after Reception." Moreover, if this manuscript is not her original composition, which I do not think it is, then in these passages it and the published *Retreat Instructions* rely ultimately on a common, previously published source or several such sources.

My summary view of the published *Retreat Instructions* is therefore as follows: These *Retreat Instructions* remain, with the very necessary qualifications I have noted, an authentic source of the general tenor of the sayings and instructions of Catherine McAuley, not in their exact wording and not because she composed all the wording of *Retreat Instructions*, which she did not, but because it is reasonable to believe, given the dates within the compiled manuscript underlying the published *Instructions*, namely, 1832–1834, that she chose the published works that were transcribed by herself or others, and were then compiled by others in the transcribed manuscript that is the basis of *Retreat Instructions*. She used these transcriptions herself, or earlier copies of them, in giving oral instructions to postulants and novices in their retreats before reception and profession of vows. Thus Catherine's intentions and "voice" can be heard in these *Instructions*, if only indirectly in her selection of the sources she or others transcribed.

Perhaps this appendix is best concluded by simply citing six principles which have been followed in the present biography and have influenced its content:

1. One cannot assume that every "instruction" or "saying" that is said to be "of Catherine McAuley"—in whatever published or unpublished form it appears—is authentic.

2. The closer one can get historically to the earliest source of an alleged saying or instruction the more accurate one can be about any claim or denial of its authenticity.

3. Accounts of Catherine McAuley's instructions and sayings presented by those who witnessed them have, by definition, greater validity than accounts written without firsthand experience or access to firsthand accounts.

4. Catherine's extended oral instructions were probably very rarely, if ever, given completely extempore, without the aid of a previously written text, and certainly not in the retreats before receptions and professions.

5. Where this is possible, knowing the date and the transcriber of a transcription or the editor or author of a manuscript or published book and how that transcriber, editor, or author worked may be crucial in deciding authenticity.

6. The important difference between an original composition and a transcription of a previously published or unpublished source needs to be acknowl-

---

38. Ibid., 88 and 105–6. These published texts do not exactly match the corresponding texts in the manuscript (MCA) which underlies the publication.

edged and maintained, even when Catherine McAuley herself is the composer, the transcriber, or the selector of a work that was transcribed, and even when the original source is not yet identified.

Finally, preserving the original wording and context of Catherine's authentic sayings and instructions—as in her letters and in other writings known to have been composed by her or by contemporary witnesses of her speech—would seem to be a courtesy one owes to her and to one's readers. The desire to modernize or otherwise alter her wording, but still present it as her wording, probably ought to be resisted. References to Catherine's sayings and instructions in this biography are cited from their earliest authentic source, and the citation given. Undocumented statements that she said this or that are probably not sufficient at this stage of McAuley research.

Bibliography

[Agnew, Elizabeth C.]. *Geraldine: A Tale of Conscience.* 3 vols. London: Charles Dolman, 1837–1839.

[Agnew, M. Clare (Elizabeth)]. *Illustrations of the Corporal & Spiritual Works of Mercy.* London: Charles Dolman, 1840.

Appleyard, Douglas S. *Green Fields Gone Forever: The Story of the Coolock and Artane Area.* N.p.: Original Writing, Ltd., 1985.

Baxter, Roger, ed. *Meditations for Every Day in the Year, Collected from Different Spiritual Writers.* 2nd ed. New York: Benziger Brothers, 1884.

Bellamy, Kathrine E. *The Steadfast Woman: The Story of Mary Francis Creedon.* [St. John's, Newfoundland]: Sisters of Mercy, n.d.

———. *Weavers of the Tapestry.* St. John's, Newfoundland: Flanker Press, 2006.

Beyond Catherine: Stories of Mercy Foundresses. Dublin: Mercy International Association, 2003.

Binns, Jonathan. *The Miseries and Beauties of Ireland.* London: Longman, Orme, Brown, 1837.

Blake, Michael. *Two Sermons: The First . . . on Palm Sunday, 1811, on the Lamented Death of the Very Rev. Thomas Betagh; The Second on . . . November [4], 1821, on . . . An Early and Religious Education.* Dublin: Richard Coyne, 1821.

Blyth, Francis. *A Devout Paraphrase on the Seven Penitential Psalms; or, A Practical Guide to Repentance.* 7th ed. Dublin: Catholic Book Society, 1835.

Bolster, M. Angela. *Mercy in Cork, 1837–1987.* Cork: Tower Books, 1987.

———, ed. *The Correspondence of Catherine McAuley, 1827–1841.* Cork: Congregation of the Sisters of Mercy, Dioceses of Cork and Ross, 1989.

———. *Catherine McAuley, Venerable for Mercy.* Dublin: Dominican Publications, 1990.

———. *Catherine McAuley, Prophet of Mercy.* Cork: D. and A. O'Leary, 1996.

———. *Venerable Catherine McAuley: Liminal for Mercy.* Cork: Printed by D. & A. O'Leary, [1998].

Bourke, Ulick J. *The Life and Times of the Most Rev. John MacHale.* New York: P. J. Kenedy, 1902.

Brennan, Bonaventure. *"It commenced with two. . . .": The Story of Mary Ann Doyle.* N.p.: Sisters of Mercy of the Northern Province, Ireland, 2001.

[Bridgeman, Mary Francis]. *Abridgment of a Guide for the Religious called Sisters of Mercy.* London: Printed for the Community by Robson and Son, 1866.

————. *A Guide for the Religious Called Sisters of Mercy.* London: Printed for the Community by Robson and Son, 1866.

Burke Savage, Roland. *Catherine McAuley: The First Sister of Mercy.* Dublin: M. H. Gill, 1949, 1955.

Butler, Alban. *The Lives of the Fathers, Martyrs, and Other Principal Saints.* 12 vols. New York: D. & J. Sadlier, 1846.

Byrne, Michael. *Tullamore Catholic Parish: A Historical Survey.* Tullamore: Leinster Leader, 1987.

Cameron, Charles A. *History of the Royal College of Surgeons in Ireland, and of the Irish Schools of Medicine.* Dublin: Fannin, 1886.

Carmichael, Ann G. "Erysipelas." In *Cambridge World History of Human Disease,* edited by Kenneth F. Kiple, 720–21. Cambridge: Cambridge University Press, 1993.

Carrigan, William. *The History and Antiquities of the Diocese of Ossory.* Vol. 1. Dublin: Sealy, Bryers & Walker, 1905.

Carroll, Mary Austin. *Life of Catherine McAuley.* New York: D. & J. Sadlier, 1866; 2nd ed., New York: D. & J. Sadlier, [1870?].

————. *Leaves from the Annals of the Sisters of Mercy.* Vol. 1–3, New York: Catholic Publication Society, 1881, 1883, 1889; vol. 4, New York: P. O'Shea, 1895.

Catholic Directory, Almanack, and Registry. . . , A Complete. Dublin: Printed for the Proprietor, 1836–1864. Cited as the *Catholic Directory.*

[Challoner, Richard, ed.]. *A Journal of Meditations for Every Day in the Year; Gathered out of Divers Authors.* Dublin: Richard Coyne, 1823.

Clear, Caitríona. *Nuns in Nineteenth-Century Ireland.* Dublin: Gill and Macmillan, 1987.

————. "Nuns in Nineteenth-Century Ireland." In *Irish Women's History Reader,* edited by Alan Hayes and Diane Urquhart. London and New York: Routledge, 2001.

Coakley, Davis. *Robert Graves: Evangelist of Clinical Medicine.* Dublin: Irish Endocrine Society, 1996.

Comerford, Michael. *Collections Relating to the Dioceses of Kildare and Leighlin.* Vol. 1. Dublin: James Duffy and Sons, 1883.

Connolly, S. J. *Priests and People in Pre-Famine Ireland, 1780–1845.* Dublin: Gill and Macmillan, 1982.

————, ed. *The Oxford Companion to Irish History.* 2nd ed. Oxford: Oxford University Press, 2002.

Convent of Our Lady of Mercy, St. Vincent's, Galway: 1840–1940. Galway: n.p., [1940].

Corish, Patrick J. "The Catholic Community in the Nineteenth Century." *Archivium Hibernicum* 38 (1983): 26–33.

————. *The Irish Catholic Experience: A Historical Survey.* Dublin: Gill and Macmillan, 1985.

Courtney, Marie Therese. "The Careful Instruction of Women." In Marie Therese Courtney and M. Loreto O'Connor, *Sisters of Mercy in Limerick,* 14–22. N.p.: Limerick Leader, 1988.

————. "Fearless Mother Elizabeth Moore." In Marie Therese Courtney and M. Loreto O'Connor, *Sisters of Mercy in Limerick,* 31–37. N.p.: Limerick Leader, 1988.

Courtney, Marie Therese, and M. Loreto O'Connor. *Sisters of Mercy in Limerick.* N.p.: Limerick Leader, 1988.

Cowper, William. "The Diverting History of John Gilpin." In *Cowper Poetical Works,* edited by H. S. Milford, 346–51. 4th ed. London: Oxford University Press, 1934.

Craig, Maurice. *Dublin 1660–1860: The Shaping of a City.* Dublin: Liberties Press, 2006.

Crawford, E. Margaret. "Typhus in Nineteenth-Century Ireland." In *Medicine, Disease and the State in Ireland, 1650–1940,* edited by Greta Jones and Elizabeth Malcolm, 121–37. Cork: Cork University Press, 1999.

Crossman, Virginia. "Workhouse." In *Oxford Companion to Irish History,* edited by S. J. Connolly, 631. 2nd ed. Oxford: Oxford University Press, 2002.

Cullen, Mary. "Breadwinners and Providers: Women in the Household Economy of Labouring Families 1835–6." In *Women Surviving: Studies in Irish Women's History in the 19th and 20th Centuries,* edited by Maria Luddy and Cliona Murphy, 85–116. Dublin: Poolbeg Press, 1989.

Customs and Minor Regulations of the Religious called Sisters of Mercy in the Parent House Baggot Street and its Branch Houses. Dublin: J. M. O'Toole and Son, 1869. Cited as *Baggot Street Book of Customs.*

Daly, Mary E. *Social and Economic History of Ireland since 1800.* Dublin: Educational Company of Ireland incorporating Longman, Browne and Nolan, 1981.

Darcy, Catherine C. *The Institute of the Sisters of Mercy of the Americas: The Canonical Development of the Proposed Governance Model.* Lanham, Md.: University Press of America, 1993.

Davis, Elizabeth M. "Wisdom and Mercy Meet: Catherine McAuley's Interpretation of Scripture." In *Recovering Nineteenth-Century Women Interpreters of the Bible,* edited by Christiana de Groot and Marion Ann Taylor, 63–80. Atlanta: Society of Biblical Literature, 2007.

Dean, Joseph Joy, ed. *Devotions to the Sacred Heart of Jesus; Exercises for the Holy Sacrifice of the Mass, Confession and Communion. . . .* Translated from the French. Dublin: Chambers and Hallagan, 1820.

[Degnan, Mary Bertrand], ed. *Retreat Instructions of Mother Mary Catherine McAuley by Sister Mary Teresa Purcell.* Foreword by Mary Bertrand Degnan. Westminster, Md.: Newman Press, 1952.

Degnan, Mary Bertrand. *Mercy Unto Thousands: Life of Mother Mary Catherine McAuley.* Westminster, Md.: Newman Press, 1957.

Dennett, Mary V. "Family History Report for the Descendants of William Armstrong Montgomery McAuley." 2010. Unpublished (photocopy).

Donnelly, Nicholas. *History of Dublin Parishes.* 17 Parts. Dublin: Catholic Truth Society of Ireland, [1904–1917].

Dublin Almanack, General Register, and Directory. Dublin: 1784–1848. Cited as the *Dublin Directory.*

Enright, Séamus. "Women and Catholic Life in Dublin, 1766–1852." In *History of the Catholic Diocese of Dublin,* edited by James Kelly and Dáire Keogh, 268–93. Dublin: Four Courts Press, 2000.

Farmar, Tony. *Patients, Potions & Physicians: A Social History of Medicine in Ireland.*

Dublin: A. & A. Farmar in Association with the Royal College of Physicians of Ireland, 2004.

Farrington, Anthony. *A Biographical Index of East India Company Maritime Service Officers, 1600–1834.* London: British Library, 1999.

Fenning, Hugh. "The Archbishops of Dublin, 1693–1786." In *History of the Catholic Diocese of Dublin,* edited by James Kelly and Dáire Keogh, 175–214. Dublin: Four Courts Press, 2000.

Fitzgerald, James. "Nano Nagle Wins Title of Ireland's Greatest Woman." *Irish Times,* June 25, 2005.

Fitzpatrick, William J. *History of the Dublin Catholic Cemeteries.* Dublin: Published at the Offices, 1900.

[Flanagan, Mary Padua], ed. *Letters of Mary Aikenhead.* Dublin: M. H. Gill, 1914.

[————]. *The Life and Work of Mary Aikenhead.* London: Longmans, Green, 1924.

Fleetwood, John F. *The History of Medicine in Ireland.* Dublin: Skellig Press, 1983.

Form of Ceremony for the Reception and Profession of the Sisters of Our Lady of Mercy. Dublin: J. Byrn, 1834; London: C. Richards, 1840.

Freeman, T. W. "Land and People, c. 1841." In *Ireland Under the Union, I, 1801–1870,* edited by W. E. Vaughan, 242–71. Vol. 5 of *A New History of Ireland.* Oxford: Oxford University Press, 1989.

French, Roger K. "Scurvy." In *Cambridge World History of Human Disease,* edited by Kenneth F. Kiple, 1000–1005. Cambridge: Cambridge University Press, 1993.

[Gaffney, Myles]. "La Regola e Le Costituzioni delle Religiose nominate Sorelle della Misericordia." *Dublin Review* 22 (March and June 1847): 1–25.

Gahan, William A. *The Christian's Guide to Heaven, or, A Complete Manual of Catholic Piety.* Dublin: M'Donnel Donnel, 1804; n.p.: Agra Press, 1834; Dublin: James Duffy, 1844. Cited as *Catholic Piety.*

Gately, Mary Josephine. *The Sisters of Mercy: Historical Sketches, 1831–1931.* New York: Macmillan, 1931.

Geary, Laurence M. *Medicine and Charity in Ireland, 1718–1851.* Dublin: University College Dublin Press, 2004.

Gilbert, John T. *History of Dublin.* Vol. 1. Dublin: McGlashan, 1854.

Doris Gottemoeller and others, eds. *Praying in the Spirit of Catherine McAuley.* Chicago: Institute of the Sisters of Mercy of the Americas, 1999.

Harden, Victoria A. "Typhus, Epidemic." In *Cambridge World History of Human Disease,* edited by Kenneth F. Kiple, 1080–84. Cambridge: Cambridge University Press, 1993.

Hardy, Anne. "Relapsing Fever." In *Cambridge World History of Human Disease,* edited by Kenneth F. Kiple, 967–69. Cambridge: Cambridge University Press, 1993.

Häring, Bernard. *The Law of Christ.* Vol. 3. Translated by Edwin G. Kaiser. Westminster, Md.: Newman Press, 1966.

[Harnett, Mary Vincent]. *The Life of Rev. Mother Catherine McAuley.* Edited by Richard Baptist O'Brien. Dublin: John F. Fowler, 1864.

Harrison, Richard S. *A Biographical Dictionary of Irish Quakers.* 2nd ed. Dublin: Four Courts Press, 2008.

Healy, Kathleen. *Frances Warde: American Founder of the Sisters of Mercy.* New York: Seabury Press, 1973.

Hearn, Mona. "How Victorian Families Lived." In Mary Daly, Mona Hearn, and Peter Pearson, *Dublin's Victorian Homes,* 61–95. Dublin: A. and A. Farmar, 1998.

Heslip, Robert. "Money." In *Oxford Companion to Irish History,* edited by S. J. Connolly, 384–85. 2nd ed. Oxford: Oxford University Press, 2002.

Holmes, Finlay. *The Presbyterian Church in Ireland: A Popular History.* Dublin: Columba Press, 2000.

An Index to the Act or Grant Books and Original Wills of the Diocese of Dublin from 1800 to 1858. Dublin: Printed for Her Majesty's Stationery Office, 1899.

Jeffery, Barbara. *Living in the Church . . . The Hardman Family Story.* N.p.: Sisters of Mercy, [2010]).

John Taylor's Map of the Environs of Dublin 1816. Edited by J. H. Andrews. Dublin: Phoenix Maps, 1989.

Jones, Greta, and Elizabeth Malcolm, eds. *Medicine, Disease and the State in Ireland, 1650–1949.* Cork: Cork University Press, 1999.

Jones, Rufus M. *The Faith and Practice of the Quakers.* Richmond, Ind.: Friends United Press, n.d.

Jung, C. G. *Memories, Dreams, Reflections.* Edited by Aniela Jaffé. Translated by Richard and Clara Winston. New York: Random House, 1963.

Keena, M. Imelda, ed. *The Letters of William [Armstrong] Montgomery McAuley.* London: Institute of Our Lady of Mercy, n.d.

Kelleher, Margaret, and James H. Murphy, eds. *Gender Perspectives in Nineteenth-Century Ireland.* Dublin: Irish Academic Press, 1997.

Kelly, James, and Dáire Keogh, eds. *History of the Catholic Diocese of Dublin.* Dublin: Four Courts Press, 2000.

Keogh, Dáire. "'The Pattern of the Flock': John Thomas Troy, 1786–1823." In *History of the Catholic Diocese of Dublin,* edited by James Kelly and Dáire Keogh, 215–36. Dublin: Four Courts Press, 2000.

———. *Edmund Rice and the First Christian Brothers.* Dublin: Four Courts Press, 2008.

Kerr, Donal. *"A Nation of Beggars"? Priests, People, and Politics in Famine Ireland, 1846–1852.* Oxford: Clarendon Press, 1994.

———. "Dublin's Forgotten Archbishop: Daniel Murray, 1768–1852." In *History of the Catholic Diocese of Dublin,* edited by James Kelly and Dáire Keogh, 247–67. Dublin: Four Courts Press, 2000.

Killerby, Catherine Kovesi. *Ursula Frayne: A Biography.* South Fremantle: University of Notre Dame Australia Press, 1996.

Kirk, Marcienne D. *Remembering Your Mercy: Mother Mary Cecilia Maher and the First Sisters of Mercy in New Zealand, 1850–1880.* Auckland: Sisters of Mercy, 1998.

Larkin, Emmet. *The Making of the Roman Catholic Church in Ireland, 1850–1860.* Chapel Hill: University of North Carolina Press, 1980.

———, ed. and trans. *Alexis de Tocqueville's Journey in Ireland, July–August, 1835.* Washington, D.C.: The Catholic University of America Press, 1990.

———. *The Pastoral Role of the Roman Catholic Church in Pre-Famine Ireland, 1750–1850.* Dublin: Four Courts Press; Washington, D.C.: The Catholic University of America Press, 2006.

LeBaron, Charles W., and David W. Taylor. "Typhoid Fever." In *Cambridge World History of Human Disease,* edited by Kenneth F. Kiple, 1071–77. Cambridge: Cambridge University Press, 1993.

Lennon, Mary Isidore. *Mother M. de Pazzi Bentley.* St. Louis: n.p., 1980.

Levin, Jeffrey. "Periodontal Disease (Pyorrhea)." In *Cambridge World History of Human Disease,* edited by Kenneth F. Kiple, 924–26. Cambridge: Cambridge University Press, 1993.

Lewis, Samuel. *Lewis' Dublin: A Topographical Dictionary of the Parishes, Towns and Villages of Dublin City and County.* Compiled by Christopher Ryan. Reprint of a portion of Vol. 1 of Samuel Lewis, *Topographical Dictionary of Ireland* (1837). Dublin: Collins Press, 2001.

———. *A Topographical Dictionary of Ireland . . . with Historical and Statistical Descriptions.* 2 vols. London: S. Lewis, 1837.

Liguori, Alphonsus M. *The True Spouse of Christ; or, The Nun Sanctified by the Virtues of her State.* Translated from the Italian by a "Catholic Clergyman." Dublin: James Duffy, 1860.

Luddy, Maria. *Women and Philanthropy in Nineteenth-Century Ireland.* Cambridge: Cambridge University Press, 1995.

———, ed. *Women in Ireland, 1800–1918: A Documentary History.* Cork: Cork University Press, 1999.

———, ed. *The Crimean Journals of the Sisters of Mercy, 1854–56.* Dublin: Four Courts Press, 2004.

———. *Prostitution and Irish Society, 1800–1940.* Cambridge: Cambridge University Press, 2007.

Luddy, Maria, and Cliona Murphy, eds. *Women Surviving: Studies in Irish Women's History in the 19th and 20th Centuries.* Dublin: Poolbeg Press, 1989.

MacLoughlin, Adrian. *Guide to Historic Dublin.* Dublin: Gill and Macmillan, 1979.

Mac Suibhne, Peadar. *Paul Cullen and His Contemporaries.* Vols. 1–3. Naas: Leinster Leader, 1961–1965.

Magray, Mary Peckham. *The Transforming Power of the Nuns: Women, Religion, and Cultural Change in Ireland, 1750–1900.* New York: Oxford University Press, 1998.

Maher, James. *The Letters of Rev. James Maher.* Edited by Patrick Francis Moran. Dublin: Browne and Nolan, 1877.

Maher, Michael, ed. *Irish Spirituality.* Dublin: Veritas Publications, 1981.

Marin, Michel-Ange. *The Perfect Religious.* 1747. Translated from the French. Dublin: Repository of St. Mary's Asylum, 1845.

Mazzonis, Querciolo. *Spirituality, Gender, and the Self in Renaissance Italy: Angela Merici and the Company of St. Ursula (1474–1540).* Washington, D.C.: The Catholic University of America Press, 2007.

M'Cready, C. T. *Dublin Street Names.* Dublin: Carraig Books, 1892.

McDowell, R. B. "Ireland on the Eve of the Famine." In *The Great Famine: Studies in Irish History, 1845–52,* edited by R. Dudley Edwards and T. Desmond Williams, 3–86. New York: New York University Press, 1957.

McEvoy, John. *Carlow College, 1793–1993.* Carlow: St. Patrick's College, 1993.

McLay, Anne. *Women Out of Their Sphere: A History of the Sisters of Mercy in Western Australia.* Northbridge, Western Australia: Vanguard Press, 1992.

McWalter, James C. *A History of the Worshipful Company of Apothecaries of the City of Dublin*. Dublin: E. Ponsonby, 1916.

Meagher, William. *Notices of the Life and Character of His Grace Most Rev. Daniel Murray, Late Archbishop of Dublin, as contained in The Commemorative Oration*. Dublin: Gerald Bellew; London: Burns and Lambert, 1853.

Milnes, Richard Monckton. "A Spanish Anecdote." In vol. 2 of *The Poetical Works of (Richard Monckton Milnes) Lord Houghton*, 281–82. 2 vols. London: John Murray, 1876.

Mitchell, James. "Father Peter Daly (c. 1788–1868)." *Journal of the Galway Archaeological and Historical Society* 39 (1983–1984): 27–114.

Monsell, J. S. *Cottage Controversy; or, Dialogues between Thomas and Andrew, on The Errors of the Church of Rome*. 2nd ed. Limerick: Goggin, 1839.

[Moore, Mary Clare], comp. *A Little Book of Practical Sayings, Advices and Prayers of Our Revered Foundress, Mother Mary Catharine [sic] McAuley*. London: Burns, Oates, 1868.

Moran, Patrick Francis. "Memoir of the Rev. James Maher, P. P." In *The Letters of Rev. James Maher*, edited by Patrick Francis Moran, i–cxii. Dublin: Browne and Nolan, 1877.

More, Hannah. "Sensibility: An Epistle to the Honourable Mrs. Boscawen." In vol. 1 of *Works of Hannah More*, 85–96. 4 vols. Dublin: D. Graisberry, 1803.

Muldrey, Mary Hermenia. *Abounding in Mercy—Mother Austin Carroll*. New Orleans: Habersham, 1988.

Murphy, Ignatius. *The Diocese of Killaloe: 1800–1850*. Dublin: Four Courts Press, 1992.

Neumann, Mary Ignatia, ed. *Letters of Catherine McAuley, 1827–1841*. Baltimore: Helicon Press, 1969.

O'Brien, Pius. *The Sisters of Mercy of Birr and Nenagh*. Ennis: Sisters of Mercy, 1994.

O'Brien, Richard Baptist. Introduction to *The Life of Rev. Mother Catherine McAuley*, by Mary Vincent Harnett, v–xxxv. Dublin: John F. Fowler, 1864.

———. *An Eight-Day Retreat, Principally Intended for the Sisters of Mercy and the Active Orders*. Dublin: John F. Fowler, 1868.

O'Connell, Daniel. *The Correspondence of Daniel O'Connell*. Edited by Maurice R. O'Connell. Vols. 1–3, Dublin: Irish University Press, 1972, 1973; vol. 4, Dublin: Stationery Office for the Irish Manuscripts Commission, 1978; vols. 5–7, Dublin: Blackwater Press, 1977, 1978.

O'Connor, John. *The Workhouses of Ireland: The Fate of Ireland's Poor*. Dublin: Anvil Books, 1995.

O'Connor, M. Loreto. "Helena Heffernan, a True Limerick Woman." In Marie Therese Courtney and M. Loreto O'Connor, *Sisters of Mercy in Limerick*, 23–26. N.p.: Limerick Leader, 1988.

O'Donnell, E. E. *The Jesuits in Dublin, 1598–1998*. Dublin: Wolfhound Press, 1999.

O'Donoghue, Mary Xaverius [Frances]. *Mother Vincent Whitty: Woman and Educator in a Masculine Society*. Carlton, Victoria: Melbourne University Press, 1972.

O'Dowd, Mary. *A History of Women in Ireland, 1500–1800*. Harlow, England: Pearson Longman, 2005.

O'Farrell, Mary Pius. *Nano Nagle: Woman of the Gospel*. Cork: Cork Publishing Limited, 1996.

Ó Gráda, Cormac. *The Great Irish Famine*. Dublin: Gill and Macmillan, 1989.

———. "Poverty, Population, and Agriculture, 1801-45." In *Ireland Under the Union, I, 1801-1870*, edited by W. E. Vaughan, 108-36. Vol. 5 of *A New History of Ireland*. Oxford: Oxford University Press, 1989.

O'Hara, Mary Nathy. *Catherine McAuley: Mercy Foundress*. Dublin: Veritas Publications, 1979.

O'Keeffe, Majella. "Mother M. Teresa White, 1809-1888." In *Beyond Catherine: Stories of Mercy Foundresses*, 92-95. Dublin: Mercy International Association, 2003.

Ormsby, Lambert Hepenstal. *Medical History of the Meath Hospital and County Dublin Infirmary.* Dublin: Fannin, 1888.

Ó Tuathaigh, Gearóid. *Ireland before the Famine, 1798-1848*. Dublin: Gill and Macmillan, 1972, 1990.

Pearson, Peter. *Dun Laoghaire: Kingstown*. Dublin: O'Brien Press, 1991.

Poor Man's Manual of Devotions. Dublin: D. Wogan, 1819.

Prunty, Jacinta. *Dublin Slums, 1800-1925: A Study in Urban Geography.* Dublin: Irish Academic Press, 1997.

Raughter, Rosemary. Introduction to *Religious Women and Their History: Breaking the Silence*, edited by Rosemary Raughter, 1-8. Dublin: Irish Academic Press, 2005.

———. "Pious Occupations: Female Activism and the Catholic Revival in Eighteenth-Century Ireland." In *Religious Women and Their History: Breaking the Silence*, edited by Rosemary Raughter, 25-49. Dublin: Irish Academic Press, 2005.

La Regola e Le Costituzioni delle Religiose nominate Sorelle della Misericordia. Rome: Congregationis de Propaganda Fide, 1841.

Rodriguez, Alonso. *The Practice of Christian and Religious Perfection*. Originally written in Spanish. Translated from the French copy of M. l'Abbé Regnier des Marais, of the Royal Academy of Paris. 3 vols. Kilkenny: John Reynolds, 1806.

Roker, Penny. "M. Mary Clare Moore, RSM." In *English Catholic Heroines*, edited by Joanna Bogle, 213-29. Leominster, England: Gracewing, 2009.

Roschini, Gabriele M. *Galleria Servitana: Oltre mille religiosi dell'Ordine dei Servi di Maria*. Rome: Pontificia Facoltà Teologica "Marianum," 1976.

Ruffing, Janet. "Catherine McAuley's Quaker Connection." *The MAST Journal* [Mercy Association in Scripture and Theology] 8, no. 1 (Fall 1997): 36-45.

Rule and Constitutions of the Religious called Sisters of Mercy. In Italian and English. Dublin: James Duffy, 1863.

Rules and Constitutions of the Institute of the Religious Sisterhood of the Presentation of the . . . Virgin Mary. Cork: James Haly, 1809.

Rutty, John. *A Treatise Concerning Christian Discipline, Compiled With the Advice of a National Meeting of the People called Quakers, held in Dublin, in the Year 1746*. [Dublin], 1752.

Sisters of Mercy, St. Louis, Missouri, ed. *Familiar Instructions of Rev. Mother McAuley.* St. Louis: Ev. E. Carreras, 1888.

Smith, M. Aquinas. "A Liverpool Pioneer in Mercy's Path: Life and Letters of Mother M. Liguori Gibson." Typescript. Liverpool: n.p., n.d.

Smith, Mary Constance. *A Sheaf of Golden Years, 1856–1906.* New York: Benziger Brothers, 1906.

Sobrino, Jon. *Christology at the Crossroads.* Translated by John Drury. Maryknoll, N.Y.: Orbis Books, 1978.

Speck, Reinhard S. "Cholera." In *Cambridge World History of Human Disease,* edited by Kenneth F. Kiple, 642–49. Cambridge: Cambridge University Press, 1993.

St. Francis of Sales. *The Spiritual Conferences.* Translated by a Member of the Order of Mercy [Mary Vincent Deasy], Sunderland. London: C. Dolman, 1853.

St. Gregory Hymnal. Revised singers' edition. Edited by Nicola A. Montani. Philadelphia: St. Gregory Guild, 1940.

Stokes, Whitley. *Projects for Re-Establishing the Internal Peace and Tranquillity of Ireland.* Dublin: James Moore, 1799.

Sullivan, Mary C. "Catherine McAuley's Theological and Literary Debt to Alonso Rodriguez: The 'Spirit of the Institute' Parallels." *Recusant History* 20 (May 1990): 81–105.

———. *Catherine McAuley and the Tradition of Mercy.* Dublin: Four Courts Press; Notre Dame, Ind.: University of Notre Dame Press, 1995.

———, ed. *The Friendship of Florence Nightingale and Mary Clare Moore.* Philadelphia: University of Pennsylvania Press, 1999.

———, ed. "The Prayers of Catherine McAuley." In *Praying in the Spirit of Catherine McAuley,* edited by Doris Gottemoeller and others, 47–75. Chicago: Institute of the Sisters of Mercy of the Americas, 1999.

———, ed. *The Correspondence of Catherine McAuley, 1818–1841.* Dublin: Four Courts Press; Washington, D.C.: The Catholic University of America Press, 2004.

Teresa of Avila. *The Collected Works of St. Teresa of Avila.* Translated by Kieran Kavanaugh and Otilio Rodriguez. 3 vols. Washington, D.C.: Institute of Carmelite Studies, 1985.

Townend, Paul A. *Father Mathew, Temperance and Irish Identity.* Dublin: Irish Academic Press, 2002.

Vicentini, Antonio M. *Il Confessore del S. Palazzo Apostolico e L'Ordine dei Servi di Maria.* Venice: Tipografia Pontificia Vesc. S. Giuseppe, 1925.

Walsh, Anne. *The Story of Ursula Frayne: A Woman of Mercy.* Mulgrave, Victoria, Australia: John Garratt Publishing, 1997.

Walsh, Dolores. *Grow Where You Are Planted: A History of Tullamore Mercy Sisters, 1836–1996.* Ferbane: Brosna Press, 1996.

Walsh, T. J. *Nano Nagle and the Presentation Sisters.* Dublin: M. H. Gill, 1959.

[Whitty, Mary Vincent]. *Mercy Women Making History, from the Pen of Mother Vincent Whitty.* Edited by Kath Burke and others. Ashgrove, Queensland: Sisters of Mercy in Queensland, 2001.

Williams, Helen Maria. "Paraphrase . . . Matt. vii. 12." In vol. 1 of *Poems,* 187–90. 2nd ed. 2 vols. London: T. Cadell, 1791.

Yeats, W. B. "Adam's Curse." In *W. B. Yeats: The Poems,* edited by Daniel Albright, 106–7, 487. London: J. M. Dent, Everyman Library, 1994.

[Young, Ursula]. *The Soul United to Jesus in the Adorable Sacrament.* Dublin: James Duffy and Sons, 1883.

Index

The Path of Mercy: The Life of Catherine McAuley was designed and typeset in Freya by Kachergis Book Design of Pittsboro, North Carolina. It was printed on 60-pound House Natural Smooth and bound by Sheridan Books of Ann Arbor, Michigan.